A Text-Book of North-Semitic Inscriptions: Moabite, Hebrew, Phoenician, Aramaic, Nabataean, Palmyrene, Jewish

George Albert Cooke

Ἀλλ' ὅμως ὁ Θεὸς διὰ τὴν τῶν πλανηθέντων σωτηρίαν ἠνέσχετο διὰ τούτων θεραπευθῆναι, δι' ὧν οἱ ἔξωθεν δαίμονας ἐθεράπευον, μικρὸν παραλλάξας αὐτά· ἵνα αὐτοὺς κατὰ μικρὸν τῆς συνηθείας ἀποσπάσας ἐπὶ τὴν ὑψηλὴν ἀγάγῃ φιλοσοφίαν.

S. Chrysostom *in Matth.* Hom. vi. 3.

· SAMVELI · ROLLES · DRIVER · S.T.P.

MAGISTRO · DISCIPVLVS

D.D.

G. A. C.

A TEXT-BOOK

OF

NORTH-SEMITIC INSCRIPTIONS

Moabite, Hebrew, Phoenician, Aramaic
Nabataean, Palmyrene, Jewish

BY THE

REV. G. A. COOKE, M.A.

LATE FELLOW OF MAGDALEN COLLEGE, OXFORD

OXFORD

AT THE CLARENDON PRESS

1903

OXFORD
PRINTED AT THE CLARENDON PRESS
BY HORACE HART, M.A.
PRINTER TO THE UNIVERSITY

PREFACE

THE present work took shape some years ago as an attempt to provide a text-book for students who offer the subject of Semitic Epigraphy in the Honour School of Oriental Studies at Oxford. The difficulty of obtaining access to inscriptions published in foreign journals, the costliness of the *Corpus Inscriptionum Semiticarum* and other works, made it desirable to prepare a collection which might bring the inscriptions conveniently within the reach of students; the texts set for the Schools were chosen to start with, and a good many more were added. The claims of other work, however, compelled me to lay aside my task for several years. Meanwhile, there appeared in 1898 Lidzbarski's *Handbuch der nordsemitischen Epigraphik*, which for the first time has dealt with the whole subject in a systematic manner. I wish to acknowledge here, with emphasis and gratitude, my obligations to the *Handbuch*; the extent of them will appear in the following pages. Lidzbarski's work has done much to supply the want which first induced me to prepare this volume; it has not, however, led me to alter my original design. I have published the texts with translations and notes; Lidzbarski, along with much valuable introductory matter, gives the texts, a glossary, and an atlas of facsimiles. This last it has not been possible to attach to my collection; within the limits laid down by the

Delegates of the Press, I have only been able to give a set of representative facsimiles and tables of alphabets, which, while not attempting to meet all requirements, will at least be sufficient to familiarize the student with the characteristic features of the different scripts.

Though English scholars have not neglected the study of Semitic Epigraphy either in their academic teaching or in their published writings—the names of the late Professors William Wright and Robertson Smith will occur to the reader in this connexion, while to many students of the younger generation Dr. Driver's pages in *Notes on the Hebrew Text of the Books of Samuel* served as their first and stimulating introduction to the subject—yet the bulk of scientific work within recent years has been done by the scholars of France and Germany. The enterprise of the Académie des Inscriptions et Belles-Lettres, and the enlightened policy of the French Government, have secured the majority of the inscriptions for the Louvre; hence it is that from Paris, in a manner possible nowhere else, the great Corpus is being issued, a work with which the eminent names of Renan, de Vogüé, Derenbourg, Halévy, Berger, Clermont-Ganneau, will always be associated. To Paris belongs the unique distinction of having recognized the study of oriental archaeology and epigraphy by the foundation of a professorship in the Collège de France, now held by M. Clermont-Ganneau, to whose original and keen researches the present work is indebted from beginning to end. For years past French scholars have been excavating and classifying the remains of Punic antiquity in the French colonies of N. Africa; in the Holy Land much excellent work is being done by the Dominican convent of St. Étienne at Jerusalem, an 'école pratique d'études bibliques,' under the accomplished direction of Père Lagrange.

In Germany the efforts of scholars have been devoted rather to the critical and grammatical examination of the documents than to the discovery of fresh material. For the Phoenician language the treatises of Schröder and Stade, though somewhat out of date, contain much that is of permanent value; on the Nabataean, Palmyrene, and other Aramaic dialects Nöldeke has written with unimpeachable authority; on points of grammar and exegesis the names of G. Hoffmann, Landau, D. H. Müller, Sachau, the two Mordtmanns, Reckendorf, Winckler (always interesting, if seldom convincing) will be of frequent occurrence in the following pages. But German scholars have also been engaged in the discovery of new material, especially in N. Arabia and N. Syria. Thanks to the courage and skill of the veteran epigraphist Julius Euting, we now possess satisfactory copies of the Nabataean inscriptions in the Ḥejaz and the Sinaitic peninsula; the Orient-Comité of Berlin has unearthed the Old Aramaic inscriptions of Zenjirli, the most important discovery since the finding of the Moabite Stone; quite recently Littmann has published the results of his exploration of the Ṣafâ inscriptions, NE. of Jebel ed-Drûz[1].

In the present work many of the inscriptions are, of necessity, the classical and familiar ones; many also are new; most of them now appear in English for the

[1] These inscriptions have also been investigated lately by Dussand and Macler, and published in their volume *Voyage archéol. au Ṣafâ etc.*, 1901.

first time. I have tried to bring the collection up to date as far as possible, and in one way or another to print the most important inscriptions which have been discovered in the last five or ten years.

My aim throughout has been not to propose novel interpretations or reconstructions of my own, but rather to give, after careful study of the various authorities on the subject, what seemed to be the most probable verdict on the issues raised, and also to bring together the chief matters of importance bearing on the texts. The frequency with which the words 'probably' and 'possibly' appear may, perhaps, be somewhat of a disappointment to the reader, as indicating an attitude of caution rather than of courage; but it is well to be reminded how seldom we can speak with positiveness on questions of grammar and interpretation where the material is so limited and where there is no contemporary literature to shed light upon the monuments. At the same time our study ought to result in doing something to reduce the limits of the possible, and discover, as precisely as we can, the extent of the probable.

To those who have helped me in the production of my book I have some special acknowledgements to make. From the Delegates of the Press I have received most generous treatment in the matter of printing. To the courtesy of the Marquis de Vogüé, President of the Commission of the C. I. S., I owe permission to reproduce Plates i and iii from the Corpus, and Plate viii from his own *La Syrie Centrale*. I am indebted to Dr. Euting for Plates iv and vii, the latter from his *Nabatäische Inschriften*; to M. Heuzey of the Louvre, for squeezes of the Nêrab inscriptions, Plates v and vi; to Dr. Budge of the British Museum, for facilities of access to the stones and seals under his charge; to Messrs. Kegan Paul, Trench, Trübner & Co. for the use of the blocks from Madden's *Coins of the Jews*. Mr. G. F. Hill of the British Museum has taken much trouble to help me with the coins, and has procured for me, by the courtesy of M. Babelon, casts of specimens in the Bibliothèque Nationale. M. Clermont-Ganneau, to whose published writings my book owes so much, has more than once given me the benefit of his opinion and advice. My former colleague, Mr. P. V. M. Benecke, Fellow and Tutor of Magdalen College, has verified and enriched several of my references to Greek and Latin authors. Above all, my grateful thanks are due to Dr. Driver for his constant encouragement. He is always ready to place his stores of knowledge at the service of his friends; and in this case he has made time, in the midst of his own work, to read my book in proof, and to offer criticisms and suggestions which have done much to improve it.

G. A. COOKE.

THE PARSONAGE, DALKEITH, N. B.,
Eastertide, 1903.

CONTENTS

PHOENICIAN: PUNIC

Malta

Asia Minor

Contents

Jewish

Coins

Seals and Gems

LIST OF PLATES

INTRODUCTION

THE inscriptions which make up the present collection are grouped under the common title of North-Semitic to distinguish them from the South-Semitic, or Sabaean and Ḥimyaritic, on the one hand, and from the Babylonian and Assyrian on the other. Geographically the area of this North-Semitic group extends from N. Syria to N. Arabia; on the East it is bounded by the Syrian desert; on the West it reaches into Asia Minor, Egypt, N. Africa, and the chief cities on the shores and islands of the Mediterranean. The languages in which the inscriptions are written belong to what may be called for convenience the Central, as distinguished from the Northern and Southern, division of the Semitic tongues[1]. This Central division is sub-divided into two main classes: i the Canaanite, which includes the Moabite, Hebrew, and Phoenician inscriptions, 9th cent. B.C.–3rd cent. A.D. and later; ii the Aramaic, represented by (*a*) the Old Aramaic inscriptions from Assyria, Babylonia, Asia Minor, and N. Syria, 8th–4th cent. B.C., (*b*) the Egyptian Aramaic, 5th–3rd cent. B.C., (*c*) the Nabataean and Palmyrene Aramaic, 1st cent. B.C.–3rd cent. A.D., a section to which we may assign the inscriptions from Têma as the earliest specimens (5th cent. B.C.) and the Sinaitic as the latest (1st–5th cent. A.D.). Some of these dialects are marked by peculiarities which, owing to local conditions, indicate a certain amount of overlapping from one class or division into another: thus the Old Aramaic spoken in the N. Syrian kingdoms of Ya'di and

[1] The Semitic languages are grouped in various ways; thus Wright, *Comp. Gr.* 12 ff., divides them into Northern i.e. Assyrian, Central i.e. Aramaic, Western i.e. Canaanite, Southern i.e. Arabic and Ethiopic. Zimmern, *Vergl. Gr.* 4 f., proposes a broader scheme, East-Semitic, i.e. Babylonian, Assyrian, and West-Semitic, i.e. Aramaic, Canaanite, Arabic, Ethiopic. The latter is preferred by König, *Hebräisch u. Semitisch* 123 f., on historical grounds, as suggesting the advance and separation of the Semitic tribes from their original home in E. Babylonia. The divisions given above are clearer for the present purpose.

Sam'al betrays several points of affinity to the Canaanite class; the Nabataean dialect, again, used for purposes of writing and commerce by the inhabitants of N. Arabia who were Arabs by race and spoke Arabic, was naturally much influenced by the language used in common speech, as appears especially in the forms of proper names; to a less degree the dialect of Palmyra, where the population was largely Arab, came under the same influence.

The chief interest of these inscriptions lies, of course, in the fact that they have preserved specimens of the North-Semitic dialects which we should otherwise know only from scattered allusions or by a process of inference very imperfect at the best. With the exception of the Hebrew and Aramaic writings of the Old Testament, there is no contemporary literature written in any of these languages. No fragments of the mythologies and histories said to have been composed in Phoenician by native writers have come down to us in the original; a few third- or fourth-hand extracts are preserved in Greek; but for the most part these Phoenician authors are names and nothing more[1]. The inscriptions, therefore, possess

[1] A cosmogony of Sidonian origin is preserved by Damascius *de Primis Principiis* 125, who borrowed it from the Greek of Eudemus, a pupil of Aristotle, and gave it a neo-Platonic interpretation. This was probably the work (*τὸ περὶ τῶν ἀτόμων δόγμα*) which is ascribed by Strabo (p. 645 ed. Müll.) to a Sidonian philosopher Mochus, who lived *πρὸ τῶν Τρωικῶν χρόνων*; his works, together with those of Theodotus and Hypsicrates, are said to have been translated into Greek by a certain Laetus (*Fr. Hist. Gr.* iv 437). Mochus, along with Hestaeus and the Egyptian Hieronymus, *οἱ τὰ Φοινικικὰ συνταξάμενοι*, is mentioned by Jos. *Ant.* i 3 9. Another cosmogony is described by Philo of Byblus (temp. Hadrian), who claims to have derived his traditions from an ancient sage Sanchuniathon (see pp. 100. 104 *n.* 2 ref.). Philo probably drew his material from various sources, and dignified it with an ancient name; see Baudissin *Stud. z. semit. Religionsgesch.* i 1–46. Native histories written by Phoenicians are cited by Josephus: (*a*) the chronicles of Tyre transl. by Menander of Ephesus (*Fr. Hist. Gr.* iv 445 ff.) *ὁ μεταφράσας ἀπὸ τῆς Φοινίκων διαλέκτου εἰς τὴν Ἑλληνικὴν φωνήν* *Ant.* viii 5 3. ix 14 2, *c. Ap.* i 18; (*b*) a list of kings from Nebuchadnezzar to Cyrus, for which he quotes *τὰς τῶν Φοινίκων ἀναγραφάς* *c. Ap.* i 21; (*c*) for the siege of Tyre by Nebuch. he gives as his authority Philostratos *ἐν ταῖς Ἰνδικαῖς αὐτοῦ καὶ Φοινικικαῖς ἱστορίαις* *Ant.* x 11 1, *c. Ap.* i 20; (*d*) for the history of Ḥiram i he refers to the Phoen. narrative of Dios (*Fr. Hist. Gr.* iv 397 ff.) *ἐν ταῖς περὶ Φοινίκων ἱστορίαις* *c. Ap.* i 17, *Ant.* viii 5 3. The sources (*b*) and (*d*) are doubtless dependent upon Menander; it is probable that Jos. derived all these extracts from the work of Alexander Polyhistor (*Fr. Hist. Gr.* iii 206 ff.). See further Meyer *Ency. Bibl.* 375^1 ff.

all the greater value; and when they are brought into relation with the languages of the Old Testament their interest is increased. Thus comparing Phoenician with Hebrew we notice at once that the resemblance is exceedingly close, both in grammatical forms and in vocabulary; in some respects Phoenician has preserved older features (e.g. the fem. in ת, the absence of vowel-letters), others are later (e.g. יתן = נתן, אלן *God*), others again are peculiar to this dialect (e.g. the 3 mas. suff. in י, א, נם, the accus. sign אית, the rel. אש, the Hif. in י), many words poetic or rare in Hebrew are common in Phoenician (see p. 23); these phenomena point to the conclusion that Phoenician and Hebrew are independent offshoots of a common ancestor, which can be none other than the ancient Canaanite, of which a few words have survived in the Canaanite glosses (15th cent. B.C.) to the Tell-el-Amarna letters[1]. It must be remembered, however, that the material is insufficient for a complete comparison[2]; and further, with the exception of 11, almost all the Phoenician inscriptions are subsequent to the 6th cent. B.C., the majority belong to the 4th cent. and later, by which time the language had probably undergone a certain amount of decay. The evidence of the Aramaic inscriptions is specially valuable because it proves the wide extent to which Aramaic was used in the Assyrian, Babylonian, and Persian empires (cf. Is. 36 11), and because it exhibits the language at an earlier stage than the literary dialects. In the Nabataean and Palmyrene inscriptions we find a dialect which is nearly related to the Western or Palestinian Aramaic of the Old Testament and of the Targums of Onkelos and Jonathan. The dates of the Old Testament Aramaic cannot in all cases be determined; parts of Ezra are probably as early as the 4th cent. B.C., Daniel was written in the 2nd cent. B.C.; the inscriptions prove that this particular type of Aramaic was used in the countries bordering upon Palestine down to the 3rd cent. A.D.[3]

[1] The words are given in the vocabulary of Winckler's edition; see also *KAT*[3] 652 f.

[2] The fullest comparison is still that of Stade, Erneute Prüfung des zwischen dem Phönicischen u. Hebräischen bestehenden Verwandtschaftsgrades in *Morg. Forsch.* (1875) 169–232.

[3] Driver *Introduction*[6] 502 ff.

All the inscriptions here collected are written in varieties of the same alphabet, commonly called the Phoenician, the archetype of Greek and ultimately of all Western writing[1]. At the earliest stage known to us the characters are very much alike, both in the Canaanite and in the Aramaic groups; in the subsequent stages each followed a process of modification on diverging lines. Thus Phoenician, after leaving the mother-country, is seen to be acquiring a more cursive and flowing style on the stones from Cyprus and Attica; the tendency becomes more strongly marked at the Punic stage; until in Neo-Punic the writing, and the language too, reached their most degenerate form and went no further, as though the possibilities of both were exhausted. The modifications of the old Hebrew writing down to the 5th or 4th cents. B.C. cannot, for lack of material, be traced in much detail; so far as we know there seems to have been little change of any marked kind. The only Hebrew inscription of considerable length earlier than the Exile is the one found at Siloam (**2**); besides this, specimens of the old Hebrew writing are furnished only by the few words engraved upon seals (**150** 6–8) and stamped upon fragments of pottery[2]. Generations after the old Hebrew writing had fallen out of use it was revived, for political reasons, in characters which closely resemble those of the Siloam inscription and the legends on seals and pottery, upon the Jewish coins (**149** C). The ancient writing was retained by the Samaritans when the Jews in general had taken to the Aramaic letters, and in an elaborated form the Samaritans use it still. The process by which the archaic Hebrew arrived at the modern square character is to be

[1] The various speculations on the origin of the Phoen. alphabet are summarized by Thatcher, art. Phoenicia *DB* iii.

[2] The recent excavations at Tell Zakariyâ and Tell eṣ-Ṣâfi, SW. of Jerusalem, conducted by Messrs. Bliss and Macalister, have produced some interesting jar-handles stamped with למלך חברן, למלך שוכה, למלך [מר?]שת; between the words is the figure of a winged scarab. These were factory-marks; למלך *belonging to the king* probably signifies that the vessel came from the royal potteries, or perhaps that it came up to the official standard of capacity; חברן &c. that it was made at Ḥebron, Sokoh &c. The other potsherds are marked with what are probably private seals, e.g. לעזר חגי, מעץ . . צפניא; a seal is engraved לרמתי יהוכל; the names are all written in two lines. See *PEFQS* 1899 and 1900; Cl.-Gan. *Rec.* iv § 1; Lidzb. *Eph.* i 54 ff. 178 ff.

traced in the development, not of the Hebrew, but of the Aramaic alphabet; and the reason is that the latter was adopted by the Jews after the Exile along with the use of the Aramaic language. The stages in this development may be followed in the Tables of the Aramaic Alphabets, Plates xiii and xiv; the most significant will be found in the Egyptian Aramaic and the Palmyrene. From this last it is but a few steps further to the square characters which appear in the Jewish inscriptions (e.g. 148 A and B), and in which the MSS. of the Old Testament are written[1].

Besides their value as specimens of language and writing, the North-Semitic inscriptions possess considerable importance for the historian. With the exception of the Moabite Stone, the Zenjirli inscriptions, and two or three others, their importance is rather incidental than primary; a few of them are dedicated to or by historical personages, a great many are dated by the reigns of kings or the eras of cities, and thus enable us to piece history together. The inscriptions cover a long period, more than a thousand years, from the 9th cent. B.C. to the 3rd cent. A.D.; and in the course of it the history which they record is not, as a rule, the history of great events or of striking figures in the drama, but the history of every-day life, its business, its honours, its religion, its commemoration of the dead. These monuments of ancient civilization have a very human interest which gives to the study of them an unexpected and refreshing zest. But when we turn to them for information on such subjects as the institutions or organizations of public life we are apt to be disappointed. For example, the little that can be gathered from the inscriptions as to the constitution of Carthage is put together on pp. 115 f., but it adds practically nothing to what we learn from Greek and Latin writers. The North-Semitic races possessed none of that genius for civic order, or for administration on a large scale, which made the Athenians so careful to inscribe their public documents 'on a pillar of stone,' and the Romans to plant the memorials of their government in every part of the empire. It is only when these races

[1] For details see Index vi under Letters, Driver *Samuel* ix–xxix, Lidzbarski *Eph.* i 109 ff. and *Jewish Encycl.*, art. Alphabet.

come under the influence of Greek and Roman institutions that we are able to glean a little about their public life. The inscriptions reveal the fact that Palmyra was organized on the model of a Greek municipality; the great Tariff was dictated by Roman common-sense and love of order; to some extent Hellenic ideas of administration had penetrated into the Nabataean kingdom, for we hear of strategoi, eparchs, and chiliarchs; the Neo-Punic colonies in N. Africa had borrowed, as it seems, some institutions of municipal life from their Roman over-lords.

Lastly, the inscriptions have much to tell us about the religious customs and ideas of the people who wrote them. Some of these ideas are the common property of Semitic religion; a good many of them, especially those connected with the relation of the god to his worshippers, and with burial and the condition of the dead, illustrate in an interesting way the ideas of the Old Testament. But again it must not be forgotten that most of the monuments belong to a period not of religious freshness and simplicity but of religious decline. The less attractive features of North-Semitic religion may be gathered from Greek and Latin authors; the inscriptions tell us little of them; but a broad comparison between this and the religion of the Old Testament shows clearly enough the depths and heights which it was possible for different peoples to reach who were bound closely together by race, by neighbourhood, and by a considerable stock of common ideas. It is the difference which polytheism and monotheism work out in their results. Nevertheless in the later periods we can trace, however faintly, something like a reaction from the prevailing polytheism in the worship of Ba'al of Heaven among the Phoenicians, and of the unnamed god 'whose name is blessed for ever' among the Aramaeans of Palmyra (pp. 45, 296 ff.); and out of the common stock of religious ideas there were some which did not altogether lie outside of the scheme of Divine revelation, and were capable of being adopted into the higher faith.

LIST OF PRINCIPAL ABBREVIATIONS

Altor. Forsch.	=Winckler *Altorientalische Forschungen.*
BAram.	=Biblical Aramaic.
CIA	=*Corpus Inscriptionum Atticarum.*
CIG	=*Corpus Inscriptionum Graecarum.*
CIL	=*Corpus Inscriptionum Latinarum.*
CIS	=*Corpus Inscriptionum Semiticarum.*
Cl.-Gan. *Ét.*	=Clermont-Ganneau *Études d'archéologie orientale.*
Cl.-Gan. *Rec.*	=Clermont-Ganneau *Recueil d'archéologie orientale.*
COT	=Schrader *Cuneiform Inscriptions and the O.T.*
Dalman *Gr.*	=Dalman *Gram. des Jüdisch-Palästinischen Aramäisch.*
DB	=Hastings' *Dictionary of the Bible.*
Del. *Assyr. HWB*	=Delitzsch *Assyrisches Handwörterbuch.*
Ency. Bibl.	=*Encyclopaedia Biblica.*
Eut.	=Euting *Nabatäische Inschriften.*
Eut. *Carth.*	=Euting *Sammlung der carthagischen Inschriften.*
Eut. *Sin.*	=Euting *Sinaitische Inschriften.*
Fr. Hist. Gr.	=Müller *Fragmenta Historicorum Graecorum.*
Gesenius, or Ges.-Kautzsch	=Gesenius-Kautzsch *Hebrew Grammar*, transl. by A. E. Cowley.
JA	=*Journal Asiatique.*
KAT^{3}	=*Die Keilinschriften und das Alte Testament*^{3}.
KB	=*Keilinschriftliche Bibliothek.*
König *Lehrgeb.*	=König *Lehrgebäude der Hebr. Sprache.*
König *Syntax*	=König *Syntax der Hebr. Sprache.*
Lidzb.	=Lidzbarski *Handbuch der Nordsemitischen Epigraphik.*
Lidzb. *Eph.* i	=Lidzbarski *Ephemeris für Semitische Epigraphik* i.
M. or Michel	=Michel *Recueil d'Inscriptions Grecques.*
Morg. Forsch.	=*Morgenländische Forschungen.*
NHWB	=Levy *Neuhebräisches u. Chaldäisches Wörterbuch.*
NPun.	=Neo-Punic.
PA. or *Pers. Ach.*	=Babelon *Les Perses Achéménides.*
PEFQS	=*Palestine Exploration Fund Quarterly Statement.*

RB	=*Revue Biblique.*
Rép.	=*Répertoire d'Épigraphie Sémitique.*
RS	=Babelon *Rois de Syrie.*
SBBA	=*Sitzungsberichte der Berliner Akademie.*
Schröder	=Schröder *Die Phönizische Sprache.*
Spic. Syr.	=Cureton *Spicilegium Syriacum.*
Vog.	=de Vogüé *La Syrie Centrale.*
Wadd.	=Waddington *Inscriptions Grecques et Latines de la Syrie.*
ZA	=*Zeitschrift für Assyriologie.*
ZATW	=*Zeitschrift für die alt-test. Wissenschaft.*
ZDMG	=*Zeitschrift der Deutschen Morgenländischen Gesellschaft.*
ZDPV	=*Zeitschrift des Deutschen Palästina-Vereins.*

On the analogy of the familiar abbreviations י׳ and וגו׳, the stroke ׳ is used to mark shortened forms; thus ח׳ denotes a word beginning with ח; ׳ח a word ending in ח.

NORTH SEMITIC INSCRIPTIONS

MOABITE

1. **The Moabite Stone.** Circ. 850 B.C. Louvre.

1 אנך·משע·בן·כמש..·מלך·מאב·הד

2 יבני | אבי·מלך·על·מאב·שלשן·שת·ואנך·מלכ....

3 תי·אחר·אבי | ואעש·הבמת·זאת·לכמש·בקרחה | בנ..[י]

4 שע·כי·השעני·מכל·ה..לכן·וכי·הראני·בכל·שנאי | עמר

5 י·מלך·ישראל·ויענו·את·מאב·ימן·רבן·כי·יאנף·כמש·באר

6 צה | ויחלפה·בנה·ויאמר·גם·הא·אענו·את·מאב | בימי·אמר·....

7 וארא·בה·ובבתה | וישראל·אבד·אבד·עלם·וירש·עמרי·את·[אר]

8 ץ·מהדבא | וישב·בה·ימה·וחצי·ימי·בנה·ארבען·שת·ויש

9 בה·כמש·בימי | ואבן·את·בעלמען·ואעש·בה·האשוח·ואב[ן]

10 את·קריתן | ואש·גד·ישב·בארץ·עטרת·מעלם·ויבן·לה·מלך·י

11 שראל·את·עטרת | ואלתחם·בקר·ואחזה | ואהרג·את·כל·העם·.

12 הקר·רית·לכמש·ולמאב | ואשב·משם·את·אראל·דודה·וא[ס]

13 חבה·לפני·כמש·בקרית | ואשב·בה·את·אש·שרן·ואת·א[ש]

14 מחרת | ויאמר·לי·כמש·לך·אחז·את·נבה·על·ישראל | וא

15 הלך·בללה·ואלתחם·בה·מבקע·השחרת·עד·הצהרם | ואח

16 זה·ואהרג·כל·.·שבעת·אלפ.·ג[ב]רן·ו..ן | וגברת·ו..

17 ת·ורחמת | כי·לעשתר·כמש·החרמתה | ואקח·משם·א..

18 לי·יהוה·ואסחב·הם·לפני·כמש | ומלך·ישראל·בנה·את

19 יהץ·וישב·בה·בהלתחמה·בי | ויגרשה·כמש·מפני·[ו]

20 אקח·ממאב·מאתן·אש·כל·רשה | ואשאה·ביהץ·ואחזה·

21 לספת·על·דיבן | אנך·בנתי·קרחה·חמת·היערן·וחמת

22 העפל | ואנך·בנתי·שעריה·ואנך·בנתי·מגדלתה | וא

23 נך·בנתי·בת·מלך·ואנך·עשתי·כלאי·האשו[ח·לם]ין בקר[בֿ]

24 הֿקר | ובר·אן·בקרב·הקר·בקרחה·ואמר·לכל·העם·עשו·לֿ

25 כם·אש·בר·בביתה | ואנך·כרתי·המכרתת·לקרחה·באסֿר

26 יֿ ישראל | אנך·בנתי·ערער·ואנך·עשתי·המסלת·בארנן.

27 אנך·בנתי·בת·במת·כי·הרס·הא | אנך·בנתי·בצר·כי·עיֿן·

28 ....ש·דיבן·חמשן·כי·כל·דיבן·משמעת | ואנך·מלכֿ

29 ת....מאת·בקרן·אשר·יספתי·על·הארץ | ואנך·בנתֿ

30 י··[מהד]בֿא·ובת·דבלתן | ובתֿ·בעלמען·ואשא·שם·את·נֿ..

31 ....צאן·הארץ | וחורנן·ישב.בה·ב..וקֿ..אשֿ.

32 ....אמר·לי·כמש·רד·הלתחם·בחורנן | וארדֿ·...

33 ....בה·כמש·בימי·ועל.דה·משם·עש...

34 ....שתֿ·שרק | ואנ..

I am Mesha', son of Kemosh- . . kịng of Moab, the Dai[2]bonite. My father was king over Moab thirty years, and I became ki[3]ng after my father. And I made this high-place for Kemosh in QRḤH, with . . . [sal]v[4]ation, because he saved me from all the . . . . . and because he made me see my desire upon all them that hated me.

'Om[5]ri, king of Israel, he afflicted Moab many days, because Kemosh was angry with his la[6]nd. And his son succeeded him; and he too said, I will afflict Moab. In my days he said . . . . [7] and I saw my desire upon him and upon his house, and Israel perished utterly for ever.

And 'Omri took possession of the [lan][8]d of Mehēdeba; and he dwelt in it, his days and half his sons' days, forty years; but Kemosh resto[9]red it in my days.

And I built Ba'al-me'on, and I made therein the reservoir (?); and I buil[t] [10] Qiryathān.

And the men of Gad had dwelt in the land of 'Aṭāroth from of old; and the king of [11] Israel built 'Aṭāroth for himself. And I fought against the city and took it. And I slew all the people . [12] the city, a gazingstock unto Kemosh and unto Moab. And I brought thence the altar-hearth of Daudoh (?), and I dr[ag][13]ged it before Kemosh in Qeriyyoth. And I caused the men of ŠRN to dwell therein, and the m[en] [14] of MḤRTH.

And Kemosh said to me, Go take Nebo against Israel. And I [15] went by night and fought against it from the break of dawn till the noontide, and I [16] took it and slew all. seven thousand m[en] and . . and women and . . [17]. and damsels, for I had devoted it to 'Ashtar-kemosh. And I took thence the . . [18]. of Yahweh, and I dragged them before Kemosh.

And the king of Israel had built [19] Yahaṣ, and dwelt therein while he fought against me. But Kemosh drove him out before me. [20] I took of Moab two hundred men, all the chiefs thereof; and I led them against Yahaṣ, and took it, [21] to add it to Daibon.

I built QRḤH, the wall of Ye'arim, and the wall [22] of the Mound; and I built the gates thereof, and I built the towers thereof; and I [23] built the king's house; and I made the sluices (?) of the reserv[oir (?) for wa]ter in the mid[st] [24] of the city. And there was no cistern in the midst of the city, in QRḤH; and I said to all the people, Make you [25] each a cistern in his house. And I cut the cutting for QRḤH with the help of [26] prisoners of Israel.

I built 'Aro'er, and I made the highway by the Arnon. [27] I built Beth-bamoth, for it was overthrown. I built Beṣer, for it was in ruins . . . [28] . . of Daibon were fifty, for all Daibon was obedient. And I became [29] king . . . . a hundred, in the cities which I added to the land. And I built [30] . . [Mehēde]ba and Beth-diblathān. And as

for (?) Beth-ba'al-me'on, I led there the ...31 ....
sheep of the land.
And as for Ḥauronān, there dwelt therein ... and 32
.... Kemosh said to me, Go down, fight against
Ḥauronān; and I went down, 33 ..../................
Kemosh in my days, and ..... from there 34
.... and I ..

The stone was discovered at Dîbân (ll. 1 f. and O.T. דיבן) in 1868. While the negotiations for its removal were going on, it was broken up by the Bedouin of the place, but not before a squeeze of the inscription had been secured while it was still intact. Two large fragments and eighteen small ones were recovered; the missing portions have been reconstructed from the original squeeze; so that the inscription can now be read in a tolerably complete text[1].

It commemorates the successful efforts made by Mesha', king of Moab, to throw off the yoke of Israel. The Moabites had been reduced to subjection by David (2 S. 8 2), but how long they remained in that state is not told. Probably in the time of Jeroboam i, or soon after, they began to revolt; for the inscription implies that some measure of independence had been gained when it states that "'Omri oppressed Moab many days' (l. 5), which no doubt means that he found it necessary to put down a rebellion. He succeeded in capturing Mēdeba and its vicinity (l. 7 f.); 'the king of Israel' also fortified 'Aṭāroth, the ancient dwelling-place of the families of Gad (l. 10 f.); Nebo and Yahaṣ became Israelite strongholds (ll. 14. 18 f.). It is interesting to find that there was a sanctuary of Yahweh at Nebo (l. 17 f.), where the Israelites must have established themselves in some numbers. 'Omri's powerful arm, however, did not reach so far as the Arnon, for the more southern cities, Dibon, 'Aro'er, Qeriyyoth, remained in the possession of Moab; but how effectually the land was subdued may be judged from the heavy tribute which 'Omri's successor, Ahab, exacted from king Mesha' (2 K. 3 4). Then, in the latter years of Ahab's reign, perhaps at the moment when he was engaged in the war against Syria (1 K. 22), Mesha' revolted. According to 2 K. 1 1. 3 5 the revolt occurred after the death of Ahab; but the inscription, with the authority of a contemporary document, corrects

[1] A recent attempt to trace the missing fragments is vividly described by Gautier, *Autour de la Mer Morte*, Genève (1901) 93–98. The text given above is based upon that of Lidzbarski *Nordsem. Epigr.* 415 f., corrected by his later investigations in *Ephemeris Sem. Epigr.* i (1900) 1–10.

this detail of the history. The king of Moab recovered the cities occupied by Israel, and strengthened various weak spots in his territory. The towns mentioned in the inscription were situated, with the exception of Ḥauronān, in the debatable land N. of the Arnon, which was nominally assigned to Reuben and Gad (Num. **32** 34–38. Josh. **13** 15–28); but Mesha''s revolt seems to have produced a durable settlement, and for the future these towns belonged to the kingdom of Moab (Am. **2** 2. Is. **15** 2 ff. Jer. **48** 1 ff. Eze. **25** 9). The inscription appears to be silent about the invasion of the allied kings recorded in 2 K. **3**, unless there is an allusion to it in l. 4. Taking the inscription to be a comprehensive summary of Mesha''s reign, as it was probably intended, we must suppose that the king of Moab ignores his reverses (2 K. **3** 24–27), just as the Hebrew history omits to mention the losses of Israel (Bennett *DB* iii 411, art. Moab).

The language of Moab, as the inscription proves, was only a dialect of Hebrew (cf. Dt. **2** 11). Such characteristic idioms as the impf. with waw conv., the inf. abs. with the fin. verb (used similarly, however, in Arabic and Syriac) אבד אבד l. 7, the use of אשר for the relative, ראה ב׳, the words הושע *save*, ירש *take in possession*, גרש *drive out*, הרג *slay*, החרים *ban*, ואעש (apoc. form), לפני, בקרב, show that Moabite was more closely akin to Hebrew than to any other Semitic tongue. The forms of the proper names point in the same direction. The following differences may be noted: הבמת זאת (Hebr. הזאת), the fem. sing. ending ת and the dual and plural ending ן (sometimes in the O.T.), שת for שנה, the conj. הלתחם (Arab. conj. viii), קיר *city*, אחז (Hebr. לכד) *take* a city, the use *in prose* of חלף *succeed* l. 6, בקע *break of dawn* l. 15, גברן and גברת l. 16 for אנשים and נשים, רחמת *damsels* l. 17. These differences are merely dialectical; some of them are related to Phoenician or Canaanite on the one side, and to Arabic[1], the language of Moab's neighbours in Edom, on the other. The words אשוח l. 9, רית l. 12, מכרת l. 25, do not occur in the O.T. The inscription is the classical example of the archaic form of Hebr. writing (cf. **2**). The scriptio defectiva is the rule, e. g. הא is used for the 3rd sing. mas. pronoun, though consonants are employed for final vowels, e. g. אבי, לפני, בי, בה, and in דיבן, דיבני; the suffix of the 3rd sing. mas. is ה׳ for ו׳; the words are divided and separated by dots as in the ancient inscriptions **2**. **61–63** (old Aram.), but also **13** and **16** (Phoen.). In general style the inscription is a real piece of literature, and indicates that Moab in the ninth cent. B.C. was not behind Israel

[1] See notes on אלתחם ll. 11. 19; מאתן l. 20; מהדבא l. 8 (?); אחז, קר l. 11; חלף l. 6.

in civilization. Finally, we have here clear evidence that not merely the language, but also the ideas, of the two nations had much in common. The religion of Kemosh was evidently very like the popular religion of Yahweh; and the manner in which the national god of Moab was regarded and spoken of finds remarkable parallels in expressions used of Yahweh in the O.T.

Among recent commentaries on the Moabite Stone the following are the most important: Bennett, art. Moab, Hastings' *Dict. of the Bible* (1900); Lidzbarski *Ephemeris* i (1900); Halévy *Rev. Sém.* (1900), see Lidzb. *Eph.* i 145; Lagrange *Rev. Bibl.* x (1901); Driver, art. Mesha, *Ency. Bibl.* (1902).

Line 1. אנך Not pronounced אנכי as in Hebr., for elsewhere in the inscr. י is written where the final vowel was sounded. In Phoen. the 1st pers. pron. is אנךְ 8 1 *n.*, in Canaanite *anuki* (Tell-el-Am. 180 66. 69), in Assyr. *anâku*, in old Aram. אנך 61 1 and אנכי 62 19. In later Aram., Arab., Eth. the form is אנא, *'ana.* משע i. e. *deliverance*, from ישע, in 2 K. 3 4 מֵישַׁע, LXX Μωσά; the latter form implies a derivative from the Hif. stem like הוֹשַׁע, מוֹשָׁעוֹת Ps. 68 21. The pronunciation, therefore, may have been either *Mesha'* or *Mosha'*. There is room for only two letters after 'כמש, so כמשמלך is not correct. Clermont-Ganneau reads כמשנר; Lidzbarski, after a fresh examination of the stone, suggests כמשכן, cf. כְּנַיָהוּ, יְכָנְיָהוּ, *Eph.* i 3 f. See l. 3 *n.* הדיבני The name דיבן ll. 21. 28 was probably pronounced *Daibon* rather than *Dibon* (O.T. דִּיבֹן, LXX Δαιβών), for the latter would not be written with the vowel letter; cf. חורנן l. 31 f. prob. *Ḥauronān*, דודה l. 12 prob. *Daudoh*. Nöldeke, however, thinks that the vowel was *ē*, *Inschr. Kön. Mesa* (1870) 33; cf. ביתה l. 25, which, as בתה l. 7 shows, could not have sounded *baitho*. But in דיבן the י is invariably written, and this is rather in favour of the former view. Dibon, Is. 15 2. Jer. 48 18. 22 &c., now *Dībān* (ديبان)[1], lay a little to the N. of the Arnon; Buhl *Geogr. alt. Paläst.* 268.

L. 2. שלשן שת Hebr. שְׁלֹשִׁים שָׁנָה; שת is therefore sing., see 6 1 *n.*, and cf. l. 8. The plur. ending ן in the O.T. (twenty-five or twenty-six times, fifteen times in Job) is mostly dialectical or late; in Aram. it is normal, e. g. 68 9. 13 מלכן רברבן.

L. 3. הבמת זאת Cf. Phoen. האדם הא 8 15. 4 6 &c., and see add. note ii p. 26. The fem. sing. ends in *ath*, as in Phoen. and occasionally in the O.T.; see add. note i p. 25. With the expression ואעש הבמת

[1] Modern forms from Kampffmeyer *ZDPV* xv–xvi (1892–3).

cf. 2 Ch. 21 11 עשה במות; a sanctuary or altar is prob. intended, rather than a literal 'high-place.' Illustrate from 1 K. 11 7. Is. 15 2. 16 12. Jer. 48 35. לכמש Kemosh was the national god of the Moabites (Num. 21 29. 1 K. 11 7. 33. Jer. 48 46 &c.), occupying among them much the same position as Yahweh among the Israelites. The name is found in compounds, e.g. l. 1 כמש[..]; *Kemosh-nadab, king of Moab*, *KB* ii 90 (=Schrader *COT* 288); כמשיחי, כמשצדק on Moab. seals, Lidzb. *Eph.* i 136 ff. The identification of Kemosh with Ares is based upon an error of Eusebius, *Onom.* 228 66 ff. ed. Lagarde. Other deities worshipped by the Moabites were עשתר כמש l. 17; בעל מען l. 30, בעל פער Num. 25 1–3, local cults of Ba'al (? of Kemosh); and possibly נבה l. 14 *n.* קרחה ll. 21. 24 f. The stone is expressly associated with the sanctuary at QRḤH ('this high-place to K. at QRḤH'), but it was found at Dibon, evidently *in situ*. We may suppose, therefore, that QRḤH was the name of a place *in the district of* Dibon (Nordlander), see l. 21 *n.* Among the Moabites Dibon may have had this extended sense, although in the O.T. it seems to be always the name of a town. QRḤH can hardly have been the acropolis of Dibon (Cl.-Gan. &c.), for this is inconsistent with the terms of ll. 21 ff. Another explanation is suggested by Lagrange, *Rev. Bibl.* x 527 f. He takes לכמש בקרחה closely together, *Kemosh-at-QRḤH*, like לבעשמם באינצם 39 1. 24 2 *n.* This expression is used of the cult of a deity transplanted from one place to another, especially to a foreign land; it would be unnatural in Moab, where Kemosh was the chief god of the whole country[1]. According to Sayce קרחה is the *Karhu* mentioned in the Karnak list of the conquests of Ramses ii, *Patr. Pal.* 237 cf. 21. The pronunciation of the word is not certain; it was either קְרָחָה or perhaps rather קָרְחֹה like יְרֵחוֹ, with the ending ־ֹה as in שִׁלֹה, גִּלֹה, and prob. דודה l. 12; Driver *Samuel* xc. בנ.. [י] Lidzb. detects traces of נ and ס, and reads בנס[ך י]שע *with a drink-offering of deliverance*; for ב cf. 2 Ch. 29 35 בנסכים. Lev. 16 3; illustrate from Ps. 116 13. Lagrange proposes בנם ישע cf. Ex. 17 15; other suggestions are

[1] Lagrange identifies קרחה with קיר חרש, קיר חרשת Is. 16 7. 11. Jer. 48 31. 36. 2 K. 3 25; regarding the latter as a corrupt form of קיר חדשה 'New town' LXX Is. 16 7. 11 (so Cheyne *Ency. Bibl.* col. 2676), and קרחה as its ancient name. But the reading of the LXX in Jer. 48 (LXX 31) 31 κειράδας B, κιδάρας A + αὐχμοῦ does not imply an original אנשי קרחה; it is merely a transliteration of קיר חרש (for קיר חרש). Qir-ḥareseth is prob. the same as Qir-Moab = the modern Kerak (Targ. on Is. and Jer. loc. cit.). Nöld. has shown that there is no etymological connexion between קרחה and Kerak, *Inschr. Kön. Mesa* 8 f. See *Expos. Times* xiii (1902) 186 f.

בםשע משע *for the deliverance of Mesha'*, Smend u. Socin *Inschr. Kön. Mesa* (1886) 17; בםת ישע *a high-place of deliverance*, Driver l. c.

L. 4. ח . לכן Perhaps השלכן (Cl.-Gan., Nöld., Lidzb.), i.e. (?) הַשָּׁלְכִן *those who attack* (?), *assailants*, lit. *cast themselves*. Neither the form (שָׁלֵךְ like גַּנָּב) nor the meaning occurs in Hebr., which uses only the Hif. and Hof. of שלך. In Arab. سلك i = *to put in*, *make to enter*, possibly in Moab. the vb. = *impel*, *assail*. The reading המלכן is less probable. הראני בכל שנאי Cf. l. 7. Ps. 59 11. 118 7 &c.

L. 5. ויענו i.e. וַיְעַנּוּ, the 3rd rad. of the ל״ו (Hebr. ל״ה) verb being retained, as in אענו l. 6. If מלך ישראל = *king of Israel* as elsewhere, ויענו must be the impf. with waw conv. introducing the predicate, *'Omri . . . he oppressed*, a very harsh construction here; see Gesenius § 111 *h*; Driver *Tenses* § 127 *a*. The rendering *was king over I.* is more suitable, although this requires על after מָלַךְ (l. 2). Perhaps the prep. was omitted by accident. יאנף Impf. of continuance in the past. The yodh seems certain (Lidzb.). For אנף cf. 1 K. 8 46 (Qal). 2 K. 17 18 (Hithp.). בארצה Cf. Num. 21 29. Jer. 48 46 מאב..עם כמוש. The ancient ה of the suff., *ahu-au-ô* Y, is preserved in Moabite; contrast Y in the Siloam inscr. 2 2–4. The form ה׳ is found in the O.T., e.g. אָהֳלֹה Gen. 9 21 &c.; Driver *Sam.* xxxv.

L. 6. ויחלפה i.e. וַיַּחְלְפֹה (Nöld.), or less probably וַיַּחְלְפֵהוּ in accordance with Hebr. usage; and similarly elsewhere in the inscr. ויחלפה = *succeeded him*; so خلف in Arab. In Hebr. the Hif. = *cause to succeed*, *substitute*, Is. 9 9. ויאמר גם הא Cf. Gen. 27 31. 1 S. 19 20–24. For הא see 3 9 *n*. After אמר there are traces of a letter, possibly ם (Lidzb.), doubtfully כ; the reading ככה or כדבר is thus very questionable.

L. 7. אבד אבד עלם i.e. אָבֹד אָבַד עֹלָם, עלם for לעלם as in poetry, e.g. Ps. 89 2. 3. 38; or אָבַד אָבַד עֹלָם, cf. Jer. 51 39 וישנו שנת עולם (Driver). וירש Either וַיִּרַשׁ or וְיָרַשׁ. The context requires a plupf. sense, for which ועמרי ירש would be the normal expression (l. 18).

L. 8. מהדבא i.e. מְהֵדְבָא (Nöld.), in the O.T. מֵידְבָא, or מְהֹדְבָא (Cl.-Gan. *Stèle de Dhiban* (1877) 55), as in the modern name مادبا; so König *Lehrgeb.* ii 345, explaining the form by the Arab. dialectical form *mâhun* = *mâ'un* 'water'[1]. Medeba (Num. 21 30. Josh. 13 9.

[1] The ה in מהדבא and in גבה l. 14 used to denote *ê* and *ô*, according to Hommel, marks an affinity with the Minaean dialect of Arabic known from the el-Öla inscrr. (NW. Arabia); *Anc. Hebr. Trad.* 276. The alleged affinity between Moabite and Minaean must be received with caution; at the same time it is natural that the

Is. 15 2 &c.) was E. of the N. end of the Dead Sea. וישב The subj., though grammatically 'Omri, must really be Israel. ימה The reading seems certain; יָמֵהּ for יָמֵיהּ *yamaih(u)* = יָמָיו *his days*. For the form with *u* cf. the Hebr. יָדֵיהוּ Hab. 3 10. גִּבֹּרֵיהוּ Nah. 2 4. עֵינֵיהוּ Job 24 23, and the Syr. ܘ̈ܗܝ', where the original *h* of the suff. is written but not sounded. For the plur. form without yodh cf. רשה l. 20. מגרלתה l. 22, contrast שעריה l. 22. בנה Prob. is also plur., *his sons* (see below); although בנה l. 6 is sing.

L. 9. בה To be completed by restoring וישב at the end of l. 8, i.e. וַיֵּשֶׁבָהּ (Nöld.). Ll. 6–9 are important for the historical setting of the inscr., although the exact bearing of some details is obscure. ויאמר גם הא וג' l. 6 points to a fresh attempt made by Ahab to assert his authority in Moab; this was prob. the immediate cause of Mesha''s revolt. וארא בה ובבתה l. 7 indicates that the revolt was successful both against Ahab (בה) and his dynasty (בתה, cf. בית אחאב 2 K. 8 18. 9 7 ff. 10 11. Mic. 6 16 &c.). וישראל אבד אבד עלם l. 7 records the final overthrow of Israel's power in Moab, marked, as we may infer from 2 K. 3 27, by the futile conclusion of Joram's expedition[1], or by the extinction of the house of 'Omri. Then in ll. 7–9 the inscr. goes back to the first stage of the revolt. This began with the recovery of Mehēdeba (l. 8 end), which had been occupied by 'Omri: 'and he dwelt in it his days and half the days of his sons, forty years.' 'Omri's reign, according to 1 K. 16 23, lasted 18 years, Ahab's 22 (1 K. 16 29), Ahaziah's 2 (1 K. 22 52), Joram's 12 (2 K. 3 1). Thus 'Omri's 'days' were 18, and 'half the days of his sons' were 18, making a total of 36, or 'forty years' in round numbers. 'Half the days' of 'Omri's sons brings us, strictly speaking, to the 18th year of Ahab; at any rate it was in the closing years of Ahab's reign, and not after his death (2 K. 1 1. 3 5), that Mesha' began his struggle for independence. But the biblical record so far agrees with the inscr., inasmuch as the Moabite rebellion continued after Ahab's death, during the reigns of his two successors (ובבתה l. 7). This second stage of the rebellion is recorded in ll. 10 ff.; 'Aṭāroth, Nebo, Yahaṣ were recovered, until Israel was finally driven out. At the close of his 18 years' struggle, Mesha' was able to commemorate his victories, and the efforts which

language of Moab should betray the influence of its Arabic-speaking neighbours. See further König *Hebr. u. Sem.* 82.

[1] 2 K. 3 27[b] seems intentionally to cast a veil over the abrupt retirement of the allies. It may have been due to superstitious dread of the god of the land after the sacrifice of Mesha''s son, or perhaps to an unexpected invasion of the Syrians. See Lagrange *Rev. Bibl.* x 538–545.

he made for the future security of his kingdom, on a triumphal inscription. The stone, be it noted, was set up in קרחה l. 3; but קרחה was not fortified till Moab's freedom had been won, and Israelite prisoners could be employed upon the works, ll. 24–26. The foregoing account to a great extent turns on the rendering of בנה l. 8 *his sons*[1], i. e. בָּנָהּ like יָמָהּ *his days* in this line. To take בנה as a sing., *his son* i. e. Ahab, raises serious chronological difficulties. It is impossible to get 40 years out of 'Omri's 18 and the half of Ahab's 22. Wellhausen makes the attempt by discarding the dates in Kings, and lengthening the combined reigns to 60 years (*Isr. u. Jüd. Gesch.*[3] 9 f.); but to do this is to dislocate the biblical chronology, and the translation of בנה *his son* is not so certain as to demand such a violent measure[2]. בעלמען l. 30 בת בעלמען Num. 32 38. Josh. 13 17. Jer. 48 23 (בית מען). Eze. 25 9 &c. Now Mâ'în (ماعين), SW. of Mâdebâ. אשוח Prob. from √שוח *sink*, so *pit* (cf. שׁוּחָה Jer. 18 20) or *reservoir* for water, l. 23. The word prob. occurs in this sense in Sirach 50 3, where אשיח בם is to be corrected to אשוח כים λάκκος ὡσεὶ θαλάσσης cod. A. See *Wisdom of Ben Sira*, Cambr. (1899) 63.

L. 10. קריתן=Hebr. קִרְיָתַיִם Gen. 14 5. Jer. 48 1 &c., now Qurêyât (قريات), S. of 'Aṭṭârûs. For the form cf. דבלתן l. 30=דבלתים, חורנן l. 31 f.=חורנים. These names are prob. not in the dual—it is difficult to see what significance the dual could have—but in the sing., with the sing. termination ־ָן, ־ָם, called by Barth a 'local ending' (*Nominalb.* 319 *n.* 5); cf. דֹּתָן 2 K. 6 13. קַרְתָּן Josh. 21 32. This ending was subsequently expanded into ־ַיִם; e. g. in Hebr. יְרוּשָׁלַיִם, חוֹרֹנַיִם &c., in Aram. שָׁמְרַיִן=שָׁמְרָן, Hebr. שֹׁמְרוֹן; similarly the Moab. צהרם= Hebr. צָהֳרַיִם. If these forms were originally duals, it is not clear how ־ַיִם, ־ַיִן could have been contracted into ־ָם, ־ָן. It is true that the dual in Moab. ended in ן, e. g. מאתן l. 20=מאתים, but the origin of this form is quite distinct. See Gesenius-Kautzsch 256; on the other hand, König *Lehrgeb.* ii 437, Wright *Comp. Gr.* 150, regard these forms as dual, and Nöldeke points ־ֵן, קִרְיָתֵן &c. ואש עטרת . . נר Cf. Num. 32 34 JE. 'Aṭâroth=modern 'Aṭṭârûs (عطّاروس),

[1] So Nordlander *Inschr. Kön. Mesa* (1896) 30 f. See Lidzbarski *Ephemeris* i 143 f.

[2] Marti has recently suggested the rendering 'he (i. e. 'Omri) dwelt therein his days, and half of my days (i. e. יָמַי for יָמָיו) his son (dwelt therein),' *Ency. Bibl.* i col. 792. This gets over the chronological difficulty, but it involves a very harsh construction. Marti rather exaggerates the awkwardness of the passage. Winckler cuts the knot by making חצי *the half* mean *the whole*! *Altor. Forsch.* ii 401–407.

about 8 miles NNW. of Dibon. For איש גד cf. איש ישראל Jud. 20 17 &c.

L. 11. ואלתחם i.e. וָאֶלְתַּחֵם=the Arab. viii conj. اِفْتَعَلَ; see Wright *Comp. Gr.* 208 f. The stem exists also in Assyr., e.g. *iktašad* 'he plundered.' בקר In Hebr. קיר = *wall*; but the meaning *town* appears in the Moab. pr. nn. קיר מואב, קיר חרשת; cf. Arab. قَرْيَة *village*. ואחזה i.e. וָאֹחֲזֶהָ; so in Arab. اخذ=*take* a city, in Hebr. לכד. At the end of the line ם is prob. to be restored.

L. 12. רית for רְאִית (ל״י), so point רִית, cf. צְבִית, אֲנִיָּה, קְרִיּוֹת (l. 13); Stade *Lehrb.* § 192 b. Cf. Nah. 3 6 רֹאִי. Eze. 28 17 רַאֲוָה. ואשב Prob. וָאָשֵׁב from שוב, Josh. 14 7; or וָאֶשְׁבְּ from שבה. אראל Of the many interpretations proposed for this word the most suitable here is *altar-hearth*, Eze. 43 15. 16 from √ארי *burn*, Arab. أَرَى whence إِرَة *hearth*+ל[א], as in כרמל, חשמל. Here אראל is in the constr. st., and in Eze. 43 15 f. it has the article; this is against treating אראל as a compound, *hearth of El*, as e.g. König does, *Lehrgeb.* ii 416. See Cheyne *Ency. Bibl.* i col. 298; Marti on Is. 29 1. The אראל was perhaps a fire-altar, i.e. a pillar surmounted by a cresset, Rob. Smith *Rel. of Sem.* 469. If אראל=*lion of El* as in 2 S. 23 20 and Is. 33 7, it is difficult to believe that this was the title of a priest, as Lidzb. takes it, *Eph.* i 278. דודה Prob. *Daudoh* (ll. 1 *n.* 3 *n.*, cf. דּוֹדוֹ Jud. 10 1), apparently a local god worshipped by the Israelites E. of Jordan[1]. As a pr. n. *Dûdu* occurs in the Tell-el-Am. letters, e.g. 44. 45; in Hebr. דָּוִד, דּוֹדוֹ, דּוֹדָוָהוּ, אלדד &c.; in Aram. דדעלה CIS ii 107; in Palm. דדא 130 2; and in the inscrr. from Ṣafâ דד[2]. The primary meaning is *loved one*, then *kinsman*, *uncle*. See Gray *Hebr. Pr. Names* 60 ff.[3] ואסחבה i.e. וָאֶסְחָבֶהָ cf. Jer. 22 19. 2 S. 17 13. Arab. سحب.

L. 13. לפני כמש Cf. לפני יהוה 1 S. 15 33. 2 S. 21 9. בקרית i.e. בִּקְרִיּוֹת Jer. 48 24. Am. 2 2 (with art.), mentioned by the latter perhaps on account of this sanctuary of Kemosh (Nöld.). It is not unlikely that Ar, the capital of Moab, was the same place; see Driver on Am. 2 2. Its site is unknown, but it must have been on the N. or NE. border of Moab. Another suggestion identifies Qeriyyoth with Rabbath-Moab, S. of the Arnon, Buhl *Geogr. Alt. Paläst.* 270. ואשב

[1] The difficult דרך Am. 8. 14 LXX ὁ θεός σου is ingeniously corrected to דֹּדְךָ by Winckler *Altor. Forsch.* i 195.

[2] Dussaud et Macler *Voyage Archéol. au Ṣafâ* (1901) 126.

[3] Winckler treats Ariel-Dôdah as a compound deity, i.e. 'nergal-Tammuz-Jahve with his consort Dodah'—an etymological extravagance; *Gesch. Isr.* ii 257 f.

i. e. וָאֹשֵׁב 2 K. 17 24. שרן if not a city, may be the שָׁרוֹן of 1 Ch. 5 16 (E. of Jordan) which is prob. the same as המישור Dt. 3 10. Josh. 13 9. 16 f. At the end of the line an א can be traced, prob. part of איש.

L. 14. מחרת Site unknown; not in the O. T. ויאמר לי כמש לך אחז Cf. l. 32. Josh. 8 1. Jud. 7 9. 1 S. 23 4 &c. נבה Num. 32 3. 38 JE (assigned to Reuben). Is. 15 2. Jer. 48 1. 22. A city on or near Mt. Nebo; Buhl 266 f. The name may point to the worship of the Babyl. god Nebo in the city or on the mountain, though not necessarily, cf. Arab. النَّبَاوَةُ *the height.* ואהלך So in Job 16 22. 23. 8; in prose only Ex. 9 23.

L. 15. בללת Pronounced בַּלֵּלָה, as Is. 15 1 בְּלֵיל. 21 11 מִלַּיִל show. מבקע השחרת (מִבְּקֹעַ) Cf. Is. 58 8 אז יבקע כשחר אורך. In Hebr. עלה is usual, e. g. כעלות הש׳ 1 S. 9 26, and with מ׳, מעלות הש׳ Neh. 4 15. צהרם Prob. sing. with the ending *ām* (l. 10 *n.*) rather than dual. In Moab. the dual ends in ןֽ׳, מאתן l. 20.

L. 16. כל Restore כלה i. e. כֻּלֹּה. After שבעת we may read [אלפ]ן גברן וגרן, and at the end of the line ו[גר]ת. גר i. e. גֵּר *resident foreigner*, *sojourner* (*stranger*, AV., RV.), or possibly, as this is not very suitable, גֻּר *young*, *child* (Lidzb.); see **20** A 15 *n.*

L. 17. רחמת i. e. רְחָמֹת cf. Jud. 5 30 רַחַם רַחֲמָתַיִם, prob. female slaves. עשתר כמש A compound deity like מלכעשתרת 10 3 *n.* עשתר was most likely a female deity, though the name is written without the usual fem. ending, as in the Babyl. *Ishtar*, the Palm. עתר (in עתרעתה 112 4), and in the Phoen. pr. n. עברעשתר **22** 1. The male עשתר (עַתְּתַר) belonged only to the S. Semites. See **4** 1 *n.* החרמתה i. e. הֶחֱרַמְתִּהָ. For the practice of *devoting* a city to the god, cf. in Israel Num. 21 2 f. JE. Dt. 2 34. 3 6. Josh. 6 17–19. The *ban* (Arab. حَرَمَ *separate, prohibit*) involved the destruction both of persons and of property, Lev. 27 28 f. See Driver *Sam.* 101 f. *Deut.* 98 f., for the idea Rob. Smith *Rel. of Sem.* 434 &c., and **79** 8 *n.* At the end of the line restore א[ת·כ]לי rather than א[רא]לי; the latter in l. 12 is sing. and has את before it.

L. 18. ואסחב·הם The pron. is here used as an accus.; cf. הִמּוֹ *eos* Ezr. 4 10. הִמּוֹן Dan. 2 35. In Bibl. Aram., as in Syr., there is no verbal suff. 3 plur.; in Syr. ܐܢܘܢ, ܐܢܝܢ are used instead.

L. 19. יהץ Num. 21 23. Dt. 2 32. Is. 15 4. Jer. 48 21 &c. The site is not known, but it lay on the E. plains, N. of the Arnon; according to Eusebius it was between Dibon and Medaba (*Onom.* 264 96 ed. Lagarde). Yahaṣ was occupied by the Israelite king at the beginning of the war, prob. as an advanced post. בהלתחמה i. e. בְּהִלְתַּחֲמֹה or

בְּהִלָּחֲמֹה following the Arab. form إِقْتِتَال inf. conj. viii. The place-names אֶשְׁתָּאֹל, אֶשְׁתְּמֹעַ are in form infinitives of conj. viii. וירשה ונו׳ Cf. of Yahweh Dt. 33 27. Josh. 24 18.

L. 20. מאתן=מָאתַיִם, pronounced מָאתַן, cf. the dual ending of the oblique cases in Arab. ـَـيْنِ, and the contraction of *ai* to *ē* in Aram. مْأَنْ, مْأَتَيْن; or the pronunciation may have been מָאתָן, like the Arab. مِأَتَان, Targ. מָאתָן. רשה Prob. *his chiefs*, =רָאשָׁיו, the plur. with suff. as ימה, בנה (?) l. 8. In Moab, as in Israel, the nation was organized in clans or families; e. g. Ex. 6 14 P. 18 25 JE. ואשאה i. e. וָאֶשָּׂאֵהוּ cf. l. 30. The suff. is sing. collective.

L. 21. לספת Inf. of יסף (l. 29), i. e. לְסֶפֶת, as לְסְפוֹת should be read in Num. 32 14. Is. 30 1. Ges.-Kautzsch 195 *n.*[1] דיבן Perhaps a district, rather than a city (l. 3 *n.*); note the expressions לספת על (cf. יספתי על הארץ l. 29) and כל ד׳ משמעת l. 28, which seem hardly applicable to a city (Nordlander 42). חערן Lit. *the woods*, prob. the royal groves or park קרחה; cf. Qoh. 2 6.

L. 22. העפל *the acropolis* of קרחה; cf. Neh. 3 27. 2 Ch. 27 3. Is. 32 14 &c. of the fortified mound within Jerusalem, 2 K. 5 24 within Samaria. שעריה Plur. with scriptio plena, cf. l. 8 *n.* מגדלתה must also be plur., i. e. מִגְדְּלֹתָהּ or מִגְדְּלֹתֶהָ (Nöld.), l. 8 *n.*

L. 23. בת מלך Cf. 1 K. 16 18. כלאי Either *both, double*, Hebr. כִּלְאַיִם, Arab. كِلَا, كِلَانِ *both*, Eth. *kel'ē*, or *sluices* from כָּלָא, √כלא *restrain.* After האש there are traces of ו; restore למין. האשו[ח · למ]ין i. e. לְמַיִן or לְמַיִן. The ב in בקרב is doubtful (Lidzb.).

L. 24. אן i. e. אַיִן. The order as in Gen. 47 13.

L. 25. המכרתת Prob. הַמִּכְרָתֹת from כרת, *cutting*, perhaps for water. In Hebr. כרת is used of *cutting* trees, and כרה of *cutting* wells or trenches. כרתי may be taken from כרה (point כָּרִתִי) whence מִכְרֶה *pit*, Zeph. 2 9; but it is difficult to see how מכרתת can come from a ל״ה verb, unless it be a peculiar Moab. form. באסרי i. e. בְּאַסְרֵי. The yodh is faintly visible. For ב *with the help of*, cf. 1 S. 14 6 and l. 28 *n.*

L. 26. ערער Num. 32 34. Dt. 2 36. Jer. 48 19 &c. The ruins 'Arâ'ir (عراعر) S. of Dibon are on the N. edge of the ravine of the Arnon (W. el Mojib). After ארנן perhaps the stroke | followed.

L. 27. בת במת Prob. the same as במות Num. 21 19 f. במות בעל 22 41 &c., situated perhaps on Mt. 'Aṭṭarûs. הרס i. e. הָרֻס 2 K. 3 25. בצר Dt. 4 43 (in Reuben) &c. 1 Macc. 5 26 ff. Βοσόρ. The site is unknown; it must have been towards the E. border of the Moab. table-land. עין i. e. עִיִּן Mic. 3 12.

L. 28. At the beginning we may conjecture [תא | ור]ש; for ריש see l. 20 *n*. Halévy suggests plausibly [חיה | בא]ש, i. e. *with the help of fifty men of D.* (l. 25), *Rev. Sém.* (1900) 292. משמעת *obedience*, cf. Is. 11 14 ובני עמון משמעתם. For the idiom see Driver *Tenses* § 189. 2. At the end of the line part of a כ can be discerned; restore מלכת[י]. In the space which follows על ריש *over chiefs* may be supplied.

L. 29. בקרן Prob. בַּקְּרָן *in the cities*. יספתי Cf. l. 21.

L. 30. Before ובת only בא can be seen, perhaps to be completed מהדבא l. 8. בת דבלתן Jer. 48 22. Num. 33 46 עלמן דבלתים. ובת בעלמען Cf. l. 9 *n*. The preceding stroke usually marks a stop; and as בעלמען was 'built' in l. 9, it seems unreasonable to take ובת ב׳ as accus. after בנתי l. 29. On the other hand if ובת ב׳ begins a new sentence as casus pendens, *and as for Beth-b.*, the construction of ואשא (cf. note on ויענו l. 5) becomes awkward. At the end of the line the usual restoration נקד is possible, meaning *breeders* of a particular kind of sheep; cf. 2 K. 3 4 (of Mesha').

L. 31. וחורנן See l. 1 *n*. 10 *n*. Is. 15 5. Jer. 48 3 ff. The city lay on the table-land S. of Wadi Kerak, but on lower ground; hence the verb ירד l. 32, and מורד ח׳ in the O.T. The word must be construed as a casus pendens. Neither ב[ן · דדן · ודדן] (Smend u. Socin) nor ב[ני · חורי] (Nöld.) can be supported by a close examination of the stone. Lidzb. suggests בת · וק. As Ḥauronān lay in the S., and outside the Israelite occupation, it is likely that these lines gave an account of campaigns against the Edomites.

L. 32. אמר לי כמש Cf. l. 14. At the end of the line Halévy (l. c.) supplies ואל [33] תחם בקר ימן רבן 'and I fought against the city many days.'

L. 33. בת. Restore וישבת i.e. וַיֵּשְׁבָהּ l. 8 f. על[א]רח prob. the name of a place.

L. 34. שרק ? meaning.

HEBREW

2. Siloam. Circ. 700 B.C. Imp. Mus., Constantinople.

1 ... הנקבה · וזה · היה · דבר · הנקבה · בעוד ....

2 הגרזן · אש · אל · רעו · ובעוד · שלש · אמת · להנק[ב · נשמ]ע · קל · אש · ק

3 רא · אל · רעו · כי · הית · זדה · בצר · מימן ....א . · ובים · ה

4 נקבה · הכו · החצבם · אש · לקרת · רעו · גרזן · על[· ג]רזן · וילכו

5 המים · מן · המוצא · אל · הברכה · במאתים · ואלף · אמה · ומא

6 ת · אמה · היה · גבה · הצר · על · ראש · החצבם

... the boring through! And this was the manner of the boring through: whilst yet . . . . . [2] the pick, each towards his fellow, and whilst yet there were three cubits to be bored [through, there was hear]d the voice of each [3] calling to his fellow, for there was a split in the rock on the right hand . . . . . And on the day of the [4] boring through the miners struck, each to meet his fellow, pick upon pick; and [5] the waters flowed from the source to the pool for two hundred and a thousand cubits; and a [6] hundred cubits was the height of the rock above the head of the miners.

This ancient Hebrew inscr. was discovered in 1880 on the right wall of the tunnel which connects the Virgin's Spring ('Ain Sitti Maryam) with the pool of Siloam (Birket Silwân, Jn. 9 7), about 19 ft. from the Siloam end. This tunnel pierces the SE. spur of the hill on which the temple of Jerusalem formerly stood. Above the inscr. the rock was dressed for a considerable space, as though it had been prepared for some more writing, or for a relievo representing the miners at work (Cl.-Gan. *Rec.* i 295. ib. ii 285 illustrn.). The inscr. describes an incident in the boring of the tunnel: the gangs which started from opposite ends successfully effected a junction, and so freed a passage for the water from the spring to the pool. The course of the tunnel is marked by two curious curves which perhaps were designed intentionally to avoid some underground obstacle, supposed by Cl.-Gan. to have been the tombs of the kings (*Rec.* ii

§ 66). A plan, showing the points where the excavators lost the direction and where they met, is given by Conder *PEFQS* (1882) 122; Stade *Gesch.* i 591; Benzinger *Hebr. Arch.* 54 &c. For an interesting parallel see the Lat. inscr. of Lambaesis (N. Afr.), CIL viii 2728, which describes the excavation of a *cuniculus* or subterranean aqueduct on similar principles.

There can be little doubt that the work was carried out in the reign of Hezekiah. We are told that, as a precaution against a possible siege (2 Ch. 32 2 ff.), he brought water from the only natural spring near Jerusalem by a channel through the rock to a place of security within the walls; 2 Ch. 32 30. 2 K. 20 20. Sirach 48 17[1]. In ancient times the city walls took in the pool of Siloam; the 'waters of Giḥon' were outside them; and the Giḥon of the O.T., as the evidence implies, was identical with the Virgin's Spring[2]. The aqueduct, therefore, and with it the inscr., may be assigned to a date about 700 B.C.[3] The character of the writing points to the same period. It belongs to the archaic stage represented by the Moabite Stone; but in general form it is lighter and more flowing than the Moabite, and some of the letters, e.g. א, ו, ז, ח, צ, are considerably different. It will be noticed that the final vowels are represented by consonants, e.g. נקבה, חיה, זה, כי, וילכו; but within the word the vowel letter is not written, e.g. צר, איש, ימן; *ô*=*au* diphth. is written *plene*, עוד (from *'aud*), מוצא, but *ō*=*ā* is written *defective*, שלש, אמת, קל, חצבם. For the suff. 3 m. sing. ו־ is used instead of the archaic ה־ (ה־ֹ), e.g. רעו. The words are separated by dots (see p. 62). The style is pure and idiomatic, and reads like a good prose passage out of the O.T. The fullest account of the inscription, and the best facsimile, are given by Guthe *ZDMG* xxxvi (1882) 725–750. Cl.-Ganneau's facsimile in *Rec.* i Pl. xvi is remarkably clear; see also Driver *Samuel* xiv ff.; Socin *ZDPV* xxii (1899) 61 ff.

[1] Καὶ εἰσήγαγεν εἰς μέσον αὐτῶν τὸν Γώγ (a corruption of ΤΟΥΔΩΡ) B. ὕδωρ A. In Hebr. the verse runs:—יחזקיהו חזק עירו בהטות אל תוכה מים : ויחצב כנחשת [l. 'בנ] צורים ויחסום הרים מקוה :.

[2] Targ., Pesh. render גיחון 1 K. 1 33 by שילוחא.

[3] Is. 8 6 can hardly refer to this invisible channel. An older water-course, which carried the water above ground down the Kidron valley into a reservoir formed by a dam across the opening of the Tyropaeon valley, was discovered by Schick some years ago (see Cl.-Gan. *Rec.* ii plan); this would agree with the prophet's reference. An ancient reservoir close to the present pool of Sil., and NE. of it, was unearthed lately by Guthe; this may have been the 'upper pool' of Is. 7 3. 36 2 and possibly the 'old pool' of Is. 22 11 (Stade 592). Other pools are mentioned in Is. 22 9. Neh. 2 14. 3 15. 16. It is impossible to identify with any certainty the details of the system of pools and channels in this quarter. See Guthe *ZDPV* v (1882) 355 ff.; Benzinger 52–54; Conder *PEFQS* (1897) 204 ff.; and for recent excavations in the neighbourhood, Bliss ib. 11 ff. 91 ff. 173 ff.

L. 1. At the beginning of the line we may conjecture הֵן *behold!* or זאת, or בים cf. l. 3. Blake (see *n.* 1 below) suggests תם; for the construction cf. Gen. 11 1. Is. 47 11. נקבה Not in the O. T.; but the vb. occurs in 2 K. 12 10 &c.=*pierce*, Arab. نَقَبَ *ib.* נקבה may be pointed נְקָבָה or נִקְבָּה, Syr. ܢܩܒܐ *hole*, Arab. نَقْبٌ *tunnel.* The word is to be translated as a verbal noun active, *piercing through*; see l. 3. דבר Cf. Dt. 15 2 וזה דבר השמטה. 19 4. 1 K. 9 15. In the lacuna there must have been a verb and a subject, e.g. *the miners were lifting up*, מניפם החצבם את (Ex. 20 25); or הניפו וגו׳.

L. 2. רעו So Jer. 6 21=רֵעֵהוּ. בעוד לה[נקב i.e. הִנָּקֵב; for the construction cf. Gen. 48 7. The נ is fairly clear (Socin l. c.), and a part of the top of ק (Lidzb. *Eph.* i 53). This restoration was proposed by Guthe l. c. 737. נשמ]ע Pf. as in 2 S. 12 22; or יִשָּׁמַ]ע.

L. 3. הית i.e. הָיָת 2 K. 9 37 Keth., rather than הָיְתָה which in this inscr. would be הָיְתָה (see above). זדה The context suggests *fissure*; but the meaning is uncertain, and the word not otherwise known. The √זוד *seethe, act presumptuously* gives no suitable sense[1]. After מימן many restore ומשמאל *and on the left*, i.e. *from S. to N.* facing the two gangs, in the direction of the tunnel. Socin in his facsimile gives אל and what are supposed to be fragments of ומ; but while the א is certain, the ל is very doubtful, and the restoration ומשמ]אל] is not sufficient to fill the gap (Lidzb. l. c.).

L. 4. החצבם *the hewers*; חצב of *hewing out* cisterns Dt. 6 11. 2 Ch. 26 10, and of *mining* Dt. 8 9. See the word in Sirach 48 17 (p. 16 *n.* 1). לקרת i.e. לִקְרַאת from קרה. וילכו Note the use of waw conv. with impf.

L. 5. מוצא *spring* of water; i.e. the Virgin's Spring, from which the tunnel starts. Cf. 2 Ch. 32 30 מוצא מימי גיחון העליון. מאתים ואלף אמה For the unusual order cf. Num. 3 50 שלש מאות ואלף. The actual length of the tunnel is 1706·8 ft. (Conder l. c. 122), very nearly 1200 cubits of 17 in.; but the 1200 is only a round number, like the 100 at the end of the line, and therefore is of no value for fixing the length of the cubit.

L. 6. גבה הצר i.e. גֹּבַהּ הַצֻּר. The thickness of the rock above the excavators is roughly calculated at 100 cubits. 'Towards the north the rock surface is 170 feet above the roof of the tunnel.' Conder l. c. 127.

[1] Blake, in the *Journ. Amer. Or. Soc.* xxii. i (1901) 52 f., suggests זָדָה from √זד which seems to have the primary meaning of *narrow* in Syr. and Arab., ܙܕ *evacuavit, privavit* (Payne Smith), زند *fill, be in straits for water*, conj. v *straitened in one's bosom* (Lane). This is possible.

PHOENICIAN

PHOENICIA

8. Byblus. CIS i. v–iv cent. B.C. Paris.

1 אנך יחומלך מלך גבל בן יחרבעל בן בן ארמלך מלך
2 גבל אש פעלתן הרבת בעלת גבל ממלכת על גבל וקרא אנך
3 את רבתי בעלת גבל [כ שמע] קל ופעל אנכלר בתי בעלת
4 גבל המזבח נחשת זן אש בח[צ]ר ז הפתח חרץ זן אש
5 על פן פתחי ז והערת חרץ אש בתכת אבן אש על פתח חרץ זן
6 והערפת זא ועמדה וה . . . ם אש עלהם ומספנתה פעל אנך
7 יחומלך מלך גבל לרבתי בעלת גבל כמאש קראת את רבתי
8 בעלת גבל ושמע קל ופעל לי נעם תברך בעלת גבל אית יחומ[לך]
9 מלך גבל ותחוו ותארך ימו ושנתו על גבל כ מלך צדק הא ותתן
10 [לו הרבת ב]עלת גבל חן לען אלנם ולען עם ארץ ז וחן עם אר
11 [ץ . . . . .] כל ממלכת וכל אדם אש יסף לפעל מלאכת עלת מז
12 [בח ועלת פת]ח חרץ זן ועלת ערפת זא שם אנך יחומלך
13 . . . . פעל מלאכת הא ואם אבל תשת שם א . ך ואם ה .
14 . . . . את ה א . . ז . . ים . ה עלת מקם ז ו . .
15 . . . . הרבת בעלת גבל אית האדם הא חרעו

I am Yeḥaw-milk, king of Gebal, son of Yehar-ba'al, grandson of Uri-milk, king [2] of Gebal, whom the lady, mistress of Gebal, made king over Gebal; and I invoke [3] my lady, mistress of Gebal, [for she hears] my voice. And I make for my lady, mistress [4] of Gebal, this altar of bronze which is in this court, and this engraved work of gold which [5] is over against this engraved work of mine, and the uraeus (?) of gold which is in the midst of the stone, which is above this engraved work of gold, [6] and this portico and its pillars and the . . . which are upon them and its roof do I, [7] Yeḥaw-milk, king of Gebal, make to my lady, mistress of Gebal; inasmuch as I invoked my lady, [8] mistress of Gebal, she has heard my voice and done kindness to me. May the mistress of Gebal bless Yeḥaw-milk, [9] king of Gebal, and grant him life and prolong his days and his years over Gebal, for he is a righteous king! And may [10] [the lady, m]istress of Gebal, give [him] favour in the eyes of the gods and in the eyes of the people of this land and the favour of the people of the lan[[11] d . . .]! Every prince and every man who shall make any addition to this alt[[12] ar or to this engraved wor]k of gold and to this portico I, Yeḥaw-milk, [13] . . . . . . set . . . . him who does that work; and if thou do not set there (??) . . and if [14] . . . . upon this place and [15] . . . . the lady, the mistress of Gebal, that man and his seed.

This is the oldest Phoenician inscr. yet found in Phoenicia itself. It belongs to the Persian age. Above the inscr. Yeḥaw-milk, in Persian dress, stands with left hand uplifted, and with the right offering a bowl to the seated goddess. The scene perhaps pictures the occasion when he dedicated the objects recorded below. A conjectural restoration of the stele standing on the two lions which were found near it is illustrated in Berger *Hist. de l'écriture*[2] 162.

L. 1. אנך The usual form of 1 sing. pron. in Phoen.; rarely אנכי CIS i 103 c. 104. 107. Though not written (cf. מפעלתן l. 2, ז, כ &c.), the final *i* vowel was prob. pronounced. In later Punic usage the final vowel seems to have been dropped in pronunciation as well as in spelling, e.g. Plautus *Poenulus* v 2 35 *anech*, Schröder xxix 18 4 אנך. Cf. 1 1 *n*. יחומלך i.e. יְחַוְּמִלְךְ *let Milk grant life* cf. תחוו l. 9 and יְחִיאֵל 2 Ch. 29 14. גבל Cf. 1 K. 5 32. Eze. 27 9. The Greeks changed the name Gebal to Βύβλος; it is now called Djebêl, about half-way between Tripoli and Beirût, where the inscr. was found in 1869. *Gubla* is frequently mentioned in the Tell-el-Am. letters, e.g. 50 2. 53. 54. 123 &c. יהרבעל *Ba'al is proud* cf. יהיר *haughty* Pr. 21 24; NHebr. (Hithp.), Aram. יהר *be haughty*. The reading, however, is uncertain. The Corp. and Lidzbarski read יחרבעל *B. rages*; Vogüé יחרבעל *B. gives joy* cf. יַחְדִּיאֵל 1 Ch. 5 24. בן בן Cf. 5 14. 27 4. CIS i 372. 391 f.; in Aram. 68 2; in Hebr. Ex.

10 2. ארמלך *fire of Milk* cf. אֲרִיאֵל 1 Ch. 6 9, and *Urumilki of Gebal* on the Taylor cylinder of Sennacherib, col. ii 50 (*KB* ii 91)—an earlier king of the same name. The occurrence of *milk* in the royal names יחומלך and ארמלך points to the cult of the patron-deity of Gebal, by tradition identified with Κρόνος, the mythical founder of the city, Philo Bybl. *Fr. Hist. Gr.* iii 568 ὁ Κρόνος . . . πόλιν πρώτην κτίζει τὴν ἐπὶ Φοινίκης Βύβλον. Milk alone as the name of the god has not been found on any inscription; it is merely a title.

L. 2. אש The Phoen. relative, pronounced as a monosyllable *ish* or *ash*, e.g. Plaut. *Poen.* v 2 56 *assamar* = אש אמר, or possibly as a dissyllable אֶשֶׁ, Plaut. ib. 1 5; Apuleius *Herb. Medicam.* 47 (48) *nesso esse sade* = נֵצָה אֶשֶׁ שָׂדֶה. The short form ש is also found, e. g. CIS i 112 b[2], and more frequently in Pun. and NPun. e.g. 41 2. 3. 55 6. 57 7. 9. 10 שלא = שֶׁלּוֹ, and in the transcriptions *si*, *se* Plaut. ib. 1 1. 8 &c. The etymology of אש is obscure. Taking ש as the original element, it is possible that א, properly a demonstrative sound, 'Deutelaut,' was added to it; cf. the א in אָז, אָנִי, אֵפוֹא, König *Lehrgeb.* ii 323; on the other hand, in the Assyr. *ša* the vowel sound followed the consonant. Whatever the relation between אש and אשר may be, in actual usage the Phoen. אש forms historically a link between the Hebr. אשר and ש. See Wright *Comp. Gr.* 119; Zimmern *Vergl. Gr.* 77. פעלתן i. e. פְּעַלְתַּנִי cf. תרגמן 4 7. יעמסן 5 5. The form of the rel. sentence is exactly like Gen. 45 4 אני יוסף אשר מכרתם אתי (Ges. § 138 *d*). The sentence has been rendered 'for whom . . . made the kingdom,' treating the suff. as = prep. and suffix, as in נתתני Josh. 15 19 &c., but ממלכת = *royal person* not *kingdom* in Phoen.; see note below. הרבת בעלת גבל The title בעלת גבל is very ancient; it was used by the inhabitants of Gebal in the fifteenth cent. B.C. of the goddess of their city, *Bilit ša Gubla* (Tell-el-Am. letters 55–110). Whether *Bilit* (בעלת) was the name of the deity, or whether it was used in an appellative sense, *mistress*, like בעל lit. *owner*, *lord*, cannot be decided with certainty[1]. Among the Phoenicians of a later age, at any rate, there is no clear evidence of a distinct goddess Ba'alath. The meaning of the expression לרבת בעלת החדרת 47 is too obscure to be decisive[2]. Probably, therefore, בעלת גבל is only the title of the chief goddess of the city, *the mistress*

[1] This goddess was, of course, a Canaanite not a Babylonian deity. But the Assyr. *Bilit* raises the same difficulty; sometimes it is used as a pr. name, sometimes as a title 'lady,' sometimes—and this illustrates the usage here—merely as a designation of Ishtar. Jastrow *Rel. of Bab. and Assyr.* 226; Zimmern *KAT*[3] 356.

[2] The NPun. pr. n. עבדבעלת is uncertain; Berger *Inscr. céram. d'Hadrumète* 2.

of Gebal; her actual name was not pronounced, perhaps out of reverence. But there can be little doubt that the Ba'alath of Gebal was 'Ashtart, just as the Ba'al of Tyre was Melqarth (**36** 1), the Ba'al of Ḥarran was Sin (p. 182), and בעלת מיפע was the title of an unnamed goddess in Sabaean (CIS iv 172 3)[1]. There is abundant evidence that 'Ashtart was the chief goddess of Gebal. The city was specially sacred to her; its coins are stamped לגבל קדשת (**149** B 11), with her symbol, the cone, standing in the temple-court (Rawlinson *Phoenicia* 146, Perrot et Chipiez *Hist. de l'Art* iii 60). Moreover, the goddess represented in the sacrificial scene above the inscr. is almost certainly 'Ashtart. In appearance, indeed, she resembles the Egyptian Isis-Hathor, having on her head the solar disk between two cow-horns[2]; but the Phoenicians borrowed some of the attributes, as well as the outward representation, of the Egyptian Isis for their own goddess. In an inscr. lately found at Memphis (1900) Isis and 'Ashtart are named together . . . לרבתי לאלם אדרת אס אלם עשתרת ולאלנם (p. 91 *n.* 1); and Plutarch has preserved the legend that Isis journeyed to Byblus (Gebal), where she was called Ἀστάρτη, *de Os. et Is.* § 15[3]. By the Greeks Ba'alath was taken to be a distinct deity, Βήλθης, Βααλτίς, and in particular the Ba'alath of Gebal was identified with Aphrodite, Ἀφροδίτη Βυβλίη, Lucian *de dea Syr.* 6[4]. In certain parts of Arabia the planet Venus had the name of *Baltht*[5]. The title רבת is given to 'Ashtart and to other goddesses; see **45** 1. **47**. **50**. **60**. **77** B. הרבת The article in Phoen. is far less common than in Hebr.; thus in **5** it occurs 7 times where Hebr. would have used it 28 times, Schröder 161. ממלכת *kingdom, sovereignty*, then generally, *royal person*, cf. l. 11. **57** 2 &c.; in contrast to ארם **5** 4. 6; and often on coins of African kings=מלך, **57** 1 *n.* וקרא אנך The ptcp. followed by the pron. as in מעל

[1] So with the Nab. דושרא lit. *lord of Shara*; the actual name of the god is unknown. Wellhausen *Reste Ar. Heid.*[2] 51; and see E. Meyer *Ency. Bibl.* 3742.

[2] Cf. Philo Bybl. ἡ δὲ Ἀστάρτη ἐπέθηκε τῇ ἰδίᾳ κεφαλῇ βασιλείας παράσημον κεφαλὴν ταύρου *Fr. Hist. Gr.* iii 569.

[3] Is. 10 4, if emended to בִּלְתִּי כֹרַעַת חַת אֹסִיר (Lagarde), may further illustrate the combination of Phoen. and Egypt. deities; Beltis is perhaps the goddess of Gebal. Cheyne *Isaiah, SBOT* 137.

[4] Cf. Philo Bybl. ὁ Κρόνος Βύβλον μὲν τὴν πόλιν τῇ θεᾷ Βααλτίδι, τῇ καὶ Διώνῃ, δίδωσι *ib.*

[5] Chwolson *Die Ssabäer* ii 22 (= En-Nedîm i iv) يوم الجمعة الزهرة واسمها بَلْتَى. Isaac of Antioch (died circ. 460 A.D.) speaks of Baaltis as a goddess common to the Osrhoenes and Arabs (*Opera* i 210 l. 98; 212 l. 129 ed. Bickell). Cumont in Pauly's *Realencyclopädie* (1896) s. v. Baltis.

אנך ll. 3. 6. שם אנך l. 12. שכב אנך 5 3; cf. in Hebr. Is. 48 13 קרא אני. Jer. 38 14 שאל אני. The idiom is more frequent in Aram., e. g. ידע אנא Dan. 2 8. In the Mishnah the ptcp. and pron. are united and form a present tense, Driver *Tenses* § 135. 4. Cl.-Gan. thinks that the words refer to the scene above 'I am (here) invoking,' *Ét.* i 11.

L. 3. אח l. 7. 28 4. 42 21 usually איח ll. 8. 15, the sign of the accus. איח was prob. pronounced *'iyyath*, later *'iyth*, *'îth=yth* in Plautus, אח in later inscrr. Nöldeke, *ZDMG* xl (1886) 738, suggests that the pronunciation was *'îûth* (*'iyûth*, *'îyôth*); but the analogy of the Hebr. form *'iwayath*, *'iyyath*, *'eth*, favours the vocalization אִיַּת. The Aram. forms יָת, ܝܳܬ, seem to be shortened from the fuller form preserved in Phoen. (61 28 *n.*); these, like the Arab. إِيَّا, presuppose an original *îyâth* (so Nöld. l. c.): König *Lehrgeb.* ii 295, Wright *Comp. Gr.* 112. קל [כ שמע] Cf. the common formula 28 7. 24 2 &c. and Ps. 116 1. 13. 17.

L. 4. המזבח נחשת זן The word denoting material (נחשת) is in apposition to the preceding noun, a familiar construction in Hebr., e. g. הבקר הנחשת 2 K. 16 17 &c., Driver *Tenses* §§ 188 (1). 191; but in accordance with Phoen. usage (l. 2 *n.*) there is no article with נחשת זן, cf. הפתח חרץ זן in this line, הערת חרץ l. 5, מרקע חרץ אז 24 1. נחשת might be explained as an accus. of limitation of the type הכרובים זהב 1 Ch. 28 18 and اَلْخَاتَمُ حَدِيدًا (Driver l. c. § 193, Wright *Ar. Gr.* ii § 44 *e*), but the former construction is far more probable in Phoenician.

Ll. 4–6. The principal objects dedicated by Yeḥaw-milk were apparently three, (1) המזבח נחשת זן, (2) הפתח חרץ זן, (3) הערפת זא. Notice that these three have the demonstrative pron., and appear again in the recapitulation l. 11 f. Attached to (2) was הערת חרץ, just as עמרה, ם ... חו, ומספנתה were attached to (3). The meaning of the second object, הפתח חרץ and הערת חרץ, is obscure. A reasonable sense is obtained for ll. 4 and 5 by treating פתח as=Hebr. פִּתּוּחַ *engraving* on a seal (Ex. 28 11 &c.), or plate (1 K. 7 37), or wall (1 K. 6 29. 2 Ch. 3 7). פתחי ז will then mean *this engraved work of mine*, i. e. the stele which bears the inscription; *over against*, *opposite to* this (על פן cf. 45 3. 1 K. 8 8. 2 Ch. 5 9), was הפתח חרץ זן, another incised stone, gilded, and surmounted by הערת חרץ set *in the midst of the stone*, i. e. prob. as a centre-piece at the top of it. What the gilded incised stone represented it is impossible to say for certain. Perhaps the stone was carved to represent a small shrine, like the façade of a temple, with the goddess standing or seated within, such as may be seen on the coins of Gebal, e. g.

Babelon *Pers. Achém.* nos. 1398, 1403, 1407 &c.; cf. the *aedicula* from Sardinia, CIS i 148, Pl. xxx. It has been suggested that פתח may mean not merely *engraved work* but *statue* or *bust*, and that the statue of the king (פתחי ז) was erected opposite to a gilded statue of the goddess (פתח חרץ ז); a position which may be illustrated from the Rosetta Stone, where the priests decree a statue of Ptolemy to be placed near the principal god of the temple, Cl.-Ganneau *Ét.* i 17. But whether פתח could be used in this sense is questionable; and even if the word is to be found in τοῖσι Φοινικηΐοισι παταΐκοισι, which Herodotus says 'the Phoenicians place at the prow of their triremes' (iii 37), this single example of doubtful significance—παταΐκοισι may refer to figures of the Egyptian god Ptah—is hardly sufficient to warrant the rendering *statue*. An obvious meaning of פתח is *door*, here a *monumental door* or *pylon* (Vogüé, Renan); this suits פתח חרץ ז but not פתחי ז, which seems to denote the stele of the inscr. What is intended by הערת, if that be the right reading, is even more doubtful. Possibly ערת is the Phoen. equivalent of the Egyptian *'ar'a*, i.e. the uraeus, or small serpent, which appears sometimes as an accessory to the winged disk and on the head-dress of gods and kings in Egyptian art. Cl.-Ganneau takes the word as a plur. denoting an uraeus-frieze of Egyptian pattern on the epistyle of the *aedicula* (הפתח); he gives several illustrations of Egyptian and Phoen. votive shrines with this decoration (l. c. 22–24). בח[צ]ר ז *in this court* is the best restoration of the text; cf. 33 2. 3. חרץ=χρυσός, זהב, 4 5. 24 1. 33 3. 5. In Hebr. חרוץ is poetical, e.g. Ps. 68 14; many words poetical, archaic, or rare in Hebr. are common in Phoen., e.g. פעל for עשה, פעם for רגל, אלף for שור, שאר for בשר, נעם for טוב, ירח for חדש &c. In this inscr. and in 4 5. 33 5 חרץ has been rendered *incision, engraving* from חרץ=*cut, sharpen* in Hebr. See 33 5 *n*. The rendering *gold* is preferable here and in 4 5. בתכת Prob.=בְּתוֹךְ cf. עלת for על ll. 11. 12. 14 &c. הערפת Prob. *gallery, portico, στοά*. Etymologically the word is the same as the Arab. غُرْفَة lit. 'eaves to catch the rain,' or 'gable from which the rain drips'; then 'the gallery below the roof,' 'upper balcony'; see Hoffmann *Ueb. einige Phön. Inschr.* 12 f. in *Abh. Gött. Ges.* xxxvi (1890). The word occurs again 10 1. 33 5. The Corp. reads, with less probability, הערכת *the row* of columns, cf. the Hebr. מערכת *a row* (of lamps) Ex. 39 37. עמדה i.e. עַמֻּדֶיהָ; cf. in Sabaean the dedication of *the peristyle of 'Umdân*, מכנתן עמדן CIS iv 240 6. וה...ם perhaps וה[ראש]ם *and the capitals*, Ex. 36 38. 38 17. וממפנתה *and its ceiling* cf. ספן in Jer. 22 14. Hag. 1 4.

L. 7. כמאש i. e. כמ+אש=כמו אשר, כאשר, 10 9. קראת Pf. 1 sing.; cf. פעלת 5 19. ימנאת 16 2. Though not written, the final *t* was pronounced; Plaut. *Poen.* v 1 1 *corathi.* Schröder 204.

L. 8. ושמע . . . ומעל Pf., prob. pronounced as fem.; cf. מנא 56 1. ימנא 27 3. חוא 54 3 (NPun.) נדר CIS i 191 2 (Pun.). In Pun. inscrr. the pf. 3 sing. fem. often ends in א (אָ-), e. g. CIS i 216 3 f. 280 2 f. &c. Contrast impf. with וְ after כאשר in Hebr., Ex. 16 34. פעל לי נעם = Hebr. עשה טוב עם Gen. 26 29. Ps. 119 65 or עשה חסד עם Gen. 24 12 &c.

L. 9. ותחוו Piel impf. 3 sing. fem. with suff. of 3 sing. mas. i. e. וּתְחַוֵּו. The same stem of the √חוח occurs in the pr. nn. יחומלך, יחובעל, יחואלן &c., cf. מְחוּיָאֵל Gen. 4 18 and perhaps חַוָּה. ותארך i. e. וְתַאֲרֵךְ; cf. 65 3. Ps. 21 5. ימו ושנתו are plur. Cf. Dt. 17 20. 1 K. 3 14. הא Pron. of 3 sing., used in this form for both genders, prob. with a difference of pronunciation, *hū'* or *hī'*, according to the gender of the antecedent; e. g. mas. האדם הא l. 15. הדבר הא 4 6. 5 10 &c. Moab. St. 1 6. 27. Old Aram. 61 30. 62 11. 22. 63 17 f. Palm. 147 ii c 6: fem. מלאכת הא l. 13. 5 11. 22. 27 2 &c.

L. 10. ותתן . . . חן לען Cf. [וי]תן לם חן וחים לען אלנם ובן אדם in the inscr. from Memphis l. 4 p. 91 *n.* 1, and the Hebr. idiom with בעיני, Pr. 3 4; also with לעיני, Ex. 7 20. Num. 25 6 &c.; cf. 62 23 קדם. אלנם Cf. 5 9. 16. 18. 22. 10 7 (constr. st.). 20 A 3. B 3 (constr. st.). *Poen.* v 1 1 *alonim valonuth*=אלנים ואלנות; the sing. occurs only in pr. nn. יחואלן, אחעלן. This אלנם is not the direct equivalent of the Hebr. אלהים, for נ does not interchange with ה; it is an independent formation with the ending ןֹ, like the Hebr. עליון, גאון; König *Lehrgeb.* ii 444. In the cases quoted אלנם has a plur. meaning *gods* (האלנם הקדשם 5 9. 22); contrast אלם, which, though plur. in form, is sing. in meaning, 33 6 *n.*

L. 11. No convincing restoration has been proposed for the beginning of the line. For the imprecations cf. 5 10–12. יסף Prob. Hif. impf. 3 sing. mas. עלת=על, after יסף 5 20. Moab. St. 1 21. 29.

L. 12. שם Ptcp., cf. l. 2 *n.* At the beginning of the next line we may restore מלך נבל פני ב to complete the construction, as in Lev. 20 5. Jer. 21 10 &c. Cl.-Ganneau l. c. restores [מלך נבל קמני ל]פעל, cf. 4 3 *n.*

L. 13. מלאכת הא. Phoen. omits the art. with the pron. in these cases, cf. האדם הא l. 15, and sometimes with the noun too, as here and 5 11 ממלכת הא. Cf. 1 3 חבמת זאת and add. note ii. The rest of the line is obscure. Cl.-Ganneau takes ואם . . . ואם as deprecative particles after the adjuration which he restores in l. 12 (קנמי), cf. Neh. 13 25, *Do not set there . . . nor.* אבל perhaps=בל *not.*

L. 14. Cl.-Ganneau suggests ת[סח]י *sweep* refuse into the sanctuary; cf. Lam. 3 45 סחי. The prohibition may be illustr. by a Gk. inscr. (B. C. 380) ἐπὶ τᾶς ἱερᾶς γᾶς κόπρον μὴ ἄγεν μηδεμίαν Michel *Rec. d'inscr. gr.* 702 21.

L. 15. זרעו In fig. sense as 4 7 *n.* 5 8. 11. 22; cf. also Ps. 21 11. זרעו is an isolated instance of the suff. ו׳ with a noun instead of the usual י׳. A verb is required at the beginning of the line, such as תקץ *may . . . cut off!* 5 9 f. 22.

Judging from this inscr., the dialect of Gebal approached nearer to Hebr. than the normal Phoen. speech. Thus the suffixed forms follow the Hebr. type, עלהם l. 6, זרעו l. 15, ימו ושנתו (plur.) l. 9, עמדיו (plur.) l. 6, מספנתה (sing.) l. 6; תחוו l. 9 with ו– for יו– cf. יְחַיֵּהוּ Ps. 41 3. The verb חוה seems to have been used at Gebal; in NPun. it occurs rather often in the form חוא, עוח &c.; in Phoen. proper it is only found in compound names. Idioms which resemble Hebr. are כאשר=כמאש l. 7, על פן l. 5 *over against*, תארך ימו l. 9, תתן חן לען l. 9 f., שם[פני ב] l. 12 f., יסף לפעל l. 11 cf. יסף לעשות 1 K. 16 33. Dt. 13 12 &c. There is a Hebr. ring about the phrase כ מלך צדק הא l. 9.

Additional note i. The fem. sing. ending in Phoenician. The ending of the fem. sing. of nouns in Phoen., whether in the absol. or constr. state, is ת׳, an archaic form which belongs also to the language of Moab, e. g. במת 1 3. מסלת 26. 28. 29. The ת׳ was prob. pronounced תָ– (in transcriptions *'aθ*), as in the names of the old Canaanite towns אֶפְרָת, בַּעֲלָת, חֶלְקַת &c., in the O. T.; for Phoen. followed the same general laws of tone as Hebr., which lengthened the vowel of *ath* under the accent. Hebrew, however, went further, and aspirated the final ת into ה, e. g. in the Siloam inscr. נקבה 2 1. הברכה, אמה 5; the transcription of some pr. names suggests that the Punic dialect did the same to a limited extent, e. g. Dido=ידידא, Carthago=קרת חדשא, Ἰμιλκών=חמלכא &c., Schröder 126. The instances of the ending א׳ with fem. nouns cited by Schröder 172 *n.* 9 are all doubtful. With regard to the fem. ending of the verb, it seems that Phoen. proper did not use a consonantal form, e. g. שמע .. ופעל 3 8. The ending א׳, developed like the Hebr. ה ָ– out of an original ת ַ–, is confined to the Punic and Neo-Punic inscrr., e. g. נדרא, נדרע *passim*, יסכא 27 3. שמעא=שמא CIS i 180 4. See Stade *Morgenl. Forschungen* (1875) 214 ff.; Wright *Comp. Gr.* 134.

Additional note ii. The forms of the demonstrative pron. in Phoenician.

Sing. (1) ז mas., sometimes fem. e.g. **3** 10. **5** 3. **7** 1. **19** 1. **42** 3 &c., and often in NPun. אבן ז **54** 1. **58** 1. Cf. the Old Aram. ז in מסכ **61** 3. ומז 4. 22, and the Hebr. זו Ps. 12 8. It does not take the art. after a definite noun; cf. Moab. הבמת זאת 1 3; *Poen.* v. 1 1 *macom esse*=מקום הזה is an exception.

(2) זן mas. **3** 4. 5. 12. Cf. Old Aram. זן **61** 1. **62** 1 and the emphatic זנת **62** 22. **63** 20. **64** 3. **68** 6. **76** c 2 (p. 185 *n.* 1); in Nab., Palm., Palest. (דֵּין) and Bibl. Aram., דנה; Eth. *zentū*.

(3) זא fem. **3** 6. 12. Cf. Old Aram. **61** 18 f. **69** 13. **76** B 5 (used as fem. of זנת); in Nab., Bibl. Aram., דא (used as fem. of דנה); Palm. דה; Eth. *zā'ĭ*.

(4) זת fem. NPun. **54** 4. **57** 3 &c.; in Plautus *syth*. Both זא and זת are, in origin, fem. formations from ז.

(5) אז mas. **11**. **24** 1. **25** 1. **30** 1, and fem. **13** 2. **15** 1. The א is a demonstrative sound, not the article.

Plur. אל **5** 22. CIS i 14 5 &c.; cf. 1 Ch. 20 8; with the art. האל **27** 3, cf. האל in the Pentateuch; in NPun. אלא, Plautus *ily*; Old Aram. אל (?) **61** 29; Egypt. Aram. אלו **74** A 2; Nab. אלה **87** 3 &c.; Palm. אלן **110** 1 &c.; Bibl. Aram. אִלֵּךְ, (אֵלֶּה Jer. 10 11); Palest. Aram. אילין; late Hebr. אֵלּוּ; Eth. *'ĕllu*.

---

4. Sidon. Tabnith. Circ. 300 B.C. Imp. Mus., Constantinople.

אנך תבנת כהן עשתרת מלך צדנם בן
אשמנעזר כהן עשתרת מלך צדנם שכב בארן
ז מי את כל אדם אש תפק אית הארן ז אל אל ת
פתח עלתי ואל תרגזן כאי אדלן כסף אי אדלן
חרץ וכל מנם משד בלת אנך שכב בארן ז אל אל תפת
ח עלתי ואל תרגזן כתעבת עשתרת הדבר הא ואם פת
ח תפתח עלתי ורגז תרגזן אל י[כ]ן לך] זרע בחים תחת שמ
ש ומשכב את רפאם

I, Tabnith, priest of 'Ashtart, king of the Sidonians, son [2]of Eshmun-'azar, priest of 'Ashtart, king of the Sidonians, lie in this coffin: [3] My [curse be] with whatsoever man thou art that bringest forth this coffin! Do not, do not [4] open me, nor disquiet me, for I have not indeed (?) silver, I have not indeed (?) [5] gold, nor any jewels of . . . only I am lying in this coffin: do not, do not open [6] me nor disquiet me, for that thing is an abomination to 'Ashtart. And if thou do at all [7] open me, and at all disquiet me, mayest thou have no seed among the living under the sun [8] nor resting-place among the shades!

The sarcophagus of Tabnith, like that of Eshmun-'azar ii (5), displays the characteristics of Egyptian workmanship; it was apparently stolen from an Egypt. tomb, for it bears the epitaph of an Egypt. general Penptaḥ. The style is that of the fourth cent. B.C.; and as the dynasty of Eshmun-'azar i and Tabnith prob. belongs to the period after the occupation of Sidon by Alexander the Great in 332, the inscr. may be assigned to the end of the century, or perhaps rather to the first decade of the next, circ. 290, and 5 to a date 15 years later; see 5 18 *n.*

L. 1. אנך See 3 1 *n.* תבנת Father of Eshmun-'azar ii, 5 1. The name, pronounced Tabnîth or Tabnêth, is preserved in that of a village near Nabatiyeh, SE. of Sidon, *Kefr Tibnîth*. It corresponds to the Hebr. Tibni, 1 K 16 21 f. LXX Luc. Θαβεννει, but hardly to the Gk. Τέννης, the king of Sidon who rebelled against the Persians and was slain in 350, for his coins bear the letters תע as the initials of his name, Babelon *PA* 1574–8. כהן עשתרת cf. 5 15. It is prob. that the dynasty was founded by a priest of 'Ashtart at Sidon; cf. 1 K. 16 31 and Jos. *c. Ap.* i 18 Εἰθώβαλος ὁ τῆς Ἀστάρτης ἱερεύς[1].

[1] עשתרת pronounced 'Ashtart, as the Gk. Ἀστάρτη (LXX &c.) proves: the chief goddess of the Phoenicians. Her cult was established at Sidon (5. 6. 1 K. 11 5. 33), at Gebal (3), at Ashqelon (Herod. i 105 τῆς Οὐρανίης Ἀφροδίτης τὸ ἱρόν . . . πάντων ἀρχαιότατον ἱρῶν ὅσα ταύτης τῆς θεοῦ, prob. alluded to in 1 S. 31 10 where בית עַשְׁתֹּרֶת is to be read, LXX τὸ Ἀσταρτεῖον; cf. the bilingual inscr. 32 1 שם בן עבדעשתרת אשקלני Ἀντίπατρος Ἀφροδισίου Ἀσκαλωνίτης), in Cyprus (e. g. at Kition 13. 20), in Sicily at Eryx (CIS i 135 לע' ארך חים = the frequent VENEREI ERYCINAI), in Gaulus (36), and at Carthage (e. g. 45 1. CIS i 255 עבד ע' האדרת . . . שמש. 263 אש בנעמה אש ע' עשתרת). The goddess of Carthage called by classical writers Coelestis, Οὐρανία (see quotation from Herodian below), was prob. none other than the Phoen. 'Ashtart; but see 48 1 *n.* As an element in compound pr. nn. 'Ashtart occurs very often. She was the goddess of fertility and generation (cf. Dt. 7 13. 28 4. 18. 51); and was identified both by Greeks and Phoenicians with Aphrodite, e. g. the common epithets Κύπρις and Κυθέρεια (of Kuthera in Crete) in Homer, and Cypria, Paphia, as titles of Venus; Λιβανῖτις was the title of Aphrodite worshipped in Lebanon (עשתרת בלבנן), Lucian *adv. indoct.* 3. There can be no doubt that the prototype of the Phoen. 'Ashtart was the Assyr. Ishtar; to a considerable

L. 2. ארן Of a mummy-case, as Gen. 50 26.

L. 3. מי את כל ארם אש תפק The construction is uncertain. Taking מי as *whosoever* and את as = אַתָּה, we may render *whosoever thou art—any man—that shalt bring forth*; cf. מן את תתגם 64 5 f. *whosoever thou art that shalt rob* (so Cl.-Gan.); but here the construction is complicated by the insertion of כל ארם and becomes very laboured. Renan may be right in explaining מי as a mistake for קנמי, *my curse be with every man*; see 5 4 *n.* תפק is prob. Hifil impf. of פוק which means (1) *bring forth, fetch out*, e.g. Is. 58 10; cf. the Aram. נפק *go forth*, in Af. *bring forth*; or (2) *light upon, find*, e.g. Pr. 3 13 ‖ מצא. 8 35. The first meaning is preferable here. According to Hoffmann פוק = primarily *to come upon by accident, break in upon, break* (*Ueber einige phön. Inschr.* 57 ff.).

L. 4. אל תפתח עלתי ll. 6. 7. 5 7. 10. CIS ii 226 2 ולא יתפתח עלידם. עלתי is prob. the prep. with suff., *upon me*, used pregnantly after תפתח lit. *open over me*; contrast 5 4 1 אל יפתח אית משכב. Less prob. עלתי is a noun (1) *inner chamber* (of the vault), the root עלה being used, as often in Assyr., in the sense of *going away*; so Winckler, *Altor. Forsch.* i 63 *n.*; or (2) *roof, lid*, lit. 'that which ascends,' cf. عِلْوٌ *upper part*, عَلَاةٌ *an elevated place*; so Hoffmann l. c. But no derivative of the verb is actually used in Assyr. or in Arab. with the meanings proposed in (1) and (2). To take עלת as = Hebr. עֲלִיָּה *upper chamber* does not suit the reference to a sepulchre. It is safer to render עלתי *upon me*. See further 5 6 *n.* תרגזן i.e. תַּרְגִּיזֵנִי Cf. 1 S. 28 15 of

degree the character of the goddesses was alike, and both filled the most prominent place in the worship of the two races. No satisfactory Semitic derivation of Ishtar-'Ashtart has yet been found; hence it has been supposed that ultimately the name is of non-Semitic origin, Schrader *COT*[2] 179, Sayce *Hibb. Lects.* 252 f. The form עשתרת with the fem. ending *t* is peculiar to the Palestinian deity. In Moabite the name occurs as עשתר with כמש 1 17; in Aram. it becomes עתר (= עתר = עשתר), e.g. Palm. עתרעתה 112 4 *n.* = 'Αταργάτις, and the pr. nn. עתרעתה CIS ii 52, עתרשמר Cl.-Gan. *Ét.* i 118. In S. Semitic (Sabaean) the phonetic equivalent is עתתר CIS iv 41 2. 46 5 &c., a male, not a female deity. 'Ashtart was not properly a moon-goddess, any more than Ishtar; but in some places she appears in this character, e.g. Lucian *de Dea Syr.* § 4 ἣν μὲν αὐτοὶ λέγουσιν, Ἀστάρτης ἐστίν· Ἀστάρτην δ' ἐγὼ δοκέω Σεληναίην ἔμμεναι (speaking of the temple at Sidon), and Herodian v 6 10 Λίβυες μὲν οὖν αὐτὴν Οὐρανίαν καλοῦσι· Φοίνικες δὲ Ἀστροάρχην ὀνομάζουσι, σελήνην εἶναι θέλοντες. 'Ashtart was sometimes represented, as we have seen (3 2 *n.*), with the Egyptian symbols of Isis and Hathor, the solar disk between two cow-horns. It has been suggested that these were misunderstood, and taken to represent the full and crescent moon; and in this way 'Ashtart came to be conceived as a moon-goddess. See Schürer *Gesch.*[3] ii 23 f.; Driver, art. *Ashtoreth*, Hastings *Dict. Bibl.* vol. i; Lagrange *Rev. Bibl.* x (1901) 550 ff.; E. Meyer *Ency. Bibl.* 3741 ff.

disquieting the dead. אי The Phoen. negative; twice in the O.T. 1 S. 4 21. Job 22 30; in Assyr. *a-a, ê, ai*. It is the usual negative in Eth., and frequently occurs in Rabbinic, e.g. אי אפשר. The pr. nn. איתמר, איזבל do prob. *not* contain this form. The other neg. in Phoen. is בל 5 3 *n*. ארלן The parallel expression in 5 5 כ אי שם בן מנם suggests that ארלן like בן must contain some such meaning as *with me*. At any rate the final ן is prob. the suff. 1 sing. in the verbal form which was sometimes used with preps.; e.g. בן, תחתנם 5 9. Hoffmann l. c. reads אר לן, which is quite possible, and takes אר as a particle strengthening the preceding negative (cf. אי בל 42 18) = the Bibl. Aram. אֲרוּ = הִנֵּה, Pal. Talm. and Midr. הרי used sometimes with merely a demonstrative force, *here*; so he renders *there is not indeed with me* (לן = לי). It is possible that S. Augustine on Ps. 123 (*Op.* iv. col. 1407 ed. Ben.) is alluding to this particle when he writes 'quod Punici dicunt *iar*, non lignum (יער), sed quando dubitant; hoc Graeci ἆρα; hoc Latini possunt vel solent dicere, "putas," cum ita loquntur, "putas, evasi hoc?"' For הנה after a negative cf. הלא הנה Hab. 2 13 and οὐχὶ ἰδοὺ Acts 2 7. Though Hoffmann's explanation cannot be regarded as certain, it is preferable to that of Halévy, who takes ארלן as = εἴδωλον. It was not the custom to bury εἴδωλα of gold and silver in sepulchres.

L. 5. מנם 5 5. 45 2 f. Prob. = Aram. مُعلْ, مُعلْتم, מָאן 65 6, lit. *vessel*, used here like the Hebr. כלי for *jewels*. Hoffmann takes the word as = *μαμμωνᾶς*, ממון, *money, valuables* (Talm.); but this does not account for the plur. form. משר Meaning unknown. בלת here apparently = בִּלְתִּי *only*. There is no exact parallel for such usage in Hebr.

L. 6. תעבת עשתרת Cf. תועבת יהוה Dt. 7 25. 17 1. 18 12 &c. Pr. 3 32. 11 20 &c. הדבר הא See 3 13 *n*. 9 *n*.

L. 7. רגז תרגזן i.e. רָגֹז תַּרְגִּיזֵנִי. In Hebr. the Qal. inf. abs. is found occasionally with the fin. vb. in a derived conjugation, e.g. Hif. עָרֹם יַעְרִם 1 S. 23 22. Nif. סָקוֹל יִסָּקֵל Ex. 19 13. יכן לך The stone-cutter has accidentally omitted the כ in these two words. The verb כון is used in Phoen., as in Arab. and Ethiop., for the Hebr. היה, in the sense *to exist, to be*; e.g. 5 8. 11. 20. 29 15. 42 3. 7. 13 &c. זרע בחים For זרע in metaph. sense cf. 61 20. 64 11. 69 12; and cf. the imprecations in 5 8–9. 11–12, and the Palm. לא יהוא לה זרע ונר עד עלמא 145 4 f. תחת שמש Cf. 5 12. The phrase is a favourite one with the author of Qoheleth.

L. 8. משכב את רפאם Again in 5 8. For משכב of a *resting-place* in the under-world cf. Eze. 32 25. For רפאם cf. Is. 14 9. 26 14. 19.

Job 26 5. Ps. 88 11 &c.; the meaning usually given is *weak ones*, √רפה *to be weak*; but, as Cheyne remarks, 'the terrible' or 'the wise' is what we should expect; see *Ency. Bibl.* art. Dead.

5. Sidon. Eshmun-'azar. CIS i 3. Date, see p. 27. Louvre. **Plate I.**

1 בירח בל בשנת עסר וארבע ר—||| | למלכי מלך אשמנעזר מלך צדנם
2 בן מלך תבנת מלך צדנם דבר מלך אשמנעזר מלך צדנם לאמר נגזלת
3 בל עתי בן מסך ימם אזרם יתם בן אלמת ושכב אנך בחלת ז ובקבר ז
4 במקם אש בנת קנמי את כל ממלכת וכל אדם אל יפתח אית משכב ז ו
5 אל יבקש בן מנם כ אי שם בן מנם ואל ישא אית חלת משכבי ואל יעמ
6 סן במשכב ז עלת משכב שני אף אם אדמם ידברנך אל תשמע
בדנם כ כל ממלכת ו
7 כל אדם אש יפתח עלת משכב ז אם אש ישא אית חלת משכבי
אם אש יעמסן במ
8 שכב ז אל יכן לם משכב את רפאם ואל יקבר בקבר ואל יכן לם בן וזרע
9 תחתנם ויסגרנם האלנם הקדשם את ממלכ אדר אש משל בנם לק
10 צתנם אית ממלכת אם אדם הא אש יפתח עלת משכב ז אם אש ישא אית
11 חלת ז ואית זרע ממלת הא אם אדמם המת. אל יכן לם שרש למט ו
12 פר למעל ותאר בחים תחת שמש כ אנך נחן נגזלת בל עתי בן מס
13 ך ימם אזרם יתם בן אלמת אנך כ אנך אשמנעזר מלך צדנם בן
14 מלך תבנת מלך צדנם בן בן מלך אשמנעזר מלך צדנם ואמי אמעשתרת
15 כהנת עשתרת רבתן המלכת בת מלך אשמנעזר מלך צדנם אם בנן
אית בת
16 אלנם אית [בת עשתר]ת בצדן ארץ ים וישרן אית עשתרת שממאדרם
ואנחן
17 אש בנן בת לאשמ[ן .ד] קדש ען ידלל בהר וישבני שממאדרם ואנחן
אש בנן בתם

לאלן צדנם בצדן ארץ ים בת לבעל צדן ובת לעשתרת שם בעל
ועד יתן לן ארן מלכם
אית דאר ויפי ארצת דגן האדרת אש בשד שרן למדת עצמת
אש פעלת ויספננם
עלת גבל ארץ לכננם לצדנם לעל[ם] קנמי את כל ממלכת וכל
ארם אל יפתח עלתי
ואל יער עלתי ואל יעמסן במשכב ז ואל ישא אית חלת משכבי לם יסגרנם
אלנם הקדשם אל ויקצן הממלכת הא והאדמם המת חרעם לעלם

In the month Bul, in the fourteenth year 14 of the reign of king Eshmun-'azar, king of the Sidonians, [2] son of king Tabnith, king of the Sidonians, spake king Eshmun-'azar, king of the Sidonians, saying, I have been seized [3] before my time, the son of a (short) number of days . . . , an orphan, the son of a widow; and I lie in this coffin and in this grave, [4] in the place which I built. I adjure every prince and every man that they open not this resting-place, [5] nor seek with me jewels, for there are no jewels with me there, nor take away the coffin of my resting-place, nor [6] carry me from this resting-place (and lay me) on a second resting-place! Yea, if men speak to thee, do not listen to their words. For every prince and [7] every man who shall open this resting-place, or who shall take away the coffin of my resting-place, or who shall carry me from [8] this resting-place, may they have no resting-place with the Shades, nor be buried in a grave, nor have son or seed [9] in their stead; and may the holy gods deliver them up to a mighty prince who shall rule over them, to [10] cut off that prince or man who shall open this resting-place, or who shall take away [11] this coffin, and the seed of that prince or of those men! May they have no root downwards or [12] fruit upwards, nor any comeliness among the living under the sun! For I am to be pitied (?); I have been seized before my time, the son of [13] a (short) number of days . . . , an orphan, the son of a widow was I. For I, Eshmun-

'azar, king of the Sidonians, son [14] of king Tabnith, king of the Sidonians, grandson of king Eshmun-'azar, king of the Sidonians, and my mother Am-'ashtart, [15] priestess of 'Ashtart, our lady, the queen, daughter of king Eshmun-'azar, king of the Sidonians—(we are they) who built the houses [16] of the gods, the house of 'Ashtart in Sidon, the land of the sea, and we caused 'Ashtart to dwell there, making (her) glorious (?); and we [17] (are they) who built a house for Eshmun, in the holy field (?), the well of Yidlal in the mountain, and we caused him to dwell there, making (him) glorious (?). And we (are they) who built houses [18] for the gods of the Sidonians in Sidon, the land of the sea, a house for the Ba'al of Sidon, and a house for 'Ashtart, the Name of Ba'al. And further, the lord of kings gave to us [19] Dôr and Yāfê, the glorious corn-lands which are in the field of Sharon, in accordance with the great things which I did; and we added them [20] to the borders of the land, that they might belong to the Sidonians for ever. I adjure every prince and every man that they open me not, [21] nor uncover me, nor carry me from this resting-place, nor take away the coffin of my resting-place, lest [22] these holy gods deliver them up, and cut off that prince and those men, and their seed, for ever!

L. 1. בבל **12** 1. **24** 2. the eighth month, November, cf. 1 K. 6 38; Assyr. *Araḫ samna*, Palm. כנן, Jewish מרחשון. The name is probably native Canaanite; its original meaning is not known. עסר For עשר, an orthographic peculiarity found only here; **42** 3. **46** 1 עשרת. In Phoen. as in Hebr. ש stands for *s* and *sh*, e.g. שמע l. 6 and ישא l. 7. שנת is plural. Phoen. uses 'in 14 years' for 'in the 14th year'; see **6** 1 *n.* and cf. the construction vi בימם **12** 1 *n.* למלכי is usually taken as inf. constr. with suff. 3 mas. sing., 'of his reign,' viz. of king Eshmun-'azar, cf. the Aram. idiom in which the suffixed noun is followed by דִּי, ד, before the genitive. The Hebr. בבאו האיש Eze. 10 3 is similar; Ges. § 131 *n.* and note [2], Schröd. 149 f. But the construction is awkward in Phoen., and the parallel which is quoted from **42** 4 ff. אחרי השאר can be otherwise explained. Lidzsb. may be right in treating מלכי as inf. constr. with י compaginis, cf. **6** 1 f. בירח...מ[לכ]י מלך ברעשתרת. In **24** 2. **26** 2 למלכי has the suff.

3 mas. sing., but the construction is different. אשמנעזר i.e. Eshmun-'azar ii, see **4** 1 f.

L. 2. בן מ' תבנת See **4** 1. דבר . . . לאמר Elsewhere peculiar to Hebr. The √ דבר l. 6 has not been found in Phoen. outside this inscr.

L. 3. נגזלת בל עתי l. 12, cf. Job 22 16 קֻמְּטוּ ולא עת. Qoh. 7 17, and the beginning of Hezekiah's hymn, Is. 38 10. The Phoen. negative בל, in Hebr. poetic, occurs again in **42** 15. **43** 6. The other negative is אי l. 5 and **4** 4 *n.*; the two are apparently combined in איבל **42** 18. 21. **43** 11. לא is not used in Phoen. The meaning of the eight following letters (again in l. 12 f.) is obscure. They may be read בן מסך ימם *the son of a* (*small*) *number of days*, cf. ימים מספר Num. 9 20 *a few days*. The word מסך prob. comes from סכך (for the form cf. מָסָךְ Ex. 26 36. מֶכֶס Num. 31 28), and means *number*, *sum*, as סָךְ in the Babyl. Aram. of the Talmud, e.g. *B. Bathr.* 21 a סך מקרי דרדקי *the number for a teacher of the young*; hence the denom. vb. סך *to sum, count up*, e.g. *B. Bathr.* 166 b (Levy *NHWB* s.v.); cf. the Syr. ܣܟܳܐ (from ܣܟܐ) *sum, limit*, and Arab. سكّ *to stop, close up*. The Hebr. סוך (שׂוך) *to fence, hedge round* Job 3 23, מסוכה *hedge* Mic. 7 4, is prob. a kindred root. With regard to בן another explanation is possible; it may be written for מן before a word beginning with מ, cf. l. 6 *n.*, **29** 13 בן מנחת (Lidzb. 312); in Himyaritic בן is the equivalent of מן *from*, e.g. CIS iv 20 4, בעמהו = מֵעִמּוֹ iv 2 9 f. If this is the case, tr. *from the* (*full*) *number of* (*my*) *days*. אזרם l. 3. Meaning unknown. The four letters occur again in an inscr. from Hadrumetum (Susa), Euting *Hadr.* 9 2 נצב מלכבעל אזרם (*Carth. In.* Anh. 6). To derive the word from אזר *to gird* (Stade *Morg. Forsch.* 225 f.) gives no sense that suits the context; on the other hand, if the root be זרם, it may have the same sense as the Arab. زَرِمَ *cease, stop short*, and אזרם, possibly an Afel form, may mean *cut off*, i.e. by disease (Winckler *Altor. Forsch.* i 67); but it is hard to say what part of the verb אזרם (Afel) can be. None of the explanations which have been proposed, e.g. Hoffmann's אָז רָם תַּם בֵּן [בֵּית] אֵל, commend themselves. The letters which follow may be read אלמת perhaps = Hebr. אַלְמָנוּת *widowhood*, here *widow*. חלת Prob. *sarcophagus*. The √ חלל = *bore, hollow out*; Arab. خلّ, hence خِلَّة *box, case*; Aram. ܚܠܬܐ *sheath*; Bab. Talm. חלתא *bee-hive*; ll. 5. 7. 11. 21.

L. 4. בנת i.e. בָּנִתִי. קנמי את כל ונו' *my curse be with every* . . . ! cf. l. 20. **4** 3 (corr.). In the Mishnah קונם is used in adjurations and imprecations, very much in the same way as קרבן (e.g. *Nedarim* 10 a), *Gittin* 45 b a man of Sidon said to his wife קונם אם איני מגרשיך 'a curse upon me if I do not divorce thee!'; the word may have been used in Phoen. for similar imprecations. It is to be explained most prob. by the Syr. ܩܢܘܡܐ *substantia*, ὑπόστασις, so *person* (from ܩܘܡ), often used in such phrases as ܩܢܘܡ ܢܦܫܟ *tu ipse*, and with the suff. simply as an emphatic pers. pron. ܩܢܘܡܝ *egomet*. In imprecations קנם will then be the object in an elliptical sentence, '(I pledge) myself, my person, with so and so (that I will avenge)...' See Wright *Comp. Gr.* 130. ממלכת **3** 2 *n.* יפתח and the vbs. which follow may be either sing. or plur. משכב A *resting-place* in the grave, as **16** 2. 2 Ch. **16** 14. Is. **57** 2, cf. **4** 8 *n.* To violate a grave was the greatest indignity that could be offered to the dead; see Am. **2** 1. Jer. **8** 1 f.

L. 5. בן Either בִּן *with me* or בָּן *with us*. The former is better suited to the context, while the latter is what we should expect from the analogy of Hebr. But the sing. suff. with demonstrative ן, though properly belonging to verbs (e.g. מעלתן **3** 2. יברכן **9** 8), may have been used in Phoen. with prepositions; cf. the form in אֵינֶנּוּ, הִנְנִי, יֶשְׁנוֹ. See note on אולן **4** 4. מנם See **4** 5 *n.* **65** 6. The five letters בנמנם are taken by the Corp. as one word בְּנִמְנָם for בְּמַטְמֹנִם *treasures* cf. μαμμωνᾶ. Stade, *Morg. Forsch.* 223, proposes בֶּן־מָנִם (from מָנֶה) *a rich man*, lit. *a son of pounds*, cf. Talm. B. *Erubim* 85 b בן מאה מנה. Both explanations are improbable.

L. 6. ואל יעמסן במשכב ז עלת משכב שני Usually rendered, 'nor superimpose upon this resting-place the chamber of a second resting-place,' taking יעמסן as impf. 3 plur. with ending ן (cf. יקצן l. 22, ישאן **33** 6), and עלת as a noun, see **4** 4 *n.* This rendering, however, is prob. incorrect. In Hebr. עמס=(1) *lay a burden upon* (על), *lade* Gen. **44** 13. Neh. **13** 15, and (2) *carry as a burden, lade oneself* Zech. **12** 3 (with suff.). Neh. **4** 11. Is. **46** 3. Each time יעמסן occurs in this inscr., ll. 5 f. 7. 21, the parallel verb in the context is ישא, just as in Is. **46** 3 העמסים . . . הנשאים cf. v. 1 and Neh. **4** 11; it is therefore most probable that יעמסן means not *lay a burden upon* (which would require the prep. על rather than ב), but *carry me as a burden*, the final ן being the suff. 1 sing. (cf. תרמן **4** 6. יברכן **9** 8. יסכרן **29** 15). Similarly in **42** 13. **43** 8 יעמס is used of an offering *carried* into the presence of the god; cf. also the pr. nn. אשמנעמס **39** 2. מלקרתעמס CIS i 941 &c. יעמסן במשכב ז can hardly mean *carry me in this sepulchre*, for the משכב, which denotes not the coffin but the sepulchre or place of burial, could not be carried away. The removal of the coffin or mummy-case is deprecated in the phrase אל ישא אית חלת משכבי, repeated three times in this context (ll. 5. 7. 21). Accordingly במשכב ז must mean *from this sepulchre*, the ב being written for מ

(מִן) before a word beginning with ם, see l. 3 *n*. The prep. ב itself cannot denote *from* (Winckler *Altor. Forsch.* i 64 f.); the instances quoted, e.g. **11** בראשת נחשת. **9** 3 בפלג לאדך. **33** 6 בכסף אלם are not conclusive. The meaning of עלת is disputed. It occurs after פתח three times in this inscr. ll. 7. 10. 20 (cf. l. 4 אל יפתח אית), and three times in **4**, ll. 4. 6. 7; similarly after יער l. 21. It is safest to take it here (l. 6), and in every case, as the prep. עלת used in a pregnant sense; thus after יעמסן, *carry me* (*and lay me*) *on a second sepulchre*, after יפתח, *open over me, over this sepulchre* i. e. *open me up* &c., exactly as the Palm. ואנש לא יפתח עלוהי גומחא *and let no man open over him this chamber* **145** 3. Note the alternative construction with the accus. l. 4 אל יפתח אית משכב ז. See **4** 4 *n*. אדמם Plur. of אדם, not found in Hebr.; ll. 11. 22. **20** A 5. **33** 4. 7. **42** 16. 17. ידברנך For suff. after דבר cf. the rare usage in O.T., e.g. Gen. 37 4 דַּבְּרוֹ. The form here is Piel impf. 3 plur., and the suff. has a demonstrative נ; cf. יסגרנם l. 19. Ps. **50** 23 יכבדנני. Gen. **27** 19. 31 תברכני. Job 7 14 תבעתני; König *Lehrgeb.* ii 443 c. ברנם This might mean *their vain talk* from בד Is. **16** 6. Jer. 48 30 &c., but it is much more likely that the stone-cutter made a mistake (cf. ll. 9. 15. 16), and intended to write בדברנם i. e. בְּדִבְרֵיהֶם. For שמע ב cf. Gen. **22** 18. 2 S. **12** 18 &c. with בקול.

L. 7. יפתח עלת **4** 4 *n*. אם איש ישא *or who shall take away*. Here and in ll. 10. 11 אם by itself=*or*, a variation from the Hebr. usage. In **42** 3 &c. אם . . . אם=*whether* . . . *or*, as in Hebr.

L. 8. יכן **4** 7 *n*. לם Prep. ל with suff. 3 plur., l. 11. Many scholars, however, take this suff. to be sing. and not plur., and suppose that it was pronounced לם -*ahim-ēm* (as *ahi-ē* י׳, the usual form of this suff.); Schröd. 153–157, see **42** 5 *n*. But in this inscr. the context does not require לם to be taken as sing. רפאם **4** 8.

L. 9. תחתנם=תַּחְתֵּיהֶם *in their stead*. ויסגרנם Piel or Hifil impf. 3 plur. mas. with suff. נם׳, *and may* . . . *deliver them up*; here followed by את *with*, instead of ביד as in O.T. האלנם הקדשם Cf. l. 22. **3** 10 *n*. Dan. 4 5. ממלכ[ת] So the text is prob. to be corrected. Cf. the mistake in ממל[כ]ת l. 11. אדר *splendid, mighty*, an epithet assumed by the Ptolemaic kings, **10** 6; cf. Ps. **136** 18 מלכים אדירים. משל Qal ptcp. where the impf. might be expected. בחם=בנם See add. note on suff. נם׳ p. 39.

L. 10. לקצתנם *to cut them off*, see add. note p. 39. The object of the inf. is expanded in the two long clauses which follow: '(even) that prince . . . . or those men (l. 11).' It is possible to put the stop at לקצתנם and take אית ממלכת וגו׳ as accus. pendens, the construction being resumed by אל יכן לם l. 11 (Hoffmann); but this is less in accordance with epigraphic style. אם *or* l. 7 *n.*

L. 11. ממל[כ]ת So correct the error of the mason. מ' הא 3 13 *n.* המת = הֵמָּה l. 22. **29** 5. **42** 17 תארםם המת. For the ending ת in המת cf. Eth. *'emûntû, 'emântû*, Assyr. *šunûti*, fem. *šinâti*, Sab. *hmt*; König *Lehrgeb.* ii 368. שרש לםם וגו' Cf. Is. 37 31. Am. 2 9. Job 18 16. For פר cf. **44** 2.

L. 12. תאר with the sense of *beauty* as in Is. 53 2. תחת שמש 4 7 *n.* נחן Apparently Nifal ptcp. of חנן i. e. נֵחָן *to be pitied*, cf. Jer. 22 23 מַה־נֵּחַנְתְּ (text doubtful); for ptcp. as gerundive cf. נורא Ps. 76 8. מהלל 18 4. It is possible (Lidzb.) that נחן may be some form (? ptcp.) connected with the √נוח and means *I am resting*; cf. נחת of *rest* in the grave **16** 2.

L. 14. בן בן refers to Eshmun-'azar, not to Tabnith; cf. **3** 1. אמעשתרת Not '*Ashtart is mother* but *handmaid of* '*Ashtart*, אמ[ת]עשתרת **16** 3, as is clear from אמאשמן CIS i 881 which must = אמ[ת]אשמן, for Eshmun could not be ' mother.'

L. 15. רבתן Cf. רבתי **3** 3. 7. אם An error for אש. בנן i.e. בָּנִינוּ. בת Plur. = בָּתֵּי.

L. 16. בת אלנם Jud. 17 5. For אלנם see **3** 10 *n.* The 'house of 'Ashtart' mentioned here is prob. the great temple of Ἀστάρτη in Sidon which Lucian visited, *de dea Syr.* § 4; see p. 27. וישרן Prob. an error for וישבן l. 17, Hifil or Piel (cf. Eze. 26 4 and ישב in Mishnah) pf. 1 plur. of ישב *and we caused to dwell.* Winckler, however, *Altor. Forsch.* i 67, prefers the text, which he renders *and we brought in*, quoting the Assyr. *šêru* (a Canaanite word), *send* or *bring in something*, often in Tell-el-Amarna letters (Winckler, Engl. Tr., p. 10*). שממארדם Meaning uncertain. The Corp. groups the letters שם מארדם *there, making* (*her*) *glorious*, i.e. מַאְדִּרִים cf. l. 19 *n.* Hoffmann explains שָׁם מְאֹד רָם in app. to עשתרת and in l. 17 to the suff. in וישבני, and illustrates the order by Ps. 47 10, and the idea by Ps. 7 18. 9 3 &c., comparing the name Semiramis = שמי רם; but it may be doubted whether שם can = nomen = numen. The rendering *of the glorious heavens* שמם אדרם does not suit l. 17. אנחן = אֲנַחְנוּ. The final vowel, though not written (cf. Aram. سمع/, later سمع), was prob. pronounced.

L. 17. אשמן Eshmun was the god of vital force and healing; hence the Greeks and Romans identified him with Aesculapius, e.g. in the trilingual inscr. **40** 1 לאשמן = ΑΣΚΛΗΠΙΩ = AESCOLAPIO. He had a shrine near Berytus, τὸ τοῦ Ἀσκληπιοῦ ἄλσος Strabo ed. Müll. 644; at Sidon his importance is implied by the name of king Eshmun-'azar. In Cyprus many pr. nn. were compounded with Eshmun, e.g. אשמנאדן

12 4. עבדאשמן 17 1 f. אשמנצלח 19 2 &c. At Carthage he had a temple which stood on the highest ground in the city, the Byrsa (cf. CIS i 252 4 עבד בת א׳). His worship was carried to the Carthaginian colonies, e.g. to Sardinia, cf. 40 and the pr. nn. עבדאשמן ib. אשמנעמס 39 2 &c. At Carthage his attributes were combined with those of 'Ashtart, e.g. עבדמלקרת כהן אשמנעשתרת CIS i 245 3 f., and in Cyprus with those of Melqarth, e.g. לאדני לאשמנמלקרת CIS i 16. The etymology of the name is obscure. According to the ancients אשמן was derived from שמני *the eighth* of the Κάβειροι[1]; recently G. Hoffmann has suggested a connexion with שָׁמֵן, אֶשְׁמָן 'the fat one,' *ZA* xi 227. The two letters before קדש are almost obliterated; the latter of the two is ר or ד. The Corp. suggests יער=יר ק׳ *the sacred grove*; שדה=שד ק׳ l. 19 *the sacred field* (Lidzb.) is more likely. Hoffmann's *holy demon* (שֵׁד) is improbable. ען ידלל Meaning uncertain; perhaps, *well of Yidlal.* וישבני Hifil pf. 1 plur. with suff. ✓ *and we caused him to dwell*, i.e. וְיִשַּׁבְנֻהוּ.

L. 18. לאלן i.e. לְאֵלֵנִי plur. constr., cf. 20 A 3. לבעל צדן *to the Ba'al of Sidon* 33 6, cf. Hesychius Θαλάσσιος Ζεύς· ἐν Σιδῶνι τιμᾶται. For Ba'al with a local designation cf. ב׳ לבנן 11. ב׳ צר 36 1. ב׳ חרן 149 A 1 ff.; in O.T. ב׳ חרמון Jud. 3 3. ב׳ חצור 2 S. 13 23. ב׳ פעור Dt. 4 3 &c. The actual name of the god was not pronounced; see 3 2 *n*. עשתרת שם בעל *'A. the name of Ba'al*, i.e. the manifestation of B. In the O.T. the Name of Yahweh is frequently used for His manifested presence (Ex. 23 20 f. 1 K. 8 16. Is. 18 7 &c.), or His Person and attributes as revealed to men (Ex. 3 15. 34 5 f. &c.). The Phoenicians, in accordance with their polytheistic tendencies, personified the attributes of Ba'al, and the name of Ba'al became a distinct deity and underwent a change of gender; the manifestation of B. became 'Ashtart his consort. Cf. תנת פן בעל *Tanith the Face of B.* in the Carthaginian inscrr.; and see further Vogüé *Mélanges d'Arch. Orient.* 53 ff., Stade *Morg. Forsch.* 196. Some authorities, however, interpret differently, pronouncing שם as שָׁם, and rendering *'Ashtart of the heaven of Ba'al*, Dillmann *Monatsber. d. Berl. Akad.* (1881) 606 ff., Nowack *Hebr. Archäol.* ii 306 f., E. Meyer *Ency. Bibl.* 3745. These scholars in l. 16 group the letters עשתרת שמם אדרם *'A. of the glorious heavens*; see note in loc. But the meaning *Himmels-Astarte Baals*, i.e. *'Ashtart the consort of* Βεελσαμην (Dillm.), can only be extracted

[1] E. g. Damascius ap. Phot. 352 b, ed. Migne iii 1305 οἱ δὲ τὸν Ἔσμουνον ὄγδοον ἀξιοῦσιν ἑρμηνεύειν ὅτι ὄγδοος ἦν τῷ Σαδύκῳ παῖς. Philo Bybl. *Fr. Hist. Gr.* iii 569 οἱ ἑπτὰ Συδὲκ παῖδες Κάβειροι, καὶ ὄγδοος αὐτῶν ἀδελφὸς Ἀσκληπιός.

from ע' שם בעל by violence; the equivalent of such a title would be עשתרת ב' ש' or ע' שמם, see p. 27. Besides the temples of 'Ashtart and Eshmun (ll. 16. 17), perhaps the gods of the royal house (Hoffm.), the king and his mother had founded temples to the patron deities of the state, Ba'al of Sidon and 'Ashtart the Name of Ba'al (l. 18). The 'house of 'A.' in l. 18 is different from the 'house of 'A.' in l. 16; the same goddess was worshipped in two temples under different aspects. יתן The Phoen. form of the Hebr. נתן, ll. **12** 3 &c., and the pr. nn. יתנבעל, בעליתן, מלכיתן &c. The form נתן, however, is implied in some names, e.g. מתן **9** 2. מתנבעל, מתנאלם &c.[1] אדן מלכם = the Ptolemaic title *κύριος βασιλέων* (Gk. inscrr.), the chief holder of royal power in the East, e.g. **10** 5 f. (Ptolemy iii). **27** 1 (Ptolemy ii). **28** 2 (Ptolemy i). **29** 4 ff. (Ptolemy vii ?); in **9** 5 Alexander the Great (Seleucid era). Here the reference is perhaps to Ptolemy ii Philadelphus; and the position of Eshmun-'azar as a subject-prince may be confirmed by Diodorus Sic. (xix 58), who mentions Phoen. kings *after* Alexander in the time of Antigonus (so Cl.-Gan. *Rec.* i 86). As illustrating Eshmun-'azar's commemoration of his suzerain's bounty, cf. what Theocritus says of Ptolemy ii, *Πολλὸν δ' ἰφθίμοισι διδώρηται βασιλεῦσιν Πολλὸν δὲ πτολίεσσι, πολὺν δ' ἀγαθοῖσιν ἑταίροις* *Id.* xvii 110 f. The death of Eshmun-'azar may have occurred about 275 B.C. His dynasty has been placed much earlier, in the Persian period; but the use of the title אדן מלכם favours the view adopted; the Persian king is always מלך מלכים, cf. **71** 3; Cl.-Gan. l.c. and *Rec.* v 223, E. Meyer l.c. 3762 *n.* See Appendix I.

L. 19. דאר The modern Ṭanṭura, on the coast, N. of Jaffa. In Assyr. inscrr. it is called *Du'ru*, Schrader *COT* 168; in the O.T. דור Josh. **12** 23 or דאר ib. **17** 11 &c. יפי Joppa, Josh. **19** 46. Jon. **1** 3 יפו. האדרת *great, glorious* ll. 9. 16 f. The idea of expanse is contained in the root (Ex. **15** 10. Ps. **93** 4 of the waves of the sea, *majestic*); so אדר is suitably applied to the wide corn-lands of שרן (Is. **65** 10. 1 Chr. **27** 29 &c.). שר = שָׂדֶה cf. **29** 9. למדת Prob. *in proportion to, in accordance with*, cf. כמדת **42** 17; from מדד

[1] Winckler *Altor. Forsch.* i 69 f. explains יתן as originally (H)ifil of נתן (cf. יוסף), subsequently used as the basis of a new Qal formation. In the same way he accounts for the Hebr. יצק, יצת, יצב &c., viz. as Qal formations from the (H)ifil of verbs פ״נ. But (1) there is no evidence for a Hifil in Hebr. with 'י for 'ה, and (2) the cognate languages show that these verbs were originally פ״ו, not פ״נ, e.g. יצב = Aram. (Targ.) יצב, Arab. وَصَبَ; יצע = Aram. יצע, cf. Arab. وَضَعَ; יצר = Aram. (Targ.) יצר, ܝܨܪ, Arab. وَصَرَ, Assyr. *eṣru*.

measure. עצמת ונ׳ *the mighty things which I did*, perhaps referring to the support given to Ptol. ii in his struggle with Antiochus i, which began about 275 B.C., Bevan *House of Seleucus* ii 233–235. The words have been transl. 'for the great tributes which I paid'; but מדה Neh. 5 4, BAram. מנדה, מדה, is a loan-word from Assyr. (*madattu*), and even if it had found its way into Phoen. through Aram., פעל is not a suitable verb to go with it; the Hebr. עשה נדר is not really parallel. ויספננם Qal perf. 1 plur. with suff. *and we added them* i.e. וִיסַפְנֻנֻם, see add. note; to take the form as Qal perf. 3 sing. with suff. does not account for the first נ. Stade, *Morg. Forsch.* 310, regards ויספננם as imperf. 3 sing. with waw conversive; but this idiom is not found elsewhere in the Phoen. inscrr. at present known (see **42** 4 *n.*); and though the נ energicum belongs to the imperf. rather than to the perf. in the cognate languages, yet a double energic נ, with the verb and in the suff. ־נם, produces a combination too clumsy to be probable. יסף עלת **3** 11.

L. 20. לכננם=לְהֱיוֹתָם Cf. **4** 7 *n.* and add. note below. נבל Prob. plur.=נְבָלִי.

L. 21. יער Piel juss. 3 sing. or plur. from ערה *lay bare, uncover*, cf. 2 Ch. 24 11 וִיעָרוּ את הארון; here followed by the prep. עלת (cf. יפתח עלת l. 7 &c. **4** 4 *n.*), unless עלת is to be taken as a noun, *inner-chamber* l. 6 *n.* לם=לָמָּה in the sense of *lest*. In dialectical or late Hebr. למה׳ preceded by the relat. has acquired this meaning, e.g. Cant. 1 7 שלמה. Dan. 1 10 אשר למה. In Aram. ܕܠܡܐ is the ordinary word for *lest*; so in BAram. די למה Ezr. 7 23, and למה alone Ezr. 4 22; Kautzsch *Gr. Bibl. Aram.* 131, see further Driver *Samuel* 123 f. In the expression לם יעמס CIS i 270 ff. (**49** 5 *n.*), לם has a prohibitive sense; cf. in Palm. למא ישבע *let him not be satisfied* **145** 7. יסגרנם l. 9 *n.*

L. 22. אל=אֵלֶּה Cf. **45** 2. 27 3 האל. יקצן Qal or Piel impf. 3 plur. with ending ־ֻן, cf. ישאן **33** 6. המת l. 11 *n.*

Additional note on the suffix of 3 plur. in Phoen. There are three forms: (1) ־הם, so far only found in Plautus *Poen.* v 1 4 *syllöhōm* i.e. שֶׁלָּהֶם, cf. Hebr. ־הֶם, Arab. ـهُمْ, Aram. ־הֹם. (2) ־ם prob. *ēm* (from *ahim*), e.g. זרעם l. 22. קלם **23** 7. מנם **43** 6. (3) ־נם, with nouns sing., e.g. אבנם **19** 3 f. ארנגם **27** 5; with nouns plur., e.g. ד[בר]נם l. 6. חברנם **42** 19. עזרנם **25** 2 (ptcp.); with the verb, e.g. לקצתנם l. 10. לכננם l. 20 (inf.). יסגרנם l. 9 (impf.). יספננם l. 19 (pf.); with preps., e.g. תחתנם l. 9. בנם ib. This suff. is compounded of ם+נ, the נ being the energic or demonstrative *nun* which is common in Arab. with the impf. (also before suffixes, e.g. *yaqṭulan-ka* and *yaqṭulanna-ka*), and appears in Hebr. occasionally, e.g. יְכַבְּדָנְנִי. In Phoen. it has been already noticed l. 6 above, ידברנך. This same נ is regularly used in the Aram. dialects with the plur. suff. attached to the verb, e.g. Bibl. Aram. ־ִ־ַנְּכוֹן, Mand. ׳ינאן, ׳ינכון, ׳ינהון (Nöldeke *Mand. Gr.* 88), Palest. Talm. ׳ינן, ׳(י)נכון, ׳(י)נון, Onk. ׳יננא, ׳נכון, ׳נינון (Dalman *Gr. d. Jüd.-Pal. Aram.* 79). It is a peculiarity of Phoen. that this נ is combined with the suff. ם, and that this ׳נם is used as a suff. with nouns and preps. See König *Lehrgeb.* ii 444, Wright *Comp. Gr.* 194.

---

6. Sidon. CIS i 4. iv cent. B.C. Louvre.

1 בירח . מפ[ע] בשת מ[לכ]
2 י מלך בדעשתרת מלך
3 צדנם כ בן בדעשתרת
4 מלך צדנם אית שרן אר[ץ]
5 [ז] ל[א]לי לעשתרת

In the month MP', in the year when king Bod-'ashtart, king of the Sidonians, came to the throne, (it was) that Bod-'ashtart, king of the Sidonians, built the plain of this land to his god 'Ashtart.

L. 1. מפ[ע] Restored after **29** 6. בשת מלכי מלך ב׳ lit. 'in the year of the reign of king B.,' i.e. prob. his first year. For the construction מלכי מלך see **5** 1 *n.*; in the latter case we find למלכי. שת (for שְׁנָת as בת for בִּנְת) is obviously singular here, as it is in such expressions as אש הא שת **27** 2, and similarly **9** 5. **10** 8. בשת שפטם **40** 2. **47** 1 . . . בשת . . בים **33** 1; so on the Moab. St. **1** 2. 8, and in Aram. **69** 1. On Phoen. coins, to denote the year, it is always שת or בשת, not שנת, e.g. Babelon *Pers. Ach.* p. 211 ff. On the other hand, שנת is the form used for the plural; thus . . בשנת . . בימם **12** 1. **13** 1. **14** 1. **23** 1 and similarly **5** 1. This is quite clear in the phrase אש המת xxxiii שנת . . **29** 5. In NPun. שנת, שענאת, is obviously plural, e.g. **53** 2. **54** 3. **56** 4. **58** 3. There are cases where בשת sing. is used, e.g. **9** 4. **10** 5. **33** 1, instead of the normal בשנת plur. **23** 6. **24** 2. **26** 2. **29** 4. 8. **30** 4; but these cases may be accounted for by the imitation of the Gk. formula ἐν ἔτει or ἔτους. Thus the usage seems to be established: in Phoen. שת was used for the sing. and שנת for the plur. (cf. Hebr. בת and בנות). The above is worked out clearly by Cl.-Gan. *Rec.* ii § 75.

L. 2. ברעשתרת Perhaps Straton i 374–362 B.C.; cf. **149** B 13, and see Appendix I. The meaning of the prefix בר is disputed. The word may be explained by the Hebr. בד plur. בַּדִּים *parts, members*. The theophorous pr. nn. which contain this prefix, e.g. ברמלקרת **39** 2. בראשמן **42** 2. ברתנת ib. 1, will then describe the individual as being under the protection of the deity, a *member* or *client* of 'Ashtart, Eshmun &c.; cf. גר **17** 2 *n*. In the same way we can account for the use of בר in a series of Carthaginian inscrr. CIS i 269–286, where it occurs, not in connection with a deity, but with the name of the donor's patron, e.g. **49** 2 f. (=CIS 269) בעלחנא אש צדן בר ארני בר אשמניתן *B. the Sidonian, the client of his master Eshmun-yathon*. This usage is explained by the old Semitic custom which allowed a foreigner to place himself under the protection of a native, a *member* of whose household he became. The donors of these inscrr. were apparently strangers (e.g. אש צדן) who availed themselves of the custom at Carthage; so Lidzbarski 134 *n*., Bloch *Phoen. Gloss.* 19 *n*. Most authorities (e.g. Corp. p. 345) take בר to be a shortened form of עבד *servant*; but this does not suit the cases where בר is used of women (CIS i 279. 280)—אמת would be the proper word—nor the cases where בר and עבד occur in the same context, e.g. ברמלקרת בן עבדמלקרת and vice versa, CIS i 203. 199. The pronunciation of ברעשתרת &c. was prob. Bod-'ashtart &c., the short vowel before ד with daghesh (... בַּד) being lengthened when בד was used in composition before another syllable; this pronunciation is supported by the Gk. form Βουδάστρατος, in an inscr. from Cos, Michel 424, Θήρων Βουδαστράτου Τύριος. A different etymology is suggested by Grunwald, *Eigennamen des A. T.* 7 *n*., who quotes the Assyr. *Pudi-ilu*, *Budu-ilu*='prince of God'(?) *KB* ii 91, *Budi-ba'al* ib. 173; this meaning of *Budu*, however, is not clearly established.

L. 3. כ בן i.e. כִּי בָנָה *for he built*; or supplying a clause before the conjunction ... (*it was*) *that he built*. Cf. **88** 3.

L. 4. שרן אר[ץ] Various restorations and renderings have been suggested; the simplest is *the plain of this land*, שרן being *a plain* between the mountains and the sea, cf. **5** 19. To *build the plain* is not a very natural expression, but it is paralleled by 1 K. 16 24 ויבן את ההר. Hoffmann, *Üb. ein. Phön. In.* 59, connects the word with אֻשַּׁרְנָא Ezr. **5** 3. 9 *walls* (Vulg.), a form which is itself equally obscure.

L. 5. ל[א]לי לע' Cf. **24** 1. CIS i 94 4. The Phoen. suff. 3 m. sing.

is √ *ℓ*, contracted from *ahi*; cf. Aram. ܐܚ̈ܐ, ܐܚ̈ܐ, ܐܚ݂. Both the Phoen. and Aram. have weakened the original *ahu* preserved in the Arab. أخ and the Hebr. אחו, אחי, אח.

7. Sidon. Sid. 4. iii–ii cent. B.C. Louvre.

1 המנחת ז אש יתן עבדמסכר רב עבר לספת

2 רב שני בן בעלצלח לאדני לשלמן יברך

This offering (is that) which 'Abd-miskar, governor of the other side of SFT, the second governor, son of Ba'al-ṣillaḥ, gave to his lord Shalman: may he bless!

L. 1. מנחת Here of an *offering* in general, as perhaps in CIS i 14 5 מנחת//אל; elsewhere 'מ is used of sacrifices, with or without blood, e.g. **29** 13. **42** 14. **43** 10. For ז with a fem. noun see **3** add. note ii. עבדמסכר Cf. חמרמסכר **59** A 5. גרמסכר CIS i 267 &c. מסכר must be the name of a deity, though it appears as the name of individuals in the Latin forms *mescar*, *misicir* &c. CIL viii **5194. 5217.** The etymology of the name is uncertain. Renan thinks of the Egypt. Sokari, who at Memphis was the god of the dead (Maspero *Hist. Anc.* 26. 412); another suggestion is that the name is pure Egypt. *mer-seḳer* 'loving silence,' a title of Hathor (cf. חמרמסכר supr.), with an elision of the *r*; Hoffmann proposes a compound of the Cyprian מרי (=מלקרת **40** 1 *n.*) + the Egyptian Σώχαρις, *Skr*, *ZA* xi 239 f.; Cl.-Gan. suggests that מסכר=מזכר (cf. **9** 6 *n.*), which may be the equivalent of Μνημοσύνη to whom a temple (*Aedes Memoriae*) was dedicated at Carthage, *Rev. Arch.* iii. t. 33, 274. This last explanation is certainly attractive. רב עבר לספת רב שני Meaning obscure. Lidzbarski 367 renders, most plausibly, 'under-prefect of Trans-LSPT,' or 'of Trans-SPT,' taking the ל as a prep. (cf. עבר לירדן) and ספת as the name of a stream (√סוף), or as = Hebr. שפה *bank*; *Eph.* i 16. 147. This rendering may be illustrated by the legend on some Cilician coins of Mazaios, מזדי זי על עברנהרא וחלך i.e. 'Mazaios governor of Trans-Euphrates and Cilicia,' **149** A 6. Cl.-Ganneau's explanation, '*rab* retired, moreover *rab* for the second time,' is less probable; it is difficult to believe that לספת = *added to this*, and שני=שֵׁנִית. Landau, *Beitr. z. Altertumsk. d. Or.* ii 13, renders 'which 'A. gave for LSPT, the over-ŠNI,' treating ר in רב as due to dittography, and reading בעבר=בַּעֲבוּר.

L. 2. בעלצלח *Ba'al prospers*, cf. רעמצלח **32** 2. אשמנצלח **35** 2; צלח is Piel. שלמן The name of this deity has been found on a

Gr. inscr. from Shêḥ Barakât, N. of Aleppo, Σελαμανης CIG 4450. 4451. The Assyr. *Shulmanu* may be the same word (Cl.-Gan. *Ét.* ii 48), but as it occurs only in pr. nn., e.g. Shalman-asar, it may be merely the title of some god; Jastrow *Rel. of Bab. and Assyr.* 189. יברך A brief petition often found at the end of a votive inscr., e.g. 9 8. 12 4. 30 6 &c.

8. Tyre. iii cent. B.C. Louvre.

1 . . . רת עלת שמאלקצדי .. נפעל הסף ז
2 באבן צר ועד כסף [numerals] טבע צר משנ.
3 . . . נדר עבדך ארנבעל השפט בן עזמלך בן
4 . . [הש]פט בן בדמלקרת השפט בן דעמלך
5 . . [השפ]ט בן עזמלך פעל אית חצי הסף ז
6 . . . ת יתן אית החצי הסף ז
7 . . . דל . . . ד שפט בן בדמלקרת
8 . . צאת . . . . . בן
9 . . . [ע]בדבעל . . .

L. 1. עלת is the prep. *upon*. The next four letters are read שמאל *the left* by Cl.-Ganneau *Rec.* i 89; but the letters are very doubtful. נפעל Nif. pf. 3 m. sing. הסף is used in the O.T. for a *sacrificial bowl* Ex. 12 22. 1 K. 7 50. Jer. 52 19. Here we must suppose that the word is used in an extended sense of a large receptacle or *reservoir*. The inscr. is carved on a small moulded cube of stone pierced with a round passage about 4½ inches in diameter; it was probably a spout through which water ran into a tank or reservoir. It seems to be the latter which is referred to as הסף, and not the stone which bears the inscr. The Hebr. סף has also the meaning *threshold*, e.g. Is. 6 4; but this meaning is not suitable here.

L. 2. באבן צר may possibly mean *in Tyrian weight*, cf. אבן המלך 2 S 14 26; but the first word is very uncertain. ועד כסף *and moreover* (?) *silver* (*shekels*). The first of the numerical signs is probably to be taken as the symbol for 1000 [symbol]; it seems to be different from the three signs which follow. This symbol [symbol] is found on the Aram. papyrus CIS ii 147; see Euting *Nabatäische Inschriften* 96 and Schröder *ZDMG* xxxix (1885) 317. The total number will be

1070. צר מבע *coinage of Tyre,* מבע lit. *stamped*; so in Arab. طَبْع *seal, imprint.* The coinage of Tyre, i.e. the Tyrian or Phoen. as distinct from the Attic standard, is frequently mentioned in the Talmud, e.g. *Bab. Qam.* 90 b מנה צורי. *Bekoroth* 49 b. Jos. *Bell.* ii 21 2 Τυρίου νόμισμα. This was the standard adopted by the Hasmonean princes, as being the native and traditional one; see Levy *Gesch. jüd. Münz.* 155.

L. 3. השפט The title only here in Phoenicia itself. At an early date, in the time of Nebuchadnezzar, we hear of a succession of *judges* at Tyre, who took the place of the king; they held office for short terms, and in one instance two ruled together for six years, Jos. *c. Ap.* i 21. Whether this precedent was followed in the third cent. is not known; cf. **17** 2. The *suffetes* at Carthage belonged to a more developed constitution. עזמלך i.e. *Milk is (my) strength*, a common name in the Pun. inscrr.

L. 4. ברמלקרת **6** 2 *n.* רעמ־מלך=רעמלך *D'om is king*, cf. **32** 2 רעמצלח בן רעמתנא צדני. These names show that רעם was a deity who had votaries among the Sidonians at the Piraeus. No further traces of him have as yet been found in Phoen.; but D. H. Müller, *ZDMG* xxx 691 f., quotes רעמם (with mimation) as a pr. name found in Himyaritic; in Arab. too pr. names are formed from the same root. The Arab. دَعْم=*prop, support*; and it is possible that רעם= *Supporter, Upholder.*

L. 5. פעל אית חצי הסף ז *made the half of this tank.* חצי again in CIS i **169** 11.

L. 6. תחצי הסף is a grammatical anomaly.

9. Umm-el-'Awâmid. CIS i 7. Date 132 B.C. Louvre.

[לארן ל]בעל שמם אש נדר עבדאלם
בן מתן בן עבדאלם בן בעלשמר
בפלג לארך אית השער ז והדלהת
אשל פעלת בתכלתי בנתי בשת 𐤗𐤗
𐤗𐤗𐤗 לארן מלכם 𐤗𐤗𐤗 ||| שת לעם
צר לכני לי לסכר ושם נעם
תחת פעם אדני בעל שמם
לעלם יברכן

To the lord Ba'al-shamem (this is that) which 'Abd-elim, [2] son of Mattan, son of 'Abd-elim, son of Ba'al-shamar, in [3] the district of Laodicaea, vowed:—even this gate and the doors [4] thereof I made in fulfilment of it (? ?); I built (this) in the year 189 [5] of the lord of kings, the 143rd year of the people [6] of Tyre, that it may be to me for a memorial and a good name [7] under the foot of my lord Ba'al-shamem [8] for ever: may he bless me!

Umm-el-'Awâmîd is a ruined site near the coast between Tyre and 'Akka.

L. 1. בעל שמם *lord of the heavens*, i.e. the god who dwells in the heavens, to whom the heavens belong[1]. Unlike the early Ba'als who were connected with the earth and with special localities, *Ba'al of heaven* had a general, universal character. He makes his appearance in the later stages of Sem. religion, during the Gk. period. The earliest texts which mention him are the Punic (3–2 cent. B.C.), 39 1 לאדן לבעשמם; CIS i 379 חנא כהן שבעלשמם (Carthage); קבר חמלכת כהן בעלשמם וגו' (a newly discovered inscr. from Carthage, Lidzb. *Eph.* i 248 *n.*); Plaut. *Poen.* v 2 67 *balsamen*. But Carthage was not the original home of the cultus. This inscr., dated 132 B.C., gives evidence for Phoenicia, and throughout the N. Semitic world ב' ש' can be traced at this and a later period; thus among the Nabataeans of Ḥauran CIS ii 163 בעשמין. 176 לבעשמן; in the Ṣafâ inscrr. בעל סמן (Littmann *Ṣafâ-Inschr.* 58. 70); in Palm. 133 1 *n.* The name implies a conception of deity which seems to have been produced by outside influences. Lidzb. l. c. suggestively notices that the Jewish title יהוה אלהי השמים Ezr. 1 2. אל השמים Ps. 136 26. אלה שמיא Ezr. 6 9 &c. מרא שמיא Dan. 5 23 &c., which begins to be used in the Persian period, and may reflect the influence of Persian religion, was circulated by the Jews of the Dispersion at the very time when ב' ש' came into vogue (3–2 cent.); and it is probable that Jewish monotheistic ideas found their way into the surrounding heathenism, as they certainly did at Palmyra (135 1 *n.*). On the other hand, when Syria came under Gk. rule, ב' ש' was readily

[1] The S. Arab. god ד̄שׂמוי is generally said to = ב' ש'; but Lidzb., *Eph.* i 243 ff., has proved that the identification cannot be sustained. The S. Arab. inscrr. do not give ד̄שׂמוי the position of ב' ש'; he is only one among other deities; and 'heaven' is never written שׂמוי in S. Arab. The Minaean form is שׂמהם, the Sabaean שמין, and 'heaven' is always sing. (Hommel *Süd-ar. Chrest.* 46). Like other Arab. names with ذو *possessor of*.., ד̄שׂמוי is an epithet, prob. = *possessor of loftiness.*

identified with Zeus, as later, under the Romans, with Jupiter; thus in 2 Macc. 6 2 ܒܥܠܫܡܝܢ = Ζεὺς Ὀλύμπιος and Ζ. Ξένιος[1]. Yet ב׳ ש׳ never occupied the predominant position of Zeus or Jupiter among the N. Semitic races[2]. Among the Nabataeans (supr.) in Roman times he never took the place of the national god Dushara; at Palmyra he was not counted among the *πατρῷοι θεοί*, and it is remarkable that the dedications which contain his name were made by private persons, and they are few in number. There is no record of any official or general adoption of his worship by a king or city. A striking reference to the god occurs in the story of Aḥiqar. Down to the fifth cent. A.D. his cult lasted in Syria, and from there passed into Armenia; see Lidzb. l. c. מתן Cf. 2 K. 11 18 מַתָּן a priest of Ba'al; *Mitinna* a king of Tyre, inscr. of Tiglath-pileser, *COT* 169; *muttun*, *mythum* &c. in Lat. inscrr., CIL viii p. 1030 a. עבדאלם Ἀβδήλιμος Jos. *c. Ap.* i 21; see 38 6 *n.*

L. 3. בפלג לארך Cf. Hebr. פלך Neh. 3 17 f., and the Assyr. *pulug(g)u* and *pulukku*, both in the sense of 'district,' 'border,' Delitzsch *Assyr. HWB* 525. 527. It is impossible to say which of the many Laodiceas in Syria is intended; perhaps L. ad mare, as distinguished from L. ad Libanum, is the most likely. Appian, *Syriaca* 57, mentions a *Λαοδίκεια ἡ ἐν τῇ Φοινίκῃ*, and there is a series of coins belonging to L. ad Libanum which bear the legend ללארכא אש בכנען 149 B 8[3]. In the Talm. a לודיקיא is mentioned, and the context implies that it was near Tyre, *Menaḥoth* 85 b: also *Siphre* (Deut.) 148 a, ed. Friedmann. The ב in בפלג is rendered 'oriundus a' by Winckler *Altor. Forsch.* i 65; but the rendering is scarcely supported, see 5 6 *n.* Cl.-Gan. takes לארך as the name of a month, *λαοδίκιος*, and explains thus: the vow was made in the middle (בפלג lit. *division*) of the month, and the building carried out at the end of it (בתכלתי), *Ét.* i 37 ff. דלהת From דל 20 A 5. Ps. 141 3 = דַּלֶּת.

[1] The שקוץ שמם of Dan. 12 11 &c. is prob. an intentional disfigurement of בעל שמם, Nestle *ZATW* (1884) 248, Driver *Daniel* 188. In *Julian* ed. Hoffmann 249 l. 8 he is mentioned along with Zeus, Hermes, Serapis.

[2] Philo of Bybl. exaggerates when he says *τοῦτον γὰρ* (*τὸ ἥλιον*) *θεὸν ἐνόμιζον μόνον οὐρανοῦ κύριον Βεελσάμην καλοῦντες*, *Fr. Hist. Gr.* iii 565 f. The identification with the sun is hardly correct.

[3] Babelon gives ללארכא אם בכנען *L. the metropolis of Canaan*, *RS* p. 84, cf. p. 86 לצר אם צדנם, 149 B 15 לצדנם אם כמב אפא כה צר; but the construction אם ב׳ is objectionable, and אש the rel. should be read, ם and ש being almost indistinguishable on the coins. It is surprising to find the same legend on coins of Berytus (Babelon *Pers. Ach.* clxlii f.); but the L. of the inscr. is not likely to have been Berytus, which was destroyed by Tryphon in 140 B.C.

For the ת artificially inserted in the plur., cf. Hebr. אֲמָהוֹת, Aram. אַמְהָן, ܐܡܗܬܐ, Arab. أُمَّهَاتٌ, and 68 16 *n.*

L. 4. אשל מעלת בתכלתי בנתי No satisfactory explanation of these words has been discovered. The translation given above is that of the Corpus; אשל = אשר לו, מעלת Pf. 1 sing., בתכלתי *in the fulfilment of it*, i.e. the vow, בנתי Pf. 1 sing. But ל by itself = לי (לו) is contrary to usage, and the suff. in בתכלתי has no direct antecedent. Another explanation is אש לְמַעֲלַת בַּת כָּלְתִי בָּנִתִי *which are for the making of the temple, I have finished; I built it . . .*, or *I have completely built.* But we should expect the forms כלת, בנת for the Pf. 1 sing., and perhaps תַּבַּת. Lidzb. proposes to treat ל before מעלת as an affirmative, the Arab. لَ, and תכלתי as a noun תִּכְלִית or תִּכְלַת with ״ compaginis, and בנתי as inf. constr. with suff., *which I have indeed made in the completion of my building*; this involves too many doubtful assumptions. בשת Sing.; see 6 1 *n.*

L. 5. לאדן מלכם 5 18 *n.* The date is reckoned by the Seleucid era which began in 312 B.C.[1] Strictly speaking the *lord of kings* was Alexander the Great (died 323 B.C.); at the time when the era was instituted, however, the reigning king was Seleucus i Nicator. 'The 180th year of the Seleucids' will be 132 B.C., and 'the 143rd year of the people of Tyre' thus makes the Tyrian era begin in 275 B.C., at which time the city, after its capture by Ptolemy Philadelphus, began to recover itself as an autonomous municipality.

L. 6. לכני i.e. לְכֹנִי لِكَوْنِي = לְחַיּוֹתוֹ סכר = זכר 56 1. שם Cf. Is. 56 5; and for שם נעם cf. שם טב 65 3, and in the Mishnah, e.g. *Berakoth* 17 a.

L. 7. מעם = Hebr. רֶגֶל. אדני *My* or *his lord.* The context makes the former more suitable.

L. 8. יברכן Cf. 7 2 *n.* The suff. shows that here and elsewhere the verb is Piel not Pual.

[1] Its starting-point was the victory of Ptolemy i Soter, the ally of Seleucus, over Demetrius Poliorcetes, son of Antigonus, at Gaza in 312 B.C. This was followed by the victory of Seleucus over Nicanor the general of Antigonus, the recovery of Babylon, and the conquest of Susiana and Media. Porphyr. Tyr. *Fr. Hist. Gr.* iii 707. See Cl.-Gan. *Ét.* i 60 ff.; Bevan *House of Seleucus* i 52. The Seleucid era was used by the Nabataeans, 97 iii *n.*, by the Palmyrenes, 110 5 *n.*, and by the Jews, who called it מנין שטרות *the era of contracts*, e.g. '*Ab. zar.* 10 a. For other designations see 1 Macc. 1 11. Jos. *Ant.* xii 5 3. xiii 6 7.

10. Ma'sûb. Date 222 B.C. Louvre.

1 ערפת כברת מצא שמש וצ
2 פלי אש בן האלם מלאך מלכ
3 עשתרת ועבדי בעל חמן
4 לעשתרת באשרת אל חמן
5 בשת א ||| ||| לפתלמים ארן
6 מלכם האדר פעל נעם בן פת
7 למים וארסנאם אלן א[ח]
8 ים שלש חמשם שת לעם [צר]
9 כמאש בן אית כל אחרי . . .
10 . . ם אש בארץ לכן לם ל . . .
11 . . . . . . עלם

The portico on the quarter (?) of the sun-rise and the north (side) [2] of it, which the Elim, the envoys of Milk-[3] 'Ashtart and her servants, the citizens of Ḥammon, built [4] to 'Ashtart in the ashērah (?), the god of Ḥammon, [5] in the 50th year of Ptolemy, lord [6] of kings, the noble, the beneficent, son of Ptolemy [7] and Arsinoë, the divine Adel[8]phoi, in the three (and) fiftieth year of the people of [Tyre]; [9] as also they built all the rest . . [10] . . . . which . in the land, to be to them for . . [11] . . . . . . ever.

Ma'sûb is situated to the S. of Umm-el-'Awâmîd, about half way between Tyre and Ptolemais ('Akka). The general purport of the inscr. seems to be this: Certain distinguished citizens of Ḥammon, a town near Tyre, build or restore a portico in the neighbouring temple of 'Ashtart at Ma'sûb, in honour of their own Milk-'Ashtart, the deity of Ḥammon. It may have been that the temple of Ḥammon was founded from that at Ma'sûb, and the restoration an act of piety towards the mother-shrine.

L. 1. ערפת See **3** 6 *n*. כברת The √כבר=*be much, great*, as in Assyr. *kabâru*, Old Aram. e.g. **61** 11. **62** 4. 9, Aram. ܟܒܪ, Arab. كَبُرَ; so 'כ may be taken as an adj. agreeing with ערפת *the great portico.*

A more expressive meaning, however, is suggested by the Assyr. *kibratu* 'a (widely) extended territory,' 'a quarter of the world,' e.g. *šar kibrat arbaʿi* 'king of the four quarters,' Schrader *COT* 247, cf. the Hebr. כברת הארץ Gen. 35 16 &c. *a distance* (lit. *a large space*) *of land*; hence we may render 'כ *quarter*. In this case כברת will be an accus. of place, defined more fully by the following genit. מצא שמש (a single term) as often in Hebr., e.g. Ex. 33 10. 1 K. 19 13. Jer. 36 10. If כברת be rendered *great*, then מצא will be accus., *on the east*, cf. Josh. 1 4. 15. 23 4. For מצא cf. Ps. 75 7 and the Old Aram. מוקא שמש 62 14.

L. 2. וצפלי Perhaps *and the north* (*side*) *of it*, צפל=צָפוֹן, נ being interchanged with ל, as לשכה and נשכה *chamber*. The ו co-ordinates the word with עד, to which also the suff. refers. For the suff. י used for the fem. (ע fem. in 3 6) as well as for the mas. cf. עברי l. 3 and CIS i 280 בר ארני . . . איש נדרא שרונת. A different meaning is suggested by Halévy *Rev. Ét. Juiv.* xii 109 f., who takes צפל as a dialectical form of טפל (cf. נצר and נטר)=*attach, add*, in Rabb. Hebr. טָפֵל *something attached, subordinate*, so וצפלי=וּטְפָלֶיהָ *and its annexes*. The first explanation is preferable. האלם appears to be a title, 'primores,' *chiefs, leaders*; cf. אֵלֵי מואב Ex. 15 15. Eze. 17 13 &c. This use of the word is perhaps to be found again on the Phoen. seal 150 5 לבעליתן אש אלם אש מלקרתרצף. מלאך Plur. constr.= מַלְאֲכֵי, in appos. to האלם. Cf. Le Bas-Waddington *Voy. Arch.* iii no. 1890 Λούκιος Ἀκκαβαίου εὐσεβ[ῶν] καὶ πεμφθεὶς ὑπὸ τῆς κυρίας Ἀταργάτης (from Kefr Hawar).

L. 3. מלכעשתרת The name of the goddess and her city occur again in inscrr. from the same neighbourhood, CIS i 8 למלכעשתרת אל חמן, and לבעליתן בן עבדחר כהן מלכעשתרת (recently discovered) Cl.-Gan. *Rec.* v 151; cf. also the Pun. inscr. CIS i 250 בדעשתרת . . עבד בת מלכעשתרת. Milk-'Ashtart is a distinct deity formed out of the combined attributes of Milk and 'Ashtart. In the combination 'Ashtart predominates, for the deity thus conceived is a goddess, not a god. Other examples of compound divinities are אשמנעשתרת CIS i 245 3 f. עשתר כמש 1 17. מלכבעל 37 1 *n.* מלכאסר ib. מלקרתרצף 150 5 &c.; see Baethgen *Beitr.* 37 ff. As the name of a god, מלך alone is not found (see, however, 50 1 *n.*); but the many pr. nn. of which מלך forms a part imply that a deity was worshipped in Phoenicia and its colonies under this title; 3 1 *n.*, Driver *Deut.* 223[1]. ועברי Not plur. constr., for this form is not written with

[1] Hoffmann, *Ueb. einige Phön. Inschr.* 26, renders *Queen-'Ashtart* (Milka-'Ashtart, but in Phoen. this would be Milkath-'Ashtart), *King Ba'al* &c. We

√ in Phoen., e.g. מלאך l. 2, בעל (prob.) l. 3, אלן l. 7; it is therefore plur. with suff. 3 fem. sing.=עַבְדֶיהָ. Cf. צמלי l. 2 *n*. בעל חמן This must prob. be rendered *citizens of Ḥammon*, cf. CIS i 120 הרנא בעלת בזנתי 'Eirene, the citizeness of Byzantium.' 309 3 בעל תברבשי; NPun. בעל המכתערם 54 2; Sab. אבעל CIS iv 86 8. 172 1; and בעלי יריחו Josh. 24 11. Jud. 9 2. If בעל be taken as a divine name, עבדי must=*her servant the Ba'al of Ḥ.*, an unsuitable expression, for Ba'al could not be termed the servant of 'Ashtart. To render *his servant B.-ḥammān's*, on the analogy of לםלכי מלך אשמנעזר 5 1, is to introduce confusion into the general sense of the inscr. A place called חַמּוֹן (*hot spring?*), near Tyre, is mentioned in Josh. 19 28 as belonging to Asher; it is prob. to be identified with Umm-el-'Awâmîd (9), where there are ruins of a Phoen. city: Guérin *Galilée* ii 141, Hoffmann l. c., Buhl *Geogr. Alt. Pal.* 229[1].

L. 4. לעשתרת באשרת This difficult phrase is usually rendered *to 'Ashtart in the ashērah*, the goddess being regarded as dwelling in her symbol, the sacred pole (בָּאֲשֵׁרָה); see Cl.-Gan. *Rec.* i 83, Robertson Smith *Rel. of Sem.* 172, Driver *Deuteron.* 202 f. We have no clear evidence, however, that the *ashērah* was the symbol of 'Ashtart. Ohnefalsch-Richter, *Cyprus, the Bible and Homer* 165. 168, explains *'Ashtart in the ashērah* as referring to an image of 'Ashtart standing in a niche in an *ashērah*, and he gives an illustration of Artemis in a similar position. But it is by no means certain that the poles or trees figured on gems &c. to which he alludes are *ashērahs*; so that this explanation has only the value of a conjecture. The most plausible solution of the difficulty is that proposed by Hoffmann l. c. The primary meaning of אשרת he takes to have been a *sign-post* set up to mark the site or the boundaries of a deity's influence; cf. Assyr. *ašru* 'place,' Aram. ܐܬܪܐ *place*, Arab. أَثَرٌ *sign, trace*, from the same root. Meaning originally the *sign* of the deity's habitation, the *ashērah* would readily be used of the *sacred precincts* or τέμενος of the god, which is exactly the sense required here; in Assyr. *aširtu, eširtu*

must take מלך, like בעל and אמן, as an appellative; but while two divine names are sometimes compounded to form a single divinity as above, the language does not favour a combination of this kind; the analogy of ordinary pr. nn. compounded with מלך requires that מלך be taken as a predicate, e. g. מלכיה *Yah is king*. *Ba'al is king* would be a suitable name for a man, but not for the god himself.

[1] Meyer, *Ency. Bibl.* 3741, renders ב' חמן *B.-ḥammān* (37 4 *n*.) i. e. the numen occupying the ḥammān of Milk-'Ashtart, *the god of the ḥammān-pillar*, who in turn has an ashērah in which dwells an Astarte, the dedication being made to the latter. This seems improbable. Would ב' חמן be called *his servant* (עבדי) in relation to אל חמן?

actually denotes a 'sanctuary' or 'temple'; so Zimmern *KAT*[3] 437 *n*. The fem. ending does not mark the gender, according to Hoffmann, but has merely a grammatical significance; it is the sign of a 'nomen unitatis' (Ges. § 122 *t*). The word *ashērah* has been read in only one other inscr., **14** 3, and there the text is uncertain. It is true that אשרה was a goddess, known in Assyria as *Ash-ra-tum*, in Arabia as *Athirat* (cf. **69** 16 *n*.), and in Canaan, 1 K. **15** 13 = 2 Ch. **15** 16. 2 K. **21** 7. **23** 4. 7; see Lagrange *Relig. Sém.* 120 ff. Here, however, באשרת cannot be treated as a divine name. אל חמן Again in CIS i 8 למלכעשתרת אל חמן from Umm-el-'Awâmîd; this shows that אל חמן is in apposition to לעשתרת.

L. 5. ארן מלכם **5** 18 *n*.; Ptolemy iii Euergetes, B.C. 247–221. בשת Sing. for the usual בשנת plur., see **6** 1 *n*.

L. 6. חארר corresponds to the Gk. μεγαλοδόξου; see **5** 9 *n*. פעל נעם i.e. εὐεργέτου; cf. **8** 8. בן פתלמים *son of Ptolemy*, i.e. of Ptolemy ii Philadelphus, B.C. 285–247. Cf. **27** 1.

L. 7. ארסנאם i.e. 'Αρσινόης. The Phoen. has transcribed the genitive; cf. **27** 2. אלן א[ח]ים i.e. אֵלֶן אַחִים cf. **8** 10 *n*., the Phoen. equivalent of the title θεῶν ἀδελφῶν in Gk. Ptolemaic inscrr., e.g. the bilingual inscr. of Canopus (B.C. 238), where Ptolemy iii is styled τοῦ Πτολεμαίου καὶ 'Αρσινόης θεῶν ἀδελφῶν, Michel **551**; see **95** 1 *n*.

L. 8. לעם [צר] See **9** 5 *n*.

L. 9. כמאש = כְּמוֹ אֲשֶׁר, see **3** 7 *n*.; lit. *according as*, introducing a fresh *item*; similarly **45** 1. 4. בן The subj. is האלם l. 2. אתרי Prob. = אחרית, here used in a concrete sense, as in **42** 4. 8. 10 אתרי השאר; Cl.-Gan. *Rec.* i 85. Hoffmann conjectures המקד[ש]ם for the missing word.

L. 10. בארץ Perhaps the land within the domain of the sanctuary of Ḥammon (Hoffm.). לכן לם ל .. Cf. **9** 6, which suggests that the line may be restored ל[סכר ושם נעם ל]עלם.

CYPRUS

11. Ba'al Lebanon. CIS i 5. viii cent. B.C. Biblioth. Nat., Paris.

a ..ו סכן קרתחדשת עבד חרם מלך צדנם אז יתן לבעל לבנן אדני
בראשת נחשת ח ... *a*

b ..טב סכן קרתחדשת

c [לב]על לבנן אדני

a . . . governor of Qarth-ḥadasht, servant of Ḥiram, king of the Sidonians, gave this to Ba'al of Lebanon, his lord, of choicest bronze.

b . . ṬB, governor of Qarth-ḥadasht.

c to Ba'al of Lebanon, his lord.

These inscriptions, the most ancient examples of the Phoen. language and writing yet discovered, are found upon eight fragments of thin bronze, which formed parts of bowls or paterae used for ceremonial purposes[1]. Six of the fragments when pieced together make up inscr. *a*; the remaining two, *b* and *c*, are considered to have belonged to a second bowl, owing to slight differences in some of the letters, e.g. א and ל. The writing is of the archaic type represented by the Moabite Stone (ix cent.) and the Old Aramaic of the Zenjirli inscrr. (viii cent.), allowing for the differences between engraving on metal and carving on stone. The Old Greek alphabet belongs to the same type; in particular, the correspondence between the ǂ i.e. ז and the † i.e. ח and the same letters in Old Greek is noticeable. On this account Lidzbarski (p. 176) is disposed to assign the inscrr. to a date not far from the period when the Greeks borrowed their alphabet from the Semites (2nd millennium B.C.), considerably earlier than the date of the Moabite Stone. Internal evidence, however, favours a later age,

[1] Fine specimens of these bowls, discovered at Nimroud, may be seen in the British Museum, Nimroud Gallery, table-cases C and D. They are the work of Phoen. artists; in some instances the artist's name is inscribed on the edge in Phoen. letters. The design and workmanship exhibit the characteristics of Egyptian art. The date of the bowls is not earlier than 700 B.C. See Brit. Mus. *Guide to Babyl. & Assyr. Antiq.* (1900) 22 f.

that of the Zenjirli inscrr. (**61–63**), the middle of the eighth cent. B.C.; and the character of the writing agrees with this.

The fragments, now in the Bibliothèque Nationale, were found in Cyprus. The dedication to Ba'al of Lebanon seems at first sight to point to Phoenicia or Syria as their original home. But the Phoen. colony in Cyprus may well have carried with them the cult of their deity from the mother-land; or if the סכן *governor* came from Phoenicia, he may have wished to remember the god of his native place, just as the Tyrian colonists at Malta made their dedication to Melqarth, the Ba'al of Tyre, **36** 1.

סכן *governor, prefect*, cf. סֹכֵן *steward* Is. 22 15. The title occurs in the Tell-el-Amarna letters, apparently as a Canaanite loan-word, *sukini = rabisi* 'officer' 237 9. The √ = *be of use, service* (Hebr.), *care for* (Assyr.). קרתחדשת i.e. *new-town*, 'Carthage.' That there was a place of this name in *Cyprus* is made certain by the mention of *Ḳarti-ḫadas(š)ti* (Assyr. ס interchanged with north-semitic ש) in the lists of Asarhaddon and Ašurbanipal, along with well-known Cyprian towns, such as Paphos, Idalion, Tamassos; *KB* ii 240. It is clear from this inscr. that the city at this period was under the dominion of the Phoen. king. Its site is unknown. An attempt is made by Schrader, *Sitzungsb. Berl. Akad.* (1890) 337–344, to identify it with Kition, the modern Larnaka. *Ḳarti-ḫadasti* occupies, he says, the place on the Assyr. lists where we should expect to find Kition; and as the name קרת־חדשת *new-town* suggests a previous 'old town,' it is probable that 'ק'ח was the Phoen. quarter of the ancient Kition. The identification he thinks to be confirmed by the discovery in Larnaka itself of an inscr. containing the words עבד' הקרתחדשתי *'Abd. the man of Carthage*, **20** B 6. This is very likely the Cyprian Carthage; but the special mention of the individual's native place rather points to the fact that his home was not in Kition but elsewhere. The bronze fragments are said to have been found on a mountain 20 miles NE. of Limassol and 10 from the sea (CIS i p. 23), at some distance from Larnaka; but this can have no bearing on the argument, for the bowls may have been removed from the place to which they originally belonged. The evidence, in fact, is not sufficient to establish Schrader's identification. עבד *servant* i.e. high official as עבד מלך בבל in 2 K. 25 8. Lidzb., ? *vassal* as in the Zenjirli inscr. **63** 3. חרם i.e. חִירָם = אֲחִירָם *brother of the exalted one*; cf. חמלך **40** 2. חמלכת ib. חיאל 1 K. 16 34 for 'אח. Ḥiram here has the title מלך צדנם *king of the Sidonians*. It is improbable that he is the Ḥiram i who was the friend of David and Solomon, for this Ḥiram is consistently called *king of Tyre* in the O.T., e.g. 2 S. 5 11. 1 K. 5 15. 9 11 &c.; and historical usage shows that מלך צר did not mean the same thing as מלך צידנים. The official title *king of the Sidonians* implies the union of Tyre and Sidon under one ruler; thus Ethba'al circ. 855 B.C. is called מלך צידנים in 1 K. 16 31 and Τυρίων καὶ Σιδονίων βασιλεύς by Josephus (*Ant.* viii 13 1 cf. Τυρίων βασ. ib. 13 2). The king of the Sidonians was virtually king of all Phoenicia, Sidonians being a general term for Phoenicians used by the people themselves (e.g. 4 1 f. 5 1 f.), by the Assyrians, by the Hebrews (e.g. Jud. 3 3. 1 K. 11 5 &c.), and by the Greeks (Homer, e.g. *Od.* 4 618. *Il.* 6 290). Another Ḥiram (*Ḫirummu*) is mentioned by Tiglath-pileser iii as paying tribute in 738 B.C. (*COT* 252). It is true he is called *of Tyre* (*Ṣurrai*); but since no king of Sidon is mentioned—if there had been one the Assyrian king would certainly not have allowed him to escape tribute—we may conclude that Sidon was at this time subject to Tyre, and Ḥiram ii king of both cities. Hence מלך צדנם would have been his full official title; and the probability is that this Ḥiram ii, who was reigning in 738, is the king alluded to in the inscr. The epigraphical evidence supports this date; for the character of the writing closely resembles that of the Old Aram. of the Zenjirli inscrr., which belong to this period, and mention Tiglath-pileser by name, 62 15 f. 63 3. 6. The third Ḥiram known to us as the contemporary of Cyrus (Jos. *c. Ap.* i 21) is altogether excluded; he could not have been called מלך צדנם, for by his time the title had long been an anachronism. The union of the two cities under the hegemony of Tyre came to an end in 701, when Sennacherib expelled Luli *šarru Ṣiduni* (= Ἐλουλαῖος king of *Tyre*, Jos. *Ant.* ix 14 2), and made Sidon subject to Assyria; *KB* ii 90. Tyre survived as a separate state with a king of its own. The above view is stated forcibly by Landau *Beitr. z. Altertumsk. d. Orients* i (1893) 17–29. אז Demonstr. pron.; add. note ii p. 26. בעל לבנן is not mentioned elsewhere; cf. הר בעל חרמן Jud. 3 3, and the Ζεὺς ὄρειος = בעל ההרים to whom a temple was dedicated at the gates of Sidon, Renan *Mission de Phénicie* 397. ארני Cf. 7 2. 12 4 &c. בראשת נ' Cf. Am. 6 6 ראשית שמנים *the best of ointments*; it is also possible to render *as the first-fruits* (ἀπαρχή) *of bronze*, cf. Ex. 23 19 &c. The ב' is *beth essentiae*.

12. Kition. CIS i 10. B.C. 341. Paris.

1 בימם ||| ||| לירח בל בשנת ־׳־ | למ[לך פמייתן מלך כתי ו]
2 אדיל ותמש בן מלך מלכיתן מלך כתי ואדיל מזבח א[ז]
3 וארום אשנם || אש יתן בדא כהן רשפחץ בן יכנש
4 לם בן אשמנאדן לאדני לרשפחץ יברך

On the 6th day of the month Bul, in the 21st year of ki[ng Pumi-yathon, king of Kition and] Idalion and Tamassos, son of king Milk-yathon, king of Kition and Idalion. This altar and two hearths (?) 2 (are they) which Bodo, priest of Reshef-ḥeṣ, son of Yakun-shalom, son of Eshmun-adon, gave to his lord Reshef-ḥeṣ. May he bless!

L. 1. vi בימם lit. *in days*, 6 for *on the sixth day*, xxi בשנת lit. *in years*, 21 for *in the twenty-first year* (see **6** 1 *n.*). This clumsy expedient is used to express the ordinal numbers which Phoen. does not possess; instinctively the noun was written in the plur. before the numerical signs; cf. **14** 1. **23** 1. **27** 1. In Hebr. and Aram. a similar usage is occasionally found, e.g. Ex. 19 15 לשלשת ימים *after three days*, i.e. *on the third day*; Dan. 12 12 *unto* 1335 *days*, i.e. *unto the* 1335*th day*; Mishnah *Berakoth* 9 b עד ג׳ שעות i.e. *to the third hour*; Mt. 20 3 ܒܬܠܬ ܫ̈ܥܝܢ; König *Syntax* § 315 m, *Lehrgeb.* ii 255 *n.* A less probable explanation is that ימם is not plur. but sing., יֹמָם, like the Aram. יְמָמָא, ܝܘܡܡܐ (Nöldeke *ZDMG* xl 721); the Aram. יממא, however, is used of *day* as distinguished from *night*, and not in such constructions as the above. בל Cf. **5** 1 *n.* למ[לך פמייתן Restored from **18** 1 f. With פמייתן cf. עבדפמי **23** 6. אמתפמי=מתפמי CIS i **55**. פמיש[מע] ib. 197 3. The form suggests that there is some connexion between פמי, clearly a divinity, and the god פעם in the pr. nn. עבדפעם CIS i 112 c[1]. c[3]. נעמפעם Eut. *Carth.* 263 2 (*namphamo* &c. in Lat. inscrr., CIL viii p. 1030 b), but the exact nature of the connexion has not been made out. It is possible that פעם forms an element in the names Pygmaios, Pygmalion (? פעם עליון)[1]; at any rate Pygmalion could be confused with Pumi-yathon, as will appear below. An

[1] It is curious actually to find the name פגמלין in Phoen. (Punic), and in combination with עשתרת, apparently as a deity. It occurs in an inscr. on a gold medallion found in a grave at Carthage, 1894, and written in the earliest type of characters. The form of the name must be due to Gk. influence. The inscr. is given in Lidzbarski 171; see also Cl.-Gan. *Rec.* v 152 *n.*

interesting side-light is thrown by Gk. historians upon Pumi-yathon (361–312 B.C.). Athenaeus Deipnosoph., *Fr. Hist. Gr.* ii 472, on the authority of the historian Daris, says that Alexander, after the capture of Tyre (332 B.C.), gave to one Pnytagoras an estate which Pasicyprus king of Amathous sold along with his crown to Pumatos of Kition, Πυμάτῳ τῷ Κιτιεῖ. There is good reason for believing that this estate was none other than Tamassos. For if we compare **26** 1 and this inscr., on the one hand, with **13** 1 on the other, we may infer that Pumi-yathon acquired Tamassos between the 8th and 21st year of his reign, and lost it between his 21st and 37th year, i.e. between 341 and 325. This agrees very well with the statement of Athenaeus that Alexander disposed of it in 332. Pumi-yathon's reign continued for some time after the latest date furnished by the inscrr. (**13** 1), as appears from his coins, stamped with his 46th year (**149** B 6). Diodorus Sic., xix 79, tells us how his reign came to an end; he was put to death by Ptolemy i Soter, who came to Cyprus ἐπὶ τοὺς ἀπειθοῦντας τῶν βασιλέων· Πυγμαλιῶνα δὲ εὑρὼν διαπρεσβευόμενον πρὸς Ἀντίγονον ἀνεῖλε. Diodorus calls him Pygmalion; but this is prob. only another name for Pumi-yathon; see Babelon *Pers. Achém.* cxxxi, Droysen *Hellenica* ii **2** 10. His death took place in 312; after this, the reckoning by the era of עם כתי began, i.e. in 311 B.C. מלך כתי ואדיל The usual title of the kings of Cyprus. כתי=Kition, on the S. coast; the importance of the town was such that 'the people of Kition,' כִּתִּים or כִּתִּיִּים, was the name given by the Hebrews to all the inhabitants of Cyprus. אדיל=Idalion, in the middle of the island, NW. of Kition. This and the following city are found in the lists of Asarhaddon and Assur-banipal, *COT* 355 ll. 13. 19.

L. 2. תמש=Tamassos, N. of Idalion; only here in the Phoen. inscrr. known. מלכיתן Cf. **13** 2. CIS i **16**. **89** &c., and on coins, **149** B 5. מזבח Cf. **3** 4.

L. 3. ארום Meaning uncertain, possibly *lions* (אֲרָיִים=אֲרָיִים), carved in stone and placed beside the altar; cf. τοὺς δύο λέοντας, dedicated to Ba'al or Zeus, in a Gk. inscr. found near Sidon, Renan *Miss. de Phén.* 397. More probably *altar-hearths*, from ארה (ארי, ארו) *burn*, Arab. إِرَةٌ plur. إِرُونَ *hearth*; אראל **1** 12. אשנם=שְׁנַיִם cf. אשן **23** 6. For the prosthetic א cf. Arab. اِثْنَانِ. ברא Cf. **14** 2 f. **31** c, frequently in Carth. inscrr. It is prob. that ברא is a shortened form of בד־מלקרת, בד־אשמן, or some such name, rather than of עבדא; see **6** 2 *n*. In Hebr. the ending would be וֹן, e.g. חנא=חַנּוּן, עבדא=עַבְדּוֹן. רשפחץ The deity רשף, *Reshef* or *Reshûf*, cf. the Assyr. (א)רְשֻׁף or (א)רְשֵׁף, occurs frequently in Cyprian inscrr. and pr. nn., e.g. רשפיתן 15 2. 23 2–6. עבדרשף 27 4; cf. מלקרתרצף 150 5. His cult was popular in Cyprus, and especially at Idalion; but beyond an allusion to his temple at Carthage CIS i 251 [עבד בת ארש[ף (the reading [עבדארש[ף in ib. 393 is uncertain), Phoen. inscrr. do not mention him outside Cyprus. In N. Syria, however, his worship was of ancient date; 61 2. 3. רשף = *flame, lightning-flash*, Ps. 78 48. Cant. 8 6; hence the god was identified with Apollo (30, Tam. 2, CIS i 89), who as *ἑκηβόλος, ἑκατηβόλος* &c. was the author of pestilence (*Il.* i 50 f.). Thus רשף may have been the Phoen. Fire-god who smites men and cattle with fiery darts (cf. Dt. 32 23. Hab. 3 5; Driver *Deut.* 368). The name always has a qualifying term, e.g. רשף־מכל (24 2. 25 2. 26 2 from Idalion), ר׳ אליית (30 3 f. from Tamassos), ר׳ אלהיתס Tam. 2 4. In these three instances the qualifying term is the name of a place or city; it is probable, therefore, that the same is the case in ר׳ חץ *Reshef of ḥṣ*, ? Issos (Cilicia). Cl.-Ganneau, vocalizing ר׳ חֻץ, takes the name to be a Phoen. rendering of Ἀπόλλων Ἀγυιεύς 'Apollo who guards the streets'; the explanation is ingenious, and may be illustrated by the Assyr. *ilu suḳi* 'the god of the streets.' The original pronunciation of רשף is preserved in the name of an Arab village near Jaffa, ارسوف *Arsûf* (cf. ארשף above) = the Seleucid *Apollonias*; *Rec.* i 176 ff. In Egyptian the god is called Raspu or Resoup; he is represented as bearded, like Apollo, and is mentioned among Asiatic deities; Müller *Asien u. Eur.* 311 f. The Corp. takes the view that ר׳ חץ = *Reshef of the arrow*, cf. Ps. 76 4 רשפי קשת; but the figure of Raspu from Egypt. monuments, given in Corp. p. 38, holds a spear, not an arrow, and for other reasons the view is improbable. יכנשלם i.e. *peace be* (*to him*); again in 14 2 (rest.), and in NPun.

L. 4. אשמנאדן See 5 17 *n*.

18. Kition. CIS i 11. B.C. 325.

1 בימם 𐤘 IIII לירח . מרפא . בשנת 𐤘 𐤗 III IIII למלך . פמייתן .
מלך . כת[י] . ואדיל . בן . מלך .

2 מלכיתן . מל[ך .] כתי . ואדיל . [ס]מלת . א[ז] . אש . יתן . ויטנא .
מנחשת . יאש . אשת . [בעלת]יתן . עב

3 [ד . בת . עשתר]ת . [בת] שמעא . ב[ן] ב[עליתן] . לרבתי . לעשתרת .
[תש]מע [. ק]ל

On the 14th day of the month Merpa, in the 37th year of king Pumi-yathon, king of Kition and Idalion, son of king Milk-yathon, king of Kition and Idalion:—This statue (is that) which Yaash, wife of [Ba'alath?]-yathon, temple-serv[ant of 'Ashtar]t, daughter of Shime'o, son of Ba'al-yathon, gave and set up of bronze to her mistress, 'Ashtart; may she hear (her) voice!

This inscr. was found and inaccurately copied by Pococke at Larnaka in 1738, with 32 others; they have all since disappeared.

L. 1. xiv בימם See **12** 1 *n*. מרפא Name of a month, according to Euting, *Sechs Phön. Inschr.* (1875), the 7th month, October. It is also called מרפאם Idal. 7 (Euting *Sits. Berl. Akad.* (1887) 422), CIS i **124** 3 (Malta), **179** 5 (Carthage). פמייתן See **12** 1 *n*. It is noteworthy that Tamassos does not occur in the king's title in his 37th year.

L. 2. [ס]מלת Fem., because the statue represented a female figure—the goddess 'Ashtart; similarly CIS i **40**. When the statue represented a male the mas. is used, e. g. **23** 2. 5. **25** 1. **27** 3; the same distinction is observed in the use of צלמא and צלמתא in Palmyrene. In the O. T. סֶמֶל occurs Dt. 4 16. Eze. 8 3. 5. 2 Ch. 33 7. 15. יתן ויטנא Perf. 3 fem.; the same formula in **23** 2. **30** 1. יטנא is Hif., cf. יקדש **28** 4. יקדשת **29** 9. 14. The initial *h* of the Hifil was weakened into the spiritus lenis and written with initial י, but prob. pronounced *i'tnî*, *iqdîsh*; cf. the similar weakening of the *h* into أ in Arabic, conj. iv; Stade *Morg. Forsch.* 208. In NPun. the Qal טנא is used in the same sense. בעל[ת]יתן So Corp.; but the reading is very doubtful.

L. 3. עבד בת ע' So restored by Berger, and adopted by Corp.; frequently in Carth. inscrr. שמעא In Hebr. שִׁמְעוֹן, a diminutive from שמע־בעל **33** 2. Adopting the text above, the husband, father, and grandfather of Yaash are mentioned. לרבתי The suff. י is here used for the 3 sing. fem.; similarly בני **27** 4.

14. Kition. CIS i **13**. B.C. 375.

1 [בי]מם ᐱ לירח זבחששם בשנת II [..למלך מלכיתן מלך כתי ואדיל סמלת ז אש יתן ו]

2 יטנא עבדאסר בן בדא בן יכ[נשלם על אשתי על...בת...בן...בן]

3 בדא לרבתי לאם האזרת כ שמ[ע קל תברך]

On the 20th day of the month Zebaḥ-Šiššim (?) in the 2nd (?) year of [......] 'Abd-osir, son of Bodo, son of Yak[un-shalom ....], set up [....] of Bodo, to his lady, the glorious (?) Mother, because she heard [...].

More than half of the inscr. has perished; but most of what is missing may be supplied with probability from the preceding inscrr. **12** and **13**.

L. 1. xx ביםם See **12** 1 *n*. זבחששם The name of a month. The text here is rather obscure, but the reading given is determined by **29** 4, where the word occurs again. Berger, *Rev. d'Assyr.* iii (1895) 69 ff., regards ששם as the name of a god, and, supposing that ש is interchanged with ס, identifies him with ססם *Sasom* in the Cyprian name עבדססם **16** 1 *n*. **27** 3 &c. The month זבחששם is then explained as the month in which sacrifices were offered to Sasom; for the constrn. cf. זבחי אלהים 'sacrifices *offered to* God,' Ps. **51** 19. But as Cl.-Ganneau justly remarks, there is no evidence that Sasom, who seems to have been a foreign deity, occupied such a place of importance in the Phoen. pantheon as to have given his name to a month in the calendar. We should therefore render זבחששם *sacrifice of sixty*, i.e. the month of the sixty sacrifices, and compare ἑκατομβαιών, the name of the first month in the Athenian calendar; *Ét.* ii § 20. The king mentioned here was either Milk-yathon or Pumi-yathon, prob. the former; for the full style of Pumi-yathon, as given in **12** and **13**, would make the line too long.

L. 2. ימנא See **13** 2 *n*. עבדאסר *Servant of Osiris*, cf. **16** 1. **18** 2 f. **36** 2 (in Gk. Διονύσιος). **27** 2 אמתאסר. **69** 9 פמסרי. ברא בן יכ[נשלם] The same names in **12** 3 f., but not the same persons. The Bodo ben Yakun-shalom who dedicated an altar in the 21st year of Pumi-yathon (341) could hardly have had a son who set up a statue early in the reign of Milk-yathon, circ. 375.

L. 3. לרבתי Cf. **18** 3. לאם For *Mother* as the title of a goddess cf. לרבת לאמא **47**. לאם לרבת לתנת CIS i 195 2. לאם רבת מן בעל 380 4, all Carthaginian. The *Mother* may have been a Phoen. goddess, or one adopted from the Gk. or Egypt. pantheon; there are traces of the worship of Demeter in Cyprus (see Cl.-Gan. *Ét.* i 154 f.). האזרת The meaning is uncertain. Perhaps the א here =ע, and the name is ptcp. f. of עזר *she who helps*, cf. **52** 5 ובאזרת for ובעזרת; but א for ע is Punic and late. If the word be derived from אזר the meaning will be *she who girds on*, figuratively *protects*;

the Piel would properly express this, Ps. 18 33. In CIS i 255 we find עשתרת הארדת i.e. (prob.) "A. the *glorious*'; it is natural to suppose that האזרת here is merely a variety of this word.

15. Kition. CIS i 44. iv–iii cent. B.C. Brit. Mus., Cyprus Room no. 47.

1 המצבת או לאשמנאדני שרדל בן עבדמלקרת בן
2 רשפיתן מלץ הכרסים

This pillar (is) to Eshmun-adoni ŠRDL, son of 'Abd-melqarth, son of Reshef-yathon, interpreter of the thrones.

This inscr. is carved on the base of a marble obelisk, about 5 ft. high, terminating in a pyramidal or gabled top. The monument is an unusually perfect specimen of the Phoen. type of *maṣṣēbah* (see the heliogravure in CIS i Tab. viii, and the illustration in Nowack *Hebr. Arch.* ii 18, Benzinger *Hebr. Arch.* 380); it may be compared with the fine specimen discovered at Larnaka (Kition) in 1894, now in the Brit. Mus., no. 31, Cyprus Room; see **21**.

L. 1. המצבת The usual word in Phoen. (rarely מנצבת **56** 1) for a gravestone or pillar erected over a tomb to commemorate the dead and perpetuate his memory among the living; cf. **16** 1. **18** 1 מצבת בחים. **19** 1. **21** 1 &c.; similarly among the Hebrews, e.g. Gen. 35 20 מצבת קברת רחל. The name of the person commemorated is usually introduced by ל, e.g. **18** 3 f. **19** 3 f. CIS i **59** 116; see further **16** 2 *n*. Thus the usage of מצבת and the form of the sentence leave little doubt as to the way in which this inscr. is to be interpreted; it records the fact the stone was erected to the memory of Eshmun-adoni ŠRDL and set up over his grave. The view, therefore, that the *maṣṣēbah* was a religious offering '(which) ŠRDL (erected) to Eshmun his lord' is not in accordance with the usage of the language; it requires אש יטנא to be supplied; and in the case of a dedication to a god the order of words would be different, as for instance in **12**. **13** and **14**. או See add. note p. 26; ז is also found after מצבת **19** 1. CIS i **61**. אשמנאדני is to be taken as a pr. name formed by a combination of Eshmun and Adon, the latter being the title of a god whose actual name was not pronounced. Similar combinations current in Cyprus are Eshmun-melqarth (CIS i 16. 23. 24) and Adonis-Osiris[1]. In these cases, however, the combination forms the name of a deity, cf. 10 3 *n*. In CIS i 42 and 43 אשמנאדני is followed by what appears to be fragments of pr. names, . . אשמנאדני־יבן 42 and . . אשמנאדני־נשב 43; here the word which follows is שרדל, evidently also a pr. name. It is prob. that in all three instances we have the individual's nomen and cognomen given, a very unusual practice (so Lidzb.). The name שרדל is found again in a Pun. inscr. CIS i 444 3 f. שרד[ל]; the etymology and pronunciation are unknown.

L. 2. רשפיתן See 12 3 *n*. It is curious to find the same name followed by the same title in 23 4 f. 6 and, according to some, in CIS i 22 [רשפ]יתן מל[ץ] כרסים. The three inscrr. prob. belong to the same period; and though in 23 4 f. 6 the son of Reshef-yathon is Adon-shemesh, yet it is conceivable that he had another son, 'Abd-melqarth, who appears here. The facts are worth noticing, but they are not sufficient to establish an identification. מלץ הכרסים The first word certainly means *interpreter* (to refs. above add CIS i 350 4 המלץ); it has this meaning in Gen. 42 23, cf. Job 33 23 and ἑρμηνευτής in Gk. inscriptions. כרסים is prob. the plur. of כרסי = Hebr. כִּסֵּא *seat, throne*; for the form cf. Old Aram. כרסא 63 7; Aram. כֻּרְסְיָא, ܟܘܪܣܝܐ; Arab. كُرْسِىّ. The title, then, may signify 'interpreter of the thrones,' i.e. dragoman to the court, whose office it was to act as interpreter between the Cyprian kings and the Persian or Greek courts.

16. Kition. CIS i 46. iv–iii cent. B.C. Bodl. Library, Oxford.

1 אנך · עבדאסר · בן עבדססם · בן חר · מצבת ·
2 למבחיי · יטנאת · על · משכב · נחתי · לעלם · ולא
3 שתי · לאמתעשתרת · בת · תאם · בן עבדמלך

I 'Abd-osir, son of 'Abd-sasom, son of Ḥor, set up (this) pillar in my life-time over my resting-place for ever; also to my wife, Amath-'ashtart, daughter of T'M, son of 'Abd-milk.

[1] Ἀμαθοῦς, πόλις Κύπρου ἀρχαιοτάτη, ἐν ὗ Ἄδωνις Ὄσιρες ἐτιμᾶτο, ὃν Αἰγύπτιον ὄντα Κύπριοι καὶ Φοίνικες ἰδιοποιοῦντο, Stephanus Byzant. ed. Meineke, p. 82.

L. 1. אנך The dead speaks in his own name. In other inscrr. of this character we find the donor[1], and once both the donor and the dead, using the 1st person (32). עבדאסר See 14 2 *n*. עבדססם Cf. 27 3. CIS i 49. 53. Tam. 2. The analogy of other proper names compounded with עבד shows that ססם is the name of a deity; it was prob. pronounced Sasom (Cypr. *apasasomose*, 'Αψάσωμος = עבדססם Tam. 2, cf. LXX Σωσομαΐ 1 Ch. 2 40) or Sesom (Σέσμαος = ססמי 28 3), or, as the Cypriote equivalent may imply, Sasm (Cl.-Gan. *Rec.* i 185, ii § 26). The fact that both here and in CIS i 53 (ע׳ בן עבדחר) 'Abd-sasom belongs to families in which Egyptian names occur, makes it probable that ססם was a foreign deity, introduced, like Osiris and Horus, from Egypt. Nothing is known of the special character of this god; Baethgen *Beitr.* 64 f. On some coins of Sinope the Aram. legend עבדססן is certified by Lidzbarski, as against Babelon's reading עבדכמו *Pers. Achém.* lxxix ff. This ססן is, however, explained by Lidzbarski as the equivalent of the Persian name Σισίνης; it is therefore not to be identified with the Phoen. ססם; *Eph.* i 106. חר Horus, the Egyptian god.

L. 2. למבחיי *during my life-time*; למן places the fact in the past, and ב gives the date; for the three preps. cf. 45 5 למבירח. 42 5 למבמחסר. There is no exact parallel in Hebr.; לְמַבָּרִאשׁוֹנָה *for what was at first* 1 Ch. 15 13 is different, לְמַב׳ being = לְ + מַה as in לְמַדַּי 2 Ch. 30 3. As a rule the מצבת was erected by the children (לאבי 18 3 f. לאבנם 19 3 f.) or a friend (32) to commemorate the dead 'among the living' בחים (e.g. 18 1); but here we have an exceptional instance of the מצבת being set up by the person commemorated during his life-time. This was done by persons who had no children to perform the pious duty, as may be seen from 2 S 18 18 ואבשלם לקח ויצב־לו בחיו את־מצבת אשר בעמק־המלך כי אמר אין־לי בן בעבור הזכיר שמי. יטנאת Perf. 1 sing., cf. 29 3 על הסמל . . . אש יטנאת לי. משכב נחתי Again in 21 5 על מ׳ נחתנם. For משכב see 5 4 *n.*; for נחת cf. Is. 30 15.

L. 3. אמתעשתרת Cf. 5 14 *n.* and 27 2 אמתאסר. CIS i 395 3 אמתבעל. ib. 446 2 f. אמתמלקרת. תאם Restored in CIS i 66 1 but not found elsewhere. עבדמלך Cf. 'Αβδιμίλκων in the Cypr. text of CIS i 89 and in 670 3. The name also occurs in the Tell-el-Am. letters, e.g. 77 37 *Abd-milki*.

In this inscr. the words are separated by dots as in 13, and the ancient inscrr. 1. 2. 61. 62. 63. It is noticeable that the tops of the letters ט, ל, ר are open.

[1] E.g. CIS i 57 'the pillar which I, Menaḥem, set up to my father.'

17. Kition. CIS i 47.

1 לעטהד בת עבדאש
2 מן השפט אשת גר
3 מלקרת בן בנחד
4 ש בן גרמלקרת ב
5 ן אשמנעזר

To 'ṬHD, daughter of 'Abd-eshmun the judge, wife of Ger-melqarth, son of Ben-ḥodesh, son of Ger-melqarth, son of Eshmun-'azar.

L. 1. עטהד The meaning of this name is unknown. It has been explained as = עֹטֶה הוֹד Ps. 104 1. 2; but this derivation is too fanciful to be likely.

L. 2. השפט See **8** 3 *n*. גרמלקרת i.e. *guest of Melqarth*, cf. גרסכן **46** 2. גרעשתרת **29** 2. 3. גרצד **31** a 1. גרססכר CIS i 267 3. גרהכל (=גֵּר הֵיכָל) ib. 112 b[1]. b[2]. The 'guest' (=πάροικος, παράσιτος) was one who placed himself under the protection of the deity; cf. in Hebr. Ps. **15** 1 יהוה מי יגור באהלך (see Cheyne in loc.), and in Arab. جار الله i.e. one who dwells in Mekka, beside the Ka'aba; the verb جار in conj. iii is used of 'dwelling beside a temple' or 'receiving under protection as a client'; similarly 'cliens Bacchi,' Hor. *Ep*. ii 2 78. It is prob. that in **20** A 15. B 10 the גרם are mentioned as a class in the list of ministers and attendants of the temple of 'Ashtart at Kition. A good illustration of the religious practice is given by a Palmyrene מצבא in the Brit. Mus., Semitic Room no. 581, which is inscribed לשדרפא אלהא טבא די יהא גיר בה הו ובני ביתה כלהן 'To Shadrapa the good god, that he might be a guest with him, he and all the sons of his house.' The religious idea of the 'guest' of a deity had its origin in the social custom of extending hospitality and protection to a stranger, and in the old Semitic right of sanctuary. Cf. **140** B 8 and בר **6** 2 *n*.; see further Robertson Smith *Rel. of the Semites*[1] 75 ff., *Kinship* 41 f.

L. 3. בנחדש i.e. 'born on the new-moon.' The name is found again in **80** 2 (Cypriote ὁ Νουμηνίων). **84**. CIS i 117 where the Greek equivalent is ΝΟΥΜΗΝΙΟΣ. The naming of children after festivals was common in early Christian times, e.g. ܒܪ ܚܕܒܫܒܐ = Κυριακός, Dominicus; ܣܘܠܩܐ i.e. born on the Ascension; ܒܪ ܨܘܡܐ i.e. born during the spring fast; Paschalis, Natalis &c.

18. Kition. CIS i 58.

1 מצבת בחים
2 אש יטנא עב
3 דאסר לאב
4 י לארכתא

The pillar among the living which 'Abd-osir set up to his father Arketha.

L. 1. מצבת בחים Cf. CIS i 116 1 מצבת סכר בחים. This inscr. proves that בחים cannot mean 'in (his) life-time' (למבחיי **16** 2), like the Gk. ζῶν, ζῶσα, and the Lat. vivus, viva, in similar cases; a son would not set up a memorial to his father while the latter was still alive. The meaning, therefore, is 'among the living'; see **15** *n.*

L. 3. עבדאסר Cf. **14** 2 *n.* The name 'Αβδούσιρος has been found on the Phoen. coast, Renan *Miss. de Phén.* 241; hence the conjecture that the Phoen. pronunciation of the Egyptian Osir was Usir. אבי It is not certain whether the form was pronounced אָבִי = Hebr. אָבִיו or אֲבִי = Aram. ܐܒܘܗܝ, Schröder 150 *n.* Nöldeke, *ZA* (1894) iv 402, thinks that the pronunciation was originally אָבִי, קְלָא, אִמִּי **21** 1. 3.

L. 4. לארכתא Possibly a Gk. name; Archytas has been suggested.

19. Kition. CIS i 60.

1 [מצב]ת ז אש יטנ
2 א אשמנצלח ו
3 מריחי לאבנ
4 ם למלכסנם
5 מהמ...

This is the pillar which Eshmun-ṣillaḥ and Mar-yeḥai set up to their father Melexenos ...

L. 1. ז Fem., see **8** add. note ii. יטנא Hif. pf. 3 plur.

L. 2. אשמנצלח Cf. בעלצלח **7** 2. רעמצלח **32** 2.

L. 3. מריחי i.e. prob. מְרְיַחֵי *Mar gives life* (Piel), **27** 3 ff. The name *Mar* has been explained by the Aram. מר, בעל=מרא, ארן; it is conjectured that, like these names, מר was originally used in an appellative sense *lord*, and afterwards as the title of a deity. A better explanation is proposed by Hoffmann, *ZA* xi 240. He regards מר in מריחי, מר ברך CIS ii 85 (? Aram.), מר מסך Cl.-Gan. *JA* viii t. i 143, as a diminutive of מלקרת; and similarly *Mar* in θεῷ Βεελμάρι *Rev. Arch.* xxix (1875) 267 inscribed on a lamp from Tyre, and in Μάρνας the Philistine god of Gaza, who appears also in Ḥauran, Διὶ Μάρνᾳ τῷ κυρίῳ Wadd. 2412 g; see also **40** 1 *n.* אשמן מארח. אבנם Cf. **27** 5, and see **5** add. note.

L. 4. מלנסנם ? = Μενίξενος.

20 A and B. Kition. CIS i 86 A and B. iv cent. B.C.
Brit. Mus., Semitic Room.

A.

1 תׄכׄלת ירח אתנם

2 בחדש ירח אתנם

3 לאלן חדש קפא II
I III

4 לבנם אש בן אית בת עשתרת כׄת קפא..

5 לפרכם ולאדמם אש על דל וקׄרׄ ʒ

6 לאׄרׄם בׄעׄרׄ אש שכנם למלכת קדשת בים זק...

7 לנערם II קפא II

8 לזבחם II קר /

9 לאשם II אש אם אית נׄעׄרׄ חלת למלכת...

10 את פרכם קפא I...

11 לנערם III קפא III

12 לגלבם פעלם על מלאכת קפא II

13 לחרשם · אש פעל אשתת אבן בׄבת מב...

14 לעבדאשמן רב ספרם ולח בים ז קר III ו . ק..

15 [לכלבם] ולגרם קר ll / ופא lll

16 . . . . אש לח בים ז קר ll ו. ב...

17 . . . .

Total (?) for the month Ethanim. [2] On the new-moon of the month Ethanim:—[3] To the gods of the new-moon QP' 2. [4] To the builders who built the house of 'Ashtart? QP' . . . [5] To the *velarii*, and to the men who have charge of the door? QR 20. [6] To?? who reside for the sacred service, on this day, Q . . . [7] To servants 2 QP' 2. [8] To sacrificers 2 QR 1. [9] To men 2 who????? for the service . . . [10] The *velarii*, QP' 1 . . . [11] To servants 3 QP' 3. [12] To the barbers officiating at the service QP' 2. [13] To the masons who made pillars (?) of stone in the house of MK . . . [14] To 'Abd-Eshmun, chief of the scribes, ?, on this day, QR 3 ?.. [15] [To 'dogs'] and temple-clients QR 3 and P' 3. [16] . . . . who?, on this day, QR 2? . . .

The two inscrr. A and B are *written* in black pigment on both sides of a stone tablet. The writing of A is in a small, close hand; that of B is in a bolder and clearer character. Many of the letters are difficult to decipher.

L. 1. תכלת *sum, total*; from כלה *be complete*. The first two letters, however, are uncertain. אתנם The month of *steady flowings*, the 7th month, Oct.–Nov.; cf. **30** 4, 1 K. 8 2 יֶרַח הָאֵתָנִים. Like the name of the month *bul* (**5** 1 *n.*), the name *ethanim* was prob. of Canaanite origin, and adopted by the Israelites from the Canaanite calendar: Benzinger *Hebr. Arch.* 201.

L. 2. בחדש *on the new-moon* i. e. the first day of the lunar month, cf. B 2. **29** 4. Ps. 81 4.

L. 3. אלן Cf. B 3, plur. constr. as in **5** 18. **10** 7. Who 'the gods of the new-moon' were is not known. The religious celebration of the new-moon was an ancient custom; see 1 S. 20 5 f. Is. 1 13. Hos. 2 13. Am. 8 5. 2 K. 4 23. קפא A coin of some kind. The four strokes, grouped like numerals, between ll. 3 and 4 may possibly indicate the 4th day of the month; or they may merely separate the previous lines from what follows.

L. 4. לבנם אש בן i. e. לְבֹנִם אֲשׁ בָּן. כת may mean *Kition*, as on coins from Sidon, **149** B 15, although כתי is the usual form.

L. 5. לפרכם Cf. l. 10; perhaps, 'those who have charge of the temple-curtains' (פָּרֹכֶת Ex. 26 31 ff. &c.), cf. Talm. *Sheqalim* 11 *b* אלעזר על פרכת, and the *velarii*, i. e. slaves who drew the curtains, in the Lat. inscrr. This explanation agrees well with what follows: 'the men in charge of the door.' For דל cf. 9 3 *n*. קר Cf. ll. 8. 14. 16. B 8. 10; a coin, here followed by the symbol for 20.

L. 6. לאדם בער Meaning and text obscure. It has been proposed to render בער *who kindles the fire*. In Hebr. the Piel is used in this sense, e. g. 2 Ch. 4 20 וְאֶת־הַמְּנֹרוֹת וְנֵרֹתֵיהֶם לְבַעֲרָם כַּמִּשְׁפָּט, cf. 13 11. איש שכנם למלכת *who reside for the work*. The construction is curious, but there is no doubt about the reading; למלכת = למלאכת l. 12. 8 11. 13. 45 2. קדשת Adj., fem. sing. For the expression מלכת ק' cf. מְלֶאכֶת עֲבֹדַת הַקֹּדֶשׁ Ex. 36 3 and 1 Ch. 9 13. 28 13 &c.

L. 9. לאשם i. e. לְאִשָּׁם cf. B 7. 46 1. In Phoen. איש (אִישׁ) is not used so frequently as אדם. אם אית נער חלת The words are unintelligible.

L. 12. לגלבם i.e. לְגַלָּבִם (Eze. 5 1), cf. גלב אלם CIS i 257 ff. and the pr. n. גלב 27 5. The barbers attached to the temple assisted at the hair-offerings, a customary form of devotion in heathen Semitic religion. Lucian, *de Dea Syr.* vi. lv, alludes to the practice of offering hair to Adonis at Byblus and P ce; it was a sacrificial act offered with the idea of attaching th ,nipper to the deity and his shrine; see Robertson Smith *Rel. of Sem.*[1] 313. The ceremonial shaving of the head was forbidden to the Israelites as a heathen practice; and the prohibition was extended to making incisions in the flesh, which also was prob. performed by these temple-barbers. See Lev. 19 27 f. 21 5. Eze. 44 20.

L. 13. חרשם For חרש cf. 22 2. 45 9. 52 6, CIS i 64 רב חרש מלכיתן. The word is generally used of workers in metal, but also of workers in stone, e.g. 2 S 5 11 ח' אֶבֶן קִיר. 1 Ch. 22 14; see also 2 Ch. 24 12. אשתת Cf. B 5. The meaning of the word is uncertain. It has been taken as = א + שָׁתֹת prosth. *pillars*, Ps. 11 3. מכ.. In B 5 אשתת מכל. Elsewhere מכל occurs with the prefix רשף as the name of the god Reshef-mukl, 24 2 &c.; מכל is prob. the name of a city (Lidzb.).

L. 14. רב ספרם Cf. הספר frequently in Carth. inscrr., e. g. CIS i 154 4. 240 ff. ולח Again l. 16. It is not unlikely that לח is an abbreviation for לח[ברם] *to the associates*, 42 2 *n*.

L. 15. [לכלבם] ולגרם Restored from B 10. Is the reference to persons or to animals? The words may be rendered *for the dogs and the whelps* (וְלִגֻּרִם), supposing that the item of expenditure is food for the temple-hounds, which in some cases were considered sacred, e.g. the hound of Isis, Adonis, &c.; so Hoffmann *Über ein. Phön. Inschr.* 17. In a Gk. inscr. from Epidaurus sacred hounds are mentioned as connected with the temple of Aesculapius (=Eshmun), Michel 1069 126 f.[1] On the other hand, כלבם and נרם may be persons: *to the 'dogs' and temple-clients*. In this case כלבם is explained by Dt. 23 19, cf. κύνες Apoc. 22 15; they were temple-prostitutes, otherwise called קְדֵשִׁים in the O.T., e.g. Dt. 23 18. 1 K. 14 24 &c.; in Assyr. *ḫarimtu, ḳadištu* (of Ishtar), Zimmern *KAT*[3] 423. The pr. n. כלב אלם CIS i 49, and such names as Kalbi-Bau, Kalbi-Marduk &c. in Neo-Babyl. contracts, may be quoted in illustration, though in these cases it is likely that כלב was used as a term not of contempt but of self-abasement, *the humble slave of the gods*. The word is found in the Tell-el-Am. letters in this sense, e.g. *kalbu-šarri* 'servant, lit. dog, of the king' 75 36. 86 19. 161 15 &c.; cf. 2 K. 8 13 עבדך הכלב[2]. It is possible that קְדֵשִׁים=כלבים originally had a similar meaning, *devoted followers*; we cannot tell. If כלבם='*dogs*' metaphorically, the נרם must be *the temple-clients*, lit. *guests*, here apparently a regular class attached to the temple and supported out of its funds; see 17 2 *n.* Or, again, נרם may be pointed נְעָרִם and mean *youths*, cf. 1 16 *n.*; but this is very uncertain.

B.

1 ⌐ עקב

2 ⌐ בחדש ירח פעלת

3 ⌐ לאלן חדש קפא ||

4 ⌐ לבעל ימם ברב שלם

5 ⌐ לנפש בת אש לאשתת מבל וש...

6 ⌐ לעבדאבסת הקרתחדשתי...

7 ⌐ לאשם · אש לקח מבנבם קפא...

8 ⌐ לרעם · אש ב??ף לכד קר || אש ב...

9 ⌐ לעלמת ולעלמת = || בזבח...

10 ⌐ לכלבם ולגרם קר || / ופא ||

11 ⌐ לנערם ||| קפא |||

12 . . . . א ||

[1] See Cl.-Ganneau *Rec.* i 235 ff.

[2] Further illustrations from Assyr. are given by Thureau-Dangin in *PSBA* xxi 133.

Continuation (?). [2] On the new-moon of the month Pa-'aloth:—[3] To the gods of the new-moon QP' 2. [4] To the ba'als of the days for the ? peace-offering. [5] To the persons of the house which is by the pillars (?) of Mikal and ... [6] To 'Abd-ubast the Carthaginian ... [7] To the men who were taken (?) from the 'dogs' (?), QP' ... [8] To the friends (?) who ... were taken (?), QR 2 which ... [9] To the virgins and virgins 22 in the sacrifice ... [10] To the 'dogs' and to the temple-clients QR 3 and P' 2. [11] To servants 3 QP' 3.

L. 1. עקב Arabic usage shows that the root had the two meanings of *follow, be behind* (conj. i) and *to pay back, recompense* (conj. iv). The name יעקב, probably in full יעקב־אל, may have had either of these two meanings originally; see Baethgen *Beiträge* 158, who compares the Palmyrene name עתעקב *Ate follows, rewards*. Hence the noun here may be rendered either *reward*, cf. עקב רב Ps. 19 12 and Pr. 22 4, or *continuation*, i. e. from the foregoing account.

L. 2. פעלת Name of a month, perhaps the 6th. It is found again in 23 1 (rest.). 29 8. Tam. 2 1.

L. 3. See A 3 *n*.

L. 4. לבעל ימם i. e. לְבַעֲלֵ יָמִם is taken to mean 'the gods who preside over the different days of the month.' ברב שלם *in magno sacrificio pacifico* (Corp.); but ברב is very doubtful. For שלם cf. שלם כלל 42 3 ff.

L. 5. The sense is obscure; נפש may be sing. collective (not plur., which would be נפשת) in the sense of *persons*, men- and women-slaves, as in Gen. 12 5. Lev. 22 11. Eze. 27 13 (with אדם). אשתת מכל See A 13 *n*.

L. 6. לעבדאבסת Cf. *Carth.* 161 6 (rest.). The name occurs in an inscr. from the temple of Osiris at Abydos, 31 *d*, and in the form 'Αβδουβάστιος in a Gk. inscr. from Sidon, Waddington 1866 *c*. There can be no doubt that אבסת is the Egyptian goddess Bast, with א prosth.; see Herodotus ii 60. 137 (temple of Bubastis). 156, and cf. the name פעל אבסת 31 *a*. הקרתחדשתי *the Carthaginian*; the Carthage in Cyprus (11 *n*.) or in Africa.

L. 7. לקח Either Qal *took* or Pual *were taken*, pf. 3 plur. מכנבם is unintelligible, unless it be a mistake for מכלבם l. 10.

L. 8. לרעם Possibly *to the friends* i. e. לְרֵעָם. The Corp. renders לכר *were taken* i. e. by lot, cf. 1 S. 10 20 f.; but this is uncertain.

L. 9. עלמת *virgins* who sang and danced in the temple rites; cf. עֲלָמוֹת תּוֹפֵפוֹת Ps. 68 26. על עלמות Ps. 46 (title). 1 Ch. 15 20.

L. 10. See A 15 *n*.

21. Kition. iv cent. B.C. Brit. Mus., Cyprus Room no. 31. **Plate II.**

1 מצבת אז אש יטנא ארש רב סרסרם לאבי לפרסי
2 רב סרסרם בן ארש רב סרסרם בן מנחם רב סרסרם
3 בן משל רב סרסרם בן פרסי רב סרסרם ולאמי
4 לשמזבל בת בעלרם בן מלכיתן בן עזר רב חז
5 ענם על משכב נחתנם לעלם

This pillar (is that) which Arish, chief of the brokers, erected to his father, Parsi, [2] chief of the brokers, son of Arish, chief of the brokers, son of Menaḥem, chief of the brokers, [3] son of Mashal, chief of the brokers, son of Parsi, chief of the brokers; and to his mother, [4] Shem-zabul, daughter of Ba'al-ram, son of Milk-yathon, son of 'Azar, chief of the pre[5]fects (?), over their resting-place, for ever.

This inscr. is written on a fine monolith of white marble with a gabled top; it belongs to the type of memorial inscrr. represented by **15. 16. 18. 19.** The stone was found in the necropolis of Kition outside Old Larnaka in 1894.

L. 1. ארש is found again in **38** 4 and often in Carth. inscrr.; on a v cent. gold ring from Syria, Levy *Siegel u. Gemmen* 53; in the form *Arisus* CIL viii 3335, *Arsus* ib. 9054; cf. עבדארש **45** 7. The √ארש Assyr. *êrêšu=desire, request*, Hebr. אֲרֶשֶׁת; possibly this is the meaning of the name here. רב סרסרם Not found elsewhere. The usage of סַרְסוֹר in Rabbinic literature gives a clue to the meaning here. Thus in *Pesikta* ed. Buber 45 *a* סרסור=*mediator* and is applied to Moses, אף הסרסור הרגיש בעבורה 'even the mediator trembled on account of it'; in the Mishnah it is used of a *negotiator* in a business transaction, e.g. *Baba Bathra* 87 *a*, cf. the Midrash on this passage, Midr. R. *Deuteron.* § 3 fol. 91 *b* ('ס applied to Moses); Talm. Jerus. *Megila* 74 *d* &c. In Arab. سُرْسُور denotes *intelligent*, *skilful*, *one who manages a business well.* Thus the earliest authority for the word is this inscr.; and there is no reason to doubt that it is a genuine Phoen. word, a technical term of Phoen. commercial life. It was probably adopted from Phoenicia by the cognate languages. Fränkel, *Aram. Fremdw. in Arab.* (1886) 186, conjectured that the Arab. سِرْسَوْر was a loan-word from Aram., but since the discovery of this inscr. he has abandoned the conjecture, *ZA* (1896) x 99. So we may render רב סרסרם *chief of the brokers*, who probably formed a merchant guild or corporation, ἀρχιπραγματευτής. In the family of Arish the office was hereditary, having been held, on the father's side, for six generations. לאבי Cf. 18 3 f. *n.* פרסי Perhaps ὁ Πέρσης, הַפָּרְסִי Neh. 12 22. The name has been found on the foot of a vase from Sidon, Cl.-Ganneau *Ét.* ii 155.

L. 2. מנחם Cf. 80 2. CIS i 87 3 (Cyprus). 102 *b* (Egypt).

L. 3. משל Cf. Euting *Carth. Inschr.* 130 4 f. מלקרתמשל.

L. 4. שמזבל Perhaps the *Name has*, or *is, carried* cf. the fem. pr. n. בעלאזבל CIS i 158 2 f. In Assyr. *zabâlu* = 'carry,' 'bring' (e. g. *KB* ii p. 235 l. 88; iii 2 p. 92 l. 53 &c.), ? = 'honour,' 'exalt,' as given in *COT*[2] 550; cf. Arab. زَبَلَ *take up and carry*. The pronunciation was prob. *zabul*; cf. the pr. n. *Zabullus* CIL viii 5987. 9947. The explanation suggested by Derenbourg, *Rev. Études Juiv.* xxx 118 ff., that שמזבל is a variation of such a name as שמביה (similarly Halévy *Rev. Sém.* iii 183 ff. 'heavenly name,' cf. Hab. 3 11) has little probability. The 'Name' may denote 'Ashtart, called שם בעל in 5 18. בעלרם Cf. 23 2 *n.*, a name belonging to the royal family of Kition. מלכיתן, also a royal name, is given to other persons, e.g. 41 6 f. (Carth.) &c. עזר Prob. shortened from עזרבעל or the like; it is found in Carth. inscrr., e.g. CIS i 453 5 f. *Carth.* 27 5 f. &c. רב חזענם Like רב סרסרם only met with here. A careful examination of the stone makes it almost certain that חזענם is the right reading, and that the indentation in the stone after ז is not a letter, but a recent mark due to an accidental blow. The reading חזיענם, given by Nöldeke, *ZA* iv 402 ff., cannot, therefore, be accepted. The meaning is doubtful. (1) The word may be connected with the Assyr. *ḫazânu* 'governor,' 'prefect,' of which the plur. is *ḫazianuti*, pointing to חזה as the root (Zimmern *ZA* vi 248); Tell-el-Am. 179 19. 147 5 *Zimridi ḫazanu ša Ziduna*, and often. This gives a suitable sense. The title may have passed from the Canaanite coast to Cyprus; Assyrian influence was predominant in both regions at various times. The ע, not used in Assyr., may be due to an attempt to express the long vowel. (2) It is natural to think of the Arab. خزن *lay up, store, guard*; خَازِن *guardian* of treasures, of Paradise Qur. 39 73. *Chief of the treasurers* would give a good sense here; but it is not likely that a pure Arab. title would be used of a local official in Cyprus. (3) Nöld., l. c., suggests חֹזֵי עֵינַיִם *eye-gazers*, i. e. *seers*, *diviners*, cf. μαντιάρχης Waddington 2795; but the construction *seers of*, i. e. *with*, *eyes* is not very natural, even if the reading חזיענם is to be accepted. (4) Halévy, *Rev. Sém.* iii (1895) 183 ff., proposes *chief of the inspectors of wells* רַב חֹזֵי עֲיָנִים; so Lidzb.(?). The plur. of עַיִן in Hebr. is עֲיָנוֹת, but the mas. form may have been used in Phoen.; Halévy compares הָעֵינָם Josh. 15 34, which is perhaps a dual. The office may be illustrated from a Gk. inscr., B.C. 333, where an official is rewarded for his services περὶ τὴν ἐπιμέλειαν τῶν κρηνῶν, Michel 105 = CIA iv 2. 169 b; cf. also ἐπιμελητὴς αἱρεθεὶς Ἔφκας πηγῆς (from Palmyra), Waddington 2571 c.; procurator aquarum, Rushforth *Lat. Hist. Inscr.* 89. It may be questioned whether חזה *seer* could be used for *inspector*; שמר *keeper* 88 7 would be a more natural term. On the whole (1) is to be preferred.

L. 5. על משכב נחתנם לעלם Cf. 16 2.

22. Kition. iv–iii cent. Larnaka.

1 לעברעשתר בן אשמנ...

2 חרש ענלת פעל זי...

To ʿAbd-ʿashtar, son of Eshmun-..., the chariot-smith; ZI... made (it).

This inscr. was found at Larnaka in 1894; see Myres and Richter *Catal. of Cypr. Mus.* 172 and Plate viii. Below the inscr. is the incised outline of a figure resembling the steering-oar (?) carved on CIS i 265, Tab. xlvii. But the figure here can hardly be meant for an oar, nor does it look like any part of a chariot. Michon, *Rév. Arch.* (1900) 458, suggests that it represents some tool, such as a plane, and compares the monument of Boitēnos Hermes, a maker of beds, κλεινοπηγός, on which his tools are carved (CIG 2135).

L. 1. עברעשתר For the usual עברעשתרת 29 2. 5 &c.; see for the form 1 17 *n*. ...אשמנ The full name was prob. compounded with עזר, ארן, or יתן.

L. 2. חרש ענלת i.e. חָרַשׁ עֲגָלֹת. For חרש a worker in metal or wood cf. **20** A 13 *n.*; and for עגלת cf. CIS i 346 3 עגלת עץ, which seems to mean (*maker of*) *chariots of wood*; a chariot is figured on a stone from Carthage illustrated in Corp. p. 397. The chariot is copiously represented in Cyprian art from the beginning of the Graeco-Phoenician period. In a private communication M. Clermont-Ganneau suggests that ... זי is the fragment of a pr. n., such as זיבקם **38** 5 &c., the name of the donor of the stele. To read מעל ז י[ברך] leaves מעל without a subj., and the stele without a donor.

23. Idalion. CIS i 88. Date circ. 386 B.C. Louvre.

1 בימם ⸗ [||| ||| ל]ירח פע[לת בש]נת ||| למלך מלכיתן [מלך כתי ו]
2 אדיל בן בעלרם · סמל או אש יתן ויטנא ת[חד]ש כל[ה] ר[שפ]
3 יתן בן עזרתבעל מלץ הכרסים לאדני למלקרת ש[מע קל]
4 פקד המפקד ז והסלמת אש למפקד [אז] אש יפקד א[דנ]ש[מש
ב]ן רשפ[יתן]
5 מלץ כרסים · ופקד הת.... סמלם בסלמת המפקד ו......אש [יפ]קד
6 עבדפמי ועבדמלקרת אשן בן [אד]נשמש בן רשפיתן מלץ כרסים
בשנת ||| |||
7 למלך מלכיתן מלך כתי ו[אדי]ל כ שמע מלקרת קלם יברכם

On the 1[6]th day of the month Pa'aloth, in the 3rd year of king Milk-yathon, [king of Kition and] [2] Idalion, son of Ba'al-ram:—This statue (is that) which R[eshef]-[3] yathon, son of 'Azrath-ba'al, interpreter of the thrones, gave and set up and entirely [renov]ated to his lord Melqarth who hears (his) voice. [4] This ? ... and the steps (?) which belong to this ? ..., which were commissioned (?), A[don]-sh[amash, so]n of Reshef-[yathon], [5] interpreter of the thrones, commissioned. And the ? .. statues on the steps (?) of the ? ... and ..... which were [com]missioned (?), [6] 'Abd-pumi and 'Abd-melqarth, the two sons of [Ad]on-shamash, son of Reshef-yathon, interpreter of the thrones, commissioned in the 6th year [7] of king

Milk-yathon, king of Kition and [Id]alion, because Melqarth heard their voice. May he bless them!

This inscr. belongs to the type illustrated by nos. **12–14**.

L. 1. ביומם See **12** 1 *n*. מעלת See **20** B 2 *n*. מלכיתן Cf. **24**. **25**. **30**. According to the chronology given by Babelon *Pers. Achém.* cxxvi, Milk-yathon reigned first from B.C. 392 to 388 and then from 387 to 361 (see **149** B 5). His third year will thus be 390.

L. 2. בעלרם **24** 1[1]. סמל Cf. **13** 2 *n*. חדש i. e. חָדָשׁ, cf. **38** 1. **46** 1. **102** 1; 2 Ch. 24 4. 12 (of the temple). 15 8 (of the altar). But this and the word following are uncertain.

L. 3. ... רשפיתן ... מלץ הכרסים See **15** 2 *n*. עזרתבעל perhaps *my help is Ba'al*; the usual form of the name is עזר בעל. מלקרת = מלך קרת *king of the city*, cf. **29** 3 &c. **36** 1 and **3** 2 *n*. This title belonged to Ba'al of Tyre, and came to be used as a pr. name; thus **36** 1 לאדנן למלקרת בעל צר. In the Gk. form of the latter inscr. the equivalent of למלקרת is ΗΡΑΚΛΕΙ ΑΡΧΗΓΕΤΕΙ. By the Greeks Melqarth was identified with Herakles, as we learn also from Philo of Byblus, *Fr. Hist. Gr.* iii 568, Μελκάθρος ὁ καὶ Ἡρακλῆς. From Tyre the cult of Melqarth spread to Cyprus (as this inscr. and **29** and the Cyprian names 'עבדמ', 'נרמ' testify), and to Egypt, Carthage, and other places; see Baethgen *Beitr.* 20 f. Melqarth is not mentioned in the O. T., but the worship of the Tyrian Ba'al introduced into N. Israel by Jezebel was most likely offered to him. שמע i. e. prob. שָׁמַע.

L. 4. Further objects dedicated to the deity. מקר המפקר has been rendered 'curavit hanc curam'; but this rendering of המפקד, while it agrees with that of מקד (cf. Ezr. 1 2), does not suit והסלמת *and the stairs* (?). Accordingly Cl.-Ganneau explains the word from Eze. 43 21, where it is ordered to burn the sin-offering בְּמִפְקַד הַבַּיִת מִחוּץ לַמִּקְדָּשׁ. The *mifqad*, then, was some place adjoining the temple,

[1] (1) Although this Ba'al-ram was the father of king Milk-yathon, he is not given the title of king either here or in **24** 1; we may conclude, therefore, that he never was king. (2) In the bilingual inscr. CIS i 89 *our prince* (ארנן) *Ba'al-ram, son of 'Abd-milk*, dedicates a statue in the reign of Milk-yathon. This Ba'al-ram is prob. to be distinguished from (1). The Cypriote version gives ὁ ϝάναξ as the equivalent of ארן, a title which belonged to princes of the Cyprian royal house, cf. Aristotle ap. Harpocration *οἱ μὲν υἱοὶ τοῦ βασιλέως καὶ οἱ ἀδελφοὶ καλοῦνται ἄνακτες, αἱ δὲ ἀδελφαὶ καὶ γυναῖκες ἄνασσαι Fr. Hist. Gr.* ii 166; also Clearchus ap. Athen. Deipnos. ib. ii 311. (3) Another Ba'al-ram was king of Kition and Idalion, as his coins testify, about B. C. 396, just before Milk-yathon; but his name has not so far been read with certainty on any inscr.; in Idal. 7 1 בעל[מלך] not בעל[רם] is prob. the right reading. See Babelon *Pers. Achém.* cxxvi–cxxx.

but outside the sanctuary; one of the gates of the city was near it, Neh. 3 31. There is nothing, however, in this inscr. to determine exactly what is meant by המפקד; but it prob. had something to do with the statue referred to in l. 2, perhaps *the pedestal* (so Lidzb. 158 *n.* 1). הסלמת The meaning of this word is also doubtful. It may be *steps*, from √סלל *to lift up, cast up*; hence סֻלָּם *ladder* Gen. 28 12. יפקד The word is uncertain; it may be Hofal pf. plur. as in l. 5. ארנשמש l. 6, only here; cf. עבדשמש CIS i 116 2 (=ΗΛΙΟΔΩΡΟϹ). 117 2. מקמשמש (name of a city) Lidzb. 316. Shamash was the sun-god; cf. in Old Aram. שמש 61 2 &c. 62 22. 64 9; in Ethiop. ሰመ.

L. 5. ופקד 3 plur.; the subject is 'Abd-pumi and 'Abd-Melqarth l. 6. A fresh dedication is mentioned here.

L. 6. עבדסמי Only found here; for סמי see 12 1 *n.* אשן בן i. e. שְׁנֵי בְנֵי. The constr. st. occurs again in 36 2 שן בן, and the abs. in 12 3 אשנם (see *n.*). The sixth year of Milk-yathon was prob. B. C. 386, unless the reckoning started from 387 when he became king a second time according to Babelon's chronology (above).

L. 7. The formula of blessing resembles that in 36 3 f. For suff. in קלם see 5 add. note.

24. Idalion. CIS i 90. Date 391 B. C. Brit. Mus., Cyprus Room no. 289.

1 מרקע חרץ אז אש יתן מלך מלכיתן מלך כתי ואדיל בן בעלרם לאלי

2 לרשף מכל באדיל בירח בל בשנת II למלכי על כתי ואדיל כ שמע קל יברך

This plating of gold (is that) which king Milk-yathon, king of Kition and Idalion, son of Ba'al-ram, gave to his god Reshef of Mukl in Idalion, in the month Bul, in the 2nd year of his reign over Kition and Idalion, because he heard (his) voice: may he bless!

This inscr. belongs to the same type as 25 and 26.

L. 1. מרקע i. e. מְרֻקָּע, again in Idal. 7 3 מרק[ע נחש]ת (Euting *Sitz.-ber. Pr. Akad.* (1887) 422). The √ רקע = *beat out thin*, of metals, e. g. Jer. 10 9 כֶּסֶף מְרֻקָּע. Ex. 39 3. Num. 17 3. Talm B. *Sheqalim* 9 *b*

רקעי זהב. The word here prob. denotes the gold-plating of the image (סמל) of the god, cf. *ἄγαλμα ἐπίχρυσον*, Herod. ii 182, and Is. **40** 19. If מרקע meant *bowl* or *vessel of beaten gold* (Corp.), the inscr. would have been written on the bowl itself, as **11**, not on a stone tablet. חרץ See **8** 4 *n*. מלכיתן . . בעלרם See **23** 1. 2 *n*.

L. 2. רשף מכל באדיל Cf. **25** 1 f. **27** 5. CIS i. **94** 4 f. מכל is prob. the name of a city, see **20** A 13 *n*.; and רשף מכל = τῷ Ἀπολῶνι τῷ Ἀμυκλοῖ CIS i 89 (Cypriote), Ἀμυκλός being a dialectical form of the classical Ἀμυκλαῖος. The Phoenicians usually tried to give the names of foreign deities a form familiar to themselves; thus 'Reshef of Mukl' was their way of representing Apollo of Amyclae in Lacedaemon. For רשף see **12** 3 *n*.; this and the following inscr. show that he was specially honoured at Idalion. The prep. in באדיל implies that the cult of the deity was transplanted from its native home; similarly בעשתם באינצם **39** 1. שחר בנרב **64** 2. **92** 3. **99** 2. In **45** 1. **55** 1, however, this appears not to be the case. בל See **5** 1 *n*. למלכי i.e. לְמָלְכִי Inf. with suff. 3 m. sing., as in **26** 2.

25. **Idalion.** CIS i 91. Brit. Mus., Cyprus Room no. 225.

1 סמל · אז · אש יתן · מלך · מלכיתן · מלך · כתי · ו[אדיל בן בעלרם
לאלי ל]ן
2 רשף · מכל · נצחת · את · סבי · היצאם · ועזרנם · . . . .

This statue (is that) which king Milk-yathon, king of Kition and [Idalion, son of Ba'al-ram], gave [to his god] Reshef of Mukl. With his ? I conquered those who came out and their allies . . . .

The general type of this inscr. resembles that of **24** and **26**.

L. 1. סמל Cf. **18** 2 *n*.

L. 2. רשף מכל Cf. **24** 2 *n*. נצחת i.e. נָצַחְתִּ or נִצַּחְתִּ. The primary meaning of נצח is *shine*, as appears from Aram. usage, e.g. Apoc. **15** 6 ܡܐܢܐ ܕܟܝܐ ܢܨܝܚܐ *raiment fine, shining*. From this comes the derived meaning *be illustrious*, *triumph*, *conquer*, e.g. Midr. Rab. *Ekah* 1 § 11 ונצח חבריה (Qal), Targ. Jon. Num. **16** 14 וּתְנַצַּח יַתְהוֹן (Pael), Dan. **6** 4 מִתְנַצַּח (Ethp.); ܢܨܚܢܐ *victory* Jud. **15** 18, נִצְחָנָא Targ. Jer. Ex. **14** 14. 25; in the O.T. cf. the late passages

Lam. 3 18. 1 Ch. 29 11: Driver *Samuel* 98 f. את Prep. as in 4 8. 5 4 &c., here prob. *with the aid of.* סבי The reading is uncertain and the meaning unknown. The first letter looks like a ס, possibly a צ, the second appears to be a ב. The Corp. reads סדי *his counsel* (i.e. Reshef-yathon's), and quotes in illustration Ps. 25 14 &c.; this is very doubtful. היצאם *those who came forth* i.e. to battle; for יצא in this sense cf. 1 S. 8 20. 2 S. 11 1. ועזרנם Cf. 5 add. note. The reference appears to be to some historical occasion, perhaps a rebellion or political revolution.

26. Idalion. CIS i 92. Date 354 B.C.

1 [סמל אז אש יתן מלך פמייתן מלך] כתי · ואדיל · בן מלך · מלכיתן

2 [מלך כתי ואדיל לאלי לרשף מכל בי]רח כרר בשנת שמן ||||||| למלכי על

3 [כתי ואדיל כ שמע קל יברך]

The son of king Milk-yathon was Pumi-yathon (B.C. 361–312), see 12. 13. 149 B 6. The missing portions of the inscr. are restored after 24 and 25.

L. 2. ירח כרר The name of this month occurs again in the NPun. inscr. 55 5. בשנת שמן למלכי Cf. 2 K. 24 12 בִּשְׁנַת שְׁמֹנֶה לְמָלְכוֹ.

27. Idalion. CIS i 93. B.C. 254. Brit. Mus., Cyprus Room no. 239.

1 בימם ||| |||| \ לירח היר בשנת ״א ״ ־| לארן מלכם פתלמיס בן פתלמי[ס ....]

2 אש הא שת ״א ״א ־ ||| |||| \ לאש כתי כנפרם ארסנאס פלדלף אמתאסר בת מב..

3 בן עבדססם בן גדעת הסמלם האל אש יטנא בתשלם בת מריחי בן אשמנא[דן]

4 על בן בני על אשמנאדן ושלם ועבדרשף שלשת בן מריחי בן
אשמנאדן בן נחמי
5 בן גלב הנדר אש כן נדר אבנם מריחי בחיי לאדננם לרשף מכל
יברכם

On the 7th day of the month Ḥiyyar in the 31st year of the lord of kings Ptolemy son of Ptolemy . . . ., [2] which is the 57th year of the men of Kition, the Kanephoroṣ of Arsinoë Philadelphos (being) Amath-osir, daughter of Mk . . ., [3] son of 'Abd-sasom, son of Gad-'ath:—These statues (are those) which Bath-shalom, daughter of Mar-yeḥai, son of Eshmun-adon, set up [4] for her grandsons Eshmun-adon and Shallum and 'Abd-reshef, the three sons of Mar-yeḥai, son of Eshmun-adon, son of Naḥmai, [5] son of Gallab, (being) the vow which their father Mar-yeḥai had vowed during his life-time to their lord Reshef of Mukl: may he bless them!

L. 1. בימם See **12** 1 *n.* חיר again in **31** *d.* **45** 5, perhaps identical with the Aram. إِيَّار, אִיָּיר Targ. Jon. Ex. **12** 39, Hebr. זִו, the second month, April–May. אדן מלכם See **5** 18 *n.* פתלמים i.e. Ptolemy ii Philadelphus, 285–247 B.C. The missing word at the end of the line is prob. פלדלף. Cf. **10** 6 f. and **29** 4 ff.

L. 2. אש הא שת i.e. אֲשֶׁר הִיא שְׁנַת. Note the pron. after the relat., a construction which occurs several times in Hebr., chiefly before an adj. or ptcp., e.g. Gen. 9 3 אֲשֶׁר הוּא חַי. Dt. 20 20. Hag. 1 9 &c.; in Aram., e.g. Dan. 7 17 חֵיוָתָא . . . דִּי אִנּוּן אַרְבַּע. Targ. 2 S. 20 19 קִירְוָא וְהִיא קַבְּהּ רַב; in Arab., e.g. Quran **43** 51 هٰذَا ٱلَّذِى هُوَ مَهِينٌ *this who is a contemptible person*; the same is found in Ethiopic. See Driver *Tenses* § 199 obs., *Samuel* 64. For שת = שנת sing. cf. **6** 1 *n.* לאש כתי The era of the people of Kition began in 311 B.C. In the previous year Pumi-yathon (**12** 1 *n.*) was put to death by Ptolemy i Soter, king of Egypt, and this brought the native dynasty to an end. For the threefold indication of date cf. **29** 4 f. כנפרם = *κανηφόρος Basket-bearer*, a title given to the virgins who carried the sacred baskets in the processions of Athene, Demeter, and Dionysos at Athens. In the cult of the Ptolemies, who were treated with divine honours (cf. **28** 2–4, **29** 5 ff.), the office of the Kanephoros was one of such dignity that in Egypt (and in Cyprus too) the year was indicated by her name; for this there is evidence from papyri, from the bilingual inscr. of Canopus (238 B. C.) l. 2 κανηφόρου Ἀρσινόης Φιλαδέλφου Μενεκρατείας τῆς Φιλάμμονος (Michel no. 551) exactly as here, and from the Rosetta Stone l. 5 κανηφόρου Ἀρσινόης Φιλαδέλφου Ἀρείας τῆς Διογένους (CIG 4697), &c., in all cases, be it noted, in connexion with Arsinoë and not with other Ptolemaic queens. From this inscr. it appears that the cult of the Ptolemies, with the κανηφορία of Arsinoë, was established in Cyprus. The name of the Kanephoros, Amath-Osir, is Egyptian (cf. עבדאסר 14 2), but she was certainly a Phoenician by race. ארסנם פלדלף (genitive) *Arsinoë Philadelphus*, the sister-consort of Ptolemy ii; the pair were worshipped as gods, cf. אלן אחים θεοὶ ἀδελφοί 10 7.

L. 3. עברססם See 16 1 *n*. נרעת Baethgen explains as *Fortune of 'Ath(e)*; cf. נר חשמם 59 C 2 and the Pun. name *Giddeneme* in Plaut. *Poen.* = נר נעם CIS i 383 1, the Palm. נדרצו Vog. 84 3, and the Hebr. גַּדִּיאֵל Num. 13 10; for the deity עתא ,עתה ,עת see 112 4 *n*. Nöldeke, however, considers that the form prob. = נרען, جَدْعان; cf. جُدَيْع, جُداعة &c., *ZDMG* xlii 471. תאל Cf. 5 22. יטנא Ifil. 3 sing. fem.; for the omission of the fem. ending cf. 3 add. note i, and 56 1 טנא. מריחי See 19 3 *n*.

L. 4. על *on behalf of*, cf. CIS i 178 על בנם . . . נדר בעלשלך. 171 6 [ככרם] מאת על בני על עבדמלקרת. בן בני See 3 1 *n*. בן is plur. constr.; בני sing. with suff. 3 sing. fem. Elsewhere this suff. is ה׳, e. g. מספנתת 3 6; in Pun. א׳, e. g. קלא CIS i 371 6, or ע׳, e. g. קלע *Carth.* 142 5 &c. שלם Cf. 28 3 *n*. נחמי Cf. CIS i 94 4 אשמנאדן בן נחמי.

L. 5. נלב See 20 A 12 *n*. כן נדר As in Arab., the copulative verb כן is used with the perf. to express a pluperfect, e. g. كَانَ خَرَجَ *he had set out*: Wright *Ar. Gr.*[3] ii § 3 (c), König *Syntax* § 122, Nöldeke *Sem. Spr.* 26. This is the only instance of the idiom so far known in Phoen. The father had registered his vow for the benefit of his three sons, but he did not live to carry it out; so this was done by their grandmother. The inscrr. CIS i 381–383 are perhaps to be understood in a somewhat similar way; thus 381 2 b י[תן] המתנת ז אש נ[דר אביא] i. e. the son gave this gift which his father had vowed; so apparently 382 אש נ[ד]רא [נד]ת נדר בעלשל[ך] and 383 [נדר] נרנעם . . . נדר מנן, the first-named carries out the vow which the second had made. אבנם . . ארנגם See 5 add. note. בחיי *during his life-time*, cf. 16 2 למבחיי *during my life-time*. רשף מכל See 24 2 *n*.

28. Larnax Lapēthos. CIS i 95. Date circ. end of iv cent. B.C.

Ἀθηνᾷ Σωτείρᾳ Νίκῃ
καὶ βασιλέως Πτολεμαίου
Πραξίδημος Σέσμαος τὸν
βω[μὸ]ν ἀνέθ[ηκ]εν
Ἀγα[θ]ῇ τύχῃ

1 לענת עז חים
2 ולאר מלכם פתלמיש
3 בעלשלם בן [ס]סמי
4 יקדש [א]ת מ[ז]בח
5 [למ]זל נעם

To 'Anath, the strength of life, and to the lord of kings Ptolemy, Ba'al-shillem, son of Sesmai, consecrated this altar. To good luck!

This bilingual inscr. is written on a rock outside the village of Larnax Lapēthos, near the ancient city of Lapēthos on the N. coast of the island.

L. 1. לענת The goddess 'Anath is met with again in Idal. 7 3 (Euting *Sitz.-ber. Berl. Ak.* (1887) 420 ff.). Her cult goes back to very early times in Syria and Palestine, and has left traces in the names of the old Canaanite towns 'Anathoth (Josh. 21 18 &c.), Beth-'anath (Josh. 19 38 &c.), Beth-'anoth (Josh. 15 59), which were the seats of her worship. The father of Shamgar was called 'Anath (Jud. 5 6)[1]. Most likely the goddess came originally from Babylonia, where Anatum was the consort of Anu (cf. עֲנַמֶּלֶךְ 2 K. 17 31): Jastrow *Rel. of Bab. and Assyr.* 153, Cheyne *Ency. Bibl.* s.v. Anath. At the same time it is curious that the Canaanites should have adopted Anatum and not the far more prominent Anu; possibly the resemblance between Anatum and ענת may be only

[1] Perhaps shortened from עבדענת; in any case an unbecoming name for an Israelite. But it is possible that Shamgar was not a 'minor judge,' but a foreign oppressor of Israel (ובן ענת is read by Cheyne l. c. in Jud. 5 6); the name 'Anath, like Shamgar and Sisera, will then be purely foreign. See Moore *Judges* 143.

accidental; E. Meyer, *ZDMG* (1877) xxxi 717 ff., and Zimmern, *KAT*[3] 353, doubt the identification. From Syria the worship of 'Anath was introduced into Egypt, prob. by the Chetas (חִתִּים), and her name appears on the monuments from the 18th dynasty downwards. She was a war-goddess, and was represented helmeted and fully armed; see the monument in the Brit. Mus., Egypt. Saloon no. 191, illustrated in W. Max Müller *Asien u. Eur.* 313. Perhaps it was as a war-goddess that 'Anath becomes Athene in the Gk. version of this inscr.; and the similarity of the two names in sound no doubt assisted the identification (cf. **24** 2 *n.*). Thus לענת עז חים='Αθηνᾷ Σωτείρᾳ; for עז חים cf. Ps. 27 1. 28 8, and **57** 1 חי חים.

L. 2. אד׳ מלכם For אדן מלכם **5** 18 *n.* פתלמיש A local variety (cf. **29** 4 ff.) of the usual form פתלמים **27** 1 &c.; here Ptolemy i Soter (B.C. 323–285). According to Diodorus Sic. xix 79, Praxippos king of Lapēthos, along with other Cyprian princes, declared for Antigonus in the struggles of the Diadochoi. Seleucus as the ally of Ptolemy i laid siege to Kerynia and Lapēthos; later on, in 312, Ptolemy himself landed in Cyprus, put Pumi-yathon king of Kition to death (**12** 1 *n.*), and then seized the person of Praxippos, thus bringing to an end the dynasty of Lapēthos. The inscr. must have been written not long after Ptolemy's victory. The Gk. here is difficult to translate. The Corp. suggests an ellipse of *νίκῃ* in l. 2, thus: 'Athenae-victoriae et (victoriae) regis Ptolemaei.' Schröder, 156 *n.*, takes the *καί* of l. 2 as belonging to the preceding word, 'and to the Victory of king Ptolemy.' The second explanation is, perhaps, preferable. For the cult of the Ptolemies, who in Egypt were associated with the ancient gods of the country, cf. **27** 2 *n.*

L. 3. בעלשלם i.e. *Ba'al requites* (Piel), CIS i 338 3; cf. אשמנשלם **35** 1. **55** 1, and שלם **27** 4. The Gk. has Πραξίδημος. On a Gk. inscr. from the same place one Πραξίδημος is ἀρχιερεὺς τοῦ ναοῦ Ποσειδῶνος τοῦ Λαρνακαίου (Waddington 2779). ססמי This name is found in 1 Ch. 2 40 סִסְמָי (LXX Σοσομαΐ, Luc. Σασαμαΐ, Vulg. Sisamoi) borne by a man of Judah descended from an Egyptian ancestor; it evidently has some connexion with the god ססם, see **16** 1 *n.* Cl.-Gan. thinks that the name in full was ססמי[חי] *Sasom-yeḥai*, thus accounting for the final י. The Gk. Πραξίδημος Σέσμαος admits of no clear explanation; perhaps Σέσμαος=Σεσμαῖος (adj.), the י in ססמי being treated as the gentilic ending. It is difficult to believe that Σέσμαος could have been written for Σεσμάου.

L. 4. יקדש Ifil perf., cf. יקדשת **29** 9. 14 and יטנא **13** 2 *n.* For the dedication of an altar cf. **3** 4 and **40** 1 מ׳ נחשת. **12** 2. **29** 10 (plur.).

34. את Usually אית as sign of accus., but cf. 8 3. 7; Cl.-Gan., however, reads קרשת 1 sing.

L. 5. למזל נעם *to good luck!*, a formula invoking a blessing; here at the end of the inscr., as in CIS i 89, where the Cypriote version has τύχαι ἀγεθαῖ. The formula occurs more often at the beginning, e.g. 29 1 משל נעם, and the frequent ἀγαθῇ τύχῃ in Gk. inscrr.; cf. the Rabbinic למז' ט i.e. למזל טוב. מַזָּל Aram. מַזָּלָא is *a star of fortune* or *fate*; the plur. מַזָּלוֹת=*signs of the Zodiac* 2 K 23 5, מַזָּרוֹת Job 38 32. In Arab. مَنَازِل plur. of مَنْزِل is used of the *stations* of the moon, e.g. Quran 10 5 'it is He who ordained ... the moon for a light وَقَدَّرَهُ مَنَازِلَ *and appointed her stations.*' Prob. מזל is a loan-word from Assyr. *manzaltu*='station,' 'abode (of God).'

29. Larnax Lapēthos 2 or Narnaka. iii–ii cent. B.C.
Discovered 1893.

1 מ ש ל נ ע ם

2 הסמל ז משאנך יתנבעל רב ארץ בן גרעשתרת רב ארץ בן עבדע[שתרת] ....סר

3 בן גרעשתרת בן שלם ... רמל אש יטנאת לי אבמקדש מלקרת ס .... ם לשמי

4 בחדש זבחשׁשם אש בשנת ⌐ I לארן מלכם פתלמיש בן ארן מלכם פתלמיש

5 אש המת לעם לפט שנת 𐤆 ⌐ III וכהן לארן מלכם עבדעשתרת בן גרעשתרת

6 רב ארץ ... רמל ובירח מפע אש בשנת IIII לארן מלכם פתלמיש בן ארן מלכם

7 פתלמיש אבחי אבי ישת במקדש מלקרת אית משפן אבי בנחשת ובירח

8 פעלת אש בשנת III II לארן מלכם פתלמיש בן ארן מלכם פתלמיש בחי

9 אבי יתת ויקדשת חית שנית בגבל שד נרנך לאדן אש לי למלקרת

10 . שבתבאת החית . מנעלת קמת עם ומזבחת לאדן אש לי למלקרת

11 על חיי ועל חי זרעי ים מד ים ולצמח צדק ולאשתו ולאדמי

12 [בחד]שם ובכסאם ירח מד ירח עד עלם כקדם ומהדלת הנחשת

13 . . . תבת וסמרת בקר אש בן מנחת חני ופעלת אנך עלת

14 . . . . . הימואפבת בכסף משקל כ[כ]ר \ ׀ / ׀ ׀ ׀ ויקדשת לאדן

15 [אש לי למלק]רת פקת ונעם יכן לי ולזרעי ויסכרן מלקרת

16 . . . . . . נעם שרש

Good fortune! [2] This statue?? Yathan-ba'al governor of the district, son of Ger-'ashtart governor of the district, son of 'Abd-'a[shtart] . . . . SR, [3] son of Ger-'ashtart, son of Shallum ? RML, (is that) which I set up for myself in the sanctuary of Melqarth, S . . . . M, for my name, [4] on the new-moon of Zebaḥ-šiššim, which is in the 11th year of the lord of kings Ptolemy, son of the lord of kings Ptolemy, [5] which is the 33rd year of the people of Lapēthos, and the priest to the lord of kings (being) 'Abd-'ashtart, son of Ger-'ashtart [6] governor of the district . . . RML.—And in the month MP', which is in the 4th year of the lord of kings Ptolemy, son of the lord of kings [7] Ptolemy, in the life-time of my father, I placed in the sanctuary of Melqarth the MSPN of my father in bronze.—And in the month [8] Pa'aloth, which is in the 5th year of the lord of kings Ptolemy, son of the lord of kings Ptolemy, in the life-time [9] of my father, I gave and consecrated many (?) animals in the border of the country of Narnaka to the lord who is mine, Melqarth; [10] ? ? the animals ? ? ? ? and altars to the lord who is mine, Melqarth, [11] for my life and for the life of my seed, day by day, and to the legitimate offspring ? and to my lord (?) [12] on the new-moons and on the full-moons, month by month, for ever as aforetime (?), and ? of bronze [13] . . . ? and a yoke of oxen (?) which is part of the offering of my grace.—And I have made upon [14] . . . . . ??

in silver, (by) weight 100 and 2 (talents?), and I consecrated (it) to the lord [16] [who is mine, Melqa]rth; ?and good be to [17] me and to my seed, and may Melqarth remember me......??

L. 1. משל נעם For מזל נעם (28 5 *n.*), a local peculiarity of pronunciation, of which other instances occur in this inscr., e.g. פתלמיש for פתלמיס, possibly סמרת for צמרת l. 13, אבמקרש for 'במ l. 3 &c. As a rule this expression is in the dat., but the nom. is found in a Gk. inscr. from the neighbourhood of Pergamum, *τύχη ἀγαθή* (Michel 1360).

L. 2. משאנך Possibly the last three letters may be the 1st pers. pron.; Cl.-Gan., *Ét.* ii § 21, reads סמל זם ש אנך *this statue is mine, (yea) mine, Yathan-ba'al.* He assumes זם to be a unique form of the demonstr. pron., and finds it twice again in l. 10; ש he takes as the rel. with suff. of 1st pron.=אשר לי, and אנך as added for emphasis after the suff. in ש (cf. in Hebr. בִּי אֲנִי הֶעָוֹן 1 S. 25 24 &c.). These are serious assumptions, especially the forms זם and שׁ. The suff. י' is nearly always written in this inscr., and the rel. here is inconvenient before אש in l. 3. רב ארץ Cf. *χωράρχης*. The office prob. dated from the establishment of the autonomy of Lapēthos. נרעשתרת See 17 2 *n.* 46 2. The line prob. should be completed with [רב ארץ בן עבדא]סר.

L. 3. שלם Cf. 27 4. רמל ... Here and in l. 6 Berger, *Rev. d'assyr.* (1895) iii 76, reads קורמל, taking it as the name of a place, Cape Krommyon, the NW. point of Cyprus. Cl.-Gan. reads פרכרמל, as a title of the רב ארץ. In the latter case, the first three letters recall the Πραξ- in the names Πραξίδημος 28, Πράξιππος 28 2 *n.*, Πράξανδρος Strabo 582 3 ed. Müll., the founder of Lapēthos—all names connected with this part of the island. ימנאת Cf. 16 2. אבמקרש Apparently אב for ב, but in l. 7 we find במקרש; cf. אבחי l. 7 for בחי l. 8. For מלקרת see 23 3 *n.* A Gk. inscr. which mentions Poseidon Larnakios has been found on the same spot (p. 81 supr.); hence it is prob. that the Gks. regarded Melqarth as a marine deity and identified him with Poseidon. The missing letters may be restored ס]כר נעם עד על[ם *a good memorial for ever.*

L. 4. For the date reckoned by the universal, local, and ecclesiastical systems cf. Luke 3 1 f. בחדש i.e. on the first day of the month; see 20 A 2 *n.* For the name of the month see 14 1 *n.* פתלמיש See 28 2 *n.* There is nothing to determine with certainty which Ptolemy is referred to here; see note on l. 12 below.

L. 5. חמת is the plur. of חא **5** 11. 22. **42** 17, the plur. being used because the number of the years is given, contrast **27** 2 אש lvii הא שת; שנת must be plur. too, like ימם before dates **12** 1 *n.* As חמת agrees with שנת, the form was evidently used for both genders. לפֹּשׁ Cl.-Gan. לפש. On coins of Ṣidqi-milk, king of Lapēthos (circ. 449–420 B.C.), the name of the city is לפש, **149** B 7; in Gk. it is written *Λάπηθος, Λάπαθος, Λάπιθος, Λήπηθις*. When the era of Lapēthos began is uncertain; see below on l. 12. כהן *priest* i.e. of the deified Ptolemy; cf. the reckoning of the year by the name of the Kanephoros of Arsinoë at Idalion, **27** 2. The latter inscr. also illustrates the threefold synchronism here.

L. 6. ממע Cf. **6** 1.

L. 7. אבחי אבי i.e. בְּחַיֵּי אָבִי, but בחי l. 8; see l. 3 *n.* אבמקרש. ישת i.e. יִשַּׁתִּ Ifil perf. 1 sing. of שית, *I set.* משמן Meaning unknown. If ש=ש=ס, we may compare מספנת *ceiling, covering* **8** 6; but this does not suggest any suitable sense. The context requires not the *overlaying* of an image but an *image* itself. ובירח The third section of inscr. begins here.

L. 8. מעלת See **20** B 2 *n.*

L. 9. יתת i.e. יָתַתִּ. חית שנית Perhaps *many animals* (Lidzb.); שנית then will = שַׂגִּית, the common Aram. word for *many* (שַׂגִּיא, שְׂגָא), e.g. Palm. **121** 5. **147** i 4. 6, used poetically in later Hebr., e.g. Job 8 7. Ps. 73 12 (שגה). Job 8 11 &c. (שגא). Cl.-Gan. renders *stray animals*, i.e. שֹׁגִית (in form like פֹּרִיָּה Ps. 128 3 &c.) from שגה, used to supply the daily and monthly sacrifices. נבל שר i.e. נֵבֶל שֹׁרֵה cf. **5** 19. 20. נרנך *Narnaka* = *Λάρναξ* near Lapēthos, cf. Nicosia = Leucosia. לאדן אש לי A more solemn and emphatic expression than לאדני; contrast לאדני (?) l. 11.

L. 10. Owing to the condition of the stone, the text and meaning of the first half of the line are quite uncertain. None of the restorations are satisfactory. Cl.-Gan. reads ושבת באת החית זם מעלת קמת זם ומזבחת and takes the general sense to be *and I made over the produce of these animals to the service of* (lit. *as serving*, ptcp. fem.) *this* QMT, *and sacrificed* (Pual ptcp.) *to Melqarth.* But the Qal of שוב, though occasionally used in Hebr. with a trans. sense (e.g. שוב שבות and Ps. **85** 5. Is. **52** 8 &c.), could hardly be used of *rendering* or *applying* a gift; if באת=תבואת it must mean *produce* of the earth, not *offspring* of cattle. Landau improves on this by reading ועלת for מעלת, *and the offerings of this foundation* (??) *and the altars to Melqarth* (*Beitr. z. Altertumsk. d. Or.* ii 47). Berger's reading חקמת עם *a rising of the people* has little probability.

L. 11. על חיי ועל חי זרעי The formula which occurs frequently in the Palm. inscrr. is very similar, e.g. על חיוהי וחיי בנוהי 135 4. 137 2. &c.; cf. 70 4. 95 2. ים מד ים *day by day* as ירח מד ירח *month by month* in the next line. מד is prob. the same as the Hebr. מִדֵּי lit. *out of the abundance of*, hence *as often as*, e.g. 1 S. 7 16 מדי שנה בשנה. Is. 66 23 מדי חרש בחרשו ומדי שבת בשבתו. ולצמח צדק Apparently *and to the legitimate offspring*; for this fig. sense of צמח *shoot* cf. Jer. 23 5 והקמתי לדוד צמח צדיק and 33 15. צדק here may be either an adj. צַדִּיק or more likely a noun צֶדֶק. ולאשתו ולארמי As they stand these words are untranslateable. See note below.

L. 12. [בחד]שם ובכסאם The words thus restored and read prob. mean *on the new-moons and on the full-moons* i.e. at the beginning and the middle of the month; cf. Ps. 81 4 תקעו בחדש שופר בכסה ליום חגנו. כקדם Perhaps *as formerly*, cf. Jer. 30 20. Lam. 5 21.

M. Clermont-Ganneau (l.c.) makes a brilliant suggestion as to the meaning of the obscure expression in l. 11 לצמח צדק ולאשתו ולארמי. His argument is as follows: (1) The ל in these words must have a different meaning from על in the same line, i.e. these words must denote not those for whose benefit (על) Yathan-ba'al made his offering, but those to whom religious service is due, like לאדן .. למלקרת in ll. 9. 10. (2) In the case of the great god Melqarth the sacrifice is to be offered daily (ים מד ים), but in the second case fortnightly, every month (בחדשם וגו'). There is, therefore, a difference of dignity between the objects of religious service. (3) The words ולאשתו ולארמי do not suggest any names of gods; but they may represent the names of some members of the Ptolemaic dynasty to whom divine honours were paid (27 2 *n.*), and the provision of the fortnightly sacrifice to them is in accordance with the Egyptian custom of celebrating a solemnity in honour of the reigning monarch on a fixed day over a month, called in Gk. and Rom. times 'the king's day.' The similarity of the letters in Phoen. makes it possible to read כלאפתר for ולאשתו, supposing a mason's error of ו for ר (though this is perhaps hardly necessary); and if a similar error of מ for נ may be admitted in the foll. word, we have the reading ולאדני. Thus the whole phrase will mean *And to the legitimate offspring* (lit. *shoot of righteousness*) *of Cleopatra and to my lord.* Two sets of historical conditions may be found to account for this remarkable and significant expression. (*a*) The inscr. may belong to the period when Ptolemy vii (vi) Philometor was engaged in a bitter struggle for power with his brother, afterwards Ptolemy ix (vii) Euergetes ii or Physkon, a struggle which considerably affected Cyprus[1]. Their mother Cleopatra, the wife of Ptolemy v Epiphanes, was regent for her eldest son from 181 to her death in 174. Yathan-ba'al thus protests his loyalty to the claims of the eldest son, *the legitimate offspring of Cleopatra* and his lawful sovereign (לאדני), Ptolemy vii (vi). The 11th year of this king will give 171–170 as the date of the inscr., and 203 B.C. as the era of Lapēthos. (*b*) A later period offers an even more suitable occasion. After the death of Ptolemy ix (vii) Euergetes ii or Physkon, his wife and niece Cleopatra iii attempted to secure the succession for her younger son Alexander, but the people refused to acknowledge him. Thereupon she sent him for safety to Cyprus, and had him appointed independent king of the island (B. C. 114). Later on, his elder brother Ptolemy x (viii) Soter ii or Lathyros was expelled by an insurrection at Alexandria instigated by his mother, and took refuge in Cyprus (B. C. 107). The situation in Cyprus at this period must have been embarrassing enough, especially for public officials like the רב ארץ at Lapēthos; and it may well be that political prudence suggested to Yathan-ba'al the equivocal expression *to the legitimate offspring of Cleopatra and to my lord*. In this case the 11th year of Ptolemy will be 107–106, and the era of Lapēthos will begin with 139 B.C. Cl.-Gan.'s correction and historical elucidation of the text are, of course, only conjectural; but the conjecture is a most suggestive one, and it is sufficiently supported to make it plausible.

L. 12. ומֹהֹרלת הנחשת might mean *and from the bronze doors*; for the construction see 3 4 *n*. The first word, however, is uncertain. Cl.-Gan. reads הדלת=δέλτος *tablet*, and takes בקדם with this sentence; but his attempt to make sense of the passage is unsuccessful.

L. 13. At the beginning of the line Cl.-Ganneau restores [אש כ]תבת *which I have written*. The next words he takes to be וסמרת בקר *and I have nailed on the wall*, comparing the Hebr. מַסְמֵר *nail*, Arab. مِسْمَارٌ (prob. a loan-word from Aram., Fränkel *Aram. Fremdw.* 89). Lidzb. reads וסמדת ב׳=וְצֶמֶד בָּקָר *and a yoke of oxen*, which agrees better with the donation of sacrificial animals in l. 9 f. בן מנחת חני Perhaps *part of the offerings of my grace*, the prep. מן being written בן before another מ, see 5 3 *n*. Cl.-Ganneau takes אש בן as=

[1] Thus Polybius, enlarging on Ptolemy's clemency towards his brother and rival, says ἔπειτα, δόξας ἐκπεσεῖν ἀπὸ τῆς ἀρχῆς ὑπὸ τἀδελφοῦ, τὸ μὲν πρῶτον, ἐν Ἀλεξανδρείᾳ λαβὼν κατ' αὐτοῦ καιρὸν ὁμολογούμενον, ἀμνησικάκητον ἐποιήσατο τὴν ἁμαρτίαν· μετὰ δὲ ταῦτα, πάλιν ἐπιβουλεύσαντος τῇ Κύπρῳ, κύριος γενόμενος ἐν Λαπήθῳ τοῦ σώματος ἅμα καὶ τῆς ψυχῆς αὐτοῦ, τοσοῦτον ἀπέσχε τοῦ κολάζειν ὡς ἐχθρόν, ὥστε καὶ δωρεὰς προσέθηκε κ.τ.λ. xl 12.

ומעלת ... אֲשֶׁר בּוֹ *on which* (*is*) *the offering*. For מנחת see 7 1 *n*. Pf. 1 sing. The fourth section of the inscr. begins here—the dedication of some metal object.

L. 14. The first part of the line cannot be understood. בכסף *of silver* like בנחשת *of bronze* in l. 7. משקל will then be in apposition to the following word denoting weight, Driver *Tenses* § 192 (1); cf. 40 1 מזבח נחשת משקל לטרם מאת. The text has כר, but this is a corn or fluid measure. It is possible that כר is an abbreviation for ככר *talent*, CIS i 171 2. 4; but the value of 102 talents of silver by the Attic standard would amount to over £2480 of our money, too large a sum to be likely. However, we do not know the value of Phoen. weights and money sufficiently well to make us reject this explanation altogether.

L. 15. מפקת Meaning unknown; *profit* has been suggested, from Aram. נפק *go forth*, but this is very doubtful. ויסכרן=וְיִזְכְּרֻנִי For the suff. cf. 4 7 תרגזן.

L. 16. The last words give no suitable sense.

80. Tamassos. Date 363 B.C. Brit. Mus., Cyprus Room no. 252.

1 סמל אז אש יתן ויטנ
2 א · מנחם · בן בנחדש בן מנ
3 חם בן ערק לאדני ל[רש]ף
4 אלית בירח אתנם בשנת
5 שלשם א — למלך מלכיתן · מלך
6 כתי ואדיל · ב שמע קל · יברך

Cypriote:

to na ti ri a ta ne to nu · e to ke ne
ka se · o ne te ke ne · ma na se se
o no me ni o ne · to i ti o i
to i a pe i lo ni · to i e le i
ta i · i tu ka i

i. e. in Greek:

Τὸν ἀ[ν]δριά[ν]ταν τό[ν] νυ ἔδωκεν
κὰς ὀνέθηκεν Μανασῆς
ὁ Νωμηνίων τῶι θιῶι
τῶι Ἀπείλωνι τῶι Ἑλεί
ται ἐ[ν] τύχαι

This statue (is that) which Menaḥem, son of Ben-ḥodesh, son of Menaḥem, son of ʻAraq, gave and set up to his lord Reshef of Eliyath, in the month Ethanim in the thirtieth year, 30, of king Milk-yathon, king of Kition and Idalion, because he heard (his) voice: may he bless!

This inscr. was found in 1885 on the site of the ancient Tamassos, between Lapēthos and Idalion. A sanctuary of Apollo has been discovered (1889) outside the town, and recent excavations at Frángissa, some 3 miles to the west, have revealed another sanctuary of the same god; Myres *Cypr. Mus. Catal.* 12. The inscr. may be compared with **12** and **18** from Kition, and with **23–26** from Idalion.

L. 2. מנחם Cf. **21** 2; Cypr. *ma-na-se-se*, perhaps for *ma-na-he-se* (Menaḥem) or *m'-na-se-se*=Μνασέας, the nearest Gk. equivalent for the Phoen. Menaḥem; Cl.-Gan. *Rec.* i 186 f. בנחדש See **17** 3 *n.*

L. 3. ערק Perhaps עֶרֶק like בֶּרֶק &c. This pr. n. possibly may be connected with the ancient Phoen. clan הָעַרְקִי Gen. 10 17. 1 Ch. 1 15, i. e. the men of Ἄρκη (Jos. *Ant.* i 6 2), at the foot of Lebanon, still called Tell ʻArqa, 12 m. N. of Tripoli. See further Schrader *COT* 104; Tell-el-Amarna letters 78 12.

L. 4. לרשף אליית Cypr. τῶι Ἀπείλωνι τῶι Ἑλείται *Apollo of Helos*, either Helos in Lacedaemon or a Cyprian city of the same name. Hesychius, *Lexicon* s. v. Zeus in Cyprus, quotes several forms which resemble Ἑλείται here, thus Εἰλήτι: Ζεὺς ἐν Κύπρῳ. Ἔλαθυς: Διὸς ἱερὸν ἐν Κύπρῳ &c. In Tam. **2** 4 f. רשף אלהיתם=Cypr. Ἀπό[λ]λωνι τῶι Ἀλασιώται, a Phoen. transcription of what is prob. the name of another Gk. town. In the bilingual inscr. CIS i 89 a third designation of the god occurs, רשף מכל Cypr. τῶ Ἀπολῶνι τῶ Ἀμυκλοῖ *Apollo of Amyclae*; see **12** 3 *n.* **24** 2 *n.* אתנם See **20** A 1 *n.*

L. 5. מלכיתן See **23** 1 *n.*

EGYPT

81. Abydos. CIS i 102. Circ. iv cent. In situ.

a

1 אנך פעלאבסת בן צדיתן בן גרצד הצרי ישב דכי

2 באן מצרם בפטרת בדמנקצת ה . נ .

b

אנך בעל[י]ח[ן] בן מנקצת . יח . . .

c

אנך מגן בן בדא . חפצבעל מנפ .

d

1 אנך עבדאבסת בן צדיתן

2 באנהגברצ || לירח חיר

a

I am Pa'ala-ubast, son of Ṣed-yathon, son of Ger-ṣed, the Tyrian, dwelling here (?), in On of Egypt, after the departure (? ?) of Bod-MNQṢTH, the man of On (?).

b

I am Ba'al-[yaḥon], son of MNQṢTH . . .

c

I am Magon, son of Bodo, . Ḥefeṣ-ba'al . . .

d

I am 'Abd-ubast, son of Ṣed-yathon . . . . . 2, in the month Ḥiyyar.

These inscrr. are a selection from those found on the walls of the temple of Osiris at Abydos (Egypt). Like the inscrr. on the colossus at Ipsambul (CIS i 111–113), and on the rocks beside the caravan-routes in the Sinaitic peninsula (108–109), they give the names, and occasionally the designations, of travellers.

a. L. 1. פעלאבסת *Bast has made*; for Bast see *d* and **20** B 6 *n*., and for the compound name with פעל cf. פעלעשתרת in the inscr. discovered at Memphis in 1900, given below[1], בעלפעל NPun. 94 2, אלפעל on coins from Byblus (**149** B 9) and in 1 Ch. 8 11 ff.; cf. עשהאל 2 S. 2 18 &c. צדיתן בן גרצד Cf. *d* and יתנצד CIS i 184 4 f. עבדצד 236 5 &c. צד (cf. Hebr. צַיִד *hunting*, צַיָּד *hunter*) is clearly the name of a deity, perhaps the god of the chase; but it is found only in compound pr. nn.[2] The deity was associated with Melqarth and Tanith at Carthage, e. g. צדמלקרת CIS i 256, צדתנת 249. It is possible that the originals of the Phoen. gods Ἀγρεύς and Ἀλιεύς mentioned by Philo of Bybl., *Fr. Hist. Gr.* iii 566, were צד וצדן i. e. *Hunter and Fisher*. The name of the city צדן is perhaps related to that of the god צד, who is supposed by some to be the Phoen. Poseidon; see Cl.-Gan. *Ét.* i 154. For גרצד cf. גרמלקרת **17** 2 *n*.; Lidzb., however, reads ברצד. ישב רכי Derenbourg's rendering (*Rev. d'Assyr.* i 93), *I dwell, crushed* (*with grief*), is most improbable. רכי has been taken as a demonstrative adv., *here*, cf. Aram. דְּיכֵי, דֵּךְ *ille*; but in Phoen. the demonstr. is ז, not ד. The reading רכי is possible; this may be an adv. of place, cf. ܠܗܠ݂ܐ, and see **4** 4 *n*., where according to Hoffmann אר is a demonstr. particle.

L. 2. באן מצרם On, Egyp. *An*, = Heliopolis in Lower Egypt; cf. Gen. **41** 45 (LXX Ἡλίου πόλεως). Eze. **30** 17; it was celebrated for the worship of the sun-god, Ra. בפטרת Possibly *after the departure*, i.e. *the decease*, *of B*. פטר has the sense *depart*, *escape*, e. g. 1 S. 19 10, and in post-bibl. Hebr. frequently occurs, in the Nifal, with the meaning *depart out of this life*, e. g. Talm. *Berakoth* 17 a ונפטר

[1] 1 המצבא [ז] יטנ[את] אנך פעלעשתרת בן עבדמלכת בן נגבעל בן עבדמלכת בן בנבעל
2 בן עבדמלכ[ת . . . על א]רתפטרמלכי לרבתי לאלם אדרת אס אלם עשתרת ולאלנם אש
3 אל[. יב]רך א[תי ואית ב]ני עבדאסר ונגבעל ועבדססם ופעלעשתרת ואת אמנם חנעשתרת
4 [וי]תן לם חן וחים לען אלנם יבן אדם

i. e. 'This erection I erected, I Pa'ala-'ashtart &c., ?son of 'Abd-malkath, ... to my mistress, the mighty god Isis, the god 'Ashtart, and to the (other) gods who [3]are (here?). May they bless [him and his] sons, 'Abd-osir &c., and their mother Ḥanni-'ashtart, [4]and give them favour and life in the eyes of the gods and the sons of men.' In l. 2 Lidzb. suggests על אֹרת סָפֶר מאלכי *on account of the protection of my journey*, supposing that מאלך = מהלך; לאלם אדרת see **33** 6 *n*.; l. 3 אל perhaps the fragment of an adv., like the Hebr. הלם, והלאה; the restoration א[תי ואית ב]ני is uncertain; l. 4 cf. **8** 10 *n*. *Rép.* i nos. 1. 58; Lidzb. *Eph.* i 152.

[2] The names Θήρων (a Tyrian, Michel 424) and Ἀψήτος (gen.) in Gr. inscrr. may be the one a translation of צד, the other a transcription of עבדצד; Cl.-Gan. *Rec.* i 187–192.

בשם טוב מן העולם. The commemoration of the dead was customary at the temple of Osiris; but this explanation of בפטרת cannot be regarded as certain. The reading of the word following is doubtful; the Corp. gives עברמנקרת; Derenbourg l. c., Lidzb. ברמנקצת, cf. מנקצת in *b*. For ה.נ. the Corp. restores האני *the man of On*; Renan האנדכי, a gentilic noun, taking דכי from the end of l. 1.

b. בעל.ח. i. e. prob. בעליחן, cf. יחנבעל 46 2 and חנבעל. ... מנקצת.יח. So Lidzb. The first word is uncertain and its etymology unknown; Derenbourg regards it as = ברמנקצת in *a*, and reads the next word as a gentilic form חתני or חתפי. Corp. מנקרתח[ם]י *Menqarth* (i. e. *Melqarth*) *protects*; cf. יַחְסִי perhaps = יַחְמְיָה *may Yah protect* 1 Ch. 7 2; Arab. حَمَى.

c. מגן Cf. 33 2 &c., a common Phoen. name. בדא See 12 3 *n*. חפצבעל *pleasure of Ba'al*; the name of another person. מנפ. may contain the name נף *Memphis*, Eze. 30 13, *of Nof* מֹנָף. It is doubtful whether the full form was מנפי, for this would require the art., as הצרי in *a*.

d. L. 1. For the two pr. nn. cf. *a*. The text followed is that of Derenbourg l. c.

L. 2. The meaning of the first group of letters is unknown. For ירח חיר cf. 27 1 *n*.

ATTICA

32. Athens. CIS i 115. Perhaps iv cent. B.C. Athens.

'Αντίπατρος 'Αφροδισίου 'Ασκαλ[ωνίτης]
Δομσάλως Δομανῶ Σιδώνιος ἀνέθηκε

1 אנך שם. בן עבדעשתרת אשקלני
2 אש יטנאת אנך דעמצלח בן דעמחנא צדני

Μηθεὶς ἀνθρώπων θαυμαζέτω εἰκόνα τήνδε,
ὡς περὶ μὲν μελέων, περὶ δὲγ πρῷρ' (ἐ)γκτετάνυσται.
ἦλθε γὰρ εἰχθρολέων τἀμὰ θέλων σποράσαι·
ἀλλὰ φίλοι τ' ἤμυναν καί μοι κτέρισαν τάφον οὖτ[η],
οὓς ἔθελον φιλέων, ἱερᾶς ἀπὸ νηὸς ἰόντες.
φοινίκην δὲ λιπ(ὼ)ν τεῖδε χθονὶ σῶμα κέκρυμμαι.

I am ŠM., son of 'Abd-'ashtart, an Ashqelonite. (This is that) which I D'om-ṣillaḥ, son of D'om-ḥanno, a Sidonian, set up.

This bilingual inscr. is written on a gravestone now preserved in the Κεντρικὸν Μουσεῖον in Athens. Underneath the Phoen. lines is carved a representation of the incident alluded to in the Gk. verses below. A corpse lies upon a bier; on the left a lion is leaping up to devour the body, on the right is a human figure with the prow of a ship in the place of the head and shoulders; it seems to be defending the corpse from the lion. The scene is perhaps intended for an allegory; the lion representing the god of the underworld eager to snatch the body, the prow or 'holy ship' (apparently personified) being possibly connected with funeral rites, which protect the dead from violation. See Wolters in *Mitth. Arch. Instituts*, Athenische Abth. xiii (1888) 310 ff. On account of the form of the Gk. letters the Corp. dates the inscr. in the second cent. B.C., Lidzb. in the fourth (?).

L. 1. אנך In this inscr. both the person commemorated and the donor of the memorial speak in the first person; see 16 1 *n.* שם. There appears to be the fragment of a letter after ם; but the full name cannot now be read. The Gk. equivalent is 'Αντίπατρος, a name specially common in the family of Herod.

L. 2. רעמצלח בן רעמחנא Δομσάλως Δομανῶ; for the deity רעם see 8 4 *n*. רעמצלח cf. בעלצלח 7 2; רעמחנא cf. בעלחנא 89 1 f. In the latter name, חנא seems to be the Perf. of חנן with the suff. of 3rd m. sing. This form of the verbal suff. is usual in NPun., e.g. פעלא 57 11, ברכא, שמאא (= שמעא) &c.; it occurs also earlier, in Pun., e.g. רפיא 40 2. Cf. the nominal suff. in א in the frequent קלא.

83. **Piraeus.** Date 96 B.C. Louvre.

1 בים ||||למרזח בשת ⅂||||\ לעם צדן תם בד צדנים בנאספת לעטר
2 אית שמעבעל בן מגן אש נשא הנו על בת אלם ועל מבנת חצר
בת אלם
3 עטרת חרץ בדרכנם 𐤆 למחת כ בן אית חצר בת אלם ופעל אית כל
4 אש עלתי משרת אית רעת ז לכתב האדמם אש נשאם לן על בת
5 אלם עלת מצבת חרץ ויטנאי בערפת בת אלם ען אש לכנת גו
6 ערב עלת מצבת ז ישאן בכסף אלם בעלצדן דרכמנם 𐤆 למחת
7 לכן ידע הצדנים כ ידע הגו לשלם חלפת אית אדמם א . ש פעל
8 משרת את פן גו

Tὸ κοινὸν τῶν Σιδωνίων Διοπείθ(η)ν Σιδώνιον

On the 4th day of the Marzeaḥ (?), in the 15th year of the people of Sidon, the community of the Sidonians resolved in assembly:—to crown [2] Shama'-ba'al, son of Magon, who (has been) president of the corporation in charge of the temple and the building of the temple court, [3] with a golden crown of 20 drachmae sterling, because he built the court of the temple and did all [4] the service (?) he was charged with:— [5] that the men who are our presidents in charge of the temple write this (our) intention upon a golden stele, and set it up in the portico of the temple before men's eyes:—that the corporation be designated [6] as surety (for it). For this stele let them bring 20 drachmae sterling of the money of the god the Ba'al of Sidon: [7] thereby the Sidonians shall know that the corporation knows how to requite the men who have done 8 service before the corporation.

The Sidonian colony, settled at the port of Athens, is referred to or implied in **34**. **35**. CIS i 116 הצדני . . . לעבדתנת, prob. also in **32**. It was no doubt a community of merchants and ship-masters, maintaining in the land of their adoption the religion and organization of their native city (see **34**. **35**). This inscr. shows, however, that they had adapted themselves to the Greek civilization in the midst of which they lived; in characteristic Greek fashion they vote a crown and monument to a deserving officer, and they record their resolution in the recognized forms used in Greek inscrr. from the fifth cent. downwards. In fact, this inscr. almost seems to be a translation from a Greek original; see CIA ii 1 b=Michel 80; CIA ii 589=M 145; CIA ii 603=M 968; CIA ii 621=M 984.

L. 1. מרזח Generally taken to be the name of a month, but the unparalleled omission of ירח before it is noticeable. Cl.-Gan. suggests that it was the name of the annual מרזח=*a solemn festival*, perhaps lasting five days (*Rec.* ii 390 *n.* iv 344); see **42** 16 *n.* בשת See **6** 1 *n.* לעם צדן The era of Sidon began when the city became autonomous in 111 B.C. This will give 96 B.C. as the date of the inscr., 9 years before Athens was taken by Sulla[1]. תם Pf. 3 m. sing., lit. *be complete*, here *has decided, resolved.* The verb governs the infins. לעטר l. 1 and לכתב l. 4, prob. also לבנת l. 5. בר צדנים must have some such meaning as *the community of the Sidonians.* In Hebr. בַּדִּים denotes *parts* of the body i.e. members (Job 18 13), or *parts* of a vine i.e. branches (Eze. 17 6). In Phoen. the sing. בר is used to describe a worshipper as a *member* of his deity, as in the pr. nn. ברעשתרת, ברמלקרת, or a stranger as a *member* of a household; see **6** 2 *n.* It is but an extension of this usage when בר is applied not to an individual but to a community; the Sidonian μέτοικοι at the Piraeus could describe themselves as בר צדנים *the Sidonian protected aliens* (Lidzb. 134 *n.*). G. Hoffmann, *Über einige Phön. Inschr.* 5 f., takes בר as a prep. בְּדֵי lit. *for the satisfaction of, for*; but this does not admit of a satisfactory construction for תם, nor does it give a natural explanation of בר in pr. nn. A Gk. inscr. from Delos illustrates this part of the text; ἡ σύνοδος τῶν Τυρίων ἐμπόρων καὶ ναυκλήρων στεφανοῖ Πάτρωνα κ.τ.λ. CIG 2271=M 998. בנאספת The Nif. ptcp. of אסף used as a noun, *gathering*,

[1] Köhler, CIA ii Suppl. 1335 b, thinks that the Gk. form of this inscr. is much older, about the second half of the third cent. B.C.; in which case the inscr. must be dated from some Sidonian era now lost to us. If the dynasty of Eshmun-'azar ceased in 275 B.C. (p. 38), the era may have started then: Meyer *Ency. Bibl.* 3763.

assembly; it corresponds to the Gk. epigraphical formula *ἐν τεῖ ἀγορᾶι τεῖ κυρίαι* CIA ii 585=M 152. לעטר Followed by a double accus. as in Ps. 8 6. 103 4. The corresponding Gk. phrase is *στεφανῶσαι (αὐτὸν) χρυσῶι στεφάνωι ἀπὸ . . . δραχμῶν ἀρετῆς ἕνεκα*, e.g. CIA iv 2 169 b=M 105 and often.

L. 2. שמעבעל i.e. *Ba'al hears*. The Gk. equivalent *Διοπείθης* i.e. *obeying Zeus* is founded on a misunderstanding of the Phoen. נשא i.e. נָשִׂיא *chief*, cf. נשיאי העדה Ex. 16 22. Josh. 9 15 &c. His term of office had elapsed, and he now receives from his late colleagues this expression of their gratitude. גו is etymologically connected with the Hebr. גוי *nation*, Aram. ܓܘܐ, Sabaean גו *community*, cf. Job 30 5 מִן־גֵּו יְגֹרָשׁוּ *they are driven far from folk*, where גֵּו should be pointed גֹּו, unless גוי be read; in Gk. inscrr. *τὸ κοινόν*. בת אלם Cf. 5 15–18 בת אלנם, and see l. 6 *n*. For על ב׳ א׳ cf. על המקדשם 46 1 *n*. מבנת A verbal noun, *building*; in Hebr. מִבְנֶה=*structure* Eze. 40 2.

L. 3. בדרכנם The prep. is ב of material; cf. 2 Ch. 9 18 (בזהב). Ex. 38 8. דרכנם is prob. an error for דרכמנם l. 6. In both places דרכמנם must be taken to represent *drachmae*; for in Gk. inscrr. of this class the sums voted are given in *δραχμαί* (i.e. silver drachmae), a larger sum for the crown and a smaller one for the stele. In this inscr., however, the sum specified in both cases is the same; and as 20 silver drachmae would be too small an amount either for the עטרת חרץ or for the מצבת חרץ, we must take דרכמנם to be *gold* drachmae. A gold drachma represented about 9*s*. 1*d*., a silver drachma about 9¾*d*. Hoffmann l.c. renders חרץ l. 5 not *gold* but *decision*; he is therefore compelled to take דרכנם l. 3 as gold drachmae and דרכמנם l. 6 as silver drachmae; but this is unnecessary and unnatural. On account of the form דרכנם, Meyer, *Entstehung d. Judenthums* 196 f., understands *darics* to be meant; *darics*, however, do not occur in Gk. inscrr. in this connexion, and it is Gk. usage (above) which is closely followed here. The fact that דרכמנם in this case is the Phoen. form of *δραχμαί* throws a valuable light on the disputed meaning of דַּרְכְּמוֹנִים in Ezr. 2 69. Neh. 7 70–72 and of אֲדַרְכֹנִים in 1 Ch. 29 7. Ezr. 8 27[1]. Both words are generally translated *darics* (R.V.); but this inscr. shows that דרכמנים was the recognized Semitic transcription of *δραχμαί*, as Lucian knew, for in the passages quoted he invariably

[1] The form אדרכנים is open to suspicion. In 1 Ch. 29 7 רבו 'וא is prob. a gloss, for the gold offering has been mentioned just before; in Ezr. (LXX 2 Esdr.) 8 27 דרכמנים is the better reading, testified by LXX A *δδονδραχμανειν*, and prob. implied by the reading of B *δδονχαμανειμ*. In the biblical passages 'ד refers not to money but to weight; a *δραχμή* among the Gks. was one-hundredth part of a *μνᾶ*.

renders δραχμάς. Moreover, the form דרכמנים corresponds with δραχμαί and not with δαρεικοί. See Kennedy, art. Money in Hastings' *Dict. of the Bible* iii 421. למחת l. 6. The context requires the meaning *of full weight*, standard current coin. The most plausible etymology of the word is that given by Hoffmann. He connects it with מחה *wipe off*, and supposes that it was used in the first place of corn-measures, 'to wipe off into the measure' i.e. 'to fill up to the full weight.' In the Babyl. dialect of the Talmud the Ethpaal of מחה is used in the sense *approved*, e.g. *Shabbath* 61 b איתמחי גברא ואיתמחי קמיע *the man* (i.e. *the physician*) *is approved and the amulet is approved*; similarly קמיע מומחה *a tested amulet* ib. 61 a. In Syr. ܐܬܒܣܝ is used of *testing* a weight or measure, e.g. Epiphanius *de Mensur. et Pond.* in *Vet. Test. ab Origene recens. fragm.* ed. Lagarde p. 48, l. 32; p. 58, l. 67; p. 51, l. 7 כר ביד חרקא דברוחקא מתתמחיא ומתחקלא (cited by Hoffmann). Hence למחת will mean *by the tested weight*, *of full weight*; the prep. is ל of norm or standard.

L. 4. איש עלתי *which was incumbent upon him*; for על in this sense cf. Num. 7 9 עבדת הקדש עלהם. Ezr. 10 4. 12. 1 Ch. 9 27 &c. The construction of the words which follow is not very clear. In l. 8 משרת is certainly a noun, *service*, from שרת *to minister*, and possibly it may be a noun here, *all the service which was laid upon him*; so Lidzb. In such a sentence the natural order would be אית כל (ה)משרת אש עלתי; but as כל in Hebr. often stands before a relative clause containing a *verb*, which is strictly its genitive (e.g. את כל אשר עשה Gen. 1 31), so here the relative clause אש עלתי מ׳, though it contains a *noun*, may be regarded as the genitive after כל. It must be admitted, however, that this is not easy grammar. Hoffmann takes משרת as an infin. with מן i.e. מְשָׁרֵת, governing אית רעת ז *because* (*he*) *administered this* . . . ; but the infin. would require a suffix in this case, e.g. מִדַּעְתִּי Is. 48 4. If משרת be a verb, it is better to take it as a ptcp. i.e. מְשָׁרֵת dependent on the suffix in עלתי, *while he administered this* . . . , an imitation of Gk. idiom, but cf. 1 K. 14 6 קול רגליה באה and Ps. 69 4 (?). אית רעת ז The word רעת may be explained in two ways. (1) It may come from the Aram. רעא *to be favourably disposed towards a person* (in Targ. רַעֲוָא, Bibl. Aram. רְעוּת Ezr. 5 17. 7 18) = Arab. رَضِيَ *to be pleased, satisfied with* = Hebr. רצה; and we may render *this* (*our*) *good pleasure*. It is not necessary, however, to assume such a strong Aramaism here; for (2) רעת may come from the same root as the Arab. رَعَى *to watch, regard, be mindful of* = Syr. ܪܢܐ *to observe, concern oneself with* (ܪܢܝܐ, ܬܪܢܝܬܐ *meditation, thought*; Targ. רְעוּ *desire*, Ps. 107 30) = Hebr. רעה, cf. Ps. 37 3. Pr. 15 14. Hos. 12 2 (?)

and רְעוּת in Qoh. 1 14 &c. Hence רעת may be rendered *intention, wish*, either governed by the preceding משרת, or placed for emphasis before its verb לכתב[1]. To connect ר׳ with לכתב is in accordance with the Gk. formula ἀναγράψαι τόδε τὸ ψήφισμα, e.g. CIA ii 311=M 124, CIA ii 176=M 109 and often, but it involves an unusual construction for כל.. משרת (supr.). לכתב הארםם The infin. is governed by תם l. 1 and הארםם is its subject. Its object must be understood, 'this decree,' if אית רעת ז be taken with משרת. נשאם לן על ב׳ א׳ i.e. the present curators of the temple. These officials may be compared with the νεωποῖαι in Asiatic sanctuaries, e.g. CIG 2656=M 453 (Halicarnassus), M 835 (ib.), CIG 2671=M 462 (Iasus).

L. 5. מצבת חרץ *a pillar of gold*, i.e. prob. a gilded stele, cf. 24 1 *n*. On the Gk. inscrr. it is always ἐν στήλει λιθίνει, e.g. CIA ii 613= M 977 and often; but here, contrary to Gk. practice, the same amount is voted both for the stele and the crown, and as the latter is specified as golden (l. 3), so the stele is to be golden (or prob. gilded) too. It is true that we do not hear of a gilded מצבת elsewhere, but such an object is not impossible in itself, and the language of the inscr. seems to demand it. Hoffmann takes חרץ as=*decision, decree* (cf. חרוץ Joel 4 14. נחרצה Is. 10 23 &c.), and as the object of לכתב. If חרץ does not mean *gold* it is simpler to give it the primary meaning of *engraving*, and to take it as the genit. after מצבת, *a stele of engraving* i.e. an inscribed stele (cf. 8 4. 5?). ויטנאי Ifil impf. 3 plur. with suff. 3 fem. sing. i.e. וְיַטְּנָאִי. ערפת *portico*, see 8 6 *n*. It corresponds to the πρόστωιον (CIA ii 613=M 977) or open pillared hall at the entrance of the temple. The custom was to place these monuments ἐν τῶι ἱερῶι τοῦ θεοῦ M 977, or πρὸ τοῦ ναοῦ M 982, or ἐν τῶι προνάωι M 546, ἐν τεῖ αὐλεῖ τοῦ ἱεροῦ M 985, ἐν τῶι ἐπιστάντι προπύλωι τῶι τοῦ τεμένους M 476 &c. עןּ אש=לְעֵינֵי אִישׁ; for the accus. instead of the prep. ל cf. פנת אלם 42 13. 48 8. The corresponding Gk. phrase is ἐν τῶι ἐπιφανεστάτωι τοῦ ἱεροῦ τοπῶι M 992, or ἐν ἱερῶι ὧι ἂν αὐτοῖς φαίνηται M 468. לכנת נו ערב *to designate the corporation as surety* (*for it*). לכנת Piel inf., governed prob. by תם l. 1, and followed by two accusatives. כנה lit. *give a title* or *cognomen* as in Aram. ܟܢܐ, Arab. كَنَى, Hebr. Is. 45 4; so in a general sense *to*

[1] The above characterization of the root رعى=ܪܥܐ=רעה is based upon Barth's study in *Wurzeluntersuchungen* (1902) 46 ff. He suggests that the primitive meaning was *to keep* (*sheep*). It must be noted, however, that the origin of the sense which √ רעה has in Ps. 37 3 &c. is far from clear. Besides the two roots above, Barth distinguishes a third, viz. رعو (ע״י) *to bind together, attach*, whence Hebr. רֵעַ *friend*.

designate. The infin. of כן *to be* is לכן 10 10, not לכנת, for which there is no analogy in ע׳ו verbs.

L. 6. ערב A noun, prob. of participial form, *surety*. In Hebr. the vb. ערב *be surety for* is followed by the accus. (Gen. 43 9. 44 32. Ps. 119 122), once by ל (Pr. 6 1); so it is better to take עלת מצבת 1 as dependent, not on ערב, but on the verb which follows; and this is more in accordance with the Gk. formula Εἰς δὲ τὴν ἀναγραφὴν τῆς στήλης δοῦναι . . . M 118 and often. ישאן i.e. יִשְּׂאֻן, the subj. being the members of the corporation. For נשא in the sense of *bringing* (an offering) cf. in Pun. CIS i 411 3 אש נשא עבראשמן, and Ps. 96 8. 1 Ch. 16 29; hence משאת *payment, tax* 42 3. 48 1 &c. בכסף The prep. ב=Gk. ἀπό; it is not ב of material as in ברדכנם l. 3. אלם בעלצדן This is a clear instance of the plur. of אל being used to denote *god*, like the Heb. אלהים; we may conclude that אלם ll. 2. 5 is also sing. in meaning. Cf. 35 2 אלם נרגל. 59 A 4 אלם הקדש, and the inscr. lately found at Memphis לרבתי לאלם אדרת אם אלם עשתרת (p. 91 *n.* 1), where אלם is connected with a female deity, and even with a fem. adj.; the plur. ארנם is used similarly, 49 3 *n.* In the following cases, פנת אלם 42 13. 43 8, עבראלם 9 1 f., מתנאלם CIS i 194 1 f. (cf. מתנאל 406 3), נלב אלם 257 4 &c., אמת אלם 378 3, the sing. meaning is most probable. Contrast the use of אלנם *gods*; see 8 10 *n*. The plur. אלם denotes a more abstract conception than the sing. אל, *godhead* as distinct from *god*: it sums up the various characteristics of the particular אל (Hoffm.); cf. the abstract plurals נעורים, זקנים, חיים (Ges. § 124 *d*). For the Ba'al of Sidon see 5 18. The order to defray the cost out of the temple treasury finds several parallels in the Gk. inscrr., e. g. τὰν δὲ γενομέναν δαπάναν ἐς τὰν ἀναγραφὰν τεισάντω τοὶ ναποῖαι ἀπὸ τῶν ὑπαρχόντων τοῖς θεοῖς χρημάτων M 1003; εἰς δὲ τὴν ἀναγραφὴν τῆς στήλης δότω ὁ ἄρχων Ἀδείμαντος Δ δραχμὰς ἐκ τῆς κοινῆς προσόδου τῶν τοῦ θεοῦ χρημάτων M 968.

L. 7. לכן *accordingly*. ירע i.e. יֵדַע. לשלם חלפת אית א׳ For the two accusatives after שלם cf. 1 S. 24 20. Pr. 13 21. חלפת *equivalent, return*, χάριτας ἀξίας, cf. Num. 18 21. 31 חֵלֶף עֲבֹדָתָם; in Aram. the verb has the meaning *substitute* (lit. *change*), e.g. *Julian Ap.* ed. Hoffm. 105 25 ܚܠܦܘܗܝ ܐܘܢ, and the frequent חֵלֶף *instead of*.

L. 8. משרת Here a noun, *service*, cf. πᾶσαν λειτουργίαν καὶ ὑπηρεσίαν ἐκτετελεκότα CIG 2786. את מן i.e. אֵת פְּנֵי lit. *with the presence, before*; את is the prep. *with*, cf. Gen. 19 27. 1 S. 2 18 משרת את פני יהוה &c. The last two lines correspond closely with the Gk. inscrr., e. g. ὅπως ἂν εἰδῶσι πάντες, ὅτι ἐπίστανται Πειραιεῖς χάριτας ἀξίας ἀποδιδόναι τοῖς φιλοτιμουμένοις εἰς αὐτούς M 145 and often.

34. Piraeus. CIS i 118. Date prob. ii–i cent. B.C. Piraeus.

מזבח ז אש ינח בנחדש בן בעליתן השפט · בן עבדאשמן
החתם · לאסכן אדר · יברך

This altar (is that) which Ben-ḥodesh, son of Ba'al-yathon the judge, son of 'Abd-eshmun the sealer, erected to Askun-adar. May he bless!

מזבח Cf. **8** 4. **12** 2. **28** 4. ינח Ifil pf. of נוח = Hebr. הֵנִיחַ 2 K. **17** 29; in Gk. ἀναθεῖναι. בנחדש See **17** 3 *n*. השפט i. e. the head of the Phoenician colony at the Piraeus, corresponding to our 'consul,' not *suffete* in the Carthaginian sense, **42** 1 *n*. החתם Either a maker of seals, or an official who seals. אסכן No doubt the same as סכן, the deity who appears in the pr. nn. Σαγχουνιάθων = סכניתן Hadr. 8 (Euting *Carth.*, Anhang Taf. 6), עברסכן CIS i 112 a. גרסכן **46**. ורסכן **52** 4 f. The name was pronounced *Sakun*, as the form אסכן implies, or *Sakkun* (Secchun CIL viii 5099), and means 'one who cares for' (cf. Assyr. *sakânu*, Tell-el-Am. 179 38. 180 13 &c.), the 'friend' or 'helper' of men; cf. the sense of סכן in Hebr., *profit, benefit*, e. g. Job **15** 3. **22** 2. **34** 9 &c. and 1 K. **1** 2. 4. Sakun was the Phoen. counterpart to the Gk. Hermes (Schröder 197 *n*.); the two Gk. inscrr. found near to this, one containing a dedication to Hermes, the other to Διὶ σωτῆρι, apparently refer to this altar. אדר is prob. an epithet, *glorious* **5** 9 *n*.; cf. the pr. nn. אדרבעל CIS i 157 1 &c., אדרמלך on a coin of Byblus, Babelon *Pers. Ach.* 1354, רשאדר the name of a town, Rusadir, also on coins (Lidzb. 370). There is not sufficient evidence that אדר was the name of a deity.

35. Piraeus. CIS i 119. Prob. iii cent. B.C. Piraeus.

'Ασεπτ 'Εσυμσελήμου Σιδωνία

אנך אספת בת אשמנשלם צדנת אש יטנא לי
יתנבל בן אשמנצלח רב כהנם אלם נרגל

I am Asepta, daughter of Eshmun-shillem, a Sidonian. (This is that) which Yathan-bel, son of Eshmun-ṣilleḥ, chief-priest of the god Nergal, set up to me.

For this form of inscr., in which the deceased speaks in the first person and the monument is set up by some one else, cf. **32**.

L. 1. אספת Perhaps the fem. of אָסָף, with a segholate termination אָסֶפֶת, pronounced אָסְפַּת, as the transcription shows. אשמנשלם Cf. בעלשלם **28** 3 *n*. In the Gk. Ἐσυμσελήμου the reduplication of the intensive stem (שלם) is not marked, cf. Δομσάλως and Δομανῶ **32**; but Βαλσιλλήχ=בעלשלך **38** 6, Balsillec CIL viii 1249. צדנת i.e. צִדֹנִית. For the omission of the art. cf. אשקלני, צדני **32**.

L. 2. יתנבל=יתנבעל (?); the ע is frequently dropped in NPun. pr. nn., e.g. מתנבל NPun. 22 3. יעזרבל ib. 13 1 f. ארנבל ib. 102 2. Perhaps, however, בל is the Babyl. *bel*, not the Phoen. *ba'al*; cf. עברבל CIS i 287, and נרגל below. אשמנצלח See **7** 2 *n*. רב כהנם ἀρχιερεύς, cf. **45** 8 (Carthage), a title almost equivalent to a pr. n., and therefore apparently רבכהנם is not in the constr. st. before the following gen.; see König *Syntax* § 285 h. The usage is, however, hardly paralleled elsewhere; it may be due partly to carelessness, and partly to the unconscious recollection of the title ἀρχιερεύς in current Gk. speech. Contrast the constructions כהן שבעלשמם CIS i 379, and כהן לאל עליון Gen. 14 18. אלם נרגל Cf. אלם בעלצרן **33** 6 *n*. It is remarkable to find the Assyr. god Nergal (see 2 K. 17 30 and Zimmern *KAT*[3] 414), the god of battle and pestilence and the dead, worshipped by Phoenicians at the Piraeus. The Phoen. colony there was evidently eclectic in its tastes; in **34** the worship of אסכן is referred to; and in the pr. nn. we find devotees of the Arabian (?) D'om (**32**), the Babylonian Shamash and Bel, and the Carthaginian Tanith (CIS i 116 לעבדתנת בן עבדשמש).

PHOENICIAN: PUNIC

MALTA

36. Malta. CIS i 122. Date ii cent. B.C. Louvre.

1 לארנן למלקרת בעל צר אש נדר

2 עבדך עבדאסר ואחי אסרשמר

3 שן בן אסרשמר בן עבדאסר כ שמע

4 קלם יברכם

Διονύσιος καὶ Σαραπίων οἱ
Σαραπίωνος Τύριοι
Ἡρακλεῖ ἀρχηγέτει

To our lord Melqarth, the Ba'al of Tyre, which thy servant 'Abd-osir and his brother Osir-shamar, the two sons of Osir-shamar, son of 'Abd-osir, vowed, because he heard their voice. May he bless them!

This inscr. is repeated in the same words on two pedestals, one at Valetta, the other in the Louvre, each supporting a small pillar. The two pillars dedicated to Melqarth (Herakles) recall the *στῆλαι δύο* which Herodotus saw in the temple of Herakles at Tyre (ii 44); cf. also Philo Byb., who says that at Tyre *ἀνιερῶσαι δὲ δύο στήλας πυρὶ καὶ πνεύματι, καὶ προσκυνῆσαι*, *Fr. Hist. Gr.* iii 566. The letters of this inscr. resemble the Tyrian and Sidonian type.

L. 1. למלקרת בעל צר See **23** 3 *n.*; similarly in Sabaean inscrr., אלמקה בעל אום 'Ilmaqqah, lord of Awwam' CIS iv 126 16, cf. 155 5. 240 5. תאלב ריםם בעל שצרם 160 3 &c. עתתר בעל מדבא 276 4. רמן בעל עלמן 140 2 f.; and see **8** 2 *n.* With the Gk. equivalent, *Ἡρακλεῖ ἀρχηγέτει*, cf. an inscr. from Delos, dated at the beginning of the second cent. B.C., where the *σύνοδος τῶν Τυρίων ἐμπόρων καὶ ναυκλήρων* use a similar designation of Herakles, *ἀρχηγοῦ τῆς πατρίδος ὑπάρχοντος* (CIG 2271 = M 998).

L. 2. עברך עבדאסר The same words in CIS i 9; for עבדאסר see 14 2 *n*. The Gk. equivalent is Διονύσιος, implying that Osiris was regarded as the counterpart of Διόνυσος. The Gk. name of אסרשמר was Σαραπίων; in this case Osiris is confused with Serapis (= Osiris-Apis), in Aram. written אוסרי חפי 72 (from Memphis). It is said that about 180 B.C., in the time of Ptolemy Philometor, the name of Serapis was first accepted for Osiris (CIG 2753 *n*.).

L. 3. שן בן i. e. שְׁנֵי בְּנֵי; see 23 6 *n*.

37. Malta. CIS i 123 a. Date uncertain. Malta. 9th–7th cent.

1 נצב מלכ
2 בעל אש ש
3 ם נחם לב
4 על חמן א
5 דן כ שמע
6 קל דברי

Pillar of Milk-Ba'al, which Naḥum placed to Ba'al-ḥammān (the) lord, because he heard the voice of his words.

The letters are of an archaic type; the W and W ll. 1. 3. 5 (but W l. 4) resemble the forms in 1. 11. 41. Lidzbarski (p. 177) considers that this points to a date before the sixth cent.; but in an isolated colony the writing may have kept a rude and undeveloped character, and therefore furnishes no sure criterion of early date.

L. 1. נצב *cippus* or *pillar*, cf. Gen. 19 26 נְצִיב מלח. The word occurs in the companion inscr. CIS i 123 b נצב מלכאסר, in 39 נצבם, 147 נצב מלכבעל לאדן לבעל חמן . . . כ שמע קל [דב]ר[י] (Sardinia), 194 and 380 נ׳ מלכבעל (Carthage), לאדן לבעל חמן נ׳ מלכבעל (Hadrumetum 9, Euting *Carth.* Anhang T. 6); in Old Aram. 61 1. 14. 62 1. 20 (with שם); and in Sabaean, e. g. Mordtmann u. Müller *Sab. Denkm.* 95. The word is identical with the Arab. نُصُبٌ pl. أَنْصَابٌ, an idol-stone to which worship was paid, e. g. *Qur.* v 92; see Wellhausen

Reste Arab. Heident. 101 f. The נצב in Phoen. was something of this kind, here a pillar of Milk-Ba'al, whose name occurs after נצב in each of the examples just given (except 89)[1]; it is thus distinguished from מצבת, which as a rule is a funeral monument. מלכבעל A deity formed out of the attributes of Milk and Ba'al in combination, cf. מלכאסר CIS i 123 b, מלכעשתרת 10 3 *n.*; the Palm. מלכבל 112 4 Μαλάχβηλος, Malagbelus, is a different name. It is curious that the pillar of one deity should be dedicated to another; but Milk-ba'al and Ba'al-ḥammān were prob. only different aspects of the same god.

L. 2. שם Cf. Gen. 28 22. 2 K. 21 7. Jer. 7 30.

L. 4. בעל חמן In the formula לרבת לתנת פן בעל ולאדן לבעל חמן this title of Ba'al occurs more than 2000 times on the votive tablets from Carthage; see also the inscr. quoted above on l. 1. It corresponds to Hammoni J(ovi) o(ptimo) m(aximo) on a Lat. inscr. from Mauretania Caesariensis, CIL viii 9018. לחמן is found alone in CIS i 404. 405, prob. for לבעל חמן; cf. עבדחמן NPun. 67 (Schröder p. 271), Ἀβδήμουνος Jos. *c. Ap.* i 17. The signification of the title is uncertain, but חמן is prob. a derivative of חמם *be hot*, whence חַמָּה *heat, sun* Is. 24 23. Ps. 19 7. Analogy is in favour of taking חמן as a noun in the genit.; but it can hardly be the name of a place, for the deity of Ḥammon (אל חמן) is Milk-'ashtart (CIS i 8) or 'Ashtart (10 4), nor a 'sun-pillar,' for the O. T. חַמָּנִים are best explained as images of Ba'al-ḥammān[2]. Hence, as no suitable meaning can be obtained from a genit. noun, it is probable that חמן is an adj., *the glowing Ba'al*, cf. בעל מרפא *the healing B.* (CIS i 41), the article which Hebr. would require being dispensed with in Phoen. (see 8 2 *n.*). The title, thus explained, does not necessarily imply that Ba'al was regarded as a sun-god—a doubtful hypothesis (see Robertson Smith, art. Baal in *Ency. Bibl.*), but it describes him as the god of fertilizing warmth, an attribute which is quite in accordance with his usual character. ארן is in a very unusual position; cf. NPun. 31 לבעל חמן אלם.

L. 6. קל דברי Cf. Dt. 5 25. Dan. 10 9. דברי i.e. דְּבָרָי(ו), following the Hebr. form; or possibly דְּבָרַי, after the Aram. מַלְכוֹהִי=מַלְכוֹי, ܡܠܟܘܗܝ; Wright *Comp. Gr.* 159. Cf. קרני 42 5.

[1] Cf. Steph. Byz. s.v. Νίσιβις . . . Σημαίνει δέ, ὥς φησι Φίλων, Νάσιβις τὰς στήλας, ὡς δὲ Οὐράνιος, νέσιβις, φησί, σημαίνει τῇ Φοινίκων φωνῇ λίθοι συγκείμενοι καὶ συμφορητοί *Fr. Hist. Gr.* iv 526.

[2] In the Palm. inscr. 136 we find a חמנא dedicated to שמש the sun-god. But this instance can hardly decide the original meaning of the ancient חמנים of the O. T. The Ἀμμουνεῖς of the Phoen. temples, mentioned by Philo Byb. as inscribed ἀποκρύφοις γράμμασι (*Fr. Hist. Gr.* iii 564), were probably חמנים.

38. Malta (Gaulus-Gozo). CIS i 132. iii–ii cent. Malta.

1 פעל וחדש עם גול אית שלש...

2 מקדש בת צדמבעל ואית מ[קדש...

3 מקדש בת עשתרת ואית מקד[ש...

4 בעת ר אדר ערכת ארש בן יאל...

5 שפט בן זיבקם בן עבדאשמן בן יא[ל...

6 זבח בעלשלך בן חנא בן עבדאשמ[ן...

7 בלא בן כלם בן יעזר שמר מחצב י...

8 עם גול

The people of Gaulus made and renovated the three(?)...,[2] the sanctuary of the temple of Ṣadam-ba'al, and the sa[nctuary..., [3] the sanctuary of the temple of 'Ashtart, and the sanctu[ary ... [4] in the time of (our) l(ord) of noble worth (?), Arish, son of Ya'el... [5] judge (?), son of Zibaqam, son of 'Abd-eshmun, son of Ya'e[l... [6] sacrificer Ba'al-shillek, son of Ḥanno, son of 'Abd-eshmu[n... [7] BL', son of KLM, son of Ya'azor, keeper of the quarry.... [8] (of) the people of Gaulus.

The inscr., though found at Malta, was prob. carried there from the neighbouring island of Gaulus, now Gozo. The writing is clear and well formed, and Carthaginian in character. The date of the inscr. is uncertain, because we do not know the era, prob. referred to in the missing portion of l. 7, from which the independence of Gaulus was reckoned. The date can hardly be later than 150 B.C., and may be earlier.

L. 1. חדש See **23** 2 *n.* עם גול Plebs Gaulitana, CIL x 7508 f. גול was pronounced with a diphthong; in Gk. Γαῦδος. שלש As the stone is broken off at this point, and it is uncertain how much of the lines is missing, we cannot tell what שלש refers to, or whether the word is complete. There are four, not three, sanctuaries mentioned in ll. 2–3.

L. 2. מקדש The inner sanctuary of the temple (בת, cf. **5** 15 f.); cf. **29** 3. 7. Eze. 48 21. Jer. 51 51. צדמבעל is generally taken as

= צלמבעל *likeness of Ba'al*, cf. מן בעל 48 1 &c., שם בעל 5 18, a goddess known to the Greeks as Σαλαμβώ or Σαλάμβας, in Lat. Salambo, and identified with Aphrodite[1], who had a temple in Gaulus, the remains of which still exist. For צדם = צלם cf. Γαῦδος = Gaulus, e.g. Strabo p. 230 ed. Müll. There is more probability, however, in the view of Hoffmann (*ZA* xi 244 f.) that צלם was a male deity whose name appears in the inscrr. from Têma 69 3 ff. 70 3, perhaps the deity of the planet Saturn, *kakkubu Ṣalmu* 'the dark' (ظلم), Delitzsch *Assyr. HWB.* 569. Hoffmann considers that צלם was associated with the sun-god among Phoenicians, and only by Greeks identified with 'Ashtart-Aphrodite. Possibly ܚܩܠ ܨܠܡ, a village near Edessa, contains the name of the deity, P. Smith *Thes.* col. 3410.

L. 4. בעת ר Cf. 42 1. ר is an abbreviation of רב or רבן; cf. חרב in CIS i 229–235 and רב ארץ 29 2. 6. The reference here, as in the case of the other officials mentioned in ll. 5? 6. 7, is not to a definite year named after the chief magistrate (... בשת שפטם 40 2 *n.*), but to the period (עת) when these persons were engaged in the active duties of their office; so Lidzb. 113 *n.* אדר ערכת Meaning uncertain. In 5 9. 10 6 אדר = *great, powerful*; ערכת has been explained by the Hebr. עֵרֶךְ a *valuation* paid for a commuted vow or due, Lev. 27 2 ff.; hence אדר ערכת is taken by the Corp. to denote *chief of the taxes*, or *assessments*, a revenue officer, or 'superintendent of public works,' cf. Aram. and Rabb. עַרְכָאָה *magistracy* (Wright *ZDMG* xxviii 143). But אדר is not a suitable word to be used as a noun for *chief*; and ערכת may be taken as a gen. of quality, in a figurative sense, *of noble worth*; for the construction cf. חכם לבב ואמיץ כח Job 9 4. רב חסד ואמת Ex. 34 6 &c. It must be admitted, however, that an expression of this kind is not customary in Phoen. inscrr. Note that ערכת is fem., while in Hebr. ערך is mas., and not used in the plural. ארש See 21 1 *n.* יאל is a divine name, as appears from יאלפעל Altib. 2 2[2]. Etymologically it may be identified with the Arab. وَائِل lit. *asylum* from وَأَلَ, *take refuge*, the god of the Arab tribe Bakr-Wâil; Wellhausen *Reste Arab. Heidentums* 64. This name occurs in Nabat. and Sin. as a pr. n. in the form ואלו and ואלת, e.g. CIS ii 214 2. 80 1. 90 2. 105, and often; in Gk. inscrr. from Ḥauran Οὐάελος &c. Wadd. 2496[3];

[1] Σαλαμβὼ ἡ Ἀφροδίτη παρὰ Βαβυλωνίοις, Hesych. *Lex.* s. v.; Σαλάμβας ἡ δαίμων [ἡ]... περιέρχεται θρηνοῦσα τὸν Ἄδωνιν, *Etym. magn.*; Salambonem omni planctu et jactatione syriaci cultus exhibuit (Heliogabalus), Lamprid. *vit. Heliog.* vii in *Scr. Hist. Aug.*

[2] Berger *JA* ix (1887) 466 ff.

[3] In Polybius Ἰόλαος; the treaty between Hannibal and Philip was ratified

in Himyar. ואל CIS iv 169 *n.*; cf. also the name of a N. Arabian king Ya'lû on Asarhaddon's cylinder, col. iii 19, Schrader *COT* 25. 208. On Edessene coins (163–167 A. D.) ܘܐܠ is the name of a king of Edessa; CIS ii p. 179. Perhaps the O.T. יואל is to be explained in this way, though the above names belong to Arab. rather than to Hebr. See Rob. Smith *Kinship* 194. 301; Gray *Hebr. Pr. Names* 153; Driver *Studia Bibl.* i 5 *n.*

L. 5. שפט Either another official (*the*) *judge*, supposing that l. 4 contained *son of . . . the*, or a pr. n. *Shafat*, common in N. Africa. זיבקם The name occurs in Punic and Neo-Punic, e. g. CIS i 251. 423 &c. and 22 2 *n.*; perhaps it is of Libyan or Numidian, rather than Phoen. origin, and equivalent to Syphax (on coins ספק). The rest of the line prob. ran *and in the time of . . . the.*

L. 6. זבח The chief officiating priest, ἱεροθύτης CIG 5752 = Mich. 554, a Maltese inscr. circa 210 B. C. For the year, or period, dated by the name of this official cf. 55 5 שת בלל חזבח (from Altiburus). בעלשלך Transcribed Βαλσιλλήχ, *balsillec* CIL viii 1249; see 35 1 *n.* The significance of שלך, found also in the name אשמנשלך CIS i 50 1. 197 4, is obscure. It is not probable that שלך = שלח, for ח is a soft guttural in Phoen., and therefore not interchangeable with ך; see 40 1 *n.* Cl.-Gan. explains שלך by the vulgar Arab. سلّك, which in the dialect of Algiers = *save, deliver, Rec.* i 165 f. חנא 39 2 and often; perhaps shortened from חנבעל or בעלחנא.

L. 7. בלא . . כלם d. λ. These names belong either to the genealogy of (ה)זבח, or to another official whose name stood in the missing part of l. 6. יעזר Short for יעזרבעל. שמר Qal ptcp., *manager, overseer*, ἐπιμελητής; the third, or, if שפט = *judge* l. 5, the fourth official named. מחצב The form of the noun points to the meaning *quarry*; cf. חצבם 2 4. 6. 1 K. 5 29. It is conjectured that the end of the line furnished the date from which the עם גול (cf. 9 5 f. 27 2 &c.) reckoned their independence. The date is unknown; but in the second Punic war Malta, and presumably Gaulus too, severed its connexion with Carthage, Livy xxi 51.

ἐναντίον δαίμονος Καρχηδονίων καὶ Ἡρακλέους καὶ Ἰολάου vii 9. 2; cf. also Diod. Sic. iv 29. Perhaps the pr. nn. *Ialnoati* CIL viii 280, *Iolitana* ib. 9341, *Iolitan(us)* ib. 9767 contain the name of the god; Nöld. *ZDMG* xlii 471.

SARDINIA

89. Caralis (Cagliari). CIS i 139. iii–ii cent. B.C. Cagliari.

1 לארן לבעשמם באינצם נצבם וחנוטם שנם || אש נדר בע
2 לחנא שבדמלקרת בן חנא בן אשמנעמס בן מהרבעל
3 בן אתש

To the lord Ba'a(l)-shamem in the Isle of Hawks: (these are the) pillars and two 2 ? which Ba'al-ḥanno, (son) of Bod-melqarth, son of Ḥanno, son of Eshmun-'amas, son of Mahar-ba'al, son of Athash, vowed.

L. 1. בעשמם i.e. בעלשמם, see **9** 1 *n.* For the quiescence of ל cf. in Nab. בעשמין CIS ii 163, לבעשמן ib. 176, in Palm. בונא **112** 2 *n.*, and in Pun. בעחנא CIS i 869 2, 'Αννίβα-ς=חנבעל, Bomilcar=בעלמלקרת, Μάκαρ=מלקרת &c.; see Schröder 100. The construction לבעשמם באינצם as in **24** 2 *n.* אינצם='Ιεράκων νῆσος, mentioned by Ptolemaeus in his description of the islands round Sardinia, *Geogr.* iii 3, ed. Müll. p. 387; in the LXX *ἱέραξ* is the usual rendering of נץ, e.g. Lev. 11 16 b. Dt. 14 14 a. Job 39 26. The Phoen. name is preserved by Pliny, Habet (Sardinia) et a Gorditano promontorio duas insulas, quae vocantur Herculis: a Sulcensi, Enosin: a Caralitano, Ficariam, *Hist. Nat.* iii 13. The island is now called San Pietro. נצבם See **87** 1 *n.* וחנוטם Meaning obscure; but evidently objects connected with the cult of the deity. In Hebr. חנט means *to embalm*, but this gives no suitable sense here. Renan (in Corp.) explains the word by the Gk. *χωνευτά*, used in the LXX for *molten images*, מַסֵּכוֹת, e.g. 1 K. 14 9 A *θεοὺς ἑτέρους χωνευτά*.

L. 2. בעלחנא **47**, cf. מלקרתחנא, רעשתנא **32** 2 *n.* שבדמלקרת The rel. ש is here used, like של in late Hebr. and ד in Aram., to express the genitival relation, in this case instead of בן; cf. **41** 2 f. רש שנגר. For ש elsewhere in Phoen. see **40** 1 ? **41** 3. **52**. CIS i 133 שעזרבעל בן מסלח (see **64** 1 *n.*). 315 ארש בן שמנגם. 316 ארש שעבדמלקרת. 317 (similarly). 379 כתן שבעלשמם. It is worth noticing that the form אש occurs along with ש in many of these inscrr. referred to; see **45** 4 *n.* אשמנעמס *Eshmun carries*, cf. בעלעמס CIS i 169, and עמסיה 2 Ch. 17 16; see **5** 6 *n.* מהרבעל A common

Pun. name, in Gk. Μέρβαλος a Tyrian king, Jos. *c. Ap.* i 21. מהר is generally explained as *gift*, Hebr. מֹהַר the purchase *price* of a wife, Gen. 34 12 &c.; this explanation, however, is not convincing.

40. Pauli Gerrei (Santuiaci). CIS i 143. ii cent. B.C.
Turin Mus.

Cleon salari(us) soc(iorum) s(ervus) Aescolapio Merre donum dedit lubens merito merente.

Ἀσκληπίῳ Μηρρῆ ἀνάθεμα βωμὸν ἔστησε Κλέων ὁ ἐπὶ τῶν ἀλῶν κατὰ πρόσταγμα.

1 לארן לאשמן מארח מזבח נחשת משקל לטרם מאת א אש נדר אכלין שחסגם אש בממלחת שמ[ע]
2 [ק]לא רפיא בשת שפטם חמלכת ועבדאשמן בן חמלך

To the lord Eshmun Merre:—the altar of bronze, in weight a hundred 100 pounds, which Cleon of ḤSGM, who is over the salt-mines (?), vowed; he heard his voice (and) healed him. In the year of the suffetes Ḥimilkath and ʿAbd-eshmun, son of Ḥimilk.

L. 1. לאשמן See 5 17 *n*. There is a mineral spring near to the place where the inscr. was found. מארח A title of Eshmun, explained by Nöldeke as the Piel ptcp. מְאָרֵחַ (note the doubled 2nd radical in the transcriptions *merre*, *μηρρη*) of ארח *wander*, *travel*, with the meaning *leader*, *guide*, cf. Eth. warĕḥa *lead*; *ZDMG* xlii 472. Lidzbarski, p. 305, suggests the Ifil ptcp. of רָוַח, cf. Hebr. 1 S. 16 23 ורוח לשאול. Job 32 20; in Aram. (Ethpa.) *alleviatus est*, e.g. 2 Macc. 13 11 = *ἀναψύχεσθαι*, *convaluit a morbo*; so מארח *he who alleviates*, *healer*, a suitable epithet for Eshmun-Aesculapius. In this case, however, the א is difficult to account for, unless it be merely euphonic. Hoffmann, *ZA* xi 238, takes מארח *Merre* as a diminutive of מלקרת, which sometimes takes the form of מר, מרי, Μαρκω, Μαρυας &c.; see 19 3 *n*. The Corp. regards מארח as = מארך scil. חיים, but in Phoen. ח is not a strong guttural, as appears from the transcriptions מארח

merre, חמלכת *himilco, imilco*, חחמלך *otmilc*, חנבעל *hannibal* &c.; see **38** 6. On the whole the first explanation seems to be the most plausible. מזבח See **28** 4 *n.* משקל See **29** 14 *n.* למרם Plur. of the Gk. weight λίτρα. The form of the symbol for 100 may be contrasted with that in **9** 4 f. **29** 14. **42** 6. אכלן = Cleon, with א prosthetic, as often in foreign names; Wright *Comp. Gr.* 45 f. שחסנם The ש is perhaps the rel. particle introducing the genit., either *son of* (see **39** 2 *n.*), or possibly *servant of* (so Corp.). The significance of חסנם is unknown; it may be a (Sardinian) pr. n., or the title of an office; possibly a transliteration of *servus sociorum*, Hoffmann l. c. Cf. **59** B 4. אש במסלחת ὁ ἐπὶ τῶν ἁλῶν, *who is over the salt mines*, though strictly this requires על instead of ב; the Corp. therefore renders *who is in the salt business*. מסלחת must be a dialectical form of ממלחת; for 'ס cf. מחצב **38** 7.

L. 2. קלא i. e. קֹלוֹ; for the form of suff. cf. **48** 5 and often. רפיא Pf. 3 sing. m. with suff. = רְפָאוֹ; cf. תברכא **48** 5 and often. The √רפא is here treated as ל״ה, the י of the root being retained before the suff., as occasionally in Hebr., e. g. הַכֵּינִי 1 K. 20 35. חַיֵּיהוּ Hab. 3 2, more frequently in the pausal forms חָסָיוּ Dt. 32 37. יֶאֱתָיוּ Job 16 22 (Ges. § 75 *u, mm*). בשת שפטם For the year reckoned by the suffetes cf. **42** 1 *n.* (Marseilles-Carthage). CIS i 170 (Carthage). **45** 5 f. (ib.). **46** 1 (ib.). **55** 5 f. (Altiburus). חמלכת . . . חמלך For 'אח, see **11** *n.*, and l. 1 *n.* above. It has been proposed to read בן as בְּנֵי, making the suffetes brothers, and providing both with a brief genealogy; but this is improbable and unnecessary (see **45** 5). The inscr. dates from after the first Punic war, when Sardinia was severed from Carthage and passed under the rule of Rome. The suffetes, therefore, were not Carthaginian; they belonged prob. to Caralis (**39**), the chief city in the neighbourhood. The form of the Latin letters is said to point to a date about 180 B.C.

41. Nora (Pula). CIS i 144. ? vi cent. Cagliari.

[מצ]
בת רש ש
נגר שהא
בשרדן ש
למה אש ל

נצבא מ
לכתן בן ר
ש בן נגד
לפסי

Pillar of Rosh, (son) of Nagid, who (dwelt) in Sardinia; Milk-(ya)thon, son of Rosh, son of Nagid, (the) Liphsite, completed it (?), (even that) which (was required) for setting it up.

The character is of an archaic type, which perhaps points to a date not later than the sixth cent. (Lidzb. 177); cf. **37** *n.* The ancient form of ת, X, occurs here.

L. 2. רש Perhaps = ראש. In Gen. **46** 21 this pr. n. is corrupt. ש נגד See **39** 2 *n.*

L. 3. נגד Prob. a pr. n.; so in Aram. CIS ii 112 (נגד?).

L. 4. שהא בשרדן It is uncommon to find the dwelling-place mentioned; cf. **81** a ישב דכי באן מצרים. Euting *Sin. Inschr.* 551 פ׳ די עמר באילת.

L. 5. שלמה Piel pf. 3 sing. mas. The ה׳ is possibly the suff. 3 sing. fem., anticipating the object in the relat. clause; to refer it to מצבת makes the construction more difficult. The subject of the vb. is מלכתן l. 6 f. שלם *complete*, perhaps with the thought of *fulfilling* a vow.

L. 6. לנצבא appears to be the inf. with suff. 3 sing. fem. of נצב; cf. Old Aram. **61** 10 לנצב, Nab. **99** 2 נצב pf., also in Palm. מלכתן For מלכיתן **12** 2 &c.

L. 9. לפסי A gentilic form of the name of a city (unknown).

GAUL

42. Marseilles. CIS i 165. Circ. iv cent. B.C. **Marseilles Museum.**

1 בת בעל[. . .] ב[עת המש]אתת אש טנ[א האשם ש על המשא]תת
עת [ר חלצ]בעל השפט בן בדתנת בן בד[אשמן וחלצבעל]

2 השפט בן בדאשמן בן חלצבעל וח[ברנם]

3 באלף כלל אם צועת אם שלם כלל לכהנם כסף עשרת ⌐ באחד
ובכלל יכן לם עלת פן המשאת ז ש[אר משקל שלשת מאת III ש]

4 ובצועת קצרת ויצלת וכן הערת והשלבם והפעמם ואחרי השאר
לבעל הזבח

5 בעגל אש קרני למבמחסר באטומטא אם באיל כלל אם צו[עת] אם
שלם כלל לכהנם כסף חמשת II[III באחד ובכלל יכן לם על]

6 ת פן המשאת ז שאר משקל מאת וחמשם אʒʒ⌐ ובצועת קצרת
ויצלת וכן הערת והשלבם והפע[מם ואחרי השאר לבעל הזבח]

7 ביבל אם בעז כלל אם צועת אם שלם כלל לכהנם כסף שקל I זר II
באחד ובצועת יכ[ן לם עלת פן המשאת ז קצרת]

8 ויצלת וכן הערת והשלבם והפעמם ואחרי השאר לבעל הזבח

9 באמר אם בגרא אם בצרב איל כלל אם צועת אם שלם כ[ל]ל
לכהנם כסף רבע שלשת זר . .[באחד ובצועת יכן לם על

10 ת] פן המשאת ז קצרת ויצלת וכן הערת והשלבם והפעמם ואחרי
השאר לבעל [הזבח

11 בצ]פר אגנן אם ציץ שלם כל[ל] אם שצף אם חזת לכהנם כסף רבע
שלשת זר II באחד וכן הש[אר לבעל הזבח]

12 [ע]ל צפר אם קדמת קדשת אם זבח צד אם זבח שמן לכהנם כסף
א[גרת]⌐ לבאחד . . . . .

13 [ב]כל צועת אש יעמס פנת אלם יכן לכהנם קצרת ויצלת
ו[ב]צועת . . . . .

14 [ע]ל בלל ועל חלב ועל כל זבח אש אדם לזבח
במנח[ת] י . . . .

15 בכל זבח אש יזבח דל מקנא אם דל צפר בל יכן לכהנ[ם מנם]

16 כל מזרח וכל שפח וכל מרזח אלם וכל אדמם אש יזבח . .

17 האדמם המת משאת על זבח אחד כמדת שת בכתב[ת . . .

18 [כ]ל משאת אש איבל שת בפס ז ונתן לפי הכתבת אש [כתב. . . .
האשם אש על המשאתת עת ר חלצבעל בן בדתנ]

19 ת וחלצבעל בן בדאשמן וחברנם

20 כל כהן אש יקח משאת בדץ לאש שת בפס ז ונענ[ש . . . .

21 פל בעל זבח אש איבל יתן את כ . . [ע]ל המשאת א[ש . . . .

Temple of Ba'al-[ ]. Ta[riff of pay]ments e[rected by the overseers of pay]ments in the time of [the lord Ḥilleṣ-]ba'al the suffete, son of Bod-tanith, son of Bod-[eshmun, and of Ḥilleṣ-ba'al] [2] the suffete, son of Bod-eshmun, son of Ḥilleṣ-ba'al, and their col[leagues].

[3] For an ox, whole-offering or prayer-offering (?) or whole thank-offering, the priests shall have ten 10 silver (shekels) for each; and for a whole-offering they shall have, besides this payment, f[lesh weighing three hundred 300 (shekels)]; [4] and for a prayer-offering (?), the ? and the ?; but the skin and the ? and the feet and the rest of the flesh shall belong to the person offering the sacrifice.

[5] For a calf whose horns are wanting (?) ?, or for a hart, whole-offering or pray[er]-offering (?) or whole thank-offering, the priests shall have five [5] silver (shekels) [for each; and for a whole-offering they shall have, besid]es this payment, flesh weighing a hundred and fifty 150 (shekels); and for a prayer-offering (?) the ? and the ?; but the skin and ? and the fe[et and the rest of the flesh shall belong to the person offering the sacrifice].

[7] For a ram or for a goat, a whole-offering or a prayer-offering (?) or a whole thank-offering, the priests shall have

1 silver shekel 2 *zars* for each; and for a prayer-offering (?) they shall h[ave, besides this payment, the ?] [8] and the ?; but the skin and the ? and the feet and the rest of the flesh shall belong to the person offering the sacrifice.

[9] For a lamb or for a kid or for the young of a (?) hart, a whole-offering or a prayer-offering (?) or a whole thank-offering, the priests (shall have) three quarters of a silver (shekel) . . *zars* [for each, and for a prayer-offering (?) they shall have, besides] [10] this payment, the ? and the ?; but the skin and the ? and the feet and the rest of the flesh shall belong to the person offering [the sacrifice].

[11] For a bird, domestic (?) or wild (?), a whole thank-offering or a ? or a ?, the priests (shall have) three quarters of a silver (shekel) 2 *zars* for each; but the fle[sh shall belong to the person offering the sacrifice].

[12] For a bird (?) or sacred first-fruits or sacrifice of game (?) or sacrifice of oil, the priests (shall have) 10 silver *a[gōrāhs* (?)] for each . . . .

[13] In every prayer-offering (?), which is carried before the gods, the priests shall have the ? and the ?; and for a prayer-offering (?) . . . .

[14] For a cake, for milk and for fat and for every sacrifice which a man is disposed to sacrifice for a meal-offering, . . . shall . . .

[15] For every sacrifice which a man may sacrifice who is poor in cattle or in birds, the priests shall have nothing [of them].

[16] Every *mizraḥ* and every ? and every religious guild, and all men who shall sacrifice . . . . , [17] such men (shall give) a payment for each sacrifice, according as is set down in the document . . . .

[18] Every payment which is not set down on this table shall be given according to the document which [. . . the overseers of payments drew up in the time of the lord Ḥilleṣ-ba'al, son of Bod-tan] [19] ith, and of Ḥilleṣ-ba'al, son of Bod-eshmun, and their colleagues.

[20] Every priest who shall receive a payment other (?) than that which is set down on this tablet, shall be fin[ed . . .].

[21] Every person offering a sacrifice, who shall not give . . . for the payment which . . . .[1].

The stone, though found at Marseilles, must have come originally from the quarries near Carthage, as its geological formation shows. In style and contents the inscr. closely resembles the group **43**. **44**. CIS i 170, which belongs to Carthage; so it is probable, but not certain, that the stone was already inscribed before it travelled to Marseilles.

L. 1. בת בעל The Corp. conjectures צפן after בעל, cf. עברצפן CIS i 265. ברצפן 108. [בעת המש]אתת Cf. **43** 1. CIS i 171 7. The missing parts of the inscr. may be restored from **43**, and from other lines of the inscr. itself. The context shows that בעת=*tariff*, but the etymology is doubtful. The word may be explained by the Arab. باع *make a covenant, stipulate*, مُبَايَعَةٌ *contract for buying* or *selling*, بَيْعٌ *buying* or *selling*, and the meaning be *agreement*; or the meaning *demand* may be obtained from the Arab. بغى, Aram. בעא *seek*. משאתת =Hebr. מַשְׂאֵת *dues, taxes*, 2 Ch. 24 6. 9. Eze. 20 40. מנא **43** 1, usually of *setting up* a statue on a pedestal (**13** 2 *n*.), or *fixing* a pillar in the ground (**16** 2 &c.). תא׳ ש על חמ׳ Cf. **46** 1. **33** 2. **55** 5. עת ר Cf. CIS i 170 1 and **38** 4. חלצבעל i.e. *B. delivers* (piel); cf. אשמנחלץ CIS i 168 2. בעלחלץ 777 5 &c. חשפט Even if the inscr. did not come originally from Carthage, it gives us some information about the Carthaginian constitution, for the colony at Marseilles would be organized on the model of the mother-state. (1) At the head of the state in Carthage were two *suffetes* (ll. 1–2. 18–19) or chief magistrates; cf. **45** 5. 6. **46** 1 (?). CIS i 170 1. 179 6 f. 196 4 f. By Gk. and Lat. writers they are called *βασιλεῖς* and *reges*, and they are generally given as two, being compared with the Roman consuls[2]. Similarly in Lat. inscrr. from N. African cities two are named, CIL viii 797. 5306; in the NPun. inscrr. from Altiburus and Maktar there are three, **55** 5 f. **59** B 4 ff. (2) The suffetes give their names to the period (עת CIS i 170, cf. **38** 4), or more usually to the year (שת **46** 1,

[1] The above translation is based upon that given by Dr. Driver in *Authority and Archaeology* 77 f.

[2] Livy xxx 7 5 Senatum itaque sufetes, quod velut consulare imperium apud eos erat, vocaverunt. Nepos *Hann.* vii 4 Ut enim Romae consules, sic Carthagine quotannis annui bini reges creabantur. In historical narratives, it is true, one 'king' is generally mentioned; but perhaps one was often away on distant duties, or one of the two may have been in some sense inferior to the other. At any rate, the comparison with the consuls is decisive.

cf. **40** 2), during which they held office. As the expression בשת שפטם suggests, the appointment was an annual one (see **45** 5 *n.*)[1]; the series of votive tablets, CIS i 199–228, were dedicated by suffetes prob. during their year of office. These tablets show that although the office was not hereditary, yet it tended to become associated with a limited number of families, of long-descended and honourable race[2]. (3) The name שפט implies that the office was magisterial, not hierarchical; thus in **45** 8 the 'chief priest' is mentioned beside the suffetes; cf. **55** 6 f. (4) Connected with the two chief magistrates were the חברם *colleagues*, who formed their council (ll. 2. 19, cf. **55** 4 and חבר היהודים **149** C). Whether these *colleagues* correspond to the γερουσία of 100 (or 104), the 'centum judices,' or to the executive committee of 30 chosen from the 100, we cannot tell. It may be assumed that the two suffetes presided over this senate (but see **45** 6 *n.*); they certainly summoned it and conducted its business[3]. (5) The office and title of *suffete* were characteristic of Carthage and of the Carth. colonies. In the latter, of course, the suffetes would not have the same importance, and prob. not exactly the same functions, as in the mother-state; they would be little more than local magistrates. They are met with in Sardinia **40**, Sicily CIS i 135, Malta ib. 124, Altiburus **55**, and in a number of N. African cities, CIL viii 7. 765. 797. 5306. 10525. The title *Judices*, given to governors or petty kings in Spain and Sardinia (Cagliari) in the Middle Ages, may be a survival from Punic times; see Ducange s. v. At the Piraeus there was a שפט, but prob. not in the Carth. sense, **34** *n.*, and cf. **8** 3 *n.* **17** 2. The chief of a Phoen. city in Phoenicia itself, or in Cyprus, was called not שפט but מלך, e. g. **3** 1. **4** 1. **5** 1. **12** 2 &c.

[1] Nepos l. c.; Zonaras, *Annal.* viii 8 τὸν γὰρ βασιλέα ἑαυτοῖς κλῆσιν ἐτησίου ἀρχῆς ἀλλ' οὐκ ἐπὶ χρονίῳ δυναστείᾳ προὐβάλλοντο. Aristotle, *Pol.* ii 11, in his parallel with the Spartan kings, who ruled for life, does not notice this point of difference; perhaps he did not believe in it. Cicero, *Rep.* ii 23, seems to imply that the Carth. *reges* were elected for life ('perpetua potestas').

[2] From any family of full civic rights, not, as in Sparta, from one family and by hereditary dignity, Aristotle l. c.; but the text is uncertain.

[3] E. g. Polybius iii 33 3. Beside the γερουσία, Polyb. mentions the σύγκλητος, x 18 1; xxxvi 2 6. The latter was probably a general assembly of the people (vi 51 6), who took a real share in the government, Arist. l. c. The γερουσία of Arist. is perhaps to be identified with the σύγκλητος of Polyb.; see Henderson *Journ. Phil.* xxiv (1896) 119 ff. Under special circumstances a military command seems to have been bestowed upon a suffete by decree of the senate, but this was exceptional; the βασιλεία and the στρατηγία are distinguished by Arist. The word שפט *judex* is in itself ambiguous; for the 104 were also called *judices*.

Ll. 3–14. A Table of Sacrifices and Dues. It appears that the sacrificial institutions of the Phoenicians had a good deal in common with those of the Hebrews, and gave expression to the same general religious ideas. Thus the chief types of sacrifice in both systems are analogous, the whole-offering, the thank-offering, the meal-offering. The Hebr. חטאת and אשם *sin-* and *guilt-offering*, however, are absent, unless something of the kind was intended by the obscure צועת, which is doubtful. The materials of sacrifice are generally alike, but in some respects the details differ: the Hebrews sacrificed domestic animals only, but the Phoenicians offered as well deer (איל), young (?) deer (צרב איל), wild-birds (? צץ), game (צד), and included milk (חלב) and fat (חלב) in the מנחת. It is to be noticed that in this inscr. oxen, sheep and goats, birds, produce are mentioned in the same order as in Lev. 1–2. Certain parts of the sacrifice are assigned to the priests and to the worshipper, as in Lev. 6 19. 7 8. 15–19. 31–34. Dt. 18 3. 4 &c.; while the relief allowed to the poor man (l. 15) may be illustrated by Lev. 5 7. 11. 12 8. 14 21 (אם דל הוא). The resemblance, however, between the two systems is a general one. Many of the sacrificial terms in Phoenician are obscure in meaning, and those which are identical with the Hebr. (e.g. כלל, שלם) may have denoted different things; at any rate they acquired different shades of meaning in the course of their separate history. See Driver *Authority and Archaeology* 78 f.

L. 3. באלף The prep. here is *beth* of reference; cf. the use of فى in Arab. (Wright *Ar. Gr.*[3] ii § 56 c); there is no exact parallel in Hebr. אלף *ox*, as in Assyr. *alpu*; in Hebr. the word is rare, and only used in the plur., e.g. Pr. 14 4. Is. 30 24. Ps. 8 8. Dt. 7 13. 28 4 ff. כלל 43 5 prob. = כָּלִיל *holocaust*, a word which in Hebr. hardly belongs to the ordinary terminology of sacrifice. It is used as a descriptive synonym of עולה, Dt. 33 10. 1 S. 7 9. Ps. 51 21; twice of the priests' מנחה, Lev. 6 15 f.; and figuratively in Dt. 13 17. Among the Phoenicians כלל was apparently the equivalent of the O.T. עולה. It was not wholly burned upon the altar[1], because part of the flesh was assigned to the priests. אם . . . אם See 5 7 *n*. צועת 43 4 f. may be connected with the same root as the Eth. ጸውዐ: (צוע) *cry out*, *invoke*, hence צועת was perhaps a sacrifice accompanied by *prayer*; it is highly precarious to make the Ethiopic root correspond to צָוַח, שִׁוַּע, as Wright does, *Comp. Gr.* 60. The Eth. ሦዐ: (שׂע),

[1] Cf. Ex. 20 24, which orders the שלמים to be slaughtered (וְזָבַחְתָּ) upon the altar, but says nothing about its being wholly burned upon it; Rob. Smith *Rel. of Sem.* 358 *n*.

whence መሥዋዕት፡ *sacrifice*, is again prob. a different root. שלם כלל may be rendered 'a שלם *of* (i. e. *accompanying*) a כלל' or 'a whole שלם.' It is probably incorrect to regard the 'ש' כ as a third kind of sacrifice, for in the second part of each direction only the כלל and the צועת are repeated. This implies that two, and not three, distinct species of sacrifice are contemplated, in which case the 'ש' כ will be a subordinate kind of כלל. Robertson Smith regards it as an ordinary sacrifice accompanying a כלל, *Rel. of Sem.* 219 *n.* It must remain uncertain what exactly the 'ש' כ was. The word שלם is of course the same as the Hebr. for *thank-* or *peace-offering*. כסף עשרת For the order cf. 2 S. 24 24. Neh. 5 15. 1 Ch. 22 13; כסף is in apposition to שקלים understood, cf. Gen. 20 16. 37 28 &c., and nominative to יכן which must be supplied before לכהנם; see Driver *Tenses* § 192 (1), König *Syntax* § 314 h. The money payments to the priests may be illustrated by CIL vi 820 pro sanguine . . et corium . . si holocaustum ✱X. עלת מן lit. *over*, here *over and above, besides*; similarly perhaps Ex. 20 3 עַל פָּנַי. שאר משקל ש' מ' lit. *flesh, a weight of* 300 (*shekels*); see Driver l. c.; משקל is in apposition to שאר, and prob. in the constr. state, as in 1 Ch. 21 25 מִשְׁקַל שש מאות; for שקלים understood after משקל cf. Num. 7 13 ff. The restoration is based on l. 6, the amount for an ox would be double of that for a calf. For שאר = Hebr. בשר see 8 4 *n.*

L. 4. קצרת ויצלת 43 8 evidently certain parts of the victim assigned to the worshipper, as the שאר was to the priests. The practice is illustrated by Lev. 7 15–19. 19 6 &c., and by a Gk. inscr. from Miletus (end of the fourth cent. B. C.) *λαμβάνειν δὲ τὰ δέρματα καὶ τὰ ἄλλα γέρεα· ἣν ἐν θύηται, λάψεται γλῶσσαν, ἰσφύν, δασέαν, ὠρήν κ.τ.λ.* Michel 726. The meaning of קצרת ויצלת is unknown. קצרת has been rendered *cuttings, prosecta*, from קצר *cut*; יצלת may be connected with the root وَصَلَ, and the Hebr. אֲצִילוֹת *joints*. The breast and right shoulder were the perquisites of the priests in the Levitical law, Lev. 7 31 f. וכן ll. 6. 8. 10 f. 43 4 bis. 5. Here we have an instance of the waw conversive in Phoen. It is used with the perfect to introduce the predicate, as it is in Hebr. (Driver *Tenses* §§ 122. 123 *a*), i. when the subject follows the verb and intervenes between it and the clause introduced by ל (לבעל הזבח); if the subject does not intervene the simple imperfect occurs, יכן לם ll. 3. 7. יכן לכהנם 13. 15: ii. when the subject precedes the verb, the sentence having commenced with the casus pendens, l. 18 כל משאת אש . . . ונתן. 43 11. l. 20 כל כהן אש . . . תענש. So far as is known at present, the idiom is found only in the small group of related inscrr., 42. 43 and

CIS i 170 (rest.). The sister idiom, the imperfect with waw conversive, has not been discovered in Phoenician; ויסמננם 5 19 cannot safely be taken as an instance. The normal tense for continuing a narrative of finished acts is the perf. with weak waw, e.g. יתן ויטנא 13 2 &c. מעל חורש 38 1. 46 1; and this construction occurs where in Hebr. the impf. with strong waw would be natural, e.g. 3 8. 5 16. 17 וישבני . . בנן. 23 5 ופקר. 29 13. 14. 33 3. The material is very limited both in extent and character, but, so far as it goes, it suggests the conclusion that the waw conversive was not used in ordinary Phoen. speech and writing. Yet it was not entirely unknown, and the few instances of its occurrence with the perf., preserved in the Carthaginian dialect, are perhaps survivals of what was once more common. The later biblical and post-biblical Hebr. shows that there was a tendency to drop the use of the waw conv., and that at last it was abandoned altogether. The same thing may have happened in Phoen., though it is not likely that at any period the idiom reached such a full development in Phoen. as in Hebrew. הערת 43 2 f., i.e. הָעֹרֹת. In Hebr. עור is mas. with a fem. ending in the plur. The עור העלה is given to the priests in Lev. 7 8; in the case of the sin-offering it was burned, Ex. 29 14. Lev. 8 17. Num. 19 5. שלבם In 48 4 and CIS i 170 2 אשלבם, ? *fatty parts*, cf. ܫܘܠܒܐ (only in the glossaries) *the fat of the hinder parts of birds*. In 1 K. 7 28 f. שְׁלַבִּים may = *cross-bars, ribs*; the exact meaning is obscure. הפעמם CIS i 170 2; see 3 4 *n*. אחרי prob. = Hebr. אחרית; see 10 9 *n*. בעל הזבח 43 2 f., lit. *owner of the sacrifice*; for בעל as a noun of relation cf. 45 9 בעל חרש, and in Hebr. Gen. 37 19 ב׳ החלמות. 2 K. 1 8. Gen. 14 13 בעלי ברית. 2 S. 1 6 &c.

L. 5. קרני i.e. קַרְנָי(ו); see 37 6 *n*. למבמחסר lit. *yet in want*, cf. Dt. 15 8. Jud. 18 10 &c.; for the accumulated preps. see 16 2 *n*. (of time). This is simpler than to take לם as = לוֹ, an isolated example of this form of the *sing*. suff. (König *Lehrg*. ii 446 *n*. 2). באטוסמא is obviously a foreign word, Gk. or Berber. Its meaning is unknown. The Corp. suggests ἀτομητός for ἀτμητός *not castrated*. איל Perhaps אַיָּל *hart* rather than אַיִל *ram*, because the latter belongs to the class specified further on, l. 7. The sacrifice of wild animals is surprising, but it seems to be implied in this Table (p. 117). The restoration of the number is based on l. 3.

L. 6. שאר משקל See l. 3 *n*. For the form of the symbol for 100 see 40 1 *n*.

L. 7. יבל i.e. יֹבֵל *ram*; in the O.T. only of the ram's-horn trumpet and of the 'year of the ram('s horn),' Ex. 19 13. Josh. 6 5. Lev. 25 13 &c. זר 43 7 a small coin, less than the quarter of a shekel l. 11. The Hebr. זֵר *border moulding* Ex. 25 11 ff., lit. 'that which presses, binds,' Aram. ܙܘܪܐ *necklace*, זירא *crown*, may possibly be connected; the √ זור = lit. *press down*.

L. 9. אמר *lamb*, Aram. ܐܡܪܐ, אִמַּר, Palm. אמריא (plur.) 147 ii a 41, Arab. إِمَّر from the Aram., Fränkel *Ar. Fremdw.* 107 f. נדא = Hebr. גדי. צרב איל 43 5. צרב = Aram. ܥܪܒܐ *sheep*, Nöldeke *ZDMG* xl (1886) 737; cf. pr. n. צרבם CIS i 380 4. The context refers to the young of sheep and goats, so צרב is prob. the young of deer, אַיָּל l. 5. A gazelle could be sacrificed by heathen Arabs, but only as a poor substitute for a sheep; Wellhausen *Reste Ar. Heidenth.* 115.

L. 11. בצפר Cf. Lev. 1 14 מן העוף. אגנן אם צץ 43 7 meaning very uncertain. אגנן is rendered *enclosure*, cf. ܓܢܐ, جُنَّة &c., √ גנן *surround, protect*; so *birds of enclosure* i. e. domestic birds. צץ may = ציץ *wing*, Jer. 48 9 (? text), Targ. ציצין Dt. 14 9. 10. Ps. 139 9 &c., Sam. Targ. Gen. 15 9 צוץ = גוזל; so perhaps *birds of wing*, i. e. wild birds. According to Athenaeus ix 47 the quail was offered to the Tyrian Baal[1]. The Hebrews as a rule offered doves and pigeons for the עולה (Lev. 1 14 cf. Gen. 15 9 JE), and חטאת (Lev. 12 6. 8), or 'birds,' of a kind not specified (Vulg. *passeres*), for purification from leprosy (Lev. 14 4). שצף, חזת Two species of sacrifice; but of what nature is unknown. שצף cannot be explained by Is. 54 8 (see Duhm or Marti in loc.); possibly חזת may have been a sacrifice in connexion with auspices, חזה, חזות *vision*, cf. Is. 28 15. 18 (perhaps of a *vision* by necromancy). See Rob. Smith *Rel. of Sem.* 202.

L. 12. על צפר The repetition of צפר and the change of preposition are to be noted; contrast 43 7–8. Perhaps צפר here means some other kind of bird than צפר l. 11 or it may = צָפִיר *he-goat*, Ezr. 8 35. Dan. 8 5 &c.; or the words צפר אם may be due to a sculptor's error. קדמת קדשת 43 9. 44 3 = Hebr. ראשית, בכורים Lev. 2 12 f. Num. 18 12 and Dt. 18 4 &c. צד 43 9 = Hebr. צַיִד *hunting* Gen. 10 9, *game* Gen. 25 28, or *food* Josh. 9 5. 14. Neh. 13 15. The latter may be intended here. זבח שמן 43 9. זבח, properly

[1] So far as date goes, there is no reason why the common domestic fowl should not have been sanctified at Carthage. It was first introduced into W. Asia by the Persians, too late to be included in the sacrificial lists of Lev. 1; but it may have reached N. Africa by the fourth or third cent. Egyptian wall-paintings represent only ducks and geese among domesticated poultry (Peters *New World* viii 36). צפר, in Phoen. 'birds for sacrifice,' has a wider sense than in Hebr. and Aram.; cf. רל צפר l. 15.

slaughter, has here the general sense of *offering*. For oil with the first-fruits see Lev. 2 14 ff.; in the Jewish system it was mingled with flour for the מנחה, but not offered separately, Lev. 2 4–6. א[גרת] Cf. 1 S. 2 36 לַאֲגוֹרַת כֶּסֶף LXX ὀβολοῦ ἀργυρίου. The *agōrāh* (=מָעָא Targ. 1 S. 2 36) was perhaps the same as the *gērah*, the 20th part of a shekel Ex. 30 13 &c., identified by Targ. and Talm. with the מָעָא *obol*, ὀβολός LXX. לבאחר Cf. למבמחסר l. 5 *n*.

L. 13. יעמס **43** 8, Nif. impf., see **5** 6 *n*. מנת אלם **43** 8 i.e. לפני אלהים. For אלם see **33** 6 *n*.

L. 14. בלל **44** 2. 7 lit. *mixed* offering in connexion with the מנחה, so *cakes* or flour mixed with oil, as in the Hebr. מנחה, Ex. 29 2. Lev. 2 4. 7 10 &c. חלב . . חלב i.e. חָלָב . . חֵלֶב *milk* . . *fat*. Neither of these formed an element in the Hebr. meal-offering; the fat was sacrificed (Ex. 23 18 JE) and burned (1 S. 2 15 f. Lev. 3 3 ff. &c.); milk was not offered at all. Among the Arabs milk was poured as a libation: Wellhausen *supr*. 114; Rob. Smith *supr*. 203. In **43** 10 only חלב occurs. אש אדם לזבח A striking case of similarity with Hebr. idiom, e.g. Hos. 9 13. Is. 10 32 &c.; Driver *Tenses* § 204. This construction, in which the inf. with ל forms the sole predicate, is freely used in later Hebr., e.g. *Aboth* 4 22 הילודים למות והמתים להחיות והחיים לדון; cf. the Syriac usage after ܠܡܐ e.g. ܠܡܐ ܠܗܘܢ ܠܡܬܠ ܡܕܡ *they can give nothing*: Stade *Morg. Forsch.* 194; Nöldeke *Syr. Gr.*[2] 216. במנחת **43** 10 the ב as in בבלל l. 3, בצועת l. 4 &c.

L. 15. דל מקנא **43** 6, cf. **45** 2. **46** 1; for דל see note above p. 117. מקנא is an accus. of limitation, *poor in respect of cattle*, like הַמְסֻכָּן תְּרוּמָה Is. 40 20. קָרוּעַ כֻּתָּנְתּוֹ 2 S. 15 32. After verbs of fullness and want the accus. is usual in Hebr.; Ewald *Synt.* §§ 281 *b* 2. 284 *c*. [מנם] From **43** 6; see **5** add. note.

L. 16. The regulations here pass from individuals (אדם l. 14. דל l. 15) to classes of men (כל ארטם l. 16. הארטם חמת l. 17); hence it is prob. that the difficult words מזרח וגו' are to be interpreted as collectives. מזרח may be connected with the Hebr. אזרח lit. *one arising* (זרח) *from the soil*, so *native*, 'a free tribesman,' here a *clan*, *society of freemen*, cf. **55** 4, where וחברנם המזבח is to be read 'וח המזרח, and **59** A 1 אש בנא . . המזרח. 16 רב המזרח. שפח belongs to the same root as the Hebr. משפחה, and may be rendered *family*. מרזח אלם Prob. *a festal gathering in honour of the gods*, θίασος; cf. the Athenian sacred *symposia*. The √רזח apparently means *cry aloud*, and the noun מַרְזֵחַ is used in Hebr. of noisy revelry (Am. 6 7) or grief (Jer. 16 5, LXX θίασον), and in Rabbinic of a banquet, esp. one in honour of a false god[1]; perhaps מרזח in 33 1 may denote the period of the annual συσσιτία. An interesting parallel to the בית מרזח of Jer. 16 5 (though the sense is different) has been found recently in the mosaic of Mâdebâ; a place called Βητομαρσεα ἡ καὶ Μαιουμας[2] is mentioned on the E. of the Dead Sea, no doubt a transcription of ב׳ מ׳, and the scene of licentious festivals; Cl.-Gan. *Rec.* iv 276. 339–345 = *PEFQS* (1901) 239. 369. 372 f. The word occurs also in Palm., בני מרזחא *members of the thiasus* 140 A 2.

L. 17. כמדת See 5 19 *n.* למדת. שת 43 11, ptcp. pass., cf. in Hebr. מול *circumcised*, לוּטָה 1 S. 21 10; König *Lehrg.* i 445.

L. 18. איבל l. 21. 43 11 a negative compounded of אי (4 4 *n.*) and בל l. 15. פס l. 20. 43 11 *tablet*, from פסס *expand*; in the Talm. פס=*plank, palisade* (Schröder 23 *n.* 3); here it is the stone which bears the inscription. ונתן Nif. pf. 3 sing. mas. of יתן with waw conv. (see l. 4 *n.*). לפי *according to the tenor of*, ל of norm; cf. in Hebr. Num. 26 54 איש לפי פקדיו &c. כתבת A different document from the פס bearing the inscription. The remainder of the line is restored from l. 1.

L. 20. ברין Meaning unknown; ב is prob. the prep., with רין cf. the Arab. رَانَ *turn aside*; so ברין perhaps *in deviation from*, Ball *Light from the East* 253. ונענש Nif. perf. with waw conv. (see l. 4 *n.*); cf. Ex. 21 22 E. Dt. 22 19.

L. 21. פל An error for כל. את Usually אית; see 3 3 *n.* על *above, beyond*; cf. Ex. 16 5. In l. 3 עלת מן.

[1] A good illustration is found in *Siphre* ed. Friedmann 47 b; the context speaks of the daughters of Moab tempting the apostate Israelites באותה שעה לעשות להם בית המקדש הרב ורשע זה מרזחים והיו קוראים להם ואוכלים; Midr. Rab. *Esther* 4 זה יושב ועושה מרזחין (of Ahasuerus).

[2] Lit. *the house of the Marzeaḥ* (i.e. orgiastic festival) *which is also the Majumas-feast.* The Gk. word Μαιουμας occurs several times in the Midrashim as מַיוּמָס *a great feast*, so called after the feast held by the pagan inhabitants of the city Majuma in Syria; Levy *NHWB* iii 99. It has been suggested that Betomarsea-Majumas was the traditional scene of the event recorded in Num. 25 1 ff.; *Rev. Bibl.* xi (1902) 150. For מרזח see further Berger *Grande inscr. dédic. à Maktar* (1899) 16 ff.; Lidzb. *Eph.* i 47. 343 f.

NORTH AFRICA

43. Carthage. CIS i 167. iv–iii cent. B.C. Brit. Mus., Semitic Room no. 490.

1 בעת המשאתת אש טנא [האשם אש על המשאתת]
2 [באלף כללם אם צועת וכן הע]רת לכהנם ותברת לבעל
הזבח . . . .
3 [בעגל כללם אם צועת וכן ה]ערת לכהנם ותברת לבעל הזבח
א . . . .
4 [ביבל אם בעז כללם אם] צועת וכן ערת העזם לכהנם וכן האשל[בם
והפעמם] .
5 [באמר אם בגדא אם ב]צרב איל כללם אם צועת וכן הערת
לכה[נם]
6 [בכל זבח אש יזב]ח דל מקנא בל יכן לכהן מנם
7 [בצפר אגנן אם] בציץ כסף זר ׀׀ על אחד
8 [בכל צועת א]ש יעמס בנת אלם כן לכהן קצרת ו[יצלת . . . . . .
9 [על כל קרמת] קדשת ועל זבח צד ועל זבח שמן . . . .
10 [על בלל ו]על חלב ועל זבח במנחת ועל [כל זבח אש אדם
לזבח . . .
11 [כל משאת אש] איבל שת בפס ז ונת[ן . . . .

Tariff of payments erected by [the overseers of payments].

[2] [For an ox, whole-offerings or prayer-offering (?), the skin shall go] to the priests, but the ? shall belong to the person offering the sacrifice.

[3] [For a calf, whole-offerings or prayer-offering (?), the skin shall go] to the priests, but the ? shall belong to the person offering the sacrifice. . . . . .

[4] [For a ram or for a goat, whole-offerings or] prayer-

offering (?), the skin of the goats shall go to the priests, but the ? [and the feet] shall go . . . .

[5] [For a lamb or for a kid or for] the young (?) of a hart, whole-offerings or prayer-offering (?), the skin shall go to the pries[ts].

[6] [For every sacrifice which one may sacrifi]ce who is poor in cattle, nothing of them shall go to the priest.

[7] [For a bird, a domestic (?) or] for a wild (?) one, 2 silver *zars* for each.

[8] [For every prayer-offering (?) wh]ich is carried before the gods there goes to the priest the ? and [the ? . . . .

[9] [For all] sacred [first-fruits], and for a sacrifice of game (?) and for a sacrifice of oil . . . .

[10] [For a cake and] for milk and for a sacrifice for a meal-offering, and for [every sacrifice which a man is disposed to sacrifice . . . .

[11] [Every payment which] is not set down on this table shall be give[n . . . .

The lacunae are supplied from **42**, which this inscr. closely resembles. An excellent facsimile is given by Ball, *Light from the East*, opp. p. 250.

L. 1. See **42** 1.

L. 2. See **42** 3 f. In contrast to **42** the שלם כלל is not mentioned here; and, instead of a money payment, the skin, which in **42** goes to the worshipper, is assigned to the priests, cf. Lev. 7 8. תברת l. 3 some part of the victim, ? *cuttings*, cf. the Arab. هَبَرَ *cut up*, بَرَا *cut out*.

L. 3. See **42** 5 f.

L. 4. See **42** 7 f. צועת **42** 2. וכן **42** 4. אשלבם So CIS i 170 2; cf. **42** 4.

L. 5. See **42** 9 f. כללם Plur.; in **42** always כלל.

L. 6. See **42** 15.

L. 7. See **42** 11. כסף In apposition to זר (**42** 7), cf. 1 Ch. 22 13 זהב ככרים מאת אלף; see **42** 3 *n*.

L. 8. See **42** 13. בנת An error for פנת. כן For the usual יכן or וכן. קצרת **42** 4.

L. 9. See **42** 12.

L. 10. See **42** 14. על זבח במנחת An abbreviated form of אש אדם לזבח במנחת.

L. 11. See **42** 18.

44. Carthage. CIS i 166. iv–iii cent. B.C.

1 . . . . ים הארבעי
2 . . . . [בל]ל שח פר יא הקדש . . . .
3 . . . . קדמת הקדש בחדרת ולחם קט[רת] .
4 . . . . . תֹד לסות עלת הקדשת יכן הלחם הא ורב .
5 . . . . ת אש כן יא ומח ותין יא לבן לקחת תשקר . .
6 . . . . . בוץ ומכסא תח וקטרת לבנת דקת שבע כם .
7 . . . . . [ב]לל וקדמת ים החמשי
8 . . . . לשת עלת החדרת נפת ע . .
9 . . . . בנם מאתם וכם . . . . . .
10 . . . . טֹ חמשת . . . .

	The fourth day.
. . . . [cak]es	plants of fair fruit, the sacred . .
. . . . first-fruits	the sacred, in the chamber, and bread, inc[ense] . . . . .
. . . . . veil (?) upon (?)	the sacred, that bread shall be, and . . . .
. . . which is fair and rich	and figs, fair (and) white, thou shalt be careful to fetch . . .
. . fine linen and a covering be[low ?]	and incense, fine frankincense, seven . . . .
. . . cakes and first-fruits.	The fifth day.
.	to set upon (?) the chamber, honey (?) . . . .
	? two hundred, and . . . . .
	. . five . . . .

An obscure and fragmentary list of religious offerings for the days of the week, perhaps during the spring festival (קדמת &c.). It may be compared with the sacrificial calendar from Cos, M. 716–718 (iii cent. B.C.); see Hicks *Journ. Hell. St.* ix (1888) 323 ff.

L. 1. ים הארבעי Cf. Hebr. יום הששי Gen. 1 31; Driver *Tenses* § 209.
L. 2. בלל See **42** 14 *n*. שח Prob. = Hebr. שִׂיחַ *shrub* Gen.

2 5 &c. פר = פְּרִי 5 12; cf. Lev. 23 40. יא l. 5 = Aram. יָאֵי *fitting, fair*, Targ. Gen. 39 6 יָאֵי בְּחֵיזְוָא. Pesh. Ps. 33 1 ܝܳܐܶܐ = נָאוָה. In Jer. 10 7 לֹא יָאָתָה is an Aramaism. הקדש l. 3. הקדשת l. 4. These forms can hardly be verbs in (H)ifil, for the (H)if. of קדש in Phoen. is יקדש 28 4. They must be adjs. with the art.; but their construction is not apparent.

L. 3. קדמת See 42 12 *n.* חדרת l. 8 *the chamber*, i.e. of the temple, like the Hebr. קֹדֶשׁ הַקֳּדָשִׁים, דְּבִיר; cf. 47 לרבת לבעלת החדרת and CIS i 124 1 חדר *a sepulchral chamber*. The Hebr. חֶדֶר has neither of these special meanings. ולחם קטרת Either ἀσυνδέτως, *bread (and) incense*, or *bread of incense* (Corp.), incense in the form of a wafer. קטרת lit. *smoke* of offerings made by fire, then the *incense-offering* (Ex. 30 8), and then, as here, the material used in this offering (Lev. 10 1 &c.). The word occurs again in CIS i 334 מכר אקטרת *the seller of incense*. Various substances used for incense are mentioned in Sabaean inscrr.; see Mordtmann u. Müller *Sab. Inschr.* 78. 81 f.

L. 4. סוית Meaning uncertain; סְוִית? *curtain, veil* = Hebr. מַסְוֶה Ex. 34 34 P. עלת Perhaps prep. *upon* l. 8. The rendering of the Corp. *upper chamber*, i.e. עִלַּת (Dan. 6 11) = עֲלִיָּה, is not probable. הקדשת l. 2 *n.* 42 12 *n.* The adj. here is fem., sing. or plur.

L. 5. מח *fat*, √מחח, whence Hebr. מֵחִים (plur. only) Is. 5 17. Ps. 66 15. In Talm. מֵיחָא is used figuratively of *choice flour*. תין Perhaps = Arab. تِين, Hebr. תְּאֵנָה. *White figs* are mentioned in Jer. Talm. *Terumoth* 43 a תאינים שחורות. לקחת תשקד For this use of the inf. with ל cf. Is. 5 2 ויקו לעשות; Driver *Tenses* § 207. The inf. of לקח takes the same form in Phoen. as in Hebr.; for other parts of the vb. cf. 20 B 7 לקח. 42 20 יקח. שקד lit. *watch, be wakeful*, Jer. 1 12. 31 27 &c.

L. 6. ברץ *byssus*, fine Egyptian linen, written *plene* because a foreign word. In Hebr. the word is met with only in late literature; its origin is uncertain. מכסא Acc. to Corp. = מכסת (cf. מקנא = מקנת 42 15) *covering*; cf. كِسْوَة the *covering* of the Ka'aba at Mekka. תח Possibly to be completed תח[ת]. לבנת λίβανος, so called from its *white* appearance. For דקת cf. Lev. 16 12 קטרת סמים דקה. כמ. is restored by Corp. כמרם *priests*, 55 7 and (Aram.) 64 1. 69 23 (rest.).

L. 8. לשת i.e. לָשִׁית. The significance of the prep. עלת is not clear in this context. נפת ? = Hebr. נֹפֶת Pr. 24 13.

L. 9. בנם may mean *among them* 5 9; '200 *sons*' for sacrifice (!) could not be mentioned in this way.

45. Carthage. iii–ii cent. B.C. Discovered 1898. Carthage Mus.

1 לרבת לעשתרת ולתנת בלבנן מקדשם חדשם כם כל אש בנ . . .
2 והחרטית אש במקדשם אל ודל מלכת החרץ ודל כל מנם א[ש . . .
3 ודל כל מנם במאזנם המקדשם אל ודל העלם אש על פן המקדש[ם
אל . . .
4 אש יבא עלת החרת שמקדשם אל כמש חגר השמרת לדר הא. . . .
5 אדרנם ועד צערנם למבירח חיר שפטם עבדמלקרת ו . . .
6 י שפטם שפט וחנא בן אדנבעל ורב עבדמלקרת בן מגן בן[. . .
7 תן בן עבדלאי בן בעליתן בן אשמנפלס ועבדארש בן עבד . . .
8 ן עבדמלקרת הרב ורב כהנם עזרבעל בן שפט רב כה[נם . . .
9 לשלך רב כהנם ובעל חרש עכברם הפלס בן חנבעל

To the ladies 'Ashtart and Tanith in Lebanon. New sanctuaries as well as all that . . . built (?) . . [2] and the sculptures which are in these sanctuaries and ? the gold-work, and ? all vessels wh[ich ? [3] and ? all vessels in ? these sanctuaries, and ? the ? which is over against [these] sanctuaries . . . . [4] which approaches the ? of these sanctuaries; as also the fence enclosing (?) that hill . . . . [5] the greatest of them even to the least of them: from the month Ḥiyyar, the suffetes (being) 'Abd-melqarth and . . . . [6]. the suffetes (being) Shafaṭ and Ḥanno, son of Idniba'al, and the Rab (being) 'Abd-melqarth, son of Magon, so[n . . . Ba'al-ya][7]thon, son of 'Abd-lai, son of Ba'al-yathon, son of Eshmun-pilles, and 'Abd-arish, son of 'Abd- . . . [so][8]n of 'Abd-melqarth the Rab, and the chief-priest (being) 'Azru-ba'al, son of Shafaṭ the chief-prie[st . . . Ba'al]-[9] shillek the chief-priest; and the master-workman (was) 'Akboram the surveyor, son of Ḥanni-ba'al.

L. 1. לרבת Sing. or plur.; see **3** 2 *n.* לעשתרת ולתנת The combination is remarkable. Cl.-Gan., *Rec.* iii 186 ff., considers that it points to a mythological connexion between the two goddesses, borrowed from the cult of Demeter and Persephone. It is possible that Tanith was associated with this cult (**47**. **48**); but ʿAshtart, usually identified with Aphrodite (**4** 1 *n*.), seems at first sight foreign to it. ʿAshtart, however, absorbed a great variety of local types, and at Carthage she may have assumed the characteristics of Demeter. In later times a temple dedicated to Ceres and Proserpine appears to have stood on or near the site of these sanctuaries[1]; but this later dedication hardly proves Cl.-Ganneau's view, for it may have been due merely to a reminiscence of the earlier sanctuaries of ʿAshtart and Tanith. בלבנן Not the Lebanon in Syria, but an eminence in Carthage, prob. so called from the *white* colour of its stone (Lidzb. *Eph.* i 21); cf. the name Λεῦκος given to the city of Τύνης (Tunis) in Diod. xx 8. For the place-name with ב see **24** 2 *n*. כם כל אש Prob.=כמאש (כמו אש)+כל, cf. כמש l. 4 and **3** 7 *n*. בנ either בָּנֻ *they built* or בנ[ם] *in them*. Cl.-Gan., l. c. § 2, adopting the latter, continues with פעל עם קרת חדשת, as **38** 1.

L. 2. חרמית Prob. plur., חַרְטִית or חֲרָטִית; √חרט=*cut*, *carve*, Aram. ܚܪܛ, Arab. خَرَطَ *peel off*, in modern usage *turn wood*. Here prob. the meaning is *sculptures*. אל See **5** 22 *n*. דל Meaning uncertain. Cl.-Gan.'s translation *conjunctim*, *item*, lit. *depending*, rests upon a questionable application of the √דלה, Arab. دَلَا *hang down*. Lidzb., l. c., renders with more probability *that which is damaged*, lit. *weak*, *poor*, supposing that repairs as well as new buildings are commemorated (**38**. **46**); this may be the meaning of דל פעמם **46** 1 *ruinous as to its steps*; elsewhere, however, in Phoen. (**42** 15) and in Hebr. דל is used of persons. מלכת For מלאכת **20** A 6. חרץ Perhaps *trench*, cf. חרוץ Dan. 9 25 (? text) and חריץ in Mishnah; so Halévy *Rev. Sém.* ix (1901) 79 ff. מנם See **4** 5 *n*.

L. 3. מאזנם Meaning unknown; *armoury* lit. *place of weapons* has been proposed (*Rép.* i 16), connecting the word with אָזֵן (√אזן) *implements* Dt. **23** 14; cf. Targ. אזינא *arms* in בית אזינן *quiver* Is. 49 2, ܙܝܢܐ *weapons* (√זין). But the construction is not evident, and נם′ may be the suff. with מאז (? sense), or a ptcp. plur. העלם Some fixed object *in front of* על פן (**3** 5) the temple; Cl.-Gan. renders *steps*, cf. עוֹלוֹת Eze. 40 26.

L. 4. יבא Sing. or plur. If העלם is the subj., יבא עלת may mean *comes* (*up*) *upon*, *ascends*, cf. Ex. 18 23. 2 Ch. 20 24. החרז Possibly connected with חרז *string together*, חרוזים *strings of beads* Cant. 1 10; here perhaps *the circle* round the precincts; so Halévy. כמש=

[1] Delattre *Bull. et mém. soc. nat. des antiquaires de France* lviii (1899) 1–26.

כמאש l. 1, as in **10** 9 introducing a further item of the dedication. In this inscr. ש is the relat. with the noun, אש with the predicate; חגר therefore must be a noun, not a verb. It means perhaps *enclosure*; the √חגר=*restrain, gird*, in Arab. حِجْر *the wall enclosing the Ka'aba*, Assyr. *igaru* 'wall.' שמרת Perhaps *watch-tower*, or *defence*. Lidzb. suggests a connexion with שָׁמִיר, سَمُرَة *thorn-hedge*, in which case חגר השמרת will be the *fence hedging* the sanctuaries. לבנן לדר הא i. e. l. 1. Cf. 2 Ch. **33** 14. After חא Halévy proposes [יקדש ם] *they have consecrated*.

L. 5. ארונם ועד צערנם Cf. Jer. **14** 3. Jon. **3** 5. The suffixes refer to the temples and their furnishings. למבירת חיר *during* or *from the month Ḥiyyar*, cf. למבחיי **16** 2. למבמחסר **42** 5 (Lidzb.); for חיר see **27** 1 *n*. Cl.-Gan. is prob. right in explaining the double mention of the reigning suffetes as an indication of a twofold date: 'when 'Abd-melqarth and . . . were suffetes [the work was begun, and lasted to the month . . .] when Shafaṭ and Ḥanno were suffetes.' The suffetes (**42** 1 *n*.) are mentioned without full genealogies, as in **40** 2 *n*. CIS i 135 6. 179 6 f.

L. 6. The י at the beginning is prob. the last letter of the name of the month, the missing sentence prob. being in the same form as the preceding one. ארנבעל is transcribed Idnibal in **60**. The constitutional position of the רב at Carthage is unknown. In **42** 1 (restored from CIS i 170) ר i. e. רַבָּנוּ is merely a title of the suffete; but in this inscr. רב, who comes after the שפטם, is a distinct official; the same must be the case with הרב in CIS i 229–235 &c. An inscr. from Tyre, lately discovered, reads עברבעל רב מאת (Cl.-Gan. *Rec.* ii 294 ff.); but whatever this may have meant at Tyre, it does not imply that the Rab was president of the 100 at Carthage (**42** 1 *n*. (4)). May the title have been given to an ex-suffete when his term of office was over, or to the members of the executive cabinet of 30 chosen from the 100? In **7** 1 f. (Sidon). **29** 2. 6 (Cyprus). **38** 4 (Gaulus) the office was that of a district governor.

L. 7. עברלאי In form resembles the Aram. אמת־אלהי=אמתלאי the mother of Abraham, *Baba Bathra* 91 a; but the Western and Punic עברלאי cannot=עבר־אלהי (Lidzb.). It may be a Numidian or Berber name. ועבדארש Apparently another official; his title and the name of his colleague prob. stood at the end of l. 6. עבדארש occurs in CIS i 537. 805, cf. **52** 2 עבארש. The prefixed עבד seems to imply that ארש was a deity, ? Ἄρης; for the name ארש see **21** 1.

L. 8. רב כהנם Cf. **35** 2 (Piraeus); evidently the office was hereditary.

L. 9. ובעל חרש Prob. *master of the workmen* (coll.), *contractor*.

As in the foregoing lines the office precedes the name. With בעל cf. בעל הזבח 42 4; חרש 20 A 13. עכברם i. e. *mouse*, cf. עכבר CIS i 178. 239 &c. Gen. 36 38 &c. הפלס i. e. הַפַּלָּס lit. *leveller*, i. e. *surveyor*, *architect*; cf. Lat. *librator*. The √פלס=lit. weigh (piel); so אשמנפלס l. 7 *whom E. weighs*; in the O. T. of *levelling* a path, e. g. Ps. 78 50. Is. 26 7.

46. Carthage. CIS i 175. Brit. Mus., Semitic Room.

1 חרש ופעל אית המטבח ז דל פעמם עשרת האשם אש על המקדשם
אש כן בשת ש . . . .
2 גרסכן וגרעשתרת בן יחנבעל בן עזרבעל בן שפט ובדעשתרת בן . . . .

The Decemvirs in charge of the sanctuaries renovated and made this slaughter-house (?) ? steps: which was in the year of the s[uffetes . . . .] Ger-sakun and Ger-'ashtart, son of Yaḥon-ba'al, son of 'Azru-ba'al, son of Shafaṭ, and Bod-'ashtart, son . . . .

L. 1. חרש ופעל Plur.; cf. 38 1. 23 2. מטבח Possibly the place where animals were slaughtered before they were sacrificed; cf. the title המטבח CIS i 237 ff. 376. The word occurs in Is. 14 21 מַטְבֵּחַ. דל פעמם Possibly *ruinous as to* (*its*) *steps*; see 45 2 *n*. The words might mean *twice* (i. e. פַּעֲמַיִם) *ruined*, G. Hoffmann quot. by Lidzb. *Eph*. i 22 *n*. 'הא' א' על המ Cf. 55 5. 42 1. אש כן בשת ש]פטם Cf. 40 2. The name of the first of the suffetes is lost; the second is Ger-'ashtart, and apparently Bod-'ashtart is the third (Corp.). But this would be very unusual (42 1 *n*. (1)); possibly Bod-'ashtart had a different title, given at the end of the line.

L. 2. גרסכן See 17 2 *n*. 34 *n*. יחנבעל Again Euting *Carth*. 230 5 f. &c.; usually חנבעל; cf. עזרבעל and יעזרבל, in Hebr. פדיה and יפדיה. בדעשתרת See 6 3 *n*.

47. Carthage. CIS i 177.

לרבת לאמא ולרבת לבעלת החדרת אש פעל חמלר בן בעלחנא

To the lady Amma, and to the lady, mistress of the inner shrine (?): which ḤMLR, son of Ba'al-ḥanno, made.

The mention of two goddesses is significant; see **45** 1 *n.* אמא is evidently the title of a deity worshipped as *Mother*, such as Rhea or Demeter; cf. Hesychius *Etym. magn.* s. v. Ἀμμάς . . . *καὶ ἡ μήτηρ, καὶ ἡ Ῥέα, καὶ ἡ Δημήτηρ.* Demeter, rather than Rhea, is prob. to be looked for here, for the worship of Demeter and Persephone was introduced *μετὰ πάσης σεμνότητος* into Carthage from Sicily as a reparation for the pillaging of their temple by Himilco during his disastrous campaign in 396 B.C.; Diodorus xiv 77. The Carthaginians would naturally adapt the new worship to their own religion, and it seems likely that the Carth. goddess Tanith (**48** 1) assumed some of the attributes of Demeter; at any rate she is called *mother* in CIS i 195 לאם לרבת לתנת and 380 לאם לרבת. Perhaps this accounts for the head of Demeter (=Tanith?) figured on the coins of Carthage; see Cl.-Gan. *Ét.* i 149 ff. For the form אמא cf. Plaut. *Poen.* iii 22 *amma* =אָם; in **14** 3 'Ashtart (?) is called *mother*. If אמא is Demeter, the other goddess is prob. Persephone, who was certainly worshipped at Carthage; a characteristic figure of her surmounts the inscr. CIS i 176, though she is not mentioned by name. The exact meaning of בעלת החדרת is obscure (see **44** 3 *n.*), possibly *mistress of the inner shrine*; cf. לאלן אקדש *to the god of the sanctuary* Costa 31 (Lidzb. *Eph.* i 39). It is prob. that חדרת corresponds to the Gk. *μέγαρον adytum*=מערת *cave*; the 'dark inner chamber, found in many temples both among the Semites and in Greece, was almost certainly in its origin a cave' (Rob. Smith *R. of S.* 183); and in the worship of Demeter and Persephone the *μέγαρα* had a special significance. The title מערת given to Ṣed-tanith in CIS i 249 עבר בת צדתנת מערת, though it is generally explained as a topographical title *Megarensis*, may well denote the goddess of the sacred cave. For בעלת see **3** 2 *n.* חמלר Cf. חמלרת CIS i 597. 787, for חמלך, חמלכת=אח־מ׳ **40** 2 *n.*; either an error or a peculiarity of spelling. בעלחנא See **39** 2 *n.*

48. Carthage. CIS i 181. Brit. Mus., Semitic Room.

לרבת לתנת פן בעל
ולאדן לבעל חמן אש
נדר בדמלקרת בן עבד
מלקרת בן חמלכת כ שמ
ע קלא יברכא

K 2

To the lady Tanith, Face of Ba'al, and to the lord Ba'al-ḥammān: which Bod-melqarth, son of 'Abd-melqarth, son of Ḥamilkath, vowed, because he heard his voice: may he bless him!

More than 2000 votive tablets of this character have been unearthed on the site of ancient Carthage, in the neighbourhood of what was once the citadel (Byrsa). The stones are often inscribed with symbols of the two deities, and the formula of dedication is in nearly all cases the same. Judging from the style of the letters, the earliest tablets belong to the same period as the sacrificial tariffs **42–44**; the latest of them must have been inscribed before the destruction of Carthage by the Romans in 146 B.C. They cover, therefore, a period of about 200 years.

L. 1. לרבת See **3** 2 *n.*; in CIS i 401 ff. לאדן (possibly by accident). תנת A female deity, as appears from the title אם which is found occasionally (p. 131). The vast number of these tablets proves that her worship was popular, though not necessarily predominant, at Carthage; it is to be noted that she always takes precedence of Ba'al-ḥammān in the formula of dedication[1]; but we cannot say for certain that she was the chief deity of Carthage, the δαίμων Καρχηδονίων (Polyb. vii 9 2). The etymology of the name is unknown; prob. it is to be looked for in Libyan or N. African, rather than in Phoenician. Nor is the pronunciation certain; *Tanith* is on the whole most likely[2], but it may have been *Tun(i)th* if Τύνης, the town near Carthage, was named after the goddess. Outside Carthage and its dependencies in N. Africa she is not found; the Sidonian called עבדתנת in an inscr. from Athens (CIS i 116) prob. had some connexion with Carthage. Tanith is never mentioned alone: in **45** 1 בלבנן follows, elsewhere פן בעל. The latter title is generally taken to mean *the face of Ba'al*, a mythic phrase perhaps denoting the self-revelation of the divine nature, cf. פני Ex. 33 14 and מלאך פניו Is. 63 9; the *manifestation* of Ba'al, we may suppose, came to be regarded as a distinct deity, cf. שם בעל **5** 18 *n.* On the other hand, Rob. Smith explains *Tanith with the Ba'al face*, i.e. the bearded, androgynous goddess, and quotes in support the title לאדן beside לרבת noticed above (*R. of S.* 459). The combinations Milk-'ashtart, Eshmun-'ashtart, Ṣed-tanith may

[1] In several inscrr. from Cirta (Constantine), e.g. those given in Corp. pp. 296 and 365 and in Lidzb. *Eph.* i pp. 40 f., Ba'al-ḥammān comes before Tanith.

[2] Cf. ΤΑΙΝΙΤΙΔΑ, said to have been found on a stone at Carthage, Corp. p. 288.

imply the same idea[1]. The character and attributes of Tanith are obscure. Some of the symbols on these tablets seem to connect her with 'Ashtart, the crescent surmounting the full moon (very common), the star, the dove, the dolphin. Two tablets (CIS i 398. 419) show the figure of a sheep, which was sacred to 'Ashtart. The commonest symbol of all, the triangle crowned by a circle with horns bent outwards, may belong either to Tanith or to Ba'al-ḥammān; Rob. Smith (l. c.) thinks that the horns are sheep-horns, pointing to 'Ashtart again[2]. We have seen that Tanith is occasionally called *Mother*, and that she was prob. assimilated to Demeter (47 *n*.); but Cl.-Ganneau seems to go too far when he alleges, on this ground, that the worship of Tanith was of foreign and Sicilian origin (*Ét*. i 149 ff.). Tanith, it is true, was rarely used in the composition of pr. names; ברתנת 42 1. צדתנת CIS i 247–249. עבדתנת ib. 116 are almost all the instances; and she has not yet been found in Carth. names transcribed into Gk. and Lat.; but this does not necessarily imply that her cult was foreign. The evidence, so far as it goes, suggests that Tanith was a native, possibly a pre-Carthaginian, deity, who, in the process of religious syncretism, so characteristic of the Semitic genius, was identified with various goddesses according to circumstances, with 'Ashtart, with Demeter, and with Artemis (CIS i 116 עבדתנת = Ἀρτεμίδωρος, from Athens). After the overthrow of Carthage, the Romans introduced the worship of Juno Coelestis (Virgo Coelestis, Coelestis) into the ruined city; but we do not know that they intended thereby to identify Juno or Coelestis with Tanith[3]; see 4 1 *n*.

L. 2. בעל חמן Prob. *the glowing B.*, see 87 4 *n*. In these inscrr. he is always the πάρεδρος of Tanith.

L. 5. קלא יברכא For the suff. 3 sing. m. cf. 40 2 *n*.

[1] Meyer, *Ency. Bibl.* 3747, after Halévy, explains פן בעל as the name of a place, like פנואל in Gen. 32 32, 'TNT of Pne-ba'al,' and supports his view by CIS i 380 לאם לרבת תנת פן בעל 'to the mother, the mistress of Pne-ba'al' (see p. 131). But the instance of פנואל seems to be too isolated to justify the inference, and analogy favours treating פן בעל as in appos. to לרבת, rather than as a genit. On the whole the first explanation given above is to be preferred provisionally.

[2] Cf. Sanchuniathon ap. Phil. Bybl. *Fr. Hist. Gr.* iii 568 Κρόνῳ δὲ ἐγένοντο ἀπὸ Ἀστάρτης θυγατέρες ἑπτὰ Τιτανίδες (? Τανιτίδες) ἢ Ἀρτέμιδες. The Persian or Babyl. Ἀναΐτις mentioned by Strabo pp. 439. 456 (codd. Ταναΐδος). 479 &c. ed. Müll., by Berosus *Fr. Hist. Gr.* ii 498, and other writers, was prob. the Babyl. Anatum rather than the Carth. Tanith.

[3] In CIL viii 999 *Dianae cael. aug.* the Virgo Coelestis is identified with Diana, cf. Tanith-Artemis; in iii 993 *Caelesti Augustae et Aesculapio Augusto et genio Carthaginis et genio Daciarum*, she is distinguished from the *genius* of Carthage, if that was Tanith.

49. Carthage. CIS i 269. Bibl. Nat., Paris.

1 לרבת לתנת פן בעל ולאדן
2 לבעל חמן אש נדר בעלח
3 נא אש צדן בד אדני בד
4 אשמניתן
5 עם קרתחדשת

Render ll. 2–5 'which Ba'al-ḥanno of Sidon, client of his lord, client of Eshmun-yathon, vowed. The people of Carthage.'

Twenty-four inscrr. of this type are given in the Corp., nos. 269–287. 288–293.

L. 2. בעלחנא As a rule the usual genealogy of the donor is not given in these inscrr., except in 271. '3 f. '7. '87. '91, where the father is mentioned. It appears that among the Semites, as among the Greeks and Romans, a slave was not allowed to have a genealogy, e. g. CIS i 236 'עבד פ, and 'בר חרי פ', בת *freed-man*, *-woman* in Nab. and Palm. inscrr. (147 ii b 12; p. 250 *n.* 1), cf. עבד אין לו חיים Talm. B. *Qiddushin* 69 a; the same must have been the case with the 'dependent foreigner' (בד אדני) of these inscrr.; Lidzb. 133 f.

L. 3. אש צדן Not אִשׁ but the relat. אש, because in four inscrr. (273. '9. '80. '81) a woman dedicates the tablet. All the tablets of this group are offered by Sidonians, who prob. occupied a subordinate position in Carth. households. For בד see 6 2 *n.* אדני With suff. 3 sing. m.; in 276. 293 אדנם, which must be the honorific plur. (cf. אלם 33 6 *n.*), as only one 'lord' is mentioned.

L. 5. The expression 'people of Carthage,' occurring here without any verbal connexion, is to be accounted for by the full term לם יעמס ע' ק' which is found elsewhere in this group, 270 ff. The meaning of the phrase is not certain, but it may be rendered 'let not the people of Carthage carry (it, i. e. the stone) away'—for building purposes. For the prohibitive לם cf. 5 21, and for עמס *carry* cf. 5 6. Another explanation is suggested by Cl.-Gan., who renders ἀτελής i. e. 'free from public burdens,' cf. *immunis perpetuus* CIL viii 2714, taking יעמס as pass.; *Rec.* iii 2. This certainly suits such a case as 274 שפט אחרש אש צדן למיעמס בן שצפם i. e. 'Shafaṭ the artisan, the Sidonian, tax-free (?), the son of Shiṣifam.'

50. Carthage. iii–ii cent. B.C. Discovered 1899.

1 רבת חות אלת מלכת שיסכהֹא
2 אתך אנכי מצלח אית אמע[ש]תרת
3 ואית עמרת ואית כל אש לא   כא
4 עֹלצא עלתי בכסף (אש) אברחת שֹלם
5 אם אית כל ארם אש עלץ עלתי
6 בר . ת הכסף ז כמ ? ת יסך אעפרת

O ladies Ḥawwath, Elath, Milkath . . ! [2] I, Maṣliaḥ, bind Am-'ashtart [3] and 'MRTH and all who belong to her; for [4] she exulted (?) over me in the matter of the money which I discharged (??) in full; [5] or every man who has exulted (?) over me [6] in . . . of this money, according to . . . the lead.

This inscr., found in the necropolis of Duimes at Carthage in 1899, is written on a small sheet of lead. It was intended, like the Gk. and Roman *tabellae devotionis*[1], to be a missive to the gods of the underworld, and to act as a spell or imprecation against the writer's enemies. These *tabellae* were rolled up and dropped down a tube, which was used also for libations to the dii inferi, into the sepulchre below. See Berger *CR* (1899) 173. 179–186; Cl.-Gan. *Rec.* iii 304–319; iv 87–97; Lidzb. *Eph.* i 26–34 (with facsimile); *Rép.* i no. 18. See also Deissmann *Bible Studies* 273 ff. for a Jewish-Greek specimen of the third cent. A.D.

L. 1. חות Cf. O.T. חַוָּה *Eve*, which according to Nöldeke and Wellhausen (see *Oxf. Hebr. Lex.* s. v.) meant originally *serpent*, cf. Arab. حَيَّة, a suitable name for the goddess of the underworld. אלת (see **60** 3 *n.*) and מלכת (in pr. nn., e. g. חמלכת, עבדמ' &c.) may be the names of infernal deities, forming with חות a triad; so Cl.-Gan., *Rec.* iv 90, who compares the *triple* Hecate. Lidzb. takes אלת מלכת as epithets of חות, *goddess, queen*, and רבת as sing. שיסכהֹא After

[1] See Wünsch *Defixionum tabellae atticae* (1897) in CIA appendix, and Michel nos. 1319–1325. The foll. is a specimen: *Φερένικος πρὸς τὸν Ἑρμῆν τὸν χθόνιον καὶ τὴν Ἑκάτην χθονίαν καταδεδέσθω· Γαλήνην, ἥτις Φερενίκου, καταδέω πρὸς Ἑρμῆν χθονικὸν καὶ Ἑκάτην χθονίαν καταδέω· καὶ ὡς οὗτος ὁ βόλυβδος ἄτιμος καὶ ψυχρός, οὕτω ἐκεῖνος καὶ τὰ ἐκείνου ἄτιμα καὶ ψυχρὰ ἔστω καὶ τοῖς μετ' ἐκείνο ἃ περὶ ἐμõ λέγοιεν καὶ βολευοίατο*, Wünsch 107 = Michel 1324. Cf. Tacitus *Ann.* ii 69.

ש a noun ought to follow; so Cl.-Gan. takes יסך as = Hebr. נֶסֶךְ, (*this is that*) *which is the libation*, the dropping of the *tabella* into the grave being equivalent to a libation. The explanation is forced, but no better one has been suggested. The reading יסכרא (סכר=זכר), favoured by Lidzb., cannot be accepted.

L. 2. אתך Probably impf. 1 sing. from תכך, whence Heb. תֹּךְ *oppression*, Aram. תִּכָּא, Arab. تِكَّة *chain, bond*, corresponding to the Gk. καταδέω *bind with magic*. מצלח Pr. n. as in CIS i 1171; in form either Hif. or Piel ptcp.

L. 3. עמרת Possibly the name of another woman beside Am-'ashtart (Berger, Lidzb.), though לא and עלצא in the foll. clauses are sing. Cl.-Gan. takes עמרת as an appellative, with some such meaning as ἐργαστήριον, as in the Gk. formula καταδῶ τὸν δεῖνα . . . καὶ τὸ ἐργαστήριον; but in this case we should expect the possessive suffix. כא = כי, as in the inscrr. from Cirta, Costa 3 2 (Lidzb. p. 433) &c.; in NPun. כח and כע (Schröder p. 264 f.).

L. 4. עלצא Hebr. עלץ = *rejoice*; so here possibly *she exulted over me*, cf. Ps. 25 2 אל יעלצו אויבי לי. Or perhaps the meaning may be *attacked*, cf. Arab. علص iii *come to blows*. Lidzb. renders *tormented*, taking עלץ as = Hebr. אלץ Judg. 16 16, with ע for א as in NPun. בכסף אש אברחת שלם So Cl.-Gan. In the inscr. אש is written over the line, prob. because it was accidentally left out after בכסף. The meaning *I have discharged* (אברחת Hif. pf. 1 sing. of ברח lit. *flee*) is conjectural, but not impossible[1]. Lidzb. reads בכספא ברחת צלמת *by her sorcery by the spirits of darkness*; כסף he supposes to = Hebr. כֶּשֶׁף, and אש he takes up into l. 3. This is very improbable; the Phoen. ס = Hebr. ש not שׁ. Money matters are frequently the occasion for these imprecations in Gk. *tabellae*.

L. 5. אם *or*, cf. 5 7 *n*.

L. 6. The line should prob. begin with a noun + ב, ? ברדת, following the construction עלצא עלתי ב' l. 4. כמ?ת It is not certain whether there was a letter between מ and ת; כמדת 42 17 might be read, at any rate כ *according to* is certain. יסך אעפרת *the 'libation' of the lead* (Cl.-Gan.). א' = ה art.; the change is prob. due to the ע following. Lidzb. suggests כמ[א] תִיַּסֵּךְ א' *as the lead is moulded*; but the Nif. form is improbable.

[1] Cf. Talm. Jer. *Git*. V 47 a אדם מבריח עצמו מן השבועה ואין אדם מבריח עצמו מן התשלומין 'a man tries to discharge himself from an oath, but he does not try to discharge himself from a payment'; Levy *NHWB* s.v. ברח.

51. **Cirta** (*Constantine*). **Costa 8.**

1 לאדן לבעל חמן ולרבת לתנת פען בעל
2 נדר אש נדר חמלכת בן בעשתרת
3 בן נבל מלך אדם בשערם בתם
4 כ שמע קלא ברכיא

The inscriptions from Cirta, now Constantine, date from the period before the Roman occupation. The writing belongs to the stage of transition from the Punic to the Neo-Punic script, and many words begin to assume forms which are characteristic of the later language. Thus the quiescent letters come into use, but not to such an extent as in Neo-Punic, e.g. פען בעל for 'פן ב, כ = כי sometimes written כא or כה. A preference is shown for strong gutturals, e.g. שמח beside שמא and שמע, בחרכא for ברכא[1]. The form of the suff. 3 m. sing. is undecided, thus מלכי Costa 18 for מלכא, קלה for קלא, ברכיא for ברכא. בעשתרת is written 'בעש, and תנת sometimes תינת i.e. Tainith or Têneth. Specimens of these inscrr. are given in the Corp. p. 365, by Berger *Actes du* 11me *congrès des Or.* (1897) § 4, 273–294, and by Lidzb. 433 f., *Eph.* i 38 ff. In general form they resemble the Carth. votive tablets, but differ from them mainly in two respects: the formula of dedication is not so stereotyped[2], Ba'al-ḥammān generally takes precedence of Tanith, and often is named alone; notices of time and place are introduced more frequently.

L. 3. מלך אדם is evidently the title of a petty king or local chieftain; cf. Costa 100 מנן בן עבדאשמן מלך אדם בשערם. The year of the king's reign is sometimes given, e.g. Costa 18 . . . מתנבעל בחמש למלכי; ib. 98 עזרבעל . . . בחמשם [שנת] למלכי; Villefosse 69 בדעשתרת . ⁖ . [א]רבעת ארבעם שת למלכי. In some inscrr. מלך אדם is the title, not of the king, but of the deity, e.g. Costa 93 לאדן לבעל חמן מלך אדם; Villefosse 69 לא' לב' ח' ולת' פן בעל מלך אדם בשרם בתם; cf. Altiburus 2 (*JA* viii t. 9. 467) לאדן ל[בעל מלך א[ד]ם]. The meaning of אדם is obscure. It can hardly be 'lord,' a variant of אדן, because

[1] Costa 75 לאדן לבעל חמן אש נדר על[כש] [2]בן חמלכת בן מ[ת]ן בחרכא [3]ושמח קלה.

[2] Note the variations in Costa 81 לאדן לאלן אקדש בעל חמן; 16 לאדן לאלן לבעל חמן; 38 לאדן לבעל אדן ולבעל חמן; 22 לאדן לבעל אדר ולרבת לתינת פן בעל. אלן, בעל אדן, בעל אדר are not different deities, but divine names regarded as equivalents of בעל חמן. Berger l. c. 282.

this word occurs previously in the dedication. Perhaps מ׳ ארם = מ׳ אֲדָמָה, 'king of the land'; so Lidzb. l. c. בשערם בתם is clearly the name of a place, perhaps of Cirta, as the inscrr. come from there, or of a city dependent on Cirta; besides the inscrr. quoted above, cf. Costa 17 לבעל חמן בשרם בתם. A group of 13 inscrr. from Carthage, CIS i 294–306, contains the expression in various forms, בשערם בתם, בשערם, בשרם, בשער, בשר &c., used apparently of a native of Cirta (?) resident in Carthage, but what the words exactly mean is not known. The name שערם possibly = שְׁעָרִים *gates*[1], and may refer to the ravines and passes of the hills in the neighbourhood of Cirta, which stood on the S. of the range which stretches across the country west of Carthage. This country was known to the Romans as the land of the Massylii, a Numidian kingdom, one of whose kings, Massinissa, figured prominently in the Second Punic War (218–201 B. C.), and died (148 B.C.) just before the destruction of Carthage. The seat of his kingdom was Cirta[2]; but that the מלך ארם of these inscrr. was a predecessor of his we cannot say.

L. 4. An interesting variation of the formula occurs in Costa 6 3 f. כ שמע קלא ברכא בים נעם [אש] בים ברך i.e. 'because he heard his voice (and) blessed him on a good day, on the day when he blessed'; cf. Is. 49 8.

52. Thugga. Brit. Mus., Semitic Room nos. 494–495.

[מ]צבת · שאטבן · בן · יפמטת · בן · פלו

הבנם · שאבנם עבארש · בן · עבדשתרת

זמר · בן אטבן · בן · יפמטת · בן · פלו ·

מנגי · בן · ורסכן

ובאזרת · שלא.... זזי · וטמן · . ורסכן

החרשם · שיר · מסדל · .. ננבסן · ואנכן · .. אשי

הנסכם שברזל · שפט · בן · בלל · ופפי · בן · בבי

[1] In a Lat. inscr. of 48–49 A. D. lately excavated at Thugga the sentence occurs: huic senatus et plebs ob merita patris omnium *portarum* sententis ornam(enta) sufetis gratis decrevit. Possibly the Pun. for *portae* would be שערם, as in these inscrr. from Cirta. Cl.-Gan. *Rec.* iii 325 *n.*; Lidzb. *Eph.* i 52.

[2] Strabo p. 706 ed. Müll. *Κίρτα τέ ἐστιν ἐν μεσογαίᾳ, τὸ Μασανάσσου καὶ τῶν ἑξῆς διαδόχων βασίλειον, πόλις εὐερκεστάτη καὶ κατεσκευασμένη καλῶς τοῖς πᾶσι, καὶ μάλιστα ὑπὸ Μικίψα κ.τ.λ.* Polyb. xxxvii 3.

This inscr. is bilingual, Punic and Berber. It was written on the E. side of a mausoleum discovered among the ruins of the ancient city of Tucca (Thugga) in Eastern Numidia; see Schröd. 257. The Pun. characters closely resemble those of 38. The monument was built evidently for a Numidian person of consequence, and the inscr. gives the names of the masons, carpenters (?), and iron-founders who erected it.

L. 1. מצבת שאמבן For the relat. in this connexion cf. מעשן עצמם שיתנמלך *the urn of the bones of Y.* Lidzb. 435; and in Palm. cf. 141 קברא דנה די עתנתן. The use of the relat. ש in this inscr. is remarkable; it has quite taken the place of the genit.; see 39 2 *n.* אמבן This and the other pr. nn. in the inscr. (exc. in ll. 2. 7) are Berber; their pronunciation and significance are unknown.

L. 2. חבנם שאבנם *the builders of the stones*, cf. 20 A 4. Three chief masons are mentioned in ll. 2–4 and their assistants in l. 5. עברשתרת . . . עבארש for עבדעשתרת . . . עבדארש (45 7).

L. 4. ורסכן The prefix as in ורוסן 55 7.

L. 5. ובאזרת Prob. for ובעזרת *and with the help of*, cf. אם האזרת 14 3 *n.* (?) שלא . . The first letter is prob. the relat.

L. 6. החרשם *the workmen*, cf. 20 A 13. שיר Possibly = שיער *of wood*; cf. St. Aug. on Ps. 123 'quod Punici dicunt *iar*, non lignum, sed quando dubitant'; see Schröd. 19.

L. 7. הנסכם שברזל *the melters, founders, of iron*, cf. CIS i 67 4 f. נסך ברזל, and ib. 327 ff. נסך החרץ. בלל Pr. n., as in 55 5.

PHOENICIAN: NEO-PUNIC

The Neo-Punic inscrr. belong to the period extending from the destruction of Carthage (146 B.C.) prob. down to the first cent. A.D. They come from ancient sites in Algeria, Tunis, and Tripoli, countries which were formerly under the dominion of Carthage or in alliance with her. The change from the Pun. to the NPun. writing began, no doubt, in Carthage itself; it was accelerated when the Pun. characters were adopted by neighbouring populations of a different race (e.g. the Numidians). Outside N. Africa, NPun. inscrr. have been found in Sardinia (60) and Sicily (CIS i 134). In appearance they are very different from the Punic inscrr. of the preceding age; the character of the writing and language shows how great had been the break with the past. So long as Carthage stood, national instinct cherished the preservation of the Phoen. mother-tongue; but under the domination of Rome there was not the same interest in keeping up the old tradition. A more cursive form of writing was adopted for greater ease and rapidity. A few letters, like ט, ס, ע, פ, are little changed; ב, ר, כ are as a rule indistinguishable, being represented by mere strokes; כ, נ, ת are generally much alike; while א, ח, ת, ם, ש become greatly debased. Thus the reading of these inscrr. is often uncertain and difficult, and the difficulty is increased by the arbitrary and irregular nature of the spelling. The use of א and ע as vowel-letters is a characteristic feature, ע=ā, and א often=ō or ā, e.g. שענאת 58 2; these letters often take the place of ה and ח, e.g. אקבר for הקבר, עוע for חוא 58 7. 3; while there seems to have been a preference for ע over א, e.g. עבן for אבן, עוע for עוא, מענע for מענא 58, but אשרם for עשרם ib. The only inscr. which throws much light on contemporary history is that of Micipsa (57). How long the NPun. speech lasted is not exactly known; it was spoken by the common people in the time of St. Augustine (see Schröd. 36); but long before that Latin had taken its place for purposes of writing.

TUNIS

53. Tunis. NPun. 123. CIL viii 793. Berlin.

Dis manib[us] sacr[um]. Gadaeus Felicis fil[ius] pius vix[it] annis LXVI *hic sit[us] est.*
Secunda Secundi fil[ia] v[ixit] a[nnis]
Saturio et Gadaeus patri piissimo posuerunt.

1 גע[ד]עי בן פלכש בן פחלען אקילא
2 עוה שענא[ת] ש[אש]ם ושאש ושהקנד
3 ע בת שקנדע אש[ת]י עוע שענת
4 פהלא לאבענהם מת קבר שעטרי וגדעי
5 ע . תכבעבדמונ . אאפהעמתרעק . . אאתמ
6 בתהנמפהלאננצתנ עוע שת הנמ . . ובדמשית
7 הע . . . . ע . . . . שעטר . . . . אקבר בשלם

Gadai, son of Felix, son of FḤL'N Aquila (?), [2] lived sixty and six years. And Secunda,[3] daughter of Secunda, his wife, lived years. [4] Saturio and Gadai made it, a grave for their father deceased (?). [5] . . . [6] . . . lived . . . [7] . . . Saturio . . . the grave, in peace.

L. 1. גע[ד]עי Restored from the Latin; cf. the Pun. name גדי CIS i 300 5. פלכש Again CIS i 151 (Sardinia, NPun.). Cl.-Gan. reads פלכם, cf. 54 2 *n.*

L. 2. שענאת=שנת plur.; see 6 1 *n.*

L. 3. עוע Pf. 3 sing. m.=חוא. The number of years is left a blank, intended to be filled up after the mother's death.

L. 4. פהלא=פעלו, Euting *ZDMG* xxix (1875) 235 f. The termination of the 3 plur., however, is not usually written, and the א may be the suff. 3 sing. m., cf. נדרא 55 1. פעלא 57 11. רפיא 40 2 &c.; the suffix will then anticipate the obj. קבר. לאבענהם is apparently a unique form for the usual לאבנם; cf. the 3 plur. m. suff. with the verb in Mandaic, לנאטינהון; Nöldeke *Mand. Gr.* § 203. מת May be ptcp. of מות, but the reading is perhaps מן.

L. 6. Euting l. c. reads at the beginning בתהנם פחלא *their house* (i.e. grave) *they made*; but 'הנ may be read ה.

54. Tunis. NPun. 66.

1 טנא אבן ז לאחתמילכת בת בעמלק
2 רת אשת יעצאתען בן שעלדיא בעל
3 המכתערם וחוא שנת ששם וחמש
4 הנכת עבנת תחת אבן זת קברת

This stone is set up to Aḥath-milkath, daughter of Bo'-melqarth, wife of Y'Ṣ'TH'N, son of She'lidi, the citizen of Makta'rim: and she lived sixty and five years. She is laid to rest (?) ? under this stone she is buried (?).

This is one of four inscrr., NPun. 66. 67. 68. 69, which follow the same type. They are given by Schröd. 271 f.

L. 1. טנא Qal ptcp. pass. אחתמילכת Again in NPun. 68 1; cf. the forms חתמלכת, חמלכת, and see 40 2 *n.* בעמלקרת for 'ברמ; so in Pun., Euting *Carth.* no. 15, cf. 'במ NPun. 86 (Schröd. 267).

L. 2. יעצאתען Cf. יעסתען 55 4. According to the facsimile, the א here is not quite in the usual form; it may be כ, in which case יעצכתען will be the same name as יעשכתען in NPun. 68 and the bilingual 69 = IASVCTA in the Lat. transcription. שעלדיא So NPun. 69, transcribed SELIDIV (genit.); in 59 B 2 f. סלדיא. Cl.-Gan., *Rec.* iii 333 *n.*, reads ש here and ז in זת l. 4 as ס. בעל המכתערם So in NPun. 67. 69. For בעל *citizen* see 10 3 *n.* Under the Romans Maktar (now مكثر) appears as Colonia (or civitas) Aelia Aurelia Mactaris or Mactaritanorum, cf. CIL viii 677 (as rest.) &c. Maktar is in the neighbourhood of Thugga (52), and has yielded a good many NPun. inscrr., see 59, and Schröd. 65 f.

L. 3. 'וחוא ונ Cf. 53 2. 3.

L. 4. The words of this line are repeated with unimportant variations in each of the inscrr. of this group. Their precise meaning is not clear. If the forms הנכת עבנת . . . קברת are verbs, they may be pass. perf. 2 sing. fem. It is possible that הנכת may be connected with

√ נח *rest*, cf. נחת 16 2; the interchange of ת with ב, though questionable in Phoen. (38 6 *n*.), is less unlikely in NPun.; Schröd., 203, thus renders *thou art laid to rest* (הֻנַּחְתָּ Hof.). עבנת in NPun. would naturally be a variation of אבנת; Schröd. suggests that it is a denominative from אבן, *thou art covered with a stone* (עֻבַּנְתָּ Pual). Another interpretation (Ewald) is *thou art shrouded, covered*, cf. the Arab. خبن *fold* or *hide in a garment*, so خَبَنَتْهُ خَبُونٌ *he is dead*. This is very uncertain. קברת is explained as = קֻבַּרְתָּ; but in each case it is doubtful how the form is to be taken. אבן זת or סת Contrast אבן ז l. 1, and see p. 26, add. note ii.

ALGIERS

55. Altiburus (Medeîna). NPun. 124. Louvre.

1 לאדן בעל חמן באלתברש נדר אש נדרא עבדמלקרת כנש בן
כנסאען . . .
2 מעריש בן תברסן ושטמן בן יכסלתן ומסהבא בן לילעי וגגם בן שסיעת ו
3 מאגמע בן תברסן ויעצמזגר בן סבג ואדנבעל בן ילל וגזר בן כנזרמן
ומעריש
4 בן לבוא חעלגם בן שטוען ויעסתאן בן מסהבא וחברנם המזבח ו
5 נסמרן בנאת ואיספן עלת מקדשם בירח כרר שת בלל הזבח בן
. . גטען ב
6 שפטם מסהבא בן יזרם ועזרבעל בן ברך וס.כסלן בן זעזבל ומביו
הצפ . אש
7 על כמר ניעטמן וכהן לבעל חמן ורוסן בן ארש כא שמע קלם ברכם
8 אש העלא [כ]א עלת או מ[נ]חת במקדש
9 אש [עבד]מלך [שם] נדרא

To the lord Ba'al-ḥammān in Altiburus: the vow made by 'Abd-melqarth KNŠ, son of KNS''N . . . [2] Ma'rish, son of TBRSN, and ŠṬMN, son of YKSLTHN, and MSHB', son of LIL'I, and GGM, son of ŠSI'TH, and [3] M'GM', son of TBRSN, and Y'ṢMZGR, son of SBG, and Idni-ba'al, son of YLL, and GZR, son of KNZRMN, and Ma'rish, [4] son of LBU', and Z'LGM, son of ŠṬW'N, and Y'ST'N, son of MSHB', and their colleagues—the [*mis*[*r*]*aḥ*]; and [5] NSMRN (?), son of 'TH (?), and 'ISFN were over the sanctuaries; in the month KRR, the year of Balal the sacrificer, son of . . GṬ'N, under (?) [6] the suffetes MSHB', son of YZRM, and 'Azru-ba'al, son of Barik, and S . KSLN, son of Z'ZBL, and MBIU the augur, who [7] was over the priests of Neiṭman (?); and the priest of Ba'al-ḥammān (being) WRWSN, son of Arish; because he heard their voice and blessed them.

8-9 . . . .

L. 1. בעל חמן באלתברש See **24** 2 *n.*, and cf. בעל חמן בשרם בתם Costa 17 (from Cirta). Altiburus is now Medéïna, where the inscr. was found. The name occurs in different forms on Lat. monuments from the same place, e. g. municipium Althiburitanum, Altuburos &c. כנש coming between the pr. n. and the patronymic, is perhaps an official designation; cf. l. 5. **34**. **45** 9. Cl.-Gan. suggests a transcription of the Lat. CENS. = *censor*, though the title would be unusual; or an equivalent for *princeps* (*gentis*), *magister* (*pagi*), local officers mentioned in N. African inscrr. (CIL viii p. 1100 f.); *Rec.* iii 31 *n.* In CIS i 417 כנש ? = כנז is a pr. n.; and it may be only a surname here. כנסאען This and most of the pr. nn. which follow are Libyan (Berber); their vocalization is unknown. Most of them end in ן (? *ân*), cf. מכפען **57** 1. For צ, formerly read in this inscr., we ought to write ס, which hitherto has not been identified in NPun. In the newly discovered inscr. from Maktar (**59**), however, the two letters are clearly distinct, [illegible] = ס, [illegible] = צ, and in this inscr. the letter is nearer to the first than to the second of these forms. So Cl.-Gan. l. c. 333 *n.*

L. 2. מעריש l. 3, cf. מרש CIS i 390, perhaps = *Marissa* in Lat. inscrr. from Numidia, CIL viii p. 1028; Berger *Journ. As.* (1887) 462. מסתבא In Lat. *Massiva.* לילעי ? = Lat. *Laelius.*

L. 3. ארנבעל See **60** 1. סבג Prob. same name as זיבקם, זיבק **38** 5 *n.*, זיוג CIS i 341. כנזרמן looks like a name from Arabia, if כנז is the same as קנז Gen. 36 11. 15. 42, and רמן is the Arabian (Sabaean) deity *Rammânu* (Hommel *Süd-Ar. Chrest.* 60), CIS iv p. 203.

L. 4. לבוא Cf. לבא CIS i 147 5 and (?) Λεββαῖος Mt. 10 3; Sin. לבאי Eut. 421. חברנם See **42** 1 *n.* The *colleagues* in this case, however, are different from the חברם who formed the council of the suffetes at Carthage; here they have no connexion with suffetes (l. 6). המזבח gives a sense which is impossible in this context; we must read המזרח (**42** 16. **59** A 1. 16), in appos. to the suff. in חברנם (Cl.-Gan.). The מזרח was an institution, prob. of pre-Roman and native origin, peculiar to N. Africa. Its character is not exactly known; most likely it partook of the nature of a religious confraternity or administrative council, possibly of an industrial guild. Cl.-Gan. thinks its Roman equivalent was *curia*, frequently alluded to in N. African inscrr. At any rate there is ample evidence that Altiburus had a municipal organization under the Romans (CIL viii 1824 municipium althiburitanum), and the מזרח may have had something to do with it. Twelve members are mentioned here by name, the first with a title or special designation (כנש). These may correspond to the African *undecim primi*[1], with a president; it is clear that the members of the מזרח were superior to the חברם, who made up the rest of the corporation.

L. 5. ונסמרן בנאת ואיספן It is uncertain whether these are the names (בן את=?בנאת) of the commissioners in charge of the sanctuaries (cf. **46** 1. **42** 1), or verbs stating the manner in which the vow (l. 1) was carried out, e. g. by the restoration or embellishment of the temples. In the latter case, איספן may be Hif. (cf. איכרמא **59** A 13), and have the same meaning as the Hebr. ספן 1 K. 7 7. Jer. 22 14; no meaning suggests itself for the other words. בירח כרר Cf. **26** 2. בלל Perhaps rather יבלל l. 3, Cl.-Gan. הזבח For the year reckoned by the name of the *sacrificer* cf. **38** 6 *n.* and Costa 105 בן כנת אזבח ('son of Kenath the sacrificer'), Lidzb. *Eph.* i 40. At the end of the line, ב may be taken with שפטם, although the usual construction is בשת ש' **40** 2. **46** 1, or שפטם **45** 5; perhaps it is the last letter of the preceding name. It is worth noticing that *three* suffetes are mentioned here, as in **59** B 4 ff.; see **42** 1 *n.*

L. 6. ברך Often in Pun. inscrr., e. g. CIS i **444** 4. **597** 4 &c. **59** B 2; in Lat. *baric*, *baricas*, *baricio* &c. CIL viii p. 1020 d. הצפ. or חצף According to Berger l. c. *the seer*, *augur*=Hebr. צפה *watchman*. Cl.-Gan. proposes הספ[ר] *the scribe*. There is a space between פ and the foll. א; no trace of a letter appears in the facsimile given by Euting *ZDMG* xxix (1875) 237.

L. 7. אש על כמר ניעמטן may be rendered *who was over the priests of Neitman*, i. e. the Egyptian goddess Neith or Nît, a manifestation of Isis; כמר plur. constr. *priests*, as in Old Aram. **64** 1 *n.*, in Hebr. 2 K. **23** 5 &c. The reading, however, is not certain, and the letters may be grouped differently. Cl.-Gan. proposes כם בן יעמטן . . for the last two words, thus providing the patronymic of מביו after the name of his office (l. 1 *n.*), but suggests no definite sense for אש על כם (l. c. 32 *n.*). ורוסן The prefix ור' as in ורסכן **52** 4. בי=כא.

L. 8. This and the foll. line are written carelessly and in another hand; their connexion with the foregoing is not clear. אש העלא Prob. *who offered up*, Hif. pf. 3 sing. m. עלה=?עלת 'a burnt-offering or a meal-offering (**42** 14 &c.) in the sanctuary.'

L. 9. Apparently 'which 'Abd-milk vowed there.' נדרא Pf. 3 sing. m. with suff. 3 sing. f.

[1] The functions of the *xi primi* (CIL viii p. 1101) are obscure. See for the above suggestions Cl.-Gan. l. c. 34 f.

56. Jol (Shershel 1). NPun. 130. Louvre.

1 סכר . . א לאשת נעמתמהרת טנא ת המנצבת רש בעת
2 עבדאשמן בן עזרבעל לאמא לתעונת אחר אש פעל ציוען
3 להחים האש שלא עזרבעל הילד שחרבעל בען שקלן
4 אמא לשרת שנת חמשם באיחשבר לטהרת נכתבת
5 ונשמרא . אתמיקנא ואידרא לים . אם עשרת
6 כמשלם . . . . . עלא הנשכבת בת שמנם שת

The memorial . . . to the woman . . . . . The pillar was set up by Rosh, daughter [2] of ʿAbd-eshmun, son of ʿAzru-baʿal, to her mother Tʿwnth, after that a monument (?) had been made [3] for the living by her husband ʿAzru-baʿal . . . Shaḥar-baʿal, son of Šqln (?), [4] his (?) mother, to minister (?) fifty years in the island of Ḥashbar (?) . . . prescribed [5] and observed (?) . . . . and the island of Dara (?) . . . ten (?) [6] . . . . . . she who is laid to rest, being eighty years old.

L. 1. סכר See **9** 6 *n.* The word which follows may be ברא, but no suitable meaning can be found for it. נעמת Perhaps *the good*; the foll. letters may be read מהרת (Derenbourg, *Comptes Rendus* (1875) 259 ff., translates *intelligent*, lit. *quick*=מְהִירָה), מהבת, or מחת. טנא Qal pf. 3 sing. fem. ת=אית Cf. **57** 3. **60** 3 f. מנצבת Cf. CIS i 159 1=מצבת **15** 1. רש Here fem.; in **41** 2 the name is mas. בת=בעת.

L. 2. לאמא=לְאִמָּהּ. פעל Qal pf. 3 sing. mas. ציוען Perhaps=צִיּוּן 2 K. 23 17; but the reading is uncertain.

L. 3. להחים Apparently=לַחַיִּים, cf. להרעת=לְרעת **57** 7. להרבת=לְרבת **60** 3, *for*, i. e. *among*, *the living*, cf. מצבת בחים **18** 1 *n.* האש Subj. of פעל l. 2. שלא=אֲשֶׁר לָהּ, cf. **57** 7. 9 f. (mas.). הילד Reading and sense doubtful. שחרבעל *whom B. seeks*; cf. שְׁחַרְיָה 1 Ch. 8 26. בען=בן. שקלן Apparently a pr. n., as in NPun. 76 5.

L. 4. The meaning of this and the foll. lines cannot be made out. Neither Euting, *ZDMG* xxx (1876) 285 f., nor Derenbourg, l. c., has anything satisfactory to propose. אמא Apparently=אִמּוֹ. לשרת ? Piel inf.; לשבת may be read. באיחשבר, like אידרא l. 5, has been taken as the name of an island (אי); cf.

אינצם **39** 1. Derenbourg explains חשבר as = Ἑσπέρα, which he supposes was the name of a small island in the lake Tritonis with a temple of Aphrodite upon it, near the harbour of Hesperides in Cyrene, mentioned by Strabo p. 710, ed. Müll. לטהרת *for the cleansing* (Derenb.); but this meaning is doubtful. נכתבת, like ונשמרא l. 5 and הנשכבת l. 6, appears to be a Nif. form.

L. 5. Derenb. reads ונשמרא ראת מי קנא and translates *and she is kept from seeing the waters of Qana*; but ראת is uncertain, and מי קנא may = מִקְנֶה (Lidzb.). עשרת Meaning doubtful: *ten* does not suit the context.

L. 6. הנשכבת Cf. משכב of the *grave*, **5** 4 *n*. שת is sing., שנת l. 4 plur.; see **6** 1 *n*.

57. **Jol (Shershel 2).** Louvre.

1 מיקדש קנאם חי חים מכפזן מלך מׄשליים
2 המילל מישר ארצת רבת ממלכאת חשב נעם
3 לא טנא ת המאש זת . . הׄאחבׄעלא קברא יעזם
4 בן ישגגזן בן בגאת בן מונזן מיקם אלם
5 זכי כרׄרׄ עלגמא . . . תמא אדׄרׄאכמאת כנםׄ
6 ות אכהנים אש עלמׄים כלא נעׄוׄכלא למח[יא]
7 ת . נם עלם עכ . . ת לח . . א . להרעת שלא . . .
8 ושעותם . . בעל . . ל . . א . . מא השם . . . .
9 רׄבׄא שלא בכל חות בנא . [מ]מעא . . .
10 רׄצאת המחקׄת שלא תבׄנם רב . . .
11 פׅעלא ארש בן עבדא . . .

L. 1. מיקדש קנאם *sanctuary of QN'M*; cf. the beginning of **42**. קנאם occurs again in NPun. 2 (Lidzb. 434) · מעל · מעקר הרעץ לקנאם ולאחיא *Mo'qar the sculptor* (?) *made* (*this*) *for QN'M and for his brothers* (or *life*?). Berger suggests that קנאם is the Egypt. deity *Ḥnûm* (*Inscr. néop. de Cherchell* (1889) 3 f.); but the opinion of Egyptologists is against the identification. חי חים *the life of* *life*; cf. לענת עז חים 28 1. מכמזן מלך משליים *Mikipsan, king of the Massilians*, i. e. of Numidia; for the pr. n. in ץ *dn* see 55 1 *n*. This can be none other than the Micipsa who appears in the history of the Roman occupation of Carthage. He was the third son of Massinissa (51 3 *n*.), and succeeded to the kingdom after the premature death of his two elder brothers. An illegitimate son of his was the notorious Jugurtha (John of Antioch *Fr. Hist. Gr.* iv 560; Diod. Sic. xxxiv 35). The seat of his kingdom was Cirta, but he was buried at or near Jol[1], where this inscr. was found; it must have been set up shortly after his death in 118 B.C. This reference to a historical personage, whose date can be fixed, is unique among the NPun. inscrr. at present known. A specimen of Numidian coinage of this period, in the British Museum, bears on the obverse the letters מן, on the reverse הת, i. e. possibly מכמזן הממלכת *Mikipsan the king*[2]; so Berger, l. c. 10, who gives an illustration of the coin.

L. 2. המילל Lit. *who is to be extolled*, an epithet of the king, probably Pual ptcp. מְיֻלָּל. In Hebr. ילל is used in Hif. *to howl*. מישר א׳ ר׳ *sovereign of broad lands*; מישר Piel ptcp. of ישר, or perhaps from שרר. ממלכאת = ממלכת *prince*; see 3 2 *n*. חשב נעם *who devises good*; cf. the Gk. title Εὐμένης.

L. 3. The previous clause from מכמזן is a casus pendens, resumed by לא=לו: *Mikipsan . . . to him Ya'asam set up this statue.* אית=ת 56 1 *n*. מאש Cf. 60 4, where the Lat. version gives *statuam*. מאאש CIS i 151 2 is apparently the same word; the etymology is unknown. קברא *his grave*. The three letters preceding are עלא ? *over him*. The erection of a statue (if the rendering be correct) over a grave was unusual; Berger compares CIL viii 211 30 *statuam posuit* (over a mausoleum), but notices that the stone which bears the inscr. does not look as if it had once formed the base of a statue.

L. 4. מזנת Possibly the Pun. form of the name Massinissa, written משתנצן on coins. מיקם אלם A title found in CIS i 227. 260–262 &c. and in a new Carth. inscr., *Rép.* i no. 13; it is prob. the equivalent of *praetor sacrorum, praefectus sacrorum* in Lat. inscrr.

L. 5. In this and the foll. lines only a word here and there can be translated. חמא may = אחמא which seems to be a pr. n. in CIS i 151 3.

[1] The burial-place of the Numidian princes was in the neighbourhood of Jol; Pomponius Mela i 6 30–1 Iol ad mare aliquando ignobilis, nunc quia Iubae regia fuit et quod Caesarea vocitatur illustris . . . ultra monumentum commune regiae gentis.

[2] Cf. the legend on coins of Juba יובעי הממלכת or מיובעי הממלכת, of Bocchus בקש הממלכת, and of Syphax ספק הממלכת (Berger l. c.).

L. 6. ואת חכהנים = ות אכהנים. פְּי לו = ? כלא. למחיא *during his life-time* (Berger); but the form is uncertain.

L. 7. עלם ? *eternity.* להרעת Cf. **56** 3 *n.*, ? *for the good pleasure which was his*; see **88** 4.

L. 9. רבא ? *his chief.* בבל חות בנא ? *during all the life of his son* (Berger).

L. 10. חמחקת ? *the inscriptions*, from חקק.

L. 11. The name of the artist who *made it.*

58. Gelma. NPun. 24. Louvre.

1 עבן ז מענע לש
2 בלת בת מעלל עו
3 ע שענת אש
4 רם ועמש א
5 שת משיכעתן בן[?]
6 בנריעל

This stone is set up to ŠBLTH, daughter of Ma'lal; she lived twenty-five years; wife of MŠIK'THN, son (?) of BNRI'L.

L. 1. עבן=אבן, see p. 140. מענע=מענא Qal. ptcp. pass.

L. 2. שבלת Perhaps=*ear of wheat*, Gen. 41 5 ff. עוע=הוא, cf. **53** 3.

L. 4. עשרם וחמש=אשרם ועמש.

L. 5. משיכעתן בנ[ן] So Lidzb.; but Schröder p. 270 reads משיכעתה, and shows ה in the facsimile, xvii 8.

L. 6. בנריעל If Schröder's reading is followed, this will be בן ריעל.

59. Maktar. Discovered 1892.

A

i

1 המזרח אש לדרת אש בנא מקדש חצרת
2 פחנת קרשם מחזת שתעת אל עמת

3 עטרת אדראת לא ולעמא ישב ארמת
4 לאלם הקידש לשאת אחת שמם בסובׄ
5 מלך חטר מיסכר רזן ימם בעל חרדת
6 על גברתם כעתבתי יתנתׄיׄ   שבעת

ii

7 סמל מרנׄ... חסיד תם . לתא עלם עבד
8 ירד בעמק הלח ואחרסת... תעת ארדת
9 ראשא צלק אתם ליטא . דל עק. צב חפערת
10 ש חרץ דערכן ולנאחן יתן נכׄתחת
11 כילן באשׁרלב פעלן ביתן   שבעת

iii

12 שׁמאת המורח אש
13 איכרמא תהמנחת
14 קרא לם מעלא מתא
15 למרתתׄ. מעׄורת

iv

16 רב מורח סהלכני בן מאנזמער
17 מעסיר בן פלכעי
18 בעלשמע בן מעסקלת
19 קערטא בן סלסמין

v

20 סהלכני בן יסתען
21 שעפרגם בן דבער
22 מתנבעל בן ברכבעל

vi

23 רופא בן מעסתיבער
24 מתנבעל בן בעות
25 בעליתן בן בובעׄ.
26 יעסכתען בן בע... ל.

vii

27 יערכני בן ארש
28 מתנבעל בן סלכני
29 ראסתיטטא בן ר..י
30 אי.נע בן מערשמא
31 סלכני בן מעסקלת
32 א... בן ארשא

viii

33 כעשא בן בעליתן
34 לקי בן געלגסת
35 עבדמלקרת בן בעליתן
36 שעפרגם בן ברכבעל
37 בעסא בן אררבעל
38 ..רולני בן מעסיסען

ix

39 ברכבעל בן דבער
40 כס.פנל בן בעלשלך
41 יסכתען בן בעליתן
42 בעלשמע בן מערוסא
43 מעסקלת
44 ברכבעל בן געגירת

x

45 ראגעטא בן הכהנת
46 אורמען בן יסתענת
47 עומזגוער בן מעסירחן

i

The *misrah* of . . . which built sanctuary, courts, [2] also a chamber (?) for the holy things, lights (?), these columns (?) at the side of (?) [3] a rich cornice (?), for themselves and their people (?) who dwell in the land :—[4] To the holy god . . . . [5] Milk-ḥaṭar-miskar, prince of the seas (?), lord of terror. [6] Upon . . . I, Yathan- . . wrote it . . .

ii

. . . .

iii

[12] Names of the *misrah* which [13] defrayed the offering. [14] Read them from top to bottom (?) [15] . . . . help.

This and the two following inscrr., B and C, were discovered in 1892 on the walls of a temple at Maktar (54 2). They were first published by Berger *Mémoire sur la grande inscription dédicatoire* . . .

à Maktar (1899); they have been treated also by Lidzbarski *Eph.* i 45–52 (1900), by Cl.-Gan. *Rec.* iii § 57 and § 3 (1900), and by Halévy *Rev. Sém.* ix (1901) 268–287. The great inscription (A) consists of ten columns, and falls into two parts: (1) Coll. i and ii, the dedication of the temple and its appurtenances, (2) Coll. iii–x, the names of those who took part in the dedication. The writing of this inscr. is, on the whole, clear and well preserved; but the meaning of Coll. i and ii is exceedingly obscure. It is noteworthy that the letters ב, ד, ר are written almost in their ancient form. Inscr. A probably belongs to an earlier date than B and C.

L. 1. המזרח ll. 12. 16. C 1. The word has been met with already in **42** 16. **55** 4. From this inscr. it is clear that the *mizraḥ* or *mazraḥ* was some kind of local council or association, in this case consisting of 32 members, including a president (רב מזרח l. 16). It was certainly a native institution, no doubt tolerated under the Roman domination; Cl.-Gan. suggests that its nearest equivalent in Latin would be *curia* or *ordo decurionum*, terms which occur in the inscrr. from N. Africa, l. c. § 3. In each instance the *mizraḥ* is mentioned in connexion with some religious act; so it may have been a religious rather than a secular association. אש לדרת *of* DRTH, perhaps a technical term describing the *mizraḥ*, ? *of the habitations*, cf. Arab. دَار *house*, Is. 38 12. If דרת were the name of a place (Lidzb. l. c., cf. דאר **5** 19), we should expect the simple prep. ב rather than אש ל; cf. **24** 2 *n*. חצרת Prob. plur. abs. To construe חצרת as a genit. after מקדש would not make good sense; the two words are to be taken ἀσυνδέτως. Cf. חצר **33** 2 f.

L. 2. פחנת Lidzb. suggests that פ=אף, as ש=אש, and ת=אית in NPun. Then חנת (cf. p. 337) may=חָנוּת, חֲנֻיּוֹת *cells* Jer. 37 16, as having an *arched* or *curved* roof; cf. Aram. ܡܫܢܝܬܐ *vaulted room*, √ חנת = lit. *bend, curve*. Hence חנת קדשם may mean *a vaulted chamber for the sacred vessels*. מחזת Perhaps = מֶחֱזָה *light, window* 1 K. 7 4 f. As the previous words seem to denote parts of the sanctuary, Cl.-Gan. renders שתעת *pillars*, Hebr. שָׁתוֹת, and אלעמת *porches, propyla*, cf. Hebr. אוּלָם. In the case of the last word, however, the rendering is made doubtful by the fact that there is a space on the stone before and after אל (facsimile in Berger l. c.); hence Lidzb. renders מחזת שתעת אל עמת *a place for the auspices* (?) *of Tat, the god of the community*. He takes תעת as = חנת rather than the Egypt. Thoth (Berger), and for עמת compares CIS i 263 עשתרת [=איש] אש בעמת אש. 264 אש בעם בת מלקרת. It may be doubted whether תעת could be substituted for the familiar חנת. Taking שחעת as = *pillars*, it is possible that אל = *these* and עמת = *beside*, Hebr. לְעֻמַּת, cf. Ex. 25 27. 1 K. 7 20. Eze. 40 18. The deity to whom the dedication is made does not appear till l. 4.

L. 3. עטרת אדראת *a crown of splendour* or *a splendid cornice*; cf. 'cum ornamentis suis' in Lat. inscrr. from this region. לא ולעמא The suffixes may refer to המזרח, *for themselves and their people*, cf. 'ad ornandam patriam' in N. African inscrr., or to חעת אל עמת if these words contain the name of a goddess. ארמת In this connexion ארץ might be expected.

L. 4. לאלם הקידש *to the holy god* = לֵאלֹהִים הַקָּדוֹשׁ; *the god of the sanctuary* would be אלן המקדש, cf. לאלן אקדש Costa 31 (Constantine) in *Eph.* i p. 39; see 83 6 *n.* No certain meaning can be given to the words which follow. שמם may = *heaven*. The last word of the line is prob. בסוב. The distinction between ס and צ (חצרת l. 1. צב l. 9. חרץ l. 10) is clear in this inscr.; see 55 1 *n.*

L. 5. מלך חטר מיסכר The name of the deity to whom the sanctuary was dedicated. The deity seems to have been a compound one (cf. מלכעשתרת 10 3), formed out of Punic and Egyptian elements, *Milk-ḥaṭar-miskar*. The temple of חטר מסכר is mentioned in CIS i 253 f. חטר is the Egypt. god Hathor, and מסכר is either an Egypt. word or Punic; see 7 1 *n.* The epithets of the deity describe him as רזן ימם i.e. *ruler of the seas* or *days* (רֹזֵן Jud. 5 3. Ps. 2 2 &c.) and בעל חרדת i.e. *lord of terror*(*s*). A Lat. dedication to Saturn has been found in the temple near to this inscr.; and it is not unlikely that Milk-ḥaṭar-miskar was a deity with the same character and attributes as Saturn. A number of votive steles to Ba'al-ḥammān, found at Maktar, exhibit the fish in various forms, pointing to the worship of a marine deity.

L. 6. על נברתם ? meaning. After נ a letter has been erased on the stone. The words which follow may be a remark of the mason: כעתבתי prob. = כְּתַבְתִּי; . . יתנ (יתנתי ?) is perhaps a pr. n. שבעת, as in l. 11, is separated by a space; its meaning is not apparent. Lidzb. suggests בעת+ש *agreement, order*; see 42 1 *n.*

Column ii is exceedingly obscure. It seems to specify the dedication of an image of the god.

L. 7. The first word is clearly סמל *image, statue*; Cl.-Gan., however, suggests that it = שמאל *on the left*. . . . מרנ Cf. the pr. nn. beginning with מר, מרברך, מריחי 19 3 *n.* The next two words possibly = חָסִיד תָּם *kind, perfect*, a description of the god, to which עלם, or אעלם, *of the world*, may also belong. עבר is perhaps the first part of a pr. n.; there seems to be a trace of letters after it in the facsimile. Lidzb. thinks that the particulars of the dedication of the סמל begin here; Cl.-Gan. reads על מעבר *on the west.*

L. 8. ירד Perhaps a verb, *brought down* (Ifil); בעמק *in the valley*; חלת? = לֻחֹת *tablets* of stone (Ex. 34 1 &c.), or *planks* of wood (Ex. 27 8 &c.), or *plates* of metal (1 K. 7 36), in a collective sense. Cl.-Gan. takes ירד as Qal ptcp., and, following out his view of the general sense, thinks that ירד בעמק refers to a part of the temple which 'descended into the valley.' He makes a new clause begin with חלת. ואחרסת? the same word as the obscure חרץ 45 4, which is some part of a temple. תעת אררת. ?=א' שתעת (l. 2) *splendid pillars* (?).

L. 9. ראשא *his* or *her head*, or *capital?*

L. 10. Cl.-Gan. reads חף ערת ש חרץ, and supposes that the words refer to 'overlaying with gold.' He compares the biblical חפה 2 Ch. 3 5 ff., and ערת in 3 5. ח' ועדכן The rendering *gold of the daric*, cf. דרכנם (for דרכמנם) 33 3, i.e. gold of standard quality, is pronounced impossible by experts in ancient coinage; see Lidzb. *Eph.* i 177.

L. 11. כילן ... פעלן? *we have finished* (Piel) ... *we have made*; Halévy renders 'we have finished our work with happiness of heart (בְּאֹשֶׁר לֵב). By Yathon. Shib'ath.' ביתן The word בת *house* is not written with the vowel letter in Pun. שבעת l. 6 *n.*

L. 13. איכרמא Berger explains by the Arab. أكرم *largiri, they paid the cost of*; this makes good sense. תהמנחת i.e. אית המנחת.

L. 14. קרא Prob. imperat. לם i.e. שמאת l. 12; Hal. takes לם as = לָמָּה *what.* מעלא מתא Lit. *upwards, downwards* (?), מתא? = Hebr. מַטָּה; cf. 5 11 f. According to Hal. מתא = מְאתָא; he renders the line, 'Read what has been adduced (lit. brought) above.'

L. 15. למרת Lit. *according to the measure* (?). מעזרת Apparently a noun from עזר *help.*

Columns iv–x. A list of the members of the *mizraḥ*, headed by the president (l. 16). The names are mostly Numidian; some are Punic, some Latin. The Latin names, it will be noticed, belong to the sons, the native ones to the fathers. This no doubt indicates that the younger generation was fast becoming latinized, a process which has become complete in other NPun. inscrr. from Maktar, where the Latin names are followed by a Latin genealogy, e.g. Marcus son of Gaius Canuleius, Publius son of Valerius Nobilis; these last belong, therefore, to a later age. With regard to the Numidian names, the pronunciation of which is in most cases unknown, the sibilant ס is characteristic, and the endings *ân* and *ath*; the latter are not sounded in the Latin transcriptions, e.g. Jasuktan = Jasucta, Galgusath = Gulussa, &c. In the Punic forms of the Latin names *a* is represented by ע, *e* and *o* by א; the ending *us* becomes א, *ius* is dropped (Berger 36).

L. 17. פלכעי Cl.-Gan. conjectures *Felicus*, *Felicio*, *Felicius*.

L. 19. קערטא = *Quartus*; or קעפטא = *Capito*.

L. 20. יסתען ? = *Islantius* (Algerian). Cl.-Gan. reads יסתענת l. 46.

L. 23. רופא = *Rufus*.

L. 26. יעסכתען Transcribed in Lat. *Jasucta* (NPun. 69, Schröd. p. 272).

L. 29. ראסתיטטא = *Restitutus*. L. 30. מערשטא = מרשטע.

L. 31. מעסקלת ? *Maskulath*, cf. *Masculus*.

L. 32. For ארשא Cl.-Gan. reads ארשם.

L. 33. כעשא ? = *Cassus*.

L. 34. לקי ? = *Lucius*. מלגסת Transcr. *Gulussa*.

L. 45. ראגעטא = *Rogatus*. הכהנת ? *the priestess*.

B

1 נבנא [כ]א המקדש ם לעטר מסכר

2 בניא יפתען בן יפשר וברך בן סלדי

3 א ומתנבעל בן ברך ומתנבעל בן בעליתן

4 .חסנן ש המקם שפטם עומזגוער

5 בן תתעי ומנדסען בן שבעטן מסולי

6 ומסיגרען בן קפסי........שמע קלם

This sanctuary was built here to ʻAṭar-miskar. It was built by Ift'an, son of Ifshar, and Barik, son of Selidi', and Muttun-ba'al, son of Barik, and Muttun-ba'al, son of Ba'al-yathon ? . of the place; the suffetes being ʻUmzgu'ar, son of Tat'ai, and Mnds'an, son of Shb'aṭn, ? and Msigr'an, son of Qfsi . . . . heard their voice.

L. 1. נבנא is not distinct in the facsimile. ם=ז. עטר מסכר Cf. A 5.

L. 2. בניא Pf. 3 pl. with suff.; cf. 52 2. ברך See 55 6 *n*. שעלדיא=סלדיא *Selidiv* NPun. 69 1 (Schröd. p. 272).

L. 4. חסם Cf. חסנם 40 1 where it is possibly a transliteration of *sociorum*. שפטם Three suffetes are mentioned here, as in 55 6. עומנועד Cf. A 47.

L. 5. מסולי Berger suggests that this is an ethnic form, meaning 'a man of Mascula' (in Numidia) CIL viii 2568 &c.; cf. חשלכי 60 2. אשקלני 32 1 &c.

C

1 המזרח אס....
2 גד היסם נדער נדרא אש ל....
3 שלא תתהא לאב ברכת מל[כ]....
4 הנדער קלא שלא עזר....

The *misraḥ*.... to Gad of the heavens (?) vowed their vow which.... his ? to the father of blessing, king (?).... the vow; his voice helped....

L. 1. המזרח A 1. אס ?=אש.

L. 2. גד היסם Perhaps rather גד השמם; for גד see 27 3 *n*. השמם corresponds with the N. African *Caelestis*. The whole expression finds a remarkable parallel in *Fortunae Caelestis sacrum* CIL viii 6943 from Cirta (Lidzb.). נדער נדרא The first is a verb, the second a noun with suff. 3 sing. m. agreeing with המזרח.

SARDINIA

60. Sulci. CIS i 149. Museum of Cagliari.

Himilconi Idnibalis . . . quei hanc aedem ex s[enatus] c[onsulto] fac[iundam] coeravit Himilco f[ilius] statuam [dedit].

1 [ח]מלכת בן · ארנבעל · בן · חמלכת
2 הפרט על · מי · טבארשא · השלכי
3 לבנאת · תהמקדש זת · להרבת לאלת
4 טינא תהמאש זת · בנא · חמלכת

Ḥimilkath, son of Idni-ba'al, son of Ḥimilkath . . . . to build this sanctuary to the lady Elath: his son Ḥimilkath dedicated this statue.

This inscr. probably belongs to the first cent. B. C.; it is among the earliest NPun. inscrr. known.

L. 1. חמלכת See 40 2 *n*. ארנבעל 45 6. 55 3, pronounced *Idnibal* (Lat. transcr.).

L. 2. The first four words prob. correspond to *qui ex senatus consulto curavit* in the Lat. version; but their exact meaning is unknown. טבארשא has a certain resemblance to τοπαρχία. השלכי Prob. *Sulcitanus, the man of Sulci*, cf. CIL 7518. The final letter is most likely י; for the form cf. חלובי *the man of Lycia* CIS i 45, and the names בזנתי Βυζάντιον, כתי Κίτιον.

L. 3. לבנאת=לבנות, implying some word meaning *curavit* in l. 2. להרבת Cf. לחים=להחים 58 3 *n*.; for רבת see 3 2 *n*. אלת Cf. 50 1 *n*. CIS i 243. 244 כהן אלת; in Aram. *Ilât* or *Allât*, see in Nab. 80 4 *n*. The Phoen. form אלת is the fem. of אל, or perhaps rather of אלן; in the latter case the vowel of the second syllable may have been long (Nöldeke *ZDMG* xlii 472)[1].

L. 4. טינא looks like the Piel of טנא, cf. כילן (?) 59 A 11. מאש The Lat. version shows that this must mean *statue*; cf. 57 3. בנא= בְּנוֹ.

[1] The identification of אלת with Ἑλλωτία—ἡ Εὐρώπη τὸ παλαιὸν ἐκαλεῖτο, ὅτι οἱ Φοίνικες τὴν Παρθένον Ἑλλωτίαν καλοῦσι *Etym. Magn.* col. 332; Ἑλλωτίς· Ἀθηνᾶ οὕτω καλουμένη, ἐτιμᾶτο ἐν Κορίνθῳ καὶ ἑορτὴ Ἑλλωτία ib. 333—is rejected by Nöldeke l. c. The forms Ἑλλωτίς, Ἑλλωτία are prob. genuine Greek.

ARAMAIC

NORTH SYRIA

61. Zenjirli: Hadad. First half of viii cent. B.C. Berlin.

1 אנך פנמו · בר · קרל · מלך · יארי · זי · הקמת · נצב · זן · להדד · בעלמי

2 קמו · עמי · אלהו · הדד · ואל · ורשף · ורכבאל · ושמש · ונתן · בידי ·
הדד · ואל ·

3 ורכבאל · ושמש · ורשף · חטר · חלבבה · וקם · עמי · רשף · פמו · אחז ·

4 ביד....הא · פלח..· ומו · אשא[ל · מן ·]אלהי · יתנו · לי · ושנם · חוו ·

5 ....ל. ארק · שערי · האל ·

6 ....ארק · חטי וארק שמי

7 וארק · ....אז · ב. רת...ימי ו.....י · יעבדו · ארק · וכרם ·

8 שם · יש[ב]..........ם · פנמו · גם · ישבת · על · משב · אבי · ונתן ·
הדד · בידי

9 חטר · חל[בבה ·]........ת · חרב · ולשן · מן · בית · אבי · ובימי · גם ·
אכל · ושתא · יאדי

10 ובימי · יתמר......קי · לנצב · קירת · ולנצב · זררי · ולבני · כפירי ·
חלבב...יקח ·

11 אש · רעיה · ויתר · הדד · [ו]אל ורכבאל · ושמש · וארקרשף · וכברו ·
נתנה · לי · ואמן . כרת

12 בי · ובימי · חלבת...ת. יהב לאלהי · ומת · יקחו · מן · ידי · ומה ·
אשאל · מן · אלהי · מת · יתר

13 לי · וארקו · ו......· קרל · אלהי · מת · פלו · נתן · הדד · מת · ל..תי
קרני · לבנא · ובחלבבתי ·

14 נתן · מת · הד[ד ·....ל]בנא · פבנית · מת · ת[ה]קמת · נצב · הדד · זן ·
ומקם · פנמו · בר · קרל · מלך ·

15 יאדי · עם · נצב · חד . . מן מן · בני · יאחז[· חט]ר · וישב · על · משבי ·
ויסעד · אברו · ויזבח ·

16 הדד · זן . . . . י . . . י . . נשי · ויזבח · . . . . . ם · . . א יזבח · הדד · ויזכר ·
אשם · הדד · או ·

17 . א · פא · יאמר · [תאכ]ל נבש · פנמו · עמך · ותש[תי · נ]בש פנמו
עמך · עד יזכר · נבש · פנמו · עם

18 [ה]דד · י . . . . זבחה זא · פתכ . . . . . [י]רקי · בה · שי · להדד ולאל ·
ולרכבאל · ולשמש

19 . . . . . . נ . [פ]נמו . . . ב . . . . . . י · ק . זא · פב . . . ה · והושבת · בה ·
אלהי · ובחלבבתה · חנאת

20 . . . . . . נתנו · לי · זרע · חבא . . . . י . . אם . . . · בני · יאחז · חטר ·
וישב · על · משבי מלך

21 על · יאדי · ויסעד · אברו · ויזבח [· הדד · זן · ויזכ]ר · אשם · פנמו ·
יאמר · תאכל · נבש פ[נ]מ[ו ·]

22 עם · הדד · ותשתי · נבש · פנמו · עם · ה[ד]ד · הא · . . . . חהן ·
זבחה · ואל · ירקי · בה ומז ·

23 ישאל · אל · יתן · לה הדד · והדד · חרא · ליתכה . . . .
אל · יתן · לה · לאכל · ברגז

24 ושנה · למנע · מנה · בלילא · ודלח · נתן · לה . . י . . . . איח . .
מודדי · מומת . . תי

25 יאחז · חטר · ביאד[י] · וישב · על · משבי · וימל[ך · . . . . וישל]ח · ידה ·
בחרב · ב . . . . . תי · או ·

26 . . . . חמס · אל · יהרג · או · ברגז · או · על · א . . . . . א · ל . . . י ·
מומת · או · על · קשתה · או · על · אמרתה ·

27 . . . . חה · ירשי · שחת · באשר · חד · איחיה · או ·
באשר · חד · מודדיה · או · באשר ·

28 חדה · איחתנ̇ה......... ירשי · שחת · ינגב איחיה · זכרי · ויקם ·
ותה · במצעה · מת · נשה
29 יאמר · אחכם · השחת · והנ...... א · ידיה · לאלה · אבה · נשה ·
יאמר · הן · אם · שמת · אמרת · אל · בפם ·
30 זר · אמר · קם · עיני · או · דלח · או...... י · בפם · אנשי צרי · פר̇גו ·
זכר · הא · לתגמרו · איחה
31 זכרו · פלכתשה · באבני · והנו ר......... ר̇ן · איחתה פלכתשנה ·
באבני · והנו · לו · שחת ·
32 באשרה · ותלעי · עינך · בא. בב̇......... על · קשתה או · על ·
גברתה · או · על · אמרתה ·
33 או · על · נרבה · את · פא · ישרה · ב.. ר........... ו · תהרגה ·
בחמ. · [או ·] בחמא · או ·
34 תחק · עליה · או · תאלב · אש · זר להרגה · י.........
מ̇ו............

I am Panammu, son of QRL, king of Ya'di, who have set up this statue to Hadad in my ? [2] There stood by me the god (?) Hadad and El and Reshef and Rekub-el and Shamash, and Hadad and El [3] and Rekub-el and Shamash gave into my hand the sceptre of ?; and Reshef stood by me; and whatsoever I take [4] in hand . . . and whatsoever I as[k of] the gods they give me, and ? ? [5] . . . . . . a land of barley ? [6] . . . . . . a land of wheat and a land of garlic, [7] and a land . . . . . . they till the land and vineyards; [8] there dwel[t] . . . of Panammu. Moreover I sat upon the seat of my father, and Hadad gave into my hand [9] the sceptre of ? . . . sword and slander from my father's house. And in my days Ya'di (?) ? did both eat and drink. [10] And in my days ? . . . to establish (?) cities and to establish (?) ., and for the sons of villages (?) ? . . takes (?) [11] each (?) ? and Hadad [and] El and Rekub-el and Shamash and Arqu-reshef did abundantly (?)

give greatness to me, and surety ? [12] with me. And in my days ? . ? to the gods, and indeed (?) they receive from my hands, and what I ask from the gods they have indeed (?) abundantly granted (?) [13] to me, and ? . . QRL, the gods indeed (?), and if Hadad gave indeed (?) to . he called me to build, and in my ? [14] Had[ad] gave indeed (?) . [to] build; and I built indeed (?), and set up this statue of Hadad, and the place of Panammu, son of QRL, king [15] of Ya'di, together with a statue . . Whoever (?) of my sons shall hold the [scept]re, and sit upon my seat and grow strong (?) and sacrifice [16] to this Hadad . . . and sacrifice . . . sacrifice to Hadad, and make mention of the name of Hadad, or [17]. shall say, May the soul of Panammu [ea]t with thee, and may the [s]oul of Panammu drin[k] with thee !—shall moreover remember the soul of Panammu with [18] [Ha]dad . . this his sacrifice . . may he look [f]avourably upon him ? to Hadad and to El and to Rekub-el and to Shamash [19] . . . [Pa]nammu . . . this . . . and I made the gods dwell in it, and in his ? I reposed (?) [20] . . they have given me a seed . . . my son shall hold the sceptre, and sit upon my seat as king [21] over Ya'di, and grow strong (?) and sacrifice [to this Hadad and remem]ber the name of Panammu (and) say, May the soul of Panammu eat [22] with Hadad, and may the soul of Panammu drink with that Ha[d]ad . . . his sacrifice let him not look favourably upon it, and whatsoever [23] he shall ask let not Hadad give him; and let Hadad pour out wrath upon him . . . suffer him not to eat, in anger, [24] and withhold sleep from him by night, and terror (?) ? to him . . . kinsman (?) . my friend (?) put to death (?) . [25] shall hold the sceptre in Ya'd[i], and shall sit upon my seat and reig[n . and pu]t his hand to the sword . or [26] . . . ? let him not slay either in anger or by . . . put to death (?) either by his bow or by his order [27] . . . shall allow to destroy after one of his kinsmen (?) or after one of his friends (?) or after [28] one of his kinswomen (?) . . . he allow to destroy, his kinsmen (?) steal my memorial, and set it up in the midst thereof (?) indeed (?) ? [29] shall say, Your brother has destroyed (?) . . his hands to the god of his father ? shall say, If (?) ? I have put these (?) orders into the mouth [30] of a stranger, say thou (?) my eye was dim or terrified or . . in the mouth of adversaries, and behold! (?) it is a memorial (?), so that ye make his kinsman (?) discontinue [31] ? and let him crush him with stones; and behold! (?) . . . his kinswoman (?), and let him crush her (?) with stones; and behold! (?) if he have destroyed [32] after him, and thine eye be wearied (?) . . . by his bow or by his might or by his order [33] or by his instigation (?), thou (?) also ? . . . thou shalt slay him ? [or] in wrath, or [34] shalt write (?) concerning him, or teach a stranger to kill him . . .

Zenjirli (زنجيرلو) is a small village in NW. Syria, rather more than half way between Antakiyeh (Antioch) and Marash. This inscription was found in 1890 at Gerjin (كرجين), half an hour NE. of Zenjirli. It is carved on a colossal statue of the god Hadad; the writing, like that of **62** and **63**, is in relief, and belongs to the archaic type represented by the Moabite Stone. The contents show that this inscr. is earlier than **62** and **63**, which date from the time of Tiglath-pileser iii (745–727 B.C.); moreover, in the latter inscrr. the Aramaic character of the dialect is more strongly marked[1].

Part i. ll. 1–15 a. Panammu acknowledges the good providence of Hadad and the other gods of his country, and records the prosperity of his reign.

L. 1. אנך In **62** 19 אִנְבִי; see **1** 1 *n.* פנמו בר קרל Panammu i **62** 5, the predecessor of Panammu ii **62** 1. **63** 2, to whom **62** is dedicated. *Panammu of Sam'al* (prob. Panammu ii) is mentioned in inscrr. of Tiglath-pileser iii, *KB* ii 20. 30. A similar name is met with in Asia Minor, in Caria, Παναμυής (Ball *TrSBA* (1888) 432), and in Isauria, *Panemou-teichos* (Ramsay *Hist. Geogr. of Asia Min.* 394 &c.). The derivation is unknown; prob., like קרל, the name is of non-Semitic origin. יאדי **62** 1. 5 &c. Ya'di was a town and petty kingdom of N. Syria, situated in the country N. of the Orontes.

[1] In connexion with these inscrr. the following abbreviations are used: Sach. = Sachau in *Mitth. aus den Orient. Sammlungen*, Heft xi *Ausgrabungen in Sendschirli* (1893). Hal. = Halévy in *Revue Sémitique* i–ii (1893–4). DHM = D. H. Müller *Altsemitischen Inschr. von Sendschirli* (1893). Nöld. = Nöldeke in *ZDMG* xlvii (1893) 96–105. Hoffm. = G. Hoffmann in *Zeitschr. für Assyriol.* xi (1897). The text above is derived from the facsimile given by Lidzbarski, *Nordsem. Epigr.*, Atlas taf. xxii, with reference to Euting's facsimile in *Ausgrab. in Sendschirli*.

Winckler, *Altor. Forsch.* i 1 ff., suggests that the well-known expressions in the Annals of Tiglath-pileser iii, *KB* ii 24 f., [*Asri*]*jâu* (*mâtu*) *Jaudâi*, [*A*]*surijâu* (*mâtu*) *Jaudi*, which are usually taken to refer to 'Azariah (=Uzziah) the Judaean,' 'A. of the *land of Judah*[1],' really refer to this יארי. The context implies that *Jaudi* was in N. Syria[2]; it speaks of nineteen districts of the city of Hamath as having revolted to *Asrijâu*, and there is little likelihood that the Judaean Azariah would have mixed in the politics in N. Syria and formed an alliance with Hamath, 150 miles N. of Palestine. According to the biblical chronology Azariah was dead at this time (about 740 B. C.), but this difficulty can be overcome[3]. Winckler's view requires that two such names as *Asrijâu* and *Jaudi* (=either יארי or יהודה) existed at the same period in different parts, a mere coincidence, perhaps. *Asrijâu*, with the divine name יהו, is more characteristic of Judaea than N. Syria; יהו, however, was not unknown in the latter region[4]. There is much to be said for Winckler's contention, but it is hardly established beyond dispute[5]. זי The Old Aram. form of די (Bibl. Aram., Nab., Palm.), used as a relative (64 14. 69 9. 70 1 &c., and on coins 149 A 6) and as a sign of the genitive (66 a. 67. 68. 76 B 3 &c.). הַקִּימַת=הקמת. נצב See 37 1 *n*. זן So in Phoen. (Gebal); see add. note ii p. 26. הדד 150 b, the chief deity of the Aramaeans; cf. "Αδωδος βασιλεὺς θεῶν Philo Bybl. *Fr. Hist. Gr.* iii 569. The statue on which the inscr. is carved represents a bearded human head with horns, the symbol of the god's power. In the O. T. his name occurs in compounds, e. g. הדדעזר 2 S. 8 3 ff.=Assyr. *Dad-'idri*; בןהדד 1 K. 20 1 (*COT* 200 f.); הדדרמון Zech. 12 11. Nothing distinctive is known of his character; but he was prob. regarded as a god of storm and thunder, for he was identified by the Assyrians as a stranger-god from the Amorite country with Rammân; see Zimmern *KAT*[3] ii 443 f. The original significance of the name may possibly be found in the Ar. هَدَّ *break, crash, growl*, هَدَّادَةٌ *thunder*; cf. Hebr. הֵד, הֵידָד *shout* (Baethgen *Beitr.* 67 f., Hal. ii 26 f.). As a personal pr. n. הדד is found in Sabaean, CIS iv 55[6]. בעלמי ? *in my youth* (בַּעֲלֻמַי) not *in my life-time* (? בְּעָלְמִי); the latter, morever,

[1] So e. g. Schrader *COT* 217 ff.

[2] Cf. also *Iaudu* in the Nimrûd Inscr. of Sargon, *KB* ii 36.

[3] See Kittel *Gesch. d. Hebräer* ii 284 ff.

[4] Thus *Iau-bi'di of Hamath*, *KB* ii 36. 56, is interchanged with *Ilu-bi'di* (of Hamath), ib. 42.

[5] It is accepted by Benzinger *Könige* 166.

[6] Possibly Hadad was known to the ancient Arabs, Wellhausen *Reste Ar. Heidenthums* 55; but Wellhausen's translation is disputed by Hoffm. 228.

is expressed by ביםי in the inscr. DHM renders *lord of waters* (בעל מי). Possibly עלמ׳ is the name of a place.

L. 2. אלהו is explained as an abstract form, אֱלָהוּתָא *godhead* (Lidzb.). The reading is uncertain. אל 62 22, Assyr. *ilu*. The name by itself is found in Sabaean inscrr., e.g. אל ועתתר Halévy no. 144 3. 150 4; elsewhere in N. Semitic inscrr. it appears in compounds, e.g. ירפאל 150 c. רשף l. 3 see 12 3 *n.*, and cf. ארקרשף l. 11. רכבאל 62 22. 63 5. The name of this deity is known so far only in this district of N. Syria; it may mean *chariot* or *steed of El* (Rekub-el), or *charioteer of El* (Rakkab-el, Rekab-el), Hoffm. 252; cf. the Palm. עגלבול 139 6 *n.* On Assyr. monuments the sun-god is sometimes represented as riding in a chariot drawn by griffins, and he is called *rakib narkabti*[1] (cf. 2 K. 23 11 מרכבות השמש and Ps. 18 11); but whether Rekub-el had any connexion with the sun-god, as his minister or attendant, we cannot tell; it is possible that he was a moon-god, for in the ancient East the moon came before the sun, as here (Lidzb. *Eph.* i 256 *n.*, cf. 112 4 *n.*). Sach. 61 f. suggests a transposition of ר and כ, and renders *cherub of El*; this is unnecessary. The pr. n. בררכב 62 1. 63 1 prob. means *son of the god Rekub-el*. שמש 62 22. 64 9 the sun-god, Assyr. *shamash*, worshipped throughout the Semitic world, e.g. in Israel 2 K. 23 11. Dt. 17 3, in Palmyra 117 5. 136 3. 6. His cult is implied by such pr. nn. as בית שמש (Hebr.), עבדשמש CIS i 116 f. (Phoen.), שמשעדרי ib. ii 87 (Aram.), לשמש 117 3. שמשגרם 145 1 (Palm.).

L. 3. חטר *branch, rod*, common in Aram., in Hebr. rare, Is. 11 1; here used for *sceptre*, Hebr. שבט. חלבבה Here and in ll. 9. 10 (rest.) this might be the name of a place not otherwise known; but in ll. 13. 19 it seems to be a fem. noun with a suffix. In each case the meaning 'blessing,' 'prosperity' (Hoffm., Lidzb.) or 'majesty' (Hal.), would suit the context. פמז i.e. פ+מה+ז, فما ذا, in ll. 4. 22 ומז, cf. מחוה=מה חוה 65 5. The conjunction פ, which is prob. to be found in אף, פל (Nöld. 103 *n.*), is used in these inscrr. like the Ar. فَ, ll. 13 f. 31. 63 18; similarly in Nab., e.g. 80 7. 10. 83 3. 94 4 &c.; in Palm. 143 5. Another form of the conjunction is פא ll. 17. 33. 62 22. אחז Peal impf. 1 sing.

L. 4. אלהו Pl. abs.=אלהין, ll. 12 f. 19. 62 23. For the omission of final ן cf. שערי l. 5. חטי, שמי l. 6. אנשי צרי l. 30. אבני l. 31. שבעי 62 3 (see note); but contrast מלכן רברבן 63 10. 13. This peculiarity finds a parallel in Assyr., which forms a plur. in *ī* (or *ē*) as well as in *âni*,

[1] Jastrow *Rel. of Babyl. and Assyr.* 461; Sach. 70.

and in Aram. dialects, e.g. Talm. דיקלי *dates*, פירי *fruits*, cf. Γεθσημανῆ = גַּת שְׁמָנֵי (Dalman *Gram. Jüd.-Pal. Aram.* § 38, 3), and in Mandaic (Nöldeke *Mand. Gr.* 162). יתנו In this dialect, and in that of Nêrab and Têma, the impf. 3 plur. ends in *û*, not, as is usual in Aram., in *ûn*, e.g. ll. 7. 12. **64** 9. 11. **65** 9. **78** B 3 (Egypt. Aram.); exceptionally in B. Aram., יֵאבַדוּ Jer. 10 11. יַחִיטוּ Ezr. 4 12. Dan. 5 10. ושאם חויו Meaning unknown. DHM takes שאם as = שְׁלָם and reads רוין = רְוָיוּתָא, lit. *peace of satiety*; but the reading is uncertain.

L. 5. ארק **62** 14 &c.; in **63** 4. **66** a (and regularly on Nineveh weights) ארקא = the later Aram. ארעא, Hebr. ארץ, Arab. أَرْض. In Jer. 10 11 ארקא occurs side by side with ארעא; in Mandaic it appears prob. as an intentional archaism, Nöld. l. c. 73. For the ק which is peculiar (Driver *Tenses* § 178) cf. רקי ll. 18. 22 = ܪܥܐ = רצה = رضى; מוקא **62** 13 = ܡܥܐ = יצא = وضا, see p. 185. שערי Hebr. שְׂעֹרִים, cf. **62** 6. 9 and see l. 4 *n*. תאל ? meaning. אל l. 29 is prob. the plur. of זן, but the article prefixed is not found in these inscriptions.

L. 6. חטי = Hebr. חטים; שמי = Hebr. שׁוּמִים Num. 11 5.

L. 7. זא **62** 9 perhaps for אַי + דִּי (DHM, Nöld.) *whatsoever*; or = Hebr. אָז, Aram. אֱדַיִן *then*. יעבדו Cf. Gen. 2 5 &c. (את האדמה). Dt. 28 39 (כרמים); in later Aram. פלח בארעא is the usual expression. See l. 4 *n*.

L. 8. DHM restores שם יש[בו ויעבדו ארק וכר]ם פנמו. גם l. 9. **62** 16, cf. אגם **62** 5, is characteristic of Hebrew; it is found on the Moab. St., 1 6, but the later Aram. does not use it.

L. 9. DHM restores [והכר]ת חרב *and he cut off*. לשן *tongue*, as the instrument of slander; cf. איש לשון Ps. 140 12. 15 3. 101 5. בית **62** 2. 7. **63** 7 ff. The scriptio plena (cf. לילא l. 24. עיני l. 30) is more frequent in **62**, which is somewhat later. ביומי = בימי **62** 18, ܒܝܘܡܝ. In Aram. the vowel of the first syllable in יומין is *ô* not *â*, as in Hebr.; cf. **65** 3. **76** A 4, constr. st. יומי **62** 11. אכל ושתא If the last word of the line be read יארי—Lidzb.'s facsimile shows traces of initial י and of ר—these words may be taken as perfs.; cf. **62** 9. DHM takes them as nouns, reading the last word אֹרוי *food and drink were abundant*, cf. l. 4 *n*. Nöld. 103 reads ורוי *and was abundant*, i. e. *abundantly*.

L. 10. Meaning very obscure. DHM regards יתמר as = יִתְאֲמַר *was appointed*, and לנצב as = לְנְצָב (cf. Solomon's נִצָּבִים 1 K. 4 7 ff.) *prefect of Q.., and prefect of the Zerart*. But לנצב may be a verb, *to set up*, and קירת *cities* **62** 4. 15; cf. הציב Dt. 32 8. Ps. 74 17. Pr. 15 25 (with גבול), 1 Ch. 18 3 (with יד). The meaning of זררי is unknown. כפירי

Perhaps *villages*; cf. Neh. 6 2 (?), כְּפָרִים Cant. 7 12. 1 Ch. 27 25. But *sons of the villages* is not a very natural expression, and possibly כפירי is the name of a tribe or place. This, however, does not suit the context of בעלי כפירי in 62 10. יקח ? impf. of לקח. The reading is uncertain.

L. 11. אש רעיה ויתר הדד (Lidzb.) ? *each his neighbour, and Hadad did richly*; but the text is very doubtful. יתר is possibly Pael of יתר l. 12. Euting's facsimile gives אשרו · יח . . · יהדד. וארקרשף The name of a god. Hoffm. 214. 252 connects ארק i. e. *'Arqu* or *'Arqt* with the √רצה=רקי (l. 5 *n.*) *be favourable*, and compares ארצו (?), רצו, apparently a divine name in Palm. (see 115 1 *n.*), ארצי and the Arab. رُضَاء (Wellhausen *Reste Ar. Heid.*[2] 58 f.). כברו i. e. prob. כְּבָרוּ *greatness*. DHM reads כבדו (for כבדותא) *honour*. נתנה Perhaps perf. 3 plur. (or sing.) with suff. 3 sing. fem.=נְתָנֻהָּ, the suff. resuming the object which precedes, *greatness they (he) gave it*. A Nifal form is improbable. DHM reads אמן כרת *a sure (covenant) they made*; אמן ? *faithfulness* occurs again in 62 21. Lidzb. reads זכרת, but neither the reading nor the form is clear.

L. 12. מת Various meanings of this obscure word are proposed: thus *gift* in l. 12 = מַתָּן; *males, male offspring* in ll. 13. 14. 62 4 = מְתִים, Assyr. *mutu*; *town, district* in l. 14. 62 10 = Assyr. *mâtu* (Winckler *Altor. Forsch.* i 107), cf. CIS ii 31 במת בבשקן *in vico Bâbsuqin*. But it seems more reasonable to give מת the same meaning throughout. Halévy regards it as an adverb, *aussitôt, forthwith*, and explains the form as a contraction of the Hebr. מתי, cf. Assyr. *maṭ*. Lidzb. renders *surely, indeed*, a meaning which suits the context in each case, and may be accepted provisionally, though its etymology is not evident. יקחו See l. 4 *n.*

L. 13. וארקו is prob. some part of the verb רצה=רקי (l. 5 *n.*); *his land* would be ארקה, like זבחה l. 18. DHM restores ו[שאל] · קרל, rendering 'and QRL asked for a male offspring; and Hadad did not give a male offspring.' This gives a suitable sense, but the rendering of מת is doubtful, and פלו (l. 31. 62 11) seems to mean *and if*, אִלּוּ=לו (Nöld. 104), rather than *and not*, לא=לו. To fill the space, ו[שאל · יאבי] is a better restoration. קרני i. e. קְרָנִי Pf. 3 sing. m. with suff., from קרא. In Lidzb.'s facsimile the ר is clear. לבנא l. 14, inf. of בנא. חלבבתי l. 3 *n.*

L. 14. מקם *place*, possibly like *τόπος* in Gk. inscrr., a *burial-place*.

L. 15. מן מן בני Part ii. ll. 15 a–24 a. Panammu invokes the blessing of the gods upon his successor if he be faithful to his religious and filial duty, and a curse upon him if he neglect it. מן מן

The first מן is perhaps the indef. pron. מַן, مَنْ, Assyr. *mannu, manu.* ויסער אברו l. 21. In Hebr. סער=*support, stay* esp. with food, e. g. Gen. 18 5; here perhaps in a more general sense, *strengthen.* אברו may be an abstr. form, אבריתא=אבְרוּ (DHM), or possibly a plur. with suff. = אַבִּירָיו *his strong ones,* Jud. 5 22. Ps. 50 13; but the latter does not give a good sense, and the form lacks support (Nöld.).

L. 16. הדד The deity is in the accus. after זבח, cf. in Sabaean עתתר . . ליזבחו CIS iv 74 11 f.; in Hebr. ל is required. The sacrifice was to be offered not to the dead, but to the god on behalf of the dead; see Lagrange *RB* (1902) xi 232 f. ויזכר אשם הדד Cf. the Hebr. idiom הזכיר שם יהוה *make mention of Yahweh's name,* i. e. to call upon, worship, Is. 26 13. Ex. 23 13. The verb here may be regarded as Afel. אשם=Arab. إِسْمٌ, Samaritan אשמא.

L. 17. מא l. 33. 62 22 = מ l. 3 *n.* [תאכ]ל נבש וגו' Cf. ll. 21 f., where the words are more legible. נבש=נפש; cf. תאלב l. 34=תאלף, اَحْفَارٌ=עִפֶּרֶת, and vice versa ברזל=فُولاذٌ &c.: Wright *Comp. Gr.* 64 f. תשתי Impf. of שתא l. 9; see l. 22 *n.* For the idea cf. Luke 22 30. עמך i. e. with Hadad. עד Prob.=עוֹד. זכר נבש . . עם The verb here and in l. 21 is Peal; contrast ויזכר אשם הדד l. 16, where the verb is Afel.

L. 18. After [ה]דד Lidzb. reads יאֹמ[ר], but the word is illegible in the facsimile. זבחה l. 22; the last letter is perhaps the suffix, *his.* Hoffm. 234 regards the form as fem, and compares שחתה 62 2; see 62 6 *n.* זא l. 19 (?), though elsewhere fem. (see add. note p. 26), is here prob. mas., like the Arab. ذا, since it appears to agree with זבחה. [י]רקי l. 22 *n.*, impf. of רקי l. 5 *n.*; cf. רצה ב in Hebr., e. g. Mic. 6 7. Hag. 1 8. שי Meaning unknown.

L. 19. ובהלבבתה חגאת *and in his prosperity I rested* (?), Lidzb., taking חגאת as Pf. 1 sing. of חגא=חנה *encamp,* cf. חגאת Pael 62 12 and מחנת 62 13 ff. But מחנה means *camp,* not as a *resting*-place, but as the place one *reaches* at the end of the day's march; so in Syr. ܡܛܐ= *incline towards, reach.* Possibly חגאת 62 12 may come from חנן *be gracious,* and חגאת be a pass. form, *I was treated graciously.*

L. 20. זרע See 4 7 *n.* The obligation of religious duty on the part of Panammu's successor is repeated; a clause expressing the possible neglect of it must be among the missing portions of ll. 20–22, to justify the imprecations in ll. 22 b–24 a.

L. 21. See ll. 15 f.

L. 22. הא in a demonstr. sense, cf. הו 78 A 3 עדנא הו *that time.* For הא after [ון] l. 21 cf. Gen. 32 3. ומן l. 4. תשתי, ירקי i. e. תִּשְׁתֵּי &c., cf. ירשי l. 27 f. תלעי l. 32. The impf. 3 sing. of these ל״י

verbs ends in ־ִי as in Palestinian Aram., Targ. &c.; contrast the Bibl. Aram. and Syr. ending ־ָא, ܳܐ.

L. 23. חרא Perhaps = חרון *wrath*. ליתכה Afel (?) impf. 3 sing. mas. with suff. 3 sing. fem. from נתך *pour forth*, in a figurative sense with חמה, אף in the O.T., e.g. Jer. 42 18. 2 Ch. 34 21. The impf. is here preceded by ל = Arab. لِ before the jussive, similarly למנע (i.e. לימנע) l. 24. לתגמרו l. 30. לכתשה (i.e. ליכתשה) l. 31, in each case with a jussive force; cf. in Sabaean ליעתורו *ut descenderent*, ולידבחו *atque ut sacrificarent* CIS iv 74 10 ff. &c., and see Hommel *Süd-ar. Chrest.* 25. This usage has not been found hitherto in Aram. Possibly it may have given rise to the impf. in ל which occurs in B. Aram., Targ. Jon., Talmud Bab., and Mandaic; but in these dialects the ל has no distinctively jussive force, and may be merely a phonetic variation of the impf. in נ (Driver *Tenses* § 204 Obs. 1). אל יתן לה לאכל Cf. 2 Ch. 20 10 for the construction. ברגז Reading indistinct, but the word is clear in l. 26.

L. 24. שנה i.e. שְׁנָה. למנע i.e. לִימְנַע Nöld. 98 *n.*, in a jussive sense; see note above. בלילא With scriptio plena, Hebr. לַיְלָה, Arab. لَيْل, but Syr. ܠܺܠܝܳܐ. דלה *terror*, as often in Targ.; but the form is not apparent; it might be inf. constr. The perf. occurs in l. 30. נתן if Peal perf., does not construe; the form must remain uncertain. For the imprecations cf. 4. 5. 64. 65.

Part iii. ll. 24 b–34. Panammu denounces those who shall attempt to injure the persons or the power of his family and successors. Such seems to be the general drift of this most obscure section. DHM thinks that the reference is to the violation of the statue; this is apparently alluded to in l. 28, but the rest of the passage deals with the treatment of persons (note the verb הרג ll. 26. 33. 34). איח appears to be a title denoting a member of the royal family, איחי אבה 62 3, like the Hebr. בני המלך 2 Sam. 13 32 ff. 2 K. 10 6 ff. 11 2 &c., and בר מלכא CIS ii 38 2 'a prince of the royal house' (?). In ll. 27. 28 איחיה is plur. with suff., l. 30 איחה is sing. with suff., while איחתה ll. 28. 31 is prob. a fem. plur. or sing. with suff. The word may be a form of אח in a special sense. מודדי l. 27 מודדיה is perhaps a noun from √ודד, Arab. وُدّ *love*, lit. *my loved one*, so *friend* (Lidzb.). מומת l. 26 seems to be Hofal ptcp. of מות. וישלח ידה בחרב Cf. Jud. 5 26 (לַיָּתֵד). Panammu appears to have in mind the wholesale assassinations of the royal family which so frequently accompany the accession of an oriental king. 62 3 shows that his fears were justified. ..חי Lidzb. suggests [בי]חי.

L. 26. חמס is some part of √חמס *be violent*.

L. 27. ירשי l. 28, i.e. יְרַשֵּׁי impf. 3 sing. mas. of רשי lit. *be able*, so perhaps *allow*, cf. רשיון *permission* Ezr. 3 7; see l. 22 *n*. שחת is perhaps inf. constr. באשר The word אשר = *place*, 62 18 (?). 64 8 אשרה *his place*. 68 6 אתרא. 76 C 4 אתר. Here and in l. 32 באשר may perhaps be taken like the Syr. ܒܐܬܪ, i.e. ܒ + ܐܬܪ, in the sense of *after*, lit. *in the place of*; so Hoffm., Lidzb. The exact meaning, however, of the expression *destroy after one of his princes* is not clear. חד must be constr. state before the gen. following, for in l. 28 it takes a fem. form before a fem. noun. For the construction cf. in Hebr. אחד העם Gen. 26 10. אחת האתנות 2 K. 4 22 &c. חד is the usual Aram. for אחד, e.g. 62 5. 63 13 &c.; in Hebr., Eze. 33 30.

L. 28. איחתה See l. 24 *n*. ינגב איחיה זכרי Here and in the foll. lines to 30 b the offender is apparently not the future king but a member of the royal house, and the offence is the removal or violation of the statue which Panammu had erected. The details and general sense are very uncertain. זכרי l. 30 (?) *my memorial*; זכר has this meaning in 62 22, Palm. דכרן 135 1, and Nab. CIS ii 169 &c.; in Phoen. סכר 9 6 *n*. ויקם Impf. 3 sing., rather than plur. as Nöld. 104. ותה Accus. particle with suff. This form is prob. preserved in ܠܘܬܗ, ܠܘܬ, but in later usage it has become ית, thus Nab. יתה 80 5, Palm. ית 121 4, BAr. יָתְהוֹן Dan. 3 12 (only here), ית in Targ. and Sam., ܝܬ in Syr. (rare). This ות, and the Phoen. אית, Hebr. את, may be accounted for by an original *'awayat* which passed into *'iwayath*, *'iyyath*, *'iyath*, *'eth*; see 3 3 *n*. במצעה *in the midst of it*, supposing that we have here the Aram. מְיצַע, מִיצְעָא *midst*, as in 62 10. 63 9 f. Hoffm. 319, however, suggests in each case the meaning *place*, מַצָּע, Arab. مَوْضِع. What the suffix refers to is not clear. נשה l. 29 Meaning unknown.

L. 29. אחכם The suff. as in לְכֹם Ezr. 5 3 &c., for the usual Aram. ־כון; cf. להם 63 18 for להון. השחת Afel, either perf. or imperat. אלה i.e. אֱלָה or אֱלָה constr. state sing.; so in Nab. 88 6. 94 3. Palm. 136 7. This is the sing. form of the plur. אלהי l. 4. For ידית cf. Ps. 44 21. הן Prob. = *if* 64 11, as in Bibl. Aram. Dan. 2 6 &c. Ezr. 4 13. The meaning of אם is not clear. שמת Perf. 1 sing. of שים. If אמרת is plur., אל may = *these*. פם l. 30, with suff. פמי 65 4; Aram. פומא, ܦܘܡܐ, Hebr. פֶּה. For the expression cf. in Hebr. שים דבר בפי פ' Num. 22 38. 23 5. 12. 16 &c.

L. 30. זר *stranger* l. 34. אמר Either perf. or imperative. Apparently the offender is supposed to make the excuse that he did not realize what he was doing. קם עיני Cf. 1 K. 14 4. רלח Perf., cf. l. 24. אנשי צרי Prob. = אנשים צרים, although, since צר = Arab. ضرّ, the dialect of this inscr. should have ק for צ, on the analogy of ארק and רקי. פחנו ? *and behold*; the reading is very indistinct, but it is supported by והנו l. 31 bis. זכר may = *memorial* as זכרי l. 28; it may also = *male*, a meaning which seems to be required for זכרו l. 31 (Lidzb.). לתנמרו Impf. 2 plur. with cohortative ל; see l. 23 *n*. נמר = *make an end*, in a trans. sense.

L. 31. זכרו Lidzb. suggests that this is an abstract form for זכרותא *mankind, men*. פלכתשה Impf. with cohort. ל 3 sing. mas. with suff. 3 sing. mas., similarly פלכתשנה with suff. 3 sing. fem. (?). כתש = *break in pieces, shatter*; in Hebr. Pr. 27 22 *to pound*, in Targ. Jon. Ex. 30 36 ותכתוש מיניה of *pounding* the incense, used in Ethpa. like the Syr. ܟܬܫ = *fight, strive*. The punishment is to be stoning, whether the offender be a man or a woman. But it is not clear what the offence is, whether the violation of the memorial, which is apparently alluded to in the preceding lines, or the attempted assassination of Panammu's successor, which seems to be the drift of what follows. אבני i. e. אבנים l. 4 *n*. שחת The form is uncertain.

L. 32. באשרה Perhaps *after him*, l. 27 *n*. תלעי Meaning doubtful. The Aram. לעי = לאי means *to be wearied*, e. g. Targ. Jon. Dt. 25 18 לעיין ומשלהיין *wearied and faint*. נברתה *his might*, cf. וּגְבוּרְתָא Dan. 2 20.

L. 33. נדבה To render *his generosity* (cf. Hebr. נדבה) does not give a suitable sense; *his instigation* is better, cf. Arab. نَدَبَ *impel, incite* (DHM). את ? *thou*, 64 5. אפ *also*, l. 17 *n*. ישרה is some part of √ ישר *be straight*. תהרגה *thou shalt kill him*. It is difficult to believe, as DHM does, that הרג can mean *destroy* (the monument).

L. 34. תחק Apparently impf. 2 sing. of חקק *inscribe* (Eze. 23 14), perhaps rather *thou shalt write of him*, or *inscribe on it*; the context is not decisive. תאלב Pael impf. of אלב = אֲלַף *learn*, ܐܠܦ *teach*; cf. נבש for נפש l. 17 *n*. להרגה Either inf. constr. *to kill him*, or impf. with ל *that he kill him*.

62. Zenjirli: Panammu. Between 745 and 727 B.C. Berlin.

1 נצב · זן · שם · ברדכב · לאבה · לפנמו · בר · ברצר מלך [יאדי].....ב·
שנת . קל . . [א]בי · פנמו ב . . ק

2 אבה · פלטוה · אלה · יאדי · מן · שחתה · אלה · הות · בבית · אבוה ·
וקם · אלה · הד[ד]...ק... משבה · על ו . . ו . . א . ושב . ו . שחת...

3 בבית·אבה·והרג·אבה·ברצר·והרג·שבעי : : : ·איחי·אבה·....·ל·
רכב·.הֹ·......בך·עלֹם.....ך·בעל·....חל.ל..מו·....

4 ויתרה · מת · מלא · מסגרת · והכבר · קירת · חרבת מן · קירת ·
ישבת·ו..נ...........קֹ...............·ש....·תשם.

5 חרב · בביתי · ותהרגו · חד · בני · ואגם · הוית · חרב · בארק · יאדי ·
וחֹל..אל פנמו בר קרל·א...·אבי...ם·ב.רֹ·אבד....

6 שאה · ושורה · וחטה · ושערה · וקם · פרם · בשקל · ושטרב.·...
בשקל·ואסנב·משת·בשקל·ויבל אבי·ברֹ....·..

7 עד · מלך · אשור · ומלכה · על · בית · אבה · והרג · אבן · שחת · מן ·
בית·אבה....מן·אצר...·ארקֹ·יאדי·מן·ב....

8 ופשש · מסגרת · והרפי · שבי · יאדי · וק[ם ·]אבי · והרפי · נשי ·
בס........·..בא.·בית·קתילת·וקנואל..ב..

9 בית · אבה · והיטבה · מן · קדמתה · וכברת · חטה · ושערה · ושאה ·
ושורה · ביומיה · ואז אכלת ושֹתֹ....

10 זלת · מוכרו · וביומי · אבי · פנמו · שם · מת · בעלי · כפירי · ובעלי ·
רכב·ו.ח.ב אבי·פנמו·במצעֹתֹ·מלכי כברֹ...[א]

11 בי · לו · בעל · כסף · הא · ולו · בעל · זהב · בחכמתה · ובצדקה · פי ·
אחז · בכנף · מ[ר]אה · מלך · אשור · ר....

12 אשור · פחי · ואחי · יאדי · וחנאה · מראה · מלך · אשור · על · מלכי ·
כבר ברש.....

13 בגלגל · מראה · תגלתפלסר · מלך · אשור · מחנת · תֹ. · מן · מוקא ·
שמש · ועֹד · מערב · ת[מן]·...

14 רבעתארק · ובנת · מוקא · שמש · יבל · מערב · ובנת · מערב · יבל ·
מו[קא · ש]מש · ואב[י ....

15 גבלה · מראה · תגלתפלסר · מלך · אשור · קירת · מן · גבל · גרגם ·
...יֹ.[וא]בי · פנמו · ברֹ · ב[רצר]..

16 שמרג · וגם · מת · אבי · פנמו · בלגרי · מראה · תגלתפלסר · מלך ·
אשור · במחנת · גם ....

17 ובביה · איחה · מלכו · ובכיתה · מחנת · מראה · מלך · אשור · כלה ·
ולקח · מראה · מלך · אשור ...

18 י · נבשה · והקם · לה · משתי · בארח · והעבר · אבי · מן · דמשק ·
לאשר · ביומי · שר ....

19 יה · ביתה · כלה · ואנכי · ברכב · בר · פנמ[ו · בצד]ק · אבי · ובצדקי
הושבני · מרא[י ...

20 אבי · פנמו · בר · ברצר · ושמת · נצב · זן · . [לאב]י · לפנמו · בר ·
ברצר · ומ.. ת · בט ...

21 ואמר · במשות · ועל · יבל · אמן · יסמ.. · מלך ·..... · ויבל · יו . א ·
קדם קבר · אבי · פ[נמו ·] ...

22 חכר · זנה · הא · פא · הדד · ואל · ורכבאל · בעל · בית · ושמש ·
וכל · אלהי · יאדי ...

23 י · קדם · אלהי · וקדם · אנש ·

This statue Bar-rekub placed to his father Panammu, son of Bar-ṣur, king [of Ya'di]: . . year . . my [fa]ther Panammu . . [2] his father; the gods of Ya'di delivered him from his destruction. There was a conspiracy (?) in his father's house, and the god Had[ad] rose . . . his seat (?) over (?) . . . destruction . . . [3] in the house of his father, and slew his father Bar-ṣur, and slew seventy 70 kinsmen of his father . . chariots . . . owner of . . . [4] and with the rest thereof indeed (?) he filled the prisons, and desolate cities he made more numerous than inhabited cities . . . . . [ye] set (?) [5] the sword against my house and slay one of my sons, I have also caused the sword to be in the land of Ya'di . . Panammu, son of QRL . . my father . . . perished . . . [6] grain and corn and wheat and barley, and a peres stood at a shekel, and a shaṭrab . . at a shekel, and an 'esnab of ? at a shekel; and my father brought . . . [7] to the king of Assyria, and he made him king over his father's house, and he slew ? of destruction from his father's house . . from the treasure . . . of the land (?) of Ya'di, from . . . [8] and he ? the prisons, and released the captives of Ya'di; and my father aro[se] and released the women of . . . . house of the women killed (?) and ? . . . [9] his father's house; and he made it better than it was before; and wheat and barley and grain and corn were plentiful in his days; and then . . . did eat and . . [10] cheapness of price (?). And in the days of my father Panammu he appointed indeed (?) ? ? and charioteers, and . . my father Panammu in the midst of the kings of ? . . [11] my [fa]ther, whether he possessed silver or whether he possessed gold, in his wisdom and in his righteousness ? laid hold of the skirt of his lord the king of Assyria . . . [12] Assyria, the governors, and the princes of Ya'di, and his lord the king of Assyria was gracious to (?) him above the kings of ? . . . [13] at the wheel of his lord Tiglath-pileser, king of Assyria, (in) the campaigns . . from the east even to the west, and [from] . . [14] the four parts of the earth; and the daughters of the east he brought to the west, and the daughters of the west he brought to the [ea]st, and [my] father . . . [15] his border, his lord Tiglath-pileser, king of Assyria, cities from the border of Gurgum . . and my [fa]ther Panammu, son of B[ar-ṣur] . . . [16] ? Moreover my father Panammu died while following his lord Tiglath-pileser, king of Assyria, in the camp, also . . . [17] and his kinsfolk bewailed him ?, and the whole camp of his lord the king of Assyria bewailed him, and his lord the king of Assyria took . . . [18] . his soul, and set up for him a ? on the way, and brought across my father from Damascus to (this) place (?) . In my (?) days . . . [19] . the whole of his house. And as for me Bar-rekub, son of Panamm[u, for the righteous]ness of my father and for my own righteousness, [my] lord made me to sit . . . [20] of my father Panammu, son of Bar-ṣur; and I have placed this statue . . to my [father] Panammu, son of Bar-ṣur . . . [21] and . said ? and concerning ? surety (?) . . king . . and ? . . before (?)

the sepulchre of my father Pa[nammu] . . . [22] and a memorial is this (?). Also may Hadad and El and Rekub-el, lord of the house, and Shamash, and all the gods of Ya'di . . . [23]. before the gods and before men!

The text given above is derived from the facsimile in *Ausgraben in Sendschirli*, and from the text as published by Lidzbarski in *Nordsem. Epigr.*

L. 1. נצב זן 61 1; for שם נצב see 87 1 *n*. ברכב 68 1 prob. a short form of בְּרְכבאל 61 2 *n*. אבה Pronounced אַבָה as appears from אבוה l. 2; the full form is אבוהי 76 A 5. D 1, in Nab. 82 2, in Palm. 110 3 &c., in Syr. ܐܰܒ݂ܽܘܗ̈ܝ. ברצר As in ברכב, the latter part of the compound is a divine name צר, which occurs in the biblical pr. n. פדהצור Num. 1 10 &c., and in the place-name ביתצור Josh. 15 58; see Gray *Hebr. Pr. Names* 195 ff.[1] מלך יאדי 61 1. After שנת Sach. reads [נ]מְלַט i. e. a Nif. form (not used in Aram.), and translates '[in remembrance] of the year when his father was delivered.'

L. 2. פלטוה One of the objects of the inscr. was to commemorate the deliverance of the king, cf. 1 3 f. For פלט, in Hebr. poetical, cf. Ps. 18 3. 44. 49. אלה יאדי Contrast אלהי יאדי l. 22. Perhaps the י at the end of אלה (constr. plur.) was left out here because יאדי follows. שחתה appears to be inf. constr. with suff., cf. l. 7. 61 27 f., and see 61 18 *n*. אלה Possibly = Hebr. אָלָה *oath*, here *conspiracy*, DHM approved by Nöld. The facsimile clearly gives אלה, but Lidzb. reads אזה, a form of the relat. particle, cf. זי (?). הות 3 sing. fem. of הֲוָא, in Bibl. Aram. הֲוַת, הֲוָת. משבה Perhaps the same word as in 61 15. 25.

L. 3. וחרג אבה ברצר *His father* is ambiguous; the suffix may refer to the murderer, another son of Bar-ṣur and brother of Panammu, or it may refer to Panammu, the murderer being some member of the royal household. The latter is preferable (DHM). שבעי For the omission of final ן see 61 4 *n*., and cf. the forms of the tens (cardinals) in Assyr. *ešrâ*, *šalâšâ*, *ḫanšâ* &c., and in Eth. *salâsâ*, *ḥamsâ* &c., and in late Syr. ܬܠܬܝ, ܐܪܒܥܝ &c. On a basalt fragment found at Zenjirli the usual form occurs with the same numerical symbols as

[1] The connexion between this divine name and the title (ה)צור *the Rock* used of Yahweh in the O.T. (Dt. 32 4. 2 S. 23 3. Is. 17 10 &c.) is not clear. Very likely there is none; the title (ה)צור seems too purely figurative to have suggested the existence of a separate deity called *Rock*. The bibl. and post-bibl. references to צור are discussed by Wiegand in *ZATW* (1890) 85 ff.

here . . [ו]מלכ · : כשלשן, Sach. 7 1. As an illustration of the massacre see Jud. 9 5. 2 K. 10 7. אחיי Apparently plur. constr.; see 61 24 *n.*

L. 4. יתרתה May be a verb (61 11 *n.*); but it is simpler to take it as a noun, cf. יִתְרוֹ Is. 44 19; the suff. will then be sing. collective, referring to those who took part in the plot. For the two accus. after מלא cf. 1 K. 18 35. Eze. 9 7 &c. מסגרת Cf. Ps. 18 46. Mic. 7 17. For מת see 61 12 *n.* חרבת Adj., cf. Eze. 36 35. ישבת Ptcp. pass. In Hebr. the Nif. ptcp. is used, e.g. Eze. 12 20 &c. חשם. DHM reads חשמו, and supposes that the speaker is the god Hadad, announcing a divine oracle.

L. 5. חר בני i.e. king Bar-ṣur; cf. Ps. 2 7. אנם See 61 8 *n.* הוית if it governs the foll. חרב must be Pael, *I caused to be, to fall*, cf. Arab. هوى *to fall*. The perf. after the impfs. in the preceding clause lays emphasis on the finality of the god's decision. פנמו בר קרל i.e. Panammu i, 61 1.

L. 6. שאה l. 9, prob. = *corn*, Assyr. *šeu*. שורה The context requires some kind of *grain*. The use of the word here throws light upon Is. 28 25 חטה שורה ושערה, and shows that it is unnecessary to regard שׂוֹרָה as a corrupt repetition of שערה. חטה ושערה Cf. חטי, שערי 61 5. 6; for prices in a time of plenty cf. 2 K. 7 1 סאה סלת בשקל וסאתים שערים בשקל. In these words the fem. ending ה (absol. state) is noticeable; cf. זנה l. 22. 63 20. 61 18 *n.*, and the usage of Bibl. Aram. and Nabataean. פרס lit. *half, a half mina*, cf. CIS ii 10 פרש, explained in the Assyr. version as 'a half mina.' In Talm. B. *Ped* viii 5 פרס, as the context implies, = חצי מנה; cf. Dan. 5 25 פְּרֵס, and see Cl.-Gan. *Rec.* i 142 f. שקל = תקל, the ש as in early Aram. inscrr. from Nineveh, CIS ii 13 f. 43, cf. שלשא ib. 3. שטרב The name of a dry (?) measure. There are traces of a letter after ב; perhaps the full form was שטרבת. אסנב Cf. סנב CIS ii 7 a, in the Assyr. version, 'two-thirds of a mina,' perhaps the Sumerian *sinibu*. משת The meaning *drink* (= מִשְׁתְּיָא Dan. 5 10) is too indefinite, and *load, something carried* (משת a fem. form of מַשָּׂא) is equally vague. Lidzb. reads משח *oil for anointing*, cf. 76 C 1 (?). 147 ii a 12 ff.; but the facsimile shows a ת. ויבל i. e. יַבֵּל Pael pf. = نقّل, ll. 14. 21. The object of the verb was prob. some such word as 'a present.' In consequence of the famine Panammu sought the protection of the Assyrian king, and no doubt had to purchase it by a gift.

L. 7. מלכת Pael pf.; illustrate from 2 K. 24 17. אבן שחת is rendered by DHM *stone of destruction*, cf. Is. 8 14 אֶבֶן נֶגֶף. Such an expression sounds too rhetorical for an inscription; moreover, אבן is an uncertain reading. מן אזר The sentence may be completed

[אלה] ארק יאדי *from the treasury of the gods of the land of Ya'di.* The reading ארק is better supported by the facsimile than Lidzb.'s אלה. The passage may be illustrated by 2 K. 16 8; cf. אצרות בית י״י 1 K. 14 26 &c.

L. 8. משש DHM renders *searched*, and compares פִּשְׁפֵּשׁ in Targ. and Talm. A better meaning, *suppressed*, may be obtained through the Assyr. *pasâsu* (פסס) = 'blot out,' 'extinguish,' esp. of sins. חרפי Afel pf. of רפי, cf. הרפה in Hebr., e.g. Cant. 3 4 אֲחַזְתִּיו וְלֹא אַרְפֶּנּוּ. Job 27 6. שבי יאדי Cf. שבי מצרים Is. 20 4. קתילת Ptcp. pass. plur. fem. The form קתל agrees with the Arab. قتل as against the Hebr. and Aram. קטל; cf. פלט Hebr., Aram. = Arab. فلت. The meaning of קואל is unknown.

L. 9. קדמתה Lit. *its former state*; cf. קדמתן Eze. 16 55. 36 11. אז *then*, or *whatever*; 61 7 *n*. אכלת cannot = אָכְלָה *food*, for the fem. ending of nouns is ה in this inscr., e.g. חטה &c. The form seems to be perf. 3 sing. fem. ושת. if these letters are correct, may be restored וְשָׁתְיַת or וְשָׁתַת *and did drink*. The subj. of both verbs is perhaps [יאדי], though in 61 9 יאדי is mas., or [ארקא].

L. 10. זלת may be explained by the Talm. זול *be cheap*, זול *cheapness*, e.g. Midr. Rab. *Qoh.* 10 c זה אוכל ביוקר וזה אוכל בזול; *Bab. Qam.* 20 a דמי שעורין בזול 'value of barley at a cheap price.' מוכרו The form is uncertain; DHM explains it as absol. st. of מוכרותא = Hebr. מֶכֶר Num. 20 19. שם The subj. seems to be the king of Assyria. בעלי רכב may well mean *charioteers*, cf. הרכב ובעלי הפרשים 2 S. 1 6; but בעלי כפירי can hardly mean *villagers, citizens of villages* (see 10 3 *n*.) in this connexion. To render *lords over chariots, lords over villages*, gives an unusual meaning to בעל *owner*, but it may be illustrated by בעלי גוים Is. 16 8. The meaning of כפירי is uncertain; see 61 10 *n*. ו.ח.ב Hal. restores ונחשב *and was esteemed* which involves a Nifal form (l. 1 *n*.); Lidzb. וחשב. במצעת See 61 28 *n*. The last letter looks like ת or ה in the facsimile; but במצעה makes no sense. מלכי כבר l. 12. כבר may be the name of a place, cf. נְהַר כְּבָר Eze. 1 1 &c., or a noun, *might*; cf. the verb כבר l. 4.

L. 11. לו . . . לו *sive . . . sive*; for לו *if* see 61 13 *n*. It is questionable whether לו could have been written for the negative לא, as many take it. The general sense appears to be, 'my father, whatever the state of his exchequer (or, however wealthy he may have been), was prudent enough to seek the patronage of a powerful suzerain.' Cf. 63 10 f. פי Not *my mouth*, which would be פמי 61 29. Lidzb. takes פ as the conjunction, and reads פיאחז; but the impf. is out of place here, and the facsimile distinctly shows the dividing dot after פי.

Possibly פי may be an unusual form of the conjunction, = פא l. 22. אחז בכנף is a figure for seeking alliance and protection, cf. Zech. 8 23. מראה From מרא 63 3 (constr. st.) with suff., cf. 76 A 7. In later Aram. the 3rd radical disappears before a suff., e. g. in Palm. מרן 126 2 &c., though it is retained in the Nab. form מראנא 81 8 &c., and in the Bibl. Aram. מָרְאִי Dan. 4 16. 21 Kethib.

L. 12. פחי must be regarded as plur. absol., not constr., and as equivalent to the Hebr. פַּחוֹת (sing. פֶּחָה), Assyr. *paḫâti* 'viceroy'; see Schrader *COT* 186. אחי יארי Prob. 'members of the royal family, lit. brethren, of Ya'di.' אח is apparently a title like אית l. 3. חנאה Possibly Pael perf. with suff. 3 sing. mas. from חנא= חנה *encamp*; 'he gave him a position in the Assyrian camp above the kings of כבר.' The suzerain was attended on his campaigns by dependent kings; cf. 1 K. 20 1. 12. 16. But the rendering *caused him to encamp* is uncertain; and as the context in 61 19 hardly admits *I encamped* as the sense of חנאת, it is perhaps better in both cases to take the forms from חנן *be gracious* (DHM), although the א is difficult to explain. על מלכי כבר Illustrate from 2 K. 25 28.

L. 13. גלגל 63 8 the same word as the Hebr. גַּלְגַּל, properly the *wheel* of a chariot, Is. 5 28. Jer. 47 3, or the *chariot* itself; illustrate from 1 K. 20 33. 2 K. 10 15. 16. The missing verb was prob. *and he caused me to ride*, or *and I ran* (63 8). תגלתפלסר So written in 2 K. 16 7; elsewhere ת׳פלאסר 2 K. 15 29. 16 10; in 63 3. 6 ת׳פליסר. For the history of this warlike and successful king see Schrader *COT* 240 ff. מחנת Prob. plur. rather than constr. sing. as in ll. 16. 17. The meaning here is *armies* or *campaigns* (DHM) rather than *camps*; cf. Jud. 4 15 f. 1 K. 22 34 &c. מחנת must be governed by some verb now lost. מוקא = מוצא, see 61 5 *n*. In Hebr. יצא is used of the sun rising, Gen. 19 23. Ps. 19 7. For מוקא . . . מערב cf. Ps. 75 7.

L. 14. רבעתאריק Cf. 63 4 מרא רבעי ארקא (plur. constr.). The latter expression shows that רבעת (Hebr. רֶבַע *one fourth*) is plur. and not sing.; cf. the Assyr. *šar kibrat irbitti* or *arba'i* 'king of the four quarters,' a title used by Tiglath-pileser and the kings before and after him; *KB* ii 2. 8. 34 &c. ובנת מוקא שמש The allusion is prob. to the transportation of subject nations, a characteristic feature of Assyrian policy. בנת may be used figuratively for 'peoples' (cf. 'daughter of Zion'), or simply *women*.

L. 15. The connexion between this and the line before was prob., 'my father rendered him military service, and his lord . . . added to his border cities &c.' (DHM). גרגם *Gurgum* or *Gamgum*, mentioned in inscrr. of Salmanassar ii, *KB* i 156. 172, a principality to the NE. of Sam'al among the border mountains between Syria and Cilicia, bounded by the districts of Kommagene (Assyr. *Kummuḫ*) and Melitene (*Milid*) on the NE. In the Annals of Tiglath-pileser iii the name occurs between *Samal* and *Milid*, *KB* ii 30. The chief town was *Marqasi* (CIS ii p. 15)=מרקש=مَرْعَش; we may conclude that the Amanus district round Mar'ash formed the kingdom of Gurgum; Sachau *Sitzungsb. Preuss. Akad.* (1892) pp. 320 ff.

L. 16. שמרג Prob. a pr. n.; cf. שמגר Jud. 5 6, and p. 80 *n.* וגם 61 8 *n.* בלגרי By metathesis for ברגלי; cf. in Mandaic ליגרא=ܪܓܠܐ, ארקבא = ܥܩܪܒܐ *scorpion*, Nöld. *Mand. Gram.* 74. בלגרי Lit. *at the feet of*; cf. for the idiom Jud. 4 10. 1 S. 25 27 &c.

L. 17. ובכיה i.e. prob. וּבַכְּיֵהּ Pael pf. 3 sing., cf. 65 5 בכתי. The construction of the words following is obscure. איחה, though sing. in form (61 30), must have a plur. meaning; it may be regarded as a sing. collective. DHM takes מלכו as=מלכותא, cf. כברו 61 11; but *his royal kinsmen* would be איחה זי מלכו. Lidzb. simplifies the difficulty by rendering *his kinsmen, the kings*; apparently treating the abstract singular form as equivalent to a concrete plur., like אלהו in 61 2 (uncertain). כלה The suff. is fem., referring back to ובכיתה מחנת מ'. For this idiomatic use of כל with suff., cf. l. 19 ביתה כלה, in Syr. ܡܕܝܢܬܐ ܟܠܗ Nöld. *Syr. Gr.* § 218, in Hebr. Is. 9 8. Jer. 13 19 &c., in Arab. اَلْبَيْتُ كُلُّهُ Wright *Ar. Gr.* ii § 82 (*a*); cf. 89 5 *n.*

L. 18. נבשה See 61 17 *n.* והקם i.e. וְהֵקִם. משתי, if correct, will=משתה *feast*, a meaning which hardly agrees with .. והקם בארח. Hal. reads משכי (√שכה), a possible alternative, and compares אֶבֶן מַשְׂכִּית Lev. 26 1. Num. 33 52, i.e. a figured stone with an image of a god; this gives a suitable sense. The reading מבכי *a weeping* (Sach. &c.) is not that of the facsimile. The passage finds a striking illustration in Gen. 50 7–13. והעבר אבי מן דמשק The subj. of the verb is Tiglath-pileser, who was engaged upon the siege of Damascus in 733–2 B.C. After 732 he returned home, and no further expedition to Syria is recorded; see Schrader *COT* 258 f. לאשר i.e. prob. to his native *place*. Panammu would naturally desire to be buried in his own country; cf. Gen. 47 29 f. 50 25. Ex. 13 19. Josh. 24 32.

L. 19. ברכב A careless spelling of ברכב. אנכי . . . הושבני The casus pendens, with the pers. pron. as subject; similarly in Hebr. Gen. 24 27 &c.; Driver *Tenses* § 197 (4). The form אנכי (61 1 אנך), a stranger to Aram., is a peculiar feature of this dialect; see

p. 185. בצדק אבי וגו' The phrase occurs again in **63** 4 f. and in the basalt fragment (l. 3 *n.*) . . [בצדק אב[י ובצדקי; cf. **65** 2. The line may be completed מלך אשור על כרסא, as in **63** 6 f.

L. 20. ושמת i. e. וְשָׂמְתְּ. After נצב ק we may restore [זכר · לאב]י *as a memorial to my father.* ומ . . ת Sach. reads ובנית.

The remainder of the inscr. is in many parts so much injured that the exact sense cannot be recovered. The general purport of l. 21 seems to be the safeguarding of the statue and sepulchre (?); ll. 22 f. probably invoke the curse of the gods upon any attempt to violate the memorial. The inscr. thus closes in the same way as **61**, but with less elaborate detail.

L. 21. אמר may be either pf. 3 sing., or impf. 1 sing. במשות Sach. connects with the Hebr. משאות *portions, gifts*, and the Phoen. משאתת **42** 1, and renders 'he gave orders in the matter of offerings.' Hoffm. derives the form from the √שית. The meaning must remain obscure. על יבל Sach. *concerning produce*, Hebr. יְבוּל. אמן Perhaps *surety*, **61** 11 *n.* ויבל ? *and he brought*, l. 6.

L. 22. זכר זנה הא The rendering given above is conjectural. For *this is a memorial* we should expect the order זנה הא זכר, as in Hebr. זה הוא בית י' 1 Chr. **21** 31. Qoh. **1** 17. The idiom is frequent in post-bibl. Hebr., and in Aram., e. g. Dan. 4 27 הֲלָא דָא הִיא בָּבֶל רַבְּתָא &c.; Driver *Tenses* § 201 (3) Obs. Normally the pronoun הוא anticipates the subject, which comes last (*this is it, Babylon*); but here the subject comes first for emphasis, and the pronoun reiterates it (*a memorial, this is it*). Similarly in Syr., the pronoun may refer either backwards or forwards to the subject; Nöld. *Syr. Gr.* § 311. מא See **61** 17 *n.* חדד וגו' See **61** 2 *n.* בעל בית *owner of the temple* (**5** 15 f.) rather than 'patron of the royal house.'

L. 23. אלהי . . אנש Cf. **69** 20 אלהן ואנש. Jud. **9** 9. 13 אלהים ואנשים.

63. Zenjirli: Bar-rekub. Same period as **62**. Imp. Museum, Constantinople.

1 אנה · ב[ר]רכב ·
2 בר · פנמו · מלך · שמ
3 אל · עבד · תגלתפליסר · מרא ·
4 רבעי · ארקא · בצדק · אבי · ובצד
5 קי · הושבני · מראי · רכבאל ·

6 ומראי · תגלתפליסר · על ·
7 כרסא · אבי · ובית · אבי · ע
8 מל · מן · כל · ורצת · בגלגל ·
9 מראי · מלך · אשור · במצע
10 ת · מלכן · רברבן · בעלי · כ
11 ספ · ובעלי · זהב · ואחזת ·
12 בית · אבי · והיטבתה ·
13 מן · בית · חד · מלכן · רברב
14 ן · והתנאבו · אחי · מלכי
15 א · לכל · מה · טבת · ביתי · ו
16 בי · טב · לישה · לאבהי · מ
17 לכי · שמאל · הא · בית · כלם
18 ו · להם · פהא · בית · שתוא · ל
19 הם · והא · בית · כיצא · ו
20 אנה · בנית · ביתא · זנה ·

I am Bar-rekub, [2] son of Panammu, king of Sam[3]'al, servant of Tiglath-pileser lord [4] of the four parts of the earth. For the righteousness of my father and for my own right[5]eousness my lord Rekub-el [6] and my lord Tiglath-pileser made me to sit upon [7] the throne of my father. And my father's house la[8]boured more than all: and I ran at the wheel [9] of my lord, the king of Assyria, in the mid[10]st of mighty kings, possessors of s[11]ilver and possessors of gold. And I took [12] the house of my father, and made it better [13] than the house of any of the mighty kin[14]gs; and my brethren the kings coveted (?) [15] all the prosperity of my house. And [16] a good house (?) my fathers, the kin[17]gs of Sam'al, did not possess; it was a house of ? [18] to them, and it was their summer house [19] and it was a winter house; so [20] I built this house.

This inscr. belongs not to a statue, like **61** and **62**, but to a building—the new palace built by Bar-rekub. It was found in 1891 on the *Tell* of Zenjirli. On the left side of the inscr. is a figure of the king in Assyrian style carved in relief, holding a lotus flower in his hand. Another fine relief of Bar-rekub has been found at Zenjirli: the king is seated on his throne, with a eunuch behind and a scribe in front of him. On the right, and at the level of the king's crown, is carved the inscr. אנה ברכב בר פנמ[ו]. In the middle of the monument, between the head of the king and that of the eunuch, is the symbol of the lunar deity, a full moon and crescent; at the right of it runs the legend מראי בעלחרן i.e. 'My lord is Ba'al of Ḥarran.' Ḥarran, in N. Mesopotamia, possessed the great temple of Sin, the Assyr. moon-god; and this was no doubt the deity whom Bar-rekub worshipped; see **64** 9 *n.* Halévy *Rev. Sém.* (1895) 392 ff.; Cl.-Gan. *Ét.* ii 213, *Rec.* ii § 40, *Album d'Ant. Or.* Pl. xlvi (facsimile).

L. 1. אנה l. 20. **68** 1. **73** A 3; contrast אנך **61** 1. אנכי **62** 19. The Aram. character of the dialect is more strongly marked in this inscr. than in the two preceding ones. ברכב The same person as the donor of **62**; he was reigning prob. in the years 732–727 B.C.

L. 2. מלך שמאל The outline of the history of Sam'al may be traced in Assyr. inscrr. for about 233 years. It is first mentioned, as a country, by Salmanassar ii (860–825 B.C.), who defeated a coalition of N. Syrian kings at the beginning of his reign, *KB* i 156 f.: Sam'al was then an independent state. It is mentioned next by Tiglath-pileser iii in 738 and 734 B.C., as a town, with a king Panammu, *KB* ii 20. 30: at this period it became tributary. Then, in 681 B.C., the provincial governor of Sam'al gave his name to the first year of Asarhaddon (681–668 B.C.), Smith *Eponym. Canon* 68; and in 670 Asarhaddon made Sam'al a halting-place on his return from Egypt. By this time it had become part of the Assyrian empire. Lastly, the name appears in two lists of Syrian towns, temp. Ašurbanipal (668–626 B.C.), which must have been written before the end of his reign, Rawlinson *Cun. Inscrr. of W. Asia* ii 53 1 l. 43; 53 3 l. 61; Sachau 58 ff. The situation of Sam'al may be inferred from the occurrence of the name in the inscrr. between Gurgum (**62** 15 *n.*) and Patin or Hamath (*KB* i 156; ii 20. 30); it lay in the country between the rivers Pyramos on the N. and Orontes on the S., at the foot of the Amanus mountains. The name has a Semitic sound, and perhaps, like the Hebr. שְׂמֹאל, means *left*, geographically *north*. In this inscr. Bar-rekub, son of Panammu ii, calls himself 'king of Sam'al' and his ancestors 'kings of Sam'al' ll. 2. 16 f., but

Panammu ii is styled 'king of Ya'di' in **62**, and likewise Panammu i in **61**. The question arises, what is the relation between the two districts or cities? Sam'al, it seems, was ruled by the dynasty of Panammu ii and Bar-rekub; Tiglath-pileser speaks of 'Panammu of Sam'al' (supr.); and we may suppose that Ya'di, which had Panammu i for its king in an earlier generation (see **61** 1 *n.*), was attached to the neighbouring state of Sam'al in the time of Panammu ii, perhaps as a reward for his fidelity to the king of Assyria. The fact that a king of Sam'al and a king of Ya'di bore the same name, though belonging to different families, may be merely accidental or due to some previous alliance by marriage (Winckler *Altor. Forsch.* i 15 ff.). It is curious, however, that Bar-rekub, if he ruled over both places, in **62** makes no mention of Sam'al, and in **63** says nothing about Ya'di. Whether Zenjirli belonged to Ya'di or to Sam'al in ancient times is not clear; for both **62** (יאדי) and **63** (שמאל) were found there. The Hadad statue (**61**), which was found at Gerjin near Zenjirli, was certainly a product of Ya'di. Winckler argues that Zenjirli and Gerjin belonged to Ya'di, and were situated near the southern border of Sam'al, the neighbouring state.

L. 3. עבד תגלתפליסר See **62** 13 *n.*; illustrate from 2 K. 16 7.

L. 4. רבעי ארקא In **62** 14 רבעתארק. ארקא is a clear instance of the emphatic state, cf. מלכיא l. 14. ביתא l. 20, and perhaps שתוא, כיצא ll. 18 f. In **61** and **62** this characteristic Aram. usage does not occur. בצדק אבי Cf. **62** 19.

L. 5. רכבאל See **61** 2 *n.*

L. 7. כרסא See **15** 2 *n.* עמל Perf. 3 sing. or ptcp., probably *laboured, toiled*, as in Aram., Arab., and late Hebr.; מן will then have a comparative sense. Bar-rekub claims that his family was the most zealous of all the princely houses in the service of the suzerain.

L. 8. ורצת בגלגל Lit. *I ran at the wheel*, i. e. followed the chariot; cf. **62** 13, and contrast 1 S. 8 11 ורצו לפני מרכבתו.

L. 9. במצעת See **61** 28 *n.*

L. 10. מלכן רברבן The form of the plur. is clearly Aram.; see **61** 4 *n.* The reduplicated form of רב is common in the Targ., רַבְרְבָא; in Syr. ܪ̈ܘܪܒܐ. בעלי כסף וגו׳ Cf. **62** 11; בעל in this sense is frequent in the O. T., e. g. Qoh. **5** 10. 12 &c.

L. 12. והיטבתה Perhaps out of spoils of the campaign; Cl.-Gan. *Rec.* ii 103.

L. 13. חד See **61** 27 *n.*

L. 14. התנאבו is a double reflexive form, Ethnafal, from אבה or from יאב (i. e. הִתְיְאִבוּ), the latter being frequent in Syr. in the Ethpa. ܐܬܐܒ, in Hebr. Ps. 119 131 יאבתי. The meaning is prob. *they wished for themselves*, i. e. *coveted*. Hoffm. compares the Assyr. Ittanafal form in *ittanabriq* 'flash forth,' and the Ethiop. reflexive with prefixed *tau* (Dillmann *Gram. Äth. Spr.*[2] 150). Sachau unnecessarily supposes an error for התנדבו. מלכיא See l. 4 *n.*

L. 15. לכל מה The ל is governed by התנאבו; מה adds a vaguely intensifying force to כל, as the Arab. ما after an indef. noun; in Palm. כלמא 147 i 12. מבת Either sing. טָבַת or plur. טָבָת.

L. 16. בי is perhaps for בית, the final ת being dropped; it is difficult to obtain sense if בי is the prep. with suff. לישה i. e. ליש *there was not*, with suff. 3 sing. mas., לישה, without the final י; cf. קרמוה 65 2 for קדמוהי. ליש is a contracted form of לא יש, cf. the Arab. لَيْسَ (inflected like a verb), Aram. לֵית, ܠܝܬ, Mand. לא ייח, and the Assyr. *lā isu* 'is not,' 'has not.' In the second Nêrab inscr. the negative shows the same tendency to assimilate itself to the word following and to lose the א, thus לאתאחזו 65 4. לשמו 6. לתהנם 8. אבהי Plur. with suff., cf. אֲבָהָתִי Dan. 2 23. For the ה inserted cf. שְׁמָהָת from שֻׁם Ezr. 5 4, and 9 3 *n.*

L. 17. בית in this and the foll. lines means *palace* more naturally than *mausoleum*. כלמו Perhaps=Assyr. *kalâmu* 'all,' 'of every kind.' 'A house of totality' will then mean 'a single house' or 'a house for everything'; it was the only palace which Bar-rekub's ancestors possessed. Another possible explanation is that כלמו stands by metathesis for מלכו=מלכות 'a royal palace,' see 62 17 *n.*; so Hoffm., Cl.-Gan., Lidzb.(?).

L. 18. להם with the suff. ־הם for ־הן; so in Egypt. Aram., e. g. במנתם 76 A 1; in Nab., e. g. להם 85 2. בניהם 89 5; in B. Aram., e. g. Jer. 10 11 and Ezr. (by the side of ־הון, but Dan. has only ־הון); and in Targ. Ps.-Jon. שתוא=Arab. شِتَآء, Hebr. סתו Cant. 2 11.

L. 19. כיצא = קיצא, cf. יכמלוך = יקמלוך 64 11. כרצי = קרצי 75 2; similarly the Arab. ضحك = Hebr. צחק, Mand. כושטא = Hebr. קשט. For the winter and summer palace cf. Am. 3 15 בית החרף, בית הקיץ, and Jer. 36 22. כיצא=Aram. קיטא, Arab. قيظ.

L. 20. ביתא See l. 4 *n.*

Additional note on the dialect of the Zenjirli inscriptions.

There can be no doubt that this dialect belongs to the Aramaic, rather than to any other branch of the Semitic family. Thus the words רברבן, קדם, סם, טרא, מטע(ה), כרסא, חד, בר, ארק, אנה; the forms אברו

61 15. כברו 11. זכרו 31. מלכו 62 17 (?); the ending ת of the fem. absol. 62 6 *n.*; the plur. ending in *n*, מלכן רברבן 63 10. 13. שלשן 62 3 *n.*, and without *n*, אלהי 61 4 *n.*; the suff. 3 sing. m. in ה׳ and 3 plur. in הם׳ 63 18 *n.*; the accus. sign ות 61 28; the relative זי; חיתה=חוה 62 2; the impf. forms ירקי, חשתי &c. 61 22 *n.* ליתכה, למנע &c. 61 23 *n.*; the use of the perf. with weak waw; the absence of the article, and the use of the emphatic form in 63;—all these forms and usages are characteristic of Aramaic. On the other hand there are features which exhibit an affinity to the Canaanite group, Hebrew, Moabite, Phoenician, e.g. אנך, אנכי, בני 61 10. 20, נם, חיה, חרג, זכר, זר, חקק, חרא, לילא, לקח, נתן; the impf. 3 plur. in *û* 61 4 *n.*; the infin. without prefixed מ; while passages abound which find illustrations or parallels in the O.T., see esp. 61 9. 16. 18. 23. 29. 62 2. 3. 4. 6. 7. 11. 13. 18. 19. 63 3. 19 with the notes. Even more significant is the way in which this dialect allies itself with Hebr. (and Assyrian) rather than with the usual Aram., in the following consonantal equations, the first three of which are also characteristic of the dialect of Nêrab, 64. 65:—

Arab.	Aram.	Hebr.	Zenj.	
ذ =	ד	= ז =	ז,	e.g. זי, זן, זנה, זהב, זכר, אחז, פמז[1].
ث =	ת	= ש =	ש,	e.g. ישב, שקל, אשר, שלשן.
ظ =	ט	= צ =	צ,	e.g. כיצא 63 19.
ض =	ק (ע)	= צ =	ק,	e.g. ארק, רקי, מוקא (61 5 *n.*).

In the last equation the alliance is with Aram., not with Hebrew. These facts point to the conclusion that the dialect belongs to an early stage of Aramaic, and differs in many respects from the later literary Aramaic, particularly in a closer resemblance to the language of the O.T. and of the early Aram. inscrr. from Nêrab, Babylon, and Egypt (61 1 *n.* 4 *n.* 5 *n.* 62 6 *n.* 63 19 *n.* &c.). It was a local dialect, with certain peculiarities of its own (e.g. פ *and*, פמז, ומז, ליש, מת?), some of which show a kinship with Arabic (e.g. פ, אשם, כל מת, זי = ذو, ודד &c.); and no doubt it was influenced by contact with Assyria. The Hittite kingdom once predominated in the neighbourhood of Ya'di and Sam'al[2], but the nature of its influence upon these petty states is not known at present.

[1] This equation is found also in the Aram. of Nineveh 66, Babylon CIS ii 65. 69–71, Asia Minor (Abydos 67, Cilicia 68. 149 A 6), Têma (Arabia) 69. 70, and Egypt 71. 74–77. It is characteristic of the Aram. of the early period, 8th–4th cent. B.C., as used in the Assyrian and Persian empires. The forms זי, זן, זנה, זא are specially significant as distinguishing the old from the later Aram. of the O.T., Nab., Palm., and Palest. dialects (see p. 26).

[2] Lagrange *Rev. Biblique* (1901) 30 f. 35 = *Rel. Sém.* (1903) 44. 50.

64. Nêrab 1. Prob. vii cent. B.C. Louvre.

1 שׂשנזרבן כמר
2 שהר בנרב מת
3 חנה צלמה
4 ואר צתׅה
5 מן את
6 תהנס צלמא
7 זנה וארצתא
8 מן אשרה
9 שהר ושמש ונכל ונשך יסחו
10 שמך ואשרך מן חין ומות לחה
11 יכטלוך ויהאבדו זרעך והן
12 תנצר צלמא וארצתא זא
13 אחרה ינצר
14 זי לך

Of Sin-zir-ban, priest [2] of Sahar in Nêrab, deceased. [3] And this is his image [4] and his couch. [5] Whosoever thou art [6] that shalt plunder this image [7] and couch [8] from its place, [9] may Sahar and Shamash and Nikal and Nusk pluck [10] thy name and thy place out of life, and with a ? death [11] kill thee, and cause thy seed to perish! But if [12] thou shalt protect this image and couch, [13] may another protect [14] thine!

The two inscrr. **64** and **65** were found in 1891 at Nêrab, a small village SE. of Aleppo. They accompany the bas-reliefs of two priests of the local sanctuary, finely executed in the Assyrian manner and singularly well preserved. No. **64** represents the priest Sin-zir-ban, with hands raised and joined in prayer; the upper part of the inscr. surrounds the head and hands, the lower part is written across the robe. The writing is not so archaic and rigid as that of the Zenjirli inscrr., while it belongs to an earlier stage than that of the inscrr. from Têma (69. 70). An indication of date is afforded by the names of the deities mentioned. They are clearly Assyrian; and 'the moon-god at Nêrab,' the chief deity of the place, can be none other than the Assyrian Sin, whose great temple was at Ḥarran. The worship of Sin had already made its way from Ḥarran to N. Syria in the time of Bar-rekub, before 727 B.C. (see p. 182); and from the same quarter it found a home at Nêrab. The temple at Ḥarran was destroyed by the Medes in 605 and restored by Nabonid in 552. Cl.-Ganneau, with much plausibility, dates these monuments from this period. He suggests that after the catastrophe of 605, Nêrab offered the hospitality of a shrine to the moon-god and his allied divinities (*Ét.* ii 222).

L. 1. ששנזרבן The first letter is not distinctly cut, but the traces are clear enough to justify the reading (Lidzb., Cl.-Gan. *Rec.* iii 106 f.). This ש must be the relative and sign of the genitive; cf. 65 1, and similarly in Phoen., at the head of an inscr., 39 2 *n.* In Aram. we should expect זי at this period (e.g. זי כספא CIS ii 70); but the usage here is perhaps influenced by the Assyr. *ša* (possessive). שנזרבן The name is Assyr., *Sin-zir-ban* 'Sin has created a son,' a suitable name for a priest of שהר = Sin, the moon-god; cf. *Marduk-zir-bâni* CIS ii 18 end. כמר 65 1. 69 23. b 2; Nab. 98 4; Syr. ܟܘܡܪܐ; NPun. 55 7 (see *n.*). The √כמר may be connected with the Assyr. *kamâru* 'lay prostrate,' hence כמר *priest*, lit. 'one who prostrates himself.'

L. 2. שהר i.e. *the moon*; Aram. סהר, סיהר, זיהר; Arab. شهر; cf. Hebr. שַׂהֲרֹנִים 'moon-shaped ornaments,' Jud. 8 21. 26. Is. 3 18; see further on l. 9. שהר בנרב *the moon-god at Nêrab* 65 1. For the expression see 24 2 *n.*; it implies that the deity was imported from elsewhere. נרב is still called النيرب. Three places of this name were known to antiquity, this one near Aleppo, another near Sermin (27½ m. SE. of Aleppo), and a third near Damascus. Nireb is mentioned in the list of Thothmes iii, *Rec. of the Past*, new ser., v 33; and Stephanus Byz. s. v. Νήραβος gives πόλις Συρίας, possibly, but not certainly, referring to the Nêrab here. It is not unlikely that Nêrab acknowledged the suzerainty of Assyria at this period, judging from the strongly marked impress of Assyr. influence on these inscriptions.

L. 3. זנה See add. note ii p. 26.

L. 4. ארצתה l. 7 ארצתא = ערשתא (Cl.-Gan. *Ét.* ii 196, Lidzb.) lit. *couch*, here *sarcophagus* 65 8, cf. Dt. 3 11 ערש ברזל; Palm. ערשא = κλίνη, Inscr. of Ṭayyibe, p. 296 *n.* 1. For the orthography cf. אשקלן = عسقلان, אתרקדש = *'Athar* (عَثَر) *is holy* CIS ii 312 (Hoffm. *ZA* xi 211), and in

Mand. אטמא=עטמא=עצם, Nöld. *Mand. Gr.* 58 *n.* For צ=ש cf. יצחק and ישחק.

L. 5 f. מן את תהגם Cf. 65 8, the indefinite rel. מן as in Nab. 94 5 מן כל די, מן די, and in Palm. 147 ii a 34. 45 ff. מן די. Cl.-Gan. finds a similar construction in 4 3 מי את כל אדם איש תפק; but see note in loc. The general sense of תהגם 65 8. 9 is clear from the context, but the etymology is uncertain. The form may be explained as the Hafel, or rather Peal, impf. of הגם=אגם *carry off by force, rob*, a root frequent in the Targums, the ה being written for א as היך for איך, הלו for אלו 73 A 1; so Hoffm. 212. Or it may be the Hafel impf. apocopated of נסא = נשא (cf. 5 5) treated as a ל״ה verb, with the ה retained in Hafel as in תאברו l. 11 (Cl.-Gan. 197 f.). The first explanation is perhaps preferable.

L. 8. אשרה Cf. 61 27 *n.* Note that ש, as in the dialect of Zenjirli, here=Aram. ת=Arab. ث; see p. 185.

L. 9. שהר ושמש ונכל ונשך 65 9. Sahar (l. 2 *n.*) is the Aram. equivalent of the Assyr. Sin, the moon-god (שהר mas.) of Ḥarran. Not only Sahar, but the other gods of Nêrab are Assyrian in origin. Thus Sin, Shamash, [Nergal], Nusku are invoked along with other deities, and in this order, by Salmanassar ii and frequently by Ašurbanipal, e.g. *KB* i 130. ii 154 f. 176 ff. 210. 216 ff. &c. In the cylinder from Abû-Habba (Sippar) Nabonid, 555–538 B.C., records how he rebuilt I-ḫul-ḫul, the temple of Sin at Ḥarran, which had been founded by Salmanassar ii and refounded by Ašurbanipal. In connexion with his work of restoration, Nabonid calls upon these same gods in the order Sin, Ningal (instead of Nergal), Shamash, [Ishtar], Nusku; *KB* iii 2 100 f. We may conclude, therefore, that along with Sin, these other deities, associated with the moon-god, were imported from Ḥarran. The god Shamash has been found already at Zenjirli, see 61 2 *n.* Nikal is no doubt the same as Ningal mentioned by Nabonid, the *n* being assimilated, and the *k* interchanged with *g*, as in *Tukulti*=תגלת in תגלתפלסר; moreover Jensen (*ZA* xi 296 f.) shows that the Sumerian Nin-gal would be pronounced by the Assyrians *Nikal* or *Nikkal*. This form actually occurs as the name of the goddess, ܒܬ ܢܝܟܠ, worshipped at Ḥarran in *The Doctrine of Addai*, ed. Phillips 24 l. 17; and the same passage enumerates the other gods, ܢܫܪܐ *the eagle*, prob. a copyist's misreading of נשך in the original, ܣܗܪܐ the moon-god, and ܫܡܫܐ the sun-god. In the inscr. of Nabonid, l. c., Ningal (= Nikal) is said to be the consort of Sin, and 'the mother of the great gods.' Nusku, the son of Sin, was a fire-god, the messenger of Bel; Jensen l. c. 295, Jastrow *Rel. of*

Bab. and Assyr. 220 f. The above argument is clearly stated by Cl.-Gan. 211–221. יסחו From נסח *tear out*, cf. ינסחוהו ורעה ושמה 69 14 (optative). Ezr. 6 11; in Hebr. Pr. 2 22. Ps. 52 7 &c. For the impf. 3 plur. in *û* for *ûn* cf. יהאבדו l. 11. יהבאשו 65 9, and see 61 4 *n*.

L. 10. מן חין *from life* rather than *from the living*, the plur. being in the absol. state, and having an abstract sense, like זקנים &c.; cf. ועד חיין *and unto life* CIS ii 163 d. ארכה בחיין Dan. 7 12. ומות לחה A second accus. of manner after the direct obj. in יכמלוך l. 11; cf. Mal. 3 24 והכיתי את הארץ חרם. Ps. 64 8 וַיֹּרֵם אלהים חץ. The meaning of לחה is unknown. Various explanations are possible: thus, *a destructive death*, Syr. ܚܒܠ *destroy; a death in full vigour*, Hebr. לח *fresh*, cf. תבא לח אלי קבר *Ber. Rab.* § 79; *an ignominious death*, Arab. لحى, ملحى *ignominious*. The general sense must be the same as יהבאשו ממתתה 65 9 f.

L. 11. יכמלוך With כ for ק cf. כיצא 68 19, קַשָּׁת = ܩܰܫܳܬܳܐ *archer* &c., Wright *Comp. Gr.* 50. ויהאבדו For the ה retained in Hafel impf. cf. יהבאשו 65 9. יהנ[סק] 69 21, and the usage in B. Aram., יְהַשְׁפִּל Dan. 7 24. תְּהַנְזִק Ezr. 4 13. The Peal of אבד occurs in 65 10.

L. 12. תנצר As in the Zenjirli inscrr., צ = Hebr. צ = Aram. ט = Arab. ظ; cf. כיצא 68 19, and see p. 185. The נ is not assimilated; cf. Ps. 61 8 &c., ינסחוהי 69 14, and contrast יסחו l. 9.

L. 13. אחרה 65 8 a curious form, not easy to account for. Hoffm., 213 ff., points it אָחֳרָה, an older form of אָחֳרָן, with ָה added to the root as in רֵעָה (from רֵעַ), לְבֵנָה, אִשָּׁה; then, he says, to this *oḥorê* was added the nominal ending ן. The addition ָה to a triliteral root is, however, a very rare occurrence, and it is doubtful whether it would be attached to such a common word as אחר. It seems much more likely that אחרה is merely the emphatic form, with ה for א, אחרה being an early form of the usual אחרנא, ܐܚܪܢܐ.

65. Nêrab 2. Prob. same date as **64.** Louvre.

1 שאגבר כמר שהר בנרב

2 זנה צלמה בצדקתי קדמוה

3 שמני שם טב והארך יומי

4 ביום מתת פמי לאתאחז מן מלן

5 ובעיני מחזה אנה בני רבע בכוו

6 י והום אתהמו ולשמו עמי מאן

7 כסף ונחש עם לבשי שמוני למען

8 לאחרה לתהנס ארצתי מן את תעשק

9 ותהנסני שהר ונכל ונשך יהבאשו

10 ממתתה ואחרתה תאבד

Of Agbar, priest of Sahar in Nêrab: [2] this is his image. For my righteousness before him [3] he gave me a good name and prolonged my days. [4] In the day that I died my mouth was not closed from words; [5] and with my eyes what do I see? Children of the fourth generation! They wept [6] for me, and were utterly distracted (?). And they did not lay with me any vessel [7] of silver or bronze; with my shroud they laid me, so that [8] for another (?) thou shouldest not plunder my couch. Whosoever thou art that shalt injure [9] and plunder me—may Sahar and Nikal and Nusk make his death miserable, [10] and may his posterity perish!

The priest Agbar is represented sitting, in the act of offering a libation before an altar. Facing him from behind the altar stands an attendant, holding a fan. The treatment of the scene recalls an Egyptian funeral rite, but the style of the figures is thoroughly Assyrian.

L. 1. שאגבר For ש see 64 1 *n*. The name *Agbaru* occurs in an Assyr.-Aram. inscr., CIS ii 42 end; cf. the name of a chief in the Amanus district, *Gabbari*, *KB* i 162. The title as in 64 1.

L. 2. בצדקתי See 62 19 *n*. 8 9. קדמוה *before him*, קדם 62 21; or the suff. cf. אבוה 62 2. 1 *n*., Palm. בנוה Vogüé 21. 80 4.

L. 3. שם טב Cf. שם נעם 9 6. והארך יומי Cf. 8 9.

L. 4. מתת Prob. perf. 1 sing., מֵתֶת. If the form were a noun, the suff. 1 sing. would be needed. לאתאחז In this inscr. ל is written for לָא, לשמו l. 6. לתהנס l. 8. 63 16 *n*. אתאחז is the Ethpeal of אחז = Syr. אחד (see p. 185) *to be closed, hindered from* .., e. g. ܦܘܡܝ .. ܠܐ ܐܬܐܚܕ Eze. 33 22, sometimes followed by ܡܢ, as here. The general sense may be illustrated by Deut. 34 7.

L. 5. מחזה אנה Oratio directa: מ׳ = מָה *what?* or *how?* For the abbreviation cf. פמו 61 3. 4. 22. חזה is the ptcp. = חָזֵה. רבע = Hebr. רִבֵּעִים Ex. 20 5. 34 7 &c. בכוני i. e. בַּכִּיוּנִי Pael perf. 3 plur.

with suff.; cf. בכיה 62 17. The perf. 3 plur. in this dialect ends in *ū*, not *ūn*, e.g. שמו l. 6, cf. קמו 61 2. נתנו ib. 20; read, therefore, בכוני not בכון. Before the suff. the נ of the 3 plur. reappears, e.g. שמוני l. 7. Hoffm. (l. c. 224) reads בכון as = בכוני; but in this inscr. the suff. is always written.

L. 6. ותום אתהמו Lidzb.'s explanation of these difficult words may be accepted provisionally (*Eph.* i 193). He takes תום as an abstr. noun used as infin. abs., and אתהמו as Ethpe. pf. 3 plur. of תום lit. *murmur*, *discomfit*, fig. *be distracted*, as in Hebr. e.g. Ps. 55 3. Hoffm. suggests בכון יוהו מאתהמו 'they wept for me—Oh woe!—the hundred of them,' taking יוהו as = *οὐαί*, Heb. הוי, אוי, Syr. ܘܘܝ, ܝܘܝ, and מאתהמו as = מְאָתֵיהֹמוֹ (cf. תְּלָתֵּהוֹן Dan. 3 23); the form of the suff. is unusual, and must be treated as a case of the separate pron. הִמּוֹ (76 B 4) being used as a suff., cf. Hebr. אֵלֵיהֵמָּה Eze. 40 16. גְּוִיֹּתֵיהֵנָּה 1 11. 78 B 2; Kautzsch *Lehrg.* ii 447. ולשמו i.e. וְלָא שָׂמוּ. מאן Cf. Dan. 5 2 מאני דהבא וכספא. 4 5 *n.* 5 5.

L. 7. למען Apparently = Hebr. לְמַעַן *in order that.*

L. 8. לאחרה לתהנס The construction gives difficulty. It is natural to suppose that אחרה and תהנס are the same forms as in 64 6. 13. Taking the ל with both words as the negative, repeated for emphasis, we may render: 'in order that thou—other one—shouldest not plunder.' But such a construction is almost intolerably harsh; the ל with אחרה may be the prep., *for another* (dat. commodi). מן את See 64 5 *n.*

L. 9. For the gods see 64 9 *n.* יהבאשו The Hafel as in 64 11 *n.* The √ באש occurs in all the cognate languages, Aram. בְּאֵשׁ, ܒܐܫ *be evil*, cf. באיש 75 2; Arab. بأس ib.; Assyr. *bîšu* 'evil'; Hebr. באש *stink.*

L. 10. ממתתה *his manner of death*; the change of persons after מן את l. 8 is curious. For the meaning cf. מרוצה *manner of running* 2 S. 18 27, and for the form cf. Targ. מְמָתָא, מְמוֹתָא; here the fem. ending is added to the root מות. אחרתה In Nab. אחר (Arab. أُخُر) is used in the sense of *posterity*, e.g. 79 2. 82 3 &c.; illustrate from Num. 24 20 וְאַחֲרִיתוֹ עֲדֵי אֹבֵד. The vivid style of the inscr. is noticeable, and recalls passages in 4. 5. 61, where similar imprecations are to be found.

BABYLONIA

66. Nineveh. CIS ii 1. End of viii cent. B.C. Brit. Mus.

a מנן — III II ב ז׳ ארקא

b IIIIIIIIIIIIIII

c חמשת עשר מנין [ב ז]׳ מלך

a 15 double (?) minas of the country.

b 15.

c Fifteen double (?) minas of the king.

The inscr. is written upon one of the bronze lion-weights found at Nineveh; CIS ii 1–14. Twelve of these weights have Assyr. as well as Aram. inscrr., and bear the names of Salmanassar, Sargon, and Sennacherib; they belong, therefore, to the viii–vii cent.

a. מנן In Babyl. written ideographically MA. NA, of Sumerian, but possibly Semitic, origin; Hebr. מָנִים from מָנֶה Eze. 45 12 &c., μνᾶ. The *mina* was the unit in the Babylonian system of weights, which was based on the sexagesimal principle; hence 60 shekels = one mina, and 60 minas = one talent. ב Prob. a symbol for *double*; CIS ii 2. 3. 4. In the Babyl. system there was a double series of weights, a heavy and a light one. The heavy mina = 982·4 grammes = 15160 grains, circ. 2⅛ lb. avoir.; the light mina was half the weight, i.e. 491·2 grammes = 7580 grains, circ. 1$\frac{1}{12}$ lb. avoir. The present weight weighs a little over 32 lb. 14 oz.; when new it prob. weighed about 33 lb. 6 oz.; its value, therefore, is that of the heavy standard. These lion-weights belong some to the one class, some to the other; the light weights sometimes have the shape of a duck. See Kennedy, art. Weights and Measures, Hastings' *Dict. Bibl.*; Benzinger *Hebr. Arch.* 180 ff.; Nowack *Lehrb. Hebr. Arch.* i 206 ff. ז׳ Sign of the genit.; 61 1 *n.* ארקא 61 5 *n.*

c. מלך In Aram. מלכא would be usual; the form is prob. due to Assyr. influence (Corp.). The 'minas of the king' corresponds to the Assyr. *mana ša šarri*, cf. Hebr. אבן המלך 2 S. 14 26 (prob. a post-exilic addition, giving the weight by the Persian standard). These weights were found among the foundations of a royal palace, underneath a colossal winged bull; most of them bear the king's name in the Assyrian versions of the inscriptions.

ASIA MINOR

67. Abydos. CIS ii 108. vi–v cent. B.C. Brit. Mus.

אספרן לקבל סתריא זי כספא *a*

A *b*

a Correct (?) according to the commissioners (?) of money.

This lion-weight, found at Abydos in Asia Minor, belongs to the Persian period, as the form of the letters shows. At this period Asia Minor was subject to Persian rule, and the Persian satraps used Aramaic in intercourse with the subject races in the west of the empire (cf. 71 *n.*). This was a trade weight officially certified to be of full standard. It weighs 25·657 grammes, i. e. originally 26 grammes = about 56 lb.; hence it appears that the standard was not the Babylonian one (66), nor the Persian silver talent of 33·6 kilogrs., but the Persian-Euboean gold talent of 25·92 kilogrs. On the back of the lion is the mark A, apparently from the Archaic Gk. alphabet; it seems to indicate that the weight was used in commerce with the Greeks.

a. אספרן is best explained as an Iranian word *uspurn* 'completeness,' 'whole' (Marti *Bibl.-Aram. Gr.* Gloss.), consequently the meaning here will be 'of full standard'; in Ezr. 5 8 &c. אָסְפַּרְנָא 'completely,' 'with exactness.' A different explanation is suggested by Hoffmann, *ZA* xi 235 f. He regards אספרן as an Aram. form of צִפֹּרֶן *nail*, with א prefixed as in אצבע, and with ס=צ as in סותא 69 13=ظُفْر; and compares the use of *supur* 'nail-sign' in Assyr., e.g. 'instead of their seal they have made their nail-sign' (*supuršunu*), *KB* iv 104. The Persian etymology, however, seems more likely in view of the date and origin of the inscr. לקבל Lit. *to meet*, so *before*, cp. in Palm. 147 i 10. סתריא Prob. = 'officials,' but the precise meaning is uncertain. Vogüé renders 'guardians' from סתר *hide*, a questionable use of the root; Levy renders 'satraps'; Geiger 'staters,' 'correct in accordance with the silver stater' (Cook *Aram. Gloss.* 23); but the weight of the lion shows that the standard was the gold talent, as Meyer points out, *Entstehung d. Judenth.* 11 *n.* The proper expression for 'officials in charge of the money' would be סתריא זי על כספא (Halévy); the Aramaic of these Persian commissioners was perhaps not very correct.

68. Cilicia. v–iv cent. B.C. In situ.

אנה ושונש בר 1
אפושי בר ברה זי 2
ושונש ואמי 3
אשולכרתי וכזי 4
צידא עבד אנה תנה 5
ובאתרא זנה משתרה אנה 6

I am WŠWNŠ, son [2] of ’FWŠI, grandson of [3] WŠWNŠ, and my mother is [4] ’ŠWLKRTI; and while [5] I am hunting here, [6] it is in this place that I am making my meal.

The inscr. is carved upon a rock SE. of Saraïdin, in the valley of the river Lamas, in the SE. of Cilicia. A facsimile is given by Nöld. l. c. infra.

L. 1. ושנש This and the other pr. nn. appear to be non-Semitic, perhaps Persian; but the forms are uncertain because the ו may be read נ. Halévy reads נ in each case, and takes נשננש as = Ξυγγενής, a dialectical form of Συγγενής (נש = ξ), אפנשי l. 2 = Ἀπάξιος; *Rev. Sém.* i (1893) 183 ff. Nöldeke reads ו, *ZA* vii (1892) 350 ff.

L. 2. בר ברה Cf. **8** 1. For ז in Cilicia = די cf. **149** A 6 and p. 185 *n.*

L. 4. אשולכרתי is explained by Halévy *Ashgal the Cretan*, or *of Cretopolis* (in Pisidia); for אשגל he compares שֵׁגָל Ps. **45** 10 &c., and takes כרתי as an ethnic form. כזי *when*, cf. Palm. **121** 3 כדי הוא חנן and l. 4. כזי, כדי more often mean *as*, e. g. **76** C 3. **94** 4 &c.

L. 5. צידא עבד Lit. *doing a hunt*; עבד ptcp. active. תנה i.e. תְּנָה *here* = ثَمَّ, as the Bibl. Aram. תַּמָּה = ثَمَّ.

L. 6. אתרא Contrast אשרה **64** 8. משתרה reading ר rather than ד; the form is Ethpa. ptcp. from שרה, and, like ܐܫܬܪܝܘ = ἀριστᾶν in the N.T., e. g. John **21** 12. 15, means *breaking* (*my*) *fast* (Nöldeke l. c.). The reading משתדה can only mean *I was cast down*, not ‘je me repose’ (Halévy).

ARABIA

69. Têma. CIS ii 113. Date prob. v cent. B.C. Louvre.

a

1 ....בשת Z|| ......
2 .. בתימ]א צלם [זי מחרם ושנגלא
3 ואש]ירא אלהי תימא לצלם זי
4 [הגם ...] שמה ביומא זן [בתי]מא
5 ....זי
6 ....
7 ....
8 ....א להן............א
9 זי [הקי]ם צלמשזב בר פטסרי
10 [בבית צ]לם זי הגם להן אלהי
11 תימא צ[דק]ו לצלמשזב בר פטסרי
12 ולזרעה בבית צלם זי הגם וגבר
13 זי יחבל סותא זא אלהי תימא
14 ינסחוהי וזרעה ושמה מן אנפי
15 תימא והא זא צדקתא זי י[הבו]
16 צלם זי מחרם ושנגלא ואשירא
17 אלהי תימא לצלם זי הגם א.
18 מן חקלא דקלן ⟵ ||| ||| ומן שימתא
19 זי מלכא דקלן |||| || כל דקלן
20 |Z .. שנה בשנה ואלהן ואנש
21 לא יהנ[פק] צלמשזב בר פטסרי
22 מן ביתא זנה ול[זר]עה ושמה
23 כמ[ריא בב]יתא זנה [לעלמא]

b

צלמשזב
כמרא

a. . . . . in the 22nd year . . . [2] [in Têm]a, Ṣalm of Maḥram and Shingala [3] and Ashîra, the gods of Têma, to Ṣalm of [4] [Hajam] . . appointed him on this day [in Tê]ma . . . . . [5] which . . . . [6] . . . . . [7] . . . . . [8] therefore . . . . [9] which Ṣalm-shezeb, son of Peṭ-osiri, set up [10] [in the temple of Ṣ]alm of Hajàm, therefore the gods of [11] Têma ma[de gra]nts to Ṣalm-shezeb, son of Peṭ-osiri, [12] and to his seed in the temple of Ṣalm of Hajam. And any man [13] who shall destroy this pillar, may the gods of Têma [14] pluck out him and his seed and his name from before [15] Têma! And this is the grant which [16] Ṣalm of Maḥram and Shingala and Ashîra, [17] the gods of Têma, have g[iven] to Ṣalm of Hajam . . : [18] from the field 16 palms, and from the treasure (?) [19] of the king 5 palms, in all [20] 21 palms . . year by year. And neither gods nor men [21] shall bri[ng out] Ṣalm-shezeb, son of Peṭ-osiri, [22] from this temple, neither his se[ed] nor his name, (who are) [23] prie[sts in] this temple [for ever].

b. Ṣalm-shezeb the priest.

The characters exhibit some archaic forms, e. g. ז and י; but as a whole they belong to the early part of the middle period of Aramaic writing. Like 61–63 the inscr. is carved in relief. It records how a new deity, Ṣalm of Hajam, was introduced into Têma by the priest Ṣalm-shezeb, who further provided an endowment for the new temple, and founded an hereditary priesthood. On one side of the stone the god Ṣalm of Hajam is represented in Assyrian fashion, and below him a priest stands before an altar, with the inscr. *b* underneath.

L. 1. בשת See 6 1 *n.* שת is in the constr. st. before the numeral as in 71 3, and often in Nab. and Palm., e. g. 78 4. 110 5.

L. 2. צלם 70 3 perhaps connected with √ظلم *be dark* (cf. Assyr. *kakkabu ṣalmu* = the planet Kêwân or Saturn, and the pr. n. *Ṣalmu-aḫi*, *KB* iv 150; see Am. 5 26), rather than abbreviated from צלם בעל *image of B.*; see 38 2 *n.* Ṣalm appears to have been an Aramaic or

N. Semitic deity, and not native to Arabia. Like בעל, he is given a local designation, ll. 10. 16. The names of the gods are here restored from l. 16.

L. 3. תימא Cf. 81 2 = תֵּימָא Gen. 25 15 = 1 Chr. 1 30 a descendant of Ishmael, Is. 21 14. Jer. 25 23. The town, now called تَيْمَاء, is situated in N. Arabia (El-Ḥejaz) in an oasis famous, even in ancient times, for its abundant and inexhaustible spring. Caravans (Job 6 19) on their way to Egypt or Assyria halted here; and the influence of commerce with these two countries is evident in this stone: the name of the priest's father is Egyptian, the figures of the god and his minister are Assyrian. לצלם זי[חגם] is governed by some verb denoting that the local gods had sanctioned the admission of this stranger deity; the Corp. suggests צדקו (l. 11) at the beginning of l. 2.

L. 4. שמה Prob. pf. 3 sing. m. with suff.=שָׂמֵהּ; the subj. will be the priest, the obj. the god.

L. 8. לחן l. 10=הֵן *if*+לְ, *then, therefore*; Dan. 2 6. 9 &c.

L. 9. צלמשזב i. e. *Ṣalm has delivered*; cf. the Assyr. *Ṣalm-mušēzib*, *Nabû-šēzibanni* Schrader *COT* 421, and the Hebr. מְשֵׁיזַבְאֵל Neh. 3 4 (Cook *Aram. Gl.* s. v.); שזב, in Targ. שֵׁיזִב, Syr. ܫܘܙܒ, is Shafel of יזב, 101 12 f. פטסרי 74 A 4 i. e. *he whom Osiris gave*, cf. the Egypt. *P'-dy-'st* 'he whom Isis gave,' *P'-dy-'Imn* 'he whom Ammon gave,' and the Bibl. פּוֹטִיפַר, פּוֹטִי פֶרַע i. e. *P'-dy-p'-R'* 'he whom the Ra gave'; see Driver, art. Potiphar, *DB* iv 23.

L. 10. חגם Prob. the name of a place where Ṣalm was worshipped; cf. الْحَجْم Yāḳût ii 886 (ed. Wüstenfeld), in Yemen.

L. 11. צדקו Pael; cf. the meaning of the noun צדקתא l. 15 *gift, endowment*, Dan. 4 24 LXX ἐλεημοσύνη, Matt. 6 1 δικαιοσύνη; Arab. صَدَقَة *alms*.

L. 12. ונבר ונו' See 64 and 65 for the adjurations.

L. 13. יחבל Pael, *destroy*; the root is found with this meaning in all the Semitic languages. סותא Perhaps the same word as مَنَارَة lit. *an elevation of land, a stone which indicates the road*, in pl. *tomb*, with ס=צ; see note on אספרן 67 (Hoffm.). In the Corp. the form is connected with the Syr. ܫܘܬܐ *found, make firm*, ܫܘܬܐܝܬ *stabilitas*; but no derivative of this root is actually used in the sense of *monument*. Winckler considers that it=the Assyr. *asumitu* 'inscribed stele,' *Altor. Forsch.* ii 76 f. (in Delitzsch *Assyr. HWB* s. v. וסם), a plausible derivation.

L. 14. ינסחוהי See 64 9 *n.*; for נ retained cf. יהנפק l. 21. תנצר 64 12 *n.* שמה l. 22. In Hebr. שֵׁם is found with almost the same meaning, *posterity*, e.g. Dt. 25 7. Ruth 4 5. 10 &c. מן אנפי Cf. 1 K. 9 7 (מעל פני). Dt. 28 63 (מעל, with נסח).

L. 15. הא זא Fem. of ܗܳܢܳܐ = Arab. هٰذَا, Syr. ܗܳܕ݂ܶܐ, Targ. הָדָא. צדקתא See l. 11 *n*. Winckler, however, regards this as a Babyl. loan-word = *sattuku* 'the regular dues or income of a temple' (Delitzsch *Assyr. HWB* 513), e.g. *KB* iii 2 32 l. 13. This is at any rate a plausible explanation, for the influence of Babylonia upon Têma, especially in religious matters, was certainly strong. See *Altor. Forsch.* i 183.

L. 16. מחרם No doubt the name of a place, like רגם. It is apparently preserved in the Arab. مُحَرَّمة near Jebel Selma, which is in the neighbourhood of Têma, Yâkût iv 425. שנגלא A deity otherwise unknown; possibly the א is the fem. ending. The name has been compared (Corp.) with that of a Babylonian goddess שנל, mentioned in the lexicon of Bar Bahlul, and stated to be the Chaldaean equivalent of Aphrodite, Lagarde *Gesam. Abhandl.* 17. Another suggestion is that Singala (*Sin-gala*) is the moon-god, Neubauer *St. Bibl.* i 224 *n*. Cf. the Palm. שגל pr. n. fem. 143 12. אשירא l. 3. Halévy suggests that אשירא=אסירא (with ש for ס as in שימתא l. 18), a form which occurs in the name of a Palm. deity רבאסירא 'Ραβασείρη (prob. *Rab-osiris*) 147 i 10. But it is possible that אשירא in spite of the י is the goddess *Ashēra*, who was certainly known in Arabia; see 10 4 *n*. and Lagrange *RB* x 549.

L. 17. .א The Corp. restores אז, with the sense *scilicet*.

L. 18. חקלא Emph. st., Targ. חֲקְלָא, Syr. ܚܰܩܠܳܐ *field*; cf. CIS ii 24. 27 דבת חקלא *record* or *tablet of the field*. This may well have been the land with which the temple was endowed, or 'the land of the priests'; see Gen. 47 22 and Lagrange *RB* x 219 who cites in illustration the Nab. חרם, 79 8 *n*. דקלן Cf. Targ. Ex. 15 27 וְשַׁבְעִין דִּקְלִין (at Elim). In the present day the value of land at Têma is reckoned by the number of palms on it; the price of a tree is said to be 20 francs. שימתא *treasury* = סימתא, ܣܺܝܡܬܳܐ. Winckler explains the word by the Babyl. *šîmtu* 'a fixing' or 'fixed portion,' so ש' די מלכא 'the king's crown estates,' *Altor. Forsch.* i 184. The Babyl. *šîmtu* does not appear to be used exactly in this sense; at the same time it must be admitted that 'treasury' is not a suitable word for what was clearly landed property consisting of date-palms.

L. 19. For the prince's contribution to the sanctuary cf. Eze. 45 17; in many Nab. inscrr. the fine for violating a tomb is ordered to be divided between the god and the king, e.g. 80 8 *n*. 81 7 f. &c.

L. 20. After the numerical symbol the Corp. restores הא or זא. אלהן 76 C 7. There is no need to render 'divine persons' i.e. members of the royal family (Halévy, Neubauer l.c. 212 *n.*).

L. 21. יהנפק For the ה retained in Hafel cf. ויהאברו 64 11 *n.*, and for the נ cf. in Nab. ינפק 79 2. 80 5 &c., and see l. 14 *n.* The form here exactly resembles יהנזיק Targ. Jon. Ex. 11 7; Dalman *Gr.* 241.

L. 23. כמריא See 64 1 *n.*

70. Têma. CIS ii 114. Circ. iv cent. B.C. Louvre.

1 [מ]יתבא זי קר
2 [ב] מענן בר עמ
3 [ר]ן לצלם אלה
4 א לחיי נפשה

The seat which Ma'nan, son of 'Imran, offered to the god Ṣalm, for the life of his soul.

The characters belong to a period late in the middle stage of Aram. writing. They are almost all of the same size, and written as it were between straight lines, like CIS ii 72 from Chaldaea; the Chaldaean manner, exemplified in the latter inscr., has perhaps influenced this style of writing (cf. 69 3 *n.*). The ז and י are archaic in form, ק is almost Nabataean, ע is shaped like a V, and א has the curious shape +ᐩ, מ is written with the two down strokes equal in length.

L. 1. מיתבא Cf. מותב 80 4, here a *seat* on which the image of the god was placed on certain days, the Lat. *pulvinar deorum*; cf. Palm. ערשא in the inscr. from eṭ-Ṭayyibe p. 296 *n.* 1, and ארכתא (Nab.) p. 255 *n.* 1.

L. 2. מענן Cf. the Nab. pr. n. מענא CIS ii 294, Euting *Nab. Inschr.* 19, and the Palm. מעני Μανναιος, e.g. Vogüé 27 4 &c. It is found in composition, e.g. מענאלהי CIS ii 118, and perhaps lies behind Μονιμος, the name of a deity associated with the sun-god at Edessa; cf. the pr. nn. معن الله (Ḥejra) and ܡܥܢܘ ܐܠܗܐ (a king of Edessa). עמרן = عَمْرَان 'Εμρανος from Ḥauran; cf. the Sinaitic עבדעמרו Eut. *Sin. Inschr.* 72, Cl.-Gan. *Rec.* ii 213; and עמרם (?) at Safâ, Dussaud et Macler *Safâ* no. 68. The root עמר, عَمَرَ = *live*, e.g. די עמר באילת Eut. *Sin. Inschr.* 551; the Arab. has also the meaning *worship*. Both pr. names have the ending *ân*, apparently usual among the Aramaeans of Arabia.

L. 3. צלם אלהא See 69 2 *n.*

L. 4. לחיי נפשה A favourite formula (with variations) in Palm. inscrr.; cf. 29 11.

EGYPT

71. Memphis. CIS ii 122. Date 482 B.C. Berlin Museum.

a

1 בריך אבה בר חור ואחתבו ברת עדיה כל וו [זי ?] חסתמח קרבתא
2 קדם אוסרי אלהא אבסלי בר אבה אמה אחתבו
3 כן אמר בשנת וווו ירח מחיר חשיארש מלכא זי מ[לכיא]
4 ביד פמן...

b חכנא *c* מ

a. Blessed be Abbâ, son of Ḥôr, and Aḥatbû, daughter of 'Adayâ, both assisted by divine favour (?)! The approach [2] before the god Osiris. Abseli, son of Abbâ, his mother (being) Aḥatbû, [3] spake thus in the 4th year, (in) the month Meḥîr, of Xerxes king of kings. [4] By the hand of Pamen . . .

b. Ḥakna.

The inscr. is written upon the base of a tablet carved with a representation of an Egyptian funeral scene. In the uppermost panel Osiris sits, attended by Isis and Nephthys; the parents of Abseli approach the deity with outstretched arms. Certain details, such as the clipped hair of the figures, betray the foreign nationality of the donor; the hieroglyphic inscr.[1] in the upper part of the tablet is evidently written by an unskilful hand. In general appearance the stone resembles 75. It belongs to the period when Egypt formed a part of the Persian empire (B.C. 525–332); and we learn from it that the Aram. settlers used their own language, which was also the language of the Persian government (cf. 67 *n.*), and at the same time adapted themselves to the religion of the country.

L. 1. בריך 75 1; the plur. would be more correct here. אבה Prob. = the Aram. אבא. חור Cf. the common Nab. pr. n. חורו (=حُورُ) 87 8. 90 5 &c., and the O.T. חור Ex. 17 10. Num.

[1] 'Offering made to Osiris, prince of Amenti, the great god, the lord of Abydos, that he may give good sepulture to (the spirit of) Aḥitobu, the matron faithful before the great god'; and behind the figure of Abba, 'the foreigner, surnamed Hitop.'

31 8. אחתבו Perhaps = אֲחָת אֲבוּהָ *sister of her father*, cf. the biblical אחאב and the Aram. אחמה (i.e. אֲחִמַּהּ) ? *mother's brother*, Levy *Sieg. u. Gemmen* p. 14 no. 20. Lidzb. illustrates from Talm. B. *Baba Bathra* 110 a רוב בנים דומין לאחי האם 'most sons are like the brothers of the mother.' עדיה Prob. the same name as the Arab. *Adi, Adiya*, عَدِيّ, عَادِيَاء; the root means *to pass, run, transgress*, cf. the O.T. עֲדָיָה 2 K. 22 1 'Yah passes by.' But the word may be read עריה. The numerical symbols must refer to the parents of the donor. חסחמה The meaning is obscure. If the word is compounded of the Egypt. *hes, hestu* and *ameh*, it will mean *favoured by the god, faithful*; cf. 75 4 חסיה plur. *those favoured* (by Osiris); in the Egypt. inscr. (p. 200 *n*. 1) *ameh* is rendered 'faithful.' It is an expression taken from the terminology of the Egypt. funeral rites. The form חמה is found on a wooden sarcophagus of the Ptolemaic period in the Cairo Museum, Cl.-Gan. *Rec.* ii 11. קרבתא The confused way in which the word is written on the stone, with ב superadded, shows that the scribe was uncertain about the form. It is probably a noun, with the sense of a 'nomen actionis,' *a drawing near*, cf. 72 1 קרבת and Ps. 73 28 קרבת אלהים לי טוב; at any rate the word denotes the 'accession' to Osiris after death. According to Egyptian belief the departed soul, if judged pure, did not merely go to Osiris, but actually became Osiris.

L. 2. אבסלי The second part of the compound resembles סַלַּי Neh. 11 8. סַלָּי ib. 12 7; the √סלה = *to weigh*. In inscr. *b* the Egyptian name is given, חכנא *Ḥakna*.

L. 3. מחיר The name of the sixth month, Jan. 26–Feb. 24, in Egyptian, in Coptic *mechir*; see Brightman *Liturgies* i. 582. חשיארש = the old Persian *Ḫshayârshâ* = אֲחַשְׁוֵרוֹשׁ Esth. 1 1 &c., in Greek Ξέρξης; he reigned from 485 to 465 B.C. מלכא זי מלכיא A common title of the Persian kings; see 5 18 *n*., and Driver *Introd.*[6] 546.

L. 4. ביד introduces the name of the scribe or sculptor, an Egyptian, פמן = *Pa-amen* 'who belongs to the god Amen'; again in CIS ii 148 3.

72. Memphis. CIS ii 123. Date v–iv cent. B.C. Louvre.

1 חתפי לקרבת בנת לאום
2 רי חפי עבד אביטב בר
3 בנת כהי עבד קדם אום
4 חרי חפי

Offering for the approach of Banith to Osiris[2]-Apis made by Abiṭab, son [3] of Banith. Thus (?) he made it before Osiris[4]-Apis.

The inscr. is written on an oblong vessel used for libations; it was found in the Serapaeum at Memphis.

L. 1. חתפי Prob. an Egypt. word *hotpit*, later *hotpi* = 'oblation.' לקרבת See 71 1 *n*. בנת An Egypt. pr. n., found again in CIS ii 148 3. The meaning is uncertain; *Pa-neit*, i.e. 'belonging to the goddess Neit,' has been suggested,' but it is questionable whether the Semitic ב is ever used to transcribe the Egypt. *p*. Maspero explains *Banit* as='leaping' in Egyptian (Corp.).

L. 2. אוסרי חפי Osiris-Apis, called by the Greeks Serapis, specially honoured at Memphis; חפי = Egypt. *Ḥapi*. It is probable that חף is to be read in Jer. 46 15 MT נִסְחַף אַבִּירֶיךָ, which many moderns correct to נָס חָף אַבִּירְךָ, after the LXX (26 15) *διὰ τί ἔφυγεν ἀπὸ σοῦ ὁ Ἆπις; ὁ μόσχος ὁ ἐκλεκτός σου κ.τ.λ.* אביטב = the Hebr. אביטוב 1 Chr. 8 11.

L. 3. כהי The context suggests the rendering *thus*; but there is no exact parallel for the form. It may be an abbreviation of הָאִי (Bab.-Aram. = *this*)+כ; see Dalman 81, Wright *Comp. Gr.* 109. The word has been rendered 'a piece of bread,' i.e. a second offering, after a Coptic noun which it somewhat resembles; but this is not probable (Corp.).

78. Elephantina. CIS ii 137. iv cent. B.C. Berlin Museum.

B	A	
כען הן צבתי	כען הלו חלם	1
כל תזבניהמו	ו חזית ומן	2
יאכלו יאנקיא	עדנא הו אנה	3
הלו לא	חמם שגא	4
שאר	[א]תחזי חז[ו]	5
קטין	מלוהי	6
	שלם	7

A. Now behold, the 1st dream I saw, and from that time I was very hot; there appeared an apparition; its words (were), 'Hail'! B. Now if ornaments (?) of all kinds thou sellest, the infants shall eat; behold, there is not a small remainder.

The above texts are written with a reed pen in Egyptian-Aram. characters on either side of a fragment of pottery. They are evidently complete in themselves, for the sentences are not broken off, but squeezed into the shape of the potsherd; the two texts form a single narrative. It was the custom to write down brief descriptions of dreams, and bring them to the temple to be interpreted.

A. L. 1. כען = קְעַן *now* in Bibl. Aram. הלו Cf. אֲלוּ in Dan. חלם Cf. τὸ πρῶτον ἐνύπνιον on a Gk. papyrus (Corp.).

L. 4. חמם = חֲמַם, ܚܡܝܡ. שנא is an adverb = שַׂגִּיא Dan. 2 12 &c.

L. 5. תחזי Prob. an error for אתחזי Ethpeal pf. (Corp.), 147 i 7. חזו i.e. חֵזוּ cf. חֶזְוָנָא דְלֵילְיָא Targ. Job 20 8.

L. 7. שלם i.e. שְׁלָם cf. Ἀπολλώνιον εἶδον· προσπορεύεταί μοι· λέγει· Χαῖρε, from the papyrus quoted above (Corp.).

B. L. 1. צבתי Plur. constr. before כל, cf. בכורי כל Eze. 44 30. The meaning is prob. *ornaments*, Targ. צִבְתָּא, ܨܒܬܐ *finery*; cf. in Palm. 119 4 תצביתהון *their ornaments*. Hoffmann (*ZA* xi 223) renders *bundles*, cf. Hebr. צְבָתִים Ru. 2 16; a less suitable sense.

L. 2. תזבניהמו Pael impf. 2 mas. or 3 fem. sing. For the suff. המו see 65 6 *n*.

L. 3. יאכלו Impf. 3 plur. without *nun*; see 61 4 *n*.

Ll. 4–6. לא שאר קטין The meaning seems to be 'there is plenty left.' שאר Prob. a noun = Hebr. שְׁאָר, cf. Nab. שארית 94 3. For לא before a noun-clause cf. לא דומיה לי Ps. 22 3. כי לא איש כמני Job 9 32 &c.

74. Elephantina. CIS ii 138. iv cent. Brit. Mus. no. 14219.

B	A	
...צחא בר חברטיסן	פעל אסמן בר....	1
...[י]תנן והן אמרו ס[הדיא]	באלו מנחמן זי הו....	2
...חרתבא ובגטף חברטי[סן]	וידניה גשוריא ס...	3

	A	B
4	ושאל על פטוסרי...	.ן לן על פוחדך אמר
5	שחומו באלו ש...	.....אבתם לה סרן ו
6	ושאל על חנ...	......לא יהב לן
7	פטחרפחרט...	.......מלכיה סרן
8	בר כומן כ...	........[פ]טנתר בר
9	....מ	........יגלף

	A	B
1	Isimen, son of . . made	. . . Ṣeḥo, son of ḤBRṬISN
2	for these comforters (?), whom he	. . . they will give (?), and if the w[itnesses ?] have said
3	and Geshuria (?) shall judge him . . .	. . . ḤRTB' and BGṬF ; ḤBRṬI[SN]
4	and he asked about Peṭosiris . . .	. . to us against PUḤDK. He said
5	Šeḥumu for these	. . . . . ? to him our prince (?), and
6	and he asked about	. . . . . . he did not give us
7	Peṭḥarpoḥraṭes . . .	. . . . of kings, our prince (?)
8	son of Kaumen	. . . . Peṭenutir, son of
9	. . . . .	. . . . shall carve (?)

The above texts are written with ink on either side of a potsherd; they probably formed part of a legal document.

A. L. 1. אסמן An Egypt. pr. n., perhaps *Isi-men*=' Isis is firm.'

L. 2. אלו l. 5 = אִלּוּ in the Mishnah, Hebr. אלה; here preceding the noun, as אִלֵּין in Dan. 2 44. 7 17 and חלין in the Pal. Talmud, see Dalman *Gram.* 82. מנחמן Perhaps = מְנַחֲמִן *comforters* in the sense of supporters or witnesses in a legal action.

L. 3. וידניה Prob. = וידיניה. נשוריא It is not certain whether this is a pr. n. or a noun.

L. 4. פטוסרי See 69 9 *n.*

L. 5. שחומו Pr. n. with ending ו' as in Nab.

L. 7. פטחרפחרט An Egypt. pr. n.='he whom the god Harpocrates gave,' Πετεαρποχράτης; again in CIS ii 147 11. The ח is used to transcribe the softer and harder aspirate (like the Arab. ح and خ) in Egyptian.

L. 8. כומן An Egypt. pr. n. *Kamen*, *Kaumenu*.

B. L. 1. צחא 77 A 4 = the Egypt. *Zeho*, in Gk. Τεώς or Ταχώς. חברטיסן Perhaps a Persian name (Corp.).

L. 5. מרן l. 7 is explained as = שרנא *our prince*. For the suff. cf. Palm. מרן **128** 3; Nab. מראנא **81** 8.

L. 6. לן = לנא *to us*.

L. 7. מלכיה Seems to be written for מלכיא, and to be part of the phrase מלך מלכיא, the usual title of the Persian kings, **71** 3 and Dan. **2** 37 (of Nebuchadnezzar).

L. 8. [פ]טנתר = the Egypt. *Peṭenuṭru* 'devoted to the gods.'

L. 9. ינלף Apparently from the Aram. נלף *to engrave on stone*; the reference is not clear.

75. Egypt; the Carpentras Stele. CIS ii 141. v–iv cent. B.C.
Museum of Carpentras (S. France).

1 בריכה תבא ברת תחפי תמנחא זי אוסרי אלהא
2 מנדעם באיש לא עבדת וכרצי איש לא אמרת תמה
3 קדם אוסרי בריכה הוי מן קדם אוסרי מין קחי
4 הוי פלחה נמעתי ובין חסיה ....

Blessed be Taba, daughter of Taḥapi, devoted worshipper of the god Osiris. [2] Aught of evil thou hast not done, and calumny against any man thou hast never (?) spoken. [3] Before Osiris be thou blessed! From before Osiris take thou water! [4] Be thou a worshipper, my pleasant one (?), and among the favoured ....

Above the inscr. an Egyptian funeral scene is carved; cf. **71**. The characters belong to a somewhat later type than those of the latter inscr.; some of them, ב, ד, ר, ע, ו, ז, י, ש, ח, א, illustrate very clearly the transition from the archaic to the square alphabet. See Driver *Samuel* xviii–xxi.

L. 1. בריכה Cf. **71** 1. תבא Egypt. pr. n. f., *ta-bai* 'she who is of the spirit.' תחפי Also Egypt., 'she who is of the god Hapi'; the mas. *Pahapi* is a common name. תמנחא i. e. תְּמַנְחָא *Monḥ* in Egypt. = 'pious,' 'perfect'; cf. the mas. מנחה זי אוסרי CIS ii 142. אוסרי אלהא Cf. **71** 2.

L. 2. מנדעם i. e. מְנַדְּעַם, so in Nab. **94** 5, cf. Mand. מינדאם (Nöld. *Mand. Gr.* 186); in Palm. מדען **147** i 5 and מדעם(א) ib. 8; in Targums מדעם and Talm. מִידֵּי (Dalman *Gr.* 90); in Syr. ܡܕܡ. The word is compounded of מַדַּע = מִנְדַּע and מא, lit. *scibile quid*; the various forms are corruptions of this (Wright *Comp. Gr.* 126). באיש See **65** 9 *n*. עבדת and אמרת 2 or 3 fem. sing. אמרת כרצי איש Prob. a variation of the idiom ܐܟܠ ܩܪ̈ܨܘܗܝ ܕ i. e. *he calumniated*, cf. Dan. 3 8. 6 25. With כרצי (so in Mand.) = קרצי lit. *morsels* cf. Syr. ܩܘܫ̈ܬܐ = Hebr. קְשָׁת, Mand. כושמא = Hebr. קֹשֶׁט. תמה i. e. תַּמָּה = ܬܡܢ may mean *there, yonder*, cf. Ezr. 5 17. 6 1, i. e. on the earth, speaking from the other world (so Nöld., Lidzb.), a somewhat artificial explanation. Lagarde suggests that תמה = Syr. ܡܬܘܡ (from ܠܐܬܘܡ), *ever*. The word cannot mean *perfect*; in Aram. this would be not תַּמָּה but תְּמִימָה, as is the rule with adjectives from ע״ע verbs.

L. 3. מין קחי Egypt. monuments and papyri frequently mention water as a last offering to the dead; illustrate from CIG 6562 εὐψύχει, κυρία, δοί(η) σοι ὁ Ὄσιρις τὸ ψυχρὸν ὕδωρ. 6717. Note the Hebraism קחי, cf. איש l. 2.

L. 4. נמעתי may be the name of an Egypt. deity, which פלחה seems to require; or it is an error for נעמתי, cf. 2 Sam. 1 26. Cant. 7 7. חסיה Perhaps the Egypt. *hosiou* 'favoured (by Osiris),' cf. חסתמח 71 1 *n*. It is also explained as = ܚܣܝ̈ܐ *pious* (plur.); but this would be written חֲסַיָּא. The line prob. ended הֲוִי שְׁלִימָה.

76. Saqqara; Papyri Blacassiani. CIS ii 145. End of v cent. B.C. Brit. Mus.

A (recto)

..... ולא ימלא בטנהם לח[ם] ...

..... איש כיבי אלהיהם ....

... ין קימיהם עד יבנון קר[יה] ....

....ע וביומן אחרנן יאכל ....

.. והי צדקה לאבוהי ויזב[ן] .....

..... ויתקלנהי בלבה ויקטל איש ל[בני]

... תך מראה וישרה בני מראה ...

.. אשה לחם ויתכנשן אלהי מצרין ...

.... שנן 33 ווו וח ....

B (verso)

1 . . . . לבני על תסהרא זי מלכא ושמע . . .
2 . . . . בר פונש הו אחר ענה מלכא . . . .
3 . . . . בר פונש מליא זי מלכא אמר וע[נה] .
4 . . . . [ק]טלת המו תהך בחרב חילך וח . . .
5 . . ף יחלף לך ושביא זי שבית בזא שנתא . . . . . .
6 . . . באלך ונרמיך לא יחתון שאול וטללך. . . . . .
7 . [בר פונ]ש על אלפי מלכא . . . . במנצ . . . .

C (recto)

1 . . . . . מלכא חעק ומשח . . . . .
2 . . זנה זי קרא . . . .
3 . [ת]תלנהי כן כזי עבדת לבנוהי . .
4 . . לולא באתר ים יקטל . . . . .
5 . . . . שעתרם בתמאי ומנח[ם] . . .
6 . . . . . ך תהך ותשלה . . . . . .
7 . . . ה עם אלהן ולחש עזור . . . . .
8 . . . י . . . ן ב . . . .

D (verso)

1 . . . . . זי ינתן לה אבוהי . . . . . .
2 . . . . . שו אלהי מצרין זי . . . . . .
3 . . . . [מצ]רין ויהוון . . . .
4 . . . מה ותאבד צדקתא ואי . . . .
5 . . . . . בו ואתנפק איש . . . . . .
6 . . . עלך בר כבוה ז[י] . . . .
7 . . [יב]רכון לקברה ול . . . .
8 . . ויאמרון לה צערי . . . .
9 . . נתה בפלג . . . . תלך ול . . . . . .

A

[1] . . . nor may their belly be filled with bread . . . [2] . . . each the pains (?) of their gods . . . [3] . . . their agreements, until they build the ci[ty] . . . [4] . . . and in later days he shall eat . . . [5] . . . righteousness to his father, and he shall sell . . . [6] . . . and let him weigh it in his heart, and let some one slay the s[ons] . . . [7] . . . his lord, and let some one release the sons of his lord . . . [8] . . . bread, and may the gods of Egypt assemble . . . [9] . . . 43 years . . .

B

[1] . . . for my sons, according to the testimony of the king, and he heard . . . [2] . . . son of Punsh, he delayed (?). The king answered . . . [3] . . . son of Punsh the words which the king said; and he answered . . . [4] . . . thou didst kill them. Thou shalt go with the sword of thy might and . . . [5] . . . shall be changed (?) for thee, and the captives which thou hast taken this year . . . [6] . . . in these; and thy bones shall not go down to Sheol, and thy shadow . . . [7] . . . [son of Pun]sh, upon the thousands (?) of the king . . .

C

[1] . . . the king, and he cried and anointing-oil . . . [2] . . . this which he called . . . [3] . . . thou shalt hang him even as thou didst to his sons . . . [4] . . . unless in the place where the sea is he kill . . . [5] . . . Sha'atram (?) in Tamai (?) and Menaḥ[em] . . . [6] . . . thou shalt go and be at ease . . . [7] . . . with the gods, and he whispered (?), Help! (?) . . . [8] . . .

D

[1] . . . which his father will give him . . . [2] . . . gods of Egypt, who . . . [3] . . . [of Eg]ypt, and they will be . . . [4] . . . and righteousness perish, and . . . [5] . . . and the man was brought out . . . [6] . . . 'LK, son of KBWH, who . . . [7] . . . [may they b]less his grave . . . [8] . . . and say to him, my (?) distress . . . [9] . . . in the midst . . .

The above texts, being written upon papyrus, do not properly come under the title of inscriptions, but they are included because they illustrate the language and writing used by Aramaic-speaking settlers in Egypt during the same period as the engraved texts of this group. The writing is of a similar type to that of **75**, but of a more cursive form, and a stage nearer to the square character; see Driver *Sam.* xxi (with facsimile). As in **75**, the language contains some marked Hebraisms. These stray leaves are too mutilated to enable us to make out their general purport; it has been suggested that they give an account of a plot against the government of the Persian king in Egypt.

A. L. 1. ימלא במנהם Cf. Job 15 2. 20 23. The 3 plur. m. suff. ends in הֹם׳, e.g. אלהיהם l. 2. קימיהם l. 3; so regularly in Nab., e.g. נפשהם **80** 2. בניהם **102** 4; Targ. Ps.-Jon. בֵּיתְהוֹם (also הוֹן׳); Bibl. Aram. רָאשֵׁהֹם Ezr. 5 10 (also הוֹן), cf. אֱלָהֲכֹם 7 17. In Palm. the form is הן׳.

L. 2. איש A Hebraism, cf. **75** 2. כיבי Perhaps = Targ. כֵּיבָא, Syr. ܟܐܒܐ, Hebr. כְּאֵב; but what 'the pains of their gods' can mean is not clear.

L. 3. קימיהם Apparently plur. of קימא, Syr. ܩܘܡܐ.

L. 4. אחרנן Plur. of אחרן, Syr. ܐܚܪܢܐ *next, following*, plur. ܐܚܪ̈ܢܐ; cf. Dan. 2 11 אָחֳרָן *another*.

L. 5. ויבן i. e. וְיִבְּנֵן, cf. in Nab. **79** 6 &c.

L. 6. יתקלנהי i. e. יִתְקְלֻנְּהִי, cf. תחלנהי C 3. For the suff. with nun energic cf. the Bibl. Aram. יְקַטְלֻנַּהּ, Pal. Aram. יעברינה (Dalman *Gr.* 308); and for the 3 sing. m. suff. in הי׳ cf. the Syr. ܘܗܝ׳ with the impf., and the Palm. יפתחיהי **145** 6. The Hebr. forms יִצְּרֶנְהוּ Deut. 32 10. יַעַבְרֻנְהוּ Jer. 5 22 are similar (Ges.-Kau. § 58 *k*). ל[בני] So Corp., cf. בני מראה l. 7.

L. 7. מראה See **62** 11 *n.*

L. 8. ויתכנשן for ויתכנשון, cf. **147** ii c 33. מצרין The dual is written with י, but the plur. without י, e.g. יומן אחרנן l. 4. שנן l. 9.

B. L. 1. חסהדא = סַהֲדוּתָא *witness.*

L. 2. פונש An Egyptian pr. n. אחר Apparently perf. 3 sing. m. ענה מלכא Cf. Dan. 2 5. 8. 20 &c.

L. 4. המו Here accus. *eos*, as in Ezr. 4 10. 23, in Dan. המון. תהך C 6, i. e. תְּהָךְ impf. of הלך; similarly in Targ. and Bibl. Aram., e.g. Ezr. 5 5 יְהָךְ.

L. 5. יחלף לך The last letter of each word is uncertain. זא Cf. **61**. 18. **69** 13.

L. 6. באלך Cf. Dan. 3 12 &c. Ezr. 4 21 &c. (אִלֵּךְ). יותתן Pe. impf. of נתח.

L. 7. אלפי Instead of אַלְפֵי *thousands*, the word may be pointed אַלֻּפֵי *chiefs*, lit. *chiliarchs*, specially an *Edomite* term, Gen. 36 15 ff.

C. L. 1. משח may be a verb *and he anointed*, or a noun *anointing-oil* as in CIS ii 44, in Palm. 147 ii a 27. משחא 122 3.

L. 2. זנה Cf. 69 22.

L. 3. תתלנהי Prob. impf. 2 sing. m. from תלה, i. e. תִּתְלְנַּהִי; for the suff. see A 6 *n*. כוי = כדי *sicut* in Nab. 80 7. 86 6, Bibl. Aram. Dan. 2 43, Targ. כד.

L. 4. לולא Dalman reads [א]לולי, like the Pal. Aram. אילולי (אילו = אין לו *if*), *Gr.* 189.

L. 5. שעתרם The form may be incomplete; a pr. n. חמאי is said to mean in Egypt. *a cat*.

L. 6. תשלה Apparently impf. of שלה *to rest*.

L. 7. אלהן Plur., cf. 69 20, and contrast אלהי 62 23. לחש Pael, as in Aram. and Hebr.; cf. Is. 26 16 (noun). עֱזוּר = ? עזור imperat. The *scriptio plena* is remarkable.

D. L. 1. ינתן So in Nab. 79 3, in Bibl. Aram. יִנְתֵּן.

L. 3. ויהוון i. e. וִיהֱוֺן.

L. 5. ואתנפק Ethp. perf.; in the Targum the Ittafal is used, e. g. אִתַּפַּק Eze. 24 6. מִיתַּפְּקָא Onk. Gen. 38 25 (with נ assimilated).

L. 6. כבות . . עלך Pr. nn.; the first is perhaps incomplete.

L. 8. צערי The י may be the suff. or sign of the plur. constr.; Targ. צַעֲרָא, Syr. ܨܥܪܐ.

L. 9. בפלג Lit. *in the division*; but the form may be mutilated.

77. Papyrus Luparensis. CIS ii 146. iv cent. B. C. Louvre.

A

1 ...[בירח] פאפי זי מת[כ]תב   נפקתה בירח פאפי

2 ...[חמר] מצרין קלבי ו   ב ו לפאפי לשרתא חמר צידן קלבי ו מצרין [קלול ו]

3 ...[מצר]ין קלול ו קלבין וו   ב וו לפאפי לשרתא מצרין קלול ו קלבין וו

4 . . . . היב לצחא בר פמת חמר מצרין מאנן ׀׀׀ ׀׀ ׀...

5 . . . . בנף קלולן ׀׀ קלבין ׀׀׀ עליך זער שר...

6 . . . .ב..ל עליך קדם עחר מ[צר]ין קלול ׀

7 . . . .מצרין קלול ׀

8 . . . .[ב]ל[י]לא מצרין קלבי ׀

9 . . . .זי בצ. נה מצרין קלול ׀

10 . . . . [ב...לפאפי] לשרתא חמר צידן קלבי ׀ מצרין [קלול ׀]

11 . . . . [ל]....בר פחה מצרין קלול ׀

12 . . . .ל[שרתא] מ[צרין קלו]ל ׀

B

1 . . . . ב ז׀׀׀ לשרתא קלול ׀ קלבי ׀

2 . . . . ב ז׀׀׀ ׀ לבגור ׀ קלבין ׀׀

3 . . . . לנקיה קדם אפתו אלהא רבא קלבי ׀

4 . . . . לנקיה קדם אסי רבתי קלבי ׀

5 ..התח ז   לשרתא חמר צידן קלבו ׀

6 ..[קלבי] ׀   ב ז׀׀׀ ׀׀ לכיחך זי הו יום לנדר לשרתא קלולן ׀׀

7 ..קלבי ׀   ב ז׀׀׀ ׀׀׀ קדם א[וסרי]....

8 . . . . עליך אנומי....

9 ..[קלול] ׀   ב ז׀׀׀ ׀׀׀ ׀׀ ל....

10 ..[קלב]י ׀   ב ז׀׀׀ ׀׀׀ ׀׀׀ ל....

11 ..פינתא   עחרנפי ה....

12 לב...א....

13 ל

A

[1] . . . [in the month] of Paophi, which is written out. [2] . . . [wine] of Egypt, qelbi 1. [3] . . . [Egypt]ian, qelul 1, qelbin 2.

. . . .

[1] Outgoings in the month of Paophi. [2] On the 1st of Paophi, for the meal, wine of Sidon, qelbi 1, Egyptian, [qelul 1]. [3] On the 2nd of Paophi, for the meal, Egyptian, qelul 1, qelbin 2. [4] Given to Ṣeḥo, son of Pamut, wine of Egypt, ma'nin 5 and . . . [5] For each person, qelulin 2, qelbin 3; on your account, a small (?) . . . . [6] . . . on your account, before 'Aḥor (?), E[gyp]tian, qelul 1. [7] . . . Egyptian, qelul 1. [8] . . . [at] night, Egyptian, qelbi 1. [9] . . . which is in . ., Egyptian, qelul 1. [10] [On the . . . of Paophi], for the meal, wine of Sidon, qelbi 1, Egyptian, [qelul 1]. [11] [To] . ., son of Peḥa (?), Egyptian, qelul 1. [12] . . . for [the meal], E[gyptian, qelu]l 1.

B

[1] On the 23rd, for the meal, qelul 1, qelbi 1. [2] On the 24th, for ? 1, qelbin 2. [3] For the libation before Apuaitu (?), the great god, qelbi 1. [4] For the libation before the lady Isis, qelbi 1. [5] For the meal, wine of Sidon, qelbi 1. [6] On the 25th of Koiḥak, which is a day for vows, for the meal, qelulin 2. [7] On the 26th, before O[siris] . . . [8] On your account ? . . . [9] On the 28th, for . . . [10] On the 29th, for . . . [11] 'Aḥor-nufi (?) . . . . . .

These texts are fragments of daily accounts kept by a steward, to be submitted to the master of the house. They were probably written during the Persian rule, and belong to a rather later date than **76**.

A. L. 1. מאפי The 2nd month of the Egyptian year, Sept. 28th–Oct. 27th; Copt. Paŏpi (see Brightman *Liturgies* 168), Gk. Παωφί, Arab. بَابَة. נפקתה A noun fem. sing. in the emph. st., or perhaps with suff. 3 sing.; cf. נִפְקְתָא Ezr. 6 4 and ܢܦܩܬܗ = τὴν δαπάνην Lk. 14 28.

L. 2. קלבי An Egypt. fluid measure; the derivation is unknown, cf. Arab. قَالَب *a mould*. The Corp. renders *lagena*. לשרתא ll. 3. 10 &c. *for the feast*; Targ. שֵׁירוּתָא, e. g. Onk. Gen. 43 16, Syr. ܫܪܘܬܐ;

from שרה lit. *to loose*, cf. משתרה 68 6. חמר צירן l. 10. B 5. Wine from Phoenicia (e.g. Beirut, Byblus) and Syria was specially esteemed in antiquity; cf. Athenaeus *Deipnosoph.* i 52 ὡς ἥδιστος ἔφυ πάντων Φοινίκιος οἶνος. מצרין Lit. *Egypt*, here Egyptian *wine*; see Gen. 40 9–11, Strabo 687 (ed. Müll.) οἶνόν τε οὐκ ὀλίγον ἐκφέρει (nome of Arsinöe), ib. 679 ὁ Μαρεώτης οἶνος &c., Pliny *Nat. Hist.* xiv 9.

L. 3. קלול It is suggested that this is the Egypt. *qerer*, *qelel* 'vessel,' Copt. κελωλ *a small vessel*. But in Aram. are found קְלָל Talm. *Para* 79 b, a stone vessel for receiving the ashes of the sin-offering, ܩܘܠܠܐ, plur. ܩܘܠܐ; whence the Arab. قلة an earthen *water-jug* (Fraenkel *Aram. Fremdw. in Arab.* 170 f.). The קלול was clearly a fluid measure; Corp. *amphora*.

L. 4. יהיב=היב Ptcp. of יהב; cf. CIS ii 147 B 2 &c. צחא Cf. 74 B 1. פמת Egypt., *of the goddess Mut*. מאנן Lit. *vessels* here *measures*; Corp. *dolia*, i.e. large wine-jars.

L. 5. נפ Apparently=נפשא *body*, *corpse*. בנפ is taken to mean *for each*, *individually*; what seems to be the full expression occurs in CIS ii 147 1 בנפא נפיא, cf. in Gk. papyri τὸ κατ' ἄνδρα τῶν σωμάτων. עליך זער The meaning perhaps is *for you* (i.e. the master) *a small* (measure of some kind).

L. 6. עחר Prob. the name of an Egypt. deity to whom the libation was offered; cf. B 11. CIS ii 136 לעחר.

L. 9. בצ . נה Restore בצענה i.e. in the city of *Tanis*, צען Ps. 78 12. 43 &c.

L. 11. פחה Probably an Egypt. pr. n. *Paḥa*.

B. L. 1. After the numeral the name of the month is to be understood; see l. 6.

L. 2. לבנור ? meaning. If it is a pr. n., instead of the numeral we must read ו as part of the name לבנורו.

L. 3. נקיה Prob.=נִקְיָה, ܢܘܩܝܐ *libation*. אפתו The name of a deity, perhaps Apuaitu (a form of Anubis), though this would be transliterated אפויתו.

L. 4. אסי רבתי See 8 2 *n*.

L. 6. כיחך The 4th month of the civil year, Egypt. *Kahika*, Arab. كيهك.

L. 8. אנוסי ? pr. n.

L. 11. פינתא If the form is complete, the meaning may be *angle*, *corner*, Targ. פִּינְיָתָא, ܦܢܝܬܐ, Hebr. פִּנָּה.

עחרנפי Perhaps = the Egypt. *Ahor-nufi* (for *-nufir*) ''Aḥor is good'; cf. A 6.

NABATAEAN

NORTH ARABIA

78. El-'Ölâ. CIS ii 332; Eut. 1. B.C. 9. At Strassburg.

1 דא נפשא די אב. בר

2 מקימו בר מקימאל די בנה

3 לה אבוהי בירח אלול

4 שנת \ לחרתת מלך נבטו

This is the monument of Ab., son [2] of Moqîmu, son of Moqîm-el, which [3] his father built for him in the month Elul, [4] the 1st year of Ḥarethath, king of the Nabataeans.

This inscr. comes from El-'Ölâ (ٱلْعُلَى), a little to the S. of El-Ḥejra (ٱلْحِجْر), where a large number of Nab. inscrr. have been found (79–93). Both places are in N. Arabia, in the Ḥejaz, S. of Têma (69 3 *n.*), and not far from the coast of the Red Sea; they are situated in what was the southernmost end of the Nab. kingdom[1].

L. 1. דא See add. note p. 26. נפשא In Nab. either fem., as here and in CIS ii 194 f. &c., or mas., 159 דנה נפש. 192 &c., frequently used of a *monument* set up over a grave; so in Aram., CIS ii 115 f.; in Palm. נפשא דה Vog. 31 1. נפשא דנה 146 1. Perhaps the word conveyed the idea of the personality (נ' lit. *soul*) of the deceased; a *nefesh* was erected for each of the persons buried in a tomb, cf. תרתי נפשתא 96 1. This idea is prob. symbolized by the pyramid standing upon a cube, such as was sometimes carved upon the rock over the inscr.; see the illustration in Vogüé *Syr. Centr.* 90. The *nefesh* is mentioned in the Talm., e.g. *Sheqalim* 5 a בונין לו נפש על קברו; cf. also ܢܦܫܐ in Syr., e.g. 1 Macc. 13 28 ܘܐܩܝܡ ܫܒܥ ܢܦܫܢ ἔστησεν ἑπτὰ πυραμίδας, referring to the monument built by Simon at Modin (Cl.-Gan. *Rec.* ii 190 f.). אב. Probably אבר.

L. 2. מקימו=مُقِيم CIS ii 215. 233; a common name in Palm., 110 f. &c.; in Gk. Μοκεῖμος, Μοκῖμος. In Nab. pr. nn. frequently end in ו', the equivalent of the Arab. ـٌ. מקימאל Compounded of מקימו and אל; cf. in Pun. מקמאל(ם) CIS i 261, and for the form, מריב

[1] The texts of 78–93, before they appeared in the Corp., were published in the valuable edition of Euting, enriched with notes by Nöldeke, *Nabatäische Inschriften* (1885).

בעל 1 Chr. 9 40. מְהֵיטַבְאֵל Neh. 6 10 &c. בנת So 99 1, cf. חנת CIS ii 224 4; but בנא 333 2 and in Palm. 122 5.

L. 3. אלול Aug.–Sept., Neh. 6 15; one of the names of the Babyl. months borrowed by the Jews after the exile. See Schrader *COT* 380.

L. 4. חרתת i. e. Aretas iv, ὁ Πετραῖος βασιλεύς (Jos. *Ant.* xviii 5 1), who reigned from B.C. 9 to A.D. 40; inscriptions (CIS ii 214 f.) and coins are dated in his 48th year. After his accession he secured the favour of Augustus, and was recognized as king (Jos. ib. xvi 10 9). Herod Antipas married his daughter (see 95 3 *n.*), but subsequently set her aside for Herodias, and thus gave Aretas a pretext to punish his son-in-law for this and other grievances (Jos. ib. xviii 5 1). At a later time, circ. A.D. 38, when St. Paul was persecuted by his ethnarch (2 Cor. 11 32), Aretas was master of Damascus; it is conjectured that the town had been made over to him by Caligula as a peace-offering[1]. He is mentioned in 20 inscrr. from El-Ḥejra (CIS ii 197–217), in the second inscr. from Petra 95, in the inscr. of Medeba 96, of Sidon CIS ii 160, of Puteoli 102, and frequently on coins. In the inscrr. he is surnamed רחם עמה = Φιλόπατρις, a title which asserts his claim to independence, in contrast to such titles as Φιλορώμαιος, Φιλοκαῖσαρ, adopted by subject kings. חרתת = Gk. Ἀρέτας for Ἀρέθας, perhaps under the influence of ἀρετή. נבטו The kingdom of the Nabataeans was centred at Petra, the former Edomite stronghold of Sela'; hence the name of the country, Ἀραβία ἡ πρὸς τῇ Πέτρᾳ i. e. Arabia Petraea. From this centre it extended northwards, at times even to Damascus (in B.C. 85 and A.D. 34–65 circ.), and southwards into N. Arabia, as far as the NE. shore of the Red Sea, 'omnis regio ab Euphrate usque ad mare Rubrum,' says St. Jerome (infr.). From the language of the inscriptions it appears that the Nabataeans were of Arab race and spoke Arabic, but used Aramaic for the purposes of writing and commerce; Nöldeke in Eut. *Nab. Inschr.* 78. Before the Hellenistic period little, or nothing, is known of them. It is probable that the *Na-ba-ai-ti*, frequently named along with other Arab tribes[2] in the Rassam Cylinder of Aššurbanipal (*KB* ii 216–222), were the Nabataeans. Whether the latter are the same as the Arab tribe called נביות in the O.T. is not altogether certain; the identification is as old as

[1] The Roman Damascene coins end with Tiberius, A.D. 34, and begin again with Nero, A.D. 62–3; in the interval Dam. was under the Nab. kings. So Gutschmidt in Eut. *Nab. Inschr.* 85; Schürer *Gesch. Jüd. Volk.*[3] i 737.

[2] E. g. the *Ḳid-ra-ai* i. e. קדר, *KB* ii 222; cf. נביות and קדר Gen. 25 13 &c., Nabataei and Cedrei in Pliny *Hist. Nat.* v 12.

Josephus (*Ant.* i 12 4 Ναβαιώθης—Ναβατηνὴν χώραν), who is followed by Jerome (*Quaest.* in Gen. 25 13 ed. Vallar. tom. iii 345) and most moderns. נְבָיוֹת looks like a fem. plur. (cf. מְנָיוֹת from מְנָת Neh. 12 47 &c.), and may possibly come from the Arab. نَبْوَاةٌ *lofty place, eminence*; its resemblance to נבטו is thus not very close, although there are analogies for the interchange of ת and ט, e. g. قتل and קטל, 62 8 *n.*[1] In the Hellenistic period the Nabataeans first appear in the time of Antigonus, 312 B.C., who sent two expeditions against them, Diod. xix 94–100. Their first known ruler was the Aretas of 2 Macc. 5 8 (τὸν τῶν Ἀράβων τύραννον), with whom Jason sought asylum in 169 B.C., for the Nabataeans were friendly to the Maccabaean family, 1 Macc. 5 25. 9 35. With the decay of the Gk. kingdoms of Syria and Egypt their power increased, and towards the end of the 2nd cent. B.C. they were consolidated under a vigorous king named Erotimus, who was perhaps the founder of the Nab. dynasty (see Jos. *Ant.* xiii 13 3. 5. 15 1. 2. *Wars* i 4 4. 8 &c.)[2]. In B.C. 85 Aretas iii was master of Damascus, and struck coins there with the legend βασιλέως Ἀρέτου Φιλέλληνος. Shortly after this the Nabataeans for the first time came into collision with the Romans under Pompey and Scaurus, Jos. *Ant.* xiv 1 4–2 3. 5 1. *Wars* i 8 1; and in the subsequent period were sometimes reduced to tributaries, sometimes allowed a measure of independence, until finally in A.D. 106, when Cornelius Palma was governor of Syria, the Nab. kingdom was absorbed into the Empire and became a Roman province[3].

The following list of Nab. kings, based upon Schürer *Gesch. Jüd. Volk.*[3] i 726–744, will be convenient for reference:

Aretas i reigning in 169 B.C.
Erotimus „ 110–100 B.C.
Aretas ii „ 96 B.C.
Obedas i „ 90 B.C.
Aretas iii circ. 85–60 B.C.
Malchus i circ. 50–28 B.C. **100*. 102.**
Obedas ii circ. 28–9 B.C. **95*.**
Aretas iv 9 B.C.–40 A.D. **78–91. 95. 96.**
Abias.
Malchus ii circ. 48–71 A.D. **92*. 93. 99.**
Rabel circ. 71–106 (?) A.D. **97*. 101.**
End of the Nab. kingdom 106 A.D.

Under the numbers marked by an asterisk further particulars will be found.

[1] The Gk. Ναβαταῖοι = Aram. נְבָטָיֵא, Lagarde *Bild. Nom.* 52.

[2] Justinus xxxix 5, cited by Schürer ib. 731. Bevan *House of Seleucus* ii 257.

[3] Dio. Cass. lxviii 14, cited by Schürer ib. 743.

79. El-Ḥejra. CIS ii 197; Eut. 2. B.C. 1. In situ.

1 דנה קברא די עבד עידו בר כהילו בר

2 אלכסי לנפשה וילדה ואחרה ולמן די ינפק בידה

3 כתב תקף מן יד עידו קים לה ולמן די ינתן ויקבר בה

4 עידו בחיוהי בירח ניסן שנת תשע לחרתת מלך

5 נבטו רחם עמה ולענו דושרא ומנותו וקישה

6 כל מן די יזבן כפרא דנה או יזבן או ירהן או ינתן או

7 יוגר או יתאלף עלוהי כתב כלה או יקבר בה אנוש

8 להן למן די עלא כתיב וכפרא וכתבה דנה חרם

9 כחליקת חרם נבטו ושלמו לעלם עלמין

This is the sepulchre which 'Aidu, son of Kohailu, son [2] of Elqasi, made for himself and his children and his posterity, and for whomsoever shall produce in his hand [3] a warrant from the hand of 'Aidu: it shall hold good for him and for whomsoever 'Aidu during his life-time shall give leave to bury in it: [4] in the month Nisan, the ninth year of Ḥarethath, king [5] of the Nabataeans, lover of his people. And may Dûshara and Manûthu and Qaishah curse [6] every one who shall sell this tomb, or buy it, or mortgage it, or give it away, or [7] let it, or frame for it any (other) writ, or bury any one in it [8] except those who are written above! And the tomb and this its inscription are inviolable things, [9] after the manner of what is held inviolable by the Nabataeans and Shalamians, for ever and ever.

L. 1. עידו **98** 1 i.e. عَائِذ, 'Αειδός Wadd. 2034 &c. כהילו i.e. كُهَيْل; in Palm. **141** 2.

L. 2. אלכסי Prob. ='Αλέξιος. ילדה ואחרה Both words are always in sing., with collect. sense. For אחר see **65** 10 *n*.

L. 3. כתב תקף **87** 3 &c. lit. *a document of confirmation*, תְּקֵף = *be strong*; cf. Esth. 9 29 (תֹּקֶף). קים Ptcp. קָיֵם. ינתן ויקבר For the construction cf. the use of the subjunct. with فَ in Arab., Wright *Ar. Gr.*[3] ii 30 f.; the impf. (or juss.) with וְ in Hebr., e.g. 2 S. 16 11

הַגִּידוּ לוֹ וִישַׂלֵּל. Is. 43 9 &c., cf. Job 19 23, Driver *Tenses* § 62; in Bibl. Aram. cf. Dan. 5 2 אמר . . . וישתון, though the pf. with ו is more usual, Dan. 5 29 &c., as in Syr., Nöld. *Syr. Gr.*[2] § 334 B.

L. 4. ניסן The 1st month, Mar. 22 to April 20, Neh. 2 1. Esth. 3 7; see 78 3 *n.* לחרתת See 78 4 *n.*

L. 5. ולעטו 81 4 &c. = Arab. لعن. The perf. is used similarly in Arab. for prayers and imprecations, e.g. لَعَنَهُ ٱللّٰهُ, Wright l.c. 3. דושרא The chief god of the Nabataeans, worshipped throughout N. Arabia, especially at Petra, and in Ḥauran at Adra'a (אדרעי) and Bostra. In Arab. the name is written ذو الشرى i.e. ذو lit. *owner, possessor* (cf. בעל) and الشرى, prob. the name of a place[1]. Wellhausen enumerates three places called Sharâ, and described by Arab. writers as remarkable either for swampy ground, or for lions, or for water, trees, and jungle. Such localities were esteemed specially suitable for a *ḥimâ* or *temenos* of a god, and Shara, wherever it may have been, was prob. a place of this kind; *Reste Ar. Heidenth.* 48 ff. Thus Dhu-sharâ lit. *owner of Sharâ* is only an appellation of the god: his actual name (p. 239 *n.* 1) was not used; cf. Dhu 'l Ḥalaṣa (Arab., 105 *n.*), Dhu Shamâwi (Sab., 9 1 *n.*), בעלת גבל (= עשתרת), בעל צר (= מלקרת), 3 2 *n.* In Sabaean both the name and title of a god are sometimes used in full, e.g. 'Athtar Dhu Gaufat (CIS iv 40 4. 41 2 f.), Almaqah Dhu Hirrân (Mordtmann u. Müller *Sab. Denkm.* 6). Dusares was worshipped at Petra under the form of a black rectangular stone[2], a sort of Petraean Ka'aba; and Epiphanius describes a feast held at Petra on Dec. 25th in honour of 'Χααβου [χααμοῦ ed. Dind. ii 484] i.e. virgin, and her offspring Δουσάρης i.e. the only son of the lord' (*Haer.* 51)[3]. By Gk. and Lat. writers Dusares was identified with Dionysos-Bacchus: Δουσάρην τὸν Διόνυσον Ναβαταῖοι ὥς φησὶν Ἰσίδωρος (Hesych. s.v.); but, as Wellhausen justly remarks, the god of a nomad race of Arabs, living in the desert, could hardly have been worshipped originally under the character of Dionysos, for Dionysos (בעל) is the

[1] Acc. to Steph. Byz. s.v. Δουσάρη, a mountain, σκόπελος καὶ κορυφὴ ὑψηλοτάτη Ἀραβίας· εἴρηται δὲ ἀπὸ τοῦ Δουσάρου. Hence, he says, the Nabs. called themselves Δουσαρηνοί.

[2] Suidas *Lex.* s.v. Θεὸς Ἄρης.

[3] If the reading is right Χααβου prob. = כעבו lit. *a die, cube*, i.e. the sacred stone, either of Dusares himself, or of a goddess-consort (such as Allât); see on the passage Rösch *ZDMG* xxxviii 643 ff. Rob. Smith holds that the Petraeans worshipped Mother and Son, each under the form of a stone (*Kinship* 292 f.; *Rel. of Sem.* 57 *n.*); Wellhausen (l.c. 50), that they conceived of Dusares as born from his *baetylion*. In his account of the cult, Epiph. may have been unconsciously influenced by Christian ideas of the Parthenogenesis.

god of agricultural, settled life. No doubt in time, under the influence of Canaanite and Aramaic civilization, Dusares assimilated the attributes of Ba'al-Dionysos[1]; and if, as there is some evidence for believing, Dusares was originally a solar deity (see Baethgen *Beitr.* 95 f.), the assimilation is not difficult to imagine. מנותו 80 4. 8. Note the ending ו׳, not elsewhere in Nab. with fem. nouns, as in Arabic a pr. n. ending in ة does not take tanwîn. מנותו is the Arab. goddess مَنَاةُ, mentioned in the Qurân, 53 20. Wellhausen, l. c. 28, explains the form as a plur. *manavâtun* and the name as = Fate, lit. *portion*, *lot* (as מנתא in Aram.), Τύχη, cf. Gad. The chief centre of the cult of Manâth was in the Ḥejaz, at the water of Qudaid, a station on the pilgrim-road between Medina and Mekka. קישה 80 4. קישא 89 9. This is the only instance known of the emph. st. in ה׳. As in the case of מנותו, nothing definite as to the character of this deity has been preserved. Eut. quotes the pr. nn. قَيْس, امرؤ القيس, عبد القيس; possibly *Ḳa-uš-ma-la-ka*, a king of Edom mentioned by Tiglath-pileser (*KB* ii 20), contains the name of the deity.

L. 6. יזבן . . יזבן Peal . . Pael, 80 4 f. 81 5. כפרא 80 1 &c., according to D. H. Müller a word imported from the Liḥyan dialect preserved in inscrr. from El-'Ölâ, *Epigr. Denkm. aus Arab.* p. 65, nos. 9. 25. 27. 29. In any case the Arab. كَفْر, usually *village*, also means *tomb*, as in Nab. The statement of Strabo (p. 667 ed. Müll.) that the Nabs. *ἴσα κοπρίαις ἡγοῦνται τὰ νεκρὰ σώματα . . . διὸ καὶ παρὰ τοὺς κοπρῶνας κατορύττουσι καὶ τοὺς βασιλεῖς* is cleverly explained by Cl.-Gan. as due to a misunderstanding of the Nab. כפרא, which suggested *κοπρία, κοπρών* to Gk. ears, *Ét.* i 146 ff. ירהן 80 5 &c. = رهن *give in pledge.*

L. 7. יותר 81 6 &c., also יאתר CIS ii 220 4, Afel impf. of אתר. יתאלף CIS ii 217 10 &c. = Arab. أُلِّفَ lit. *join*, so *compose* (books), a different sense from that of the Aram. אלף, ילף *teach, learn.* אנוש The form as in Hebr. and BAram. Dan. 4 13 Kt. The word is used in this dialect, as also in BAram. (אֱנָשׁ), with an indeterminate sense, *every man, no man, any one*, τις, e. g. 86 6. 89 5. 90 3. 94 5; similarly in Targ. Onk., e. g. Lev. 13 2. 18. 24; cf. Palm. אנש 147 i 11.

L. 8. לחן i. e. לָהֵן = לָא הֵן *except* 88 3. 94 5. Dan. 2 11. 3 28 &c.; cf. לחן די יתוא 90 4. עלא Cf. עֲלָּא מִנְּהוֹן Dan. 6 3 and עילא in Pal.

[1] Thus coins of Bostra (iii cent. B. C.) bear the figure of a wine-press, and the legend Ἄκτια Δουσάρια or Δουσάρια alone; see further Mordtmann *ZDMG* xxix 104 f.

Aram., for the usual ܟܬܒܗ. כתבה has the suff. 3 sing. m. חרם 81 3. 86 2. 94 3–5, Af. ptcp. מחרם 86 3, hence מחרמתא 102 1 f. *chapel*; in Palm. חרמן 112 4 = ἀναθέματα; in Sabaean חרמת = *sanctuary* (*Sab. Denkm.* 70), similarly מחרם CIS iv 74 15. The √ حرم conveys the idea of a sacred thing *prohibited* to human use, hence حَرَامٌ *sanctuary*; see 1 17 *n.*, p. 68, and Lagrange *Rel. Sém.* 181–187.

L. 9. חליקת 81 3. 86 2 &c. = خَلِيقَةٌ *nature, character.* שלמו 81 4. 86 3 &c., a people nearly related to the Nabataeans; Steph. Byz. s.v. Σαλάμιοι ἔθνος Ἀράβιον· σάλαμα δὲ ἡ εἰρήνη· ὠνομάσθησαν δὲ ἀπὸ τοῦ ἐνσπονδοι γένεσθαι τοῖς Ναβαταίοις. In the Talm. they are mentioned together, e. g. Jer. *Shebi'ith* vi fol. 36 b ערביא שלמייא נבטייא; see Neubauer *Géogr. du Talm.* 427 for other references. In the Targ. שַׁלְמָאָה = הַקֵּינִי, e. g. Onk. Num. 24 21 f., &c.

80. **El-Ḥejra.** CIS ii 198; Eut. 3. B. C. or A. D. 1. In situ.

1 דנה כפרא די עבדו כמכם ברת ואלת ברת חרמו
2 וכליבת ברתה לנפשהם ואחרהם בירח טבת שנת
3 תשע לחרתת מלך נבטו רחם עמה וילען דושרא
4 ומותבה ואלת מן עמנד ומנותו וקישה מן יזבן
5 כפרא דנה או מן יזבן או ירהן או ינתן יתה או ינפק
6 מנה גת או שלו או מן יקבר בה עיר כמכם וברתה
7 ואחרהם ומן די לא יעבד כדי עלא כתיב פאיתי עמה
8 לדושרא והבלו ולמנותו שמדין 5 ולאפכלא קנס
9 סלעין אלף חרתי בלעד מן די ינפק בידה כתב מן יד
10 כמכם או כליבת ברתה בכפרא הו פקים כתבא הו
11 והבאלהי בר עבדעבדת
12 עבד

This is the tomb which Kamkâm, daughter of Wâilat, daughter of Ḥaramu, [2] and Kulaibat her daughter made for themselves and their posterity: in the month Ṭebeth, the ninth year [3] of Ḥarethath, king of the Nabataeans, lover of his people. And may Dûshara [4] and his throne (?), and Allât of 'Amnad, and Manûthu, and Qaishah curse him who shall sell [5] this tomb, or who shall buy it, or mortgage it, or give it away, or take out [6] from it body or limb, or who shall bury in it any other than Kamkâm and her daughter [7] and their posterity; and any one who shall not do according to what is written above, he shall be charged [8] from Dûshara and Hubalu and from Manûthu with 5 curses, and to the magician (?) with a fine [9] of a thousand *sela's* Ḥarethite; saving him who shall produce in his hand a writ from the hand [10] of Kamkâm or Kulaibat her daughter concerning the said tomb; and the said writ shall hold good. [11] Wahb-allâhi, son of 'Abd-'obedath, [12] did the work.

L. 1. עברו The mas. form is used in 3 plur. pf. and impf., though the subj. is fem., cf. **86** 1. יתקברון **93** 2. כמכם Pr. n. fem. = كَمْكَامْ an Arab. gum, Sab. כמכם (*Sab. Denkm.* 83), κάγκαμον. The genealogy is here reckoned through the mother and grandfather (חרמו), and the grave is set apart by a mother and daughter for themselves and their children, the family *sacra*, with the exclusive right of burial, being thus transmitted through women independently of their husbands; cf. **86**. From **91** it appears that married women could hold property and bequeath it on their own account. Sometimes it is the father who provides for the burial rights of his daughters and their children, e. g. **81**. **90**; but as a rule the family grave descends in the male line, e. g. **79**, esp. **89**. These facts point to the independent position held by women among the Nabataeans, testified further by the Nab. coins, upon which women figure prominently; and to the survival of the old rule of female kinship, along with the later system of transmission through males (Nöld. in Eut. *Nab. Inschr.* 79 f., Rob. Smith *Kinship* 313 ff.). ואלת **90** 2 i. e. وَائِلَةْ fem., Οὐαελαθη Wadd. **2055**; in Sin. the name is mas., Eut. **504** &c. חרמו i. e. حَرَامْ, cf. حَرِيمْ.

L. 2. כליבת i. e. كُلَيْبَةْ fem. of كُلَيْبْ. לנפשהם The suff. הם is mas. and fem. in Nab.; see **76** A 1 *n.* טבת i. e. טֵבֵת the 10th month, Dec. 17–Jan. 15, Assyr. *Tibituv*, **78** 3 *n.*; Esth. **2** 15. Thus in the 9th year of Aretas iv the first half of Ṭebeth fell in B.C. 1, the second in A.D. 1.

L. 3. וילע Impf. **86** 8; pf. **79** 5.

L. 4. מותבה **94** 3 f. (after ודושרא) = ܡܘܬܒܗ *his throne*, מותב = מושב,

70 1 (מיתבא, see *n.*), cf. Apoc. 12 5. The *throne* of D. has been explained as the platform on which his shrine was built; Cl.-Gan. identifies it with his altar, and thinks that the altar-throne was none other than the black squared stone worshipped at Petra (p. 218), *Rec.* iv 247–250[1]. It seems, however, more likely that the explanation of the term is to be found in the ritual scenes depicted on Bab.-Assyr. tablets, where the god is seated in his shrine facing the altar; e.g. the tablet of Nabû-pal-iddina illustrated in the Brit. Mus. *Guide to Bab. and Assyr. Ant.* (1900) Pl. xxii. Thus ומותבה is practically the same as *his shrine*; see 94 3 *n.* אלת i. e. اللات *Allât*, the chief goddess of the ancient Arabs; cf. CIS ii 185 אלת אם אלהיא. She is mentioned with Al-'Uzza and Manât in Qur. 53 20. Arab writers say that her *ḥimâ* (79 5 *n.*) was the rich valley in which the town of Ṭâif lay, 60 miles SE. of Mekka; while the inscrr. show that her worship extended northwards to Ḥejra, Ḥauran (98. 99), as far as Palmyra (117); it reached also to Carthage and the Pun. settlements, see 60 3 *n.* The name אֱלָת with a final long vowel due to contraction (not the fem. ending), means *goddess*, and is prob. contracted from أَلْإِلَاهة (fem. of أَلْإِلَاه = الله) — ال الت — اللات, the middle stage of the contraction appearing in the 'Αλιλάτ of Herod. iii 8. The expression אלת אלהתהם *A. their goddess* in 99 1 seems to show that the original meaning of the name was in time forgotten. As to the character of the deity, there is some reason to think that she was a sun-goddess (so Wellh. *Reste Ar. Heid.* 33); in Sabaean *Ilâhat of Hamdân* אלהת המדן had solar attributes, *Sab. Denkm.* 66 f. But in Palm. 117 6 she is distinct from שמש; by Herod. (l. c.) and others she is called Οὐρανίη[2]; and in Ḥauran and at Palmyra her Gk. equivalent was 'Αθήνη[3]. This rather implies that she was an astral or sky deity, possibly the moon-goddess beside Dûshara the sun-god, if such was his original character (79 5 *n.*). In ancient Babylon Allatu was goddess of the nether regions (Jastrow *Rel. of Bab. and Assyr.* 104 &c.), but

[1] On some early Gk. vases the god is represented seated on his altar. Cl.-Gan. quotes Gk. inscriptions from Shêḥ Barakât near Aleppo (*Ét.* ii § 4) to Ζεὺς Μαδβαχος = מרבחו (?) בעל = Ζεὺς βωμός on an inscr. lately found in the same district, *Rec.* iv § 28. The evidence is hardly convincing enough to support the far-reaching identification above.

[2] Herod. says, the Arabs ὀνομάζουσι δὲ τὸν μὲν Διόνυσον 'Οροτάλ, τὴν δὲ Οὐρανίην 'Αλιλάτ. Origen *contr. Cels.* v 37 οἱ 'Αράβιοι τὴν Οὐρανίαν καὶ τὸν Διόνυσον μόνους ἡγοῦνται θεούς. Arrian *Exp. Alex.* vii 20 Ἄραβας δύο μόνον τιμᾶν θεούς, τὸν Οὐρανόν τε καὶ τὸν Διόνυσον.

[3] 'Αθήνη in Gk. inscrr. from Ḥauran = אלת, Wadd. 2203, 2308 &c. The son of Zenobia, והבלת, was called in Gk. 'Αθηνόδωρος.

there is no evidence that אלת had this character in Phoen. or Arab. religion (see 50 1 *n.*). מן עמנר or עמנר The name of a place; cf. אלת די בצלחר 99 1 f.

L. 6. נת . . שלו . . עיר Arab. words: جُثَّة *corpse*, شِلْو *member of the body*, غَيْر *another*.

L. 7. מאיתי עמה 81 7 i.e. מֵאִיתַי עַמֵּה, cf. מאיתי עלוהי CIS ii 217 7. The first letter is the Arab. conj. فَ, cf. מקים l. 10 and often.

L. 8. הבלו Though the prep. is absent, this is prob. the ancient god هُبَل, cf. בנהבל 102 5 (?); for the omission of the prep. cf. לנפשהם ואחרהם l. 2. שמרין Perhaps to be connected with حَمْدَم which sometimes = *to curse*, the Aram. equivalent of the Arab. لعن; cf. CIS ii 211 8 לענת iiii *four curses*. לאפכלא Possibly the name of some religious or secular institution, Lidzb. 145 *n.* Nöld. suggests that the form is an error for לאכפלא *in double* (*amount*); cf. מאיתי עלוהי כפל CIS ii 217 7. The word has been found recently in a Palm. inscr. following the name of a person בעל . . . בר ירחבולא אפכלא די עזיזו אלהא where it is clearly a priestly title, perhaps (after the Assyr. *Abkallu*) = 'magician' (see p. 295 *n.* 1), and in the Minaean (?) inscr. from Warka אפכל? = أفكل in the same position, Hommel *Süd-Arab. Chrest.* 113. Lidzb., *Eph.* i 203, proposes doubtfully the rendering *administrator*. קנם 89 8 = *fine*, as in Targ., e.g. Ps.-Jon. Ex. 21 30 קְנָסָא דְמָמוֹנָא. The resemblance to κῆνσος, *census*, is prob. only accidental; *census* does not = *fine*, and a Lat. word is not likely to have become naturalized in this connexion (Nöld.).

L. 9. סלעין In Targ. סלעא = Heb. שקל, e.g. Onk. Ex. 30 13 סִילְעָא בְּסִילְעֵי קוּדְשָׁא, Syr. ܣܶܠܥܳܐ, Gk. στατήρ; here silver drachmae. חרתי An indeclinable adj. formed from חרתת, حارِثِيّ from حارِثة, 'authorized, issued by Aretas.' The coins of Aretas iii, Obodas, and Aretas iv (at the beginning of his reign) are heavier in weight than those of the later kings. This double threat of divine curses and a fine in money is a peculiar feature of the El-Ḥejra inscrr.; cf. 69 19 *n.* Lidzb., p. 143, has pointed out the remarkable parallel afforded by a number of Gk. sepulchral inscrr. from W. Asia Minor, especially by those from Lycia[1]. The custom of specifying a fine for violating a tomb spread widely from Lycia over the Roman Empire, and in this way may have reached the Nabataeans.

[1] See Hirschfeld in *Königsberger Studien* i (1887, 83–144). The foll. is a specimen, from Pinara, circ. 3 cent. B.C. (Hirschfeld, p. 107) ἐὰν δέ τις παρὰ ταῦτα ποιήσῃ, ἁμαρτωλὸς | ἔστω θεῶν πάντων καὶ Λητοῦς | καὶ τῶν τέκνων καὶ προσ-|αποτεισάτω τάλαντον ἀργυρίου | καὶ ἐξέστω τῶι βουλομένωι | ἐγδικάζεσθαι περὶ τούτων.

L. 10. בכפרא הו Eut. renders (*who are*) *in the said grave*; but it is better to refer the prep. to כתב *a writing . . . in connexion with* &c.

L. 11. והבאלהי **93** 7 i.e. وَهْبُ اللّٰهِ, the name of the sculptor; the י' is the sign of the genit. עבדעבדת Compounded with the name of king Obodas; cf. עבדמלכו **97** ii. עבדחרתת **82** 5. עבדרבאל CIS ii 304. The origin of these names may have been due to the deification of kings after death (see **95** 1 *n.*); in some cases, perhaps, the second name belonged to a venerated ancestor, or to a tribe (cf. Arab. Abd-Ahlihi), Wellhausen *Reste* 4.

81. El-Ḥejra. CIS ii 199; Eut. 4. A. D. 4. In situ.

1 דנה כפרא ובססא וכונא די עבד חושבו בר
2 כפיו בר אלכוף תימניא לנפשה וילדה וחבו אמה
3 ורופו ואפתיו אחותה וילדהם חרם כחליקת חרם
4 נבטו ושלמו לעלם ולען דושרא כל מן די יקבר בכפרא דנה
5 עיר מן די עלא כתיב או יזבן או יזבן או ימשכן או
6 יוגר או יהב או יאנא ומן די יעבד כעיר מה די עלא
7 כתיב פאיתי עמה לדושרא אלהא בחרמא די עלא
8 לדמי מנמר סלעין אלף חרתי ולמראנא חרתת מלכא כות
9 בירח שבט שנת עשר ותלת לחרתת מלך נבטו רחם
10 עמה

This is the tomb and the base and the foundation (?) which Ḥûshabu, son [2] of Kafiyu, son of Alkûf, the Têmanite, made for himself and his children and Ḥabu his mother, [3] and Rûfu and Aftiyu his sisters and their children, an inviolable place, after the manner of what is held inviolable [4] by the Nabataeans and Shalamians, for ever. And may Dûshara curse every one who shall bury in this tomb [5] any other than those written above, or shall sell it, or buy it, or pledge it, or [6] let it, or give it away, or lend it temporarily! And any one who shall do otherwise than what is above [7] written, he shall be charged to the god Dûshara, in connexion with the above inviolable place, [8] at the full price of a thousand *sela's* Ḥarethite, and to our lord the king Ḥarethath the same amount. [9] In the month Shebaṭ, the thirteenth year of Ḥarethath, king of the Nabataeans, lover of [10] his people.

L. 1. בססא = *βάσις*, Syr. ܒܣܝܣ, ܒܣܣܐ, in Targ. בָּסִים. כונא Some part of the building, but the exact meaning is unknown. If taken from √כון, כַּוְנָא (כַּוָּנָא) would mean something 'straight,' 'fixed'; but the word may be Gk., hardly, however, *χώνη melting-pot, funnel*, as proposed in Corp. A good many terms connected with building and sculpture were introduced into Aram. from Gk., e. g. תיטרא *θέατρον* CIS ii 163 2, Palm. בסלקא 119 3. חושבו i. e. حُوَشِّبُ.

L. 2. כפיו Cf. Arab. كَفِىٌّ *equal, sufficient.* אלכוף Corp. suggests a compound of אל and כפף [כוף], 'incline, O El.' תימניא From תימא 69 3 *n.*, as بَهْرَانِيّ from بَهْرَاءُ (Nöld.); cf. 85 2 *n.* חבו In Arab. perhaps حُبّ *love*, cf. חבימו 98 3.

L. 3. רופו Nöld. compares رَأَف *to pity*; but ? רומו. אפתיו 98 3 is not otherwise known. The Corp. compares פתא, פתי *to be wide, open.* אחותה Plur. with suff. 3 sing. m.; cf. אחותהם 85 3 and in Egypt. Aram. CIS ii 150 8 (as here). חרם כחליקת See 79 8. 9 *n.*

L. 4. נבמו ושלמו See 79 9 *n.*

L. 5. ימשכן 86 4 &c.; Syr. ܡܫܟܢ *to pawn* or *mortgage*; in 79 6 &c. ירהן.

L. 6. יהב i.e. יְהַב, יֶהֱב, the rarely used impf. of יהב; in 79 6 &c. ינתן. יאנא Prob. a verb from إِنَى, أَنَاءٌ *time* (Nöld.).

L. 8. לדמי מגמר Lit. 'according to a price of totality.' דמי is plur. constr., for Aram. uses only the plur., ܕܡܝܐ, ܕܡܝܢ; cf. CIS ii 217 7 כפל דמי אתרא דנה *double the price of this place.* מגמר is prob. a noun مُجْمَر from جمر iv *to unite, collect, reckon up*, rather than a pass. ptcp. מְגַמַּר, מֻגְמַר, which would not agree with the plur. דמי. סלעין See 80 9 *n.* מראנא See 62 11 *n.* חרתת מלכא The regular order in Nab., 85 10. 92 4 &c., as in BAram. Dan. 3 1. 5 1 &c., and late Hebr. Dan. 1 21. 1 Chr. 29 29.

L. 9. שבט i. e. שְׁבָט Zech. 1 7, the 11th month, Assyr. *šabaṭu*; 78 3 *n.* עשר ותלת This is the usual order in Nab. (with a fem. noun), cf. עשר ושבע 82 4. 93 6. 99 3; similarly in Palm. 147 ii b 20 עשר ושת, in Mandaic (Nöld. *Mand. Gr.* 189), and in Phoen. 5 1 and NPun. In Syr. the ten follows the unit.

82. El-Ḥejra. CIS ii 201; Eut. 5. A. D. 8. In situ.

1 דנה כפרא די עבד מלכיון פתורא
2 על חנינו הפסתיון כלירכא אבוהי
3 ולנפשה וילדה ואחרה אצדק באצדק בירח ניסן
4 שנת עשר ושבע למראנא חרתת מלך
5 נבטו רחם עמה עבדחרתת פסלא
6 בר עבדעבדת עבד

This is the tomb which Malkiôn Pathôra made [2] over Ḥunainu Hephaestiôn the chiliarch his father, [3] and for himself and his children and his posterity, each legal kinsman: in the month Nisan, [4] the seventeenth year of our lord Ḥarethath, king [5] of the Nabataeans, lover of his people. ʻAbd-ḥarethath the mason, [6] son of ʻAbd-ʻobedath, did the work.

L. 1. מלכיון = Μαλχίων Wadd. 1910 &c. פתורא Cognomen of the father, = *table* in Aram., e.g. Targ. Onk. Ex. 25 23. D. H. Müller suggests that the name = τραπεζίτης; but this would be פְּתוֹרָיָא (Nöld.).

L. 2. על 91 2, instead of the usual ל, implies that the father was already dead. חנינו 95 1 حُنَيْن = Ὀυαῖνος Wadd. 2048 &c. הפסתיון i.e. Ἡφαιστίων. כלירכא = χιλίαρχος.

L. 3. אצדק באצדק A legal phrase frequently occurring in these inscrr., 86 2. 88 2 &c. In form אצדק is an adj. with the elative א (أَصْدَق), though without the significance of the elative in Arab. (compar., superl.); the ב is distributive, as in שנה בשנה Dt. 15 20. חדש בחדש 1 Chr. 27 1. Literally, אצדק may be rendered *authorised*; it conveys the idea of *legal right*, perhaps also of *kinship*; Nöld. is inclined to give the latter as the original sense, and compares the Syr. ܐܙܕܩܐ *relatives, kinsmen* (Payne Smith *Thes.* col. 1085). At any rate in usage the phrase denotes 'haeres quisque in vice suâ,' 'jure haereditatis' (Corp.), 'all who have claims as kindred'; thus אחרה ואצדקה CIS ii 220 1 f. לילדהם ואצדקהם 215 2. די יתקברון בה א׳ בא׳ 219 2 f. כל אנוש אצדק וירת 86 3.

L. 5. עבדחרתת See 80 11 *n*. פסלא 88 9 &c. i.e. פַּסָּלָא, or פָּסְלָא, ܦܣܠܐ.

83. El-Ḥejra. CIS ii 202; Eut. 6. A. D. 15. In situ.

1 דנה כפרא ואונא די
2 עבד מנעת בר אביץ לנפשה
3 ובנוהי ובנתה וילדהם בשנת
4 עשרין וארבע לחרתת מלך
5 נבטו רחם עמה

This is the tomb and habitation which [2] Mun'ath, son of Abyas, made for himself [3] and his sons and his daughters and their children: in the [4] twenty-fourth year of Ḥarethath, king [5] of the Nabataeans, lover of his people.

L. 1. אונא = Syr. ܐܘܢܐ *a lodging, inn,* so *mansion, abode,* e.g. Jn. 14 2 ܒܒܝܬ ܐܒܝ ܐܘܢܐ ܣܓܝ ܐܝܬ; a somewhat poetical expression to be found in an inscr. By Ephraem it is used of *mansions of the dead* ܐܘܢ̈ܐ ܕܡܝ̈ܬܐ.

L. 2. מנעת 101 3 i.e. ܡܢܥܬ, Μόναθος Wadd. 2429. אביץ i.e. ابيض.

84. El-Ḥejra. CIS ii 204; Eut. 7. A. D. 16. In situ.

1 דנה כפרא די עבד תימאלהי בר
2 חמלת לנפשה ויהב כפרא דנה לאמה
3 אנתתה ברת גלהמו מן זמן שטר
4 מוהבתא די בידה תעבד כל די תצבא
5 מן 26 באב שנת 25 לחרתת מלך נבטו
6 רחם עמה

This is the tomb which Taim-allâhi, son of [2] Ḥamilath, made for himself; and he has given this tomb to Amah [3] his wife, daughter of Gulhumu, from the date of the deed [4] of gift which is in her hand, (that) she may do (with it) whatever she pleases: [5] from the 26th of Ab, the 25th year of Ḥarethath, king of the Nabataeans, [6] lover of his people.

L. 1. חימאלהי i. e. تَيْمُ ٱللّٰهِ *slave of Allah*, Θαιμάλλου (gen.) Wadd. 2020; frequent in Sin., e. g. 108.

L. 2. חמלת Mas., 87 2 ff. fem., = حَمْلَة or حِمَالَة (*sword-belt*, حمل *to carry*); cf. Ἀμέλαθος Wadd. 2393 &c.

L. 3. אנתתה From אנתת (= אנשת, Syr. ܐܰܢ̱ܬ݁ܬ݂ܳܐ *att-thâ*) with suff. 3 sing. m.; contrast אתתה CIS ii 194. In Palm. the forms are אתת, emph. איתא, with suff. אתתה; in Pal. Aram. איתת, איתתא &c., with suff. איתתתיה and איתתיה, plur. נשין, נשיא (cf. נשי 62 8); Dalm. *Gr.* 159. גלהמו Cf. the name of the Arab tribe جُلْهُمَة. שטר 93 5. שטרי 94 4, Palm. 147 i 8, the usual Aram. word for a *bill* or *bond*, e. g. שְׁטַר חוב *a bill of debt*, hence the NHebr. שְׁטַר מִקָּח וּמִמְכָּר.

L. 4. תצבא 87 5. 147 ii c 50. For the form תצְּבָא cf. יְחַוֵּא 90 4.

L. 5. אב The 5th month; see 78 3 *n*.

85. **El-Ḥejra.** CIS ii 205; Eut. 8. A. D. 25. In situ.

1 דנה כפרא די עבדו ושתי ברת בגרת
2 וקינו ונשנכיה בנתה תימניתא להם כלה
3 כלה ולשמית ועשפא.....אחותהם בנת
4 ושתי ו....כלה די יתקברון......דנה
5 די עלא....כלה בכפרא דנה פקים על
6 ושתי בנתה. . . . .
7 . . . חאין . . . .
8 . . . .
9 פאיתי עמה לאלהי סלעין מאה חרתי
10 ולמראנא חרתת מלכא כות בירח איר שנת
11 𐢭 𐢬 IIII לחרתת מלך נבטו רחם עמה

This is the tomb which Washti, daughter of Bagarath, [2] and Qainu and Nashankiyah (?) her daughters, the Têmanites, made for themselves, each [3] one of them, and for Shamiyath and .... their sisters, daughters [4] of Washti .... that they be buried .... this [5] who are above .... in this tomb; and it shall hold good for [6] Washti, her daughters ... [9] and he shall be charged to my god a hundred *sela's* Ḥarethite, [10] and our lord Ḥarethath the king the same amount: in the month Iyar, the [11] 34th year of Ḥarethath, king of the Nabataeans, lover of his people.

L. 1. ושחי The name is read distinctly in l. 4. It can hardly be the same as the O.T. ושחי, which is of Persian (Zend) origin. בגרת 97 ii i.e. بُجْرَة, بَجْرَة *corpulent*, Βάγρατος Wadd. 2562.

L. 2. קינו 87 2 fem., in Sin. mas., e.g. Eut. 4. 557 &c.; in Arab. قَيْن is the name of a tribe, Hebr. קַיִן Num. 24 22. Jud. 4 11. נשכביה Similarly in Sin., e.g. Eut. 51. 190 &c. (mas.); cf. שכביה Eut. 162. בנתה Plur.; cf. 80, where the grave is provided by a mother and her daughter. Here the sisters of the foundresses are to have the use of the tomb; see 80 1 *n*. תימניתא i.e. תֵּימָנָיְתָא; see 81 2 *n*. כלה כלה are distributive.

L. 6. The illegible lines no doubt contained the usual imprecations.

L. 9. אלהי Either plur. or sing., with suff. מאה The smallness of the fine is remarkable; contrast 81 8. Eut. suggests that a metal plate, specifying a heavier penalty, was attached to the inscr. subsequently. In some cases traces of such tablets are still to be seen.

L. 10. איר 86 9 &c., i.e. Apr.–May; Assyr. *airu*, Palm. איר, Syr. ܐܝܪ, Rabb. אִיָּר; see 78 3 *n*.

86. El-Ḥejra. CIS ii 206; Eut. 9. A.D. 26. In situ. **Plate VII.**

1 דנה קברא די עבד כהלן אסיא בר ואלן לנפשה וילדה ואחרה
2 אצדק באצדק עד עלם ואיתי קברא דנה חרם כחליקת חרמא
3 מחרם לדושרא בנבטו ושלמו על כל אנוש אצדק וירת די לא
4 יזבן קברא דנה ולא ימשכן ולא יוגר ולא ישאל ולא יכתב
5 בקברא דנה כתב כלה עד עלם וכל אנוש די ינפק בידו כתב מן כהלן
6 פקים הו כדי בה וכל אנוש די יכתב בקברא דנה כתב מן כל די עלא
7 פאיתי עמה לדושרא כסף סלעין אלפין תלת חרתי ולמראנ[א]
8 חרתת מלכא כות וילען דושרא ומנותו כל מן די יעיר מן כל
9 די עלא בירח איר שנת תלתין וחמש לחרתת מלך נבטו רחם עמה
10 אפתח בר עבדעבדת וחלפאלהי בר חמלגו פסליא עבדו

This is the sepulchre which Kahlân the physician, son of Wa'lân, made for himself and his children and his posterity, [2] each legal kinsman, for ever. And this sepulchre is an inviolable place after the manner of the inviolable sanctuary [3] which is inviolably dedicated to Dûshara among the Nabataeans and Shalamians. It is incumbent upon every legal kinsman and heir that he do not [4] sell this sepulchre, nor pledge it, nor let it, nor lend it, nor write [5] in respect of this sepulchre any deed, for ever. But every man who shall produce in his hand a writ from Kahlân, [6] it shall hold good according to what is in it. And every man who shall write on this sepulchre any writing other than what is above, [7] he shall be charged to Dûshara in money three thousand *sela*'s Ḥarethite, and to our lord [8] the king Ḥarethath the same amount. And may Dûshara and Manûthu curse every one who shall change aught of [9] what is above! In the month Iyar, the thirty-fifth year of Ḥarethath, king of the Nabataeans, lover of his people. [10] Aftaḥ, son of 'Abd-'obedath, and Ḥalaf-allâhi, son of Ḥamlagu, the masons, did the work.

L. 1. כחלן .. ואלן i.e. كَهْلَان .. وَأْلَان.

L. 2. אצדק באצדק See 82 3 *n*.

L. 3. מחרם Afel ptcp; cf. 69 16 (a place), and 79 8 *n*. ירת i.e. יָרֵת or יָרֵת = Hebr. יֹרֵשׁ.

L. 4. ימשכן See 81 5 *n*. יכתב ב' Nöld. renders 'make any written contract for the use of this grave.'

L. 6. מן כל די עלא Corp. renders as above, and the similar phrase with עיר elsewhere (e. g. 81 5), supports this. Nöld., however, regards מן here as the Arab. من لِلْبَيَانِ (من *explanatory*), and renders 'a writing *of the same kind as* all that is above.' This usage is more distinct in 89 2. 5.

L. 8. יעיר Pael, = Arab. يُغَيِّرُ *he shall change*; cf. غَيْرٌ *another*, עיר.

L. 10. אפתח i.e. أَفْتَحُ. חלפאלהי i.e. خَلَفُ ٱللّٰهِ *compensation from Allah*; often abbreviated خَلَف 89 1; cf. 'Αντίγονος, Palm. חליפי p. 301 *n*. 1 = 'Αντιόχου. 118 1. חמלגו Nöld. suggests حَمْلَجَ (the vb. = *to make fast* a line) as an equivalent.

87. El-Ḥejra. CIS ii 207; Eut. 10. A.D. 27. In situ.

1 דנה קברא די עבד ארוס בר פרון לנפשה ולפרון אבוהי
2 הפרכא ולקינו אנתתה ולחטיבת וחמילת בנתהם וילד חטיבת
3 וחמילת אלה ולכל מן די ינפק בידה תקף מן ארוס דנה או
4 חטיבת וחמילת אח[ו]תה בנת פרון הפרכא
5 די יתקבר בקברא דנה או יקבר מן די יצבא
6 בתקפא די בידה כדי בכתבא הו או אצדק באצדק
7 בי[ר]ח ניסן שנת תלתין ושת לחרתת מלך נבטו רחם עמה
8 אפתח בר עבדעבדת ווהבו בר אפצא וחורו בר אחיו פסליא
9 עב[ד]ו

This is the sepulchre which Arûs, son of Farwân, made for himself and for Farwân his father [2] the eparch, and for Qainu his wife, and for Ḥaṭibath and Ḥamilath their daughters, and the children of the said Ḥaṭibath [3] and Ḥamilath, and for every one who shall produce in his hand a warrant from the said Arûs, or [4] Ḥaṭibath and Ḥamilath his sisters, daughters of Farwân the eparch, [5] to be buried in this sepulchre, or to bury whom he pleases, [6] in virtue of the warrant which is in his hand, according to what is in that writ, or each legal kinsman. [7] In the month Nisan, the thirty-sixth year of Ḥarethath, king of the Nabataeans, lover of his people. [8] Aftaḥ, son of 'Abd-'obedath, and Wahbu, son of Afṣa, and Ḥûru, son of Uḥayyu, the masons, [9] did the work.

L. 1. ארוס The termination perhaps indicates a Gk. name. פרון i. e. فَرْوَانُ. Arab. words in ـَانُ do not take tanwîn, hence this name does not end in ו.

L. 2. הפרכא 93 1 = ἔπαρχος, cf. Sin. הפרכיה = ἐπαρχία 107, the ה as in Syr. ܗܘܦܪܟܐ, ܗܘܦܪܟܝܐ. קינו 85 2 n. אנתתה i. e. the wife of Farwân, and step-mother of Arûs. חמלת ,חטבת i. e. حَاطِبَةُ, حَامِلَةُ (84 2 n.).

L. 3. אלה 94 3 prob. אִלֵּה, plur. of דנה, דא; see add. note p. 26. תקף 79 3 n.

L. 4. אחותה An error for the plur. אחותתה. Other errors in this inscr. are ביח l. 7. עבו l. 9.

L. 8. אפתח 86 10 *n.* חבו i.e. وَهْبٌ. אפצא 93 8 i.e. أَلْفَى; the name occurs in the Liḥyan dialect, Müller *Ep. Denk. aus Ar.* nos. 30. 32. חורו 90 5 i.e. حُوْرٌ, Hebr. חור Ex. 17 10 &c., Gk. Οὖρος Wadd. 2270 &c. אחיו i.e. أُخَيٌّ dimin., *little brother.*

88. **El-Ḥejra.** CIS ii 208; Eut. 11. A.D. 27 (?). In situ.

1 דנה כפרא די עבד שלי בר רצוא
2 לנפשה וילדה ואחרה אצדק באצדק
3 ודי לא יתקבר בכפרא דנה להן אצדק
4 באצדק ודי לא יתזבן ולא יתרהן כפרא
5 דנה ומן די יעבד כעיר די עלא פאיתי
6 עמה לדושרא אלה מראנא [כסף סלעין] אלף
7 חרתי בירח ניסן שנת 𐢭 ... \
8 לחרתת מלך נבטו רחם עמה אפתח
9 פסלא עבד

This is the tomb which Shullai, son of Raḍwa, made [2] for himself and his children and his posterity, each legal kinsman; [3] and that no one is to be buried in this tomb except each legal [4] kinsman, and that this tomb is not to be sold or mortgaged. [5] And whoever does otherwise than is above, he shall be [6] charged to Dûshara, the god of our lord, [in money] a thousand [*sela's*] [7] Ḥarethite. In the month Nisan, the ... year [8] of Ḥarethath, king of the Nabataeans, lover of his people. Aftaḥ [9] the mason did the work.

L. 1. שלי 93 4 probably=Συλλαῖος (ὁ τῶν Ναβαταίων ἐπίτροπος Strabo 663 ed. Müll.). This presupposes a form سُلَى or شُ, from سل, which, however, is not known. Prop. nn. of the form فُعَلَى are fem., e.g. سُلْمَى; Nöld. prefers a form سُلَّاءُ. רצוא=رَضْوَاءُ; in which case, though not known in Arab., it will be one of the few mas.

names of the form نَغْلَاءُ, fem. of أَنْغَلُ (Nöld.). Wellhausen takes it as = رُضَاء, the name of an ancient Arab deity, and compares the Palm. names חים רצו 115 1. נר רצו Vog. 84 3; *Reste Ar. Heid.* 58 f. Cf. perhaps *Risuil* (? = רצואל) CIL v 4920.

L. 3. לחן 79 8 *n*.

L. 4. יתזבן Ethpa. This unusual form (for יזדבן) appears to have been current; cf. מתזבנא ptcp. fem. 147 ii c 33 and 94 4 *n*.

L. 6. אלה if it qualified דושרא, would be אלהא; see 61 29 *n*.

L. 7. Eut. fills the lacuna with ڪ ↗ i. e. 15, making a total of 36. The Corp. would add two or three strokes, making 38 or 39.

89. **El-Ḥejra.** CIS ii 209; Eut. 12. A. D. 31. In situ.

1 דנה כפרא די עבד חלפו בר קסנתן לנפשה ולשעידו ברה
2 ואחוהי מה די יתילד לחלפו דנה מן דכרין ולבניהם ואחרהם
3 אצדק באצדק עד עלם ודי יתקברון בכפרא דנה ו... שעידו דנה
4 ומנועת וכנושת וריבמת ואמית ושלימת בנת חלפו דנה ולא רשי
5 אנוש כלה מן שעידו ואחוהי דכרין ובניהם ואחרהם די יזבן כפרא דנה
6 או יכתב מוהבה או עירה לאנוש כלה בלעדהן יכתב חד מנהם לאנתתה
7 או לבנתה או לנשיב או לחתן כתב למקבר בלחד ומן יעבד כעיר דנה פאיתי
8 עמה קנס לדושרא אלה מר[אנא כס]ף סלעין חמש מאה חרתי
9 ולמראנא כות כנסחת דנה יהיב בבית קישא בירח ניסן שנת ארבעין
10 לחרתת מלך נבטו רחם עמה רומא ועבדעבדת פסליא

This is the tomb which Ḥalafu, son of Qos-nathan, made for himself and for Sha'idu his son [2] and his brothers, as many male children as shall be born to the said Ḥalafu, and for their sons and their posterity, [3] each legal kinsman, for ever; and that there be buried in this tomb . . . the said Sha'idu, [4] and Manû'ath and Kenûshath (?) and Ribamath (?) and Umayyath and Shalimath, daughters of the said Ḥalafu. And no man shall be allowed, [5] either Sha'idu, or his brothers male, or their sons, or their posterity, to sell this tomb, [6] or write a (deed of) gift or anything else to any man, with the sole exception that one of them write for his wife, [7] or for his daughters, or for a kinsman, or for a son-in-law, a deed of burial. And whoever does otherwise than this, he shall be [8] charged with a fine to Dûshara, the god of [our] lord, [in mon]ey five hundred *sela's* Ḥarethite, [9] and to our lord the same amount, according to the copy hereof deposited in the temple of Qaisha. In the month Nisan, the fortieth year [10] of Ḥarethath, king of the Nabataeans, lover of his people. Rauma and 'Abd-'obedath, the masons.

L. 1. חלפו i.e. خَلَفٌ 86 10 *n.* קסנתן=*Qos gives*, cf. Κοσνατανος in a Gk. inscr. from Memphis (200–150 B.C.), where Κοσγηρος, Κοσβανος, Κοσμαλαχος &c. also occur; Miller *Rev. Archéol.* (1870) 109 ff. קס was apparently the name of an Edomite deity, cf. Ḳaušmalaka, Ḳaušgabri, Edomite kings, Schrader *COT* 150; and the Edomite Κοστόβαρος Jos. *Ant.* xv 7 9 f. In Sin. the name קוסעדר is found, Eut. 423, though the reading is not quite certain; and in Hebr. ברקוס Ezr. 2 53. It is natural to compare קישא l. 9 (79 5 *n.*), but Nöld. is against the identification, *ZDMG* xli 714. שעידו i.e. سُعَيْدٌ *Fortunatus*, cf. שעדו (سَعْدٌ) Sin. 106, Palm. 127 3, and שעודת 95 3.

L. 2. מן דכרין An Arabism, cf. l. 5 אנוש כלה מן שעידו and 86 6 *n.* מן . . מה=ما . . من; Wright *Ar. Gr.* ii § 48 *g.*

L. 4. מנעת Cf. مَنِيعَةٌ pr. n. fem.=*defended*, and מנעת 83 2. The two names which follow are uncertain. אמית Prob. dimin. أُمَيَّةٌ from أَمَةٌ *handmaid.* שלימת i.e. سَلِيمَةٌ, ܫܠܡ, cf. שלמו (fem.) CIS ii 210 2. רשי i.e. רַשַּׁי 90 3; Targ., Talm. רַשַּׁאי *one to whom something is allowed.*

L. 5. אנוש כלה 94 5 i.e. אִ' כֻּלֵּהּ=*every one*; cf. כְּתָב כֻּלֵּהּ CIS ii 219 5, and ܡܪܝܐ ܟܠܗ, ܟܠܗ ܡܕܝܢܬܐ Nöld. *Syr. Gr.*[2] § 218; see 62 17 *n.*

L. 6. או עירה=او غَيْرَهَا, lit. *or* (any deed) *other than it.* בלעדהן Lit. *except if*; 80 9.

L. 7. נשיב i.e. نَسِيبٌ=*kinsman* in the male line; but as these would naturally have the right of burial, the meaning here may be a descendant in the female line, a daughter's child; Rob. Smith

Kinship 315 f. בלחור In CIS ii 215 6 בלחוד, Targ. בִּלְחוֹד *only, alone*, to be taken with בלעדהן; cf. 90 6.

L. 8. קנם 80 8.

L. 9. נסחת See p. 189, = نُسْخَة; Assyr. *nisḫu* 'excerpt' (*ZA* iv 267); cf. the late Rabbin. נוסחא *a variant, another reading*. The word appears to be of N. Semitic origin, rather than native to Arab., the fem. ending in نسخة being equivalent to the Aram. emph. st.; see Fränkel *Aram. Fremdw.* 251. יהיב For יהיבא. קישא See 79 5 *n*.

L. 10. רומא 91 2 perhaps رُوَمَاءُ, or abbrev. from رُوَمَانُ, a common name.

90. El-Ḥejra. CIS ii 212; Eut. 14. A.D. 35. In situ.

1 דנה כפרא די עבד עבדעבדת בר אריבס לנפשה
2 ולואלת ברתה ולבני ואלת דא ובנתה וילדהם די יתקברון בקברא הו
3 ולא רשין ואלת ובניה די יזבנון או ימשכנון או יוגרון כפרא דנה או
4 יכתבון בכפרא הו כתב כלה לכל אלוש לעלם להן די יהוא כפרא הו לואלת ולבניה
5 ובנתה ולילדהם קים לעלם וקם על ואלת ובניה די הן יהוא חורו אח עבדעבדת
6 דנה בחגרא ויהוא בה חלף מות די יקברון יתה בקברא דנה לחודוהי
7 ולא ינפק יתה אנוש ומן די יעיר ולא יעבד כדי עלא כתיב
8 פאיתי עמה למראנא כסף סלעין אלפין תרין חרתי בירח
9 טבת שנת ארבעין וארבע לחרתת מלך נבטו רחם עמה
10 אפתח בר עבדעבדת פסלא עבד

This is the tomb which 'Abd-'obedath, son of Aribas, made for himself, [2] and for Wa'ilath his daughter, and for the sons of this Wa'ilath and her daughters and their children, that they may be buried in the said sepulchre; [3] and neither Wa'ilath nor her sons shall be allowed to sell or pledge or let this tomb, or [4] write in respect of this tomb any deed for any man, for ever; but that the said tomb shall hold good for Wa'ilath and for her sons [5] and her daughters and for their children for ever. And it is incumbent upon Wa'ilath and her sons, if Ḥûru, brother of this 'Abd-'obedath, be [6] in Ḥejra, and the fate of death befall him, to bury him, and none but him, in this sepulchre; [7] and no man shall take him out. And whoever shall change (this provision), and not do according to what is above written, [8] he shall be charged to our lord in money two thousand *sela's* Ḥarethite. In the month [9] Ṭebeth, the forty-fourth year of Ḥarethath, king of the Nabataeans, lover of his people. [10] Aftaḥ, son of 'Abd-'obedath, the mason, did the work.

L. 1. אריבס Hardly an Aram. name; possibly Ἀρύβας.

L. 2. ואלת See 80 1 *n*.

L. 3. רשין 89 4 *n*.

L. 4. אלוש An error for אנוש. לחן 79 8 *n*.

L. 5. קים The ptcp. goes with יהוא l. 4. חורו Perhaps a merchant who was often absent from home (Nöld.).

L. 6. חגרא=الحِجْر, the emph. st. in Aram. representing the Arab. art., lit. 'the guarded, forbidden place.' In the Targg. and Talm. חגרא occurs as a name of various places; the חגרא mentioned in *Jebamoth* 116a as the home of a Jew living at Neharde'a (Babyl.) may be El-Ḥejra (Nöld.). A good many Jews were settled in the N. of the Ḥejaz. חלף מות Lit. 'a mortal change.' לחודוהי Lit. *he alone*; cf. בלחוד 89 7.

91. El-Ḥejra. CIS ii 213; Eut. 15. A. D. 36. In situ.

1 דנה כפרא די עבדו ענמו בר גזיאת וארסכסה

2 ברת תימו אסרתגא על רומא וכלבא

3 אחיה פלענמו תלת כפרא וצריחא דנה

4 ולארסכסה תלתין תרין מן כפרא וצריחא

5 וחלקה מן גוחיא מדנחא וגוחיא

6 ולענמו חלקה מן גוחיא מד[נ]ח ימינא

7 וגוחיא די בה להם ולילדהם אצדק באצדק

8 בי[ר]ח טבת שנת 𐢫𐢫𐢨 לחרתת מלך נבטו

9 רחם עמה אפתח בר [עבדעבדת] פסלא עבד

This is the tomb which 'Ânimu, son of Guzayath, and Arisoxe, [2] daughter of Taimu the *stratēgos*, made over Rauma and Kalba [3] her brothers;—and to 'Ânimu (belongs) the third part of this tomb and vault, [4] and to Arisoxe two-thirds of the tomb and vault; [5] and her portion of the niches is the east side and the niches (there); [6] and 'Ânimu has his portion of the niches on the south-east, [7] and the niches which are in it;—for them and for their children, each legal kinsman. [8] In the month Ṭebeth, the 45th year of Ḥarethath, king of the Nabataeans, [9] lover of his people. Aftaḥ, son [of 'Abd-'obedath], the mason, did the work.

L. 1. עגמו 140 B 1. Arab. names like غَانِمٌ, غَنَم are suggested as equivalents. Ἄναμος, common in Ḥauran, prob. stands for أَنْعَمُ = אנעם (CIS ii 191 1) rather than for עגמו. נזיאת The Arab. would be جَزِينَةُ or جُزَيْنَةُ; the mas. form occurs, جَزَى. ארסכסה Nöld. suggests that this is an abbreviation, Ἀριστοξη for Ἀριστοξένη; for the omission of τ cf. אסרתגא l. 2; the Corp. merely transliterates *Arsaxa*. She was the wife of 'Ânimu; note in this inscr. the predominance of the woman (80 1 *n*.).

L. 2. תימו = تَيْم, CIS ii 203 1 &c. על 82 2 *n*. רומא 89 10. כלבא An Aram. name = ܟܠܒܐ, cf. Phoen. כלבא CIS i 52 1; see 92 2 *n*.

L. 3. אחיה i. e. אַחֻיַהּ; the suff. refers to ארסכסה. צריחא 94 1 = ضَرِيح lit. *excavation*, so *underground chamber*, in poetry *a grave*; the vb. = 'to dig a grave.' Cf. in Hebr. צריח Jud. 9 46. 49 (see Moore in loc.). 1 S. 13 6, and the use of מערה in Gen. 23 9. 20. For the arrangement of an ancient Arab tomb see Wellhausen *Reste* 179.

L. 4. תלתין תרין Cf. רבע שלשת *three-quarters* 42 11.

L. 5. נחיא Sing. נחא CIS ii 211 1 ff., plur. נחין 94 1 = *loculus* or *niche* for a corpse. In Palm. the form is גמחא 145 3. גמחין 144 7, which suggests the Assyr. *kimaḫḫu* 'grave,' 'coffin' (Winckler *AF* ii 61, Del. *Assyr. HWB* 587); hence the word is prob. of foreign origin. For the quiescence of the מ cf. אַרְגְּוָן and the Aram. אַרְגְּוָן, ܐܪܓܘܢܐ. מדנחא i. e. מַדְנְחָא, ܡܕܢܚܐ, from דנח *to rise*, of the sun; in Heb. מזרח. For the interchange of נ and ר cf. סָגָן and ܣܓܢܐ, נבוכדנאצר and נבוכדראצר &c.; Wright *Comp. Gr.* 67. The Arab. ذَرِيح (Wellh. *Reste* 65), prob. the god of the rising sun, comes from this root.

L. 6. מרח An error for מדנח; other errors are בית for בירת l. 8, בר for (?) בר עבדעבדת l. 9.

92. El-Ḥejra. CIS ii 218; Eut. 21. A.D. 39. In situ.

1 דנה מסגדא די עבד
2 שכוחו בר תורא לאערא
3 די בבצרא אלה רבאל בירח
4 ניסן שנת חדה למלכו מלכא

This is the cippus which [2] Shakuḥu, son of Thôra, made to A'ra [3] who is at Boṣra, the god of Rabel. In the month [4] Nisan, the first year of Mâliku the king.

L. 1. דנה מסגדא So usually, but CIS ii 176 'רא מ. The √ سجد = *to prostrate oneself*; as used in Nab., מסגדא means, not 'the place where one prostrates' (مَسْجِد *mosque*), but 'an object before which one prostrates'; the verbs used with it are די עבד (frequently), די קרב 101, די הקים 97 i, די בנה ועבד CIS ii 188 (corr. by Dussaud et Macler *Voy. Arch.* no. 30). The *mesgida* was, in fact, a votive stele or column, in this case carved in relief under a canopy upon the face of the rock, but sometimes standing by itself in the sacred enclosure; thus 97 is a hexagonal column ornamented with busts, fillets, &c., CIS ii 185 is a square pillar with a moulding and plinth, 190 a pillar 6 ft. high. In the case of 188 the *mesgida* is a squared stone now serving as the abacus of a pillar in the narthex of an ancient church, and still the object of local veneration; see Dussaud et Macler l. c. 161 f. The *mesgida* was more than a memorial stone, it was dedicated to a deity, as here to A'ra, 101 to Dûshara and A'ra, CIS ii 190 to Dûshara. Perhaps it was regarded as a kind of votive altar, not, however, intended for sacrifice; 97 is shaped very much like a Gk. altar, 188 may have been originally an altar table or base. At any rate the monument was supposed to represent the person who erected it, and to plead for him before the deity. See Lagrange *Rel. Sém.* 206 f.

L. 2. שכוחו Prob. Aram., from שכח *to find*. The form פעולו is rare in Nab. names. תורא Also Aram., תּוֹרָא = *ox* (Hebr. שׁוֹר); for the animal name cf. כלבא 91 2. The dedication perhaps implies that the donor came from Bostra. אערא Again in 101, and with the description די בבצרא; the god is not otherwise known. Dussaud and Macler, *Voy. Arch.* 169 f., take אערא as the Aram. form of אֵצֶר, one of the sons of Se'ir, Gen. 36 21 &c. This would correspond to the Arab. اذر, which, however, is not the name of a tribe. Lidzb., *Eph.* i 330, suggests that the root is غفر, which in Aram. would become עער, and, to avoid the double guttural, אער, אערא; cf. ضعف = ܐܥܦܐ *double*, Driver *Tenses* 223. In this case אערא will correspond to the Roman Abundantia, Ops; غَفْرَاء *wealth, plenty*. Possibly the name ארעא gives the clue to the mysterious 'Οροτάλ mentioned by Herodotus as the consort of 'Αλιλάτ (see p. 222 *n.* 2); Cl.-Gan. *Rec.* ii 374. 'Οροτάλ may = ארעא אלהא; but the τ is not easy to account for, and Cl.-Gan. has since offered a better explanation[1].

L. 3. די בבצרא 101 7 f.; cf. די בצלחד . . לאלת 99. The idiom די ב׳ indicates the transference of the worship from Bostra, in the N. of the Nab. kingdom, to El-Ḥejra. For the idiom see **24** 2 *n.* אלה רבאל *the god of Rabel*; contrast עבדת אלהא *the god 'Obedath* **95** 1. For a god as patron of an individual cf. אלת חמיש **95** 2. לאלה קציו 100 2. אלה שעידו CIS ii 176 4. דושרא אלה מראנא **88** 6. 101 6 f. (ε)ἰς θεὸν ['Α]μέρου Duss. et Macl. 205. רבאל may be either the king of that name (see **97** iii *n.*), or a private person, for the name is not uncommon. If Rabel here is king R., then מלכו מלכא l. 4 must have come after him, and reigned between A. D. 96—the latest year of Rabel (ii) known from inscrr.—and A. D. 106, when the Nab. kingdom was absorbed into the Roman province of Arabia; so Duss. et Macl. 171 f., who regard this מלכו as Mâliku iii (iv). But there is nothing in this inscr. to prove that Rabel was more than a private individual; and if he were a king, he may have been an earlier R. (see on **97** iii) and not necessarily Rabel (ii), for the expression 'A'ra the god of R.' may imply that a devotion to this deity was by ancestral custom especially connected with the name and family of R. (Cl.-Gan. *Rec.* iv 178 f.; Schürer[3] i 742).

L. 4. מלכו i. e. Mâliku ii, son of Aretas iv Philopatris, **99** 3, the last Nab. king but one, A. D. 48–71 circ. He is mentioned by Jos. as contributing troops to the army of Vespasian in A. D. 67 for the Jewish war (*War* iii 4 2). It was during his reign that Damascus passed into the hands of the Romans, prob. under Nero, see p. 215 *n.* 1. The name מלכו = مَالِكُو was pronounced Mâliku, as appears from the form Μαλίχας[2]; in Jos. Μάλιχος or Μάλχος; cf. Μάλχος Jn. 18 10. There is not sufficient reason for supposing that מלכו was a successor of Rabel, usually considered the last Nab. king; see note above.

[1] 'Οροτάλ (= Διόνυσος ap. Herod.) is the actual name of the god otherwise called by the title Dûshara (p. 218); see *Rec.* v § 24.

[2] *Periplus maris Erythraei* (written circ. A. D. 70) Λευκὴ κώμη, δι᾽ ἧς ὁδός ἐστιν εἰς Πέτραν πρὸς Μαλίχαν, βασιλέα Ναβαταίων, Müll. *Geogr. Gr. Min.* i 272.

93. El-Ḥejra. CIS ii 221; Eut. 24. A. D. 49. In situ.

1 דנה כפרא די עבד עידו הפרכא בר עבידו
2 לה ולילדה ולאחרה ודי יתקברון בכפרא
3 דנה אפתיו אם עידו דנה ברת חביבו
4 ונאתת אנתתה ברת שלי ומן די ינפק
5 בידה שטר מן יד עידו דנה וכפרא דנה
6 עביד בירח אדר שנת עשר וחדה למלכו
7 מלכא מלך נבטו עבדעבדת בר והבאלהי
8 והנאו בר עבידת ואפצא בר חותו פסליא עבדו

This is the tomb which 'Aidu the eparch, son of 'Ubaidu, made [2] for himself and for his children and for his posterity; and that there may be buried in this tomb [3] Aftiyu, mother of the said 'Aidu, daughter of Ḥabîbu, [4] and Na'ithath his wife, daughter of Shullai, and whoever shall produce [5] in his hand a deed from the hand of the said 'Aidu. And this tomb [6] was made in the eleventh year of king Mâliku, [7] king of the Nabataeans. 'Abd-'obedath, son of Wahb-allâhi, [8] and Hâni'u, son of 'Obaidath, and Afṣa, son of Ḥuthu, the masons, did the work.

L. 1. עידו 79 1 *n.* הפרכא 87 2 *n.* עבידו 140 B 1 = عُبَيْد, Ὄβαιδος Wadd. 1977.

L. 3. אפתיו 81 3 *n.* חביבו = حَبِيب, Syr. ܚܒܝܒ, Gr. Ἄβιβος, Ἄβειβος Wadd. 2099 &c.

L. 4. נאתת in Arab. probably would be نَائِتَة from نات *pacillare* (Nöld.). שלי 88 1 *n.*

L. 5. שטר 84 3 *n.*

L. 6. מלכו See 92 4 *n.*

L. 7. והבאלהי 80 11 *n.*

L. 8. הנאו 97 i = هَانِئ, prob. Ἄνεος, Ἀναῖος Wadd. 2185. 2021 &c. אפצא 87 8 *n.* . חותו Perhaps = حَوَّات, or حُوت = Αὖθος Wadd. 1986 &c.

94. Petra 1. CIS ii 350. Circ. 1st cent. A.D. In situ.

1 קברא דנה וצריחא רבא די בה וצריחא זעירא די גוא מנה די בה
בתי מקברין עבידת גוחין
2 וכרכא די קדמיהם וערכותא ובתיא די בה וגניא וגנת סמכא ובארות
מיא וצהותא וטוריא
3 ושארית כל אצלא די באתריא אלה חרם וחרג דושרא אלה מראנא
ומותבה חרישא ואלהיא כלהם
4 בשטרי חרמין כדי בהם פפקדון דושרא ומותבה ואלהיא כלהם די
כדי בשטרי חרמיא אנו יתעבד ולא יתשנא
5 ולא יתפצץ מן כל די בהם מנדעם ולא יתקבר בקברא דנה אנוש
כלה להן מן די כתיב לה תנא מקבר בשטרי חרמיא אנו עד עלם

This sepulchre, and the large vault within it, and the small vault inside, within which are burying-places fashioned into niches, [2] and the wall in front of them, and the rows (?) and the houses within it, and the gardens and the garden of the ? , and the wells of water, and the ridge (?), and the hills (?), [3] and the rest of all the entire property which is in these places, is the consecrated and inviolable possession of Dûshara, the god of our lord, and his sacred throne (?), and all the gods, [4] (as specified) in deeds relating to consecrated things according to their contents. And it is the order of Dûshara and his throne (?) and all the gods that, according to what is in the said deeds relating to consecrated things, it shall be done and not altered. [5] Nor shall anything of all that is in them be withdrawn; nor shall any man be buried in this sepulchre save him who has in writing a contract to bury, (specified) in the said deeds relating to consecrated things — for ever.

The façade of the tomb, carved with Gk. columns, Egypt. cornice, and Assyr. battlements, like some of the tombs at El-Ḥejra, exhibits the style of Nab. monuments belonging to the 1st cent. A.D.; see

Vogüé *JA* viii (1896) 486. A ground-plan of the two chambers and the atrium in front of them is given ib. xi (1898) 140 f. A good description of Petra and the re-discovery of the inscr. is given by Lagrange, *RB* vi (1897) 208 ff.

L. 1. צריחא **91** 3 *n.*; cf. the use of מערתא in Palm., **144** 3 and Vog. **67** 2 קברא ומערתא די בנה. נוא מנה Cf. נו מן **147** ii c 47; here נוא has final א as in Dan. **3** 6 &c. (Arab. جاء *intrare*), elsewhere in Nab., נו. בתי מקברין Cf. בת מקברתא Palm. Vog. **64** 1. מקברין is a noun (מְקְבַר or מַקְ׳); the sing. מקברתא occurs in **96** 1 &c. Note the double plur. of a compound term; cf. שטרי חרמין l. 4. עבידת נוחין Lit. *a work of niches*, describing בתי מקברין; for נוחין *loculi* see **91** 5 *n.* Two *loculi* exist in the tomb; prob. it was intended to make more if required.

L. 2. כרכא *the wall* surrounding the atrium in front of the tombs; √כרך = *surround*, cf. ܟܪܟܐ *fenced city*. ערכותא Plur. of ערכתא, prob. *rows* of pillars or arcades; cf. Hebr. מערכה *a row* Ex. **39** 37. Vogüé explains by ערכת **3** 6, but ערפת is prob. to be read there. גניא *Gardens* near a tomb were common in antiquity, e. g. John **19** 41 and the Roman *cepotaphia* i. e. a grave with fields and gardens round it; Marquardt *Das Privatleben der Römer*[2] 369, quoted by Barth *Hebraica* xiii (1897) 275[1]. גנת סמכא Possibly *a garden of reclining* (גִּנַּת סְמָכָא), i. e. a garden for funeral feasts. As Nöld. remarks, it is better to give גנת the same meaning as גִּנַּיָּא, rather than derive it from וְנָא *to lie down* (*ZA* xii 3 f.), though it is tempting to compare ܣܡܟ ܒܡܣܡܟܐ *convivio accumbe* &c., Payne Smith *Thes. Syr.* coll. 2662 and 744. צהותא The meaning of this and the foll. word is very uncertain. The Arab. صَهْوَةٌ = (1) *a cave from which water wells forth*, so here perhaps *water-tank* (Barth), cf. صُهْوَةٌ *fish-pond*; or (2) *the ridge of a mountain, a tower on a hill-top*; cf. the place-names Ṣahwet el-Ḫidr, Ṣahwet el-Belâṭ in Ḥauran (Baed. *Paläst.*[5] 205 f.). Either meaning may be right here; but since in **95** 2 צהות is more suitably rendered by (2), the latter rendering may be adopted in both places: it is unlikely that the same word would have different meanings in the two inscrr. Cl.-Gan. renders *roof* in **95** 2, and here *terrace*, i. e. the upper part of the tomb. Nöld.'s *dry places*, from ܨܗܐ *be thirsty*, is not probable. טוריא *Rocks* or *rocky heights*; or possibly low *walls surrounding* the wells and tank, cf. تَوْرٌ *circle*, or تَارَ *go round*, דור, תור.

[1] Strabo mentions the gardens and wells for irrigating them at Petra, πηγὰς ἀφθόνους . . . εἴς τε ὑδρείαν καὶ κηπείαν p. 663 ed. Müll. Cl.-Gan. *Rec.* ii 93. 129.

L. 3. אצלא Prob. = أَصْل *landed property*, lit. *root*, *lineage*; أَصِيلَة *a man's whole property*. The precise meaning of most of the foregoing terms is not clear, nor is the disposition of the various appendages of the tomb. Vogüé (*JA* xi 143 f.) includes them all within the atrium in front. Some of them may be placed there, 'the portico with its buildings' (ערכותא ובתיא), the wells and tank (?)—a conduit has been discovered in one corner of the atrium; but it may be doubted whether the space (77 by 66 ft.) is sufficient for *the houses*, *the gardens*, *the hills* &c., the most obvious meaning of בתיא, גניא, טוריא. These may have been outside the precincts; די באתריא אלה 'which are in these places' suggests, not the enclosed space, but localities outside of it. Perhaps the general plan resembled that of the Roman garden-tombs (supr.), with their *area* in front of the sepulchre, their *aediculae*, pavilions, wells, *taberna* &c. (Barth l. c.). Winckler suggests the arrangement of a Moslem mosque-tomb, and, disregarding the natural meanings of the words, takes גניא, גנת ס' to mean a covered cloister and shrine; *AF* ii 60 ff.   אלה 87 3 *n*.   חרם 79 8 *n*.   חרג = Arab. حَرَج *that which is forbidden*, *unlawful*. The two nouns are so closely connected that they govern a common genit. (Nöld.).   אלה מראנא 88 6 &c., 'our lord,' either Aretas iv (78 4 *n*.) or one of his immediate predecessors, Obodas ii, Malchus i.   ומותבה 80 4 *n*. The form with ה, and the absence of ו from the foll. חרישא, are against taking מותבה as the name of a deity. Nöld. favours the explanation that מותבה (وثب) = *his council*, seated round the god; cf. مَجْلِسَة *council*. Cl.-Gan.'s rendering *she who is seated*, i. e. his Πάρεδρος (*Rec*. ii 131), and Winckler's, *his spouse* (Ethiop. *wasaba* iv = 'to marry'), are etymologically improbable.   חרישא Ptcp. pass. emph. st. agreeing with מותבה, prob. = حرس *guard*, *watch*, so *protected*, *holy*.

L. 4. שטרי Plur. constr., 84 3 *n*. These documents were no doubt preserved in the temple archives.   פקדון Nom. = ܦܘܩܕܢܐ, as דכרן Palm. Vog. 74 = ܕܘܟܪܢܐ; Hebr. פִּקָּדוֹן, זִכָּרוֹן.   אנו Plur. of הא, apoc. from אִנּוּן; BAram. הִנּוּן, הִמּוֹן, הִמּוֹ; Talm. אִינְהוּ (pl. of אִיהוּ). Elsewhere in Nab. הם CIS ii 210 6; in Aram. המו 76 B 4.   יתשנא Cf. Ezr. 6 11. Dan. 6 9. 18. In this dialect the ת stands before the sibilant, e. g. יתזבן 88 4 *n*.

L. 5. יתפצין Ethpa. impf. of פצין = فصّ *extract*, *disjoin*, in iv *to separate* a part and give it away.   מנדעם 75 2 *n*.   אנוש כלה 89 5 *n*.   לחן 79 8 *n*.   תנא CIS ii 69 perhaps = Targ. תְּנָאָה, Syr. ܬܢܝܐ *agreement*, *contract*; in Nab. תְּנָא may have been written for דַּנֵּי. Winckler explains by the Assyr. *dannitu* 'a piece of writing.' מקבר Inf. constr. 89 7 (Lidzb.); or a noun l. 1.

95. Petra 2. El-Mer. CIS ii 354. A. D. 20. In situ.

1 דנה צלמא די עבדת אלהא די עבדו בני חנינו בר חטישו בר
פטמון .....
2 תלוך בר ותרא אלה חטישו די בצהות פטמון עמהם על חיי חרתת
מלך נבטו רחם ע[מה ושקילת]
3 אחתה מלכת נבטו ומלכו ועבדת ורבאל ופצאל ושעודת וחגרו
בנוהי וחרתת בר חג[רו בן בנה]
4 ..... בשנ]ת 3||| ||| ||| לחרתת מלך נבטו רחם עמה עלה שלם

This is the statue of the divine 'Obedath, which the sons of Ḥunainu, son of Ḥoṭaishu, son of Paṭmon, made . . . . . [2] Teluk, son of Withra, the god of Ḥoṭaishu, who is on the ridge (?) of Paṭmon, their ancestor (?); for the life of Ḥarethath, king of the Nabataeans, lover of his pe[ople, and Shuqailath] [3] his sister, queen of the Nabataeans, and Mâliku and 'Obedath and Rabel and Peṣael and Sha'ûdath and Ḥigru his children, and Ḥarethath, son of Ḥig[ru his grandson] [4] . . . . . in the 29th year of Ḥarethath, king of the Nabataeans. Peace be upon him!

The inscr. was found at Petra in an artificial grotto, now called El-Mer, once used as a sanctuary. De Vogüé *JA* xi (1898) 129 ff.; Cl.-Gan. *Rec.* ii § 73.

L. 1. עבדת אלהא The statue was that of 'Obedath, one of the Nab. kings. It was a custom among the Nabs. to deify kings after their death: e. g. Uranius, quoted by Steph. Byz., *Ὄβοδα, χωρίον Ναβαταίων, Οὐράνιος Ἀραβικῶν τετάρτῳ, ὅπου Ὀβόδης ὁ βασιλεύς, ὃν θεοποιοῦσι, τέθαπται* *Fr. Hist. Gr.* iv 525 (cf. Tertullian *Ad nat.* ii 8 . . . Obodan et Dusarem Arabum); and among the Palmyrenes, 121 3 אלהא אלכסנדרוס קסר. 122 3 אלהא [הדרי[נוס; cf. 10 7 *n.*, 80 11 *n.* The king here was a predecessor of Aretas iv (l. 4), i. e. prob. Obedas ii,

28 to 9 B.C. He is mentioned by Strabo (663 f. ed. Müll.) in connexion with the campaign of Aelius Gallus against S. Arabia, 25–4 B.C., and by Josephus in the later period of Herod's reign, when Syllaeus his ἐπίτροπος was a suitor for Salome (*Ant.* xvi 7 6. *War* i 24 6), and at the time of Herod's expedition against Trachonitis (*Ant.* xvi 9 1. 4). חניתו 92 2. חמישו = Ὀταισος, Ὀτασος Wadd. 1984. 2226; cf. חֻשִׁים 1 Chr. 3 22. Neh. 3 10 &c. פטמון Perhaps from פטם *be fat*, or فطم wean, cf. فَاطِمَة; for the ending cf. זכרון, מקרון. An Egypt. derivation, Pet-ammon (69 9 *n.*), is not so likely. At the end of the l. either another set of donors was mentioned, or there was a verb, still governed by בני חניתו, describing the association of the new cult of 'Obedath with that of the family god of Ḥoṭaishu (Cl.-Gan.).

L. 3. ותרא Cf. O.T. יִתְרוֹ (Midianite), יֶתֶר, יִתְרָא, and the Minaean ותראל Glaser 299 3 (Hommel *Süd-ar. Chrest.* 116), Οὔιθρος Wadd. 2537 *h*[1]. Yaquṭ mentions a village in Ḥauran, وَتْر N. of Bostra, in Nab. country. אלה חמישו See 92 3 *n.* In these cases the god is not named as a rule; here it was prob. Dûshara, אלה מראנא 88 6. בצהות The Arab. صهوة means both *fountain* and *crest of a hill, tower upon a hill.* In 94 2 צהותא may have the former sense; the latter would be suitable here. Cl.-Gan., however, explains צ' as the *roof* of the house, where the statue or altar of the family god was set; cf. Strabo (p. 667) ἥλιον τιμῶσιν ἐπὶ τοῦ δώματος ἱδρυσάμενοι βωμόν (of the Nabataeans), 2 K. 17 12. עמים The context implies *kinsman, ancestor.* פטמון was great-grandfather to the בני חניתו; hence both here and in 99 2 Cl.-Gan. gives עם the specific sense of *great-grandfather.* But though this was the relationship in both cases, it is hardly expressed by the word עם, which at most implies *kinsman*; cf. Arab. عَمّ *paternal uncle*, and the O.T. names אליעם, עמינדב &c., Gray *Hebr. Pr. N.* 51 ff. In רחם עמה the meaning is certainly *people*, not *ancestors*; Schürer *Gesch.*[3] i 738. על חיי

[1] The name occurs in the foll. inscr. on an altar (disc. 1895) from Kanatha (Josephus), now el-Qanawât, NE. of Bostra, in Jebel Ḥauran:

נדר וצעד אל בני ותרו רחמי גרא שלם
קציו בר חנאל אמנא שלם

'Vowed and sacrificed (?) by the family of the Benê Withro, lovers of Gad. Greeting! Qaṣiu, son of Ḥann-el, the master-workman. Greeting!' צעד is explained by Cl.-Gan. as Pael of صعد = *to mount*, أَصْعَدَ = O.T. שלח in Saadya's version; *Rec.* iii § 10. The vb. صعد is not actually used in the sense *to sacrifice*, nor is נדר found in Aram. inscrr. with the meaning *to vow*. Hence Lidzb. prefers to read נדר וצעדאל as pr. nn. (*Ephem.* i 74), though the names do not occur elsewhere. אל = Arab. آل CIS ii 164 f. גרא = Τύχη, whose cult was popular in Ḥauran. See also *Rep.* no. 53.

חרתת Cf. **102** 3 and לחיי נפשה **70** 4; see **29** 11 *n*. חיים here practically = *σωτηρία*. שקילת So restored by Vog. Shuqailath must have been the second wife of Aretas iv, and, as we learn from this inscr., his sister too. Her name appears on copper coins at the closing period of Aretas' reign. His first wife was Ḥuldu (**102** 4), associated with him for at least 20 years. Probably the second marriage took place not long before this 29th year of the king's reign. There was another queen Shuqailath[1], perhaps the daughter of this one, sister-consort of Malchus ii (**92** 4) and mother of Rabel (**97** iii *n*.).

L. 3. The six children are prob. those of the first marriage. The first three are all dynastic names. מצאל Cf. the Palm. מציאל Euting *Epigr. Misc.* 131, either mas. or fem., cf. Φασηέλης, Οὐλπία Φασαιέλη Wadd. 1928. 2445. שעודת Prob. fem., as names of this form usually are, e.g. מנועת **89** 4. כמולת CIS ii **225**; for the name cf. שעידו **89** 1 *n*. If these were princesses, one of them may well have been the unnamed wife of Herod Antipas (p. 215). בנוהי Not necessarily *sons*, but *children*, cf. Palm. קברא דנה בנא אלהבל . . להון ולבניהון Vog. **37**, and prob. בנידם **102** 4. At the end of the line Cl.-Gan. restores [חנ]רו דנה.

[1] Mentioned in an inscr. lately found at Petra, De Vogüé *JA* viii (1896) 496 f.: שנישו אח שקילת מלכת נבטו בר . . . Cl.-Gan. has acutely discerned that אח = not *brother*, but *grand-visier*; cf. Strabo p. 663 ed. Müll. *ἔχει δ' ὁ βασιλεὺς ἐπίτροπον τῶν ἑταίρων τινά, καλούμενον ἀδελφόν* (*Rec.* ii 380).

MOAB

96. Medeba. CIS ii 196. A. D. 37. Vatican Museum.

1 דא מקברתא ותרתי נפשתא די
2 עלא מנה די עבד עבדעבדת אסרתגא
3 לאיתיבל אסרתגא אבוהי ולאיתיבל
4 רב משריתא די בלחיתו ועברתא בר עבדעבדת
5 אסרתגא דנה בבית שלטונהם די שלטו
6 זמנין תרין שנין תלתין ושת על שני חרתת
7 מלך נבטו רחם עמה ועבידתא די
8 עלא עבידת בשנת ארבעין ושת לה

This is the sepulchre, and the two monuments [2] above it, which 'Abd-'obedath the *stratēgos* made [3] to Aithi-bel the *stratēgos* his father, and to Aithi-bel [4] chief of the camp at Luḥîthu and 'Abarta, son of the said 'Abd-'obedath [5] the *stratēgos*, in the seat of their jurisdiction which they exercised [6] twice, for a period of thirty-six years, in the time of Ḥarethath, [7] king of the Nabataeans, lover of his people; and the above work [8] was executed in the forty and sixth year of his (reign).

It is a peculiarity of this inscr. that the words are separated.

L. 1. מקברתא See **94** 1 *n*. תרתי נפשתא **78** 1 *n*.

L. 2. עלא מנה i.e. עֵלָּא מִנֵּהּ, cf. Dan. 6 3 and Palm. ד לעל מנה Eut. *Epigr. Misc.* **5** 3 f. אסרתגא Cf. CIS ii **195**, where a *nefesh* is erected (עבד) by יעמרו אסרתגא to his brother, the son of עבישו אסרתגא (A. D. 39). The inscr. **195** comes from Umm-er-Reṣaṣ, 16 miles SE. of Medeba. These two inscrr., which are almost contemporary, indicate that the Nab. *stratēgos* was the governor of a small district, and that the office was to some extent hereditary [1]; cf. **97** ii *n*. It is not impossible that both these *stratēgoi*, 'Abd-'obedath and Ya'amru, may have assisted the wife of Herod Antipas in her

[1] Strabo says of the Nabs. κατὰ πρεσβυγένειαν καὶ βασιλεύουσιν οἱ ἐκ τοῦ γένους καὶ ἄλλας ἀρχὰς ἄρχουσι p. 666 ed. Müll.

flight to her father Aretas iv at Petra; she was passed on, says Josephus, from one *stratēgos* to another, *κομιδῇ τῶν στρατηγῶν ἐκ διαδοχῆς Ant.* xviii 5 1. The castle of Macherus would prob. have been in the district of Ya'amru; the boundary between the two governors was perhaps the W. Zerqa Ma'in. Cl.-Gan. *Rec.* ii 202.

L. 3. איתיבל i.e. אִיתִיבֵל *Bel has brought* (i.e. the new-born), Afel of אתא, cf. the Syr. pr. n. ܐܝܬܝܐܠܗܐ, Nöld. *ZA* (1891) 149 *n.*; or, אִיתַיבֵל *Bel exists*, cf. אִיתַי אֱלָהּ Dan. 2 28 and אִיתִיאֵל Neh. 11 7. אִיתַי 1 Chr. 11 31. *Bel* is the Babylonian deity (p. 269), and not another form of the Canaanite *Ba'al*. The only other Nab. name in which בל has been found is בנתבל **102** 5, and that is uncertain; in Palm. בל and בול are frequent in pr. nn. The second איתיבל was grandson of the first; it was a custom to repeat family names at this interval in the genealogy.

L. 4. משריתא **140** B 3. **122** 5, Syr. ܡܫܪܝܬܐ *camp, army*; in Targ. שרא=*encamp*. לחיתו must have been within the jurisdiction of the *stratēgos*, and therefore near Medeba. The name suggests מַעֲלֵה הַלֻּחִית Is. 15 5. Jer. 48 5; but according to the *Onomasticon* (136 23 ed. Lag.) this was between Areopolis (Rabbath-Moab, Rabba) and Zoar = Ṣarfa, to the N. of Wadi Kerak (Buhl *Geogr.* 272), and therefore too far south[1]. עברתא Site unknown; evidently a fort commanding a *pass* in the highlands near Medeba or the *ford* of a river. The name recalls the O. T. הר העברים=the Nebo range, Num. 27 12. In Roman times there were several camps in the neighbourhood; e. g. cohors tertia . . in ripa vadi Apharis fluvii in castris Arnonensibus, *Notitia dignitatum* xxx.

L. 6. וזמנין תרין Cf. וְזִמְנִין תְּלָתָה Dan. 6 11. תרתין זבני CIS ii 186 3. Palm. זבנן סגיאן **121** 5.

L. 7. עבידתא Noun formed from Pe. ptcp. pass., cf. **94** 1. Ezr. 4 24 &c. עבידת בית אלהא; see Marti *Gr. Bibl. Aram.* 86.

[1] If מ׳ הלוחית = Tal'at Helsa, on W. slope of Mt. Nebo, some 5 or 6 m. NW. of Medeba, this would answer to the conditions; but the grounds on which Conder (*PEF Mem., East. Pal.* i 228. 253), followed by G. A. Smith (*Map of Pal.*), bases the identification, are extremely questionable; see Driver *Exp. Times* (1902) 460.

DAMASCUS

97. Ḍumêr. CIS ii 161. A.D. 94. Louvre.

Col. ii	Col. i
בגרת אם אדרמו אסרתגא	[דנה מ]סגדא די הקים
ונקידו מן על טעמא	[ה]נאו בר חרי גדלו ברת
בני עבדמלכו	

Col. iii

אסרתגא בירח איר
שנת X 9 ʒ במנין ארהומיא
די הו שנת X 3 לרבאל
מלכא

C	B	A	F
נקידו ברה	אדרמו ברה	הנאו	...לענו אתתה

Col. i [This is the c]ippus which Hâni'u set up, the freedman of Gadlu, daughter [ii] of Bagarath, mother of Adramu the *stratēgos* and Neqîdu, by adoption sons of 'Abd-mâliku [iii] the *stratēgos*, in the month Iyar, in the year 405, by the reckoning of the Romans, which is the 24th year of king Rabel.

The place now called Ḍumêr (ضمير) was the first station on the Roman road from Damascus to Palmyra. The inscr. is written on the sides of a hexagonal column, a little over 3 ft. high, resembling a Greek altar. Round the upper part is a series of busts, each with a name below it (A B C F); two busts (D E) are missing.

Col. i. מסגדא See 92 1 *n.* הנאו 93 8 *n.* בר חרי Lit. *filius libertatis*, so *libertus*; in Hebr. cf. בן חורים Qoh. 10 17; in Palm. 147 ii b 12 קלקיס בר חרי קיסר, and the inscr. found at South

Shields (Lidzb. 482) רגינא בת חרי ברעתא חבל[1]. In Syr. ܚܪܪ Pa. = *set free*, and similarly the Pi. of חרר in NHebr., whence חר *freeman*.

Col. ii. בגרת See 85 1 *n*. אדרמו=أَدْرَم *toothless*. נקידו Cf. נְקוֹדָא Ezr. 2 48=Neh. 7 50 &c. מן על Lit. *on the ground of, by reason of*; cf. על in 147 i 6 על צבותא אלן. טעמא To be explained by the Syr. ܛܥܡܐ *a graff*, ܐܛܥܡ *he graffed*; hence used of adoption (Cl.-Gan. *Rec*. i 61). בני עבדמלכו It is clear that Hâni'u was both the freedman and husband of Gadlu[2]. Their sons were adopted by 'Abd-mâliku, prob. a kinsman of Gadlu, in order to secure a social position which their father could not give them. It would seem that 'Abd-mâliku transmitted his own office to the elder of the two sons, cf. 96 2 *n*. For עבדמלכו see 80 11 *n*.

Col. iii. איר 85 10 *n*. The sign of the numeral 4 is unusual. The date is given by the Seleucid era, which began in 312 B. C.; see 9 5 *n*. במנין ארהומיא i.e. בְּמִנְיַן אַרְהוֹמָיֵא, for the orthography cf. Clement's ܐܪܗܘܡܝܐ *Thes. Syr*. s. v.; מנין lit.=*counting*. The reference, as Cl.-Gan. l. c. 71 f. has shown, is to the Seleucid era reckoned, not by the old style or Macedonian calendar, which was on the lunar system, but by the Roman or Julian calendar (solar), which had been introduced recently into Syria. רבאל Rabel, the last Nab. king (92 3 *n*.), known only from inscrr. (e.g. 95 2 *n*. 101 9) and coins[3].

[1] The Lat. part of this inscr. runs: D[is] m[anibus]. Regina liberta et conjuge Barates Palmyrenus natione Catuallauna an[nis] xxx. The stone, now in the Free Library, S. Shields, was found in the neighbouring Roman camp.

[2] The relation was not unknown: Cl.-Gan. quotes Orelli 3024 Ti. Claudius Hermes . . Claudiam M. Titi filiam . . patronam optimam, item conjugem felicissimam—id. 3029 D. M. Lucretiae Eutychidi, Lucretius Adrastus conjugi et patronae dulcissimae. Cf. preceding note.

[3] The name occurs in an inscr. lately found (1897) at Petra; see Cl.-Gan. *Rec*. ii § 58, *Album* Pl. XLV; Schürer *Gesch*.[3] i 732. 742 f.

[דנה צ]למא די רבאל מלך נבטו
. . . . . . ת מלך נבטו די הקים לה
. . . . . . נר ? ים ? ? י רבא חרתה
. . . . . . בירח כסלו די [הו] שטרא
. . . [שנת] xvi לחרתת מלכא [מלך נבטו]

This statue must have belonged to another king Rabel, for his father's name ended in ת, and he was succeeded by a king Ḥarethath, who reigned at least for 16 years; Rabel, the last Nab. king, is therefore out of the question. On the strength of a passage in Steph. Byz. which says that Antigonus the Macedonian was slain by Rabilus the king of the Arabians, Cl.-Gan. dates this inscr. 70–69 B. C., correcting Antigonus to Antiochus (i. e. A. xii). Josephus, however, clearly implies that the Arabian king who defeated and slew Antiochus at Cana was Aretas (*Ant*. xiii 15

This inscr. tells us that his reign began in A. D. 71; the latest inscr. is dated in his 26th year, i.e. A. D. 96 (p. 255 *n.* 1); the Nab. kingdom came to an end in A. D. 106. Rabel, as this inscr. from the NE. of Damascus shows, must have ruled over an extensive territory.

The series of busts and inscrr. is not complete. It began with Hâni'u in the centre, and followed from the left with Adramu, the eldest son, and then with Neqîdu. Whose wife was represented by F, to the right of A, is not certain; the Corp. restores עבדמלכו for E; the remaining name at D was prob. נדלו.

1. 2)—i. e. Aretas iii. There is evidently some confusion in the statement of Steph. Byz. (*Fr. Hist. Gr.* iv 525). It is not at present clear where this king Rabel is to be placed.

ḤAURAN

98. **Ḥebran.** CIS ii 170. A. D. 47. Louvre.

1 בירח תשרי שנת שבע לקלדיס
2 קיסר
3 דנה תרעא די עבד מלכו בר
4 קצ[יו] כמר אלת שלם קרי

In the month of Tishri, the seventh year of Claudius Caesar: this is the gate which Mâliku, son of Qaṣ[îu], priest of Allath, made. Call a greeting!

L. 1. תשרי The 7th month, Sept.–Oct.; in **123** 5 = Ὑπερβερεταῖος. קלדיס Claudius, Jan. 41–Oct. 54 A. D. The inscr. dates from the interregnum (44–52) between Herod Agrippa i and ii, when Ḥauran and Trachonitis were governed directly by the Roman imperial power. For קלדיס the more correct form would be קלודיס, as אורליס in Palm.

L. 2. קיסר The form with י is derived from the Gk. Καῖσαρ, in Palm. usually קסר **121** 3 &c.

L. 4. קציו **99** 2 is everywhere the name of a person, not of a god, **100** 2 *n.* כמר See **64** 1 *n.* אלת **80** 4 *n.* קרי Imperat.; cf. the Arab. formula قرا عليه السلام.

99. **Ṣalḥad.** CIS ii 182. A. D. 65. In situ.

1 דנה ביתא די בנה רוחו בר מלכו בר אכלבו בר רוחו לאלת אלהתהם
2 די בצלחד ודי נצב רוחו בר קציו עם רוחו דנה די עלא
3 בירח אב שנת עשר ושבע למלכו מלך נבטו בר חרתת מלך נבטו רח[ם] עמה

This is the temple which Rûḥu, son of Mâliku, son of Aklabu, son of Rûḥu, built to Allath their goddess [2] who is in Ṣalḥad, and whom Rûḥu, son of Qaṣîu, ancestor (?) of the said above-named Rûḥu, had established. [3] In the month Ab, the seventeenth year of Mâliku, king of the Nabataeans, son of Ḥarethath, king of the Nabataeans, lover of his people.

L. 1. רוחו 140 B 2 = Arab. رَوِح *joyous*, Ῥουαῖος Wadd. 2034. אכלבו = Arab. أَكْلَبُ *rabidus*. אלת אלהתהם See 80 4 *n.* and cf. אלהתא CIS ii 336 3; the suff. as in שלטונהם 96 5.

L. 2. די בצלחד 92 3 *n.* This idiom implies that the worship of Allath at Ṣalḥad was introduced from some other place (24 2 *n.*); this appears to have been done by an ancestor of the Rûḥu who now builds a temple for the goddess. צלחד is the present صلخد, in Yaquṭ صرخد, situated on one of the southernmost heights of Jebel Ḥauran. It has been identified with the O.T. סלכה Deut. 3 10. Josh 12 5 &c., mentioned along with Edre'i as marking the S. frontier of Bashan. נצב The pf. to be rendered by plupf.: the introduction of the worship would take place before the building of the temple (Lidzb. 150 *n.*). קציו 98 4. 100 2. עם רוחו may be rendered *with R.*, i. e. the introduction of Allath was the joint enterprise of R. son of Qaṣîu and R. son of Mâliku. But in 95 2 עם = *kinsman, ancestor* (*great-grandfather*, Cl.-Gan. *Rec.* ii 373 f.), and this seems to be the meaning here. The worship of Allath had been established at Ṣalḥad for three generations, or about 100 years, before the date of the inscr., i. e. at a period which corresponds with the occupation of this region by the Nabataeans after the capture of Damascus by Aretas iii in B.C. 85 (see p. 216). It is possible, as Cl.-Ganneau points out, that the קציו of Bostra (100 2) was the קציו of this inscr., evidently an important person; if this was the case, the father introduced his family god (prob. אערא 92 2 *n.*) at Bostra, the son did the same for Allath at the neighbouring Ṣalḥad.

L. 3. אב The 5th month, July–Aug. מלכו 92 4 *n.* Between the death of Aretas iv in A.D. 40 and the reign of Malchus ii we must probably insert the reign of Abias, ὁ Ἀράβων βασιλεύς Joseph. *Ant.* xx 4 1. Hence the accession of Malchus ii cannot be placed earlier than about 48 A.D. (Schürer 739); his 17th year will then be A.D. 65.

100. **Bostra.** CIS ii 174. Circ. 40 B.C. Louvre.

1 די קרב נטראל בר
2 נטראל לאלה קציו
3 בשנת ∕׀ למלכו מלכא

Offered by Naṭar-el, son of Naṭar-el, to the god of Qaṣîu; in the 11th year of king Mâliku.

Bostra, in Gk. Βοστρά, now بُصْرَى, was the chief city of Ḥauran in the 1st cent. A.D. The Nabataeans made it a great centre for commerce with Palmyra, Babylonia, and the south. Cf. **125** 5.

L. 1. נטראל i. e. *El keeps*, Ναταρήλος Wadd. 2351; an Aram. name.

L. 2. אלה קציו See **92** 3 *n.*; the god was perhaps אערא, the patron of the family (**99** 2 *n.*).

L. 3. מלכו The inscr. is evidently an early one, judging from the rude and somewhat archaic style of the writing. Hence the king will be the earlier rather than the later Mâliku (**92** 4), i. e. Malchus i (Schürer 735, not ii), circ. 50–28 B.C., who appears again in **102**. His relations with Herod the Great are described by Josephus (*Ant.* xiv 14 1–2. *War* i 14 1–2). He refused Herod assistance at the time of the Parthian invasion B.C. 40, and was subsequently fined by Ventidius for the support which he gave to the invaders (Dio Cass. 48 41). Part of his territory was made over by Antony to Cleopatra; after a time the tribute was withheld, and by Antony's order Herod made an expedition into the territory of the Nabataeans, and in the end succeeded in inflicting a severe defeat upon Malchus, B.C. 32–31 (Joseph. *Ant.* xv 5. *War* i 19). The last that we hear of him is in connexion with a plot against Herod, which led to the death of the aged Hyrcanus (*Ant.* xv 6 2–3).

101. Imtân. A. D. 93. In situ.

דנה מסגדא
די קרב
מנעת בר
גדיו ל
דושרא ו
אערא אלה
מראנא די
בבצרא בשנת
𐢮 III לרבאל
מלכא מלך

11 נבטו די

12 אחיי וש

13 זב עמה

This is the cippus offered by Mun'ath, son of Gadiyu, to Dûshara and A'ra the god of our lord who is in Boṣra, in the 23rd year of king Rabel, king of the Nabataeans, who brought life and deliverance to his people.

Imtân lies SE. of Bostra. The inscr. was discovered by Dussaud and Macler; *Voy. Arch.* (1901) no. 36. See also *Rep.* nos. 83 and 86.

L. 1. מסגדא See 92 1 *n.*

L. 3. מנעת See 88 2 *n.*

L. 4. גדיו In Sin. Eut. 93. 95 &c.; in Palm. גדיא = Arab. جُدَىّ.

L. 6. אערא See 92 2 *n.* 3 *n.* אלה מראנא *the god of our lord* i. e. of the king, as in 88 6. 89 8.

L. 9. רבאל 97 iii *n.*

L. 12. For the title cf. CIS ii 183 . . . רבאל . . די אחיי עמה ו (25th year) and the inscr. below[1]. It may point to some historical act of deliverance, or perhaps rather (like the רחם עמה of Aretas iv) to a patriotic policy at a time when the independence of the Nab. kingdom was threatened by Rome; cf. the Hellenist title Σωτήρ. In the earlier inscrr. of the reign Rabel has no such title; it is omitted, however, in 97 iii (24th year) possibly for political reasons. אחיי Af. of חיי, cf. the pr. n. חייאל CIS ii 224 7. For שיזב see 69 9 *n.*

[1] Duss. et Macl. no. 62; *Rép.* no. 86:—

a דנ[ה] ארכותא די עבד עליו
בר גשם לשיע אלקום [אלה]
b א בשנת עשרי[ן ו]שת לרבאל מלכא מל
ך נבטו די אחיי ושזב עמה

D. et M. explain ארכותא as = Lat. *arca*, i. e. sarcophagus. Cl.-Gan. thinks of part of a building, *Rec.* iv 175; but it is prob. that أَرِيكَة *couch, bridal seat* = סיתובא 70 1 *n.*, Lidzb. *Eph.* i 332. At the end of the next l. Cl.-Gan. plausibly reads לשיע אלקום [אלה]א *to the god She'a-alqûm*; the reading is brilliantly confirmed by 140 B 4 *n.* The 26th year of Rabel was A. D. 96.

ITALY

102. Puteoli. CIS ii 158. A. D. 5. **Naples Museum.**

1 דא מחרמתא [די ח]דתו ,...... ת ועלי נחשא .....

2 .... ל.... ומרתי די מתקרא זבדת ......

3 .... צי צידו בר עבת מן דילה על חיי חרתת מלך נ[בטו ודי]

4 [ח]לדו אתתה מלכת נבטו ודי בניהם בירח אב שנת ⁄ I [III
למלכותה]

5 ... אתר זמן אבני מחרמתא קדמיתא די עבד בנהבל בר בם....

6 [בשנת III] III II למלכו מלך נבטו יהבו בגו מחרמתא דא

This is the sanctuary [which] .... restored, and 'Ali the copper-smith .....[2] ...... and Marthi, who is called Zubdath ....[3] .... Ṣaidu, son of 'Abath, at his own expense, for the life of Ḥarethath, king of the N[abataeans, and of] [4] Ḥuldu his wife, queen of the Nabataeans, and of their children, in the month Ab, the 14th (?) year [of his reign] [5] ... after the time when the former sanctuaries were built (?), which Ben-hobal, son of Bm ... made [6] [in the 8th (?) year] of Mâliku, king of the Nabataeans, they placed within this sanctuary.

L. 1. מחרמתא See **79** 8 *n.* חדתו **23** 2 *n.* עלי = Arab. عَلِيٌّ, Sin. עליו, 'Αλεῖος Wadd. 2520. נחשא *a worker in bronze*, Syr. ܢܚܫܐ, or possibly, *diviner*.

L. 2. מרתי Cf. Palm. **120** 1 = Μάρθειν (fem.). די מתקרא Ethpe. ptcp., cf. **128** 2. זבדת = Arab. زُبْدَة.

L. 3. צידו = Arab. صَاعِدٌ, cf. Palm. צידא **137** 2. עבת Perhaps from √ عبث *to play*. מן דילה i. e. ἐκ τῶν ἰδίων, cf. Palm. מן כיסה **116** 4. **122** 6. על חיי ח׳ **95** 2 *n.* The usual title רחם עמה is omitted.

L. 4. חלדו **95** 2 *n.*, cf. O.T. חֻלְדָּה 2 K. 22 14 (fem.) and חֹלֶד *weasel* Lev. 11 29; so in the Mishnah חולדא, Arab. خُلْدٌ. בניהם Prob. *children*, not merely *sons*; **95** 3 *n.* אב **99** 3 *n.* To fill up the space three units are required, and prob. למלכותה, Corp.

L. 5. זמן 84 3 constr. st. before a verbal clause. אבני Prob. pf. 3 plur. fem.; but the form is not clear: it has been explained as contracted from אתבני, or as an internal pass. מחרמתא ק׳ Both plur. fem. בנתבל Either בְּנָה־בֵל (96 3 *n.*) or בְּנָ־הֻבַל, Hobal being an old Arab deity, هبل at Mekka, the chief god of the Ka'aba; see Baethgen *Beitr.* 113. For compounds with בנא cf. O.T. בנהדד (בנה־דד?), בניה &c.

L. 6. The Corp. supplies בשנת and two units to fill the lacuna. למלכו i.e. Malchus i, 100 3 *n.* The inscr. is too mutilated to enable us to make out the general sense with certainty. It appears that Ṣa'du in the 14th year of Aretas iv dedicated some object for the life of the king and his family, and deposited it (l. 6) in the recently restored sanctuary, which had been built some 50 years before. This inscr., like CIS ii 157 (also from Puteoli), is a witness to the extent and enterprise of Arabian commerce during the prosperous days of the Nab. kingdom. Nab. merchants had established themselves and the worship of their native deity on the shores of Italy, at the important harbour of Puteoli (cf. Acts 28 11. 13).

NABATAEAN: SINAITIC

The Sinaitic inscriptions are written in the Nabataean dialect and script [1]. Most of them are to be seen on the rocky sides of the Wadi Mukatteb ('covered with writing'), through which one of the ancient trade routes passed; they occur also in other valleys of the Peninsula, e. g. W. 'Aleyyât, W. Leja', W. Ferân, W. Ma'ârah. For the most part they consist of proper names with short formulae of greeting (שלם פ'), or blessing (בריך פ'), or commemoration (דכיר פ'), varied in different ways. Very few are dated (see **107. 108** *n.*); but from the character of the writing, a ruder and more cursive form of the normal Nab., we may conclude that they belong to the first four centuries A. D.; not later, for by the 6th cent., when Cosmas Indicopleustes travelled through this region, their origin was already forgotten [2]. It may be explained in the manner suggested by Euting. The caravans which brought merchandise from India to the markets of Egypt and the Levant travelled up from S. Arabia by the Red Sea coast, and then struck inland through the passes of the Sinaitic Peninsula. For the stage from S. Arabia to El-'Ölâ or El-Ḥejra they would have an escort of Himyarites; for the next stage, from El-'Ölâ to Petra, a Nab. escort would take them through Nab. territory. Here the caravans would be joined by Nab. clerks, writers, customs officers; and these were the authors of the inscriptions. When their services were not wanted they would spend their leisure with the Bedouin and their camels at the pasture-grounds. This explains how the inscriptions are found both along the trade routes and in out-of-the-way valleys which only lead to pasturage. Euting has published the standard collection of Sin. inscrr., numbering 677; *Sinaïtische Inschriften*, 1891.

[1] A few are in Greek, Arabic, and Latin.

[2] Ὅθεν ἐστὶν ἰδεῖν ἐν ἐκείνῃ τῇ ἐρήμῳ τοῦ Σιναίου ὄρους ἐν πάσαις καταπαύσεσι, πάντας τοὺς λίθους τῶν αὐτόθι, τοὺς ἐκ τῶν ὀρέων ἀποκλωμένους, γεγραμμένους γράμμασι γλυπτοῖς Ἑβραϊκοῖς, ὡς αὐτὸς ἐγὼ πεζεύσας τοὺς τόπους μαρτυρῶ. ἅ τινα καὶ τινὲς Ἰουδαῖοι ἀναγνόντες διηγοῦντο ἡμῖν λέγοντες γεγράφθαι οὕτως, ἄπαρσις τοῦδε, ἐκ φυλῆς τῆσδε, ἔτει τῷδε, μηνὶ τῷδε, καθὰ καὶ παρ' ἡμῖν πολλάκις τινὲς ἐν ταῖς ξενίαις γράφουσιν Migne *PG* lxxxviii 217; Lidzb. 91.

103. Eut. 519. W. Mukatteb.

שלם אוישו בר פציו בטב \

Greeting! Uwaisu, son of Faṣiyyu; good luck!

The inscr. begins with a greeting and ends with a farewell. שלם Lit. *peace* (106); similarly in Egypt. Aram. CIS ii 152, and in Nab. at El-Ḥejra ib. 253 &c. אוישו = أُوَيْس dim. of אושו = أَوْس *gift*, both common names in Sin.; cf. אושאלהי Eut. 566. אושלבעלי 104, and the frequent Αὖσος Wadd. 2034 &c. The pr. nn. in Sin. are generally Arabic, seldom Aramaic. פציו Found in various forms, מצי, מציאו, חמצא &c.; the Arab. would prob. be فَصِيّ. בטב Lit. *in good*, similarly at El-Ḥejra CIS ii 243 &c.; cf. הֱיֵה בְטוֹב Qoh. 7 14.

104. Eut. 559. W. Mukatteb.

שלם עבדדושרא בר תנתלו
ואושלבעלי בר גרמלהי בר חיטמו

Greeting! ʿAbd-dushara, son of Thantalu, and Aus-albaʿali, son of Garm-allâhi, son of Ḥaiṭamu.

תנתלו Cf. the Arab. تُنْتُلَة *rotten egg*, from تَنْتَلَ *to soil oneself*. אושלבעלי See 103, *gift of the Baʿal*, elsewhere אושאלבעלי. The ל or אל is the Arab. art., cf. אלבעלו 105. אלאברשו Eut. 548. אלאחרשו 539 &c. The combination of Arab. and Aram. in this name is noteworthy. גרמלהי = גרמאלהי Eut. 79 &c., Garmallae (dat.) CIL x 2638; cf. גרמאלבעלי 106 &c. The prefix גרם, which occurs frequently before the name of a deity in Sin., may = جِرْم *body* (cf. Hebr. גֶּרֶם *bone*), so *member of Allah* &c.; cf. the Phoen. ברעשתרת 6 2 *n.* Another suggestion is that the word = *fear*, like the Eth. *gĕrăm*; in modern Abyss. many names begin with *germa* (Cook *Aram. Gloss.* s. v.). חיטמו Nöld. quotes the Arab. names خَطْمَة, خَطْمَاء *with a large nose.*

105. Eut. 327. W. Ferân.

שלם ואלו בר חלצת קדם אלבעלו

Greeting! Waʾilu, son of Ḥâliṣat, before the Baʿal.

ואלו See 38 4 *n.* (יאל). חלצת Like ואלו, a very common name in these inscrr.; it is found also at El-Ḥejra CIS ii 307 and in Ḥauran, 'Αλασαθός Wadd. 2042. 2047 (but according to Nöld.=עלשת, *ZDMG* xlii 474). Wellhausen suggests a derivation from خَلَصٌ, خَلَصَة *a creeping plant* resembling the vine, which is prob. the meaning of Dhu 'l Ḥalaṣa, the name of a heathen Arab deity. חלצת itself cannot be the name of the god used as the name of a man, because ذو الخلصة is merely a title, 'of the creeping plant' (which perhaps had wreathed itself round the sacred stone), the actual name of the deity not being uttered (see on דושרא 79 5); *Reste Ar. Heid.* 47 f. The pronunciation of חלצת was prob. خَالِصَة. קדם אלבעלו *before the Ba'al* (104 *n.*); prob. supply in thought 'may there be remembrance,' as in CIS ii 338 דכרן עריש מן קדם דושרא. For the ellipse here cf. ib. 320 F מן קדם דושרא ומנתו and Eut. 437 קדם דשרא וא[לבעלו ?] במישו בר ואלו.

106. Eut. 186. W. 'Aleyyât.

דכיר בטב ושלם
שעדו בר
גרמאלבעלי
עד עלם V
ש·

Remembered in welfare and peace be Sa'adu, son of Garm-alba'ali, for ever! . . .

שעדו CIS ii 231 &c., Palm. 127 3 (in Gk. σοαδου), also in the Sin. names שעדאלהי 107 and שעדאלבעלי; שעדלת 140 B 2. שעדו = Arab. سَعْد *happiness, good fortune.* גרמאלבעלי 104 *n.*

107. Eut. 463. A. D. 189. W. Mukatteb.

בריך ואלו בר שעדאלהי
דא בשנת 6666 ל להפרכיה די
בה אחרבו ע[רב]יא ארעא

Blessed be Wa'ilu, son of Sa'ad-allâhi. This (was written) in the year 85 of the Eparchy, in which the Arabs (??) devastated (?) the land.

שעראלהי See 106 *n*. A similar sign for 20 occurs in an early Arab. inscr. from Ḥarran given by Vogüé in *Syr. Centr.* 117; for the usual Nab. form see 97. 101. The date is reckoned from the Eparchy (87 2 *n*.), i. e. the establishment of the Roman *governorship* over Arabia in A. D. 106 (see p. 216). This reckoning was known as the Era of Bostra (March 22, 106 A. D.)[1], and was used throughout the province of Arabia. אחרבו ע[רב]יא So read by Eut., Lidzb. (or עריא *the strangers*, *Eph.* i 339), supposing an allusion to some Bedouin attack upon the oases of Sinai. Cl.-Gan., however, prefers אחרפו ע[נ]יא—a reading certainly justified by Euting's copy, Taf. 26—and renders the line 'in which the poor of the land were allowed to glean (the fruit)'; אחרפו he explains as = أَخْرَفُوا (conj. iv), or pass. أُخْرِفُوا *allow* or *be allowed to gather fruit*, and ע[נ]יא as constr. st. = עניי with א as in Palm. הֵיָא, בנָא (but see below), cf. ענוי ארץ Am. 8 4 &c. He finds in the words thus interpreted a religious institution, analogous to the Jewish Sabbatical year, which assigned at fixed yearly intervals the fruit-gleanings to the poor; see *Rec.* iv § 33 = *Rép.* no. 129. There is absolutely no evidence, however, that such an institution ever existed; and it may be doubted whether אחרפו, an Ofal, passive, form, would be used in Nab. instead of the usual Ethp.; خرف means only 'to gather fruit fallen on the ground.' In the *Rev. Bibl.* xi (1902) 137 it is proposed to read אחרבו עניא א' *the wells of the land were dried up*, עניא for עיניא; the objection to this is that the plur. constr. in Nab. does not end in א (Lidzb. *Eph.* i 339). The inscr. has recently been examined afresh on the spot by Fathers Jaussen and Savignac of Jerusalem; their investigations confirm Eut.'s reading אחרבו, *RB* xi 467.

108. Eut. 457. A. D. 210–211. W. Mukatteb.

דכיר תימאלהי בר יעלי שנת מאה ע |
דמין על תלתת קיסרין

Remembered be Taim-allâhi, son of Ya'ali! The year one hundred (and) 6, equivalent to (the year of) the three Caesars.

[1] So in Gk. inscrr., e. g. ἔτους . . τῆς Βοστρηνῶν [scil. ἐποχῆς], or ἔτους . . τῆς ἐπαρχίου[-ας] Wetzstein *Ausgew. Inschr.* (*Abh. Berl. Akad.* 1863) 111. 112.

תימאלהי See 84 1 *n*. יעלי = يَعْلَى. דמין i.e. דָּמְיָן ptcp. pl. fem. of דמא agreeing with שנין understood; the usual prep. after דמא is ל. The 106th year of the Era of Bostra = 210–211 A.D. During this year the Emperor Septimius Severus died (Feb. 4th, 211), and both his sons Caracalla and Geta became joint emperors; the year, therefore, was remarkable for having witnessed three Caesars on the throne. With תלתת קיסרין cf. the form AVGGG (i.e. tres Augusti) on Lat. inscrr. (Cagnat *Cours d'épigr. Lat.*[3] 373); it is possible that קיסרין may be the equivalent of the official title Augustus. Cl.-Gan., *Rec.* iv § 32 = *Rép.* no. 128, interprets the date differently; for the numeral, which is irregular in form (see **107**), he reads על, and מרין for דמין. Supposing דמין to be an error for מרין *lords*, or *our lords* (=מרינא), he renders 'the year 100. For (the salvation of) our lords, the three Caesars.' But it may be doubted whether an inscr. of this fugitive, personal character would be written *for the sake of* (על) such august beneficiaries; analogy leads us to expect merely a date after the pr. nn. Moreover, there are historical objections; the 100th year (Bostra) = 204–205 A.D.; it would thus fall well within the reign of Severus (198–211 A.D.)[1], and though Caracalla became joint emperor in 201, he and his brother did not share the imperium with their father till 210–211.

109. Eut. 410. W. Mukatteb.

דנה סוסיא די
עבד שעדלהי בר אעלא

This is the horse which Sa'd-allâhi, son of A'lâ, drew.

Rude drawings sometimes accompany the Sin. inscrr.; cf. the pictures on the rocks near Têma and El-Ḥejra, Eut. *Nab. Inschr.* 8 f. In this case Sa'd-allâhi has drawn his horse; cf. Eut. 416. סוסיא The form is Aram., cf. ܣܘܣܝܐ. אעלא = أَعْلَى *most illustrious*.

[1] The fact that in several Lat. inscrr. from Africa Geta is styled Augustus before 209 (CIL viii p. 974) is not sufficient to support Cl.-Gan.'s contention.

PALMYRENE

Palmyra, called in Gk. Πάλμυρα, in the O. T. and in the native inscriptions Tadmor[1], lay 150 m. NE. of Damascus in an oasis of the Syrian desert. Its situation afforded a meeting-place for the trade which crossed from E. to W., or came up from Petra and S. Arabia. The city existed for commerce. The 'chief of the caravan,' the 'chief of the market,' appear in the inscriptions among the principal citizens, **116. 121**, holding magistracies and imperial posts; influential trade-guilds witness to the importance of the local industries, **126**; the splendour and wealth of the city may be judged from the ruins of temples, streets, and tombs which still exist. The prosperity of Palmyra began to rise probably about the time when the Romans established themselves on the Syrian coast; for political reasons it was desirable to keep the direct route between the Euphrates and the Mediterranean in the hands of a vassal power. Probably in the reign of Augustus Palmyra became a part of the Roman empire, but the exact date is not known; later on it received special favours from Hadrian, who visited the city about 130 A. D. and granted it the privileges of the *jus Italicum*, perhaps also the rank of a colony[2], and adorned it with new buildings; from his time it took the name of Hadriana Palmyra, הדרינא תדמר **147** ii. With the Romans on the one side and the Parthians on the other, the Palmyrenes had a difficult part to play[3], but they always knew how to use the rivalry of the two empires for the advancement of their trade, and in the later Parthian wars both their policy and their active services were attended with signal success. For 150 years, from 130–270 A. D., Palmyra's fortunes were at their height. Under Odainath and Zenobia, during a brief period, the state held a foremost place in the Eastern empire; after Zenobia's overthrow in 273 it fell into decay and never recovered.

[1] 2 Chr. 8 4 is the earliest reference to the city. The original source had תמר, a place in Judah, 1 K. 9 18 Kt.; this was altered by the Chronicler or a later scribe to תדמר (so in 1 K. 9 18 Qeri) evidently with a view to increasing the extent of Solomon's kingdom. Jos. says that the Syrians pronounced the name *Thadamora*, Θαδάμορα, *Ant.* viii 6 1: the Arabs call it تَدْمُر.

[2] By the 3rd cent., at any rate, it had become a colony, **121. 127**.

[3] Pliny 5 21 Palmyra urbs . . . privata sorte inter duo imperia summa, Romanorum Parthorumque, et prima in discordia semper utrinque cura.

As a vassal of Rome, Palmyra enjoyed a liberal measure of military and civil independence. It was allowed to use the native language for official purposes, and, like other communities in the Asiatic and Syrian provinces[1], to farm the customs for the benefit of the community, independently of the sovereign power (**147**). The organization of the city was that of a Greek municipality under the empire. The government was vested in the Council and People (בולא ודמס), and administered by civil officers with Greek titles, the proedros (פלהדרותא, title of the office), the grammateus (גרממטוס), the archons (ארכניא), the syndics (סדקיא), the dekaprotoi (עשרתא); see **147** i and **122**. Along with these there was, at least in the 3rd cent., a *Ras* or *head* of the state (ריש **125**), virtually a prince, chosen from the leading family, of senatorial rank (סנקלטיקא **125**) and Roman appointment. The office was handed on by Septimius Ḥairân (**125**) to his son Sept. Odainath, who received even higher rank, the consular dignity (הפטיקא **126**). After his death, Odainath was actually styled *king of kings* (**130**), but no inscription contains the title during his life-time. See Mommsen *Provinces of the Rom. Emp.* ii 92–112.

The language spoken at Palmyra was a dialect of Western Aramaic[2]. In some important points, indeed, the dialect was related to Eastern Aram. or Syriac, e. g. the plur. in ־ֵא, חגרא **113** 3. מלכא **130** 1; the dropping of the final *ī* and *ū* in אבוה, אחוה, בנוה (but אבוהי &c. also occur), נחת **113** 4. אקים **113** 3. **130** 4 (but אקימו **114** 2); the adverbial ending *âîth*, שכחית **121** 6; the infin. ending *ā*, מתחשבו **147** ii c 4; also the words מטל **121** 6. חנן **121** 3. כלמא **147** i 12. עמרא *life* **121** 6. עלתא **135** 1. תמלילא **117** 5 &c. But the relation to Western (Palestinian) Aram. is closer. Specially characteristic are the following features: the impf. with י, not as in Syr. and the E. dialects with נ or ל; the plur. in ־ַיָּא; the rel. די as in Bibl. Aram. and in the Targ. Ps.-Jon. (Dalman *Gr.* 85); the conj. בדילדי; the pers. pron. דנה, דה, אלן; כות **121** 6 &c.; the distinction between ש and ס, as in Bibl. Aram., e. g. סניאן and 'ש, סחר **121** 5. 6. **147** i 4. The bulk of the population of Palmyra was of Arab race, hence many of the proper names are Arabic, and several Arabic words occur, e. g. מגר **112** 3. חרם **112** 4. פחר **136** 6. The technical terms of municipal and administrative life are mostly Greek; even under the Roman government the Greek terminology

[1] See Dessau *Hermes* xix 528 ff.

[2] Like the Egypt. Aram. and Nabataean. Cf. Epiphanius *Haer.* 66 13 [PG xlii 48] Ἄλλοι δὲ δῆθεν τὴν βαθυτάτην τῶν Σύρων διάλεκτον σεμνύνονται, τήν τε [τὴν] κατὰ τὴν Παλμύραν διάλεκτον, αὐτήν τε καὶ τὰ αὐτῶν στοιχεῖα· εἰκοσιδύο δὲ ταῦτα ὑπάρχει.

was retained, e. g. אסטרטגיא, אכסניא, בולוטא, נמס, דנמא, חינמנא, הפקא, נמוסא, תגמא, and the titles mentioned above. The Latin words in the inscriptions are קלניא, קסר, קטריא, לגיונא, דוקרנא. On the characteristics of the dialect see Nöldeke *ZDMG* xxiv 85–109, cited as Nöld.

The inscriptions are often given in a Gk. version after the Palm.; and as a further result of Roman influence many natives bore Latin in addition to Aram. names. The writing is a modified form of the old Aram. character, and in many respects approximates the Hebr. square character. A noteworthy feature is the diacritic point which is often used, as in Syr., to distinguish ר from ד. The letters א, ב, ד, ו, ם, ג, ר often have ligatures binding them to the letter which precedes or follows; נ has a final form. The words are sometimes separated, and occasionally the end of a clause is marked by the full stop ✥. The inscriptions belong to the first three centuries A. D.; the earliest is dated B. C. 9 (141), the latest Aug. 272 A. D. (Vog. 116; see p. 293). The standard collection is that of de Vogüé *Syrie Centrale* 1868, cited as Vog.; supplementary collections are those of A. D. Mordtmann *Neue Beiträge z. Kunde Palmyras* 1875, cited as Mordtm.; Clermont-Ganneau *Études* i § 9; Sachau *ZDMG* xxxv 728 ff.; D. H. Müller *Palm. Inschr.* 1898; J. Mordtmann *Palmyrenisches* 1899 &c.

HONORARY INSCRIPTIONS

110. Vogüé 1. A. D. 139. In situ[1].

1 בולא ודמס עבדו צלמיא אלן תרויהון

2 לאעילמי בר חירן בר מקימו בר חירן מתא

3 ולחירן אבוהי רחימי מדיתהון ודחלי אלהיא

4 בדילדי שפרו להון ולאלהיהון בכל מבו כלה

5 ליקרהון בירח ניסן שנת //// ⊃— 33 ⊃—

Ἡ βουλὴ καὶ ὁ δῆμος Ἀαιλάμειν Αἱράνου τοῦ Μοκίμου τοῦ Αἱράνου τοῦ Μαθθᾶ καὶ Αἱράνην τὸν πατέρα αὐτοῦ εὐσεβεῖς καὶ φιλοπάτριδας καὶ παντὶ τρόπῳ φιλοτείμως ἀρέσαντας τῇ πατρίδι καὶ τοῖς πατρίοις θεοῖς τειμῆς χάριν ἔτους νυʹ μηνὸς Ξανδικοῦ. Wadd. 2586.

[1] The Palmyrene inscr. are all *in situ* except where otherwise stated.

The Council and People have made these two statues [2] to A'ailami, son of Ḥairân, son of Moqîmu, son of Ḥairân, (son of) Mattâ, [3] and to Ḥairân his father, lovers of their city and fearers of the gods, [4] because they were well-pleasing to them and to their gods in everything whatsoever: [5] to their honour. In the month Nisan, the year 450.

The honorary inscrr. (**110–132**) are written upon Corinthian columns which were ranged along the principal streets, or stood in the courts and porticos of the temples. On the column there is generally a bracket for the bust to which the inscription refers.

L. 1. בולא ודמס i. e. בּוּלֵא וְדֵמֹס. אלן Plur. of דנה, regularly in Palm.; see add. note ii p. 26. תרויהון Lit. *the two of them*, תַּרְוַיְהוֹן (= תְּרֵיהוֹן), cf. **111** 2 and the Palest. forms תרווייהון, תרוויהון, Dalman *Gr.* 98.

L. 2. אעילמי 'Ααιλάμεις. The name is Arab., and may be explained as a diminutive of the elative form with the ending ـِيّ ('relative'), i.e. أُعَيْلَمِيّ from علم *know*, cf. أُزَيْهِر from ازهر &c. As the Gk. form shows, the pronunciation does not strictly represent the Arab.; perhaps this is due to the influence of Aram., which rarely recognizes dimin. forms; cf. also Χεεῖλος = كُهَيْل, Σεμίας = سُعَيْمِيَة &c. The pr. n. Αἴλαμος Wadd. **2086** is similarly explained as = عَيْلَم (J. Mordtmann *Palmyrenisches* 15 f.). חירן = حُيَيْرَان an ancient name in the tribe of the Beni Hamdân (Blau *ZDMG* xxviii 75), very common in Palm. מקימו **78** 2 *n.*[1] מתא The preceding בר is left out, as frequently in Palm.—a strong proof of Gk. influence; see the Gk. version. מתא is abbreviated from some form like מת בול (= מתן־בול).

L. 3. ר' מ' **111** 3 f. i.e. רָחִימֵי מְדִיתְהוֹן. מדיתא (**147** ii b 7 &c.) = מדינתא (from דין); in Palm. and Syr. *city*, πάτρις; in Bibl. Aram. *province*. For the assimilation of נ cf. אתת (= אנשת), and in foreign words סרקיא **147**. סקלטיקא Vog. **21** (p. 285 *n.* 1).

L. 4. בדילדי **113** 4 f. &c. *on account of*, frequent in Palest. Aram. but not in Syr., Dalman *Gr.* 187. בדיל is Hebraized בשל Jonah 1 7 (= באשר ל v. 8). 12. Qoh. 8 17. מבו An error for צבו lit. *purpose*, *intention*, as in Syr. with a vague sense, *matter*, *thing*, Dan. 6 18; plur. צְבְוָתָא **147** i 6.

[1] Final *î* in Palm. is represented in Gk. by εις, ει, ειν, e. g. בריכי **111** 2 Βαρείχειν; also medial *î*, e. g. מקימו Μοκείμου and Μοκίμου, זבידא Ζεβείδαν **118** 2. Where י = diphth. *ai* the Gk. writes αι, as here, חירן Αἵρανος, בידא **118** 3 Βαιδâ &c.; Nöld. 88 f.

L. 5. שנת Constr. st. before the number. The name of the month in the Gk. version comes from the Macedonian calendar. The date is reckoned by the Seleucid era which began Oct. 312 B.C.; see **9** 5 *n*. **97** iii *n*.

111. Vog. **2.** A.D. 139.

בולא ודמס עבדו צלמיא אלן

תרויהן לבריכי בר אמרשא בר

ירחבולא ולמקימ[ו] ברה רחימי

מדיתהון ודחלי א[לה]יא ליקרהון

בירח ניסן שנת //// ק 33 ק

Ἡ βουλὴ καὶ ὁ δῆμος Βαρείχειν Ἀμρισάμσου τοῦ Ἰαριβωλέους καὶ Μόκιμον υἱὸν αὐτοῦ εὐσεβεῖς καὶ φιλοπάτριδας τιμῆς χάριν . . . Wadd. 2587.

The Council and People have made these two statues [2] to Bariki, son of Amri-sha, son [3] of Yarḥi-bôlē, and to Moqîm[u] his son, lovers [4] of their city and fearers of the g[od]s: to their honour. [5] In the month Nisan, the year 450.

The form is identical with that of the preceding inscription.

L. 2. בריכי i.e. *Benedictus*. אמרשא An abbrev. for אמר שמשא (see the Gk.) *Shamash has promised*, cf. the O.T. אמריהו 1 Chr. **24** 23 &c., and the Sab. יתעאמר *KB* ii 54; for שא = שמשא cf. חימשא, אלחשא Vog. **34**. Prob. the Hebr. pr. n. בעשא (=בעלשא) is to be explained in this way; see S. A. Cook *Expos. Times* x (1899) 525 ff.

L. 3. ירחבולא Derived from the name of the Palm. deity ירחבול **121** 6 *n*.; cf. **115** 5 *n*. The nom. of Ἰαριβωλέου would end in -ης, cf. בונא **112** 2 Βωννέους; hence the final vowel in both names was pronounced *ē*, cf. בולא = βουλή; Nöld. 90.

112. Vog. **3.** A.D. 140.

צלמא דנה די אצ[ט]לי בר חירן שבא בר

חירן בונא שבת די עבדת לה בולא די

מגד לה. ח... לעלמא ו.. מל. תא ואקם

4 . חר[מן] ל[מ]לכב[ל ולג]ד תימי ולעתרעתה

5 [א]לה[יא] טב[יא] בת.די..ת ליקרה בירח

6 [תמוז שנ]ת //// ⸢⸣33⸢⸣ / ϕ

Ἡ βουλὴ Ἀστάλειν Αἱράνου τοῦ Σαβᾶ τοῦ [Αἱρά]νου τοῦ Βωννέους ἐπαγγειλάμενον αὐτῇ ἐπίδοσιν αἰωνίαν [εἰς] θυσίαν κατ' ἔτος ἀναθέματα [Μαλα]χβήλῳ καὶ Τύχῃ Θαιμεῖος καὶ [Ἀτερ]γάτει πατρῴοις θεοῖς τειμῆς καὶ μνήμης χάριν ἔτους ανυ' πανήμου. Wadd. 2588.

This statue is that of Aṣṭali, son of Ḥairan, (son of) Sabâ, son [2] of Ḥairân, (son of) Bônnē, (son of) Shabbath, which has been made to him by the Council to whom [3] he presented . . . for ever . . . . and set up [4] consecrated things to Malak-be[l and to the Fort]une of Thaimi and to 'Athar-'atheh, [5] the good gods . . . . . . to his honour. In the month [6] Tammuz, the year 451.

L. 1. אצטלי An Ethpe. form from צלא ? *pray*; cf. אתפני 118 1. שבא Sometimes סבא, prob. = Talm. שבא, Nab. שבי CIS ii 215, from شب *befall*, cf. Βαρσαββᾶς Acts 1 23; Dalman *Gr.* 143 *n*.

L. 2. בנא Perhaps = בול נא[א] *Bôl is dear*, or = בולנא Vog. 95 2 from בול ענא or בול לנא; but see 143 6 *n*. The Gk. form with double ν shows that ל has been assimilated; cf. בעשמם 39 1 and 111 3 *n*. שבת may be a cognomen.

L. 3. מגר 123 4 = مَجَّدَ *to make a generous gift*; in Aram. the noun is used, מַגְּדָא *a costly gift*. After מגר some word corresponding to ἐπίδοσιν is to be supplied; Vog. מתנא.

L. 4. חרמן See 79 8 *n*. מלכבל A solar deity who stood at the head of the Palm. gods, as the inscr. below shows [1]. The Gk. and Lat. transcriptions Μαλαχβῆλος, *Malachibelus*, *Malagbelus* indicate

[1] Rom. 2, in the Capitoline Mus., A. D. 236.

עלתא דה למלכבל ולאלהי תדמר

קרב טבריס קלודיס פלקסי

ותדמריא לאלההון שלם

Soli sanctissimo sacrum. Ti. Claudius Felix et Claudia Helpis et Ti. Claudius Alypus fil[ius] eorum votum solverunt libens merito Calbienses de coh[orte] iii.

מַלְכְּבֵל = מַלְאַךְ בֵּל *messenger of Bel* (Lidzb. *Eph.* i 256 f.) rather than מַלְכְּבֵל *Bel is king*. The god Bel came from Babylon. The name is not found on public inscrr., but only on small tesserae, and often accompanied by the symbol of the sun with rays, e. g. Vog. 132 ff. בל יברך לבני חלא &c. 143. As a sun-god Bel could easily be adapted to שמש, undoubtedly the chief god of Palmyra; he was further identified with Ζεύς, Wadd. 2606 a, **140** A 2 *n*. Lidzb. suggests that the native שמש was interpreted as מלאך בל, the *messenger*, or the revealer of Bel. If this is correct we can understand how שמש, בל, מלכבל are all really the same chief deity, under various aspects. Malak-bel is sometimes associated with 'Agli-bôl, the latter, as the moon, being named before the sun, **139** 6 *n*., cf. **61** 2 *n*. ו[לג]ד תימי or ו[ג]ד. Cl.-Gan. reads [ג]ד, in appos. to מלכבל (*Rec.* iii 244 f.), but the Gk. has καί. The two deities are named together on a Palm. seal, מלכבל נדתימי Mordtm. no. 88. גד תימי = Τύχη Θαιμεῖος, gen. of Θαιμεῖς (Nöld. 88), the patron deity of the clan תימי[1]. The name תימי = תֵּיְם *slave* requires, like עבד, the name of a god to complete its meaning, e. g. תימאלהי **84** 1. The worship of Gad-Tyche was widely popular in Syria and Ḥauran; cf. the pr. nn. גדעתה Vog. 143, גדרצו ib. 84, and **27** 3 *n*. עתרעתה 'Ατεργάτις, the great goddess of the Aramaeans. The chief centres of her cult in Syria were at Hierapolis in Mesopotamia and Damascus[2]; outside Syria her most famous temple was at Ashqelon[3]. Another temple occupied an ancient shrine at 'Ashtaroth-qarnaim, the 'Ατεργάτιον at Karnion 2 Macc. 12 26, τὸ τέμενος ἐν Καρνάιν 1 Macc. 5 43; both here and at Ashqelon Atergatis took the place of an earlier Astarte. The name is compounded of עתר = עתתר = עשתרת and עתה. As עַתְּתַר (*mas.*) the deity was worshipped in S. Arabia (see **4** 1 *n*.). There are traces of the form עתר among the Aramaeans, e. g. the pr. n. עתרשור Cl.-Gan. *Ét.* i 118 (עתרעזה CIS ii 52 is doubtful); it was known to Strabo, who writes it 'Αθάρα[4], the θ being a softening of the original doubled letter; cf. Hesych. 'Ατταγάθη

[1] Cf. בל ברך לבני תימי Mordtm. no. 60.

[2] Strabo p. 636 ed. Müll. ἡ Βαμβύκη ἣν καὶ Ἔδεσσαν καὶ Ἱερὰν πόλιν καλοῦσιν, ἐν ᾗ τιμῶσι τὴν Συρίαν θεὸν τὴν 'Αταργάτιν. Her name occurs on coins of Hierapolis, Babelon *Pers. Ach.* pp. liii. 45. For Damascus see Justin xxxvi 2 Nomen urbi a Damasco rege inditum, in cuius honorem Syri sepulcrum Athares [MSS. Arathis] uxoris eius, pro templo coluere deamque exinde sanctissimae religionis habent.

[3] Diod. ii 4. Near Askalon is a temple of the goddess ἣν ὀνομάζουσιν οἱ Σύροι Δερκετοῦν κ.τ.λ.; her image was that of a woman with a fish-tail. See Schürer *Gesch. Jüd. Volk.*[3] ii. 23 f.

[4] P. 667 'Αταργάτιν δὲ [ἐκάλεσαν] τὴν 'Αθάραν· Δερκετὼ δ' αὐτὴν Κτησίας καλεῖ.

'Αθάρη παρὰ τῷ Ξάνθῳ *Fr. Hist. Gr.* iv 629. A hint as to the nature of the deity is given by an inscr. of Ašurbanipal, *KB* ii 220 f., which mentions a N. Arabian tribe as worshippers of *Atar-samaim* i. e. Atar of the heavens. The second part of the compound, עתה, עתא, or עתי[1], occurs frequently in pr. nn., e. g. זברעתה, ברעתה, עתנורי, and with a mas. verb, e. g. עתנתן, עתעקב; but whether עתה was a male or female deity is not clear. The Syr. ܥܬܐ of Adiabene was a goddess (Cureton *Spic. Syr.* ܝܛ 9); in a Gk. inscr. from Batanaea, Wadd. 2209, a god Ἔθαος is named, perhaps = עתא. The usual Gk. transcription is -γαθη[2]. Of the nature of this deity nothing certain is known. As 'Athar-'atheh was specially connected with Hierapolis, it is possible that 'Atheh was the Phrygian god Attis = Adonis, whose cult was established there; 'Athar-'atheh will then represent a union between the Syrian goddess and the youthful god of foreign origin (Lagrange *RB* x 559 f. = *Rel. Sém.* 132, following E. Meyer, Hommel &c.); at any rate עתרעתה denotes 'Ashtart who has assumed the attributes of 'Atheh, cf. מלכבל above. At Ashqelon she was a fish-goddess, but her worship seemed to Herod. to be that of 'Αφροδίτη οὐρανίη (i 105), and such no doubt was her character at Palmyra; cf. an inscr. from Delos quoted by Schürer l. c. 24 'Αγνῇ 'Αφροδίτῃ 'Αταργάτι. In the Talm. her name is תרעתא *Ab. Zar.* 11 b; in Gk. and Lat. it is often Δερκετώ, Derceto.

L. 6. Πάνημος = תמוז, the 10th month, July.

113. Vog. 4. A. D. 247.

1 צלמא דנה די יולים אורלים

2 זבידא בר מקימו בר זבידא עשתור

3 בידא די אקים לה תגרא בני שירתא

4 די נחת עמה לאלגשיא ליקרה בדיל

5 די שפר להון בירח ניסן שנת ע ⊂—

/// y —⊃ 33

[1] The differences are merely orthographical; Lidzb. *Ephem.* i 84 (against Cl.-Gan.).

[2] Athenaeus viii 37 . . . Γάτις ἡ τῶν Σύρων βασίλισσα . . . ὑπ' ἀγνοίας δὲ τοὺς πολλοὺς αὐτὴν μὲν 'Ατεργάτιν ὀνομάζειν . . .

Ἰούλιον Αὐρήλιον Ζεβεῖδαν Μοκίμου τοῦ Ζεβεῖδου Ἀσθώρου Βαιδᾶ οἱ σὺν αὐτῷ κατελθόντες εἰς Ὀλογεσιάδα ἔνποροι ἀνέστησαν ἀρέσαντα αὐτοῖς τειμῆς χάριν Ξανδικῷ τοῦ ηνφʹ ἔτους. Wadd. 2599.

This statue is that of Julius Aurelius [2] Zebîda, son of Moqîmu, son of Zebîda, (son of) ʽAshtôr, [3] (son of) Baida, which has been set up to him by the merchants of the caravans [4] who went down with him to Ologesias: to his honour, because [5] he was well-pleasing to them. In the month Nisan, the year 558.

L. 2. זבידא i. e. *Donatus*, cf. זברבול, זברנבו 133 1; O.T. זָבוּד, זַבְדִּי, זְבַדְיָהוּ, זַבְדִּיאֵל, N.T. Ζεβεδαῖος; Arab. زبد *gift*, Aram. זבד *to present*. עשתור Mas. form of עשתרת; the full form would be בר ע׳, cf. the name of the Jewish proselytes בֵּי(ת) בר עשתור Talm. J. *Bikk.* 64 a. The long *ô* has, of course, nothing to do with the Massor. punctuation עַשְׁתֹּרֶת; it is an original long vowel, represented sometimes by ֻ, e. g. Phoen. עוֹלָם Οὐλῶμος, Assyr. *Ḫirummu* חִירָם &c. The name here was prob. borrowed from the Phoenicians; cf. עבדעשתר 22 1 *n.* and עסתורנא 143 2. See Hoffmann *Über ein. Phön. Inschr.* 6. 22 *n.*

L. 3. בידא Perhaps abbr. from זבידא. אקים Afel pf. 3 plur., the final vowel being quiescent, as in the Syr. ܐܩܝܡܘ; cf. נחת l. 4 and p. 264. תגרא 147 i 7. ii c 16, i. e. תַּגָּרָא plur. emph., with the ending א‎ַ (shortened from אֵי—), as in Syr. ܬܓܪ̈ܐ, from תגר Pa. *to sell*. For the form cf. עברא 126 4. מלכא 180 1; it was prob. common in the spoken language (see p. 264). בני שירתא 114 2 lit. *sons of the caravan*, συνοδία (Lk. 2 44); cf. 116 2 רב ש׳ συνοδιάρχης, and Syr. ܫܝܪܬܐ, Arab. سيّارة; the Aram. word is perhaps borrowed from Arab. (Fraenkel *Aram. Fremdw.* 180). For בני ש׳ cf. בני מריתא 122 4.

L. 4. נחת Pf. 3 plur.; see l. 3 *n.* אלִגְשִׁיָא Vologasias, a town on a tributary (Νααρσάρη, Ptolemaeus) of the Euphrates, about 55 m. SE. of Babylon, and 62 Rom. miles S. of Seleukeia and Ktesiphon, founded by Vologasus I, who became king of the Parthians in A. D. 51. This able ruler succeeded in diverting the trade of Palmyra towards his new city, whence it was carried by river to Charax, the great emporium of the Persian Gulf (114. 115).

114. Vog. 5. A.D. 155.

1 [צל]ם מרקס אלס תיד[רוס די מתקרא

2 שם]עגד די אקימו לה בני שירתא די

3 [סלק]ת מן כרך אספסנא בדילדי עדרה

4 [בכל צב]ו [כל]ה ליקרה ברבנות שירת[א]

5 [די זבדע]תא בר זבדלא ידי בירח אב שנת //// ⟵ 333y/

. . . . [ἡ Σπασίνου] Χάρακος συνοδία βο[ηθή]σαντα αὐτῇ παντὶ τρόπῳ διὰ Ζαβδεαθοῦς Ζαβδελᾶ τοῦ Ἰα[δδαίου] συνοδιάρχου. Ἔτους ϛξυʹ μηνὸς λώου. Wadd. 2590.

[Stat]ue of Marcus Aelius Theod[ōros who is called [2] Shem]a'-gad, which has been set up to him by the members of the caravan which [3] [cam]e up from Karak Hispasina, because he helped it [4] [in everyth]ing [whatso]ever: to his honour; the chief of the caravan being [5] [Zabde-'a]thē, son of Zabd-ila, (son of) Yaddai. In the month Ab, the year 466.

L. 1. The restoration is that of J. Mordtmann *Palmyrenisches* 17 f., based upon Mordtm.'s copy. תידרום Again in Sachau no. 1, Cl.-Gan. *Rec.* iii 157.

L. 2. שמענר Cf. the Phoen. שמעבעל 38 2. בני ש׳ See 118 3 *n.*

L. 3. [סלק]ת 115 2. The outward journey to the Euphrates was called *going down* נחת 118 4, the return journey *coming up*. כרך אספסנא = Σπασίνου Χάραξ, the great mercantile town at the mouth of the Tigris, near the modern village Bassra, founded first by Alexander the Gt. and called Alexandria, then after its destruction by a flood called Antioch, prob. after Antiochus the Gt., and finally re-founded by Ὑσπασίνης, an Arab chief who made it the capital of a small kingdom and gave it his name, early in the 2nd cent. כרך, כרכא 115 is Aram., from כְּרַךְ *surround*, ܟܪܟܐ *fenced city*, *citadel*, cf. כרכא 94 2 and *Kerak* the capital of Moab. כ׳ אספסנא = *the fortress* or *city of Hispasina*; in ordinary pronunciation the first syll. was dropped, as appears in the Gk. Spasinou Charax (115 Gk. version). עדרה i. e. עֲדָרֵהּ.

L. 4. בכל צבו כלה So restored by Reckendorf *ZDMG* xlii 397 *n.*;

110 4; cf. the Gk. ברבנות Lit. *in the chieftainship*, 'ר being the title of the office of 'רב ש 115 2.

L. 5. זבדלא = זבד אלא, cf. זבדלה 140 A 3. ידי 115 &c. Ἰαδδαῖος. The doubled letter indicates a pet name, which is also abbreviated from some such form as ידיעבל; cf. בני Vog. 34 Βέννιος from . . . בנה, זבי 130 Ζαββαῖος from . . . זבד, מקי Vog. 116 Μακκαῖος from מקימו; Lidzb. *Eph.* i 76. אב Λῶος, the 5th month, July–August.

115. Vog. 6. A.D. 193.

צלמא דנה די תימרצו בר תימא בר מקימו
גרבא רב שירתא די עבדו לה בני שירתא די סלקו
עמה מן כרכא בדילדי חסכנון זוז דנרין די דהב
עתיקין תלת מאה ושפר להון ליקרה וליקר ידי
[ועבד]בול בנוהי [ב]ירח ניסן שנת ע ⸗ ////

Τὸν ἀνδρ[ιάντα ἀ]νέστησαν [Θαιμαρ]σᾷ Θαιμῆ τοῦ [Μο]κίμου τοῦ [Γ]α[ρβᾶ συν]οδιάρχῃ οἱ σὺ[ν αὐτῷ ἀ]ναβάντε[ς ἀπὸ] Σπασίνου Χάρ[ακος ἀφειδήσαν]τι αὐτο[ῖ]ς χρυσᾶ παλαιὰ δηνάρι[α] τριακόσια ἀναλ[ω-μ]ά[τ]ω[ν καὶ ἀρέσ]αντι αὐτοῖς εἰς τειμὴν [αὐτοῦ] καὶ Ἰαδδαίου καὶ Ἀβδιβώλου υἱῶν αὐτοῦ ἔτους δφ′ Ξανδικοῦ. Wadd. 2596.

This statue is that of Taim-arṣu, son of Taimē, son of Moqîmu, [2] (son of) Garbâ, chief of the caravan, which has been made to him by the members of the caravan who came up [3] with him from Karak, because he saved them (their) expenses, three hundred denarii of gold, [4] ancient currency, and was well-pleasing to them: to his honour, and to the honour of Yaddai [5] [and 'Abdi]-bôl his sons. In the month Nisan, the year 504.

L. 1. תימרצו 140 A 5 Θαιμάρσας, and prob. *Themarsa* (in an African inscr., Cl.-Gan. *Rec.* iii 165) = *slave of Ruḍâ*, رضاء, an ancient Arab god; 88 1 *n.*, and p. 295 *n.* 1 (ארצו).

L. 2. גרבא Vog. גבבא after Wadd. 2591 Γαββᾶ, which, however, is prob. to be emended Γαρβᾶ; for גרבא cf. 147 ii b 27 and גריבא Vog. 141, Hebr. גָּרָב 2 S. 23 38 &c., = *scabby*.

L. 3. כרכא 114 3 *n*. חסכנון 121 5 Pa. pf. with suff. ־נון from חסך, ܚܣܟ, Hebr. חשך *to hold back, spare*, here followed by two accusatives, lit. *he held them back from expense*, i.e. he paid their expenses himself; hence the word comes to = ἀφειδεῖν *to bestow lavishly*. זוד i.e. זְוָד *expenses for a journey*, e.g. לְמִיתַּן לְהוֹן זְוָדִין לְאוֹרְחָא Onk. Gen. 42 25. The Gk. equivalent is ἀναλώματα. דנרין = δηνάρια, with Aram. pl. ending.

L. 4. עתיקין *ancient*, i.e. belonging to an earlier currency, heavier in weight; παλαιὰ δηνάρια. In 1 Chr. 24 22 'ע occurs as an Aramaism.

L. 5. עבדבול *servant of Bôl*, the Palm. god; cf. the divine names ירחבול 121 6. עגלבול 139 6, and the pr. nn. ירחבולא 111 3. זבדבול 140 A 6 &c. The form is peculiar to Palm. It has been explained as 'the god of the month Bûl,' or as a dialectical form of בל *Bel* in מלכבל 112 4 or of בעל in ב' שמן 122 6; but the Palm. *ô* could not have arisen from *'a* (Nöld. *ZDMG* xlii 474), and the first explanation is very doubtful.

116. Vog. 7. A.D. 257–8.

1 צלמא דנה די יולים אורלים
2 שלמלת בר מלא עבדי רב שירתא
3 די אקימת לה בולא ודמס ליקרה
4 די אסק שירתא מגן מן כיסה
5 שנת y ק— 333 y //// [illegible]

Ἡ βουλ[ὴ καὶ ὁ δῆμος Ἰ]ούλιον Αὐρήλιο[ν ...... τὸν καὶ Σαλμάλ]λαθον Μαλῆ τοῦ [Ἀβδαίου ἀ]ρχέμπορον ἀνακομίσα[ντα τὴν] συνοδίαν προῖκα ἐξ ἰδίων τειμῆς χάριν ἔτους θξφ'. Wadd. 2603.

This statue is that of Julius Aurelius [2] Salm-allath, son of Malē, (son of) 'Abdai, chief of the caravan, [3] which the Council and People have set up to him to his honour, [4] because he brought up the caravan gratis, at his own expense. [5] The year 569.

L. 2. שלמלת = שלם אלת. For אלת see **117** 6 *n.*; and for the abbreviation cf. ותבלת Vog. **21**. עברלת **94**. אמתלת Lidzb. p. 221. מלא In Gk. Μαλῆς (nom.), -ῆ (gen.), -ῆν (acc.) **122** 1, the Aram. א‍ֵ‍ representing the Gk. η(ς), **111** 3 *n.*; for the name cf. Talm. מלאי, Lk. **3** 31 Μελεά, Nab. מלא CIS ii **215**, possibly connected with √מלא *be full*, cf. the pr. n. ימלא Vog. **85**; Lidzb., however, suggests that מלא is abbr. from מלכי, cf. *μαλχεα* Chron. 458 (Tischendorf on Lk. **3** 31).

L. 4. אסק i.e. אַסֵּק Af. of סלק; cf. **114** 3 *n.* מן i.e. סְנָן Lit. *emptiness*, Arab. مَجَّانًا, used like the Hebr. חִנָּם in the sense *for nought*, e.g. Targ. Job **1** 9. מן כיסה Lit. *out of his purse* **117** 5. **122** 6, cf. Nab. מן דילה **102** 3.

117. Vog. **8.** A.D. 129.

[צלמא דנה די.... די אקימו בני....]
כלהון ליקרה בדיל [די שפר להון]
ועבד הו ולשמש אחוהי באכ...
ק ה עמודין שתא ושריתהון ס
ותטליליהון מן כיסהון ליקר שמש
[ו]אלת ורחם אלהיא טביא בירח
אדר שנת //// ⊃ 33

[This statue is that of ... which the sons of ... have set up] ² all of them to his honour, because [he was well-pleasing to them], ³ and made, himself and Lishamsh his brother ... ⁴ .. six pillars and their beams ⁵ and their coverings, at their own expense, to the honour of Shamash ⁶ [and] Allath and Raḥâm, the good gods. In the month ⁷ Adar, the year 440.

L. 3. לשמש i.e. *Belonging to Shamash*, cf. Λισάμσου (gen.) Wadd. **2458**. For the form cf. Phoen. Λεάσταρτος (Jos. *c. Ap.* i 18), Arab. لله, Hebr. לָאֵל Num. **3** 24 *Belonging to El*, לְמוֹאֵל Prov. **31** 1. At the end of the line J. Mordtmann suggests באכ[סדרא] *in this exedra*; Lidzb. ב[א]סלקא *basilica* **119** 3 *n.*

L. 4. עמודין שתא It is a peculiarity of Palm. that the numeral follows its noun, cf. **115** 3 f. **119** 3. We gather from this inscr. that the colonnades which lined the streets of Palmyra were built by degrees at the cost of public-spirited citizens. שריתהון **133** 1; Targ. שָׁרִיתָא *beam*.

L. 5. תטלילהון = Syr. ܬܛܠܝܠܐ *covering* from ܛܰܠܶܠ, 183 1. שמש For the worship of Shamash at Palmyra see 136, and 61 2 *n*.

L. 6. אלת See 80 4 *n*. and 116 2 *n*. רחם The name of a god, the attribute *Compassionate* being personified and treated as a distinct divinity, cf. רחמא 139, elsewhere רחמנא 138; the pronunciation was prob. רַחָם, רַחָמָא i. e. رَحَام, Nöld. 89. The deity occurs in Sabaean, e. g. רחם סנת *Raḥâm Sujuḥ* CIS iv 40 5; similarly רחמן = الرحمن ib. 6 3.

L. 7. אדר The 12th month, Δύστρος, Feb.–March.

118. Vog. 9. A. D. 162.

צלֿ[ם ח]ליפי בר אתפני בר חליפי
[די] עבד לה חליפי [ב]ר חגגו בר מלכו
[בדי]ל די [שפ]ר לה ליק[ר]ה יאשמה...
... בעמודא דנה למקמו ועלוהי
... ן תֿנכֿרי יחא בירח [אד]ר שנת
/// ק 333 ק ////

Stat[ue of Ḥa]lîfi, son of Ethpani, son of Ḥalîfi, [2] [which] has been made to him by Ḥalîfi, son of Ḥaggâgu, [s]on of Mâliku, [3] [be]cause he was [well-pleas]ing to him, to his honour: . . . [4] . . . on this pillar to set up, and upon it [5] . . . while (?) he shall live. In the month [Ad]ar, the year 473.

L. 1. חליפי Cf. חלפו 89 1 *n*. אתפני For the form cf. אצטלי 112 1.

L. 2. חגגו 140 A 3 = حَجَّاج, cf. חגגא *Rép*. no. 148 and חגי Lidzb. 270, Phoen. חגי, חגת, Hebr. חגי *festal* (?), LXX Ἀγγαῖος.

L. 4. למקמו If the reading is correct, an infin. לְמִקְמוּ, as in Syr. ܡܩܡܘ, Nöld. 104.

L. 5. כרי יחא Reading uncertain; perhaps impf. יֵחֵא, Nöld. ib.

119. Vog. 11. A. D. 179.

צלמא דנה די שריכו בר חירן בר עלינא
צפרא די אקימת לה בולא ליקרה

3 ועבד בסלקא דנה עמודין שבעא
4 ותצביתהון כלה ועבד כנונא די נחשא
5 בירח אדר שנת ///// 𐡚 3333 𐡚

Ἡ βουλὴ Σόραιχον Αἰράνου τοῦ Ἀλαινῆ Σεφφερᾶ εὐσεβῆ καὶ φιλόπατριν καὶ φιλότειμον τειμῆς καὶ εὐνοίας χάριν μηνὶ Δύστρῳ τοῦ ϛυʹ ἔτους. Wadd. 2594.

This statue is that of Soraiku, son of Ḥairân, son of ʿAlainê, [2] (son of) Ṣepperâ, which the Council has set up to him, to his honour. [3] And he made this basilica with seven pillars [4] and all their decoration; and he made the brazier of bronze. In the [5] month Adar, the year 490.

L. 1. שריכו 120 2. 146 2 an Arab. name, شَرِيك *friend, companion*; cf. סריכו 129 4. עליתא Cf. Arab. عِلْيَان *tall*, Hebr. עלין.

L. 2. צפרא Σεφφερᾶ, cf. Hebr. צִפּוֹר LXX Σεπφώρ Num. 22 2 &c.

L. 3. בסלקא Lidzb. 238 renders most plausibly *basilica*; the word is prob. to be read in 117 3. In both inscrr. *pillars* are mentioned in the context.

L. 4. תצביתהון = Syr. ܬܨܒܝܬܐ *ornament*, e.g. Pesh. Esth. 2 3. 9. 12, from √צבת 143 10; see also p. 301 *n.* 1. כנונא None of the meanings of *κανών* suits the context; nor is the rendering *base* (כנונא=כַּנָּא) probable. Most likely the word = Syr. ܩܘܢܢܐ *cooking-pot, bowl, pan,* PSm. *Thes.* col. 1762; cf. Hoffmann *Auszüge Syr. Akt. Pers. Märt.* 37 *n.* 312 f. ܘܐܡܣ ܩܘܢܢܐ ܡܢ ܚܝܠܐ ܐܝܟ ܕܢܘܪܐ ܕܚܡܝܡ ܡܫܩܘܡܐ.

120. Vog. 13. A.D. 179.

1 צלמתא דנה [די] מרתי ברת יד[א בר והבלת]
2 בר שמעו[ן] די אקים לה שרי[כו בר חירן בעלה]
3 די מלחת ליקרה בירח אדר ש[נת ///// 𐡚]
4 𐡚 3333

Μάρθειν Ἀλεξάνδρου τοῦ καὶ Ἰαδῆ τοῦ Οὐαβαλλάθου τοῦ Συμώνου Σόραιχος Αἰράνου ἀνὴρ αὐτῆς μνήμης ἕνεκεν. Μηνεὶ Δύστρῳ τοῦ ϛυʹ ἔτους. Wadd. 2592.

This statue is that of Marthi, daughter of Yad[ē, son of Wahab-allath], [2] son of Shim'on, which has been set up to her by Sorai[ku, son of Ḥairân, her husband], [3] because she was ? : to her honour. In the month Adar, the y[ear 4]90.

L. 1. צלמתא Fem., because the statue is that of a woman; cf. Phoen. סמלת **13** 2 *n.* דנה, however, keeps its mas. form; contrast נפשא דה Vog. **31**. מרתי Cf. N.T. Μάρθα and **102** 2. ידא Ἰαδῆς, cf. ידי Ἰαδδαῖος **114** 5 *n.*

L. 2. שמעון Like מרתי, a Jewish name. These persons prob. belonged to the Jewish colony in Palmyra, or were related to Jewish families there. שריכו See **119** 1 *n.*

L. 3. מלחת Perhaps = Arab. مَلُحَتْ *she was pleasant*, instead of the usual שפר; cf. the Arab. pr. n. مُلَيحة (Nöld. 106). But the omission of לַהּ (the prep. always follows שפר) makes this explanation doubtful.

121. Vog. **15.** A.D. 242–3. **Plate VIII.**

1 צלם יולים אורלים זבדלא בר מלכו בר מלכו
2 נשום די הוא אסטרטג לקלניא במיתויתא די
3 אלהא אלכסנדרוס קסר ושמש כדי הוא תנן
4 ק[ר]ספינוס הינמונא וכדי אתי לכא ית לגיניא
5 זבנן סגיאן והוא רב שוק וחסך רזאין שגיאן
6 ודבר עמרה שכיתית מטלכות סהד לה ירחבול
7 אלהא ואף יולים ≡≡≡ די ספא ורחים מרתא
8 אקים לה בולא ודמוס ליקרה שנת ע ב— 33 ב— ////

Ἡ βουλὴ καὶ ὁ δῆμος Ἰούλιον Αὐρήλιον Ζηνόβιον τὸν καὶ Ζαβδίλαν δὶς Μάλχου τοῦ Νασσούμου στρατηγήσαντα ἐν ἐπιδημίᾳ θεοῦ Ἀλεξάνδρου καὶ ὑπηρετήσαντα παρουσίᾳ διηνεκεῖ Ῥουτιλλίου Κρισπείνου τοῦ ἡγησαμένου καὶ ταῖς ἐπιδημησάσαις οὐηξιλλατίοσιν ἀγορανομήσαντά τε καὶ οὐκ ὀλίγων ἀφειδήσαντα χρημάτων καὶ καλῶς πολειτευσάμενον ὡς διὰ ταῦτα μαρτυρηθῆναι ὑπὸ θεοῦ Ἰαριβώλου καὶ ὑπὸ Ἰουλίου ═══ τοῦ ἐξοχωτάτου ἐπάρχου τοῦ ἱεροῦ πραιτωρίου καὶ τῆς πατρίδος τὸν φιλόπατριν τειμῆς χάριν ἔτους δνφ'. Wadd. 2598.

Statue of Julius Aurelius Zabd-ilâ, son of Mâliku, son of Malikû, [2] (son of) Nassûm, who was *stratēgos* of the Colony at the coming [3] of the divine Alexander Caesar; and he served when [4] C[r]ispinus the governor was here, and when he brought hither the legions [5] many times; and he was chief of the market, and spent money in a most generous manner; [6] and he led his life peaceably (?); on this account the god Yarḥi-bôl has borne witness to him, [7] and also Julius ———, who fosters and loves the city: [8] the Council and People have set (this) up to him, to his honour. The year 554.

L. 1. זבדלא 114 5 *n.* The *stratēgos* had another name beside this, Zenobios (Gk. text); cf. 128. Here and in 128. 127 all three *stratēgoi* are called Jul. Aurelius in addition to their native names; the emperors [Aurelius] Antoninus Pius and M. Aurelius no doubt made these names popular.

L. 2. אסטרטג One of the chief civil magistrates. Another title for the executive officials of the municipality was ארכניא 147 i 2 ἄρχοντες; both were equivalent to the Rom. *duumviri* (Cagnat *Cours d'épigr. lat.*[2] 150); contrast the Nab. אסרתגא 96 2 *n.* קלניא 127 4. At what period Palmyra received the Jus Italicum and the title of Colonia is not known; probably it was under Hadrian, when he visited the city in 130–1 A. D. (see p. 263). במיתויתא An infin. noun, of the form مَفْعُولَة (see Barth *Nominalb.* 257), from אתא, i. e. מִיתוּיְתָא = Pal. Syr. ܡܐܬܝܘܬܐ *adventus* Mt. 24 3: Pesh. ܡܐܬܝܬܗ.

L. 3. אלהא = the title *divus*, given to the emperor after his death; cf. 95 1 *n.* 122 3. אלכסנדרוס i. e. Severus Alexander 222–235 A. D. He stayed at Palmyra prob. in 230–1 A. D., during the indecisive campaign against the Persians under Ardashir or Artaxerxes; see Mommsen *Provinces* ii 90. שמש Pa. 128 3. תנן = Syr. ܬܢܢ; cf. תנה תנה 68 5.

L. 4. הינמונא 147 ii b 15. 24 = ἡγεμών i. e. praeses provinciae. אתי i. e. אַתִּי, Targ. O. Gen. 39 14 אַיְתִי, Af. of אתא. לבא = Pal. Syr. ܚܣܐ. ית The old accus. particle is not found in Palm. elsewhere.

In this dialect the object is usually not marked by any sign, though ל occasionally appears, e. g. עַל יברך לבני חלא Vog. 132.

L. 5. זבנן סניאן i. e. זְבְנִן סַנְיָאן, cf. זְבְנִין שַׁגִּין 147 i 6; ז׳ is the plur. of זְבַנְתָּא (= זבנתא), Syr. ܙܒܢܐ, ܐܙܒܢ fem. *time*; Reckendorf *ZDMG* xlii 394 *n*. Palm., Syr., Mand. (זיבנא) use the form with ב, other Aram. dialects have מ, e. g. זמנין in Nab. 98 6 *n*. Note the form שניאן in this line; see p. 264, and cf. 148 a. 13. רב שוק ἀγορανομήσαντα, i. e. praepositus annonae. שוק = *street*, O.T. and Targ.; then *broad place, market*, Talm. וחסך רזאן ש׳ οὐκ ὀλίγων ἀφειδήσαντα χρημάτων, lit. 'he spared (others from) many expenses'; for חסך Pa. see 115 3 *n*. Vog. gives רזאן = וזין 123 5, accepted doubtfully by Nöld. 97. Mordtm., however, reads רזאן, which may be derived from رزأ *to make a person poorer in something* (two accus.); hence مُرَزَّأ *one who has been reduced*, i. e. by his generosity, so *generous*, and רזאן δαπαναλ. In the S. Arab. inscrr. from Ma'rib רזא has the sense of *bestow, expend* (Lidzb. *Eph*. i 239).

L. 6. ודבר עמרה שכיתית καὶ καλῶς πολιτευσάμενον. For דבר ע׳ (Pa.) cf. the Syr. ܠܡܕܒܪܘ ܕܟܝܐ ܠܡܥܡܪܗ *to lead a pure life* (Cureton *Spic. Syr.* ܡܐ 21), no doubt a rendering of the Gk. idiom βίον ἄγειν, *vitam agere*. עמרה *his life*=the Syr. ܡܥܡܪܐ *victus, modus vitae*, from ܥܡܪ *habitavit*. Mordtm. reads עמרהי זכיכית *his life purely*; but except in the case of אבוהי, אחוהי, חיוהי, בנוהי, עלוהי, the 3 sing. mas. suff. in Palm. ends in ה—; and as he allows that the letters יי look like ש in his squeeze, we may read עמרה שְׁכִיתִית, or ע׳ שְׁכִ׳ (Nöld. 103). The Syr. ܫܟܐ *quievit* (cf. Hebr. שקט) would give the rendering *quietly* for שכ׳; but the expression is jejune, and the reading שְׁפִירָיִת καλῶς is more likely to be right: Reckendorf l. c. 395 *n*. 1. Note the Syr. adverbial ending *âîth*, p. 264. מטלכות i.e. מְטֻל כְּוָת 147 i 6 *on that account*. The combination is not found in other Aram. dialects; but מטל is common in Syr. and Pal. Aram., cf. מטול ד, מ׳ כן *because* Targ. Ps.-Jon. Lev. 8 15; כְּוָת is also used in Pal. Aram. for *according, as* (Dalm. *Gr*. 178), cf. Nab. 81 8 (*accordingly*) and Syr. ܐܟܘܬ, ܟܘܬ. ירחבול Cf. θεῷ μεγίστῳ Ἰεραβ[ώ]λῳ in an inscr. from Egypt (Coptos), Cl.-Gan. *Rec*. ii 118. The god's approval was perhaps conveyed by an oracle; cf. ἐπιμελητὴς αἱρεθεὶς Ἔφκας πηγῆς ὑπὸ Ἰαριβώλου τοῦ θεοῦ Wadd. 2571 c. The name of the deity is composite, like עגלבול, מלכבל, and the first part of it suggests a moon-god (ירח); but what evidence there is implies a sun-god, e. g. CIL iii 1108 Deo soli Hierobolo &c., and ירחי = Ἡλιόδωρος p. 301 *n*. 1; J. Mordtmann *Palmyren*. 44 f. Further light on the subject may be expected from a Palm. inscr.

discovered at Ḥomṣ, not as yet published; *RB* xi 410 *n.* 7. Cf. the pr. n. ירחבולא 111 3 *n.*

L. 7. Both in the Palm. and Gk. texts a name has been erased after *Julius*; it was prob. *Philippus*, i.e. Jul. Philip, an Arabian from the Trachonitis, who was praefectus praetorio = ἔπαρχος τοῦ ἱεροῦ πραιτωρίου (Gk. text) in A. D. 242–3, the year of this inscription. He instigated the murder of Gordian iii, and succeeded him as emperor (A. D. 244–249). ספא i.e. סָפֵא ptcp. lit. *gives to eat, nourishes*; cf. Targ. Ps.-Jon. Num. 11 18 מַן יְסַפִּינָנָא בִּישְׂרָא 'who will give us flesh to eat?' מרתא So Mordtm., rather than מרתה *his city*; elsewhere the form is מריתא. Cf. ורקתא 131 1.

L. 8. אקים Prob. plur., 113 3 *n.*

122. Vog. 16. A. D. 131.

1 [בולא ודמס עבדו צלמא דנה למלא הגרפא]
2 בר ירחי [לשמש?] רעי די הוא גרמטוס די תרתיא
3 וכדי את[א תנן] הדרינס אלהא יהב משחא
4 לבני מד[יתא ול]אסטרטו[יא] ולאכסניא די א[ת]א
5 עמה . . . . . [מש]ריתה בכל מדען ובנא הכלא
6 ופרנאי . . [ותצב]יתה כלה מן כיסה לבעל שמ[ן]
7 ולדר . . . . ה ד . . . . . מן בני ידיעבל
8 ב[ירח] . . . ן שנת [////] ק 33 //

[Ἡ βουλὴ καὶ] ὁ δῆμος Μαλῆν τὸν καὶ Ἀγρίππαν Ἰαραίου καὶ Ῥααίου γραμματέα γενόμενον τὸ δεύτερον ἐπιδημίᾳ θεοῦ Ἀδριανοῦ ἄλιμμα παρασχόντα ξένοις τε καὶ πολείταις ἐν πᾶσιν ὑπηρετήσαντα τῇ τε τῶν στρατευμάτων ὑπο[δοχ]ῇ καὶ τὸν ναὸν τὸν [τοῦ Ἡ]λίου σὺν τῷ . . . ναιω . . . [καὶ τ]αῖς ἄλλα[ις] . . . το . . . Wadd. 2585.

[The Council and People have made this statue to Malē Agrippa], [2] son of Yarḥai, (son of) [Lishamsh?] Ra'ai, who was secretary for a second time; [3] and when the divine

Hadrian ca[me here], he gave oil [4] to the people of the ci[ty and to] the *strator*[*es*] and to the strangers who ca[m]e [5] with him . . . his [ca]mp with everything. And he built the temple [6] and . . . [and its decor]ation, all of it, at his own expense, to Ba'al-sham[in] [7] and to . . . . of the Benê Yedî'a-bel. [8] In [the month] . . . the year [4]42.

The above text is based upon the restoration of Cl.-Gan. *Ét.* ii § 9; cf. Mordtm. 22 ff., J. Mordtmann *Palmyren.* 19 50.

L. 2. ירחי An abbreviation of ירחבולא 111 3. לשמש The ל is barely visible; cf. 117 3 *n.* גרמטוס γραμματεύς 147 i 2 = the Rom. title *scriba*. The Palm. ו = Gk. ευ, as in סלוקוס 123. בילומא 124. די תרתיא = Syr. ܕܬܪ̈ܬܝܐ, emph. form of ܬܪ̈ܬܝܢ; the form actually met with in Syr. is ܕܬܪ̈ܬܝܬܐ, Hexapl. Is. 61 7. Jer. 33 1 &c. ܕܬܪܬܝܬܐ ܨܡ (Nöld. 102 and *Syr. Gr.* 96).

L. 3. וכדי וגו' See 121 2 f.

L. 4. בני מדיתא Cf. בני שירתא 118 3 *n.* אסטרטור[יא] = *stratores*, 'equerries,' Cl.-Gan.; אסטרטו[מא] = στράτευμα, G. Hoffmann; אסטרטו[יא] = στρατιῶται, Vog. אכסניא = ξένοι, formed with the adjectival ending *āi* from ξένος. א[ת]א Plur., like אקים 113 3.

L. 5. After עמה Cl.-Gan. reads [ופרנס מש]ריתה *and supplied his camp* (see 132 3 *n.*); cf. the Gk. ὑπηρετήσαντα τῇ τε τῶν στρατευμάτων ὑποδοχῇ. For משריתה cf. 96 4. בכל מרען ἐν πᾶσιν. מִרְעָן = מרעם 147 i 8. 11 &c. = מנרעם 75 2 *n.* חכלא 147 i 10 היכלא.

L. 6. ופרנאי So Cl.-Gan., admitting that the ר may be ד, and that the י is indistinct. The Gk. fragment . . . ναιω he restores [προ]ναίῳ, and the Palm., פרנאיסה or פרנאינה *its pronaos* or *vestibule*. ותצביתה 119 4. לבעל שמן The Gk. text of Wadd. given above is to be corrected τὸν [τοῦ] Διὸς σὺν τῷ κ.τ.λ. The reading לבעל שמן, adopted by Cl.-Gan. and J. Mordtm., is conjectural; Lidzb. prefers לבריך שמה *Eph.* i 257 *n.*

L. 8. The month may be [ניס]ן Vog.

123. Vog. 17. A.D. 254.

1 בולא ודמוס ליולים אורלים

2 ענא די מתקרא סלוקוס בר

3 עזיזו עזיזו שאילא די שמש ושפר

4 להון באסטרטגותה ומגד לבולא

5 זוזין רבו ליקרה בירח תשרי שנת

6 σ / y 333 ⸺ y σ

Ἡ β[ουλὴ καὶ ὁ δῆμος Ἰ]ούλιον Αὐρή[λιον Ὄγγαν τὸν καὶ] Σέλευκον [δὶς τοῦ Ἀζίζο]υ τοῦ Σεειλᾶ δυα[νδρικὸν φιλοτεί]μως στρατ[ηγήσαντα κ]αὶ μαρτυρηθέν[τα καὶ φιλ]οτειμησάμεν[ον τῇ αὐτῇ] κρατίστῃ βουλῇ Ἀτ[τικὰς] μυρίας τειμῆς ἕνεκεν ἔτους ϛξφ′ Ὑπερβερεταίῳ. Wadd. 2601.

The Council and People to Julius Aurelius [2] 'Ogga, who is called Seleukus, son [3] of 'Azîzu, (son of) 'Azîzu, (son of) She'eilâ, who served and was well-pleasing [4] to them in his office of *stratēgos*; and he presented to the Council [5] ten thousand drachmae: to his honour. In the month Tishri, the year 566.

L. 2. ענא Prob. an abbreviation of ענלבולא (Lidzb.), as ירחי from ירחבולא. די מחקרא 102 2. סלוקוס For the additional name see **121** 1 *n*., and cf. **122** 2 *n*.

L. 3. עזיזו = عَزِيز *strong*. The name is found in Egypt. Aram. CIS ii 136, in Nab. ib. 311 B, in late Hebr. עזיזא Ezr. 10 27, and elsewhere in Palm. In the inscr. given on p. 295 עזיזו is the name of a god = Ares. שאילא Σεειλᾶ, with the consonantal value of א preserved; contrast the Talm. שילא (Dalm. *Gr.* 124) and the Syr. ܫܝܠܐ = Σίλας (i. e. שאילא) Acts 15 22. The meaning is the same as that of the O.T. שָׁאוּל. שמש **121** 3.

L. 4. מגד See **112** 3 *n*.

L. 5. זוזין = drachmae, Ἀττικάς (Gk. text). The drachm was a quarter of a shekel in Jewish money; thus 1 Sam. 9 8 רבע שקל כסף is rendered by the Targ. וזוא חדא דכספא. The Attic drachm was the universal silver unit in the East; after the Roman conquest it was adopted as practically equivalent to the Roman denarius, hence in Josephus δραχμὴ Ἀττική or Ἀτθίς always = denarius. The value of the drachm-denarius was about $9\frac{1}{2}$*d*. תשרי Ὑπερβερεταῖος = Sept.–Oct., the 7th month.

124. Vog. 20. A.D. 258–9.

1 לאורליס ורוד הפקא
2 ובילוטא תדמריא עבד
3 בלעקב בר חרשא ליקרה
4 שנת ע 333

Αὐρήλιον Οὐορώδην ἱππικὸν καὶ βουλευτὴν Παλμυρηνὸν Βηλάκαβος Ἁρσᾶ τὸν φίλον τειμῆς χάριν ἔτους οφʹ. Wadd. 2604.

To Aurelius Worod, knight [2] and councillor, of Tadmor, made by [3] Bel-ʻaqab, son of Ḥarshâ, to his honour. [4] The year 570.

L. 1. ורוד **127** &c., a name of Persian origin, borne by several Arsacid kings. הפקא Here with an Aram. ending, in **129** 3 הפיקס ἱππικός. For the ending א׳ = ος cf. הפטיקא **126**. סנקלטיקא **125**. אפטרפא **127**.

L. 2. בילוטא *βουλευτής*, cf. **122** 2 *n.* תדמריא Adj. sing.; the plur. has the same form, see Rom. 2 on p. 268, l. 3. The vowel in the second syll. was *ō*, e.g. תדמור **125**; the Arab. تَدْمُر, however, has preserved what was prob. the original pronunciation.

L. 3. בלעקב **140** B 8 probably *Bel follows* (? ptcp.); this is the meaning of עקב both in Arab. and Syr. The name occurs in a Gk. inscr. from Coptos, Βηλάκαβος (as here), Cl.-Gan. *Rec.* ii 118; cf. עתעקב Vog. 32 &c. חרשא Ἁρσᾶ = ܚܪܫܐ *enchantment.*

125. Vog. 22. A.D. 251.

1 צלמא דנה די ספטמיוס חירן בר
2 אדינת סנקלטיקא נהירא ורש
3 תדמור די אקים לה אורליס
4 פלינוס בר מריא פלינא רעי פלחא
5 דבלגיונא די בצרא ליקרה בירח
6 תשרי די שנת ע 333 ///

Σεπτίμιον Αἱράνην ’Οδαινάθου *τὸν λαμπρότατον συν-κλητικὸν ἔξα[ρχον* Παλμυ]ρηνῶν Αὐρήλι[ος Φίλινο]ς [Μα]ρ. ‘Ηλιοδώρου . . . . . *στρατιώτης* λεγ[εῶνος Κυρηνα]ϊκῆς *τὸν πάτρωνα τειμῆς καὶ εὐχαριστίας χάριν ἔτους γξφ'*.

This statue is that of Septimius Ḥairân, son [2] of Odainath, the illustrious senator and chief [3] of Tadmor, which has been set up to him by Aurelius [4] Philinus, son of Marius Philinus, (son of) Ra'ai, the soldier [5] who was in the legion of Bostra: to his honour. In the month [6] Tishri of the year 563.

L. 1. ספטמיוס חירן was at this time the head of the house of Odainath, the leading family of Palmyra, which by the 3rd cent. had acquired almost the position of a reigning dynasty; see p. 264. This Sept. Ḥairân appears to have been the first of his race to receive the title of *Ras* l. 2, in addition to his Roman rank as a senator. He was the son of Odainath the senator [1]; and though the relationship is nowhere stated, it is prob. that he was the father of the famous Sept. Odainath (126), the grandson bearing the same name (see footnote) as the grandfather according to Palmyrene custom. Vogüé suggests that the name Septimius was given to the family by the Emperor Sept. Severus (193–211 A.D.), in recognition of their services during the Parthian wars; it was also borne by Sept. Worod (127), who was probably connected with the family of Odainath by alliance or otherwise; cf. 129 3. 130 2.

L. 2. אדינת Cf. the Arab. diminutive أُذَيْنَةٌ *a little ear.* סנקלטיקא = *συγκλητικός of senatorial rank.* נהירא *λαμπρότατος* = clarissimus, a title which went with the dignity of senator; see Cagnat l.c. 89. 131. ריש *Head* i.e. prince; Arab. رَأْسٌ, Syr. ܪܫܐ, in the same sense; cf. רשה 1 20.

L. 4. רעי 122 2 ‘Ραaίου. The Gk. here gives ‘Ηλιοδώρου. פלחא = *στρατιώτης*, from פלח *work, serve*; cf. פלחה 75 4 *worshipper*.

L. 5. דבלגיונא So Mordtm., as there is no diacritic point over the first letter. Vog.'s reading רב לגיונא is, moreover, inconsistent with the Gk.: the donor is merely *στρατιώτης*. For ד in Palm. cf. דנבת for רבנת Vog. 71. דענה 83 a 3 (corr.). 105 3. דשנת 18. The legion stationed at Bostra was the iii Cyrenaic; hence the restoration of the Gk. text. בצרא The capital of the Province of Arabia; 100 *n*.

[1] Vog. 21: קברא דנה בנא אדינת סקלטיקא בר חירן והבלת נצור לה ולבנוה[י] ולבנאבנוהי לעלמא. The Gk. has Τὸ *μνημεῖον* . . *ἔκτισεν* . . *Σεπτίμιος* ’Οδαίναθος ὁ *λαμπρότατος συνκλητικὸς κ.τ.λ.*

126. Vog. 23. A.D. 258.

1 צלם ספטמיום אדינת
2 נהירא הפטיקא מרן די
3 אקים לה תגמא די קיניא
4 עברא דהבא וכספא ליקרה
5 בירח ניסן די שנת y — 333 y ////

Σεπ[τίμιον 'Οδαίναθον] τὸν λαμ[πρότατον ὑπατικ]ὸν συντέ[λεια τῶν χρυσοχ]όων καὶ ἀργ[υροκόπων τ]ὸν δεσπότην τειμῆς χάριν [ἔτ]ους θξφ' μηνεὶ Ξανδικῷ. Wadd. 2602.

Statue of Septimius Odainath, [2] the illustrious consul, our lord, which [3] has been set up to him by the guild of smiths [4] who work in gold and silver: to his honour. [5] In the month Nisan of the year 569.

L. 1. ס' ארינת 125 1 *n.* 130. The famous prince under whom Palmyra reached the summit of its fortunes (p. 263). He came to the front by the effective aid which he gave to the Romans in the Persian wars, especially in the defeat of the Persian king Sapor. After this event, during the rivalries for the purple, he took the side of Gallienus, and to the end, whatever his ultimate intentions may have been, maintained his allegiance when the latter became emperor. Gallienus, much engaged in the affairs of the West, practically left the East to the government of Odainath, who became, 'not indeed joint-ruler, but independent lieutenant of the emperor for the East' (Mommsen *Provinces* ii 103); see 130 1 *n.* In the local administration of Palmyra Sept. Worod (127 ff.) acted as his viceroy and imperial procurator; while Odainath himself, by a series of brilliant victories over the Persians, succeeded in re-establishing the frontiers and prestige of the Eastern empire, A.D. 264–5. He was assassinated in A.D. 266–7 at Hemesa[1]. His authority passed to his wife Zenobia

[1] His eldest son Herodes; 'non Zenobia matre, sed priore uxore genitus' (Treb. Pollio *Trig. Tyr.* § 16), was killed at the same time. The same authority states that Odainath left two sons by Zenobia, besides Wahb-allath, Harennianus and Timolaus. The statement is open to question; other authorities know of only one son, who succeeded his father. Mommsen l. c. 106 *n.*

(181) and their son Wahb-allath, who endeavoured not merely to maintain but to surpass the extensive powers held by Odainath.

L. 2. נהירא הפטיקא *λαμπρότατος ὑπατικός*=vir clarissimus consularis. At this period, and up to the time of Diocletian, the title denoted not the office of consul but the consular rank. Note the progression of dignities in the family (p. 264). מרן 130 4 *δεσπότης*. The name does not necessarily imply a *king* or *ruler*, because in 128 it is given to a procurator (Sept. Worod); cf. מרתחון 181 4 *τὴν δέσποιναν*, of Zenobia.

L. 3. תגמא=*τάγμα*, Syr. ܛܰܓܡܳܐ *ordo*; here the Gk. equivalent is *συντέλεια*. קיניא i. e. קִינַיָּא plur.

L. 4. עברא i. e. עָבְדֵי̇א ptcp. plur. constr. For the ending see חגרא 118 3 *n.*

127. Vog. 24. A. D. 263.

ספטמיס וורוד קרטסטס אפטרפא
דוקנרא די אקים ליקרה
יוליס או[ר]ליס נבובד בר שעדו חירא
אסטרגא די קלניא רחמה
שנת ע ⊃— 333 ⊃— //// בירח כסלול

Σεπτί[μιον Οὐορώδην τὸ]ν κράτιστον ἐπίτροπ[ον Σεβαστοῦ δ]ουκηνάριον Ἰούλιος Αὐρή[λιος Νεβό]βαδος Σοάδου τοῦ Αἱ[ρᾶ] *στρατηγὸς τῆς λαμπροτάτης κολωνείας [τ]ὸν ἑαυτοῦ φίλον τειμῆς ἕνεκεν ἔτους δοφʹ μηνεὶ Ἀπελλαίῳ.* Wadd. 2607.

Septimius Worod, most excellent *procurator* [2] *ducenarius*, which has been set up to his honour [3] by Julius Au[r]elius Nebu-bad, son of So'adu, (son of) Ḥairâ, [4] *stratēgos* of the Colony, his friend. [5] The year 574, in the month Kislul.

L. 1. ספטמיס וורוד 128. 129. The inscrr. and statues dedicated to his honour show that he was one of the most distinguished citizens of Palmyra at the time of its greatest prosperity, in position next to the prince himself. He held an imperial office under the emperor Gallienus (128 2 f.), as well as the highest local dignities. A Gk.

inscr. (Wadd. 2606 a) mentions that he was the chief of a caravan and defrayed the cost of the return journey, and *agoranomos* (**121** 5 *n.*), and *stratēgos* i. e. chief magistrate, and president of the banquets of Bel (*συμποσίαρχον τῶν . . . Διὸς Βήλου ἱερέων*). He was viceroy, *argapetes* (**129** 2 *n.* **126** 1 *n.*), of Odainath. The inscrr. say nothing about his family; the name ספטמיס may indicate an alliance with the reigning house (**125** 1 *n.*), while ורוד (**124** 1 *n.*) perhaps points to a Persian or Armenian origin (Vog.). אפטרפא ד׳=*ἐπίτροπος δουκηνάριος*, procurator of the second class (ducenarius), an imperial revenue officer.

L. 3. נבובר Prob. contracted from נבו עבר; J. Mordtm. would read נבחבר **184** 2. In Palm. the god Nebo is met with only in pr. nn., e.g. זבדנבו **188** 1. ברנבו **184** 2; in Aram. pr. nn. it is frequent, e.g. נרנבו CIS ii 139 B, 2. נבוסרדן=Assyr. *Nabû-šar-iddin* ib. 29. שעדו See **106** *n.* חירא An Arab. name, cf. חירן **110** 2.

L. 4. רחמה i. e. רָחֲמֵהּ lit. *his lover*, **129** 5. **140** B 8.

L. 5. כסלול 'Απελλαῖος=Jewish כסלו, the 9th month, Nov.–Dec.

128. Vog. **25.** A.D. 263.

1 צלמא דנה די ספטמיוס
2 ורוד אפטרפא דוקנרא די
3 קסר מרן די אקים לה
4 בולא ודמוס ליקרה
5 בירח ניסן די שנת ע 𐡿 333 𐡿 ////

'Η *βουλὴ καὶ ὁ δῆμος Σεπτίμιον* [Ο]*ὐορώδην τὸν κράτιστον ἐπί*[*τρ*]*οπον* [*Σεβ*]*αστο*[*ῦ τοῦ κυρίου*] *δουκη*[*νά*-*ριον . . . . τειμῆς χ*]*άριν* [*ἔτους δοφ' μηνὶ Ξ*]*αν*[*δικῷ*]. Wadd. 2606.

This statue is that of Septimius [2] Worod, *procurator ducenarius* of [3] Caesar, our lord, which has been set up to him by [4] the Council and People: to his honour. [5] In the month Nisan of the year 574.

See on **127**.

L. 3. קסר i. e. Gallienus. The official in Lat. inscrr. is called procurator Augusti. מרן See **126** 2 *n.*

129. Vog. **26.** A. D. 264.

ספטמיוס ורוד קרטסטוס אפטרפא
דקנרא וארגבטא אקים יולים
אורלים ספטמיוס ידא הפקוס
בר אלכס[נד]רוס חירן סריכו ליקר
רחמה וקיומה בירח סיון די
שנת y⊃333⊃y

Σεπτίμιο[ν] Οὐορώδην *τὸν κράτιστον ἐπίτροπον Σεβαστοῦ δουκηνάριον καὶ ἀργαπέτην* Ἰούλιος Αὐρήλιος *Σεπτίμιος* Ἰάδης *ἱππικὸς Σεπτιμίου* Ἀλεξάνδρου *τοῦ* Ἡρώδου *ἀπὸ στρατιῶν τὸν φίλον καὶ προστάτην τειμῆς ἕνεκεν ἔτους εοφʹ μηνεὶ Ξανδικῷ.* Wadd. 2610.

Septimius Worod, most excellent *procurator* [2] *ducenarius* and commandant, (this statue) has been set up to him by Julius [3] Aurelius Septimius Yadē, knight, [4] son of Alexander Ḥairân, (son of) Soraiku, to the honour [5] of his friend and patron. In the month Sivan of [6] the year 575.

L. 2. ארגבטא *ἀργαπέτης*, a Persian word, compounded of *arg* ارگ 'fortress' and *bed* بذ 'lord' or 'chief,' hence 'commander of a fortress.' The title is actually found in Persian at this period (Nöld. 107); in the Targ. it appears as ארקבטא 2 Chr. 28 7; in Wadd. 2606 a it seems to be paraphrased by *δικαιοδότης τῆς μητροκολωνίας*. The office was an exceptional one in this case, owing to the unique position of Odainath as practically emperor of the East. A deputy became necessary for the local administration of Palmyra; hence the military command of the city as well as the chief civil authority was committed to Sept. Worod.

L. 3. ידא **120** 1 *n*. הפקוס Cf. הפקא **124** 1 *n*.

L. 4. סריכו Cf. שריכו **119** 1 *n*.

L. 5. קיומה A verbal noun of the form פְּעוּל, Syr. ܩܝܘܡܐ, lit. *one who stands up* (to protect &c.)=the Lat. patronus, Gk. *προστάτης*. In the Pesh. it occurs in the sense of *prefect*, e. g. 1 K. 4 5. 7; in 3 Esdr. 2 12 ܩܝܘܡܐ ܕܝܗܘܕ = *ὁ προστάτης τῆς* Ἰουδαίας. סיון The 3rd month, May–June. The Gk. text gives *Ξανδικός* i. e. ניסן, April.

180. Vog. 28. A.D. 271.

1 צלם ספטמיום אדי[נת] מלך מלכא

2 ומתקננא די מדיתא כלה ספטמיא

3 זבדא רב חילא רבא חבי רב חילא

4 די תדמור קרטסטא אקים למרהון

5 בירח אב די שנת ע — 3333 //

Statue of Septimius Odai[nath], king of kings, [2] and restorer of the whole city. The Septimii, [3] Zabdâ, general in chief, and Zabbai, general [4] of Tadmor, the most excellent, have set (it) up to their lord. [5] In the month Ab of the year 582.

L. 1. ס׳ אדינת See 126 1 *n.* מלך מַלְכַּא 113 3 *n.* is an oriental title borrowed from the Persian kings, 71 3 *n.* There is no evidence that it was adopted by Odainath himself; this inscr. was not erected till after his death, at a time when his generals were organizing a revolt against Rome[1]. It is perhaps not without significance that there is no Gk. version of this inscr.; the Romans would scarcely have allowed Od. to be called 'king of kings' had the title been publicly exhibited in a language which they could understand. That Od. assumed the title of king is not unlikely (*Hist. Aug.* xxiv 15 2 adsumpto nomine regali); but that he ever usurped the name of *Augustus*, or received it from the emperor as Treb. Pollio asserts[2], is not borne out by the evidence. As a reward for his distinguished services Od. received from Gallienus the title of *αὐτοκράτωρ* or *imperator* in 264 A.D., a dignity which no doubt implies a position beyond that of a governor or vassal-king; it was probably this which gave rise to Pollio's statement. The absence of *Augustus* from the coins of Od., and the designation *vir consularis*, *ὑπατικός* (126 2), only possible for a subject, are sufficient, in Mommsen's opinion, to prove that the assumption of the imperial title is imaginary. After the death of Od., Zenobia is called *βασίλισσα*, and her son Wahab-allath governed Egypt under Claudius with the title *βασιλεύς*. In 270 A.D. his coins

[1] A Gk. inscr. lately found at Palmyra is dedicated [βασ]ι[λ]εῖ [βα]σιλέων, and may refer to Od.; but the text is too fragmentary to justify definite conclusions. Cl.-Gan.'s reconstructions in *Rec.* iii § 36 can hardly be supported; see 126 1 footnote.

[2] *Vit. Gallieni* 10 Odenatus rex Palmyrenorum optinuit totius Orientis imperium. Ib. 12 Gallienus Odenatum participato imperio Augustum vocavit.

display *v(ir) c(onsularis) R(omanorum) im(perator) d(ux) R(omanorum)*, and his head appears beside Aurelian; in an inscr. from Byblus (CIG 4503 b, Vog. p. 32) Aurelian and Zenobia are mentioned together as *Σεβαστός* and *Σεβαστή* [1]. Then, during the year 270–1, the breach with Rome becomes apparent. In Palmyra Zenobia is still *βασίλισσα* (181 = Wadd. 2611, cf. 2628 [2]), but in distant quarters, as in Egypt, both she and her son claim the dignity of *Augustus*; Wahab-allath (5th year) begins to issue coins, struck in Alexandria, without the head of Aurelian and bearing the imperial title, and Zenobia's coins bear the same. The assumption marked a definite rejection of all allegiance to Rome; it was strenuously avenged by Aurelian, the true Augustus, in 273. See Mordtm. 26; Mommsen *Prov.* ii 103 f. *n.*; Cl.-Gan. *Rec.* iii § 28; Bury's Gibbon i Appendix 18. 19.

L. 2. מתקננא A verbal noun formed from Pael ptcp. of תקן *make straight, establish*, with the ending *ān*, i. e. מְתַקְּנָנָא. It is the equivalent of *κτίστης*, a title used by the Arsacid kings; in Syr. ܡܬܩܢܢܐ is used in the same sense, and of God as *conditor, stabilitor*. Cl.-Gan. (l. c.) proposes to make the whole title מ׳ די מדיתא כלה = the technical *corrector totius provinciae*. מ׳ may well mean *corrector*, but Roman titles are avoided in this inscr., and native ones ostentatiously substituted. ספטמיא *Σεπτίμιοι*, in 181 ספטמיוא, with the Gk. plur. ending, cf. קרטסטוא 181. Perhaps they were related to the family of Odainath, 125 1 *n.*

L. 3. Cf. 181 2 f. זבדא *Ζάβδας*, like זבי *Ζαββαῖος* and זבדי 133 1, is abbreviated from some name beginning with זבד, cf. זבדלא for זבד אלא; see 114 5 *n.* זַבַּי occurs in the O. T., Ezr. 10 28. Neh. 3 20; cf. בתזבי 181 1.

L. 4. קרטסטא Plur., referring to the two generals; either for קרטסטוא, or a plur. in אֵ֫—, like מלכא l. 1. אקיטו = אקים 118 3 *n.*

L. 5. אב i. e. July–August; 181 4.

181. Vog. 29. A.D. 271.

1 צלמת ספטמיא בתזבי נהירתא וחדקתא
2 מלכתא ספטמיוא זבדא רב חילא
3 רבא וזבי רב חילא די תדמור קרטסטוא
4 אקים למרתהון בירח אב די שנת ע 3333 //

[1] This may have been allowed to pass, for *Augusta* was an honorary title, while *Augustus* belonged to an office.

[2] Διὶ ὑψίστῳ καὶ ἐπηκόῳ ἡ πόλις ὑπὲρ σωτηρίας Σεπτιμίας Ζηνοβίας τῆς λαμπροτάτης βασιλίσσης μητρὸς τοῦ λαμπροτάτου βασιλέως Οὐαβαλλάθου Ἀθηνοδώρου.

Σεπτιμίαν Ζηνοβίαν τὴν λαμπροτάτην εὐσεβῆ βασίλισσαν Σεπτίμιοι Ζάβδας ὁ μέγας στρατηλάτης καὶ Ζαββαῖος ὁ ἐνθάδε στρατηλάτης οἱ κράτιστοι τὴν δέσποιναν ἔτους βπφ' μηνεὶ Λώῳ. Wadd. 2611.

Statue of Septimia Bath-zabbai, the illustrious and the pious, [2] the queen. The Septimii, Zabdâ, general [3] in chief, and Zabbai, general of Tadmor, the most excellent, [4] have set (it) up to their mistress. In the month Ab of the year 582.

L. 1. צלמת 120 1 *n.* בתזבי For the form cf. בתעבידה Vog. 84, בתחנא, בתחתב &c.; for זבי see 130 3 *n.* The queen is better known by her Gk. name *Ζηνοβία*, which perhaps marks relationship with *Ζηνοβίος*; several persons of this name are mentioned in the inscriptions. נהירתא ח' = *clarissima pia*; see 125 2 *n.* זרקתא = צְדִיקְתָא; for the omission of י cf. מרתא 121 7: here perhaps the *i* was pronounced short in a shut syllable. The final א can be faintly traced on the stone.

L. 2. After the death of Odainath in 266–7 Zenobia succeeded to his position, and practically governed the state on behalf of her young son Wahab-allath = Athenodōrus (p. 291 *n.* 2). Not content with pursuing her husband's policy, she determined to make Palmyra mistress of the Eastern empire; see 130 1 *n.* Under her general Zabdas, the Palmyrenes possessed themselves of Egypt in 270, garrisons were pushed even into the W. of Asia Minor, and Zenobia still professed to be acting in concert with the Roman government. But when Aurelian became emperor (270), he detected at once the object of this aggressive policy and took strong measures to arrest it. At the end of 270 Egypt was recovered for the Empire by Probus, but not without a struggle. The Palmyrenes were now in open conflict with Rome. Towards the close of 271 Aurelian marched through Asia Minor, overthrowing Zenobia's forces in Chalcedon, and capturing Ancyra and Tyana, and passed into Syria. The main army of the Palmyrenes in vain endeavoured to check his advance at Antioch; they were driven to Hemesa (now Ḥomṣ), where a great battle was fought; again, under Zabbai and Zenobia herself, they were defeated, and compelled to fall back upon their native city. Undeterred by the 70 miles of desert, Aurelian led his army up to Palmyra and laid siege to it. In the spring of 272 the city surrendered; Zenobia and her son were captured on the banks of the Euphrates as they were flying to Persia for help; the queen was carried a prisoner to Rome to grace the conqueror's triumph. A few months later, in the autumn of 272[1], the Palmyrenes again revolted; Aurelian instantly returned, surprised the city, and without mercy destroyed it in the spring of 273.

L. 2. קרטסטיא, ססטטיא For the plur. forms see **180** 2 *n.*

L. 4. מרתותן See **126** 2 *n.*

132. Eut. 102. A.D. 21.

1 צלם חשש בר נשא בר בולחא חשש די

2 עבדו לה בני כמרא ובני מתבול מן די קם

3 ברשהון ועבד שלמא ביניהון ופרנס

4 ברמנהון בכל צבו כלה רבא וזערא

5 ליקרה בירח כנון שנת III ⊂—3—⊂ III

Μάλιχον Νεσâ τοῦ Βωλλâ τοῦ ἐπικαλουμένου Ἀσάσου φυλῆς Χομαρηνῶν Παλμυρηνῶν ὁ δῆμος εὐνοίας ἕνεκα. Wadd. 2578.

Statue of Ḥashash, son of Nesâ, son of Bôl-ḥa Ḥashash, which [2] the Benê Komâra and the Benê Mattā-bôl have made to him, because he stood up [3] at their head and made peace between them, and superintended [4] their agreement (?) in everything whatsoever, the great and the small: [5] to his honour. In the month Kanûn, the year 333.

L. 1. חשש Ἀσάσου, בני חשש Mordtm. no. 57; cf. Arab. حُسَاس *bad fortune.* The Gk. Μάλιχον = מלכו is difficult to account for; perhaps it is not correctly copied. נשא **147** i 3 prob. abbreviated from נשאל Νασαήλου Wadd. 2070 c. בולחא **144** 4 prob. = בול אחא *B. is brother* (Lidzb.), or = בול לחא *B. washes away* (*sin*), Syr. ܚܠܐ, cf. ܚܘܚܠܐ Wright *Martyrol.* 10 (*Journ. Sacr. Lit.* ser. 4, vol. 8). Cl.-Gan. rightly corrects ΚΩΜΑ in the Gk. text to ΒΩΛΛΑ, *Rec.* ii § 33.

L. 2. בני כמרא i.e. φυλὴ Χομαρηνῶν, again in Cl.-Gan. *Ét.* i 118 (inscr. G); cf. **140** A 3 and the pr. n. Χόμρου (gen.) Wadd. **2389**. The Gk. forms point to כֻּמְרָא, cf. Targ. כּוּמְרָא, Syr. ܟܘܡܪܐ *priest.*

[1] The latest inscr. is dated Aug. 272, Vog. 116.

In the Palm. text the 'בני כ are the joint donors of the statue; in the Gk. they are the tribe to which Bôl-ḥa belongs, and the dedication is made by ὁ δῆμος. Cl.-Gan. l. c. rightly renders the Gk., 'of the tribe of the Palmyrene Chomarenians'; the expression Παλμυρηνῶν ὁ δῆμος = 'the People of the Palmyrenes' is unsupported. Possibly, as Cl.-Gan. suggests, the mention of ὁ δῆμος without the usual ἡ βουλὴ καί implies that the local senate was not yet in existence; it may not have been constituted till the time of Hadrian (circ. 130 A. D.), and the grant of the *jus Italicum*. This inscr. is dated A. D. 21, and after 141 (A. D. 9) is the second oldest known. בני מתבול i. e. Μαθθαβωλίων φυλή Wadd. 2579, not named in the Gk. text; מתבול = מתן בול. בריל די = מן די 110 4 *n*.

L. 3. פרנס In Syr. ܦܪܢܣ = *administravit, aluit, curam gessit*; in the Targ. it is used for *nourish, feed*, e. g. Eze. 34 8 = רעה; cf. 122 5 *n*. The rendering given above is indefinite, owing to the uncertain sense of the following word.

L. 4. ברמתהן Evidently not Aram. It is perhaps a noun (with suff. *ân*) from the Arab. برم *twist*, in conj. iv *to twist two threads*, so *to make firm, consolidate*; thus ابرم العقد *he established the contract*. Prof. Margoliouth, in a private communication, suggests a connexion with the Persian فرمان *mandate, order* &c., 'firman,' which gives a fairly good sense: 'he administered their government.' בכל צבו כלה 110 4 &c.

L. 5. כנון The 8th month, Δῖος, Jewish מרחשון, Oct.–Nov. This inscr. was published by Euting *Sitzungsb. Berl. Akad.* (1887) 410.

VOTIVE INSCRIPTIONS

133. Eut. 4. A.D. 67.

1 עמודיא אלן חמשא ושריתהון ותטלילהון קרב זבדי בר
זבדנבו קחזן די מן בני מעזין לבעל שמן אלהא טבא
2 ושכרא על חיוהי וחיי בנוהי ואחוהי בירח אלול שנת
/// y ⊃ 333 ⊃ ///

These five pillars and their beams and their coverings Zabdai, son of Zabd-nebu, (son of) Qaḥzân, who is of the Benê Ma'ziyân, offered to Ba'al-shamin, the good ² and bountiful god, for his life and the life of his sons and his brothers; in the month Elûl, the year 378.

L. 1. שריתהון ותט׳ See 117 4. 5 *n.* קרב Cf. 70 1. 136 3. Rom. 2 (p. 268 *n.* 1). זבדי Cf. זבדא 130 3 *n.* זבדנבו 127 3 *n.* קחזן An Arab. pr. n. from قَحَزَ or قَحْزَنَ *push, strike.* מעזין The name of a tribe, in Arab. prob. مَعْزِيَان or مُعْزِيَان Nöld. ap. Eut. *SBBA* (1885) 669 ff., where this inscr. is published. לבעל שמן Elsewhere in Palm. 134, where he is called מרא עלמא, and the inscr. on p. 296 *n.* 1 = Ζεὺς μέγιστος κεραύνιος, and in 122 6 (rest.). In name and attributes the *Lord of Heaven* transcends all other deities. He was not, however, included among the national gods of Palmyra (see 112 4), or officially recognized in public documents; and though he probably had a temple there, his worshippers seem to have been few. See 9 1 *n.*

L. 2. שכרא i.e. שָׂכָרָא 140 B 4, lit. *giving reward,* Hebr. שָׂכָר *reward, wages* (שכר Pi. not used). The אלהא שכרא is a god שמשלם שכר טוב לצדיקים Talm. B. *Berakoth* 4 a, quoted by Lidzb. *Eph.* i 202; cf. the Minaean pr. n. ישכראל Hommel *Süd-ar. Chrest.* 113. 136. In the inscr. below the word is written סַכָּרַיָּא plur.[1], as סכרים for ש in Ezr. 4 5. על חיוהי ונו׳ Cf. 29 11 *n.* אלול Aug.–Sept.

[1]
1 [ל]ארצו ולעזיזו אלהיא טביא וסכריא עבד בעל...
2 בר ירחבולא אסכלא די עזיזו אלהא טבא
3 ורחמנא על חיוהי וחיא אחוהי בירח תשרי
4 שנת 500 דכיר ירחי [illegible]

[1] To Arṣu and 'Azîzu, the good and bountiful gods, (this) has been made by Ba'al..., son of Yarḥi-bôlē, augur (?) of 'Azîzu, the good and compassionate, for his

184. Vog. 73. A. D. 114.

1 לבעל שמן מרא עלמא עבדו
2 נבחבד וירחבולא בני ברנבו
3 בר נבחבד בר [מ]לא ארנבי על
4 [ח]ייהון וחיי [בנ]יהון ואחיהון
5 בירח אב שנת ////ↄ—3 y ↄ

To Ba'al-shamin, lord of eternity, (this) has been made by [2] Nebu-zebad and Yarḥi-bôlē, sons of Bar-nebu, [3] son of Nebu-zebad, son of [M]alē Arnabi, for [4] their [l]ives and the life of their [so]ns and their brothers; [5] in the month Ab, the year 425.

L. 1. בעל שמן 183 1 *n.* מרא עלמא Similarly in the inscr. from eṭ-Ṭayyibe (near Palmyra)[1]; cf. *Deus Aeternus* of Jup. Dolichenus, *Opt. Max. Caelus Aeternus Iuppiter* in Lat. inscrr. of this period. But, as Lidzb. has pointed out, the other possible meaning of the title, *lord of the world*, is prob. implied at the same time, and influenced by the Jewish רִבּוֹן שֶׁל עוֹלָם, רִבּוֹן הָעוֹלָמִים. The latter formula has made its way into Islam as رَبُّ العَالَمِين; cf. the *šar kiššati* 'lord of all things,' assumed by the Assyr. kings (*Eph.* i 258).

L. 2. נבחבד 127 3 *n.* ירחבולא 111 3 *n.*

L. 3. ארנבי So Vog.'s copy; ? from أرنب = *a hare.* Mordtm. 28, however, reads אכנבי *Acnebiensis*; J. Mordtm. compares the family

life and the life of his brothers: in the month Tishri, the year 500. Remembered be Yarḥai the sculptor.' ארצו Vog. 189, cf. רצו 115 1 *n.* עזיזו = Ares, the god of the Edessenes, ܥܙܝܙܐ ܚܝܠܬܢܐ Cureton *Spic. Syr.* ܦܐ 24. Ἄρης, Ἄζιζος λεγόμενος ὑπὸ τῶν οἰκούντων τὴν Ἔδεσσαν Σύρων Ἡλίου προπομπεύει Julian Apost. *Orat.* iv 154. Deo Azizo p(uero conserva)tori CIL iii 875. Θαῖμος Ἀζείζῳ ἐποίησα Wadd. 2314. אפכלא 80 8 *n.* probably borrowed from the Assyr. *abkallu* 'a specially wise man,' *KB* vi 320; Delitzsch *Assyr. HWB* 9. Here the word is a priestly title, such as temple magician; the Arab. أَنْكَل gives no suitable sense. See *Rép.* no. 30; Cl.-Gan. *Rec.* iv § 37; Lidzb. *Eph.* i 201 ff. 349.

[1] Διὶ μεγίστῳ κεραυνίῳ ὑπὲρ σωτηρίας Τρα[ιανοῦ] Ἀδριανοῦ Σεβ[αστοῦ] τοῦ κυρίου Ἀγαθάγγελος Ἀβιληνὸς τῆς Δεκαπόλεος τὴν καμάραν ᾠκοδόμησεν καὶ τὴν κλίνη[ν] ἐξ ἰδίων ἀνέθηκεν. Ἔτους ἐμυ' μηνὸς Λῴου (= 134 A. D.).

לבעל שמן מרא עלמא קרב
כפתא ושרשא אגתנגלס

כפתא = a vaulted niche for a statue; Vog. 70. שרשא See 70 1 *n.* The inscr. is in the Brit. Mus.

τῶν Χεννάβα (*ZDMG* xxxv 747 f.); but if 'א is a gentilic name we should expect אכנביא. Lidzb., *Eph.* i 198, reads אכלדי (surname or title), which is supported by Mordtm.'s facsimile; the name thus written has been found recently in an inscr. published by Sobernheim (Lidzb. l. c.).

L. 4. This line, omitted from Vog.'s copy, is supplied by Mordtm.

135. Vog. **75.** A.D. 125.

1 לבריך ש[מה] ל[ע]למא
2 טבא ור[ח]מנא
3 עבד פרנך בר חרי
4 לשמש בר שמשגרם
5 נרקיס בר חרי מלא
6 ברפא על חייהן וחיי
7 בניהן בירח כסלול
8 שנת //// ך 3 ך y //

To him whose na[me] is blessed for [e]ver, [2] the good and the com[p]assionate, [3] (this altar) has been made by Parnak, freedman [4] of Lishamsh, son of Shamsi-geram, [5] (and by) Narcissus, freedman of Malē, [6] (son of) Borefâ, for their life and the life of [7] their sons: in the month Kislûl, [8] the year 437.

L. 1. לבריך שמה לעלמא A common formula in Palm. dedications; grammatically the phrase 'בריך ש' לע (138) is treated as a single adj., and ל prefixed. It is remarkable that, like other epithets of the Palm. gods (cf. 134 1 *n.*), this has a distinctly Jewish character; cf. ברוך שם כבודו לעולם Ps. 72 19, also 113 2. Dan. 2 20, and the Hebr. or early Samaritan inscr. ברוך שמו לעלם Lidzb. 440. Out of reverence the actual name of the deity was not used (cf. p. 21), and can only be conjectured: most likely it was בל=מלכבל=שמש (112 4 *n.*). Though avoiding it in this formula the Palmyrenes did not object to use בל in pr. nn. (זבדבל, ידיעבל, עבדבל &c.), any more than the later Jews, who read אדני for יהוה, objected to such names as ישעיהו, יותנן &c. In Gk. the title is rendered Ζεὺς ὕψιστος καὶ ὑπήκοος Vog. 101. 124 &c.; it implies a monotheism such as appears sporadically in the worship of

Ζεὺς ὕψιστος, Θεὸς ὕψ. from the 1st cent. onwards[1]. The spread of monotheistic ideas was in part due to the Jewish Diaspora, whose influence no doubt made itself felt in Palmyra (cf. pp. 45. 278. 296).

L. 3. פרנך Sachau, *ZDMG* xxxv 737, suggests Φαρνάκης as an equivalent; cf. the Pers. פרנוג = Saturn, and the O.T. פַּרְנָךְ Num. 34 25. Vog. reads פרנר; Mordtm. פרד. בר חרי See 97 i *n*. Strictly the phrase = *son of a freeman*, ܒܪ ܚܐܪ̈ܐ, i.e. *liber* not *libertus* = ܡܫܚܪܪܐ, but in ordinary speech it was used in the latter sense.

L. 4. שמשגרם 145 1? *Shamash has appointed*, ܓܪܡ; in Gk. Σαμσιγέραμος Wadd. 2564, Σαμψιγέραμος a king of Hemesa, Jos. *Ant.* xviii 5 4.

L. 5. נרקים Νάρκισσος, a common name for a freedman in the time of the Empire. Here נ׳ is the joint donor of the altar; the conjunct. ו must be supplied.

L. 6. ברפא Cf. בורפא Vog. 109 = בול רפא.

186. Oxoniensis 1. A.D. 85. Ashmolean Mus., Oxford.

1 [ב]ירח אלול שנת /// ק 3333[3]
2 [ק] ע / חמנא דנה ועלתא דה
3 [ע]בדו וקרבו לשמש חביד[א]
4 בני מלכו בר ידיעבל בר נשא
5 די מתקרא בר עבדבל די מ[ן]
6 פחד בני מגדת לשמש
7 אלה בית אבוהן על
8 חייהון וחיי אחיה[ו]ן
9 ובניהון

[In] the month Elul, the year 396, [2] this sun-pillar and this altar [3] have been [m]ade and offered by Lishamsh and Zebîd[a], [4] sons of Mâliku, son of Yedî'a-bel, son of Nesâ, [5] who was called son of 'Abd-bel, who was o[f] [6] the family of the Benê Migdath, to Shamash, [7] god of their father's house, for [8] their life and the life of their brothers [9] and their sons.

[1] Thus Gk. inscrr. from the Bosporus (Tanais) contain the remarkable expression εἰσποιητοὶ ἀδελφοὶ σεβόμενοι θεὸν ὕψιστον, cf. Acts 10 2. 22. 18 43. 50 &c. Jos. *Ant.* xiv 7 2. See Schürer *SBBA* (1897) 200 ff., and *Gesch.*[3] iii 123 f.

L. 1. אלול The 6th month, Aug.–September.

L. 2. חמנא A pillar dedicated to שמש, standing beside the altar; see **87** 4 *n.*, and cf. מזבחות הבעלים והחמנים אשר למעלה מעליהם 2 Chr. 34 4. עֲלָתָא *altar*, common in Syr.

L. 4. ידיעבל **140** A 6, in **122** 7 the name of a tribe, Ἰεδειβῆλος, cf. O.T. יְדִיעֲאֵל 1 Chr. 7 6 &c., and Sab. ידעאל (Hommel *Süd-ar. Chrest.* 101); ידיע perhaps = مُحَجَّل *notable, illustrious one.* נשא **147** i 3 = Νεσᾶ.

L. 6. פחר Vog. 32. 33 = فَخِذ lit. *thigh*, cf. Gen. 46 26 &c., *a subdivision of a tribe.* The word implies a clan whose descent is reckoned by the male line, just as the Arab. *baṭn* is a clan of female ancestry; see Rob. Smith *Kinship* 33 f. מגרת The name comes from the √ مجد **112** 3 *n.*; cf. the Sin. pr. n. מגדיו, Syr. ܡܓܕܝ (Lidzb. 305), the Edomite מגדיאל Gen. 36 43, Sab. מגדעל. שמש The sun-god, whose worship was predominant at Palmyra, as appears from numerous pr. nn. and dedications, e.g. **117** 5 *n.*, Vog. 108 לשמש אלהא טבא, the inscrr. on tesserae, e.g. Vog. 135 שמש שרן רבא, see further on מלכבל **112** 4 *n.*; ירחבול **121** 6 *n.* was also worshipped in connexion with the sun. The great temple of the sun-god is still the most imposing building among the ruins of Palmyra.

L. 7. אלה בית אבוהן Cf. **61** 29. **95** 2.

187. Vog. 76. A.D. 135.

1 לבריך שמה לעלמא עבד שלמן בר נשא
2 צידא ברק על חיוהי וחיי בנוהי
3 X בירח ניסן שנת //// ⟵ 33 y // X

To him whose name is blessed for ever (this) has been made by Shalman, son of Nesâ, [2] (son of) Ṣaïda, (son of) Baraq, for his life and the life of his sons. [3] In the month Nisan, the year 447.

L. 1. שלמן Again in Vog. 33 a. 49 &c., Σαλαμάνης Wadd. 2147, in Nab. CIS ii 294. 302 = Arab. سَلْمان, Assyr. *Šalamanu* Schrader *COT* 441. The name is not distinctively Jewish.

L. 2. צידא From ציד *to hunt*, **102** 3 *n.* ברק Either nomen or cognomen, in Sab. ברקם, Pun. *Barcas*, surname of Hamilcar, Hebr. ברק Jud. 4 6 ff.; cf. אברוק **140** A 6.

L. 3. The cross at the beginning and end of the line may be the Christian symbol, somewhat disguised. It is questionable, however, whether the cross was used in this way in the first half of the 2nd cent.; nor is it likely that a Christian would write such an inscr. upon a pagan altar, though in itself the formula in l. 1 might not be objectionable, 135 1 *n.* The inscr. may have a Jewish origin; the name ברק has a Jewish sound; but no Jew would 'make' a Palm. altar.

188. Vog. 79. A.D. 256.

1 בריך שמה לעלמא [טבא]
2 ורחמא מודא...ה ד...ח
3 לשמש לרחמנא די ק[ים]הי
4 בימא וביבשא וע[ניה]
5 די קרההו ו......חה
6 בירח אלול שנת [ע—] 333 y //

Blessed be his name for ever, [the good] [2]and the compassionate! offered in thanksgiving by... (son of) [3]Lishamsh, to the compassionate one who de[liv]ered (?) him [4]by sea and land, and an[swered him] [5]who invoked him, and...... [6]In the month Elûl, the [5]67.

L. 1. בריך וגו' 135 1 *n.*

L. 2. רחמא 189 3 is perhaps a mistake for the usual רחמנא l. 3. מודא Afel ptcp. of ידא (אודי) *confess*, used in votive inscrr. with the special sense of *giving thanks* for some benefit, e.g. Vog. 101 עבד ומודא *εὐχαρίστως ἀνέθηκεν.*

L. 3. ק[ים]חי i.e. קַיְּמֵהּ Pael of קים, so Vog. Nöld. (99), however, restores ק[רי]חי = ܩܪܝܗܝ, which has the support of the Syr. form. As in Syr., the final י was prob. not pronounced, hence it is usually not written, e.g. עניה l. 4. Vog. 92. 103. קריה 103. In l. 5 קרההו is a form contrary to all analogy, and is prob. incorrectly copied.

L. 4. יבשא . . ימא Cf. Gen. 1 10. וע[ניה] The restoration is based on Vog. 92 &c. די קר[א] לה ועניה; in Gk. *εὐξάμενος καὶ ἐπακουσθεὶς ἀνέθηκεν κ.τ.λ.*

L. 5. אלול 186 1 *n.*

139. Vog. **93.** Circ. A. D. 230.

1 מודן כל יום נדרבול
2 ומקימו בּני דדא בר
3 מקימו דנאל לרחמא
4 טבא ותירא על חייהון ·
5 . תיא דנה ו... ילהון
6 כלה.. י לעגלבול ומלכבל אלן
7 .... שנת ע ק 33 . .

Giving thanks every day, Nadar-bôl [2] and Moqîmu, sons of Dada, son [3] of Moqîmu, (son of) Daniel (?), (dedicate this) to the compassionate one, [4] the good and the merciful, for their life. [5] . . . . this and their . . . . . [6] all of it . . . to the gods (?) 'Agli-bôl and Malak-bel [7] . . . . the year 54 . .

L. 1. מודן Ptcp. plur.; **188** 2 *n.* נדרבול ? *Bôl has vowed.*

L. 2. דדא Δάδος Wadd. 2081 &c. = عمّ *paternal uncle*; cf. the pr. n. חלא Eut. 103 1 &c. = خال *maternal uncle.*

L. 3. דנאל ? = Hebr. דָּנִיֵּאל, in Nab. CIS ii 258. But such a form in Palm. may be questioned; Nöld. (88) reads חנאל ="Αννηλος Wadd. 2320 &c. רחמא **188** 2 *n.*

L. 4. רחמא . . ותירא = the Assyr. *rêmênu taiâru* (Lidzb. 153 *n.*); the latter word = *pitiful* (√תור) in Assyr., see Delitzsch *HWB* 604 f. 703. In *Eph.* i 79, however, Lidzb. suggests חיבא, as in Mand. with ראחמאנא.

L. 5. Perhaps read [וח]יא [ב]נהו[ן] ובנ[ת]יהון כלה, J. Mordtm. from his father's copy, and Cl.-Gan. *Rec.* ii § 37. The only objection is that the sign after חייהון l. 4 usually marks the end of a clause. If דנה is right, the preceding word ought to be a sing. noun; the suff. הון must refer to the donors.

L. 6. The suggested reading [כר]י *as well as to 'Agli-bôl and M.*, carrying on לרחמא l. 3, is doubtful because it ignores the full stop at the end of l. 4. עגלבול The Palm. moon-god, associated with Malak-bel, the solar deity (**112** 4 *n.*), e. g. **140** A 2. Vog. **140**, and the inscr. below [1] from a stele which represents the god as a young Roman

[1] Rom. 1, in the Capitoline Museum: 'Αγλιβώλῳ καὶ Μαλαχβήλῳ πατρῴοις θεοῖς καὶ τὸ σίγνον ἀργυροῦν σὺν παντὶ κόσμῳ ἀνέθηκε Τ. Αὐρ. 'Ηλιόδωρος 'Αντιόχου

warrior, with a large crescent attached to his shoulders (cf. *Syr. Centr.* pl. 12. 141). The meaning of the name is uncertain; the √עגל = *be round*, in Pa. *to roll*, so perhaps *chariot of Bôl*, in Aram. עֲגַלְתָּא, [illegible] *chariot*; cf. רכבאל 61 2 *n.* אלן Apparently for אלהן 69 20. 76 C 7; we should expect אלהיא.

140 A and B. Littmann 1 and 2. A—A. D. 29; B—A. D. 132. Discovered 1900.

A

1 [בירח] שבט שנת ///כ—33 עלתא דה [עבדו]
2 [בני] מרזחא אלן לעגלבול ולמלכבל אלה[יהון]
3 ..בי בר עתנורי עודו וחגגו בר זבדלה כמרא
4 [ונ]בוזבד בר מלכו מתנא ותימו בר עגילו רבבת
5 [ו]מלכו בר ירחבולא חתי וירחבולא בר תימרצו
6 אברוק וזבדבול בר ידיעבל אלהו ועגילו בר
7 נורי זבדבול ומלכו בר מקימו תימעמד

In the month Shebaṭ, the year 340. This altar [has been made] [2] by the following [members of] the *thiasos* to ʽAgli-bôl and Malak-bel [their] gods:—[3] . . bai, son of ʽAthē-nûri (son of) ʽAudu, and Ḥaggâgu, son of Zabd-ilah (son of) Komâra, [4] [and N]ebu-zebad, son of Mâliku (son of) Mathna, and Taimu, son of ʽOgêlu (son of) Rabâbat, [5] [and] Mâliku, son of Yarḥi-bôlē (son of) Ḥattai, and Yarḥi-bôlē, son of Taim-arṣu [6] (son of) Abrôqa, and Zabdi-bôl, son of Yediʽa-bel (son of) Alihu, and ʽOgêlu, son [7] of Nurai (son of) Zabdi-bôl, and Mâliku, son of Moqîmu (son of) Taimo-ʽamad.

'Αδριανὸς Παλμυρηνὸς ἐκ τῶν ἰδίων ὑπὲρ σωτηρίας αὐτοῦ καὶ τῆς συμβίου καὶ τῶν τέκνων ἔτους ζμφ' μηνὸς Περιτίου.

1 לעגלבול ומלכבל וסמיותא די כספא ותצב
2 יתה עבד מן כיסה ירחי בר חליפי בר
3 ירחי בר לשמש שעדו על חיוהי וחיא
4 בנוהי בירח שבט שנת 547

סמיותא = *a standard*, *σημεῖον*, signum. תצביתה 119 4 *n.* ירחי Note = *'Ηλιόδωρος*; cf. 122 2 = *'Ιαραῖον*. חליפי 86 10 *n.*

These inscrr., engraved on small altars, were first published by Littmann, *Journal As.* (1901) ii 374–390.

L. 1. שבט The 11th month, Jan.–February; cf. p. 302 footnote.

L. 2. בני מרזחא The idiomatic expression for *members of* a guild, cf. בני שירתא 118 3 *n.*, and the O.T. בני קרח ,בני הנביאים. For מרזחא see 42 16 *n.*; the existence of religious symposia at Palmyra is proved by the inscr. Wadd. 2606 a *συμποσίαρχον τῶν . . . Διὸς Βήλου ἱερέων* (127 1 *n.*). לעגלבול ולמלכבל 139 6 *n.*

L. 3. Restore prob. חבי = חבאלהי. עתנורי Already known in Palm.; cf. Cl.-Gan. *Ét.* ii 96 and 112 4 *n.* עודו = عَوْذ, Αὖδος, a name common in Sin.; cf. عوذ مناة Wellhausen *Reste* 6. חננו 118 2 *n.* זבדלח 114 5 *n.* כמרא 132 2 *n.*

L. 4. נבוזבד 127 3 *n.* מתנא Prob. abbreviated from מתנבול, cf. 132 2 *n.*; Lidzb., *Eph.* i 344, compares the Pun. מתנא=מתנאל[ם], and the Talmudic מתנה = מתניה. חימו Cf. 112 4 *n.* עגילו 'Ογήλου Vog. 70 1; for the √ עגל see 139 6 *n.* רבבת = رَبَابَة, from رَبَاب, *a white cloud*; cf. the fem. pr. n. רבבם in Sab. (Lidzb.).

L. 5. ירחבולא 111 3 *n.* חתי Perhaps abbreviated from the well-known Arab. pr. n. حَاتِم. תימרצו 115 1 *n.*

L. 6. אברוק Prob. a variation of the name ברק 137 2, cf. the Talm. בְּרוֹקָא *flashing light* (cf. סַאִיר); the latter form is found in Palm., Lidzb. *Eph.* i 206 inscr. D. Littmann explains the name as = ابو رُواق, and compares the name of the place أُمّ رَوَاق. ידיעבל 136 4 *n.* אלהו Cf. the Ṣafaïte אלה, Littmann *Zur Entziff. d. Ṣafâ-Inschr.* 39, where the Gk. "Αλειος, 'Αλλέου, and the Arab. 'Ulaiha are suggested as possible parallels. The fem. form אלהת used as a mas. pr. n. also occurs in Ṣafaïte, e. g. Littmann ib. 57.

L. 7. נורי Abbr. from some such name as נורבל Vog. 124; cf. the Talm. נורי = נוריה. תימעמד Vog. 124 Θαιμοαμέδου.

B

1 [ת]רתן עלותא אלן עבד עבידו בר ענמו

2 [ב]ר שעדלת נבטיא רוחיא די הוא פרש

3 [ב]חירתא ובמשריתא די ענא

4 לשיעאלקום אלהא טבא ושכרא די לא

5 שתא חמר על חיוהי וחיי מעיתי

6 ועבדו אחוהי ושעדלת ברה בירח

7 אלול שנת ||||ᑐ—33||| ודכיר זבידא בר

8 שמעון בר בלעקב גירה ורחמה קדם

9 שיעאלקום אלהא טבא ודכיר כל

10 . מעיד עלותא אלן ואמר דכירין

11 . . א אלן כלהון בטב

These two altars have been made by 'Ubaidu, son of 'Ânimu, [2] [s]on of Sa'd-allath, the Nabataean, of the Rûḥu tribe, who was a horseman [3] in the fort and camp of 'Ana, [4] to She'a-alqûm, the good and bountiful god, who does not [5] drink (?) wine, for his life and the life of Mu'ithi [6] and 'Abdu his brothers, and Sa'd-allath his son; in the month [7] Elûl, the year 443. And remembered be Zebîda, son [8] of Shim'on, son of Bel-'aqab, his patron and friend, before [9] She'a-alqûm the good god; and remembered be every one [10] . . visits (?) these altars, and says, 'Remembered be [11] all these . . for good!'

The inscr., though written in Palm., is thoroughly Nabataean in character. The donor of the altars, the deity to whom they are dedicated, and most of the pr. nn. are all Nabataean.

L. 1. עלותא = ܥܠܘܬܐ. עבידו 93 1 *n.* ענמו 91 1.

L. 2. שעדלת = שעד־אלת; see 106 *n.* רוחיא i. e. a member of the family of רוחו 99 1. 2 *n.* פרש Not a member of the equestrian order, הפקא ἱππικός, but simply a soldier in the cavalry.

L. 3. חירתא = ܚܝܪܬܐ *camp*, cf. Arab. حَيْر *sheep-fold*; but perhaps this is the name of a place الحيرة, on the Euphrates. משריתא 96 4 *n.* ענא The name of a place; Littm. suggests Ἄναθα, now عانة, on the Euphrates.

L. 4. שיעאלקום A Nab. inscr. from Ḥauran contains a dedication to this deity, see p. 255 *n.* 1; in the Ṣafâ inscrr. he is frequently mentioned as שעהקם, e. g. ורשר ובעל־סמן ונר־עור ושעדהקם (=אלת) הלת ם Littm. *Ṣafâ-Inschr.* p. v. The name = شَيْعُ القَوْمِ *protector of the people*, the god *who accompanies the people*, prob. the special deity of the caravan; for the conception cf. Ex. 23 20. 23. 33 14 f. Is. 63 9. שכרא 138 2 *n.*

L. 5. שתא, or משתא Af. ptcp. *who does not allow wine-drinking*, inserting a letter at the beginning of the line. The worshippers of this deity were prohibited from the use of wine, very likely as a protest against the Dionysiac cult of Dûshara (see 79 5 *n.*)[1]. Similarly in the O.T., the Nazirite vow and the principles of the Rechabites (Jer. 35) were protests against the degenerating influence of Canaanite civilization. As a custom among the Nabataeans, abstinence from wine is mentioned by Diodorus xix 94 3[2]; it was inculcated in Arabia before the time of Mohammed (Robertson Smith *Prophets* 84. 388). מעיתי A Nab. pr. n., Dussaud et Macler *Voy. Arch.* no. 59, in the Gk. version Μοειθου; similarly Wadd. 2483. The form מעיתי is endearing and diminutive, cf. חביבי, עוזי, מלכי, זברי &c. (Lidzb. *Eph.* i 218); the Arab. equivalent is مُغيث from غاث *to succour*, cf. the Palm. pr. names יעת, יעתו i.e. يغوث (*Rép.* no. 85), עות 143 2.

L. 7. אלול Aug.–September.

L. 8. בלעקב 124 3 *n.* נירה For גר *guest* in Phoen. and Palm. see 17 2 *n.* Here, however, the word must denote not the receiver, but the giver of hospitality; cf. the pr. n. Κοσγηρος from Memphis, not 'Kos is client' but 'K. is patron,' K. being a deity (Nöld. *SBBA* (1882) 1187 *n.*). Thus גר like جار denotes both sides of the relation; it has the double sense of the German *Gastfreund*. The Gk. equivalent of נירה ורחמה would be τὸν αὐτοῦ ξένον καὶ φίλον *his host and friend* CIG 2502 &c., cf. רחמה וקיומה 129 5; Cl.-Gan. *Rec.* v 45 f. Zebîda discharged the obligations of hospitality towards the Nab. soldier at Palmyra. רחמה 127 4 *n.*

L. 10. מֹעיר or עיר Ptcp. Afel or Peal of עור = عَاذَ, conj. v تَعَوَّذَ *to visit*; Lidzb. l. c. 346. At the beginning of the line די is to be restored. Another proposed reading is די לא מעיר or יעיר *who does not change* (86 8 *n.*); but there is hardly room for לא. ואמר Ptcp., i. e. וְאָמַר.

L. 11. At the beginning of the line Cl.-Gan. restores שמא *names*, pl. constr. or emph.—a doubtful form; Lidzb. better אנשא or גבריא.

[1] Cl.-Gan. ingeniously discovers a parallel in the struggle between Dionysos and the fabled 'anti-bacchic' king of the Arabs, Lycurgos (cf. [θε]ῷ Λυκούργῳ Wadd. 2286 a); the scene of the legend is placed in Arabia. *Rec.* iv 398 ff.

[2] Νόμος δ' ἐστὶν αὐτοῖς μήτε σῖτον σπείρειν μήτε φυτεύειν μηδὲν φυτὸν καρποφόρον, μήτε οἴνῳ χρῆσθαι μήτε οἰκίαν κατασκευάζειν.

SEPULCHRAL INSCRIPTIONS

141. Vog. **30 a.** B.C. 9.

1 קברא דנה די

2 עתנתן בר כהילו די

3 בנו עלוהי בנוהי

4 כהילו וחירן בנוהי

5 די מן בני מיתא

6 בירח כנן שנת /// ⊃— ////

This sepulchre is that of [2] 'Athē-nathan, son of Kohailu, which [3] has been built over him by his sons [4] Kohailu and Ḥairân, his sons, [5] who are of the Benê Maitha. [6] In the month Kanûn, the year 304.

The characteristic form of the Palm. sepulchre is that of the tomb tower. One of these, called Kasr eth-Thunīyeh, is 111 ft. high, 33½ ft. square at the base, 25 ft. 8 in. square above the basement. It contains six stories, and places for 480 bodies. Opposite the entrance is a hall (cf. **143** 8) with recesses for coffins; it has a richly panelled ceiling; underground is an immense vault (cf. **143** 1). Illustrations of this and another well-preserved tower are given in Wm. Wright's *Palmyra and Zenobia* (1895) 81. 85. Within the towers are found the busts so characteristic of Palm. art (cf. **142** 3). The form of these monuments is of Asiatic origin; but the decoration is in the Roman style. The inscriptions outside the towers are often bilingual, within they are Palm. alone.

L. 2. עתנתן See **112** 4 *n.* כהילו **79** 1 *n.*

L. 3. בנוהי In the corresponding inscr. (Vog. **30 b**) on the N. side of the tomb, this is twice written ברתי = ברה *his son*; but the form with the final vowel is so singular that בנוהי is prob. to be preferred as correct (Nöld. 98).

L. 5. בני מיתא Vog. **32** 4, the name of a clan; cf. **132** 2. **133** 1. **136** 6.

L. 6. כנן The 8th month, Oct.–November. The facsimile gives דנן, which is to be corrected to כנן. This is the oldest Palm. inscr. known. The writing is rather more archaic and angular than that of the later inscrr., especially the form of ת. Palm. writing shows extraordinarily little variation during the period of 280 years for which we have specimens.

142. Chediac i (Cl.-Gan. *Ét.* ii § 5). A.D. 94. Qaryatên (between Damascus and Palmyra).

1 בת עלמא דנה עבד מתני בר נורבל בר מלכו
2 בר תימצא על נורבל אבוהי ועל נבי אמה ליקרהן
3 וליקר בנוהי די עלמא צלמיא אלן די מתני בר
4 נורבל בר מלכו בר תימצא בר מתני בר בונא בר
5 מתני די מתקרה מהוי ודי נורבל אבוהי ודי
6 נבי אמה בירח אב שנת ////ק—ץ /

This house of eternity has been made by Matnai, son of Nûr-bel, son of Mâliku, [2] son of Taim-ṣa, over Nûr-bel his father and over Nabbai his mother, to their honour, [3] and to the honour of his sons, for ever. These statues are those of Matnai, son [4] of Nûr-bel, son of Mâliku, son of Taim-ṣa, son of Matnai, son of Bônnê, son [5] of Matnai who is called Mahûi, and of Nûr-bel his father, and of [6] Nabbai his mother. In the month Ab, the year 406.

L. 1. בת עלמא Frequent in Palm. as a term for the grave, e.g. **148** &c., in bilingual inscrr. *μνημεῖον αἰώνιον, αἰώνιος τάφος* Vog. **36** a, b; cf. in the O. T. בית עלמו Qoh. 12 5, in Pun. CIS i **124** חדר בת עלם, and among the Christians of Edessa ܒܝܬ ܥܠܡܐ. The idea may go back to the Egyptians, who, according to Diodorus, called the graves of the dead *ἀϊδίους οἴκους* (i **51** 2). מתני Prob. an abbreviation from מתן־בול. נורבל Vog. **124** *Νουρβῆλον*, cf. עתנורי **140** A 3.

L. 2. תימצא Vog. **33** b, cf. אמתצא Vog. **51**. The divine name צא perhaps=צא[ר]=רצו (Lidzb.), **115** 1 *n.* נבי occurs elsewhere, Lidzb. 321; the name is evidently abbreviated, but the derivation is obscure.

L. 3. די עלמא An unusual expression for לעלמא **112** 3 or עד עלמא **145** 5; but cf. ליקרהון די בת עלמא Vog. **34**.

L. 4. בונא **112** 2 *n.*

L. 5. מתקרה Usually מתקרא; for the variation cf. זבדלה and זבדלא, ברעתה and ברעתא &c. מהוי Again in the inscr. given by Cl.-Gan. *Rec.* iii 183=*Eph.* i 85; the derivation is obscure.

143. **Müller 46.** A.D. 193. **Qaryatên.**

מערתא דה די בת עלמא עבד
פציאל בר עסתורגא בר עות
בר לשמש בר לשמש לה שקקן
תרתן חדא על ימינא כדי אנת
עלל פאחרתא מקבלא
חבידא בר מען בר בולנורעתה
שקקא כדי אנת עלל על שמלא

אכסדרא דנה מקבלא די
מערתא די מקבל בבא חפר
וצבת שוען בר תימא בר
אבגר לה ולבנוהי ולבני
בנוהי הדי רחמת לה שגל
ברת לשמש בר עשתורגא בר
פציאל בירח אדר שנת חמש
מאה וארבע

This vault of the eternal house has been made by [2] Faṣai-el, son of 'Astôr-ga, son of 'Auth, [3] son of Lishamsh, son of Lishamsh, for himself, two corridors, [4] the one upon the right as thou [5] art entering, and the other lying opposite. [6] And Zebîda, son of Ma'n, son of Bôl-nûr-'athē, [7] (has made) the corridor as thou art entering on the left.

[8] This *exedra* on the opposite side of [9] the vault, which lies opposite to the door, has been digged [10] and ornamented by Sau'an, son of Taimē, son [11] of Abgar, for himself and his sons and his grand[12]sons ? ? to him Shegal, [13] daughter of Lishamsh, son of 'Ashtôr-ga, son of [14] Faṣai-el. In the month Adar, the year five [15] hundred and four.

L. 1. מערתא 144 3 the burial cave, excavated in the side of a hill, entered by the door of the tomb tower (p. 306), Vog. 36 &c., τὸ σπηλαῖον Wadd. 2626; in Hebr. מערה Gen. 23 19 f.

L. 2. פציאל Φασαιλη Wadd. 2445; so Lidzb. 479, instead of פחיאל D. M. Müller *Palm. Inschr.* 19, where this inscr. was first published (1898). עסתורנא l. 13. Lidzb. suggests that the form is abbreviated from עשתור גרם (see 135 4 *n.*). For the form עשתור see 118 2 *n.*; for the interchange of ס and שׂ cf. ס and שׂ in 121 5. עות=غَوْث, Γαῦτος Wadd. 2019 &c.; the full name is עותאלהי Eut. *Sin.* 72 &c.; see 140 B 5 *n.*

L. 3. שקקן So Lidzb. Cf. Syr. ܫܩܩܐ *via angusta*, pl. ܫ̈ܩܩܐ; in Targ. שְׁקָקָא=*street.*

L. 5. עלל Ptcp. sing. of עלל *enter*; cf. 147 ii c 16. פ׳ The conjunction ﬞ, here in Palm., as in Nab. and Old Aram., 61 3 *n.* מקבלא i.e. מַקְבְּלָא Afel ptcp. fem. abs. state, from קבל *to meet*; so the infin. לקבל=*before, in the presence of* 67. 147 i 10, in Afel *to be opposite* (144 6).

L. 6. מען=the Arab. pr. n. مَعْن; in Nab. and Sin. מענו, in Gk. Μάνος, Μάννος Wadd. 2042 &c. 2584. בולנורעתה Cf. עתנורי 140 A 3. נורבל 142 1. Lidzb. (500) suggests that this may be the full form of the abbreviated names בנא, בולנא.

L. 8. אכסדרא 144 6 ἐξέδρα, i.e. a hall with recesses, such, for example, as the fore-court of the great temple at Ba'albek, which has recesses or chambers on each side; see the plan in Baedeker *Paläst.*[3] 343. Here the *exedra* is the hall with recesses for coffins, in the centre of the tomb tower, leading to the vault; see p. 306. In the Targ. and Talm. א׳=a porch, or covered passage before a house, e.g. Judg. 3 23=τὴν προστάδα; *Tamid* 28 b אכסדראות של בנין *ex. of masonry* round the temple-court. מקבלא here is mas. emph. state, as in 144 6.

L. 9. בבא Not otherwise found in Palm., common in Targ. and Talm., rare in Syr. The Arab. باب is derived from this word; see Fraenkel *Aram. Fremdw.* 14.

L. 10. צבת Pael, cf. the noun תצביתתהן in 119 4 &c. שען Prob.=Σανάνου Wadd. 2537 a, cf. سَوْغ, سُوَاغ *first watch of the night.*

L. 11. אבגר Ἄβγαρος Wadd. 1984 d &c., ܐܒܓܪ a common Syr. pr. n.=*lame.*

L. 12. הרי ? meaning. Lidzb. (503) suggests מדי *which* 147 i 4 &c.= Bibl. Aram. מָה דִי, and renders רחמת *she bore* (a denomin. vb. from רְחִמָא *love*). The word may be read רחקת *she gave birth to*, Arab. دحق; this is to be preferred. שגל A common fem. pr. n. in Palm.; cf. perhaps שגלא 69 16 *n.*

L. 14. אדר Feb.–March.

144. Nöld. A. D. 188. Imp. Mus., Constantinople.

1 בירח כנון שנת ע [numeral signs]
2 אחבר לשמש בר לשמש
3 בר תימא מן מערתא
4 דה לבונא בר בולחא
5 בר בונא בר יקרור
6 אחברתה מן אכסדרא מקבלא
7 גמחין תמניא מן ימינך
8 ארבעא ומן סמלך ארבעא

In the month Kanûn, the year 500. [2] Lishamsh, son of Lishamsh, [3] son of Taimĕ, has given a share of this vault [4] to Bônnĕ, son of Bôl-ḥa, [5] son of Bônnĕ, son of Yaqrûr. [6] I have given him a share of the *exedra* lying opposite, [7] eight niches, on thy right hand [8] four, and on thy left four.

The inscr. was published by Nöldeke *ZA* (1894) pp. 264–267.

L. 1. כנון **141** 6 *n.*
L. 2. אחבר Afel of חבר *to join, associate*; cf. l. 6.
L. 3. מערתא **143** 1 *n.*
L. 4. בולחא **132** 1 *n.*
L. 5. יקרור = ܥܩܘܪܐ *toad*; cf. the pr. nn. חלדה Vog. 74 *weasel*, עכבור *mouse*, قنفذ *hedge-hog* &c.

L. 6. אחברתה i.e. אַחְבַּרְתֵּהּ Af. pf. 1 sing. with suff., cf. the infin. Vog. 71 לאחבורא בה איש = κοινωνὸν αὐτοῦ προσλαβεῖν in the Gk. version. מקבלא Af. ptcp. mas. emph.; אכסדרא is mas., **143** 8; cf. בסלקא **119** 3 (Cl.-Gan. *Ét.* i 130).
L. 7. גמחין *loculi*; see **91** 5 *n.* (Nab. גוחיא).

145. Cl.-Gan. I (*Ét.* i 121). ii–iii cent. A. D. Louvre.

1 חבל שמשגרם בר נורבל
2 מראגרא והו בנא קברא דנה
3 ואנש לא יפתח עלוהי גומחא

4 דנה עד עלמא לא יהוא לה

5 זרע וגר עד עלמא ולא יקשט

6 למן די יפתחיהי עד עלמא

7 ולחם ומן למא ישבע

Alas! Shamshi-geram, son of Nûr-bel [2] Mar-agra. And he built this sepulchre. [3] And let no man open over him this niche [4] for ever! Let him have no [5] seed or fortune for ever, nor let there be any prosperity [6] for him who shall open it, for ever, [7] and with bread and water may he never be satisfied!

L. 1. חבל An interjection of grief very common in funeral inscrr. and on busts (p. 306); in the Talm. חֲבַל, חֲבִיל, Dalman *Gr.* 192. שמשגרם 135 4 *n.*

L. 2. מראגרא Cognomen or title; if the latter, perhaps=ܡܳܪܶܐ ܐܰܓܪܳܐ *dominus mercedis*, i. e. qui militibus stipendia pendet, *paymaster*; *Thes. Syr.* col. 30. Cl.-Gan. suggests the general sense of *treasurer*, *Ét.* i 123.

L. 3. אש Cf. 69 20; אנש in Nab. 86 6. 90 7 &c. For similar prohibitions see 4. 5. 61. 64 f. 69. לא יפתח עלוהי See 5 6 *n.* גומחא 91 5 *n.*

L. 5. גר *fortune*, as in the pr. nn. גר רצו Vog. 84. גר עתא 143 &c. יקשט The root=*be firm, right* in Aram.; hence קְשׁוֹט, קֻשְׁטָא, Syr. ܩܽܘܫܬܳܐ=*truth, righteousness* &c. Taking the verb here in a neuter sense, we may render 'let there be no right to him who'; for the construction cf. Hebr. יִיטַב לְ, יֵרַע לְ &c.

L. 6. יפתחיהי For the form cf. the Syr. ܢܶܦܬܚܽܘܗܝ.

L. 7. מן=מין 75 3, *bread and water*, i. e. the elementary necessaries of life. Winckler renders *bread and manna*, i. e. food for the dead, or divine food, ambrosia, which is his explanation of מָן in Ex. 16 15; *Altor. Forsch.* ii 322 f. It is much more likely that מן here=מין, although the form is unusual. למא must have the sense of a prohibitive negative. It may be explained on the analogy of the Hebr. למה (Driver *Samuel* 123 f.) as meaning *wherefore?* = *let . . not*; in Aram. when connected by די with the preceding clause it comes to mean *lest*, דִּי לְמָא, ܕܰܠܡܳܐ, in Targ. Onk. and Pesh.=Hebr. פֶּן, e. g. Gen. 42 4. Num. 16 34 &c.

146. Constantine: Afr. I. ii–iii cent. A. D.

D[is] m[anibus] s[acrum]. Suricus Rubatis Pal[murenus] sag[ittarius centuria] Maximi [vixit] ann[is] XLV mi[lit]avit an[nis] xiii. CIL viii 2515.

1 נפשא דנה די
2 שריכו בר רבת
3 תדמוריא קשטא
4 קטרי מֹאכסמוס
5 בר שנת 33 ←
6 חבל

This monument is that of Soraiku, son of Rubat, the Palmyrene archer, century of Maximus, 45 years old. Alas!

L. 1. נפשא See **78** 1 *n.* Here נ׳ takes a mas. pronoun; in Nab. either mas. or fem.

L. 2. שריכו **119** 1 *n.* רבת=رُوبَة, Nöld. 89.

L. 3. קשטא *sagittarius*=Syr. ܩܶܫܛܳܐ or ܩܶܫܬܳܐ; the ט and ת (Hebr. קשת), the ק and כ, are interchanged in this word, Nöld. 97. Besides this inscr. there is further evidence that a contingent of Palm. archers served in the Roman army in Africa. An inscr. discovered by Prof. Flinders Petrie at Coptos contains a dedication to the Palm. god Ἱεραβ[ώ]λῳ=ירחבול, made by Αὐρήλιος Βηλάκαβος Ἱερα[ῖος or -ου] οὐηξιλλάριος Ἀδριανῶν Παλμυρηνῶν Ἀντωνινιανῶν τοξότων. In *Rec.* ii § 42 Cl.-Gan. rightly shows that Ἀδρ. Παλμ.=הדרינא תדמר **147** ii. The fame of the Palm. archers was remembered by Jewish tradition; according to the Talm. 80,000 of them assisted at the overthrow of the first temple, 8000 at that of the second! Neubauer *Géogr. du Talm.* 303.

L. 4. קַטְרִי *centuria.* For the assimilation of נ in foreign words according to the law of Semitic speech cf. סִקְלֵטִיקָא=συνκλητικός p. 285 *n.* 1, אַגַתַנְגְלֹס = Ἀγαθάνγελος inscr. of eṭ-Ṭayyibe p. 296 *n.* 1, אַלְכְּאַנְדְרוֹס **147** i 2, סרקיא ib. 11, and, in native words, the common מדיתא = מדנתא &c. מאכסמוס Nöld. (p. 86) notes this as a unique instance of the vowel letter א representing ă; to avoid the anomaly he corrects the reading to קטריא מכסמוס. In the original א is uncertain, perhaps erased.

TARIFF

147. A.D. 137. In situ.

The following plan shows the arrangement of the inscription:—

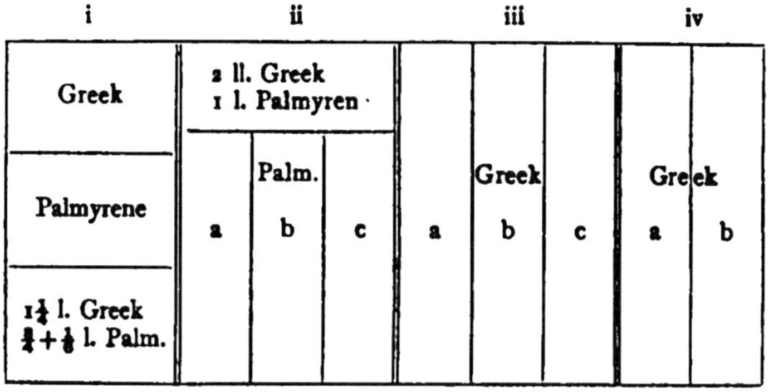

Greek Text.

i.

1 Ἔτους ημυ' μηνὸς Ξανδικοῦ ιη' δόγμα βουλῆς.

2 Ἐπὶ Βωννέους Βωννέους τοῦ Αἱράνου προέδρου, Ἀλεξάνδρου τοῦ Ἀλεξάνδρου τοῦ

3 Φιλοπάτορος γραμματέως βουλῆς καὶ δήμου, Μαλίχου Ὀλαιοῦς καὶ Ζεβείδου Νεσᾶ ἀρχόν-

4 των, βουλῆς νομίμου ἀγομένης, ἐψηφίσθη τὰ ὑποτεταγμένα. Ἐπειδὴ ἐ[ν τ]οῖς πάλαι χρόνοις

5 ἐν τῷ τελωνικῷ νόμῳ πλεῖστα τῶν ὑποτελῶν οὐκ ἀνελήμφθη, ἐπράσ[σετ]ο δὲ ἐκ συνηθείας, ἐν-

6 γραφομένου τῇ μισθώσει τὸν τελωνοῦντα τὴν πρᾶξιν ποιεῖσθαι ἀκολούθως τῷ νόμῳ καὶ τῇ

7 συνηθείᾳ, συνέβαινεν δὲ πλειστάκις περὶ τούτου ζητήσεις γείνεσθ[αι με]ταξὺ τῶν ἐμπόρων

8 πρὸς τοὺς τελώνας· δεδόχθαι, τοὺς ἐνεστῶτας ἄρχοντας καὶ δεκαπρώτους διακρείνοντας

9 *τὰ μὴ ἀνειλημμένα τῷ νόμῳ ἐνγράψαι τῇ ἔνγιστα μισθώσει καὶ ὑποτάξαι ἑκάστῳ εἴδει τὸ*
10 *ἐκ συνηθείας τέλος, καὶ ἐπειδὰν κυρωθῇ τῷ μισθουμένῳ, ἐνγραφῆναι μετὰ τοῦ πρώτου νό-*
11 *μου στήλῃ λιθίνῃ τῇ οὔσῃ ἀντικρὺς [ἱ]ερ[οῦ] λεγομένου Ῥαβασείρη, ἐ[πι]μελεῖσθαι δὲ τοὺς τυγχά-*
12 *νοντας κατὰ καιρὸν ἄρχοντας καὶ δεκαπρώτους καὶ συνδίκ[ους τοῦ] μηδὲν παραπράσσειν*
13 *τὸν μισθούμενον.*

(Aramaic text, ll. (1–11) 14–24.)

25 Γόμος *καρρικὸς παντὸς γένους· τεσσάρων γόμων καμηλικῶν τέ-*
26 λος *ἐπράχθη.* (Aramaic text, ll. (12, 13) 26–7.)

ii.

[Ἐπὶ *αὐτοκράτορος* Καίσαρος *θεοῦ* Τραιανοῦ Παρθι]-*κοῦ υἱο*[ῦ *θε*]*οῦ* [Νέρουα *υἱωνοῦ* Τραιανοῦ Ἀδριανοῦ Σεβαστοῦ *δημαρχικῆς ἐξουσίας τὸ κα' αὐτοκράτορος τὸ β' ὑπ*]*άτου τὸ γ' πατρὸς πατρίδος ὑπάτω*[*ν* Λ. Αἰλίου Καίσαρος *τὸ β'* Π. Κοιλίου Βαλβίνου].

(Aramaic text, 1 line, and columns a, b, c.)

iii a.

(1–47 = Aram. ii a 1–31.)

1 *παρὰ τ*[*ῶν παῖδας εἰσαγόντων εἰς* Πάλμυρα]
2 *ἢ εἰς τὰ ὅ*[*ρια*
3 *ἀγόντω*[*ν*
4 *παρ' οὗ ἂ*[*ν*]
5 *μ* *ους*
6 *παρ' οὐ*[*ετερανοῦ ?*] *οιε*
7 *κἂν τὰ σώμα*[*τα*] *οτο* [*ἐξ*
8 *ἄγηται ἑκάστου σώμα*[*τος*

9 ὁ αὐτὸς δημοσιώνη[ς
10 πράξει ἑκάστου γόμο[υ καμηλικοῦ]
11 εἰσκομισ[θέ]ντος
12 ἐκκομισθ[έντ]ος [γόμου καμηλικοῦ]
13 ἑκάστου vacat
14 γόμου ὀνικ[οῦ ἑκάστο]υ εἰ[σκομισθέντος ἢ]
15 ἐκκομισθέν[τος]
16 πορφύρας μηλωτῆ[ς] ἑκά[στου δέρμα]-
17 τος εἰσκομισθέν[τ]ος [πράξει]
18 ἐκκομισθ[έντο]ς
19 γόμου κ[αμηλικοῦ] μύρου [τοῦ ἐν ἀλαβάσ]-
20 τροις ε[ἰσκομισθέντος πράξει]
21 καὶ το
22 ἐκ[κομισθέντος]
23 γ[όμου καμηλικοῦ μύρου τοῦ ἐν ἀσκοῖς]
24 αἰγείοις [εἰσκομισθέντος πράξει]
25 [ἐκκομισθέντος] [γόμου ὀνικοῦ μύρου
26 τοῦ ἐν ἀλαβάστρ]οις
27 [εἰσκομισ]θέν[τος πράξει]
28 [ἐκκομισ]θέν[τος]
29 γόμου ὀνικοῦ μ[ύρου τοῦ ἐν ἀσκοῖς]
30 αἰγείοις εἰσκομ[ισθέντο]ς πρ[άξει]
31 ἐκκομισθέντος π[ρ]άξ[ει]
32 γόμου ἐλεηροῦ το[ῦ ἐν ἀσκο]ῖς [τέσσαρ]-
33 σι αἰγείοις ἐπὶ καμήλ[ου εἰσκομισθέν]-
34 τος vacat
35 ἐκκομισθέντο[ς]
36 γόμου ἐλαιηροῦ τοῦ ἐ[ν ἀσκο]ῖς δυ[σὶ αἰ]-
37 γείοις ἐπὶ καμήλ[ου εἰσκομισθέντος]
38 πράξει
39 ἐκκομισθέντ[ος]
40 γόμου ἐλε[ηροῦ τοῦ ἐπ' ὄνο]υ ε[ἰσκομισθέν]-

41 το[ς πράξει]
42 ἐκ[κομισθέντος]
43 γόμ[ου τοῦ ἐν ἀσκοῖς τ]έσσ[αρσι]
44 αἰγείοις [πρά]ξει * ιγ´
45 ἐκκομι[σ]θέ[ντος] * ιγ´
46 γόμου κ [τοῦ ἐν] ἀ[σ]κοῖς δυσὶ αἰγείοις
47 ἐπὶ κ[αμήλου εἰσ]κομισθέντος πράξει * ζ.

iii b.

(21=Aram. ii a 41?; 27–30=ii a 46–49; 31–45=ii b 1–12.)

Of the first 18 lines only unimportant fragments remain.

19 λλης vacat
20 μηλουτσ σ ης
21 [θ]ρέμματος η εσ ο
22 δ θ
23 δ εαδ εου ε
24 ὁ αὐτὸς δ[ημ]οσιώνης ἑκάσ
25 παρ' ἑκ[άστο]υ τῶ[ν τὸ] ἔλαιον κατα[κομιζόντων?]
26 πον [πωλού]ντων
27 ὁ αὐτ[ὸς δημοσιώνης] πρά[ξει] λει
28 ος
29 [λαμβά]νουσιν π
30 ἀσσάρια ὀκτώ ιη
31 [ἀσ]σάρια ἓξ ἐν καστ ἀσσς´
32 [ὁ αὐτὸς δημ]οσιώνης πρ[άξ]ει ἐργαστηρίων
33 παντοπωλ[εί]ων σκυτικῶν
34 ἐκ συνηθείας ἑκάστου μηνὸς
35 καὶ ἐργαστηρίου ἑκάστου vacat * α
36 παρὰ τῶν δέρματα εἰσκομιζόν[των
37 ἢ πω]λούντων ἑκάστου δέρματος ἀσσά[ρια δύο]
38 ὁμοίως ἱματιοπῶλαι μεταβόλοι πωλ[οῦν]-
39 τες ἐν τῇ πόλει τῷ δημοσιώνῃ τὸ ἱκανὸν τ[έλος?]
40 χρήσεος πηγῶν · β´ · ἑκάστου ἔτους * ω´

41 ὁ αὐτὸς πρά[ξ]ει γόμου πυρικοῦ οἰνικοῦ ἀχύ-
42 ρων καὶ τοιούτου γένους ἑκάστου γόμου
43 καμηλικοῦ καθ' ὁδὸν ἑκάστην ✱ α'
44 καμήλου ὃς κενὸς εἰσαχθῇ πράξει ✱ α'
45 καθὼς Κίλιξ Καίσαρος ἀπελεύθερος ἔπραξεν.

iii c.

(22–24 = Aram. ii b 22. 23.)

The first half (about 20 lines) is almost entirely obliterated.

21 νέτω vacat
22 ὃς ἂν ἅλ[ας] η ἐν Παλμύροισι
23 Παλμυρη[ν]ῶν παραμετρησάτω [τῷ δημο]-
24 σιώνῃ ε[ἰς ἕκ]αστον μόδιον ἀσσά[ριον]
25 ὃς δ' ἂν οὐ παραμετρησ[άτω]
26 ον ἔχων το δημο
27 παρ' οὗ ἂν ὁ δ[ημοσι]ώνης [ἐνέ]-
28 χυρα λά[βῃ]
29 ἀποδω σινο αβρει
30 δημο ηιου διπ[λοῦ] ο ἱκανὸν λαμβα-
31 νέτω περὶ τ[ο]ύτου πρὸς τὸν δημοσιώνη[ν]
32 τοῦ διπλοῦ ε[ἰσα]γέσθω vacat
33 περὶ οὗ ἂν ὁ δημ[ο]σιώνης τινὰ ἀπαιτῇ περί τε
34 οὗ ἂν ὁ δημοσιώ[νης] ἀπό τινος ἀπαιτῆται περὶ
35 τούτου δικαιοδο[τείσ]θω παρὰ τῷ ἐν Παλμύ-
36 ροις τεταγμένῳ vacat
37 τῷ δημοσιώνῃ κύρι[ον] ἔ[σ]τω παρὰ τῶν μὴ ἀπ[ο]-
38 γρα[φομένων ἐ]νέχυρα [λ]α[μβάνει]ν δι' ἑαυτοῦ ἢ
39 υτατα [ἐνέ]χυρα ἡμέρα[ι]
40 [ἐξέστω τῷ δημ]οσιώνῃ πωλεῖν
41 [ἐν τόπῳ δημ ?]οσίῳ χωρὶ[ς]
42 δόλου πο ἐπράθη
43 ἢ δοθῆναι ἔδει π ειν τωδ καθὼς

44 καὶ στιν τοῦ νόμου τω vacat

45 λιμένος π [πη]γῶν ὑδάτων Καίσαρος

46 τῷ μισθωτῇ εντος παρασχέσ[θαι]

iv a.

(27 = Aram. ii b 43; 34–37 = ii b 45–48; 41–57 = ii c 3–22.)

1 ἄλλῳ μηδενὶ πράσσειν διδό[ν]αι λαμ[βάνειν]

2 ἐξέστω μήτε τι ωφσ ανθρ [μή]-

3 τε τινι [ὀν]όματι τοσ π

4 τοῦτο ποιήσῃ ηε

5 δ[ι]πλοῦν

[four lines illegible]

10 Γαίου

11 αντι

12 μετα[ξ]ὺ Παλ[μυρηνῶν]

13 νους ἐστὶ

14 γείνεσθαι κλ οι

15 εσ σατο μ

16 ὅσα δὲ ἐξ

17 ω

18 α εισπ

19 τω α ωνη

20 τῷ τελών[ῃ] θω vacat

21 οἳ δ' ἂν ε [ἐ]ξαγ

22

23 σ ας

24 καθ' ἣν ανλογ (?)

25 τοῦ δὲ ἐξάγω αι

26 αδωσε

27 ἐρίων

28 θαρ

29 π ειλ

30 γ διαγ

31 οροι ματου μὲν ορι
32 αγωγις ✱ · ϛʹ · τοῦ δὲ θʹ
33 ἀξιοῦντος το νου εἰ καὶ μὴ σ
34 [ἰτ]αλικῶν ἐξαγ[όντω]ν πράσσειν ὕστ[ερον ὡς συν]-
35 εφωνήθη μὴ ι [α]ὐτῶν ἐξαγό[ντων] [δι]-
36 δόσθαι vacat
37 μύρου τοῦ ἐν ἀσκο[ῖς αἰγεί]οις πρά[ξει ὁ τελώνης]
38 κατὰ τὸν νόμο[ν] οὔτε
39 τημα γέγονεν τῷ προτε ε εικ
40 [ὥσπερ ἐν τῷ] ἐσφραγισμένῳ νόμῳ τέτακται vacat
41 τὸ τοῦ σφάκτρου τέλος εἰς δηνάριον ὀφείλει λο[γεύε-σθαι]
42 καὶ Γερμανικοῦ Καίσαρος διὰ τῆς πρὸς Στατείλι[ον ἐπισ]-
43 τολῆς διασαφήσαντος ὅτι δεῖ πρὸς ἀσσάριον ἰτα[λι-
44 κὸν] τὰ τέλη λογεύεσθαι τὸ δὲ ἐντὸς δηναρίου τέλο[ς]
45 συνηθείᾳ ὁ τελώνης πρὸς κέρμα πράξει τῶ[ν δὲ]
46 διὰ τὸ νεκριμαῖα εἶναι ῥειπτουμένων τὸ τέλο[ς οὐκ ὀφείλεται]
47 τῶν βρωτῶν τὸ κα[τὰ] τὸν νόμον τοῦ γόμου δην[άριον]
48 εἴστημι πράσσεσθαι ὅταν ἔξωθεν τῶν ὅρων εἰσά[γη-
49 ται] ἢ ἐξάγηται vacat τοὺς δὲ εἰς χωρία ἢ ἀπὸ τῶν
50 [χω]ρίων κατακομίζοντας ἀτελεῖς εἶναι ὡς καὶ συνεφώ-
51 νησεν αὐτοῖς vacat κώνου καὶ τῶν ὁμοίων ἔδ[ο]-
52 ξεν ὅσα εἰς ἐμπορείαν φέρεται τὸ τέλος εἰς τὸ ξη-
53 ρόφορτον ἀνάγεσθαι ὡς καὶ ἐν ταῖς λοιπαῖς γείνεται πόλεσι
54 καμήλων ἐάν τε κεναὶ ἐάν τε ἔνγομοι εἰσάγωνται ἔξωθεν
55 τῶν ὅρων ὀφείλεται δηνάριον ἑκάστης κατὰ τὸν
56 νόμον ὡς καὶ Κουρβούλων ὁ κράτιστος ἐσημι-
57 ώσατο ἐν τῇ πρὸς Βάρβαρον ἐπιστολῇ.

iv b.

[About 30 lines almost entirely illegible.]

5 [ἑ]ταίρω[ν]

30 τὰς συνφων

31 τελώ[ν]ην γείνεσθαι [τὸ ἐκ τοῦ]

32 νόμο[υ] τέλος πρὸς δηνά[ρ]ιον φ[ημί ? λογεύεσθαι]

33 ἐννόμιον συνεφωνήθη μὴ δεῖν πράσσε[ιν]

34 ε [τ]ῶν δὲ ἐπὶ νομὴν μεταγομένων

35 ν θρεμμάτων ὀφείλεσθαι χα-

36 ρίσασθαι τὰ θρέμματα ἐὰν θέλῃ ὁ δη[μοσιώνης]

37 ἐξέστω.

Palmyrene Text.

i.

14 (1) דנמא די בולא בירח ניסן יום ⊃— y/// שנת

////⊃— 33 y/// בפלהדרותא די בונא בר

15 (2) בונא בר חירן וגרמטיא די אלכסדרס בר אלכסדרס בר

פלפטר גרמטוס די בולא ודמס וארכוניא

16 (3) מלכו בר עליי בר מקימו וזבידא בר נשא כד הות בולא

כנישא מן נמוסא אשרת

17 (4) מרי כתיב מן לתחת בדילדי בזבניא קדמיא בנמוסא די

מכסא עבירן שנין חיבן

Decree of the Council, in the month Nisan, the 18th day, the year 448, during the presidency of Bônnē, son [2] of Bônnē, son of Ḥairân, and the secretaryship of Alexander, son of Alexander, son of Philopator, secretary of the Council and People, and the archons (being) [3] Mâliku, son of 'Olai, son of Moqîmu, and Zebîda, son of Nesâ. When the Council was by law assembled, it established [4] what is written below—

18 (5) מכסא לא אסקו והוו מתגבין מן עידא במרען די הוא
מתכתב באגוריא די

19 (6) מכסא והוא גבא היך בנמוסא ובעידא ומטלכות זבנין
שגין על צבותא אלן

20 (7) סרבנין הוו ביני תגרא לביני מכסיא אתחזי לבולא די
ארכוניא אלן ולעשרתא

21 (8) די יבנן מרעם די לא מסק בנמוסא ויכתב בשטר
אגריא חדתא ויכתב למרעמא

22 (9) מרעמא מכסה די מן עידא ומדי אשר לאגורא וכתב
עם נמוסא קדמיא בגללא

23 (10) די לקבל היכלא די רב אסירא ויהוא מבטל לארכוניא
די הון בזבן זבן ועשרתא

24 (11) וסדקיא די לא יהוא גבא אגורא מן אנש מרעם יתיר

Whereas in former times by the law of taxation many goods liable to [5] taxation were not specified, but taxes were levied on them by custom, according to what was written in the contract of [6] the tax-collector, and he was in the habit of making levies by law and custom, and on this account many times about these matters [7] disputes arose between the merchants and the tax-collectors—It seemed good to the Council of these archons and to the Ten [8] that they should make known what was not specified in the law, and (that) it should be written down in the new document of contract, and (that) there should be written down for each [9] article its tax which is by custom, and what they have established with the contractor, and they have written it down together with the former law on the stele [10] which is in front of the temple of Rabaseirē;—and that it be made the concern of the archons who shall be (in office) at any time, and of the Ten, [11] and of the syndics, that the contractor do not demand any further levy from any man.

(Greek text, 1½ l.)

26 (12) טעון קרס די כלמא גנם כלה לארבעא טעונין די גמלין

27 (13) מכסא גבי

ii.

(Greek text, 2 ll.)

נמוסא די מכסא די למנא די הדרינא תדמר ועינתא די מיא...קיסר

a.

(1–31=Greek iii a; 41=iii b 21?; 46–49=iii b 27–30.)

1 מן מעלי עלימיא די מתאעלין לתדמר

2 או לתחומיה [יגבא מכס]א לכל רגל ד 3//

3 מן עלם די..ן ב........[ל]מפק[נא] ⊃— //

4 מן עלם ומת[ן] די יזבן....⊃—

5 והן זבונא ומעל..ין יתן לכל רגל ⊃— //

6 הו מ[כסא יג]בא [מ]ן טעון גמלא די יבי[שין]

(Greek text.)

[12] A waggon-load of any kind of goods whatsoever, at four camel-loads [13] the tax shall be levied.

ii.

(Greek text.)

The law of the taxes of the custom-house of Hadriana Tadmor, and the wells of water ...... Caesar.

a.

From importers of slaves who are imported into Tadmor [2] or its borders the [tax-collector shall levy] for each person 22 denarii. [3] From a slave who .... [for] export, 12. [4] From a slave-veteran who shall be sold .... 10; [5] and if the buyer .... he shall give for each person 12. [6] The said t[ax-collector shall l]evy from a camel-load of dry

7 למעלנא......... די טעון גמלא ד / [// ?]
8 מן [טעון גמלא] למ[פקנא] ד ///
9 מן ט[עון] חמרא למעלנא [ולמפקנא]....
10 מן א[רג]ונא מלטא לכל מ[שך למעלנא]....
11 ולמ[פ]קנא אסרין У ///
12 מן טע[ון ג]מל[א] די משחא בשימא [די]
13 מתאעל [ב]ש[טיפת]א ד 3 У
14 ולמא ד..... ל. וסא דנה
15 למפקנ[א]. כ. ן... [ג]מל לטעונא ⟵ ///
16 מן טעון גמלא די [מ]שחא בשימא [די יתאעל]
17 בזקי[ן די] ע[זי ל]מ[על]נא ד ⟵ /// ולמפק[נא ד У //]
18 מן ט[עון חמר די] משחא [בשימא ד]י יתאעל
19 בש[טיפ]תא [למעלנא ד] ⟵ /// ולמפקנא ד У //
20 מן טעון חמר [ד]י משחא [בשימא] די
21 יתאעל בזקי[ן]........[למ]פקנא ד У //
22 מן טעון די מש[חא די בזק]ין ארב[ע]

goods, [7] for import .... of the camel-load, 3 (?) denarii. [8] From [a camel-load] for ex[port], 3 denarii. [9] From a donkey-l[oad], for import [and for export}.... [10] From purple fleeces, for each s[kin, for import] .... [11] and for export, 8 assarii. [12] From a cam[el-lo]ad of sweet oil [which] [13] is imported [in] the f[lask], 25 denarii. [14] And for what ...... this [15] for export ...... [c]amel, for the load 13 denarii. [16] From a camel-load of sweet oil [which is imported] [17] in goa[t-s]kins, for im[por]t 13 denarii, and for expor[t 7 denarii]. [18] From a [donkey-loa]d [of sweet] oil which is imported [19] in the fl[as]k, [for import] 13 [denarii], and for export 7 denarii. [20] From a donkey-load of [sweet] oil which [21] is imported in skin[s] ... [for ex]port 7 denarii. [22] From

די עז למעלן טעון ג[מל]א ד 𐡛 ///

ולמפקנא ד 𐡛 [///]

מן טעון די מ[שחא] די [בז]קין תרתן די עז

למעל[ן] ט[עונ]א די גמלא ד [ע //] ולפקנא ד [ע //]

מן טעו[ן] חמר די משח למ[עלנא] ד ע // ולמפקנא [ד ע //]

מן טעון דהנא די בזקין א[רבע] די עז די

טעון גמל מעלנא ד 𐡛 /// ול[מפק]נא ד 𐡛 ///

מן טעון דהנא די בזקי תרת[ן די] עז

לטעון גמל למעלנא ד ע // ולמ[פקנא ד ע //]

מן טעון [דה]נא די חמר למעלנא [ד ע // ולמפקנא] ד ע //

מן טעון [נוני]א מליחיא לטעונא די [גמלא]

[למעלנא ד] 𐡛 ומן מפק מנהון ....

........א לטעונא די גמלא לם...

........א די טעון חמרא למעלנ[א]

.........נא יגבא מכסא ד ///

a load of oi[l which is in] four goat-[ski]ns, [23] for import, the ca[mel]-load, 13 denarii, [24] and for export 1[3] denarii. [25] From a load of o[il] which is [in] two goat-[sk]ins, [26] for import, the camel-l[oa]d, [7] denarii, and for export [7] denarii. [27] From a donkey-load of oil, for im[port] 7 denarii, and for export [7 denarii]. [28] From a load of fat which is in f[our] goat-skins, which [29] is a camel-load, import 13 denarii, and for [expo]rt 13 denarii. [30] From a load of fat which is in tw[o] goat-skins, [31] for the camel-load, for import 7 denarii, and for ex[port 7 denarii]. [32] From a donkey-load of [fa]t, for import [7 denarii, and for export] 7 denarii. [33] From a load of salted [fish], for the [camel]-load, [34] [for import] 10 [denarii], and from an exporter of any of them ... [35] ... for the camel-load ... [36] ... of the donkey-load, for import [37] ... the tax-

38 ....יא ד־־ו

39 ....מן אם

40 ....יא......[אס]רין //

41 ....שאמריא למע[לנא].....רשא חד אסרא חד

42 מן [טעו]נא גמלא א........//

43 ....מן ארב א........[א]סרין..//

44 מן..................ד

45 א.............ממן די יהוא מזבן משחא

46 בשימא אסרין...אף יגבא מכסא מן איתא מן

47 מן די שקלא דינר [או] יתיר דנרא חד מן איתא

48 ומן מן די שקלא אסרין תמניא

49 יגבא אסרין תמניא

ii b.

(1–12=Greek iii b 31–45; 22. 23=iii c 22–24; 43=iv a 27; 45–48=iv a 34–37.)

1 ומן מן די שקל[א] אסרי[ן ש]תא

2 יגבא אסרין [ע /]

3 אף יגבא........ודי ח[נ]תא ופטפלא

collector shall levy 3 denarii [38] . . . 10 denarii . . [39] . . . from . . [40] . . . 2 assarii [41] . . . lambs, for im[port] . . . one head, one assarius. [42] From a camel-[loa]d . . . 2 [43] . . . from ? . . assarii . . 2. [44] From . . . [45] . . . from one (?) who shall sell sweet oil [46] assarii . . Also the tax-collector shall levy from women, from [47] one who has taken a denarius [or] more, one denarius from the woman. [48] And from one who has taken eight assarii [49] he shall levy eight assarii.

ii b.

[1] And from one who has taken [s]ix assarii [2] he shall levy [6] assarii. [3] Also he shall levy . . . and of the shop and

4 ....פ̇.........היך עדתא
5 [לכל] ירןח] מן חנותא ד /
6 [מן כל] משך די [י]תאעל או יזבן למשכא אסרין //
7 ... ימנתיא די הפכין במדיתא יהן מוס מכסא
8 [לתש]מיש עינן תרתן די מ[י] די במדיתא ד y /// —
9 [י]נבא מכסא לטׄעונא די חטא וחמרא ותבנא
10 ו[כ]ל מדי דמא [להון לכ]ל גמל לארח חדא ד /
11 לגמלא כדי יתאיעל סריק ינבא ד /
12 היך [די] גבׄ[א] קלקיס בר חרי קיסר
13 ס̇..........סׄא די תדמר ועינתא די מיא
14 ומל....יב. [מ]דיתא ותחומיה היך
15 א [מכס]יא [די] אׄגר קדם מרינס היגמונא
16 ....טען די גמלׄא ד //// ומפקן ד ////
17 מ[ן]........מׄלטׄא לׄכל משך למעלנא ד //// ולמפקנא ד ////
18 [אף] ינב[א מכסא] מן גנסיא כלהון היך די כתיב מן לעל

general store [4] ... according to custom, [5] [every] mon[th] from the shop 1 denarius. [6] [From every] skin which shall be imported or sold, for the skin 2 assarii. [7] ... clothiers (?) who shall barter in the city, their tax shall vary. [8] For the use of two wells of wa[ter] which are in the city, 800 denarii. [9] The tax-collector shall levy for a load of wheat and wine and straw [10] and suchlike, for each camel, for one journey 1 denarius. [11] For the camel when it is brought in empty he shall levy 1 denarius, [12] as Kilix, freedman of Caesar, levied. [13] ... of Tadmor and the wells of water [14] ... the town and its borders, as [15] .. the [taxes] for [which] they (?) contracted before Marinus the governor. [16] ... the camel-load, 4 denarii, and export, 4 denarii. [17] From ... a fleece, for each skin, for import 4 denarii, and for export 4 denarii. [18] [Also the tax-collector shall l]evy from goods of all kinds

19 ...טב..עא באסרא חד למדיא די קסטן

20 עשר ת[שת]...מא די. יתבעא יתן [לה]ן לתשמישא

21 .לא....תשע לכל מדא מן נמ[וס]א דנה ססטרטין ////

22 מן יהוא לה מלח בתו[מר].......מאר

23 ת[דמרי]א יכילנה ל....א די מא (?) באסרא חד

24 ....אי........קי..היגמונא

25 ..חשבן מב.......בני תדמריא ל.י

26 ...קס מכס[מס] קי[סר]

27 חיב לא הוא........סא..גרבא

28 אלקמס וחת.....נמוסא יפרע מ[כס]א

29 משתתף ד......אדי...יהוא

30 פרע למכסא מן די מעל רגלין לתדמר

31 [או] לתחומיה ומפק לכל רגל י..

32 ו..י........[מ]פק יפרע למכ[סא ד]ינרין //

33 ...די....[על]ם וטרן.ד y ///

34 ...לכל.....מיא דנה.......

as it is written above. [19] . . . one assarius for the modius of costus-roots. [20] [Six]teen . . . what shall be desired, he shall give [to th]em for use. [21] . . . nine for every modius by this l[a]w, 4 sestertii. [22] Whoever shall have salt in Tad[mor] . . . [23] the T[admoren]es, he shall measure it . . . at one assarius [24] . . . the governor. [25] . . a reckoning . . . the Tadmorenes . . [26] . . . cus Maxi[mus] Cae[sar], [27] he is not liable . . . [28] Alkimus . . . the law, he shall pay the t[ax], [29] participating . . . he shall [30] pay to the tax-collector. Whoever imports any persons into Tadmor [31] [or] its borders, and exports (any), for each person . . . [32] . . . [ex]port, he shall pay to the tax-col[lector] 12 [denarii] [33] . . . who . . . [sla]ve-veteran . . 8 denarii [34] . . . for

35 .. מעלנ...... ה וד ב— ומפקנ[א] ע //

36 .... מן די מפק עלם ומרן

37 .. חשבן .... כתיב בנמוסא

38 .... פרע ד ע ////

39 ... מ....... לא כתיב בדיל[די]

40 מרעם לא ... או ל ....

41 לא דמיא ....

42 ומעלן מב ....

43 ודי עמרא .... נא די אפק ד ///

44 תדמ[ר].. מכסא .... פרעא תהוא.עמרא

45 דיא .... מכסא למפקנא בתר..

46 כות הוו ספו[ן]....לא ע מרא. איטליק[א]

47 [י]הוא פרע ..... למפקא

48 משחא ב[שימא די] בזקין די עז יהוא מכסא

49 .... בדילדי בטען די

ii c.

(3–22 = Greek iv a 41–57.)

1 כתב די טעא מכס[א].....בן

each ... this ... [35] .. import ... and 10 denarii, and export, 7 [36] ... whoever exports a slave-veteran [37] .. a reckoning ... written in the law [38] ... pay 9 denarii [39] ... is not written, because [40] anything ... [41] is not like ... [42] and import ... [43] and of wool ... which he exports, 3 denarii. [44] Tadmor .. the tax ... she shall pay. The wool [45] of (?) ... the tax for export afterwards [46] as they have agreed ... Italian modius, [47] shall he pay ... to the exporters. [48] [Sweet] oil [which] is in goat-skins shall the tax-collector [49] ... because by mistakes in the

ii c.

[1] document which the tax-collector committed ... [2] ... in

2 מן . . שו בנמוסא . חיפא ד —— ע
3 מכסא די קצבא אפי דנר חיב
4 למתחשבו היך די אף גרמנקוס קיסר
5 באגרתא די כתב לסטטילס פשק די
6 הא כשר די . . מכסיא אפי אסר איטלקא
7 גבן ומדי גו מן דנר חיב מכסא היך
8 עדתא ע[ר]פן יהא גבא
9 פגרין די משתדן מכס לא חיבין
10 לטעמתא הי בנמ[ו]סא לטעונא אקימת
11 די יהוא מתג[ב]א דנר
12 מדי יהוא מ[תאעל] בר מן תחומא או מאפק
13 מן די מפק ל[קרי]א [או] מעל מן קריא
14 מכס לא חיב היך די אף הוו ספון
15 אסטרביליא ומדי דמא להון אתחזי די
16 לכל די עלל לחשבן תגרא יהוא מכסא
17 היך ליביש היך די הוא אף במדינתא

the ? law, 15 denarii. [3] The tax on slaughtered animals by the denarius must [4] be reckoned, as also Germanicus Caesar, [5] in the letter which he wrote to Statilius, explained that [6] it was indeed right that . . the taxes (should be) levied by the Italian assarius, [7] and what is under a denarius, the tax-collector must according to [8] custom levy in small coin. [9] Dead bodies which are thrown away are not liable to taxation. [10] As to victuals, it (is said) in the law: For a load I have ordained [11] that a denarius shall be levied, [12] whenever it shall be imported from without the borders, or exported; [13] whoever exports to the [villages or] imports from the villages [14] is not liable to taxation, as also they agreed. [15] Pine-cones and such-like, it seemed good that [16] for all that comes into the market the tax shall be [17] as for dry goods, as has been also

18 אחרניתא

19 גמליא הן טעינין והן סריקין יהן

20 מתאעלין בר מן תחומא חיב כל

21 גמל דנר היך בנמוסא והיך די אשר

22 קרבלון כשירא באגרתא די כתב לברברס

23 על גלדיא די גמליא חסא.ן כפרו די מכס

24 לא נבן 𐡹 עשב[י]א . . . . ותא אתחזי די יהון

25 יהבין מכ[סא] בדילדי אית בהון תגרתא

26 מכסא די עלימתא היך די נמוסא מחא פשקת

27 הו מכסא יג[בא מכ]סא מן עלימתא די שקלן דנר

28 או יתיר לאי[תא דנר]א והן חסיר תהוה שקלא

29 מדי הו[ת] שקלא [יגבא מן] צלמי נחשא אדרטיא

30 אתחזי די יתגבא היך [מן נח]שא ויהוא פרע צלם

31 בפלגות . . . וצלמין . . ן טען 𐡹 על מלחא

32 קש . . . [א]תחזי לי די באתר די דמס תהוא

(the rule) in [18] other cities. [19] Camels, whether they be brought in laden or empty [20] from without the borders, each camel is liable [21] for a denarius, as is in the law, and as [22] the excellent Corbulo established in the letter which he wrote to Barbarus [23] about the camel-skins ? ? that they do not levy [24] a tax. Herbs . . . it seemed good that they should [25] pay the ta[x], because they are an article of merchandise. [26] The tax of female slaves, as I clearly (?) explained the law, [27] the said tax-collector shall le[vy the t]ax from female slaves who take a denarius [28] or more, for (each) wo[man a denari]us, and if she take less, [29] what she has taken [he shall levy. From] images of bronze, statues, [30] it seemed good that (the tax) be levied as [from bron]ze, and the image shall pay [31] half . . . and images . . . a load. For salt [32] . . . it seemed

33 מתזבנא באתר די מתכנשין ומן מן ת[גרא]
34 יזבן לחש[בנ]ה יהוא יהב למדיא אסר איטלקא
35 היך בנמוסא ואף מכסא [מ]לחא די הויא
36 בתדמר היך בה.........אפי אסר יהוא
37 מתקבל ולמ[די]א יהוא מזבן היך עידא
38 ....[מכ]סא די ארגונא ברילדי
39 ק..........ארבעא ופלג.....
40 ....מלכין....ת וחיטא
41 ....ד די יהוא
42 ..א............יהוא מתגבא
43 מכסא היך די נמ[וסא].....על ∽ למעלן שלחא
44 אסרין // אשב .....[ינ]בא ולממפקנא
45 למעונא.......[כות א]ף הוו ספן
46 ענא ת.ו....ה......מן תחומא.פהן
47 ....א מכסא חיב או הן לגו מן
48 ....על... מדיתא למגז מכס לא חיב
49 מ........[ח]נותא ומן די היך יהון הון

good to me that in the public place it be [33] sold, in the place where they assemble; and whoever of the merchants [34] shall buy (it) at its reckoning, he shall give for the modius an Italian assarius, [35] as is in the law, and also the tax of (?) the salt which is [36] in Tadmor, as . . . by the assarius it shall be [37] admitted, and by the mo[di]us it shall be sold, according to custom [38] . . . the [ta]x on purple, because [39] . . . four and a half . . . [40] . . . kings (?) . . . ? [41] . . . which shall be [42] . . . shall be levied, [43] the tax as the law . . . For import, skins (?) [44] 2 assarii . . . [he shall l]evy, and for export [45] ? . . . [as al]so they have agreed. [46] Sheep (?) . . . from the borders . . . [47] . . . the tax is liable, or if below [48] . . . the city, to shear, a tax is not liable [49] . . . the shop and because, as they shall

. . . . מכסא . . . . א היך בנמוסא דנר . . א . . . נא . . . . .
מכסא לא יהוא מתגבא אלא ל . ן די יהוא מתאעל . . . . .
[תד]מר אן יצבא מכסא יהוא

be (?) [50] . . . the tax . . . as in the law a denarius . . . the tax shall not be levied except . . shall be brought in . . . [Tad]mor, if he wish, the tax shall be.

The most valuable commentaries on this inscription are those of Reckendorf, *ZDMG* xlii (1888) 370–415, and of Dessau, *Hermes* xix (1884) 486–533 (Gk. text). With this Tariff are to be compared the Gk. Tariff of Coptos A. D. 90, Hogarth in Flinders Petrie *Koptos* (1896) 27 ff., and the Lat. Tariff of Zarai, CIL viii 4508. The T. of Palmyra is that of a local *octroi*, the T. of Zarai refers to an imperial *douane* at the port, the T. of Coptos is distinct from both.

i.

L. 1. דגמא די בולא The Senate promulgates this important decree (*δόγμα*) on its own account, without reference to Rome. The earlier tariff, however, of which this is only a readjustment, was in all essentials drawn up by the Roman authorities, see ii b 12. 15; c. 5. 22. בְּפְלֶהֶדְרוּתָא The office of *πρόεδρος*; ל is written instead of ר especially after פ, cf. the Talm. פלהדרין and פרהדרין *προέδριον*, פלטרין *πραιτώριον* &c.

L. 2. גרמטיא The office of *γραμματεύς*, גְרַמַטוּס 122 2 *n*. אלכסדרס with נ assimilated, cf. 146 4 *n*., but without the assimilation in 121 3; cf. סקלטיקא Vog. 21, but סנק׳ 125 2. ארכוניא *ἄρχοντες*, probably the same as *στρατηγοί* in 3rd cent. inscrr.; see 121 2 *n*.

L. 3. עליי 'Ολαιοῦς (gen.) = عَلِيّ. נשא 132 1 *n*. כר הות וגו׳ *βουλῆς νομίμου ἀγουμένης*. For מן נמוסא cf. מן עידא *by custom* l. 5 &c. The vowel of the first syllable of נמוסא coming before the *ό* was prob. *ŏ*, as in Gk.; but in Syr. ܢܳܡܽܘܣܳܐ, in Arab. نَامُوس. אַשְׁרַת ii c 21, Afel of שרר, Syr. ܐܰܫܰܪ lit. firmum fecit.

L. 4. מדי ii c 7. 27, מא די a 14, in Bibl. Aram. מָה דִּי Dan. 2 28 &c., Talm. מה ד. בדילדי 110 4 *n*. וְבְנַיָּא קַדְמַיֵּא *ἐν τοῖς πάλαι χρόνοις*. זבנא *χρόνος* is mas., but ז׳ *πλειστάκις* l. 6 is fem., 121 5 *n*. Distinguish between מַכְסָא *tax*, cf. מֶכֶס Num. 31 28, and מָכְסָא, ܡܳܟܣܳܐ *tax-collector* l. 6 &c. עֲבִידָן Plur. of עבידתא 96 7, here in the sense of *articles* i.e. of merchandise. שְׁנַיִן Cf. 121 5 סניאן and שניאן. חַיָּבִן מַכְסָא The adject. absol. governing the accus., as often in Syr.; cf. בָּתִּים מְלֵאִים כָּל־טוּב Deut. 6 11.

L. 5. לא אַסִּקוּ Afel 3 plur. mas. from סלק *go up*, rather than Pual אֻסַּקוּ. The subj. is indefinite, lit. *they did not bring* (*them*) *up* i. e. on to the tariff; Gk. *οὐκ ἀνελήμφθη*. וְהֲוֹו or וְהֲוָו Perf. 3 plur. mas., although used with a fem. subj. עבידן, a grammatical solecism. מִתְגְּבַיִן Mas., if it is to agree formally with והוו, but מִתְגַּבְיָן if it is to be of the same gender as עבידן. The pass. construction is used elsewhere with this vb., e. g. ii c 11. 42. 50; נבא = *collect*, *exact* tribute. מן עֲיָדָא *by custom*, ܥܝܳܕܳܐ. The expression is varied, thus היך .. בעידא l. 6. היך עידא ii c 37. היך עָדְתָא ii b 4. במדען די Lit. *at the rate of anything which*; מדען = מדעמא l. 8 (see note). אַמִּיכָא דֻּ *μισθώσει* = שְׁטַר אַגְרָא l. 8. אגר, ܐܓܰܪ = *to hire*, of taxes *to collect*, *farm* ii b 15, אָגוֹרָא l. 11 *the contractor*. In Palmyra, as elsewhere in the Rom. empire, the taxes were not collected by state officials, but by persons who entered into a contract to raise them. As a self-governing state within the empire, Palmyra was allowed to levy its own taxes and reap the profits. In the same way subject kings and tetrarchs levied taxes within their territories, e. g. Herod Antipas in Galilee, Mt. 9 9 &c.; see Schürer *Gesch.*[3] i 475 ff. In the Gk. version the collector is called ὁ *τελωνῶν* l. 6. ὁ *μισθούμενος* 10. 13. *τελώνης* iv a 20 &c. *μισθωτής* iii c 46. *δημοσιώνης* iii a 9; cf. *μισθωταί* in the T. of Coptos l. 2.

L. 6. מַכְסָא This system of farming out the taxes naturally led to abuses. The *publicani* were notorious for their extortions and dishonesty, e. g. Lk. 3 12 f. 19 8 &c. In the Talm. the מוכסין appear in a very unfavourable light, e. g. *Baba Qama* 113 a; for a typical instance of injustice at Askelon in the time of Ptolemy Euergetes see Jos. *Ant.* xii 4. 5. The absence of any fixed scheme of rates was a fruitful source of disputes, as at Coptos, Hogarth l. c. 28. In the promulgation of this tariff at Palmyra we have a rare instance of an attempt to deal with abuses by cancelling the loose system of taxation 'by custom,' and specifying fixed rates in detail; cf. Tacitus *Ann.* xiii 50. 51. וְהֲוָא נָבֵא The subj. is the preceding מכסא. מטלכות 121 6 *n*. צְבְוָתָא 110 4 *n*.

L. 7. סַרְבָּנִין or סַרְ׳ from סרב *to scold, dispute*. In the Targ. סַרְבָּן is an adj. (Barth *Nominalb*. § 207 d), and the noun is סַרְבָּנוּתָא, ܣܪܘܒܘܬܐ. תַּגָּרָא ii c 16. 113 3 *n*. אתחזי Elsewhere the construction is אתחזי די ii c 24. 30; so here די ought to be followed immediately by the verb, א׳ די יבנון ארכניא ועשרתא, as in the Gk. *δεδόχθαι τοὺς ἐνεστῶτας ἄρχοντας καὶ δεκαπρώτους διακρείνοντας* (Reckendorf 397). As it stands די can only be rendered as the gen. sign. עֲשַׂרְתָּא Emph. st. of עֲשַׂרָא; numbers denoting a company or college take this form in Syr., e. g. ܬܪܥܣܪܬܐ *the Twelve* (Nöld. *Syr.*

Gr. § 151). The *δεκάπρωτοι decemprimi* were specially concerned with the revenue.

L. 8. יבנון Af. impf. of בין, i. e. יְבִינוּן lit. *cause to understand.* מְפַּק Af. ptcp. pass., rather than a ptcp. Hofal, *τὰ μὴ ἀνειλημμένα*; the pass. ptcp. (קְטִיל) in the Aram. dialects is frequently used of past time, especially in Syr. and in the Talm., e. g. ܟܬܝܒ *γέγραπται*: Nöld. *Syr. Gr.* § 278 a, Dalman *Gr.* 231. Other instances of the pass. ptcp. in the Tariff are מְבַטַּל (not מְבַטְּל) l. 10. מַאשַׁק (not מְאַשַּׁק) ii c 12. נבי l. 13. נבן ii c 7. ויכתב The pass. of the tenses is normally expressed by the reflexive stems in the Aram. dialects, hence we should prob. point יִכְּתֵב Ethpeel (cf. מִתְכְּתֵב l. 5), and, with the same assimilation of ת (ד), יִזַּבַּן Ethpa. ii a 4 &c., מִזַּבַּן (or מְזַבַּן Pael ptcp. pass.) ii c 37 (cf. מתזבנא ii c 33); see Duval *Rev. Ét. Juiv.* viii 57–63. Others, however, such as Sachau *ZDMG* xxxvii 562 ff., Wright *Comp. Gr.* 225, regard יכתב and the ptcps. in the note preceding as Hofal or Pual forms, יְכֻתַּב &c., on the analogy of Hofal forms in Bibl. Aram., e. g. הָתְקְנַת, הוּסְפַת Dan. 4 33 &c. But, as Duval points out, these forms are artificially modelled upon the Hebrew, and prob. were never used in actual speech, certainly not in the vulgar dialect of Palmyra. Moreover in Bibl. Aram. these forms were only used for the *Perf.* 3 pers.; for the impf. and for the other persons the reflexive is employed to express the passive. Duval further tries to explain אשר and כתב l. 9 as passives, but in spite of the difficulty of the construction it is better to treat them as actives. שְׁטַר אַגְרָיָא l. 5 *n.* 84 3 *n.* למרעמא מ׳ *ἑκάστῳ ἴδει*; see 75 2 *n.*

L. 9. ומדי אשר לא׳ וכתב The Gk. has *καὶ ἐπειδὰν κυρωθῇ τῷ μισθουμένῳ, ἐνγραφῆναι.* This, however, is not the strict meaning of the Palm. מדי may = *when*, e. g. ii c 12, like the Syr. ܡܐ ܕ whenever, but elsewhere it = *that which*, e. g. l. 4. The two verbs must be taken as active, אַשַּׁר Afel of שרר (not Ofal, see above), and since כתב cannot be pronounced as Ethpeel, it must be Peal; the verbs may be either 3 plur. defectively written (118 3 *n.*), or 3 sing. with 'the Council' understood as the subject. The perf. וכתב cannot = *and that they should write*; this would require ויכתב or יכתב; the latter is read by Bevan, correcting the text, *Daniel* 215. בגללא Lit. *a round*, so generally of drafted stone, e. g. אֶבֶן גְּלָל Ezr. 5 8. 6 4; the Gk. has *στήλη*.

L. 10. היכלא *ἱεροῦ*. רב אסירא *Ῥαβασείρη*, apparently a divine name (p. 198). Both the Palm. and the Gk. texts imply that the new tariff was to be exhibited not merely in the same place but on the same stone as the old. Hence it ought to be possible to compare the new with the old, point by point; but the fragmentary state of both texts renders this difficult, the more so as we cannot tell for certain where the new ends and the old begins. The new code appears to extend from ii a 1 to ii b 12; it is not unlikely, as Reckendorf argues, that the old code begins at ii b 13, which R. restores נמוסא די מכ]סא די תרמר]; references to it are found in ii b 15. 28. 37. 49. c 1 f. 19 ff. The following table gives such comparisons as can be made out:

	Old Tariff	*New Tariff*
Slaves	ii b 30–36.	ii a 1–5.
Sweet-oil	b 48–49.	a 12–21. 45.
Victuals	c 10–14.	b 9–10.
Camels	c 19–22.	b 11.
Women	c 26–29.	a 46–b 2.
Purple	c 38.	a 10.

מְבַטַּל Pael ptcp. pass., ἐπιμελεῖσθαι τοὺς ἄρχοντας. The ptcp. is used impersonally with ܠ and pers. pron. in the sense *it concerns*, ܡܒܛܠ ܠܗ; this construction is frequent in Aram. דִּי חָזֵה The ptcp. used of the future. בזבן זבן Cf. Jn. 5 4 ܙܒܢ ܘܙܒܢ.

L. 11. סרקיא συνδίκους. For the assimilation of נ cf. 146 4 *n*. נָבֵא Peal ptcp.

L. 12. טען γόμος, a *qaṭûl* form like לבושא; in Syr. ܛܥܢܐ *load, freight*, Targ. מַטְעֲנָא. קרס καρρικός = *carrus*. כָּלְמָא Here an adj.; in Syr. ܟܠܡܐ ܕ = *whosoever, as often as*; in Palest. Aram. כל מה = כלום *something, anything*, in questions and after negatives, Dalman *Gr.* 90. גְמַלִין A camel-load = about 6 cwt.

L. 13. גְּבֵי Peal ptcp. pass., ii c 7 גבן, cf. in Bibl. Aram. גְּלִי, Dan. 2 30. קְרֵי Ezr. 4 18.

ii.

לִמֵנָא ܠܡܐܢܐ, λιμένα accus. of λιμήν *portus*, 'custom-house.' חַדְרִינָא תרמר See p. 263 and 146 3 *n*.

a.

L. 1. מַעֲלֵי Afel ptcp. plur. constr. from עלל *enter*, in the Tariff with the meaning *to import*, εἰσάγειν, εἰσκομίζειν, as opposed to אַפֵּק Afel from נפק, *to export*, ἐκκομίζειν. עֲלִימַיָּא Lit. *youths*, i.e. slaves, παῖδας, cf. עֶלֶם 1 S. 20 22; Targ. עֲלֵימָא, fem. עֲלֵימְתָא; Syr. ܥܠܝܡܐ, ܥܠܝܡܬܐ. The fem. plur. עלימתא ii c 26 = *harlots*. מִתְאַעֲלִין Ettafal ptcp.

L. 2. לְתְחוּמַיָּה Plur. with suff., ii b 14. 31, τὰ ὅρια; sing. תחומא. רגל l. 5, plur. ii b 30 רגלין, = Arab. رَجُل *a man*; ἑκάστου σώματος iii a 8. ד is the initial of דנר δηνάριον (represented in the Gk. by ✱), originally, as its name implies, the equivalent in silver of ten copper asses. Its value at this period was 4 sestertii (ii b 21) or 16 asses, i. e. about 9½*d.* Government dues and official payments were calculated on the Roman denarius-as system, see ii c 3 ff.; Kennedy *DB* iii 429.

L. 3. מַפְּקָא Emph. st. of מַפְּקָן b 16 *export*, as opposed to מַעְלָן, מַעְלְנָא *import*.

L. 4. עלם ומרן b 33. 36 = the Roman *mancipia veterana*, a class of slaves, distinguished from *mancipia novicia*, who by Roman law were not only free from taxation, but did not need to be 'declared.' Contrary to the usual practice, at Palmyra these slaves were sold; Dessau l. c. 505. יִזְבַּן b 6 Ethpa.; see i 8 *n*.

L. 5. זְבוּנָא Cf. אֲגוֹרָא i 11.

L. 6. הו ii c 27 ὁ αὐτός = Syr. ܗܘ, which frequently comes to be used merely as a rendering of the Gk. article; Nöld. *Syr. Gr.* 173.

L. 9. טען חֲמָרָא γόμος ὀνικός = half a camel-load.

L. 10. אַרְגְּוָנָא מַלְּמָא πορφύρας μηλωτῆς, i. e. wool died with purple; the form אַרְגְּוָנָא occurs in Dan. 5 7 &c., Syr. ܐܪܓܘܢܐ. In the old law, ii c 38, 'purple' alone is mentioned, without details. מְשַׁךְ = [δέρμα]τος iii a 16 f.

L. 11. אסרין Plur. of אִסָּרָא l. 41 ἀσσάριον Mt. 10 29. Lk. 12 6, Mishnah אִיסָּר, Syr. ܐܣܪܐ = *assarius*, a by-form of *as*, but apparently not of the same value. For the *as* was $\frac{1}{16}$th of a denarius (supr.); while the *assarion* was $\frac{1}{24}$th of a silver denarius, according to the Mishnah, e.g. האיסר אחד מעשרים וארבעה בדינר כסף Talm. Jer. *Qiddushin* 58 d. In the 2nd cent., therefore, there was a considerable difference in value between the Hellenistic *assarion* and the official Roman *as*, which in this inscr. is called אסר איטלקא ii c 6. 34; see Schürer *Gesch.*[3] ii 54, Kennedy, l. c.

L. 12. מִשְׁחָא בְּשִׂימָא ii b 48 f. μύρον, oil for anointing, distinguished from משחא l. 22 *oil*; cf. Lk. 7 46 ܡܫܚܐ ἔλαιον and ܡܫܚܐ ܕܒܣܡܐ μύρον.

L. 13. בְּשַׁטִּיפְתָא [τοῦ ἐν ἀλαβάσ]τροις; cf. Mt. 26 7 ܫܛܝܦܬܐ ܕܡܫܚܐ ܕܒܣܡܐ ἀλάβαστρον μύρου.

L. 17. בְּזִקִּין דִּי עֲז ἐν ἀσκοῖς αἰγείοις. זקין, sing. זִקָּא, is fem.; בְּזִקִּין תַּרְתֵּין l. 25.

L. 19. בשטיפתא Perhaps rather בשטיפיא mas.

L. 22. טען די משחא γόμου ἐλαιηροῦ iii a 32.

L. 26. ולפקנא An error for ולסמ׳.

L. 28. דהנא Syr. ܕܘܗܢܐ, Targ. דּוּהֲנָא and דִּיהֲנָא *fatness*, Arab. دُهْن *fat*.

L. 32. The odd numbers in the foregoing lines (13–32), 26, 13, 7, imply that 1 denarius was charged on the beast (see ii c 21), and 24, 12, 6 on the freight. In the Rom. imperial tariff (Zarai, see p. 332) beasts were not taxed, 'pecora in nundinium immunia.'

L. 33. נתיא מליחיא or נתא Cf. Neh. 13 16 וְהַצֹּרִים . . מְבִיאִים דָּאג וְכָל־מֶכֶר.

L. 41. אִמְרַיָּא (Schröder), Syr. ܐܶܡܪܳܐ, Targ. אִמְּרָא, Arab. إِمَّر.

L. 46. איתא l. 47, cf. ii c 26–29. אִיתְּתָא, אִתְּתָא, is the form in the Targ., = אִנְתְּתָא; the vowel of the 1st syllable is short, in spite of the vowel letter. Elsewhere in Palm. the form is אתתה *his wife*, e. g. Vog. 33 a. The women here referred to are ἑταῖραι; for references to their taxation in antiquity see Dessau 517, and cf. in the tariff of Coptos ll. 19 f. Γυναικῶν πρὸς ἑταιρισμὸν δραχμὰς ἑκατὸν ὀκτώ (see p. 332).

L. 47. דִּנְרָא ii c 3 &c. 115 3. The transcription דינר (only here) is exceptional.

L. 48. תְּמַנְיָא Fem. with the mas. אמרין.

ii b.

L. 3. חנותא The reading in l. 5 is certain, lit. *a vaulted room*; cf. Hebr. חָנוּת *cell*, in plur. Jer. 37 16, and Syr. ܚܳܢܘܬܳܐ = Hebr. לִשְׁכָּה 2 K. 23 11; generally *a shop, bazaar*, sometimes (e.g. Jer. 37 16 Aq.) as here = ἐργαστήριον iii b 32. 35. פטפלא παντοπωλείων σκυτικῶν (*shoemakers*) iii b 33; the Aram. equivalent of the latter word is lost. For פט' see 146 4 *n*.

L. 6. יִזַּבַּן Reflexive, i 8 *n*., the same form as יתאעל.

L. 7. ימנתיא Perhaps to be restored [ח]ימנתיא ἱματιοπῶλαι iii b 38; נתתיא is a possible reading. די הָפְכִין μεταβόλοι, lit. *who change*, i. e. trade. יהון c 19 = יְהוֹן c 49 = יֶהֱוֹן 76 D 3. מוּם מִכְסָא Lit. *they shall be unsteadiness* (i. e. *unsteady*) *in taxation*, i. e. *their tax shall be undetermined*, the noun (Syr. ܡܽܘܡܳܐ) in appos. instead of an adj.; cf. the Hebr. idiom, Driver *Tenses* § 189. 2. The Gk. has τὸ ἱκανὸν τ[έλος] iii b 39.

L. 8. לְתַשְׁמִישׁ Targ. תַּשְׁמִישָׁא, Syr. ܬܫܡܫܬܳܐ. מ[ין] must be taken as a sing. = מין; there is not room, according to Reckendorf, for the restoration מ[יא] l. 13. The amount of the tax obviously implies more than a single use of the wells; the Gk. has χρήσεος πηγῶν β′ ἑκάστου ἔτους ✱ ω′ (i. e. 800 denarii) iii b 40. Palmyra was renowned for its supply of water; thus Pliny 5 21 'Palmyra urbs nobilis situ divitiis soli et aquis amoenis.'

L. 9. חמא Syr. ܫܘܚܠܐ, Targ. חִמִּין. Possibly here the word is plur. חִמְּא.

L. 10. מדי here includes the relat., *that which,* ii c 29. The old law corresponding to ll. 9. 10 appears to be given in ii c 10–14.

L. 11. כדי יִתְאַיְעַל i.e. ὃς (=די with the subjunct.) εἰσαχθῇ iii b 44. In the old law the tax was charged on laden and unladen camels (ii c 19–22), in the new only on the latter, because for a laden camel the tax was charged on the freight; cf. ii a 32 *n.*

L. 12. קִלְקִיס Κιλιξ, prob. an imperial chief commissioner of taxes in the province of Syria. The final ξ is divided and the vowel transposed; Reckendorf compares קְסוֹרְיָא = ἰξορία in the Midrash R. בר חרי 97 i *n.* 186 5.

L. 15. אגר Prob. 3 plur. m.; cf. i 9 *n.*

L. 19. Before באסרא perhaps [יִתְּבְ]עֵא l. 20, Reckendorf. מדיא l. 21 מדיא=*modius.* קֻסְטוֹן=κόστος a root used as spice, Syr. ܩܘܣܛܘܣ, ܩܘܣܛܐ, also, as here, ܩܘܣܛ.

L. 20. עֲשַׂר וְשֵׁת 81 9 *n.* The thing numbered must have been fem.

L. 21. סַסְפַּרְסִין Plur. of סַסְפַּרְסָא.

L. 22. מלח ὃς ἂν ἅλας, see the regulations of Corbulo ii c 31–37. For the salt-tax cf. 1 Macc. 10 29 τῆς τιμῆς τοῦ ἁλός. 11 35. There are salt-lakes in the neighbourhood of Palmyra.

L. 23. ת[דמרי]א From the Gk. Παλμυρη[ν]ῶν iii c 23. יְכִילֶנֵּה Afel impf. 3 sing. m. of כול, with nun energic, παραμετρησάτω ib.; the Syr. form is ܢܟܝܠ. The lacuna following may be supplied ל[כל מדי]א ε[ἰς ἕκ]αστον μόδιον iii c 24.

L. 25. חֲשְׁבַּן l. 37. ii c 16. 34, cf. ii c 4; Syr. ܚܘܫܒܢܐ. בני The form is uncertain.

L. 29. מִשְׁתַּתְּפִין Ethpeel ptcp., lit. *binding himself to, associating*; in Syr. the reflexive takes the form ܐܫܬܘܬܦ, act. ܫܘܬܦ, Duval *Gr. Syr.* 81 f.

L. 30. פָּרַע Peal ptcp.; cf. fem. פָּרְעָא l. 44. רגלין ii a 2 *n.*

L. 33. עלם ומרן ii a 4 *n.*

L. 43. עמרא ܥܡܪܐ, ἐρίων iv a 27.

L. 45. למפקא בָּתַר=ἐξαγ[όντω]ν πράσσειν ὕστ[ερον ὡς συν]εφωνήθη (כְּוָת חֲזוּ סִפְּחִין) iv a 34 f. בתר, from ב and אֲתַר *place,* is a prepos.; the Gk., however, suggests an advb. Lidzb. takes בתר כות together, *after that.*

L. 46. ספחן c 14. 45=σύμφωνοι, cf. Dan. 3 10 סיפניה=συμφωνία.

L. 47. מַפְּקָא Afel ptcp. plur. mas.=αὐτῶν ἐξαγό[ντων] iv a 35; for the plur. ending cf. חגריא i 7 *n.*

L. 49. טִעֲנָן ܛܥܢܐ.

ii c.

L. 2. חיםא or ציםא. The Gk. has [ἐν τῷ] ἐσφραγισμένῳ νόμῳ.

L. 3. קָצָבָא In Syr. ܢܟܘܣܐ = *slaughterer*; τὸ τοῦ σφάκτρου τέλος iv a 41. אַפֵּי דִּנָר εἰς δηνάριον iv a 41, cf. אַפֵּי אַסַּר l. 6. πρὸς ἀσσάριον iv a 43; in Syr. אפי is preceded by a prepos., e.g. ܠܘܬ ܐܦܝ. See ii a 2 *n*.

L. 4. לְמִתְחַשְּׁבוּ The inf. ending as in Syr.; cf. the infin. ending ות in Bibl. Aram., e.g. הִתְנַדָּבוּת Ezr. 7 16. לְחוֹרְשׁוּתַי Dan. 4 15 ('binding forms'), and in Targ., Dalm. *Gr.* 228. Germanicus Caesar, the nephew and adopted heir of Tiberius, was sent on a special mission to the East, A.D. 17–19, with command of all the provinces beyond the Hellespont. During his administration he succeeded in establishing excellent relations, in which no doubt Palmyra was interested, between the Roman and the Parthian powers. Statilius, like Barbarus l. 22, was prob. an imperial procurator of the province of Syria; cf. b 12 *n*.

L. 5. פסק l. 26, Pael ܦܣܩ *exposuit*.

L. 6. הא, like the enclitic ܗܘ in Syr., is here used to give emphasis; cf. the use of הו in Vog. 36 b דכרנא דנה די הו יקר בית עלמא *this monument which is a tomb of honour*; also הי in l. 10 למעמתא הי. אסר איטלקא See i 11 *n*.

L. 7. גְּבֵן Peal ptcp. pass. plur., agreeing with מַכְסַיָּא l. 6 which was prob. preceded by יְהוֹן. גו מן ἐντός iv a 44, lit. *within*. In other dialects גו usually takes a prep., e.g. ܡܢ ܓܘ &c.; cf. אפי l. 3 *n*., and בר *outside* l. 12 = Syr. ܠܒܪ. In l. 47, however, we find לגו מן.

L. 8. קֶרְמָן κέρμα iv a 46, cf. Jn. 2 15 ܩܘܪܡܛܝܗܘܢ = τὰ κέρματα. Here קרמן is the small copper coinage struck locally; for higher values the imperial coinage was used. יְהוֹן = יְהֵא.

L. 9. פגרין The Gk. has τῶ[ν δὲ] διὰ τὸ νεκριμαῖα εἶναι ῥειπτουμένων iv a 45 f. The reference is to the bodies of old or sick animals which could not be brought to the slaughter-house. מִשְׁתְּרַיִן Ethpe. ptcp. of שרא.

L. 10. לְמַעְמְתָא τῶν βρωτῶν, Syr. ܡܥܣܡܬܐ or ܡܥܣ' *taste, a repast*. אַקִימֵת Af. pf. 1 sing.

L. 12. מדי = ܡܛܠ ܕ i 9 *n*., ὅταν iv a 48. מַאְפַּק Afel ptcp. pass.; as a rule the א is not retained in this form. תְּרוּמָא Sing., or תְּרוּמַיָּא plur., cf. l. 7 *n*.

L. 13. מַפַּק = מַאְפַּק. לְקִרְיָא = ܩܘܪܝܐ plur., εἰς χωρία iv a 49.

L. 15. אִסְטְרֹבִילַיָּא = στρόβιλοι, here = κώνου iv a 51; the kernel of the fir-cone is still esteemed in Syria as an article of food. The 'similar' fruits would prob. be nuts and almonds.

L. 16. עָלֵל For the uncontracted form cf. עָלְלִין Dan. 4 4 &c. Kt., עָלִּין Qerî. תְּטַלֵּל Dan. 4 9; similarly in Talm. עללין, חששין &c., Dalman *Gr.* 274. This form is specially common in the case of עלל. לְחֻשְׁבַּן תַּגָּרָא Lit. *everything that enters into the reckoning of the merchants*, ὅσα εἰς ἐμπορείαν φέρεται iv a 52.

L. 17. יְבִישׁ Syr. ܝܒܝܫ, ξηρόφορτον; cf. ii a 6.

L. 19. סריקין See ii b 11 *n*.

L. 22. קרבלן The famous Gnaeus Domitius Corbulo, consular legate of Cappadocia and afterwards of Syria A. D. 57–66, in the reign of Nero. קְשִׁיטָא = κράτιστος as a title.

L. 23. וְגַלְדַיָּא Syr. ܓܶܠܕܳܐ, Arab. جلد *skin*, once in Hebr., Job 16 15; perhaps the camel-hides used for packing merchandise. על . . . די Prob. אתחוי intervened, as די implies; cf. l. 31 f.

L. 24. Reckendorf proposes עִשְׂבַּ[יָּ]א [דִי אָסְ]וָתָא *herbs of the physicians*; cf. *Baba Bath.* 74 b הדוא עישבא סמתרי הוה *that herb serves for plaisters*.

L. 26. עֲלִימָתָא ἑταιρῶν iv b 5; cf. ii a 46–b 2. נמוסא Perhaps an error for בנמוסא. מחוא Nöld. conjectures מַחְוֵא Afel ptcp. *showing*, as a correction.

L. 29. אַנְדְּרִיַּטַיָּא ἀνδριάντες, Syr. ܐܰܢܕܪܝܰܢܛܐ, Targ. אַנְדַּרְטָא *idol*. The word here is a further description of צלמי נחשא.

L. 31. במלנות l. 39. The word is perhaps incomplete; ? ו for ב.

L. 34. למדיא אסר The price seems too small; perhaps it is the amount of the tax, not the cost of a bushel of salt.

L. 35. הָוְיָא Ptcp. fem.

L. 38. ארנונא See a 10.

L. 43. שלחא The rendering is uncertain, *honey-comb* or *skin*—the Syr. ܫܠܚܳܐ has both meanings; or *weapons*, Targ. שִׁילְחָא, Arab. سلاح, Hebr. שֶׁלַח.

JEWISH

148 A. Benê Ḥezîr. Chwolson 6. Circ. i cent. B.C. In situ.

1 זה קבר והמש[כ]ב לאלעזר חניה יועזר יהודה שמעו[ן] יוחנן

2 בני ים.....ב..ף ואלעזר בני חניה

3 ...מבני חזיר

This is the tomb and resting-place of Eli'azar, Ḥanniah, Yô'azar, Yehudah, Simeon, Yôḥanan, sons of . . . . . . and Eli'azar, sons of Ḥanniah . . . of the sons of Ḥēzîr.

This inscr. is written over the entrance of the so-called Tomb of St. James at the foot of the Mt. of Olives, opposite the SE. angle of the Temple-area. The writing exhibits a form of Hebrew which is advancing towards the square character. Thus א, ה, ל, ע, ר are very near to their later forms; ב, ד, ח, ם still resemble the Nab. and Palm. types; ו and ז are indistinguishable; נ has a final form, and when י follows joins on to it with a ligature; in the case of בני all three letters are thus united; cf. the use of the ligature in Palm. The form of י is peculiar, ٦; this is different from the Nab. and Palm. forms, and resembles the archaic ⅄, without the two lower strokes. A somewhat similar י appears in Jewish ossuaria. Facsimiles of this and the following inscr. are given by Driver *Samuel* xxiii and xxv.

L. 1. Chwolson, *Corp. Inscr. Hebr.* 66, supplies the art. before קבר, following de Vogüé; the facsimile shows no trace of it. If the art. is written with משכב, as appears to be the case in spite of Lidzb.'s text (p. 485), it is required with קבר. The reading משכב is not quite certain; the last letter looks more like ד or ר than ב; for the word see 4 8 *n*.

L. 2. Chwolson reads בני יוסף בן . . . ב . . . [וליו]סף. But יוסף is very doubtful; the fifth letter may be ס, it is certainly not ו.

L. 3. בני חויר In 1 Chr. 24 15 חֵזִיר is the ancestor of a priestly family, in Neh. 10 21 חֵזִיר is one of the ראשי העם. It is not unlikely that the persons mentioned in the inscr. belonged to the priestly family of Ḥēzîr; de Vogüé conjectures further that Simeon, Yô'azar, and Eli'azar were the high-priests of the same names, belonging to the family of Boethos, who held office in B.C. 24–5, 4, and 4 ff., respectively

(Schürer *Gesch.*[3] ii 217). The tomb is an imposing one, with an architectural façade in the Gk. style. It may be dated in the 1st cent. B.C. or A.D.; most probably it was executed in the reign of Herod the Gt. It cannot be later than A.D. 70, for a tomb on such a scale could not have been designed after the destruction of Jerusalem. The evidence of the writing is not decisive, but Meyer considers that it points to a date earlier than the 1st cent. B.C., *Entsteh. d. Judenth.* 143.

B. **Kefr Bir'im.** Chwolson 17. ii or iii cent. A.D. In situ.

יהי שלום במקום הזה ובכל מקומות ישראל יוסה הלוי בן
לוי עשה השקוף הזה תבא ברכה במעיוש.

Peace be upon this place and upon all the places of Israel! Yôseh the Levite, son of Levi, made this lintel. May a blessing come upon his works!

This inscr. is written over the door of a ruined synagogue at Kefr Bir'im, a village near Ṣafed in Galilee. The writing has a more finished and formed character than that of A; it is obviously later. The architectural style of the ruins perhaps belongs to the 2nd half of the 2nd cent. A.D. (Renan); Lidzb., however, suggests the 4th cent. (*Jewish Ency.* i 444). The א has a form which is characteristic of later inscrr., with the left limb descending perpendicularly. The ו and י are mere strokes, and only differ in the slight slope of ו to the left. The ז has a short stroke to the right, ʌ; ם takes a final form ן. It is to be noticed that the *scriptio plena* is employed throughout. יוסה This form, a diminutive of יוסף, occurs in the recently discovered Hebr. mosaic at Kefr Ḳenna in Galilee, Lidzb. *Eph.* i 314; it appears also in the Jer. Talm. יוסה and יוסא, otherwise usually יוסי; in the Bab. Talm. יוסף. The form seems to be Palestinian. שקוף = the O.T. משקוף Ex. 12 7. 22 f. מעיוש The stone-cutter left out the ש after ע and then added it to the end of the word. After ש is a perpendicular stroke, the meaning of which is not evident.

ARAMAIC, PHOENICIAN, AND JEWISH COINS

149 A 1–6. Aramaic Coins: Tarsus. iv cent. B. C. Brit. Mus.
Plate IX A 1–6.

The coins nos. 1–6 were struck in Cilicia. The legend בעלתרז connects them with Tarsus, the most important city of the province, and under the Persian empire a great military and naval depot. This money was issued by Persian satraps, not as governors for the use of their provinces, but as military commanders for the payment of their troops when occasion required. Thus, for example, after the occupation of Cyzicus in 410, Pharnabazus gave his soldiers two months' pay and large sums to the chiefs of the allied fleet (Xen. *Hellen.* i. 24–26). Besides the satraps on special occasions, various towns and petty dynasties who acknowledged the suzerainty of Persia, all of them, it is to be noticed, near the shores of the Mediterranean, were allowed to coin money of their own (e. g. B 1–3. 5–7. 9. 10. 13); and this local money was current simultaneously with the imperial coinage. See Babelon *Pers. Ach.* xxii f.

A 1.

Tarsus.

Æ. *Obv.* בעלתרז *Ba'al of Tarsus.* Type: the god seated on the diphros, wearing the himation over the left shoulder and about the lower limbs, his right hand resting on a sceptre: linear circle.

Rev. כלך פרנבזו *Cilicia, Pharnabazus.* Type: a bearded male head wearing a crested Athenian helmet, perhaps the head of Ares: linear circle. Persian stater. Hill *Brit. Mus. Catal. of Gk. coins of Lycaonia, Isauria, and Cilicia* (1900), p. 165, no. 21; Babelon *PA* no. 169.

For the term בעל תרז see 5 18 *n*. Pharnabazus belonged to an Iranian family which was closely connected with Hellespontine Phrygia, and produced the satraps who governed this province; he succeeded his father Pharnacus in 413 B. C. Outside his own province, in Cilicia, he conducted military operations at three periods, B. C. 398–394, 391–389, 379–374, to the last of which his coins are generally assigned. After years of preparation (391–389), the expedition against Egypt took place; Pharnabazus had for his colleague in the command Datames (nos. 2–4), who afterwards succeeded him, and this association accounts for the close similarity between the coins of the two satraps. Pharnabazus appears to have introduced the remarkable types of the heads of Ares (?) and Arethusa (no. 2). פרנבזו is a Persian name, cf. תריבזו (Hill l. c. 164, no. 12); the final ו is explained by Marquart, *Philologus* liv 494 Anm. 35, as the vulgar-Persian ending of the genitive from which the normal *š* has fallen away, *Farnabāzō* being = *Frana(h)bāzauš*. Instead of כלך some of the coins have חלך (never on the coins of Datames); for the interchange of כ and ח cf. אנכי and אנחנו, חָרִיץ and كَرِيص &c. (König *Lehrg.* ii 458).

The Carpentras stele 75 affords the nearest parallel to the Aram. characters on coins 1–6.

A 2.

Tarsus.

Æ. *Obv.* Type: head of Arethusa with streaming hair and fillet, wearing earrings and necklace: circle of dots.

Rev. תרדמו *Tardamu.* Type: as no. 1, with circle of dots. Persian stater. Hill l. c. 167, no. 30; *PA* no. 183.

The *obv.* type is found also on coins of Pharnabazus; it was copied from the famous Arethusa coins of Kimon of Syracuse (see Hill *Coins of Ancient Sicily* 106 f.). The reading of the satrap's name is not certain, owing to the similarity of ד and ר; it may be תרדמו or תדרמו. The satrap belonged to a Karian family, and *Tardamū* was probably the original form of his name in Karian, with the ending *amū* as in Παναμύης, Ἐξαμύης; the Gk. form Δατάμης, well known from the historians, probably represents the Iranian pronunciation of the name (Marquart l. c. 493)[1]. Datames succeeded (circ. 386) his father Kamissares in the satrapy which comprised 'partem Ciliciae juxta Cappadociam quam incolunt Leucosyri' (Corn. Nep. *Dat.* i, corrected by Meyer to 'partem Cappadociae juxta Ciliciam,' *PA* xxxix). His coins were struck in Cilicia in 378, under the same circumstances and in the same mints as those of Pharnabazus, at the time when the troops of the Great King were being equipped for the expedition against Egypt. Datames succeeded Pharnabazus in the command of this war. In 369 he laid siege to Sinope, and struck coins of Sinopean type with the legend ΔΑΤΑΜΑ (*PA* no. 200; Bevan *House of Seleucus* i 80. 82). After taking part in the great revolt of the satraps in 362, he was assassinated towards the close of the same year.

[1] For other explanations see Hill l. c. lxxix; Babelon *PA* xxxviii.

Tarsus. A 3.

Æ. *Obv.* בעלתרז Type: Ba'al of Tarsus seated on the diphros to right, wearing the himation about the lower limbs; his right hand holds a sceptre surmounted by an eagle with spread wings, his left an ear of corn and a bunch of grapes; beside him is the thymiaterion; below the diphros a lotus flower: the whole enclosed by a circle with projections.

Rev. תרדמו Type: the satrap Tardamu wearing the Persian head-dress, an under-garment with sleeves, a cloak, and Persian trousers; on his knees is a quiver; he holds in both hands an arrow, which he examines; before him is a bow, and in the field above the winged disk of Ormuzd: circle of dots. Persian stater. Hill l.c. 167, no. 32; *PA* no. 187.

The *obv.* type is meant to suggest that the god is seated in his temple, the projections round the circle being intended to represent columns. The *rev.* type indicates that the satrap is preparing for the campaign against Egypt.

Tarsus. A 4.

Æ. *Obv.* בעלתרז Type: as in 3, but the face and upper part of the body are turned to the front, and the diphros is seen in three-quarters view: circle as in 3.

Rev. תרדמו Type: the satrap Tardamu on the right, with his name in front, wearing a long chiton and himation, his right hand raised before his face in the attitude of adoration. On the left the figure of Ana, his right hand pointed towards Tardamu, the left lowered; the name אנא, not visible in this specimen, is usually written behind; between them the thymiaterion: the whole enclosed by a linear square, bordered with dots on the top and two sides, with antefixa along the top. Persian stater. Hill l.c. 168, no. 35; *PA* no. 193.

The *rev.* type is variously interpreted. The two figures are evidently in a temple; Babelon takes them to be two deities, Ba'al of Tarsus on the right, Ana on the left. But the figure on the right is represented in the act of adoration, like Yeḥaw-milk in 8, and the name in front seems to signify that this is the satrap (Hill l.c. lxxx). Nothing is known of the god אנא; it is not probable that he is the Assyr. Anu.

Tarsus. A 5.

Æ. *Obv.* בעלתרז Type: as in 1, but here the god holds in his right hand an ear of corn and a bunch of grapes, his left rests upon a lotus-headed sceptre; under the diphros the ringed cross.

Rev. מזדי *Mazdai.* Type: lion attacking stag; the whole within a sunken square. Persian stater. Hill l. c. 169, no. 38; *PA* no. 201.

The *rev.* type is borrowed from Cyprus; it was the regular emblem of Kition (B 2. 3. 5. 6), and was probably adopted by Mazaeus at the time of the expedition which aimed at restoring Evagoras ii to the throne of Salamis (Diod. xvi 42), and probably used Kition as a convenient basis of operations (Hill l. c. lxxxii). Although Mazaeus is not mentioned in connexion with this war, yet he may have directed it and supplied the funds, for Cyprus belonged to the same satrapy as Phoenicia, where he was engaged in putting down a rebellion. It is to be noticed that the sunken square is also characteristic of the coinage of Cyprus, cf. B 1–7. Mazaeus was the greatest of the western satraps; he governed Cilicia from 361 to 333, and united under his rule Cilicia, Syria and Mesopotamia. The disastrous battle of Arbela, which gave to Alexander the empire of the Persian kings, only brought Mazaeus fresh advancement; he threw himself into Babylon with the wreck of his forces, and upon Alexander's approach surrendered the city (330); he was rewarded with the satrapy of Babylonia, and died in 328; see Bevan l. c. 245. The coins of Mazaeus, classified by Six in the *Numism. Chron.* (1884) *Le satrape Mazaïos*, are numerous and varied; for 30 years he issued money in Cilicia, and concurrently in Syria for 15 years under the Persian king, and for 3 years in Babylon under Alexander the Great.

Tarsus. A 6.

Æ. *Obv.* בעלתרז Type: Ba'al of Tarsus as in 1, holding a lotus-headed sceptre in his right hand; in the field to left an ear of corn and a bunch of grapes, and the letter ג; under the diphros the letter מ: circle of dots.

Rev. מזדי זי על עברנהרא וחלך *Mazdai who is over the Country beyond the River and Cilicia.* Type: two lines of walls, each with four towers one above the other; above a lion bringing down a bull: circle of dots. Persian stater. Hill l. c. 170, no. 48; *PA* no. 238.

The letter מ under the diphros has been explained as the initial of מלך; perhaps it merely indicates 'a moneyer or other subordinate of Mazaeus' (Hill lxxxiv). The letter נ may be a mint-mark. The *rev.* type of the lion and bull is an emblem of Tarsus; the walls below probably represent the fortifications of the city, rather than the Cilician Gates (Six, Babelon); they suggest an enclosure rather than a passage. The form of the relat. זי occurs in the Cilician inscr. 68; see also p. 185. The 'Country beyond the River' (i. e. Euphrates) was N. Syria, the term being used from the standpoint not of Cilicia but of Persia, as עבר הנהר in Neh. 2 7. 9. 3 7. Ezr. 8 36, עֲבַר נַהֲרָה Ezr. 4 10. 5 3 &c. Cf. 7 1 *n.*, and for חלך see no. 1 *n.*

149 B 1–15. **Phoenician Coins.** v–ii cent. B. C. Brit. Mus., and Bibl. Nat., Paris. **Plate IX B 1–15.**

Cyprus, Kition. B 1.

Æ. *Rev.* לבעלמלך (*Coin*) *of Ba'al-milk.* Type: lion seated, with open jaws; the whole within a sunken square bordered with dots. Persian stater: Brit. Mus. Cf. *PA* no. 647 (a tetrobol).

The reign of Ba'al-milk i is to be placed between the defeat of Xerxes in B. C. 479 and the occupation of Kition by the Athenians in 449. In the disaster of 479 the Persian fleet almost entirely perished, and with it the princes of Cyprus and Phoenicia; hence Xerxes found it necessary to send for the Tyrian Ba'al-milk to become king of Kition and found a new dynasty. The Tyrian origin of Ba'al-milk is shown by the type which he introduced upon his coinage, the figure of the Tyrian Herakles (Melqarth), as on the *obv.* of this coin; cf. B 4–6.

Kition. B 2.

Æ. *Rev.* לעזבעל *Of 'Az-ba'al.* Type: lion devouring a stag; border and square as 1. Persian stater: Brit. Mus. *PA* no. 670.

After the brief occupation of Kition by Kimon in 449 B. C., the Athenians evacuated the city, and 'Az-ba'al succeeded his father Ba'al-milk i as king from 449 to 425. His coins bear the Tyrian Herakles on the *obv.* (see B 1); but on the *rev.* a new type appears, the lion devouring the stag, an emblem of the Persian triumph over the Athenians. 'Az-ba'al was the first to style himself 'king of Kition and Idalion.'

Kition. B 3.

AR. Rev. לבעלמלך *Of Ba'al-milk.* Type: as B 2. Persian stater: Brit. Mus. *PA* no. 679.

Ba'al-milk ii was the son and successor of 'Az-ba'al; he reigned from B.C. 425 to 400.

Kition. B 4.

AR. Rev. [ל]מלך דמנכ *Of king Demonicus.* Type: the bearded Herakles, with lion-skin on shoulders, marching to right; his left hand holds in front of him a bow, his right brandishes a club; sunken square. Persian stater: Bibl. Nat. *PA* no. 695.

Demonicus reigned at Kition from B.C. 388 to 387. He owed his position to the protection of Athens; and the fact that the Athenian domination in Kition did not last longer than the expedition of Chabrias in 388 accounts for the shortness of his reign. Demonicus himself was an Athenian, and the influence of Athens appears on his coins. They are the work of Greek, not oriental, engravers, hence the figure of Herakles differs noticeably from the figure on the coins of the native dynasty (cf. B 5. 6); the *obv.* type is a reproduction of the statue of Athene Promachos, erected on the Acropolis after Marathon to express defiance of the Persians; and on some of his coins Demonicus uses the Gk. language, the only king of Kition to do so. דמנכ = Δημόνικος; the omission of נ is due either to accident or to the difficulty of transcribing a foreign name.

Kition. B 5.

N. Obv. Type: the bearded Herakles, wearing a lion-skin on his head; his left hand, covered with another lion-skin, holds a bow in front, his right brandishes a club above his head; in the field the ringed cross: circle of dots.

Rev. [ל]מלך מלכיתן *Of king Milk-yathon.* Type: lion devouring stag; sunken square with border of dots. Hemi-stater: Bibl. Nat. *PA* no. 699.

Milk-yathon, king of Kition and Idalion (**12–14. 26. 30**), was the son of Ba'al-ram (**23–25**), and reigned from B.C. 392 to 361. In the series of inscrr. which refer to him a break occurs in the 4th year of his reign, i.e. 388, the date of the Athenian investment and the usurpation of Demonicus. When the Athenians abandoned Kition, Milk-yathon was restored by the Persians. He was the first king of Kition to mint gold coins.

Kition. B 6.

Æ. *Obv.* Type: as B 5.

Rev. [למלך פמ[יתן *Of king Pumi-[yathon]*. Type: as B 5; in the field to right 𐤍 𐤍 (i.e. year 40). Hemi-stater: Bibl. Nat. *PA* no. 722.

Pumi-yathon, king of Kition, Idalion, and Tamassos (12. 18. 26), was the son and successor of Milk-yathon. He reigned from B.C. 361–312, for at least 47 years; see p. 56.

Lapēthos. B 7.

Ꝛ. *Obv.* לצדקמלך *Of Ṣidqi-milk.* Type: head of Athene to left, wearing Corinthian helmet and earrings, her hair arranged symmetrically down her neck.

Rev. [ל]צדקמלך Type: head of Athene to front, wearing close-fitting helmet ornamented with two bull's ears and two cristae; her hair arranged symmetrically on each side of her head; a necklace round her throat; the whole within a sunken square. Persian stater: Brit. Mus. *PA* no. 783.

Ṣidqi-milk (cf. O.T. צִדְקִיָּהוּ, Sab. צדקאל Hal. 193 1, Hommel *Süd-Ar. Chr.* 106), king of Lapēthos, reigned from about B.C. 449 to 420. He began to reign after the departure of the Athenians in 449 (see on B 1 and 2), when the Persians recovered possession of the island. The helmet of Athene in *rev.* recalls Herodotus' description of the armour of the Chalybians in the host of Xerxes, *ἐπὶ δὲ τῇσι κεφαλῇσι κράνεα χάλκεα· πρὸς δὲ τοῖσι κράνεσι, ὦτά τε καὶ κέρεα προσῆν βοὸς χάλκεα· ἐπῆσαν δὲ καὶ λόφοι* vii 76.

B 8.

Laodicea of Libanus.

Æ. *Rev.* On the right ΒΑΣΙΛΕΩΣ ΑΝΤΙΟΧΟΥ, on the left [ל]לאדכא אש בכנען *Of Laodicea which is in Canaan.* Type: Poseidon facing, half naked, wearing the chlamys, his right hand holding a patera, his left leaning on the trident; in the field to left ΛΛ, on the right a mint-mark. Chalkous (= ⅛ of an obol): Bibl. Nat. Babelon *Rois de Syrie* no. 660.

The *obv.* has the bust of Antiochus crowned with a diadem. Λαοδίκεια ἡ πρὸς Λιβάνῳ (Strabo 643 ed. Müll.), so called to distinguish it from Λαοδίκεια ἐπὶ τῇ θαλάσσῃ, was an important city of Coele-Syria, founded by Seleucus Nicator on the plain SE. of

Hemesa in the region of the upper Orontes. The coin bears the name of Antiochus iv Epiphanes, B. C. 175–164. For the reading אש instead of אם (Babelon) see p. 46 *n.* 3; the title אם *metropolis*, lit. *mother*, occurs on coins of Sidon, e. g. B 15, and of Tyre לצר אם צדנם *RS* p. 86, but probably not on the coins either of Laodicea or of Berytus. It is interesting to find the biblical name כנען = Phoenicia on these coins, cf. Is. 23 11. Zeph. 1 11. Josh. 5 1 LXX &c.; it occurs besides only on the coins of Berytus which have the legend ללארכא אש בכנען (p. 46 *n.* 3).

Byblus. B 9.

Æ. *Rev.* [אל]פעל מלך גבל *El-pa'al king of Gebal.* Type: lion devouring bull, the body of the bull incused, the head in relief: circle of dots. Graeco-asiatic stater: Bibl. Nat. *PA* no. 1344.

Of the kings of Gebal under the Persian empire two, Yeḥaw-milk and Uri-milk, are mentioned in 3, but the exact date of their reigns is not known. The two later kings of Gebal, El-pa'al (cf. אֶלְפַּעַל 1 Chr. 8 11 ff.) and 'Az-ba'al (B 10), whose coinage is illustrated here, were reigning probably in B. C. 360 and 340 respectively, at any rate shortly before the Greek conquest, for Alexander would not have allowed them to issue money in their own names. The type of the lion and bull is an acknowledgement of the Persian supremacy (cf. A 6).

Byblus. B 10.

Æ. *Rev.* עזבעל מלך גבל *'Az-ba'al king of Gebal.* Type: lion devouring bull: circle of dots. Graeco-asiatic stater: Brit. Mus. *PA* no. 1357.

See on B 9 above.

Byblus. B 11.

Æ. *Rev.* ΒΑΣΙΛΕΩΣ (right) ΑΝΤΙΟΧΟΥ (left). Type: the Phoen. Kronos (see p. 20) with six wings, standing to left, holding a sceptre in the right hand; on his head-dress a four-branched ornament (see Philo Bybl. *Fr. Hist. Gr.* iii 569); in the field above לגבל *Of Gebal*, below קדשת *the holy*: circle of dots. Chalkous: Bibl. Nat. *RS* no. 671.

The *obv.* has the bust of Antiochus crowned with a diadem. This is a specimen of the bronze coinage of Gebal under the Seleucids. The 'king' is Antiochus iv Epiphanes, 175–164 B. C. For the epithet קדשת in connexion with Gebal see p. 21.

Tyre. B 12.

Æ. *Rev.* Type: an owl, holding under its left wing the Egyptian crook and flail; in the field to right the number 35 (i. e. year): circle of dots. Attic didrachm: Brit. Mus. *PA* no. 2022.

The series of Tyrian coins of which this is a specimen reflects the disturbances of the period from B.C. 312 to 275. In 312 Tyre was taken from Antigonus by Ptolemy, the ally of Seleucus; coins were struck at once, and continued for 3 years (*PA* nos. 2007–2013). Then there comes a break for 20 years; in 287 Tyre passed into the hands of Seleucus; the period was too disturbed for the minting of money. Then the coins begin again in the 23rd year and continue till the 37th (*PA* 2014–2022; Cl.-Gan. *Ét.* i 59 f.). This brings us to 275, when Tyre was recaptured by Ptolemy ii Philad., and started a new era as an autonomous city (9 5 *n.*). Thus the years numbered on the coins are in fact the years of Ptolemy, beginning with his capture of the city in 312, and closing with his recapture of it in 275. The *rev.* type is noticeable: the owl is Greek, the crook and flail are Egyptian, the symbols of Osiris; the combination indicates the range of the mercantile relations of Tyre, and the influence of Athens and of Egypt upon the city. The *obv.* type, Melqarth riding on a sea-horse with a dolphin below, is a native emblem, symbolizing the claim of Tyre to the empire of the sea. A special interest attaches to the Tyrian coins of this size and value; they were used by the Jews, who had no coinage of their own, as 'the sacred shekel' for the payment of religious dues (Ex. 30 13. Lev. 5 15. 27 3. 25. Num. 7 13. 86 &c. P); it is expressly enjoined in the Talm. that these dues are to be paid in Tyrian money, e.g. B. *Bekoroth* 49 b כולם בשקל הקדש במנה צורי. See Kennedy *DB* iii 422; cf. also 8 2 *n.*

B 13.

Sidon.

Æ. *Obv.* A Phoenician galley at sea, with oarsmen; in the field above ||| (i. e. year 3): circle of dots.

Rev. Type: the Persian king, Artaxerxes iii Ochus, in his chariot, driven by his charioteer, followed on foot by an attendant who holds in his right hand a sceptre terminating in an animal's head, and in his left an oinochoë; in the field above the letters עב: circle of dots. Quadruple Phoen. shekel: Brit. Mus. Cf. *PA* no. 1607 (12th year).

This coin is assigned by Babelon to Straton ii, king of Sidon from B. C. 346 to 332; the letters עב are the initials of his name עבדעשתרת (*PA* clxxxv). The coins of this king closely resemble those of his predecessor, Straton i 374–362 B. C., which also have the initials עב in the field of *rev.*

Byblus. B 14.

Æ. *Rev.* לגבל קדשת *Of Gebal the holy* on left; on right a legend of which only the letters י . ת . עש can be deciphered. Type: 'Ashtart (cf. 8) to left, her hair falling on her neck, robed in a tunic, with a peplos covering the upper part of the body and the arms; the right hand raised and extended, the left holding a long sceptre terminating in a ball: circle of dots. Hemi-chalkous: Bibl. Nat. *PA* no. 1373.

This is a specimen of the autonomous coins of Gebal, belonging to a later period than B 11, after the reign of Antiochus v.

Sidon. B 15.

Æ. *Rev.* לצדנם | אם כמב | אפא כת | צר *Of the Sidonians, metropolis of Kambe, Hippo, Kition, Tyre.* Type: a steering oar. Hemi-chalkous: Brit. Mus. *PA* no. 1620.

This is a specimen of the autonomous coins of Sidon, dating from the middle of the ii cent. B. C. לצדנם is a rendering of the Gk. ΣΙΔΩΝΙΩΝ *RS* nos. 682 ff., cf. לצר = ΤΥΡΙΩΝ ib. nos. 674 ff. For אם see B 8 *n.* The towns mentioned are those which Sidon claimed as her colonies; כמב, on some coins written כבב (*PA* no. 1619), was the primitive name of Carthage, אפא = Hippo on the N. coast of Africa; see *RS* cx, *PA* clxxxvi. Here Sidon calls herself the mother-city of Tyre, but on the Tyrian coins of the time of Antiochus iv we find the relations reversed, לצר אם צדנם *RS* p. 86. In earlier days צדנם included both cities; see p. 54.

149 C. Jewish Coins. ii cent. B. C. to ii cent. A. D. Brit. Mus.

The native Jewish coins, with Hebr. inscrr., appear at three periods: (1) the period of the Hasmonaean princes, from John Hyrcanus to Mattathias (Antigonus), i.e. from 135 to 37 B. C.; (2) the First Revolt against the Romans, 66–70 A. D.; (3) the Second Revolt, 132–135 A. D. Their appearance thus marks the efforts that were made to maintain or assert the independence of the nation; and in agreement with the spirit of these movements the coins are stamped with legends in the archaic character which had long ago fallen out of use, and given way to the square character developed in Aramaic. The writing varies so little during the 170 years that it affords no indication of date. The following forms of letters are characteristic of the coins:

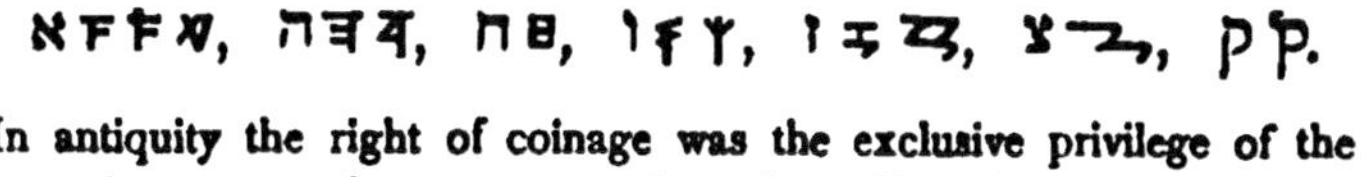

In antiquity the right of coinage was the exclusive privilege of the sovereign power; it was a sure sign of rebellion if any subject state took upon itself to issue money. Under the Seleucid kings certain semi-independent towns were allowed to issue bronze pieces bearing the head of the king on one side and the name of the city on the other, e.g. B 8 and 11; and a privilege of the same kind was bestowed upon the Jewish state by Demetrius ii (145–138 B.C.), and afterwards confirmed to Simon the Maccabee by Antiochus vii Sidetes (138–129 B.C.): 'I give thee leave to coin money for thy country with thine own stamp' (ποιῆσαι κόμμα ἴδιον νόμισμα τῆς χώρας σου) 1 Macc. 15 6. The concession implied that Judaea was recognized as a free state under the suzerainty of Syria. To what extent Simon availed himself of the privilege is not known, and it was soon withdrawn (1 Macc. 15 27). If he issued money at all it would have been in bronze, not in silver; but, according to the view adopted here, no coins, whether bronze or silver, can be assigned to him. His son and successor, John Hyrcanus (135–104 B.C.), was the first Jewish prince to issue money in his own name. The following is a specimen of his small bronze coins:

a

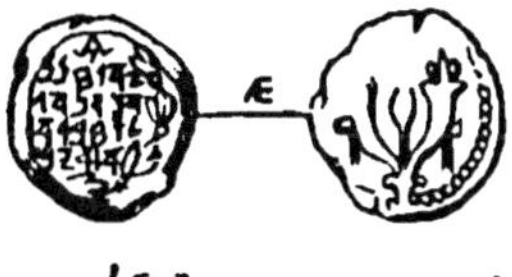

Obv. יהוחנן הכהן הג[ד]ל וחבר ה[י]הודים A.

Rev. A double cornucopiae with a poppy head in the centre.

The A at the beginning of the legend is taken to be the initial of Alexander ii Zebina (128–122? B.C.), the nominal over-lord of Hyrcanus; it may indicate the alliance between the two in 128, Ἀλέξανδρος . . . φιλίαν ποιεῖται πρὸς Ὑρκανὸν τὸν ἀρχιερέα Jos. *Ant.* xiii 9 3; possibly, however, it denotes the 'year 1' (Madden *Coins of the Jews* 81). The letter is not found on the later coins of Hyrcanus.

The two cornua-copiae he prob. adopted from Zebina, on whose coins they first appear. The official title of Hyrcanus is 'the high priest,' though in character he was more of a secular prince than a religious pontiff; the Jewish commonwealth regarded itself not as a kingdom but as a church, and the priest at the head of it was not an autocrat, but the chief of a community. The earlier coins of Hyrcanus are issued jointly by him and the community; his later coins, however, are issued in his name alone י׳ הכהן הגדל ראש חבר היהודים. Nestle (*ZATW* 1895, 288–290) has suggested that ראש חבר = ἐθνάρχης, used of Simon 1 Macc. **14** 47. **15** 1. 2, but without sufficient grounds. The precise meaning of חבר היהודים is disputed. In Hebr. חֶבֶר = *company, association*, Hos. **6** 9 חבר כהנים. It is natural, therefore, to regard ח׳ הי׳ as a corporation or college within the Jewish nation, the *γερουσία* or senate mentioned in 1 Macc. **12** 6. Judith **4** 8 &c.; so Madden 77, Wellhausen *Isr. u. Jüd. Gesch.*[3] 282 *n.* But it seems that the *γερουσία* (= the later Sanhedrin) was not of sufficient importance at this period to be named upon the coins. The Pun. חברם, referred to by Renan in this connexion, were not the senate but the *colleagues* of the suffetes, **42** 2. 19. **55** 4. The general opinion is that ח׳ הי׳ = *the community of the Jews*, as similar or equivalent terms were in use, e.g. חבר עִיר *a city community* Mishnah *Berakoth* 30 a, τὸ πλῆθος τῶν Ἰουδαίων 1 Macc. **8** 20, τὸ ἔθνος τῶν Ἰ. ib. **12** 3; Reinach *Monnaies Juives* 23, Kennedy, art. Money *DB* iii, Schürer *Gesch.*[3] i 269. Kennedy makes the attractive suggestion that חבר = τὸ κοινόν; the LXX renders בית חבר Pr. **21** 9 ἐν οἴκῳ κοινῷ, cf. **25** 24, and elsewhere uses κοινωνέω, κοινωνός to render derivatives of חבר. The expression τὸ κοινόν has various meanings; thus in Jos. *Vita* 12. 49 &c. τὸ κοινὸν τῶν Ἱεροσολυμιτῶν is apparently the executive authority of the δῆμος, = τῶν Ἱερ. οἱ πρῶτοι ib. 7; in classical Gk. τὸ κοινόν = *respublica*, and is often used of Gk. states or cities, e.g. τὸ κ. τῶν Κρηταιέων Michel 439, τὸ κ. τὸ Ταρμιανῶν ib. 1188–1190. We do not know enough of the constitution of the Jewish state at this time to determine exactly the relation between τὸ κοινόν and חבר.

The following are specimens of the coins of Alexander Jannaeus (103–76 B.C.), whose long reign was marked by much violence and bloodshed, and by an increasing cleavage between the adherents of the Maccabees and the party, including the Pharisees, which cherished the traditional ideals of Judaism. The high-priesthood in the person of Alexander became thoroughly secularized. His Jewish name Jannaeus, Talm. ינאי i.e. יני, is contracted from יְנָתָן, יְהוֹנָתָן.

b

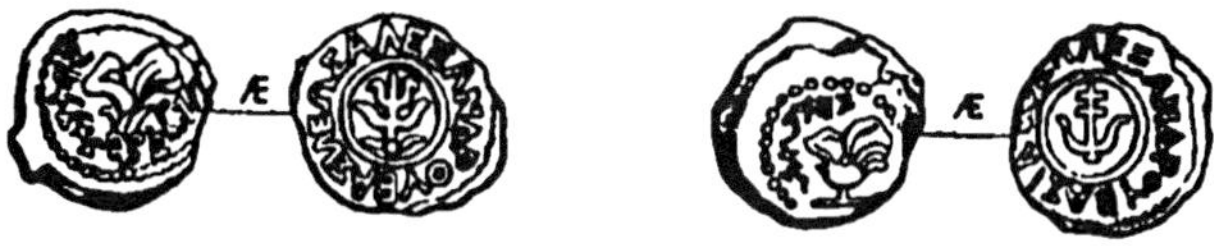

Obv. יהונתן המלך Type: a half-opened flower.

Rev. ΒΑΣΙΛΕΩΣ ΑΛΕΞΑΝΔΡΟΥ round a circle. Type: an anchor with two cross-timbers.

c

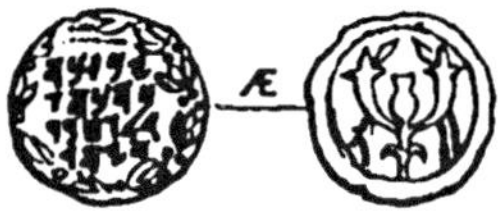

Obv. ינתן הכהן הגדל וחבר היהוד[ים] within a wreath.

Rev. Double cornucopiae with a poppy head in the centre.

Jannaeus issued a double series of coins, regal and pontifical. The interest of the regal series (*b*) lies in the appearance of המלך for the first time on Jewish coins, and in the use of the Gk. legend on the reverse. The adoption of these novelties was probably one of the causes which led to a breach with the Pharisees. The anchor on *b*, and the double cornucopiae on the pontifical coins *c*, are borrowed from the Seleucid kings, and illustrate the continued influence of their coinage.

The following is a specimen of the coins of Antigonus-Mattathias, B. C. 40–37, the last prince of the Hasmonaean dynasty:

d

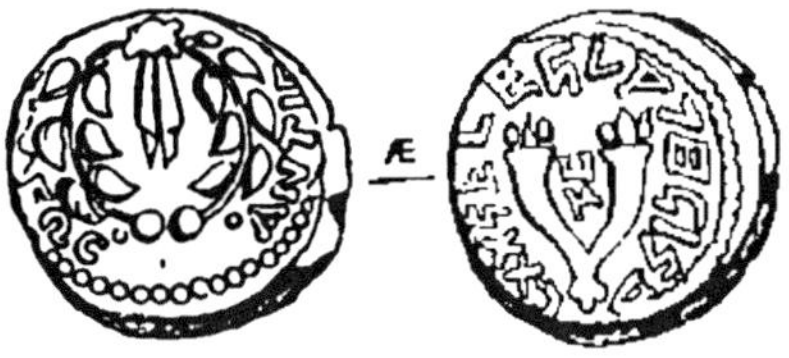

Obv. [ΒΑΣΙΛ]ΕΩΣ ΑΝΤΙΓ[ΟΝΟΥ] round a wreath.

Rev. מתתיה כהן גדל חבר יה Type: a double cornucopiae, with שא i. e. *year 1* in the centre.

After having been a prisoner in Rome, Antigonus attempted to obtain the kingdom in B.C. 42, but was defeated by Herod. With the help of the Parthians, however, he succeeded in taking Jerusalem in B.C. 40, and was made king. Not long afterwards Herod, who had received the nominal title of king of Judaea through Roman influence, laid siege to Jerusalem and, aided by the Roman general Sosius, captured it in 37; Antigonus was ignominiously executed with the axe. These coins show that he had adopted the name of Mattathias, the founder of his dynasty; they are the first Jewish coins which bear a date.

Coins of the First Revolt, A. D. 66–70. **Plate X 1–5.**

e (1)

AR. *Obv.* שקל ישראל Type: a broad-lipped chalice, on either side a pellet, above the cup the letter א = *1*.

Rev. ירושלם קדשה Type: a flowering lily.

f (2)

AR. *Obv.* חצי השקל Type: a chalice with jewelled rim, above the cup the letters שב = *year 2*.

Rev. ירושלים הקדושה Type: a flowering lily.

g (3)

AR. *Obv.* שקל ישראל Type: as *f*, above the cup the letters שד = *year 4*.

Rev. ירושלים הקדושה Type: as *f*.

h (4)

Æ. *Obv.* לגאלת ציון Type: as *f*.

Rev. שנת ארבע Type: a *lûlab* with an *'ethrog* on either side.

i (5)

AR. *Obv.* שקל ישראל Type: as *f*, above the cup the letters שה = *year 5*.

Rev. ירושלים הקדושה Type: as *f*.

These coins have been usually attributed to Simon Maccabaeus (142–135 B.C.), e.g. by Madden 65 ff., and others; but there is now a general agreement among experts that they belong rather to the period immediately preceding the fall of Jerusalem in A. D. 70. It will be observed that the shekels are dated from the first year to the fifth; if they belong to Simon's reign, which lasted 7 years (1 Macc. 13 14 f. and 16 14), the two years at the close must be left without coins; no reason can be found for the increasing rarity and entire cessation of the shekels in the fifth year. Moreover, it is difficult to believe that, if Simon had issued silver coins, his successors would not have done the same; but the Hasmonaean princes, in accordance with their constitutional position under the suzerainty of Syria, only minted bronze money; and their money bears the names of the princes, while the shekels, in striking contrast, have no name to show who issued them. On technical grounds of style and fabric they are related to the tetradrachms of Nero and Vespasian minted at Antioch, and not to the Seleucid silver coins of the Maccabaean period. The issue of such coins with the legend *Jerusalem the holy* is in itself an assertion of independence; it proves that the Jews were in revolt against the sovereign power; and since there was only one other occasion when the independence of Jerusalem was not constitutional but usurped, viz. in 132–135 A. D., and the coins of the latter age are well known in detail, there remains the period of the First Revolt against the Romans in 66–70 A. D. The shekels and half-shekels must have been coined by the executive authority of Jerusalem which undertook the defence of the city and the conduct of the war. The fact that they appear in considerable numbers during the first three years, and then become rarer, until they cease altogether with the exceedingly rare shekel of the fifth year (Apr. to Aug. A.D. 70), agrees exactly with the history of the revolt from its successful start to its gradual collapse. See Kennedy, art. Money in *BD* iii, whose arguments are incorporated above, and Schürer *Gesch.*[3] i 762 ff. Reinach, *Mon. Juives* 47 f., suggests that the coins were especially designed for the payment of the temple tax, the shekel for two persons (cf. Mt. 17 24–27), the half-shekel for one, and to take the place of the Tyrian tetradrachms (or staters) and didrachms which had formerly been used for this purpose (cf. on B 12).

e (1) The chalice probably represents the temple vessels. The broad rim is characteristic of shekels of the first year, so also the pellets, probably intended for jewels, and the letter א alone without ש = שנת. The dating of the coins is perhaps imitated from the Tyrian staters, but cf. *d*. ירשלם קדשה Note the *script. defect.*, and the absence of the article. The legend is perhaps copied from that on the Tyrian staters, Τύρου ἱερᾶς καὶ ἀσύλου; the minting of these staters at Tyre ceased in A. D. 56, so that probably it would have been necessary in A. D. 66 to provide fresh coins of the same value for use in Jerusalem (Reinach).

h (4) This is a specimen of the *bronze* money of the fourth year; varieties of the legend on the reverse are שנת ארבע חצי and שנת ארבע רביע; it is supposed that these coins represent ⅛, ½, ¼ shekels respectively, and that they were siege tokens to be redeemed by silver money when the relief came. This explanation, however, is uncertain, for there are silver shekels (*g* 3) and half-shekels of the fourth year, beside these supposed tokens. The chalice shows that they belong to this period. לגאלת ציון *Belonging to the redemption of Zion*, cf. לנבל B 11. 14 &c., and לחרות י׳ *k*; less prob. ל = *at the time of*. The *lûlab* לוּלָב lit. *palm branch* was a bundle of myrtle and willow with a palm leaf, the *'ethrog*, אֶתְרֹג a citron, carried in each hand at the feast of Booths; Lev. 23 40.

Coins of the Second Revolt, A. D. 132–135. **Plate X 6–9.**

j (6)

Æ. *Obv.* שמעון נשיא ישראל in three lines within a laurel wreath.
Rev. שנת א[חת לגאל]ת ישראל Type: a vase with two handles.

k (7)

AR. *Obv.* שמעון within a wreath.
Rev. לחרות ישראל Type: a palm branch. Restruck on a denarius-drachm of Trajan.

l (8)

Æ. *Obv.* שמעון Type: a palm tree.
Rev. [ש]ב לחר[ות] ישראל Type: a vine leaf.

m (9)

AR. *Obv.* שמעון Type: a conventional figure of the Beautiful Gate of the Temple (?); above, a star.
Rev. לחרות ירושלם Type: a *lûlab* with *'ethrog*. Restruck tetradrachm of Antioch.

The evidence for the course of events which led to the Second Revolt in the 16th year of Hadrian is conflicting; it seems probable, however, that the rebuilding of Jerusalem as a heathen city, with the name Aelia Capitolina, was begun during Hadrian's visit to Syria in 130 A.D. He was again in Syria in 131, and his visit was commemorated by coins which bear the inscr. *adventui Aug(usti) Judaeae*. The foundation of a temple to Jupiter Capitolinus on the site of the Jewish temple is probably to be connected with this occasion (Schürer *Gesch.*[3] 680 ff.); but whether the temple was founded before or after the revolt, the policy of Hadrian had been sufficiently coercive to incite the Jews to revolt. The fuel was ready to be ignited when Bar-Kokba applied the spark. The Jewish leader at once signalized his rebellion by issuing coins in his own name, 'Simon, the prince of Israel' (*j*), and in the name of 'Eliazar the priest,' who appears on the coins of the first year, and seems to have been joint-leader. Simon is called by Christian writers Bar-Kokba (Βαρχωχέβας) = בַּר כֹּכְבָא *son of the star*, alluding to Num. 24 17, but by Rabb. writers בַּר כּוֹזִיבָא or בן כ׳, Kôzêba being the name either of his father or his native town, probably the latter; *Chosiba* was a well-known place on the road to Jericho. He claimed to be the Messiah, and he received the support even of the great Rabbi Aqîba, who applied to him the prophecy of Num. 24 17, e.g. Jer. *Ta'anith* 68 d דרך כוכבא מיעקב. The revolt spread widely throughout Palestine; it was finally suppressed by the Roman general Jul. Severus; Jerusalem was recaptured, and Simon's cause collapsed with the fall of Beth-ther, now Bittir, 3 hours SW. of Jerusalem, where he and his followers made their last stand, in the 18th year of Hadrian, 134–5 A.D.

j (6) The types on these coins represent either objects connected with the Temple and its worship, vase or sacrificial flagon, lyre, trumpets, or the characteristic products of the country, vine-leaf (*l*) palm (*k*, *l*), grapes. This coin and *l* are dated the 1st and 2nd year of the revolt. Beside these bronze coins there is a silver issue, dated in the same way.

k (7) The silver coins of this period are all, probably without a single exception (Kennedy), imperial denarii, drachms, and tetradrachms, restruck with Jewish types and legends. Sometimes, as in *m*, no trace of the original appears, but very often, as in this case, the legend of the imperial coin can still be read in part. לחרות י *Of the emancipation of Israel*; cf. *h* n. חֵרוּת is a noun from חרר, in Syr. ܚܐܪܘܬܐ; for the root see 97 i *n*.

m (9) The signification of the type is not certain. The star above the Temple probably alludes to Simon's pretensions.

SEALS AND GEMS

150.

Plate XI gives some specimens of Aram., Phoen., and Hebr. seals, dating from the 8th cent. B. C. onwards. The seals afford interesting illustrations of the archaic character; they are all chosen from the British Museum collection, Semitic Room cabinet.

I

למלכרם *Belonging to Milk-ram*, on an ivory brooch found underneath a colossal bull in the palace of Nimroud. The inscr. is Phoen. rather than Aram. (Levy *Siegel u. Gemmen* 5 no. 2); pr. nn. compounded with מלך are exceedingly common in Phoen., e. g. מלכיתן **12** 2 &c. יחומלך, ארמלך **8** 1 &c.; for the second part of the compound cf. the pr. n. רמבעל CIS i 99 1. The Egypt. style of the cartouche and the ornament above it is in favour of Phoen. (cf. p. 27) rather than Aram. workmanship. The writing is very early, prob. 8th cent., the date of the building of the palace at Nimroud.

2

CIS ii 75. A seal in the form of a cylinder. The treatment and costume of the figures are Assyrian. In the centre is the eunuch worshipping the god Hadad, who wears a crown with rays, and holds in his right hand what may have been intended for a flower. Behind the eunuch is a priest, assisting or initiating him. The inscr., which is in Aram., and belongs prob. to the 7th cent., runs as follows: לאכדבן בר גברד סרסא זי הקרב להדד *Belonging to Akdban, son of GBRD, the eunuch, who made offering to Hadad.* אכדבן is explained by Levy as derived from כדב = Hebr. כזב with א prosth., and meaning lit. *the false one, callidus*. Sachau reads אכברו *the strong one* (*ZA* 1891, 432); but comparing the fifth letter with the ר in הקרב it will be seen that the former reading is prob. right. גברד According to Sachau l. c. *Gabbarud* = Assyr. *garparuda* or *galparuda*. Another suggestion is made in *JA* (1892) xix 565 that the name = גֵּר בָּרֻד *client of Barud* (a deity). For זי see **61** 1 *n*. הקרב Afel, as in Dan. and Ezr. = *bring an offering*; for the ה retained in Afel, contrary to ordinary Aram. usage, cf. **61** 29. **62** 4. 18. **64** 11. **65** 3. **97** i, and Bibl. Aram. הדד See **61** 1 *n*. Macrobius describes the image of Hadad as surrounded with rays and holding a flower in his hand, *Saturn.* I 23.

3

CIS ii 77. A cylinder seal from Assyria. The worshipper, attended by winged deities or genii, is offering his devotions to the god *Ilu* in the form of a disc with wings and a human head (?). Two rays descend from under the wings of the disc, one of them touches the worshipper. In the centre is a figure which is taken to represent the flowing water of a mystic fountain. The inscr. is in Aram., and dates from the 8th–7th cent.:—ירפאל בר הרעדד *Yirp-el son of Hor-'adad.* The pr. n. ירפאל may = יִרְפְּאֵל Josh. 18 27 i.e. יִרְפָּא אֵל *El will heal*, cf. רְפָאֵל 1 Chr. 26 7. But since רפא does not occur in Aram., Levy (p. 7) takes ירפ' to be the Afel of רפי, and explains *El will set free.* The engraver has turned א the wrong way both times. הרעדד The last two letters look alike; the ר is closed at the top, but in the word בר it is open, hence הרעדר *Horus helps* may be right; עדר = עזר, as כרב in אכרבן no. 2 may = כזב, though ד = ז is remarkable in Aram. of the 8th cent. The reading הרעדר, however, is uncertain; the right-hand stroke of ר in בר is slanting, but in the last letter of the pr. n. it is perpendicular. How הרעדר is to be explained, if that is the correct reading, is not clear.

4

CIS ii 94. An Aram. seal of the 5th cent., Persian period. לתמכאל בר מלכם *Belonging to Tamak-el, son of Milkom.* תמכאל = *El holds, sustains*, again in Phoen., Cl.-Gan. *Sceaux et cachets* no. 23; the verb תמך *hold fast* is well known in Hebr. and is used in the Targ. The explanation suggested in the Corp. תָּם כָּאֵל *perfect as El*, is most improbable. Notice the beginning of a ligature at the foot of ר following ב.

5

Levy no. 18, p. 31. A Phoen. seal with the inscr. לבעליתן איש אלם איש למלקרתרצף *Belonging to Ba'al-yathon, a man of the gods* (?), *who belongs to Melqarth-reṣef.* איש אלם Possibly אלם may have a sing. meaning, as in the pr. n. מתנאלם (?) 33 6 *n.*, but the expression *man of the gods* i.e. *divine servant* is unusual, and it may be more correct to render *the nobleman*; for אלם as a title cf. 10 2 *n.*, and for the idiom cf. the Hebr. אִישׁ רֵעִים Prov. 18 24 lit. *a man of friends*, i.e. *a friendly man*, איש דברים Ex. 4 10. מ' רצף A complex divinity; see 10 3 *n.* רצף = רשף 12 3 *n.* Date, 5th–4th cent.

6

Levy no. 7, p. 39. A seal with Hebr. inscr. לעבר אלאב בן שבעת עברמתת בן צרקא *Belonging to the servant of Eli'ab, son of Shib'ath. The servant of Mattath, son of Ṣedoqa.* Here apparently two persons have combined to adopt a common seal. It is probable that עבר־אלאב are two words, *servant of Eli'ab*; and similarly עבר־מתת *servant of Mattath*. For אלאב cf. the O.T. אֱלִיאָב 1 S. 16 6. Other seals of slaves are Levy no. 8 לשבניו עבר עזיו and no. 9 לאביו עבר עזיו. A slave does not give his genealogy; see p. 134. שבעת Cf. the O.T. שֶׁבַע 2 S. 20 1. מתת Prob. abbreviated from מתתיה, cf. 149 C *d*. צרקא Cf. the O.T. צָדוֹק, צָדֹק 1 K. 1 26 &c. Date, 7th–6th cent.

7

Levy no. 11, p. 42. A scarab of green jasper in Egyptian style, with Hebr. inscr. לזכר הושע *For a memorial of Hôshê'a.* The form of the ז is to be noticed; it occurs on the coins of Eliazar the priest (pp. 359 and 353). The curve in the shaft of כ is an indication of later date. The Hebr. name הושע has been found recently at Tell ej-Judeideh on a Jewish seal, Lidzb. *Eph.* i 183. Above the inscr. is engraved the figure of a winged sphinx, with the *pshent* head-dress. Date, 8th–4th cent.

8

Levy p. 54. A Hebr. seal on both sides of a crystal. On one side is engraved in Egypt. style the figure of the god Harpocrates sitting on a lotus flower; on the other is the inscr.:—לעשיו בן יוקם *Belonging to 'Asiyu, son of Yôqim.* The words are separated by small strokes. For עשיו cf. the O.T. עֲשָׂיָה 2 K. 22 12. עֲשִׂיאֵל 1 Chr. 4 35. עֲשָׂהאֵל 2 S. 2 18; the final יו is a fragment of יהוה, cf. עזיו above, and the form עשיהו on a Jewish seal, Cl.-Gan. *Rec.* iii § 32. יוקם Abbrev. from יְהוֹיָקִים 2 K. 23 34. Date, 5th–4th cent.

INDEX I

NORTH-SEMITIC

[The following special abbreviations are used where necessary: d. = deity, n. = noun, pr. = pronoun, pre. = preposition. The words and forms are those mentioned in the notes.]

INDEX II

ARABIC

INDEX III

SYRIAC

INDEX IV

GREEK

INDEX V

BIBLICAL REFERENCES

𝔊 = LXX, 𝔖 = Syriac, 𝔗 = Targum, 𝔗 Psj. = Targum Pseudo-Jonathan.

GENESIS.

1 10 300
31 97. 125
2 5 126. 166
4 18 24
9 3 78
21 8
10 9 120
17 89
11 1 17
12 5 69
14 5 10
13 119
18 101
15 9 Sam. 𝔗 120
18 5 168
19 23 178
26 103
27 99
20 16 118
22 18 35
23 9. 20 237
19 f. 308
24 12 24
27 179
25 13 215
15 197
28 120
26 10 170
29 24
27 19. 31 35
31 8
28 12 75
22 104
32 3 168
32 133
34 12 109
35 16 49
20 60
36 11. 15. 42 145
15 ff. 210
21 238
38 130
43 299
37 4 35
19 119
28 118
38 25 𝔗 210
39 6 𝔗 126
14 𝔗 279
40 9–11 213
41 45 91
42 4 𝔗 311
23 61
25 𝔗 274
43 9 99
16 𝔖 212
44 13 34
32 99
45 4 20
46 21 111
26 299
47 13 13
22 198
29 f. 179
48 7 17
50 7–13 179
25 179
26 28

EXODUS.

3 15 37
4 10 361
6 14 13
7 20 24
9 23 12
10 2 20
11 7 𝔗 199
12 7. 22 f. 342
22 43
39 𝔗 78
13 19 179
14 14. 25 𝔗 Psj. 76
15 10 38
15 49
27 𝔗 198
16 5 122
15 311
22 96
34 24
17 10 200. 232
15 7
18 23 128
25 13
19 13 29. 120
15 55
20 3 118
5 190
24 117
25 17
21 22 122
30 𝔗 Psj. 223
23 13 168
18 121
19 54
20 ff. 37
20. 23 304
25 11 ff. 120
23 𝔗 226
27 154
26 31 ff. 67
36 33
27 8 155
28 11 22
29 2 121
14 119
30 8 126
13 121. 351
13 𝔗 223
36 𝔗 171
33 10 49
14 f. 132. 304
34 1 155
5 f. 37. 106
7 190
34 126
36 3 67

INDEX VI

GENERAL

APPENDIX

I

The Phoenician Inscriptions of Bostan esh-Shêḫ, Sidon.

These inscriptions, which repeat the same text six or seven times with slight variations, were found in 1900 and 1901 at a short distance to the N. of Ṣaida, near the Nahr el-Auwali. They are written upon the inner faces of blocks of stone which formed part of the inclosure or foundation of the temple of Eshmun; being built into the masonry, like the inscribed bricks in Assyrian buildings, they were not intended to be exposed to view. The most complete text, repeated with slight changes on the same block, is that published by Macridy-Bey and Père Lagrange in *RB* (1902) 498–526, with a facsimile. A text practically identical and almost as complete has been published, with two plates, by Berger, *Mém. sur les inscrr. de fondation du temple d'Esmoun à Sidon*, 1901, from one of the stones now in the Louvre, which also possesses the fragment of another of the series (*Rép.* nos. 287. 288). The inscriptions are discussed at length by Clermont-Ganneau in *Rec.* v § 41, who has done much to clear up the difficulties which they present. The following text is based upon that of Berger:—

1 מלך בדעשתרת מלך צדנם בן בן
2 מלך אשמנעזר מלך צדנם בצ
3 דן ים שמם רמם ארץ רשפם צד
4 ן משל אשבן וצדן שד אית [כל?]
5 הבת ז בן לאלי לאשמן שר קד
6 ש

King Bod-'ashtart, king of the Sidonians, grandson [2] of king Eshmun-'azar, king of the Sidonians, (reigning) in Si[3]don by the sea, Shamim Ramim, the land of Reshafim, Sid[4]on of Mashal, 'ŠBN, and Sidon on the plain—the whole (?) [5] of this temple built to his god, Eshmun, prince of Qa[6]desh.

This text must be carefully compared with **4** and **5**; the writing is of the same general character and period.

L. 1. מלך בדעשתרת See **6**; Bod-'ashtart was the successor of Eshmun-'azar ii (**5**). בן בן The father is not mentioned because he never was king; contrast **5** 13 f.

L. 2. אשמנעזר i. e. Eshmun-'azar i. Both Bod-'ashtart and Eshmun-'azar ii were grandsons of this king, the former being the son of a younger brother or sister of Tabnith (**4**). The genealogy will thus be as follows:—

Eshmun-'azar i

Tabnith = Am-'ashtart   X = Y

Eshmun-'azar ii   Bod-'ashtart

בצדן The prep. denotes that Bod-'ashtart claimed sovereignty *in* or *over* (cf. משל ב **5** 9) Sidon; so Torrey *Journ. Amer. Oriental Soc.* xxiii 156–173 (with facsimile). The interpretation of the following words is difficult; but Torrey and Cl.-Gan. are prob. right in regarding them as the names of various places round about Sidon. The places are enumerated *ἀσυνδέτως* (cf. **149** B 15), with ו before the last in the list, as sometimes (though not usually) in Hebrew, e.g. Gen. **5** 32. **13** 2. **14** 1 &c.; Gesenius, p. 509 *n*.

L. 3. צדן ים *Sidon of the sea*, the maritime Sidon, as distinguished from צדן שד l. 4. שמם רמם Lit. *high heavens*. The words suggest the *Σαμσηρούμος* or *Ὑψουράνιος* of the cosmogony of Sanchuniathon (Philo Bybl. *Fr. Hist. Gr.* iii 566); so Lagrange. The expression recalls the שמם אדרם in **5** 16 f.; and although 'High-heavens,' 'Glorious-heavens,' do not seem very obvious names for terrestrial localities, yet such they probably were (Cl.-Gan.). In both cases this explanation suits the context. Cl.-Gan. suggests that שמם אדרם was the name of the place where the tomb of Eshmun-'azar ii was found, S. of the Nahr el-Ḳamle, at a distance from the ancestral burying-place; this may have been the special domain of Am-'ashtart, the queen-mother and priestess of 'Ashtart (**5** 14 f.). ארץ רשפם For the god Reshef see **12** 3 *n*.; like בעל he was the tutelary of several cities, and thus the plural of his name would come into use. In Phoen. the plur. of בעל is found in בעל ימם **20** B 4 *n*., but not in the manner common in the O.T. The only other divine names found in the plur. in Phoen. are אלנם (p. 24, cf. אלחי **61** 12 &c.) and אלם (p. 99).

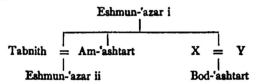

L. 4. צדן משל *Sidon-Mashal* or *S. of Mashal.* One of the texts (Lagrange A) reads במשל. Cf. the O.T. place-names מָשָׁל 1 Chr. 6 59. מִשְׁאָל Josh. 19 26. 21 30, and the modern Arab. names derived from مشل. אשבן might be divided and translated *who built*; but the context requires another place here. In the genealogies Gen. 36 26. 1 Chr. 1 41 אֶשְׁבָּן is the name of an Edomite chief. וצדן שר The waw is read by Lagrange; Berger gives מ, but Cl.-Gan., after an examination of the original, decides in favour of ו. The word שר (Lagrange, Berger with ? שר) is prob. to be taken as = שדה *field* (5 19. 29 9), here in the sense of *country* or *plain*, the *inland* as distinguished from the *maritime* Sidon, l. 2 f.; the term is used by Ezekiel in connexion with Tyre, בנותיה אשר בשדה 26 6. At the end of the line Cl.-Gan. proposes כל instead of של (Berger); this improves the sentence.

L. 5. הבת ז בן Cf. 5 15 ff.; but this temple is not to be identified with the one founded by Eshmun-'azar ii, which perhaps was at שמם אדרם; at any rate, the temple built by Bod-'ashtart stood outside the present Sidon, near the Nahr el-Auwali. לאלי לאשמן Cf. לאלי לעשתרת 6 5 in the inscr. of Bod-'ashtart; also 24 1 f. שר קדש Either *holy prince* or *prince of Qadesh* (Cl.-Gan.); hence we must certainly restore לאשמן שר קדש in 5 17 (see p. 37). In the latter case, קדש is further defined by ען ידלל בהר i.e. 'Qadesh of the well of Yidlal in the mountain,' prob. Lebanon. Cl.-Gan. suggests with much probability that both Eshmun-'azar ii and Bod-'ashtart brought the worship of Eshmun from an ancient, venerated shrine, Qadesh, into their new temples at Sidon.

The date of this Sidonian dynasty has been much disputed. Lagrange would assign it to the Persian period and the time of Xerxes; but against this is the title אדן מלכם 5 18, which belongs to the Ptolemaic, not the Persian, kings; see p. 38. Cl.-Gan. suggests ingeniously that Eshmun-'azar i is none other than the Abdalonymus of the classical historians, who was placed on the throne of his ancestors, under romantic circumstances, by Alexander the Great after the occupation of Sidon in 332 B.C. The story is told by Diod. Sic. xvii 47, but wrongly referred to Tyre. With the change of his fortunes the king may have changed his name, as was frequently done. It is probable, in any case, that the date proposed on p. 27 is substantially correct; and the epigraphical evidence agrees with this. On the other hand, this inscr. shows that Bod-'ashtart is not to be identified with Straton i 374–362 B.C., as is suggested, with hesitation, on p. 41.

II

Aramaic Papyrus from Elephantina. MS. Aram. c. 1 (P) in the Bodleian Library.

By the courtesy of the Secretary of the Society of Biblical Archaeology, I am allowed to reprint the text of this papyrus which has been published with a translation, notes, and facsimile by Mr. A. E. Cowley, Fellow of Magdalen College, Oxford, in the May number of the Society's *Proceedings* (vol. xxv Parts 4 and 5, pp. 202 ff., 1903). The papyrus was purchased by Prof. Sayce at Elephantina, and brought by him to the Bodleian Library in 1901. It arrived in three small rolls; these have been ingeniously pieced together, and now form a leaf 13½ × 9¾ inches, which contains the longest and most continuous text of the kind hitherto published. The following is Mr. Cowley's text and translation:—

1 ....ר̇ בר יתמא ל... נתנת לי כסף
2 ......פ̇...ב̇ני פתח כסף שז לו וירבה עלי כסף חלרן וו
3 לכסף שז לירחא עד יום זי אשלמנהי ל[ך] ותהוה מרבית
4 כספך חלרן ווו...לירח ו וירחא זי לא אנתן לך בה
5 מרבית יהוה ראש וירבה ואשלמ[נה]י לך ירח בירח
6 מן פרסי זי יתנון לי מן אוצרא ותכתב לי נבז על כל
7 כסף ומרבי זי אהוה משלם לך והן לא שלמת לך כל
8 כספך ומרביתה עד ירח תחות שנת..ווו ווו יעקף כספך
9 ומרביתה זי ישתאר עלי ויהוה רבה עלי ירח לירח
10 עד יום זי אשלמנהי לך
11 שהדיא
12 עקבן בר שמשנורי
13 קצרי בר יההדר̇י
14 מחסיה בר ידניה
15 מלכיה בר זכרי̇ה̇
16 כתב ספרא גמריה בר אחיו על פם שהדיא זי על ספרא זנה

[This is the agreement between X and Y] bar Yathma. You have given me the sum of [2].......... PTḤ the sum of ŠZ for himself (?), for which interest shall be due from me at the rate of 2 ḤLR [3] per ŠZ per month, till the day on which I repay it to you. The interest of your loan (to me) shall be ... ḤLR per month. Any month in which I fail to give you [5] interest, it is to be (added to the) principal, and to bear interest. I agree to pay it to you month by month [6] out of my pay which they give me from the treasury, and you shall give me a written receipt (?) for all [7] money and interest which I pay to you. If I fail to repay to you the whole of [8] the principal, with the interest thereon, by the month of Thoth in the year [? 1]6, I am to be held liable for double (?) the principal [9] and interest outstanding, and to continue to pay interest (on it) month by month [10] till the day when I repay it to you. [11] Witnesses:—[12] 'Uqban b. Shemesh-nuri. [13] Qoṣri b. Yah-hadari. [14] Maḥaseiah b. Yadoniah. [15] Malkiah b. Zekariah. [16] The document was written by Gemariah b. Aḥio in the presence of the witnesses who(se names) are appended hereunto.

The language and writing exhibit the usual characteristics of Egyptian Aramaic (pp. 185. 200). The interest of the text lies in the fact that it is a Jewish document of early date; the witnesses and the writer bear Jewish names. These Jews were evidently engaged in business as bankers or money-lenders. They write in Aramaic, probably because it was the official language of the Persian empire. The date of the document may be placed in the Persian period, certainly not later than 300 B.C., and probably 150 years earlier (cf. **72. 76**), as Mr. Cowley is inclined to believe. The legal form resembles that of the agreements written in cuneiform with Aram. seals attached, CIS ii 64–66, belonging to the 6th–5th cents. B.C.; no. 66 is dated 450 B.C. We have, then, a very early piece of evidence for a settlement of Jews in Upper Egypt; indeed, after the allusion of Jeremiah to the Jews 'dwelling in the land of Pathros,' i.e. Upper Egypt (44 1. 15; Schürer *Gesch.*[3] iii 19 ff.), this is the earliest contemporary reference. And this document does not stand alone. Mr. Cowley is publishing in the next number of the *PSBA* 6 ostraka,

5 of which come from Elephantina and belong to the same period, and refer to the same names, probably also to the same persons, as the papyrus.

L. 1. ...ל Mr. Cowley conjectures לאמר as on Ostrakon 1.

L. 2. בני . . פּ Perhaps פּני . . . בּ. שז l. 3, reading certain; probably the name for a sum of money. Mr. Cowley compares the Babyl. *soss*=60 shekels=1 maneh; Prof. Sayce thinks it is a Persian word. חלרן or חלרן Perhaps=Babyl. *ḫalluru*, a coin used in reckoning the amount of interest in cuneiform contracts (see Sayce ap. Cowley).

L. 3. מרבית *interest*; cf. Lev. 25 37; תרבית Lev. 25 36. Eze. 18 8. For ancient ideas and legislation on the subject of interest see Driver, *Deut.* 266 f.

L. 4. The numeral may have been 6 or 8. After לירח the stroke somewhat like a ! is prob. a mark of punctuation.

L. 5. ראש *principal*; cf. the usage in Lev. 5 24 ושלם אתו בראשו, and Talm. B. *Sanhedr.* 3 b ממון שאינו משתלם בראש 'money which is not paid as capital.' ירח בירח Cf. the idiom יום ביום in B Aram. Ezr. 6 9 and late Hebr. Ezr. 3 4. 1 Chr. 12 23 &c.

L. 6. פרסי In the Mishnah פרס is frequent in the sense of *salary, income.* מן אוצרא The debtor was apparently in a government office. נבז after תכתב must mean a document, Mr. Cowley suggests 'receipt' and a Persian derivation.

L. 7. מרבי here without the final ת (ll. 3. 5), from a ל״י verb, is strictly the fem. of מַרְבֶּה Barth *Nominalb.* § 248.

L. 8. תחות The first Egyptian month, Aug. 29–Sept. 27; Copt. Thŏouth, Gk. Θώθ. In the space after שנת must have stood the symbol for 10 or 20; analogy suggests that the reference is to the years of a king's reign. יעקף The root عقف=*bend, curve*, so with עלי l. 9 *shall return upon me*, i.e. *shall be required of me*. Mr. Cowley suggests *shall be doubled against me*; 'if the debt was not paid, or if any interest was outstanding, the debtor was to pay interest on double the accumulated sum at the rate previously settled' (l. 2).

L. 12. עקבן Cf. the O. T. יעקב. שמשנורי Not a Jewish name; cf. the Palm. שמשגרם (p. 298), עתנורי (p. 303), נורבל (p. 307).

L. 13. יהודרי i. e. *Yah is my glory*; if the reading is right the form is unusual; cf. אֶלְעוּזַי *El is my strength* 1 Chr. 12 5 and יוֹכֶבֶד in PC (Gray *Hebr. Pr. N.* 156).

L. 14. מחסיה Cf. מַחְסֵיָה Jer. 32 12. 51 59. ידניה Cf. O.T. דנאל.

L. 15. מלכיה . . זכריה Both common in O.T.

L. 16. For גמריה cf. 2 Sam. 6 3. 4, Gray l.c. 36, Driver *Sam.* 204.

ADDENDA

Page 36, line 14 below, *add* see Appendix I.
Page 123, line 3 above, *add* **Plate III.**
Page 147, line 1 above, *add* **Plate IV.**
Page 186, line 1 above, *add* **Plate V.**
Page 189, line 6 below, *add* **Plate VI.**
Page 344, line 9 above, חלך Cf. the Assyr. *Ḫilakku* = Cillcia. In Eze. 27 11 Halévy proposes to read חלך *Cilicia* for חילך.

PHOENICIAN Cyprus. No. 21

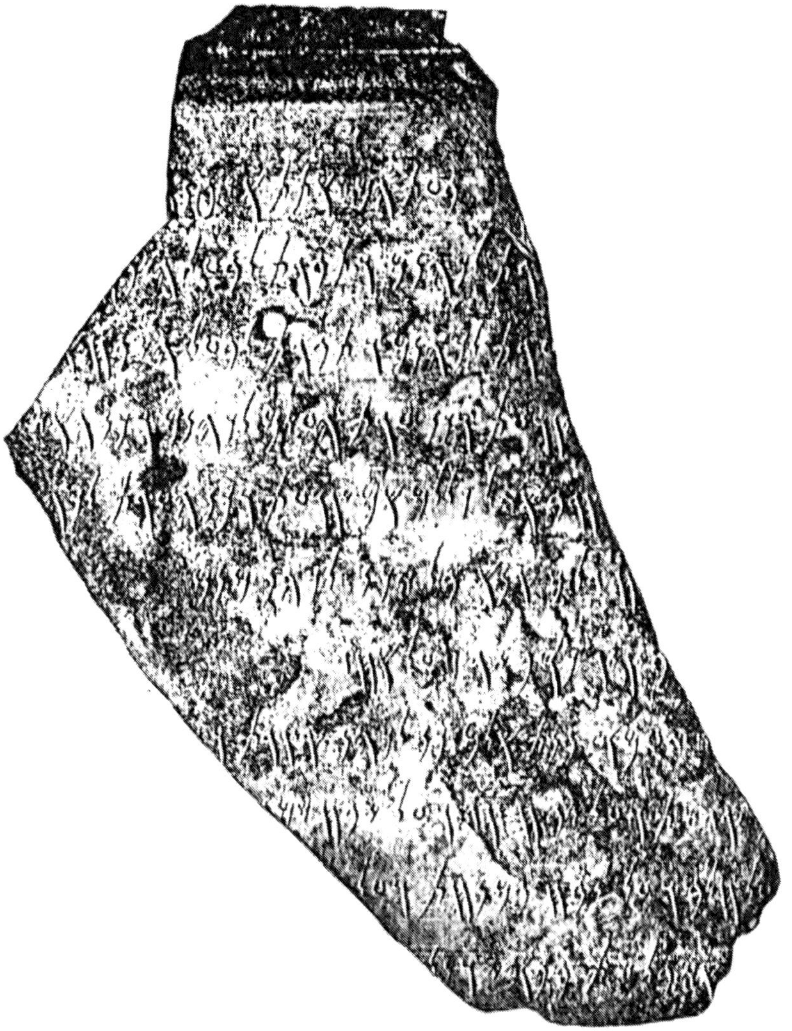

PUNIC Carthage. No. 43

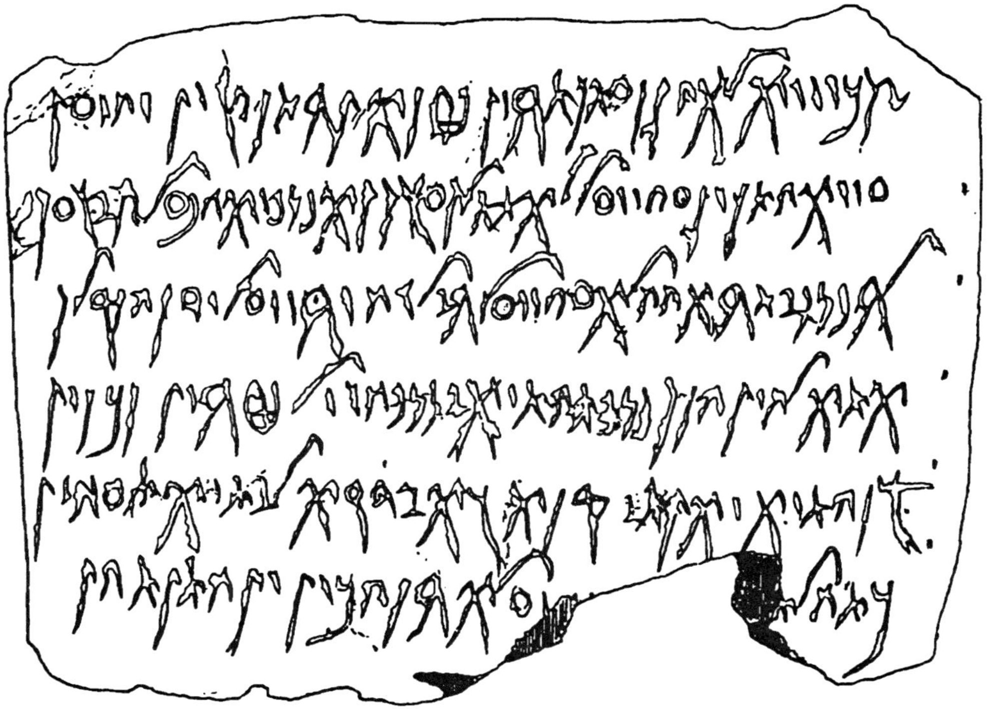

NEO-PUNIC Jol (Shershel 1). No. 56

ARAMAIC Nērab. No. 64

PLATE VI

Plate VII

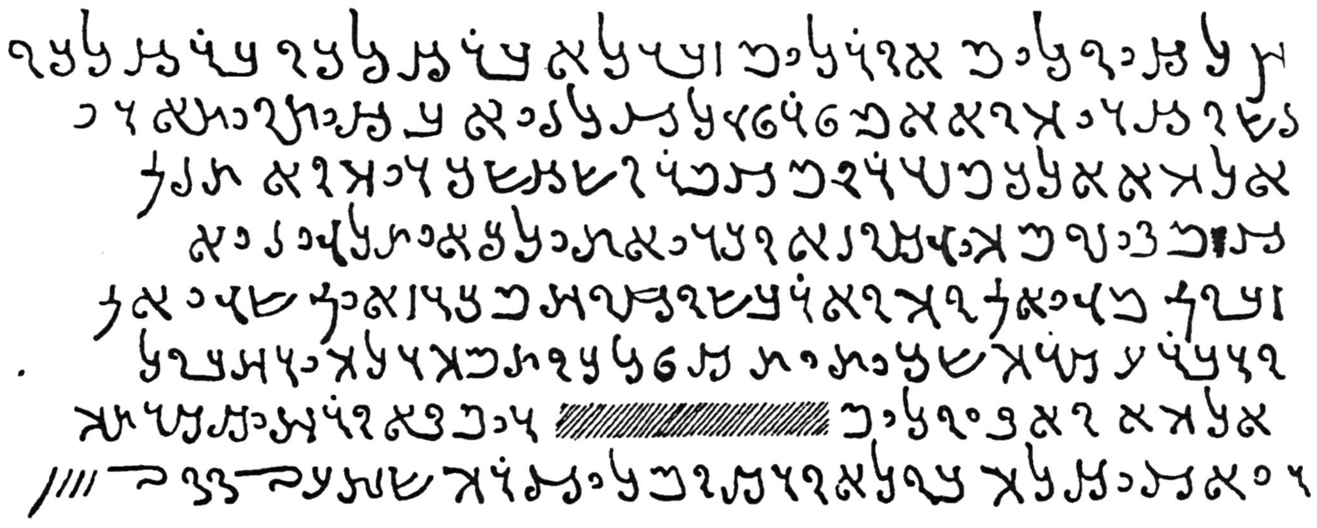

PALMYRENE

Palmyra. No. 121

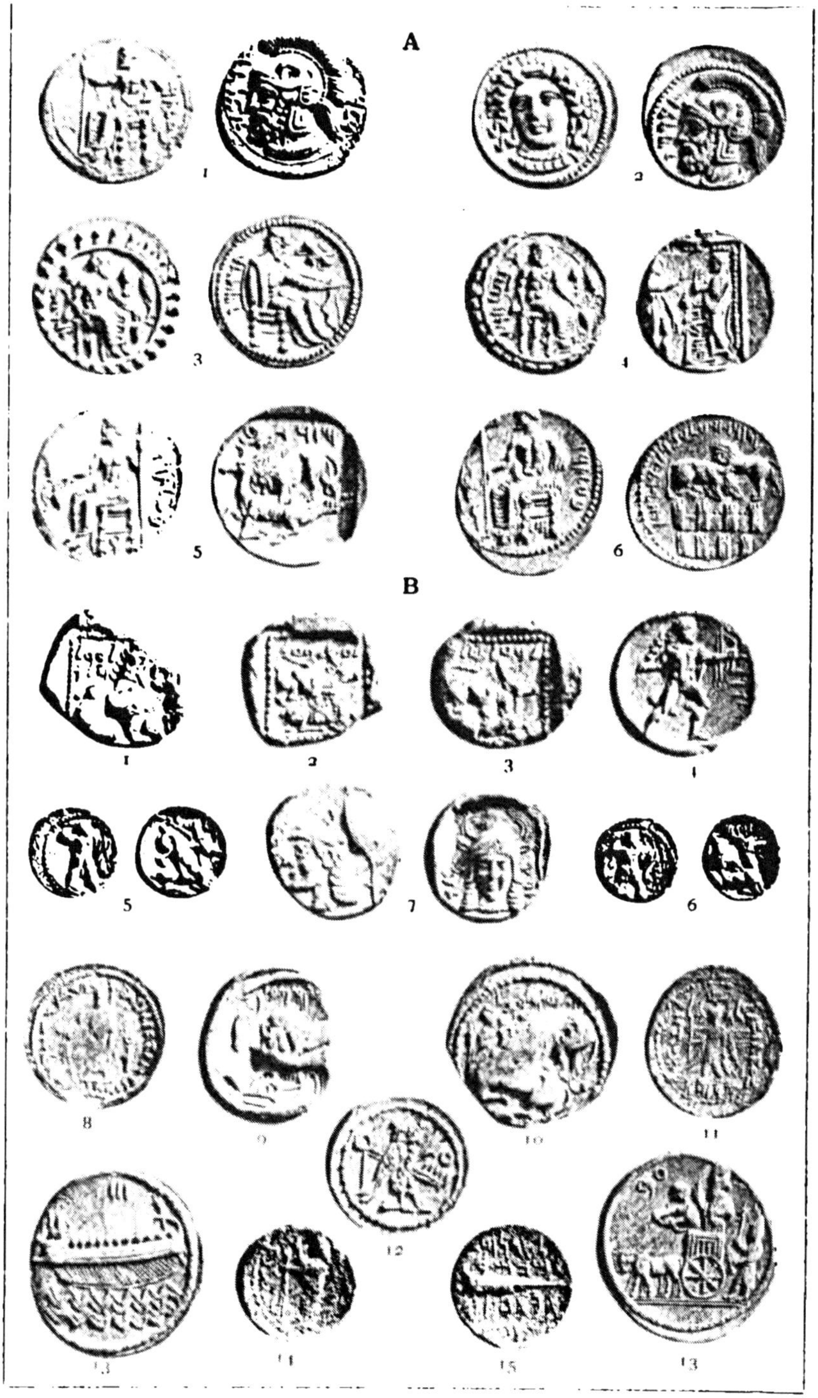

CILICIAN AND PHOENICIAN COINS

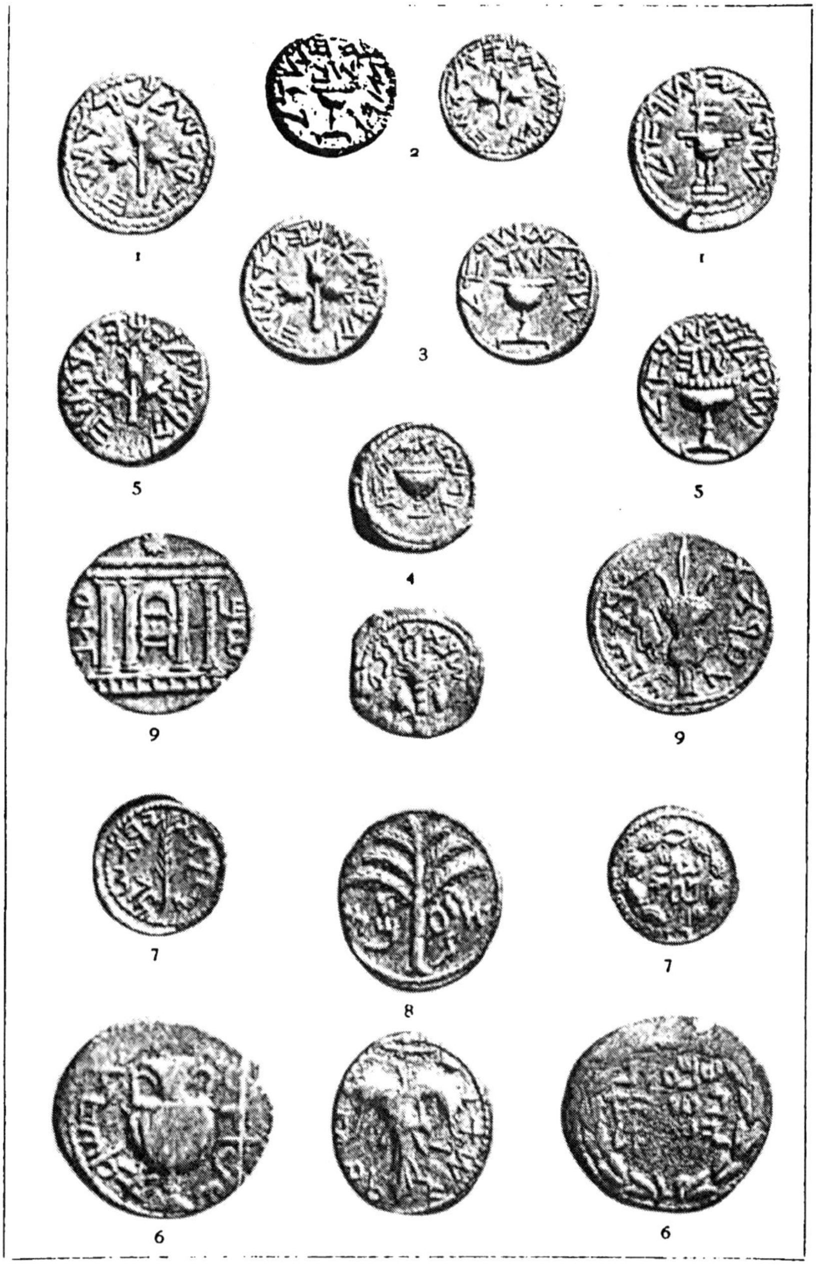

JEWISH COINS

PLATE XI

SEALS AND GEMS

PHOE

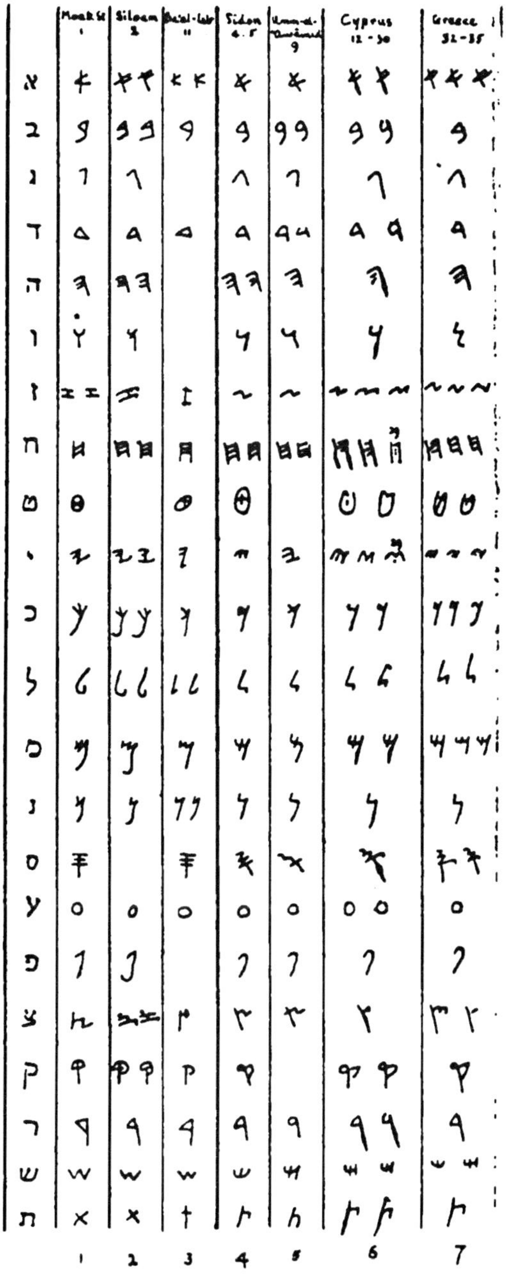

Moab St. 1
Siloam 2
Ba'al-Leb. 11
Sidon 4.5
Umm-el-'Awamid 9
Cyprus 12-30
Greece 32-35
א
ב
ג
ד
ה
ו
ז
ח
ט
י
כ
ל
מ
נ
ס
ע
פ
צ
ק
ר
ש
ת
1
2
3
4
5
6
7

	Moab & 1	Siloam 2	Ba'al-lub 11	Sidon 4.5	Umm-el-ʿawāmīd 9	Cyprus 12-30	Greece 31-35
א							
ב							
ג							
ד							
ה							
ו							
ז							
ח							
ט							
י							
כ							
ל							
מ							
נ							
ס							
ע							
פ							
צ							
ק							
ר							
ש							
ת							
	1	2	3	4	5	6	7

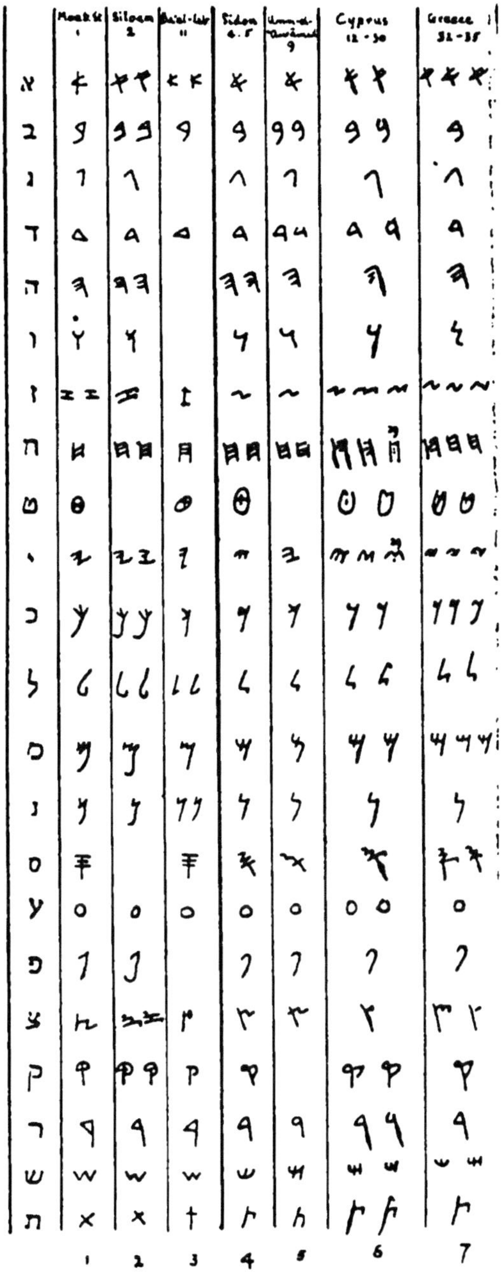

PLATE

ARAMAIC
N Syria
Asia Minor
Arabia
Egypt
Zenjerli
Nerab
Abydos
Teima
Memphis
Memphis
Carpentras
Papyri

NABATAEAN
PALMYRENE
Hejra
Petra
Hauran
Hauran
Sinaitic
א
ב
ג
ד
ה
ו
ז
ח
ט
י
כ
ל
מ
נ
ס
ע
פ
צ
ק
ר
ש
ת
1
2
3
4
5
6
7
8 - 9

LaVergne, TN USA
16 September 2010
197305LV00004B/119/P

9 781146 621236